SHIP REGISTRATION

LLOYD'S SHIPPING LAW LIBRARY
Series Editors: Hatty Sumption and
Clare Ambrose

LLOYD'S SHIPPING LAW LIBRARY

Offshore Construction
Law and Practice
Stuart Beadnall and Simon Moore

Laytime and Demurrage
Seventh edition
John Schofield

The Law of Ship Mortgages
Second edition
David Osborne, Graeme Bowtle and Charles Buss

Berlingieri on Arrest of Ships
Sixth edition
Francesco Berlingieri

Merchant Shipping Legislation
Third edition
Aengus R.M. Fogarty

CMR
Contracts for the International Carriage of Goods by Road
Fourth edition
Andrew Messent and David A. Glass

London Maritime Arbitration
Fourth edition
Clare Ambrose, Karen Maxwell and
Michael Collett

The York–Antwerp Rules
The Principles and Practice of General Average Adjustment
Fourth edition
N. Geoffrey Hudson and Michael D. Harvey

Admiralty Jurisdiction and Practice
Fifth edition
Nigel Meeson and John A. Kimbell

General Average
Law and Practice
Third edition
F. D. Rose

*The Law of Tug and Tow and Offshore
Contracts*
Fourth edition
Simon Rainey

[For more information about this series, please visit: www.routledge.com/Lloyds-Shipping-Law-Library/book-series/LSLL]

SHIP REGISTRATION

LAW AND PRACTICE

EDWARD WATT

LL.B. (Edin.), LL.M (Lon.), Dip. L.P., N.P.
Solicitor and Notary Public
Addleshaw Goddard LLP, Edinburgh

CONSULTING EDITOR
RICHARD COLES

T.D., LL.B. (Hull)
Visiting Senior Research Fellow
Institute of Maritime Law
University of Southampton

THIRD EDITION

informa law
from Routledge

Third edition published 2019
by Informa Law from Routledge
2 Park Square, Milton Park, Abingdon, Oxon OX14 4RN

and by Informa Law from Routledge
711 Third Avenue, New York, NY 10017

Informa Law from Routledge is an imprint of the Taylor & Francis Group, an informa business

© 2019 Edward B. Watt

The right of Edward B. Watt to be identified as editor of this work has been asserted by him in accordance with sections 77 and 78 of the Copyright, Designs and Patents Act 1988.

All rights reserved. No part of this book may be reprinted or reproduced or utilised in any form or by any electronic, mechanical, or other means, now known or hereafter invented, including photocopying and recording, or in any information storage or retrieval system, without permission in writing from the publishers.

Whilst every effort has been made to ensure that the information contained in this book is correct, neither the author nor Informa Law can accept any responsibility for any errors or omissions or for any consequences arising therefrom.

Trademark notice: Product or corporate names may be trademarks or registered trademarks, and are used only for identification and explanation without intent to infringe.

First Edition published by Informa 2002

Second Edition published by Informa Law 2009

British Library Cataloguing-in-Publication Data
A catalogue record for this book is available from the British Library

Library of Congress Cataloging-in-Publication Data
Names: Coles, Richard M. F. | Watt, Edward, author.
Title: Ship registration : law and practice / by Edward Watt; consulting editor,
    Richard Coles.
Description: Third edition. | Milton Park, Abingdon, Oxon; New York, NY:
    Informa Law from Routledge, [2019] | Series: Lloyd's shipping law library |
    Includes index.
Identifiers: LCCN 2018012866 | ISBN 9781138244917 (hbk) | ISBN 9781315268200 (ebk)
Subjects: LCSH: Ships—Registration and transfer. | Ships—Nationality. |
    Flags of convenience. | Ships—Registration and transfer—Forms.
Classification: LCC K4158 .C65 2019 | DDC 343.09/65—dc23
LC record available at https://lccn.loc.gov/2018012866

ISBN: 978-1-138-24491-7 (hbk)
ISBN: 978-1-315-26820-0 (ebk)

Typeset in Times
by Apex CoVantage, LLC

Printed and bound by CPI Group (UK) Ltd, Croydon, CR0 4YY

For Cameron and Hamish

CONTENTS

Foreword	xi
Preface	xiii
Acknowledgements	xv
Table of cases	xvii
Table of legislation	xix
Table of conventions	xxv

CHAPTER 1	THE LEGAL CONCEPT OF SHIP REGISTRATION	1
CHAPTER 2	DUTIES OF THE FLAG STATE	14
CHAPTER 3	THE LEGAL REQUIREMENTS OF SHIP REGISTRATION	27
CHAPTER 4	INTERNATIONAL REGISTERS	45
CHAPTER 5	BAREBOAT CHARTER REGISTRATION	62
CHAPTER 6	FACTORS INFLUENCING CHOICE OF FLAG	74
CHAPTER 7	BAHAMAS	88
CHAPTER 8	BARBADOS	97
CHAPTER 9	BERMUDA	109
CHAPTER 10	BRITISH VIRGIN ISLANDS	117
CHAPTER 11	CAYMAN ISLANDS	128
CHAPTER 12	CYPRUS	142
CHAPTER 13	GIBRALTAR	153
CHAPTER 14	HONG KONG	161

CHAPTER 15	ISLE OF MAN	169
CHAPTER 16	JAMAICA	176
CHAPTER 17	LIBERIA	184
CHAPTER 18	MALTA	197
CHAPTER 19	MARSHALL ISLANDS	206
CHAPTER 20	NORWAY	216
CHAPTER 21	PANAMA	222
CHAPTER 22	SINGAPORE	232
CHAPTER 23	ST VINCENT AND THE GRENADINES	239
CHAPTER 24	UNITED KINGDOM	249
CHAPTER 25	VANUATU	261

Appendices		269
Statistics		271
I	Leading flags of registration by tonnage	273
II	Ownership of the world fleet, 2017	275
III	Paris MOU – White/Grey/Black Lists	277
IV	STCW White List	280
Legislation and Conventions		283
V	Extracts from UK Merchant Shipping Act 1995	285
VI	Extracts from UK Merchant Shipping (Registration of Ships) Regulations 1993	301
VII	Geneva Convention on the High Seas	325
VIII	Extract from UN Convention on the Law of the Sea 1982	333
IX	UN Convention on Conditions for Registration of Ships 1986	338
X	International Convention on Maritime Liens and Mortgages 1993	346
Forms		353
XI(a)	Bahamas forms	355
XI(b)	Cayman Islands forms	363
XI(c)	Gibraltar forms	396
XI(d)	Isle of Man forms	410
XI(e)	Liberia forms	429
XI(f)	Malta forms	438
XI(g)	Marshall Islands forms	444

XI(h)	Norway forms	457
XI(i)	Singapore forms	475
XI(j)	UK forms	488

Index 511

FOREWORD

One of the most important decisions a ship-owner or a bareboat charterer will take is where to register their vessels. Combined advances in technology and port State control mean that the scrutiny and publicity of flag State performance has never been greater and is now inescapable. It is also true that with over 70% of the world's fleet now registered under an open or international register (such as Liberia, Panama or the Marshall Islands) the historic criticism that these are 'flags of convenience' seeking to evade an owner's obligations is simply not true. A complex number of factors influence an owner's decision as to where to register their ships. These include restricted cabotage (in some domestic markets such as USA, Japan or Brazil one needs to fly their flag to operate); the locality of the administration of the flag; reputation (those operating under a flag with a good reputation and on the so-called White Lists are far less likely to be inspected or detained when visiting a port); the cost of operation; availability of insurance; naval protection; and the type of ship being registered, among many others.

This third edition of *Ship Registration: Law and Practice* is an invaluable guide for owners, advisors, flag administrations and others seeking to understand the whole process and responsibilities of ship registration. As well as covering the essential concepts, flag State duties, procedural requirements and the factors influencing where to register, the volume details the registration process for the most commonly used flags.

The shipping industry is evolving fast and with ever-increasing scrutiny. Environmental, safety, manning and technological issues are becoming ever more important and it is vital therefore that owners make the right decision when undertaking one of the most funda-mental tasks of ship-ownership – where to register. This book assists in the task greatly.

GUY PLATTEN
Secretary General
International Chamber of Shipping

PREFACE

The purpose of this book remains to introduce the reader to the legal concepts surrounding the registration of ships and as a source of reference upon ship registration worldwide. It seeks to explain a global practice both from the perspective of customary international law and individually from a domestic viewpoint in certain chosen jurisdictions. It aims to provide an objective assessment of the issues arising from the use of what are still commonly known as 'flags of convenience'. It is hoped to explain in an unbiased way – such as with reference to Port State Control inspection and compliance statistics – the various reasons why the continuing and widespread pejorative usage of that term is now entirely misconceived.

The book considers the history and legal theory of a register of ships and examines in detail the practice and procedures in a number of leading flag States. As before, the individual national chapters have been set out, as far as possible, in a common format to enable the practitioner or ship-owner to gain quick access to the relevant material and to compare easily the requirements of one jurisdiction with another.

Since the publication of the second edition of this work in 2009 our world and previously assumed constants in domestic politics and international relations have changed dramatically and in unforeseen ways. Developments affecting the subject-matter – such as the influences of shifting attitudes towards globalisation, the impact of technology on the operation of the vessels themselves, heightened requirements of safety and security and environmental protection, together with demands for ever-greater transparency in offshore jurisdictions and beneficial ownership structures – deserve a new edition to remain contemporary.

Unchanged since 2009 is the dominance of the three leading open registries of Panama, Liberia and the Marshall Islands both in terms of tonnage and number of vessels. The use of technology, such as the provision of electronic certificates to vessels, is now being embraced by some registers and to varying degrees. One expects this will in time become the norm and may change the way we understand the process, if not the legal nature, of the documentation of ships. Where possible, mention is made in the individual national chapters of the use of technology including the ability of a register to receive documents electronically and to issue certification in this way.

New analysis is included in respect of the developing jurisprudence from two cases decided by the International Tribunal of the Law of the Sea, concerning the meaning of the principle of "genuine link" and the true supervisory role of a flag State, for which judgment in the later decision was delivered since the publication of the second edition. The introductory legal chapters have been expanded to discuss the duties of a flag State in this particular light and also consider the effect of the Maritime Labour Convention and developments including the Recognised Organisation Code and the IMO Instruments Implementation Code.

A new chapter is included for the British Virgin Islands as a Category 1 registry within the Red Ensign Group. Due to the size of their respective merchant fleets the national chapters for Belize, Luxembourg and Madeira have been discontinued in this edition. In the interest of brevity and focus in the national chapters, the detailed consideration of company formation requirements, double taxation treaties, taxes and fee structures, and radio accounting authorities for each jurisdiction has been removed or abbreviated. The number of forms reproduced in the appendices has also been given more focus, and limited to those typical and representative of the major flag States and certain of those from the Red Ensign Group.

Mindful of the benefits of a combined source of reference, new statistical content is also found in the provision of the Paris MOU white–grey–black lists as an essential barometer of flag State performance, updated analysis of the merchant fleet of the world by registry and by beneficial ownership, and the STCW white list is included for the first time.

The book is not intended to provide formal legal advice upon any particular situation. Errors or inconsistencies among the myriad contributors from each national jurisdiction, ingathered over a prolonged period, are mine alone. I have attempted to state the law in this dynamic area as I understood it on 1 March 2018.

E.W.
Edinburgh
14 March 2018

ACKNOWLEDGEMENTS

I would like to thank first of all Richard Coles for the opportunity to become involved in this project in 2008. Ten years on, Richard has asked me to pick up the ball and run with it and I am privileged to do so. In addition to his consulting role in this edition, Richard has contributed five of the national chapters, including the Cayman Islands content in view of his close association with that registry in the commercial and luxury yacht arena, culminating in his appointment for some years now as a member of the Cayman Islands Shipowners Advisory Council – Yacht Committee.

We both wish to recognise and thank the following individuals and organisations for their kind assistance, without which it would not have been possible to produce this book:

Mr. John Aune, Deputy Director and Ms. Exie Tomlinson-Panton, Registrar of Shipping, Cayman Registry

Captain Raman Bala, Director, Virgin Islands Shipping Registry

Mr. Peter Buhagiar, Chief Registrar and Mr. Gordon Cutajar, Assistant Registrar of Ships, Malta Merchant Shipping Directorate

Ms. Yvonne Dawkins, UK Ship Register

Captain Peter Green, Principal Registrar, Barbados Maritime Ship Registry

Mr. V. Hariharan, Partner, Haridass Ho & Partners, Singapore

Mr. Seymour Harley, Registrar of Ships, Maritime Authority of Jamaica

Mr. Cliff Lui, Managing Associate, Addleshaw Goddard LLP, Hong Kong

Mr. Greg Maj, Chief Registrar, LISCR LLC, New York

Ms. Rainelda Mata-Kelly, Law Offices Rainelda Mata-Kelly, Panama

Ms. Carolyn Moree, Deputy Director and Registrar, Bahamas Maritime Administration

Mr. John Ramage, Chief Operating Officer, International Registries (UK) Ltd, London

Ms. Dee Rescigno and Captain Michael Decharles, Vanuatu Maritime Services Ltd, New York

Ms. Tone Olsen Riesnes, NIS-NOR, Norway

Mr. Edward Robinson, Registrar of Shipping, Bermuda Shipping and Maritime Authority

Mrs. Joanna Welch, Associate, Gateley plc, London

Mr. Dick Welsh and Mr. Cameron Mitchell, Isle of Man Ship Registry

Ms. Caitlyn Wilson, Legal PA, Addleshaw Goddard LLP, Edinburgh

Ms. Yinca Williams, Legal Department, Office of the Commissioner for Maritime Affairs of St Vincent and the Grenadines, Geneva

Mr. John Wolf, Managing Partner, and Mr. Damien Magee, Senior Associate, Campbells, Cayman Islands and British Virgin Islands

International Maritime Organisation

Paris MoU on Port State Control

United Nations Conference on Trade and Development, *Review of Maritime Transport* series

United Nations Treaty Collection

Finally, my heartfelt thanks to Sinéad for everything accomplished at home and for our boys that was done while I worked on this edition, for your calm patience and support.

TABLE OF CASES

Angel Bell, The [1979] 2 Lloyd's Rep 491 ....1.3

Assunzione, The [1954] P150...1.14

Chartered Mercantile Bank of India v Netherlands Steam Navigation Co Ltd 27
    (1883) 10 QBD 521 .... 1.14, 1.32

Chevron North America, The [2002] 1 Lloyd's Rep 77...5.1, 5.25

Chung Chi Cheung v The King [1939] AC 160...1.31

Cunard SS Co v Mellon, 262 US 123 (1923)..3.5

Curtis v Wild [1991] 4 All ER 172..3.39

European and Australian Royal Mail Company Ltd v Peninsular and Oriental Steam
    Navigation Com (1866) 14 LT 704 ....3.42

Giuseppe di Vittorio, The [1998] 1 Lloyd's Rep 136...5.3

Global Marine Drilling Co v Triton Holdings Ltd, 23 November 1999 (unreported),
    Outer House, Court of Session 3.41

Hartwig v United States 19 F 2d 417 (1927) 3.9

Il Congreso del Partido [1978] QB 500..5.25

Indian Grace, The [1998] 1 Lloyd's Rep 1..1.38

Industrial Investment Corp of India Ltd v Bombay Offshore Supplies & Services Ltd
    (20 February 1993) Dubai Court of Cassation No. 331/1992....................................3.41

KeyBank National Association v The Ship "Blaze" [2007] 2 NZLR 271 ....1.33

Lauritzen v Larsen 345 US 571 (1953) 1.32, 3.4

Liechtenstein v Guatemala (Second Phase) [1955] ICJ Rep 4
    (The Nottebohm Case) 3.11–3.17, 3.33

Liverpool Borough Bank v Turner (1860) 29 LJ Ch 827 ....1.33

Longshoremen v Ariadne Shipping Co, 397 US 195 (1970) 3.5

M/V "Virginia G" Case, Panama v Guinea-Bissau, Merits, ITLOS
    Case No 19, ICGJ 452 (ITLOS 2014) 3.32, 3.33, 3.34, 3.36, 4.2

M/V "Saiga", The Case (Saint Vincent and the Grenadines v Guinea), 4 December 1997

M/V "Saiga", The (No.2) Case (Saint Vincent and the Grenadines v Guinea),
    ITLOS Case no 2, 1 July 1999.. 3.27 3.28, 3.34, 3.36

McCulloch v Sociedad Nacional de Marineros de Honduras, 372 US 10 (1963) 3.5

Muscat Dhows Case, France v Great Britain, Award, (1961) XI RIAA 83, ICGJ 406
    (PCA 1905), 8 August 1905, Permanent Court of Arbitration 3.3

Naim Molvan v Attorney General for Palestine [1948] AC 351 .... 1.1, 1.4

Perks v Clark [2001] 2 Lloyd's Rep 431 .... 3.38, 3.41

R (on the application of Miller) v Secretary of State for Exiting the European Union
    [2017] UKSC 5...3.2

R v Goodwin [2006] 1 WLR 546 ....3.42

R v Bolden and Dean [1998] 2 Cr App R 171... 1.5, 1.19

TABLE OF CASES

Ripon City, The [1897] P 226 ....1.38
Sea Eagle, The [2012] 2 Lloyd's Rep 37...3.39
Spector v Norwegian Cruise Line Ltd 545 US 119 (2005) 1.32, 3.5
St Machar, The (1939) 65 Ll L Rep 119 ....3.38
Steedman v Scofield [1992] 2 Lloyd's Rep 163..3.42
Stolt Loyalty, The [1995] 1 Lloyd's Rep 598...5.1
Virginius Case, The (1874) 76 Parliamentary Papers (Spain No.3) 299 .... 3.1, 3.28
Von Rocks, The [1998] 2 Lloyd's Rep 198 ....3.38, 3.41
Wells v The Owners of the Gas Float Whitton (No. 2) [1897] AC 337 ....3.38
Wildenhus's Case, 120 US 1, 12 (1887)..3.5

TABLE OF LEGISLATION

Act for the Registration of British Vessels
  1845 .... 1.37
Act of 12 June 1987 No.48 establishing
  a Norwegian International Ship
  Register (Norway) 20.3, 20.5,
                                                      20.18
  s 1 .... 3.43, 20.4
  s 3 .... 20.3
  s 4 .... 20.8
Acte de Navigation 1793 (France) 1.15
Aliens Restriction (Amendment) Act 1919
  s 5 .... 24.15
Amendment Law 108(I)/2005 (Cyprus)
  s 3(a) 12.15
Amendment Law 169(1)/2004 (Cyprus)
  s 4 .... 12.15
Associations Law, Title 5 (Liberia) 17.7
Basic Law of the HKSAR (Hong Kong) 14.2
Beneficial Ownership (Companies)
  Regulations 2017 (Cayman Islands) ... 4.27
Beneficial Ownership (Limited Liability
  Companies) Regulations 2017
  (Cayman Islands) 4.27
British Nationality Act 1981 .... 9.6. 13.6,
                                                      15.6, 24.6
British Overseas Territories Act 2002
  s 1 .... 9.1, 10.6
Business Companies Act (Amendment
  of Schedules) Order 2017, SI 2017/17
  (BVI) 10.28
Business Companies Act 2004 (BVI) 10.28
  ss 161–168 .... 10.28
Business Corporation Act (Liberia) 6.5, 6.21,
                                                      17.7, 17.11
Business Corporations Act
  (Marshall Islands) 19.7
Companies Act (2006, Revised Edition,
  Cap. 50) (Singapore) 22.7

Companies (Amendment) Law 2017
  (Cayman Islands) 4.27
Companies Act (Cap. 191) (Vanuatu) 25.7
Companies Act (New Zealand) 25.7
Companies Act 1929 .... 17.7
Companies Act 1930 (Gibraltar) 13.7
Companies Act 1948 .... 25.7
Companies Act 1967 .... 25.7
Companies Act 1994 (St Vincent and
  the Grenadines) 23.7
Companies Act 2004 (Jamaica) 16.6, 16.7
Companies Act 2006 .... 24.7
  s 859A 24.29
Companies Law (2016 Revision)
  (Cayman Islands)
  s 183 .... 11.6
Companies Ordinance (Cap. 32)
  (Hong Kong) 14.6
  Pt XI 14.8, 14.12
Companies Ordinance (Cap. 622)
  (Hong Kong)
  Pt 16 .... 14.6, 14.7, 14.12
Consolidated Act no. 856 of 1 July 2010
  (Denmark)
  s 46 .... 1.16
Council Directive 95/21/EC established
  common criteria for control of
  ships by port States and
  harmonising procedures on
  inspection and detention
  throughout the EU 2.22, 2.25, 2.27
Council Directive 99/35/EC in relation
  to ro-ro ferries and high-speed
  passenger crafts 2.27
Council Directive 2005/35/EC on Ship
  Source Pollution 2.25
Council Directive 2009/15/EC in relation
  to Recognised Organisations 2.27

TABLE OF LEGISLATION

Council Directive 2009/16/EC of the
European Parliament and of the
Council on port State control..............2.27
art 24..2.27
Council Directive 2009/17/EC in
relation to vessel traffic monitoring....2.27
Council Directive 2009/20/EC in relation
to insurance for maritime claims........2.27
Council Regulation (EEC) No 2137/85
on the European Economic Interest
Grouping 9.6
art 1..24.6
Council Regulation (EC) No 417/2002
on the accelerated phasing-in of
double hull or equivalent design
requirements for single hull
oil tankers 2.25
Criminal Justice (International
Co-operation) Act 1990
s 19..1.5
Disabilities Act of 1990 (USA) 3.5
Dominica International Maritime Act 2002...... 1.8
European Economic Interest Grouping
Regulations 1989, SI 1989/638.............9.6
Finance Act 2000
s 22..24.18
Sch 22 ....24.19
Finance Act 2005
s 93..24.19
Hong Kong (British Nationality)
Order 1986......................... 9.6, 10.6, 13.6,
15.6, 24.6
Hovercraft Act 1968 (Application)
Order 1986 (IOM)...............................3.43
Immigration Restriction (Commonwealth
Citizens) Act 1945 (Jamaica)..............16.5
Inland Revenue Ordinance (Cap. 112)
(Hong Kong)......................................14.12
International Business Companies
(Amendment and Consolidation) Act,
Chapter 149 of the Revised Laws of
St Vincent and the Grenadines 2009
(St Vincent and the Grenadines).........23.7
s 67..23.8
s 108..23.10
s 180..23.19
International Business Companies
Act 1991 (Barbados) 8.7
International Companies Act (Vanuatu).......25.7,
25.16

Labour Code (Panama)
art 266...21.18
Law 2687/53 for the Protection of
Foreign Capital (Greece)....................6.11
Law No. 5 of 1997 (Panama)..................21.10
Law No. 8 of 1925 (Panama)....................21.3
Law No. 11 of 1973 (Panama) 21.3, 21.11
Law No. 14 of 1980 (Panama).......21.3, 21.24,
21.27
Law No. 18 of 2015 (Panama)..................21.9
Law No. 32 of 1927 (Panama)..................21.7
Law No. 43 of 1984 (Panama).......21.3, 21.24,
21.27
Law No. 47 of 2013 (Panama)..................21.9
Law No. 55 of 2008 (Panama).......21.3, 21.24,
21.27
Law No. 57 of (Panama) 21.1, 21.3, 21.13
art 70...5.23, 5.28
art 78...5.31
Law No. 83 of 1973 (Panama)..................21.3
Law No. 234 of 14 June 1989
(Italy)......................................5.10, 5.22
Law of the Flag Act (Flaggenrechtgesetz)
(Germany)..5.18
Liberian Code of Laws 1956 .... 1.8
Limited Liability Companies
(Amendment) Law 2017
(Cayman Islands)................................4.27
Maritime Act (Cap. 131) (Vanuatu)...........5.29,
5.30, 25.3
s 8..25.12
s 17(1)..25.4
s 31..25.8
s 31(1)(d) 5.28
s 31(2A)..5.27
s 31(3)..5.30
s 31(4)..25.8
s 31(5)..25.8
s 31(6)..25.9
Maritime Act (Liberia)
s 51..6.5
Maritime Act (Norway)............................20.18
Maritime Act 1990 (Marshall Islands)..........19.3,
19.12, 19.24
s 103..19.3
s 203...19.4, 19.6
s 260..19.12
s 270..19.13
s 271..5.28
s 272..5.23

xx

TABLE OF LEGISLATION

Maritime and Port Authority of Singapore Act
1996 (Singapore) 22.2
Maritime Law (Liberia), Title 21 .... 5.30,
17.3, 17.23
  s 51(1) 17.4
  s 51(2) 17.4
  s 51(2)(a) 17.4
  s 51(3) 17.4
  s 51(6) 17.4, 17.5
  s 51(7) 17.4
  s 57(1) 1.36
  s 85 .... 5.23
  s 89 .... 17.10
  s 91 .... 5.28
  s 94 .... 5.23
Maritime Regulations (Liberia) 17.20, 19.3
  Ch X 17.13
Maritime Regulations (Marshall Islands)
  Ch 7 .... 19.15
Maritime Regulations Order No. 25
of 1990 (Vanuatu) 25.3
  s 40 .... 25.11
Merchant Shipping (Amendment)
Act 1990 (Malta) 5.21, 18.6
Merchant Shipping (Categorisation
of Registries of Overseas Territories)
Order 2008, SI 2008/1243 .... 10.2
Merchant Shipping (Categorisation of
Relevant British Possessions)
Order 2003, SI 2003/1248 .... 9.4
Merchant Shipping (Certification,
Safe Manning, Hours of Work and
Watchkeeping) Regulations
(2004 Revision) (Cayman Islands) ... 11.11
Merchant Shipping (Fees and Taxing
Provisions) Law of 2010 (Cyprus) 12.3
Merchant Shipping (Fees and Taxing
Provisions) Laws of 1992–2007
(Cyprus) 12.3
Merchant Shipping (Fees) Regulations
2012 (Bermuda) 9.22
Merchant Shipping (Manning and STCW)
Regulations 2014 (Isle of Man) 15.11
Merchant Shipping (Manning,
Training (Gibraltar) and Certification
for Seafarers) Regulations 2006
(Gibraltar) 13.3
Merchant Shipping (Maritime Labour
Convention) (Medical Certification)
Regulations 2014 (Cayman Islands) ... 11.11

Merchant Shipping (Masters and
Seamen) Laws 1963 to 2002 (Cyprus). 12.19
Merchant Shipping (MLC) Regulations
2012 (Bahamas) 7.9
  reg 2.5.2 .... 7.17
  reg 4.2 .... 7.17
Merchant Shipping (Officer Nationality)
Regulations 1995, SI 1995/1427 .... 24.15
Merchant Shipping (Port State Control)
Regulations 1995, SI 1995/3128 .... 2.22
Merchant Shipping (Port State Control)
Regulations 2011, SI 2011/2601 .... 2.22
Merchant Shipping (Qualified Owners
of Manx Ships) (Relevant Countries)
Regulations 2007 (Isle of Man) 15.7
Merchant Shipping (Registration of
Ships) Regulations 1993,
SI 1993/3138 .... 4.5, 5.7,
24.3, App VI
  reg 1(2) 5.4
  reg 2(5) 1.37
  reg 6(1) 1.38
  reg 7 .... 24.6
  reg 7(1)(a) 4.5
  reg 7(1)(f) 4.5
  reg 8 .... 24.6
  regs 11–16 .... 6.32
  reg 22 .... 24.22
  reg 24 .... 24.20
  reg 28(1)(a) 24.22
  reg 28(1)(b) 24.22
  reg 33 .... 24.25
  reg 36(1) 24.25
  reg 36(5) 24.25
  reg 57 .... 24.27
  reg 59 .... 1.38, 9.24, 24.28
  reg 63 .... 24.31
  reg 68 .... 24.21
  reg 69 .... 24.21
  Sch 4 .... 1.35
Merchant Shipping (Registration of Ships)
Regulations 1996 (Singapore)
  reg 3 .... 1.16
Merchant Shipping (Registration
of Ships) Regulations 2003
(Bermuda) 9.3, 9.4
  reg 5(1) 9.6
  reg 5(2) 9.7
  reg 47 .... 9.24
  reg 55 .... 9.20

TABLE OF LEGISLATION

Merchant Shipping (Registration
of Ships)(Amendment) Regulations
2017, SI 2017/879 ....24.25
Merchant Shipping (Registration of
Ships, Sales and Mortgages) Laws of
1963 to 2005 (Cyprus) 12.3
s 5(1)(a)..6.5
s 5A(1) 12.15
s 23B..5.3
s 23J..5.27
s 23J(3) 5.30
s 23(2)...12.27
s 23C..12.16
s 23D..12.16
s 23N..12.17
Merchant Shipping (Registration)
(Fees and Charges) Regulations
(Hong Kong)...14.3
Merchant Shipping (Registration)
(Ship's Names) Regulations
(Hong Kong)...14.3
s 3..14.4
s 11(4) 14.6
Merchant Shipping (Registration)
(Tonnage) Regulations (Hong Kong) 14.3
Merchant Shipping (Registration)
Act 1995 (Gibraltar)............................13.3
Merchant Shipping (Registration)
Act 1995 (Gibraltar)
s 7(1)(b) 13.11
s 7(3)(a)..13.6
s 7(3)(b) 13.6
s 32..13.11
s 33(1)..13.14
Sch 2 ....13.6
Merchant Shipping (Registration)
Ordinance (Cap. 415)
(Hong Kong)..............................14.3, 14.4
s 2..3.43
s 11(1)(b) 14.7
s 20(2)...14.8
s 68..14.6
s 84..14.8
Merchant Shipping (Safe Manning,
Hours of Work and Watchkeeping)
Law of 2000 (Law 105(I)/2000)
(Cyprus) 12.19
Merchant Shipping (Safety of
Commercial Sailing and Motor
Vessels) Regulations 2004, SI 2004/6 . 10.32

Merchant Shipping (Salvage and Pollution)
Act 1994
Sch 4 ....3.38
Merchant Shipping (Standards of Training,
Certification and Watch-keeping)
Regulations 2015, SI 2015/782........24.13
Merchant Shipping (Training and
Certification) Regulations (Malta) 18.10
Merchant Shipping (Training,
Certification and Manning)
Regulations 1998 (Singapore)...........22.15
Merchant Shipping (Training,
Certification, Manning and
Watchkeeping) Regulations 2011
(Bahamas) 7.9
Merchant Shipping (Vessels in
Commercial Use for Sport or Pleasure)
Regulations 1998, SI 1998/2771........6.36
Merchant Shipping Act (1854)
Amendment Act 1880
s 2..1.37
Merchant Shipping Act (Bahamas)
s 2..5.3
Merchant Shipping Act (Chapter 179)
(Singapore)
s 13(1)..1.36
Merchant Shipping Act (Malta)
s 84A..5.3
s 84B..5.21
s 84M..5.27
s 84W(1)..5.16
Merchant Shipping Act 1854 ....1.37
Merchant Shipping Act 1894 ....1.13
s 1..1.12
s 2..1.12
s 742..3.38
Merchant Shipping Act 1970
(Commencement No. 12)
Order 1995, SI 1995/1426 ....24.15
Merchant Shipping Act 1973 (Malta)........18.3,
18.20
art 4 ....18.7
art 5 ....18.19
art 12 ....18.19
art 14 ....18.17
art 15 ....18.17
art 16(5) 18.19
art 19A 18.20
art 28(2) 18.23
art 38(3) 18.22

art 39 ....18.22
art 84C 18.7
art 84G 18.7
art 84H 18.7
art 84I 18.7
art 84M 18.7
art 84P 18.8
art 84T 18.8
art 84W 18.8
Pt IIA 18.6

Merchant Shipping Act 1976
     (Bahamas) 7.3, 7.7, 7.9
  s 3(4) 7.6
  s 3(5) 7.15
  s 13(1) 7.18
  s 26 ....7.15
  s 57(1) 1.37

Merchant Shipping Act 1982 (St Vincent
     and the Grenadines) 23.3

Merchant Shipping Act 1988 ....1.13, 4.5
  s 2 ....1.13

Merchant Shipping Act 1995 ...... 1.4, 1.33, 9.4,
                                   11.2, 15.3, 24.3,
                                            App V
  s 1(1) 1.8
  s 6(1) 1.4
  s 8 ....24.4
  s 17(1) 5.3
  s 17(1) 24.9
  s 18 ....24.3
  s 85(2) 24.15
  s 308 ....24.4
  Sch 1 ....1.39, 5.16

Merchant Shipping Act 1996
     (Act 7 of 1996, Cap. 179)
     (Singapore) 22.3, 22.25

Merchant Shipping Act 2001 (BVI) 10.3
  s 3(1) 10.3
  s 4(1) 10.6
  s 4(2) 10.7
  s 5 ....10.7
  s 6(1) 10.7
  s 7 ....10.5
  s 11(3) 10.4
  s 111 ....10.11
  s 13(1) 10.19
  s 14(1) 10.19
  s 20(2) 10.17
  s 27(1) 10.22
  s 27(2) 10.22

ss 21–35 ....10.8
s 28 ....10.8
s 28(3) 10.8
s 33 ....10.9
s 36 ....10.21
s 36(6) 10.21
s 83 ....10.26, 10.27
s 414 ....10.19

Merchant Shipping Act 2002 (Bermuda) 9.3
s 23 ....9.4
s 31 ....9.4
s 31 ....9.8
s 32 ....9.8
s 36 9,6

Merchant Shipping Law (2016 Revision)
     (Cayman Islands) 11.3, 11.25
s 2 ....11.21
s 4(1) 11.6
s 4(2) 11.6
s 5 ....11.6, 11.7
s 6 ....11.7
s 7 ....11.5
s 13(1) 11.18
s 14(1) 11.18
s 27(1) 11.21
s 27(2) 11.21
ss 21–35 ....11.8
s 28 ....11.8
s 28(1) 11.8
s 28(3) 11.8
s 33 ....11.9
s 36 ....11.20
s 36(6) 11.20
s 419 ....11.18

Merchant Shipping Registration
     Act 1991 (Isle of Man) 15.3
s 45 ....15.6, 15.7

Navigation Act of 1793 (France) 3.8

Navigation Code (Italy)
     art 156 ....5.22

Norwegian Act re Working Hours
     on Ships 4.42

Norwegian International Ship Register Act 4.42

Norwegian Maritime Code of
     24 June 1994 No.39 ....20.3, 20.5
s 33 ....3.43

Norwegian Seamen's Act 4.42

Oil Pollution Act 1990 (USA) 2.25

Order no.1053 of 26 August 2013
     (Denmark) 5.21

TABLE OF LEGISLATION

Registered Business Company Act
 2002 (Liberia) 17.7, 17.11
Regulation of 18 June 2009 No. 666
 (Norway)...20.9
Ship Registration Act 1992 (NZ)
 s 2...5.3
 s 2(1)...3.43
Shipping (Amendment) Act 2007
 (St Vincent and the Grenadines).........23.3
Shipping (Training Certification,
 Safe Manning, Hours of Work and
 Watchkeeping) Regulations 1998
 (Jamaica)................................16.15, 16.16
Shipping Act (Bahamas)
 s 33(3)..5.28
 s 33(4)..5.27
Shipping Act 1994 (Barbados)..............8.3, 8.9
 s 8...8.4
 s 8(11)...8.4
 s 9(2)..8.10
 s 10...8.4
 S 27(2) 8.22
 s 38...8.11
 s 47(4)..8.10
 s 47(5)..8.11
 S 49...8.23
 S 86(1) 8.16
Shipping Act 1998 (Jamaica)...........16.2, 16.21
 s 18...16.12
 s 19...16.13
 s 20(2)..16.5
 s 29...16.27
 s 32...16.2
 s 43...16.26
 s 69...16.25

 s 80..16.25
Shipping Act 2001 (Canada)
 s 46..1.16
Shipping Act 2004 (St Vincent
 and the Grenadines)............................23.3
 s 5A(1)..5.2, 23.11
 s 5B(1) 5.27, 23.11
 s 5B(2) 5.31
 s 5D(1)...23.12
 ss 91–103 ....23.14
Shipping and Maritime Authority
 Act 2016 (Bermuda)..............................9.2
Shipping and Navigation Act 1784.............1.15
 s 3...1.10
 s 19...1.26
Shipping Corporation Act (Barbados) 8.7
Shipping Registration Act 1981 (Australia)
 s 3...5.3
 s 8...1.16
Shipping Registration Act 1981 (Australia)
 s 12...1.16
Telecommunications Act 2006 ....10.16
Tonnage Tax (Training Requirement)
 (Amendment) Regulations 2017,
 SI 2017/882......................................24.18
Tonnage Tax (Training Requirement)
 Regulations 2000, SI 2129/2000.......24.18
Utility Regulation and Competition
 Law 2016 (Cayman Islands).............11.17
Vanuatu Maritime Act, Cap. 131 ....1.8
 s 16..1.8
Virgin Islands Constitution Order 2007,
 SI 2007/1678.......................................10.1
Virgin Islands International Business
 Companies Ordinance.........................25.7

xxiv

TABLE OF CONVENTIONS

Athens Convention relating to the Carriage of
Passengers and their Luggage
by Sea 1974 ....24.9, 24.22
Code for Recognized Organizations
2015...2.10
Code for the Implementation of Mandatory
IMO Instruments 2007
Code for the Implementation of Mandatory
IMO Instruments 2011 ....2.8
Code of International Standards and
Recommended Practices for a
Safety Investigation into a Marine
Casualty or Marine Incident 2010 ......2.10
Convention on the High
Seas 1958........................ 3.14, 3.22, 3.30,
App VII
art 2 .... 1.2
art 5 .... 1.2, 1.25, 1.30, 2.6, 3.13,
3.17, 3.18, 3.24
art 6 ....5.11, 5.12
art 10 ....1.30, 2.6
Hague Convention Abolishing the
Requirement of Legalisation for
Foreign Public Documents 1961 ....12.25
International Convention for the Control
and Management of Ships' Ballast
Water and Sediments 2017 ....2.10
International Convention for the
Prevention of Pollution from
Ships, 1973 as modified by the
Protocol of 1978 ....2.8, 2.25, 4.34, 6.31,
10.31, 11.30, 12.5
Annex I reg 4 ....2.12
Annex II reg 10 ....2.12
International Convention for the Safety
of Life at Sea 1974 .... 1.6, 2.8, 2.25,
2.34, 2.35, 4.34,
6.31, 6.35, 7.5, 10.31,

11.30, 11.31, 12.5, 12.26,
13.20, 14.10, 18.12, 19.18
reg XI-1/3 ....1.27
reg XI-1/5 ....4.28
regs 1-5 ....6.35
reg 6 ....2.12
reg 13(b) 18.12
International Convention on Civil Liability
for Bunker Oil Pollution Damage
2001 .... 12.25, 24.9, 24.22
International Convention on Civil
Liability for Oil Pollution
Damage 1969 ....24.9, 24.22
International Convention on Load Lines
1966 .... 1.6, 2.8, 6.35, 12.5
art 3 ....7.23
art 13 ....2.12
art 87 ....6.35
International Convention on Maritime
Liens and Mortgages 1993 ....5.33, 5.34,
App X
art 16 ....5.33
International Convention on Salvage 1989
art 1(b) 3.39
International Convention on
Standards of Training,
Certification and Watchkeeping
for Seafarers 1978 .... 2.8, 2.37, 2.38,
2.39, 4.34, 6.24,
6.35, 7.9, 7.10, 8.13, 8.14,
9.16, 10.11, 10.12, 11.11,
12.19, 12.20, 13.17, 15.11,
16.15, 16.18, 17.10, 18.10,
18.11, 19.17, 21.17, 22.16,
23.14, 23.15, 24.13, 25.11, 25.12
art 8 ....25.11
art 9 ....6.35
reg 1/10 .... 8.13, 8.15, 14.10, 23.15, 25.12

xxv

TABLE OF CONVENTIONS

International Convention on Tonnage
  Measurement of Ships 1969........2.8, 3.46,
                10.29, 11.28,
                16.26, 18.12, 22.22
  art 3(1) 1.6
  art 7...2.12
International Convention Relating to
  the Arrest of Sea-going Ships
  1952...3.39
International Convention relating to the
  Limitation of Liability of Owners
  of Sea-going Ships 1957......................3.39
International Management Code
  for the Safe Operation of
  Ships and for Pollution
  Prevention 2002 ....1.6, 2.29, 2.30,
                2.31, 2.32, 2.33
International Regulations for
  Preventing Collisions at
  Sea 1972 ....2.8. 10.31, 11.30
International Ship and Port Facility
  Security Code 2.34, 2.35, 2.36
Maritime Labour Convention
  2006.............. 4.34, 4.35, 4.36, 6.13, 6.23,
                7.5, 7.9, 11.11, 24.22, 24.33
Nairobi International Convention
  on the Removal of Wrecks
  2007...24.9, 24.22
United Nations Convention on
  Conditions for Registration
  of Ships 1986 ....1.18, 4.37, 3.19, 5.13,
                5.24, 5.25, App IX

art 2...5.24
art 7.....................................3.19, 3.20, 3.22
art 9...3.19, 3.20
art 9(2)...3.22
art 10....................................3.19, 3.21, 3.23
art 11 ....5.25
art 11 ....5.5
art 11(1) 5.25
art 11(2)(h)..5.25
art 11(2)(i)...5.25
art 11(5) 5.25
art 12...5.5, 5.25
art 12(1) 5.25
art 12(2) 5.25
art 12(3) 5.25
art 12(4) 5.25
art 87..3.19, 3.20
United Nations Convention on the Law of the
  Sea 1982 ....3.18, 3.22, 3.26, 3.27,
                4.2, App VIII
  art 25 ....2.16
  art 87...2.1
  art 91 .... 3.18, 3.24, 3.28, 3.29, 3.30, 3.34
  art 92 ....3.30
  art 94 ....2.2, 3.18, 3.30, 3.36
  art 217 ....2.3, 2.6
  art 218 ....2.16
  art 292 ....3.27
United Nations International Convention
  on Maritime Liens and Mortgages
  1993......................................5.5, 5.11, 5.14
  art 16 ....5.14, 5.27

xxvi

CHAPTER 1

The legal concept of ship registration

the freedom of the open sea . . . is a freedom of ships which fly, and are entitled to fly, the flag of a State.[1]

General principles

1.1 To display a flag is an ancient symbol of loyalty and affiliation. Ships of all kinds across the world – as diverse as massive container vessels, oil tankers, offshore support fleets, luxury yachts, drilling units and dumb barges – have at least one thing in common. They fly a national flag and display a 'home' port of choice. In the twenty-first century such a tradition may seem rather antiquated, like flag signals at the Battle of Trafalgar or communication by semaphore, yet remains an essential and practical ingredient of international law and commerce. The instant visual identification of the nationality of a ship in this way whilst underway is to allow any vessel to transit international waters, the high seas, unhindered. Consistent with this purpose, tradition dictates that the national flag does not require to be flown when a ship is alongside in port because, at that time, she is subject to the jurisdiction of the adjoining land.

1.2 The freedom of the high seas is one of the fundamental principles of public international law. The 1958 Geneva Convention on the High Seas, Article 2, provides that "The high seas being open to all nations, no State may validly purport to subject any part of them to its sovereignty."[2] Such freedom means the unrestricted access of vessels belonging to all nations, to all parts of the sea that are not included in the territorial sea or internal waters of a State. Land-locked countries are not excluded from this freedom – a treaty of 1921 enshrines the principle that a State with no sea border may yet be a flag State that can register ships under its jurisdiction and any named place within that territory may be the port of registry for such vessels.[3] Land-locked countries with ship registries include Austria, Bolivia, Ethiopia, Luxembourg, Mongolia and Switzerland. In order that the principle of unrestricted access to the high seas should not lead to a situation of anarchy

---

1 *Naim Molvan* v. *Attorney General for Palestine* [1948] AC 351, 369 *per* Lord Simonds.

2 The idea of the freedom of the seas is attributed to the Dutch lawyer Grotius, whose treatise *Mare liberum* was published in 1608 in response to Portuguese claims of sovereignty over tracts of seas in the East Indies. Grotius' theory is based on the principle that the high seas are avenues of commerce not capable of appropriation by any single nation.

3 League of Nations 'Declaration recognising the Right to a Flag of States having no Sea-coast', signed in Barcelona, 20 April 1921.

and abuse, international law lays down rules providing a framework for the exercise of that freedom, and looks to individual States to ensure and enforce compliance with those rules through the jurisdiction exercised over their national vessels.

1.3 A cardinal rule is that jurisdiction over a vessel on the high seas rests solely with the State to which the vessel belongs. A second rule, which is a corollary of this essential principle, is that all vessels using the high seas must possess a national character. Nationality is attributed to vessels flying the flag of a State in which the vessel is publicly registered. Article 5 of the High Seas Convention provides that "Ships shall have the nationality of the State whose flag they are entitled to fly." This language is echoed in the decision of Donaldson J (as he then was) in the case of *The Angel Bell*.[4] The case concerned a dispute between cargo interests and the mortgagee of a Panamanian vessel. The question arose as to the proper law of the mortgage. The Commercial Court held that "A ship is, in effect, a floating piece of the nation whose flag it wears . . . *prima facie*, mortgages either of foreign land or ships will be governed by the law of their situs or flag."[5]

1.4 A ship possessing no nationality – a stateless ship – enjoys no protection in international law. She is unable to engage in lawful trade since ports will deny entry to her. The UK Merchant Shipping Act 1995 provides that clearance shall not be granted for any ship until the Master has declared to a customs officer the name of the nation to which he claims that the ship belongs.[6] If a ship attempts to proceed out to sea without such clearance, she may be detained until the declaration is made. The earliest UK legislation to the same effect was in 1784.[7] Furthermore, a stateless ship is liable to seizure. The case of *Naim Molvan* v. *Attorney General for Palestine*[8] concerned the vessel *Asya*, which was attempting to land Jewish settlers contrary to the Immigration Ordinance in force in Palestine in 1948. The vessel was carrying no papers and was arrested by a British destroyer 100 miles from the Palestine coast, flying no flag to which she was entitled – although when approached she hoisted the Turkish flag and, when boarded, the Zionist flag. The Palestinian court ordered the forfeiture of the vessel even though she had been seized on the high seas. On appeal, the Privy Council rejected the proposition that the principle of freedom of the high seas extended to a ship possessing no nationality and accepted as a valid statement of the law the following passage from Oppenheim's *International Law*:

> In the interest of order on the open sea, a vessel not sailing under the maritime flag of a State enjoys no protection whatever, for the freedom of navigation on the open sea is a freedom for such vessels only as sail under the flag of a State.[9]

1.5 The principle that an unregistered ship enjoys no protection under international law extends to a deprivation of the rights established under criminal laws of those on board her on the high seas. In the case of *The Battlestar*[10] the Court of Appeal found that the

---

4 [1979] 2 Lloyd's Rep 491.

5 The distinction between the public and private law usage of this metaphor or legal fiction should be recognised. See further para. 1.31 below.

6 Merchant Shipping Act 1995, s.6(1).

7 Shipping and Navigation Act 1784, s.32 'Ships leaving Port without Certificates to be forfeited'.

8 [1948] AC 351.

9 6th edn, Vol. 1, p. 546.

10 *R. v Bolden and Dean* [1998] 2 Cr App R 171.

owners of a yacht discovered on the high seas in possession of almost 1,500 kg of cannabis resin were not able to plead an abuse of process or unlawful boarding of their vessel by UK customs authorities, because – although showing the home port of Delaware and holding a Certificate of American Ownership – searches in the US Coastguard, federal and State records revealed the yacht to be unregistered in the United States. This case concerned UK legislation in which the offence of drug trafficking applies expressly to UK-registered ships and to "a ship registered in no country or territory".[11] By contrast, enforcement powers cannot be exercised by the UK Customs & Excise against a ship which is registered in any other State without the express request for assistance or permission from the flag State. These circumstances demonstrate well the difference between documentation and registration, which shall be discussed further below.

1.6 The term generally used to describe the attribution of national character to a vessel is registration, meaning the entry of the particulars of the vessel in the public records of a State. For the purpose of many international shipping Conventions, registration in a particular State is a sufficient connecting factor to regard the vessel as possessing that State's nationality.[12] In terms of the International Safety Management Code 2002, for example, the 'Supervising Administration' is defined as "the Government of the State whose flag the ship is entitled to fly".[13] In the International Convention on Load Lines 1966, the 'Administration' is "the Government of the State whose flag the ship is flying".[14]

1.7 Every State may maintain registers in which the particulars of merchant vessels possessing the nationality of that State and flying its flag are entered. Individual nations fix the conditions for the entry of ships in their registers and such entry is generally a precondition for the possession of that State's nationality, the hoisting of the national flag and the issuance to the vessel of documents attesting to its nationality.[15]

1.8 There is a very broad consistency of the statutory language used across flag States large and small in this area. For example, the Liberian Maritime Law[16] provides:

> no vessel engaged in foreign trade shall fly the flag of the Republic of Liberia or be accorded the rights and privileges of a Liberian vessel unless such vessel shall be registered in accordance with the provisions of Chapter 2 of this Title.

The Vanuatu Maritime Act[17] and the Dominica International Maritime Act 2002[18] are in similar terms. For the purposes of the UK Merchant Shipping Act 1995, a British ship is one registered in accordance with that legislation.[19]

1.9 What began historically as a local practice has developed and extended to become the multinational basis of mutual recognition for vessels from every corner of the globe.

---

11 Criminal Justice (International Co-operation) Act 1990, s.19.

12 See, e.g., International Convention on Tonnage Measurement of Ships 1969, Art. 3(1); International Convention on Load Lines 1966, Art. 4(1).

13 Adopted pursuant to the International Convention for the Safety of Life at Sea (SOLAS), 1974.

14 As amended by the Protocol of 1988, Art. 2(2).

15 See further, Chapter 3.

16 Title 21, Liberian Code of Laws 1956, as amended, s.50.

17 Vanuatu Maritime Act, Cap. 131, s.16.

18 Section 29(1) "No Vessel subject to Chapter 1 shall be documented or re-documented under the laws of Dominica or be awarded the rights and privileges of a vessel of Dominica unless that vessel is registered in accordance with the provisions of this Part."

19 Merchant Shipping Act 1995, s.1(1).

The registration of ships has its origins in the laws of imperial Rome[20] and was widespread in the City States of mediaeval Italy. At that time, the name of the ship would have been registered, together with the name of her owner and tonnage, and fraud in such matters could lead to confiscation of the vessel. With reference to the early development of the Italian law merchant, Holdsworth[21] mentions that "the equipment, licensing, loading and registry of ships, the nature and variety of papers which trading ships must carry . . . occupy a large space in the statutes of the Italian towns". In England, the registration system goes back to the seventeenth and eighteenth century Navigation Acts, beginning with a statute of Charles II in 1660.[22] Here can be seen for the first time the compulsory requirement to notify to a government official the characteristics of a vessel, its owners, where it was built – "and that upon such Oath, he or they shall receive a Certificate . . . whereby such Ship or Vessel may for the future pass and be deemed as a Ship belonging to the said Port". That is, a certificate of registration.

1.10 Registration of UK vessels of greater than 15 tons of burden became compulsory, on pain of forfeiture, in 1784.[23] The object of the Navigation Acts was to prevent foreign-owned vessels taking advantage of the commercial privileges enjoyed by vessels flying the British flag; by the late eighteenth century they also sought to restrict entitlement to the flag to ships built within the British dominions.[24]

1.11 The expressions "nationality", "documentation", "flag" and "registration" are often used as if they were interchangeable. This is not simply a question of lay misusage. Imprecise employment of these terms in international Conventions can lead to considerable confusion in the application and interpretation of the law of the sea. It is therefore proposed here to explain the meaning of these four terms, by reference to their function.

Nationality

1.12 A vessel may be considered as possessing the nationality of a State even though she is unregistered, possesses no documents evidencing that nationality, nor flies the flag of that State. The UK Merchant Shipping Act 1894 defined a British ship purely in terms of ownership, regardless of whether or not she had been registered as the Act required:

1. A ship shall not be deemed to be a British ship unless owned wholly by persons of the following description . . .; namely,
    British subjects;
    Bodies corporate established under and subject to the laws of some part of Her Majesty's dominions, and having their principal place of business in those dominions.
2. (1) Every British ship shall . . . be registered under this Act.

---

20 See Williams, 'The Function of Evidence in Roman Law', *Law Magazine and Review* 203 (4th Series); Rienow, *The Test of the Nationality of a Merchant Vessel* (1937).

21 5 *A History of English Law* 73.

22 12 Car. 2, c.18.

23 Shipping and Navigation Act 1784, 26 Geo. 3, c.60, ss. 3 and 32. The long title of this legislation is "An Act for the further Increase and Encouragement of Shipping and Navigation". Section 3 provides that vessels shall "be registered in Manner herein-after mentioned; and that the Person or Persons claiming property therein shall cause the same to be registered, and shall obtain a Certificate of such Registry from the Collector and Comptroller of His Majesty's Customs".

24 For the history of British ship registration, see *Abbott's Law of Merchant Ships and Seamen* (14th edn, 1901).

1.13 The effect of these provisions was to make compulsory the registration of all British-owned ships in the register of British ships provided that in the case of bodies corporate they did not have their principal place of business outside Her Majesty's dominions. Concealment of the British character of such a ship, as for example by sailing her under a foreign register and flag, subjected the vessel to forfeiture.[25] Influenced no doubt by the dramatic increase in the use of foreign flags by domestic shipping companies, after almost 100 years on the statute book, following the amendment of the Merchant Shipping Act 1894 by the Merchant Shipping Act 1988, British character can only be assumed by registration.[26]

1.14 Prior to the enactment of the 1894 Act, this question was considered in *Chartered Mercantile Bank of India* v. *Netherlands Steam Navigation Co Ltd*.[27] This was a collision case concerning a Dutch-registered ship owned and controlled by British subjects through a Dutch subsidiary of an English company, in the judgment of which it was considered "absurd to suppose that the mere fact of carrying the Dutch flag, makes her [i.e., the defendant's ship] a Dutch ship. Pirates carried the flag of every nation, but they were hanged by every nation notwithstanding."[28] This judgment of the English Court of Appeal makes very clear that the motivation for the registration of the vessel in the Netherlands was to enjoy trading routes to Java. The shareholders of the Dutch ship-owning company and the English ship-owning company, which were the owners of the two vessels involved in the collision, were identical. In these circumstances, the court asked "whether the mere fact of obtaining a register in Holland and carrying the Dutch flag makes her a Dutch ship", and Brett LJ found that:

> the mere fact of her being registered in Holland for the purpose of carrying on a Dutch trade . . . does not prevent her from being a British ship . . . If she belong absolutely and entirely to English owners, she is an English ship before she is registered, and whether she is registered or not.[29]

1.15 In the course of history, a number of connecting factors have been put forward as the appropriate test of a vessel's nationality. A statute of George III[30] required every British ship to be of British build; the French Acte de Navigation of 1793 contained a similar provision in respect of French ships. A British ship had to be crewed by British nationals until the middle of the nineteenth century. In the twentieth century, a 1982 report by the United Nations Conference on Trade and Development (UNCTAD) on Conditions for the Registration of Ships[31] listed 28 countries which still required their vessels to be manned entirely by nationals and a further 24 countries which stipulated that key personnel and/or a given percentage of the crew be nationals.

---

25 Legitimate 'dual' registration of a British ship elsewhere, such as through bareboat charter registration into a foreign registry, has always been anathema to UK practice. The inconsistency in principle is that bareboat charter into the UK Register is permitted. See further Chapter 5.

26 Merchant Shipping Act 1988, s.2. This section is now substantially re-enacted in the Merchant Shipping Act 1995, s.1.

27 (1883) 10 QBD 521, approved in the context of choice of law aspects of the judgement in *The Assunzione* [1954] P150.

28 *Per* Brett LJ, at p. 535.

29 *Ibid*, at p. 536: "it has always been held, and it seems to me to be the law, that she cannot evade liability if she is a British ship by the mere fact of her owner omitting to register her as a British ship".

30 Shipping and Navigation Act 1784.

31 TD/B/AC. 34/2, 22 January 1982, considered further at para. 1.18.

1.16 The nationality of the ship-owner, whether a natural person or a body corporate, is often advanced as the criterion for determining a vessel's nationality. In the case of ownership by individuals, the requirement of certain States is that those individuals be nationals, and in many cases resident nationals or domiciled nationals. For example, Australian law requires the registration of any ship which is owned by an Australian national, or where the majority of the owners of shares in the ship are Australian nationals.[32] The Canada Shipping Act requires registration of vessels owned by Canadian citizens or permanent residents.[33] The Danish Merchant Shipping Act states succinctly "in order for a ship to be considered as Danish and fly Danish flag, the owner of the ship shall be Danish".[34] In Singapore, the legislation describes two categories of persons qualified to be owners of ships registered there – citizens of Singapore and bodies corporate incorporated in Singapore.[35]

1.17 In the case of ownership by bodies corporate, national legislation may simply require that the ship be owned by a legal entity incorporated in the relevant jurisdiction without regard to the nationality of the persons participating in the entity or its effective seat of management. In this way, the postal address of a company's registered office may be considered by the national legislation to suffice as the qualification or minimum nexus between the flag State and the beneficial owner of a vessel.[36] To be sure, in many instances that is so regardless of the nationality of the shareholders of the corporate entity. As an example, for the purposes of the Liberian Maritime Law, vessels otherwise qualified are eligible for registration if owned by a corporation formed and registered in Liberia. Some countries stipulate that shares in ship-owning companies be owned wholly or in a stated percentage by national citizens. Others (including Liberia and the Marshall Islands) permit foreign incorporated companies to be registered locally as such in the country of the register, often described as a foreign maritime entity or equivalent terminology, for the purpose of attaining the requisite national ownership qualification and entitlements.

1.18 The 1982 UNCTAD report on Conditions for Registration of Ships,[37] as a precursor to the 1986 UN Convention of that name, mentioned 46 countries at that time imposing some requirement for equity participation in ship-owning companies by national citizens – of these, 40 countries then insisted upon majority participation by nationals. The report listed nine countries (People's Republic of China, Ethiopia, the former German Democratic Republic, Ghana, Haiti, Iraq, Mexico, the former USSR and the Yemen People's Democratic Republic) requiring 100% equity participation by nationals. Additionally, the report indicated that management requirements (either with regard to the nationality of management personnel or to the location of the seat of management in the flag State) were applied by at least 52 countries. By 2012 UNCTAD listed only five major flag States (Belgium, Denmark, Germany, India and Japan) as almost exclusively used by national owners.

---

32 Shipping Registration Act 1981 ss. 8 and 12.
33 Canada Shipping Act 2001, s.46, that is, unless registered in any other foreign State.
34 Consolidated Act no. 856 of 1 July 2010, s.1(1).
35 Merchant Shipping (Registration of Ships) Regulations 1996, reg. 3.
36 See further Chapter 6 for a snapshot analysis of the major flags of the world's merchant fleet according to the nationality of their underlying beneficial owners.
37 *Op. cit.*

1.19 Twenty years on from the 1982 *travaux preparatoires* context and analysis, by 2002 the equivalent data revealed that of the 35 largest registered merchant fleets only Denmark and Norway showed a majority of ownership by their nationals and then both by adopting the model of second or international registries.[38] Indeed, the move from national ownership as the norm has been dramatic. Until 1995 less than half of the world's merchant fleet was foreign-flagged.[39] From a proportion of 50.6% in 1995, the share of non-domestic registration of such tonnage rose in the following ten years to 65.1% in 2005 and reached 70.01% by January 2017.[40]Facing the facts of such statistics, the view is increasingly gaining ground that the only universally applicable test for determining a vessel's nationality is the fact of her registration – or, in a limited range of cases, documentation not accompanied by registration – in a particular State.[41]

Documentation

1.20 In practice 'documentation' is used to refer to the issuance by the competent authorities of a State to a ship-owner of a document evidencing a vessel's nationality and attesting to her right to fly the national flag of that State. Although registration and documentation generally go hand in hand, this is not always the case and the two concepts should not be confused. Registration generally involves the public recognition and protection of the ship-owner's title to the vessel as well as the conferment of nationality; whereas documentation, on the other hand, is chiefly concerned with granting and evidencing the entitlement of the ship-owner to fly the national flag.[42]

1.21 An example of registration and documentation not being either simultaneous or synonymous is demonstrated when an application to register a vessel is first made to the Panamanian flag State. At this first stage of the registration procedure, the vessel is issued with a document known as a patente de navegación, generally by a Panamanian consular authority. This document, which entitles the vessel to fly the Panamanian flag for a period of up to six months, may be issued in respect of suitably qualified ships on the basis of an application by the owner and payment of the necessary taxes and fees, without any requirement for production of evidence of the owner's title to the vessel or the recording thereof in the Panamanian public registry, which may take place at any time during the validity of the patente. The case of *The Angel Bell*[43] arose in such circumstances, where the vessel was provisionally registered but these additional formal requirements meant that the issuance of documentation was not perfected at the time of her loss, resulting in the dispute between the cargo interests and the mortgagee as to the proper applicable law.

---

38 See further Chapter 4.

39 Commercial seagoing vessels 1,000 GRT and above.

40 UNCTAD, *Review of Maritime Transport* – UNCTAD/RMT/2012, Figure 2.4; UNCTAD/RMT/2017, Table 2.3.

41 See *R v Bolden and Dean (The Battlestar) op. cit.*

42 In the case of *Saint Vincent and the Grenadines v Guinea (The Saiga)(No.2)* before the International Tribunal for the Law of the Sea, discussed further in Chapter 3, the period of validity of the provisional certificate of registry on board the vessel had expired, raising the question of whether the registration and hence the nationality of the vessel had also therefore lapsed.

43 *Op. cit.*

1.22 In so-called 'dual' or 'parallel' registration situations, which arise when a vessel registered in one State receives entitlement to fly the flag of another State on the basis of a bareboat charter arrangement with suitably qualified persons in the latter State, the distinction between documentation and registration becomes crucial. This matter will be discussed in detail in Chapter 5.

1.23 When distinguishing documentation and registration it is useful to consider the following principles:

(1) Although registration is often a precondition of the right to fly a particular flag, this is not invariably so. Documentation, however, is the only allowable and internationally accepted evidence of the right to fly a flag, without which there can be no recognition on the high seas or in a port State of the national character of a ship.

(2) Registration generally involves ascertainment of the owner's title to the vessel and the recognition and protection of other rights *in rem* in the ship, for example, mortgages. Registration is therefore evidence, generally conclusive, of title; documentation does not provide conclusive evidence of title, merely national character.

1.24 Two categories of documentation are almost universally adopted, each fulfilling a separate function. A certificate of registry is evidence of the ownership and nationality of a ship, accurate according to the records of the flag State on the date of issue. A certificate of registry in practice does not provide evidence of any mortgage or other encumbrance which has been granted or exists over the ship, and is in some jurisdictions issued only once, upon first registration of a vessel with the flag State; in other jurisdictions the certificate of registry requires to be renewed at intervals. A transcript of registry, on the other hand, is a publicly accessible document which will show according to the records of the flag State on any given date of issue upon application, both the registered owner and the presence of any properly registered encumbrances.[44] In this way, the intended purchaser of a vessel is well advised to investigate not only the certificate of registry, but also to procure an up-to-date transcript of registry prior to any acquisition.

Flag

1.25 The flying of the national flag is visual evidence and a symbol of a ship's nationality. As previously mentioned, in the words of the 1958 Convention on the High Seas: "Ships have the nationality of the State whose flag they are entitled to fly."[45] The national flag of the vessel should be flown from the stern whenever identification of the vessel's national character may be required – this would certainly be the case when sailing through national waters of a State, or passing through shipping lanes or traffic separation schemes and, of course, in circumstances where the national laws of the ship require that the flag be flown. However, outside these cases where the hoisting of the flag is necessary or useful to aid identification, there seems to be no obligation in international law for the vessel's national flag to be flown at all times on the high seas.[46]

---

44 The forms of certificates of registry and transcripts of registry are normally prescribed by statute or subordinate legislation of each State. See further, para. 1.35 *et seq.*

45 Article 5.

46 See H. Meyers, *The Nationality of Ships* (1967).

1.26 'Flag' is also used as a shorthand for the allocation of nationality to a vessel and the assumption of exclusive jurisdiction and control by a State over the vessel.[47] With or without the physical presence of a flag on board or on display, the convention of marking the home port of registry on the stern of all merchant vessels makes the task of identifying the nationality of a vessel in practice a relatively simple one at any given moment. The compulsory marking of the name of the vessel and her home port on the stern is found in legislation as early as 1784.[48]

1.27 To the details of the vessel's name, flag and home port one may add the further identifier of the IMO number allocated to the ship as a means of verification. The permanent and visible marking of vessels in this way became compulsory by resolution of the Diplomatic Conference on Maritime Security in December 2002.[49]

Registration

1.28 Registration means the entering of a matter in the public records. We have seen that registration is generally – but not always – not only a precondition for, but also considered to be the essential objective test of a vessel's nationality. This is the public law function of registration, as opposed to its private law function. The distinction between public law and private law was first made by the jurists of ancient Rome. According to Justinian: "Publicum ius est quod ad statum rei Romanae spectat; privatum quod ad singulorum utilitatem [public law is that which has to do with the constitution of the Roman State; private law, that which has to do with individuals]."[50] In this analysis, private law had to do with adjusting the relations and securing the interests of individuals and settling disputes between natural persons, whereas public law concerned the framework of government, the functions of public officials and the adjustment of relations between individuals and the State.

1.29 Among the public law functions of registration we may therefore include:

(1) the allocation of a vessel to a specific State and its subjection to a single jurisdiction for the purposes, for example, of safety regulation, security aspects, crewing and discipline on board;
(2) the conferment of the right to fly the national flag;
(3) the right to diplomatic protection and consular assistance by the flag State;
(4) the right to naval protection by the flag State;
(5) the right to engage in certain activities within the territorial waters of the flag State – for example, coastal fishing, trading or in the case of a pleasure yacht, cruising between the ports of the flag State;
(6) in case of war, for determining the application of the rules of war and neutrality to a vessel; and

---

47 Dr Frank Wiswall, *Bareboat Charter Registration, Legal Issues and Commercial Benefits* (International Chamber of Commerce 1988).

48 Shipping and Navigation Act 1784, s.XIX provides for marking "in white or yellow letters, of a length of not less than four inches, upon a black ground, on some conspicuous part of the stern . . . the name by which such ship or vessel shall have been registered, and the port to which she belongs, in a distinct and legible manner".

49 Amending SOLAS Regulation XI-1/3 for cargo ships >300GT and passenger ships >100GT, entering into force on 1 July 2004.

50 Digest I.i.

(7) publicity itself, the provision of searchable, verifiable and authoritative information within the public domain.

1.30 It is with these functions that public international law and the majority of international Conventions on the law of the sea are concerned – imposing obligations upon their signatories to take responsibility for their subject-matter. Thus, Article 5 of the 1958 Convention on the High Seas provides: "the State must effectively exercise its jurisdiction and control in administrative, technical and social matters over ships flying its flag". In Article 10 of the same Convention it is provided: "Every State shall take such measures for ships under its flag as are necessary to ensure safety at sea." In other words, as discussed further below, the adoption of a vessel by a flag State government brings with it responsibilities.[51]

1.31 It is useful in this context to reiterate the principle with which this chapter began, namely that it is the combination of the international status of the high seas and the inherent mobility of the assets themselves which requires each flag State to assert their authority in this way. International law has been described as a structure of normative conduct, providing a degree of order such as to allow society to maximise the common good, and the application of substantive norms to otherwise lawless areas are a good example of this theory in practice.[52] Brierly explains:

> The justification of this principle is simply that *some* law must prevail on ships . . . It is needless to explain it by regarding ships as floating portions of a state's territory, a metaphor which, if pressed, would lead to the absurd result that the waters surrounding a ship from time to time would be territorial waters.[53]

The 'floating territory' theory is attributed to Jeremy Bentham's epigram – a ship is an ambulatory province[54] – but this analysis can lead to difficulties. The Privy Council rejected the idea in an appeal concerning a murder on board a vessel in the case of *Chung Chi Cheung* v. *The King*:

> However the doctrine of extraterritoriality is expressed, it is a fiction, and legal fictions have a tendency to pass beyond their appointed bounds and to harden into dangerous facts. The truth is that the enunciators of the floating island theory have failed to face very obvious possibilities that make the doctrine quite impracticable when tested by the actualities of life on board ship and ashore.[55]

---

51 See further Chapter 2.

52 Higgins, *Problems and Process* (OUP 1994), Ch.1.

53 Brierly, *The Law of Nations* (OUP 1982), p. 152.

54 *Traités de legislation civile et penale* (1802), vol. 1, p. 332.

55 [1939] AC 160. Their lordships also contemplated an alternative scenario: "Similarly, in the analogous case of an embassy. Is it possible that the doctrines of international law are so rigid that a local burglar who has broken and entered a foreign embassy and, having completed his crime, is arrested in his own country, cannot be tried in the Courts of the country? It is only necessary to test the proposition to assume that the foreign country has assented to the jurisdiction of the local Courts. Even so, objective exterritoriality would, for the reason given above, deprive our Courts at any rate of any jurisdiction in such a case. The result of any such doctrine would be not to promote the power and dignity of the foreign sovereign, but to lower them by allowing injuries committed in his public ships or embassies to go unpunished". In the context of our modern day debate concerning truth in politics and in the media it is interesting to find analysis of extraterritorial jurisdiction continuing in these terms: ". . . for many reasons it is an objectionable term. It introduces a fiction, for the person or thing is in fact within, and not outside, the territory: it implies that jurisdiction and territory always coincide, whereas they do so only generally; and it is misleading because we are tempted to forget that it is only a metaphor, and to deduce untrue legal consequences from it as though it were a literal truth."

1.32 For the private law aspects of ship registration, such as the application of civil or commercial law on board, and governing the choice of law relating to the vessel itself and the property on board, the metaphor can be useful.[56] For cases of collision between two vessels of different nationalities, the metaphor causes difficulty in application. Similarly, the English courts have described the theory as "a very common and fruitful source of error, viz. the error of identifying ships with portions of the territory of the States to which they belong" particularly in the context of collision cases[57] as compared to being a useful tool to determine the applicable law in commercial disputes between parties to a contract of affreightment.[58]

1.33 If it may be said that public law sees the ship in the dynamic sense of a floating community carrying with it the sovereignty of the State whose flag she flies, private law sees the ship in the static sense of a chattel, an item of moveable property over which one or more persons may have rights which the law considers worthy of protection. The distinction between the public law and private law functions with reference to the statutory precursors of the current UK Merchant Shipping Act have been explained by the Court of Appeal in this way:

> There are two points of public policy which may be suggested in these acts relating to shipping: the one a policy regarding the interests of the nation at large, relating to the question who shall be entitled to the privileges of the British flag . . .; the other policy being similar to that which gave rise to the acts for the registration of titles to land – the object being to determine what should be a proper evidence of title in those who deal with the property in question.[59]

1.34 On this basis, the private law functions of registration therefore include:

(1) the protection of the title of the registered owner; and
(2) the protection of the title and the preservation and ranking of priorities between persons holding security interests over the vessel, such as mortgagees.

1.35 The determination of the procedures for registration and the matters and interests which may be recorded in the register are of course a question for the law of each State. Classically these details will include the vessel's dimensions and tonnage, a description of the main engines, and the name and address of the registered owner. The first statutory form of a certificate of registry is found in the UK Shipping and Navigation Act of 1784, the requirements of which includes details of the name and residence of the owner, the name of the vessel, the name of the Master, the date and place of construction, the number of masts and decks, and the measured dimensions and tonnage of the vessel. To this day,

---

56 See also the analysis of the US Supreme Court in *Spector v Norwegian Cruise Line Ltd*, distinguishing between the "internal affairs and operations" of a vessel as contrasted with statutory requirements "that concern the security or well-being of United States citizens", discussed in Chapter 3.

57 *Chartered Mercantile Bank, op. cit.*, Lindley LJ at p. 544.

58 In *Lauritzen v Larsen* 345 US 571 (1953) the US Supreme Court notes that "authorities reject, as a rather mischievous fiction, the doctrine that a ship is constructively a floating part of the flag State, but apply the law of the flag on the pragmatic basis that there must be some law on shipboard, that it cannot change at every change of waters, and no experience shows a better rule than that of the state that owns her".

59 *Liverpool Borough Bank v Turner* (1860) 29 LJ Ch 827, 830 *per* Wood, V-C, more recently cited with approval by the High Court in New Zealand in *KeyBank National Association v The Ship "Blaze"* [2007] 2 NZLR 271 at 277.

the information provided by the ship-owner upon first registration forms the basis of the detail later to be included in the vessel's documentation issued by the registry thereafter.[60] In the present day case of British ships registered in the UK, Schedule 4 of the Merchant Shipping (Registration of Ships) Regulations 1993 lists the various details relating to the owner and the ship which are to be entered on the register.[61] These include the nationality or place of incorporation of the owner and the IMO number or HIN for the vessel.

1.36 Similarly, the legislation in Singapore describes that the Registrar shall enter in the register the name of the ship and the port to which it belongs, the ship's build and other particulars descriptive of the identity of the ship, the particulars respecting its origin and the name and description of its owner and, if there are more owners than one, the proportions in which they are interested in the ship.[62] For vessels registered in Liberia, a demonstrably authorised representative of the owner must take an oath declaring the name of the vessel, its net tonnage, the place where built, the date when built, the name and residence of any other owner and his citizenship, each owner's proportion and the name of the declarant and his citizenship.[63]

1.37 The number of part-owners who may appear on the ship register varies from State to State. The property in a British ship is divided into 64 shares[64] and subject to the provisions of the UK Merchant Shipping Act relating to joint owners, not more than 64 persons or bodies corporate may be registered at the same time as owners of any one ship. Under the Codice della Navigazione property in Italian ships is divided into 24 shares, or carats (*carati*). Bahamian ships are divided into 64 shares;[65] Cypriot ships are divided into 100 shares.[66] The historical reason for the choice of 64 shares as the number of co-owners is uncertain.[67] Now adopted by many registries worldwide, particularly those of former British colonies, while the basis for this number of shares is a matter of speculation, the historical development of this usage can be more easily identified. Sixty-four shares first appeared in UK legislation in the Act for the Registration of British Vessels 1845. The UK Merchant Shipping Act of 1854 allowed up to 32 separate owners and in 1880 this number was increased to allow 64 separate owners of a UK ship.[68]

1.38 The nature of the property interests, or rights *in rem*, which may be entered in the register also varies between individual States. A right *in rem* is "a right acquired by one over a thing".[69] In the UK, only ownership title and mortgages may be recorded. It

---

60 See further Chapter 3 in relation to individual flag State requirements and procedures in practice.

61 SI 1993/3138, as amended. Extracts are provided in Appendix VI.

62 Merchant Shipping Act (Chapter 179) s.13(1).

63 Liberian Maritime Law, Title 21, s.57(1).

64 Merchant Shipping (Registration of Ships) Regulations 1993, reg. 2(5).

65 Merchant Shipping Act 1976 (Chapter 268, as amended), s.6.

66 Merchant Shipping (Registration of Ships, Sales and Mortgages) Laws of 1963 to 2005, s.4(3)(a).

67 Lloyd's Register 'Infosheet' No. 25, 4 August 2003 suggests the early historical sub-division of a ship by its owners into moieties – resulting in shares of a half, a quarter, a 16th, a 32nd and finally a 64th. Some commentators have suggested that the number is arbitrary and without historical significance. Other theories include the basis that Victorian ships had 64 ribs, that Roman galleons had 64 oarsmen, or that the number was the result of a 36% tax imposed on ownership for the purpose of naval protection.

68 Merchant Shipping Act (1854) Amendment Act, 1880, s.2.

69 Gorrell Barnes J in *The Ripon City* [1897] P 226 at p. 242. For a comprehensive historical review and analysis of the legal nature of an *in rem* claim in the English courts, see the speech of Lord Steyn in *The Indian Grace* [1998] 1 Lloyd's Rep 1.

is also possible to register a notice of mortgage intent, which secures the priority of a mortgagee for 30 days pending full registration of the mortgage itself.[70] Other jurisdictions permitting such prior notice to be recorded include Bermuda, the British Virgin Islands and the Isle of Man. No notice of any trust, express, implied, or constructive may be entered in the register in the UK.[71] In other countries, arrests (precautionary seizures by financial creditors or those entitled to a maritime lien) may be entered on the register.

1.39 As concerns ownership, registration ensures that the ship-owner's title is valid against third parties; as concerns mortgages, registration not only gives notice of the creditor's interest in the vessel and thus protects that interest against third parties, it also fixes the ranking priority between competing mortgagees. Schedule 1 to the UK Merchant Shipping Act 1995[72] provides:

> Where two or more mortgages are registered in respect of the same ship or share, the priority of the mortgagees between themselves shall . . . be determined by the order in which the mortgages were registered (and not by reference to any other matter).

1.40 In some jurisdictions, registration of the mortgage may in fact and law be creative of the security interest, rather than the date of its execution between the parties. Care must also be taken to ensure that company law requirements are fulfilled in the jurisdiction of incorporation of the owner entity such as to preserve the validity of charges granted by that company although also entered in a specialist register abroad.

---

70 Merchant Shipping (Registration of Ships) Regulations 1993, reg. 59.
71 *Ibid.*, reg. 6(1).
72 Schedule 1, para. 8(1).

CHAPTER 2

Duties of the flag State

Introduction

2.1 As discussed in Chapter 1, international law looks to individual flag States to ensure compliance with the rules it lays down for the exercise of the freedom of the high seas. The corollary of the principle of the freedom of the seas, as previously mentioned, is that States must take responsibility for the operations of the vessels sailing on the high seas bearing their flag. The practical enforcement of this statement of principle presents considerable difficulties. The United Nations Convention on the Law of the Sea (UNCLOS) 1982[1] provides that such freedom is exercised by States under the conditions laid down by this Convention and by other rules of international law; in particular, the freedom of the high seas must be exercised by all States "with due regard for the interests of other States".

2.2 Article 94 of UNCLOS describes in some detail, using the imperative "shall", the obligations of the flag State in the effective exercise of jurisdiction and control over its ships in administrative, technical and social matters. These obligations extend to the maintenance of a register of ships, the assumption of jurisdiction under its internal law over ships on its register, their Masters, officers and crews and the taking of the necessary steps to ensure safety at sea, including regular surveys. In a more widely drawn provision, the article continues to narrate the requirement of each State "to conform to generally accepted international regulations, procedures and practices, and to take any steps which may be necessary to secure their observance".

2.3 Article 217 of UNCLOS obliges flag States to ensure compliance by their vessels with international rules and standards as well as laws and regulations adopted in accordance with the Convention for the protection of the marine environment from pollution. States must adopt the necessary laws and regulations for the implementation of these international precepts and provide for their effective enforcement irrespective of where a violation occurs. In particular, flag States must prohibit their vessels from sailing except in compliance with international rules and standards, ensure that their vessels carry the necessary certificates issued pursuant to those rules and standards and periodically inspect those vessels to ensure that the certificates are in conformity with the actual physical condition of the asset. The same article also provides for the investigation by flag States of violations by their vessels of international rules and standards and for the stipulation by flag States of penalties adequate in severity to discourage violations.

---

1 Article 87. For the full text of the Articles referred to in this section, see extracts reproduced at Appendix VIII.

2.4 It is the lack of any effective mechanism for the enforcement of these well-intentioned but practically toothless requirements against flag States who do not themselves enforce or observe compliance by the ship-owners registered with that State, which has drawn the greatest criticism and concern. While the imperative of maintaining and improving standards is well understood, the challenge for the international community is how to enforce against not only sub-standard vessels but also sub-standard flag States.[2]

Implementation of mandatory instruments

2.5 The perceived need for stricter application of internationally recognised rules and standards after the *Exxon Valdez* disaster in 1989 led to the establishment of the IMO Subcommittee on Flag State Implementation (FSI) in 1992. The FSI Subcommittee encouraged the adoption of a significant number of resolutions of the IMO Assembly in the fields of safety, pollution prevention and port State control. Following the *Prestige* casualty in November 2002 a letter to the Secretary-General of the United Nations was jointly submitted by Greenpeace International, the International Transport Workers' Federation and the World Wide Fund for Nature calling for the establishment of a task force to address the stated problem of the lack of a genuine link between a ship and the State of her registration, and the lack of adequate implementation and enforcement by certain flag States. As a result, the Consultative Group on Flag State Implementation was convened in May 2003 and included representation from the IMO, the International Labour Organization, the UN Food and Agriculture Organization, the United Nations Environment Performance, UNCTAD and the OECD.

2.6 The Report of the Secretary-General, published in March 2004, made clear that despite certain differences of opinion among the members of the Consultative Group as to the causative effect of open registers or flags of convenience as such upon sub-standard vessels and their operators, the primary responsibility for enforcement of standards rests with the flag State rather than the port State.[3] That outcome is also the clear intention of Article 5 and Article 10 of the 1958 Convention on the High Seas and Article 94 and Article 217 of UNCLOS.[4] The solutions which the Report suggests include the mandatory audit of flag State controls and their measures of implementation of international Conventions. The Report concludes that port State control measures cannot counteract the failure of flag States to meet their obligations under international law, and that compliance can only be ensured through an adequate system of sanctions imposed by the States parties to the international Conventions which are being breached in their observance by others.

2.7 Following the recommendations of the FSI Subcommittee, procedures for the Voluntary Member State Audit Scheme were adopted by the IMO in December 2005. These procedures aim to provide a comprehensive and objective assessment of flag States' compliance with their treaty obligations and are described as "a tool to achieve harmonized and consistent global implementation of IMO standards".[5] The first States to complete the Voluntary Audit were Chile, Denmark, UK and Liberia. In 2007 the IMO

---

2 In other words, *quis custodiet ipsos custodes?*
3 General Assembly, 59th session, A/59/63.
4 See further, Appendix VII and Appendix VIII.
5 A.974 (24).

adopted a revised Code for the Implementation of Mandatory IMO Instruments,[6] intended as the audit standard against which participants shall be assessed, of which a failure to satisfy is intended to form the basis for the imposition of sanctions or penalties against non-compliant States for their failures to implement international standards on board their merchant ships and by their ship-owners.

2.8 This Code was further revised in November 2011, the recitals to which describe:

REAFFIRMING that States, in their capacity as flag States, have the primary responsibility to have in place an adequate and effective system to exercise control over ships entitled to fly their flag and to ensure that they comply with relevant international rules and regulations in respect of maritime safety, security and protection of the marine environment.[7]

The 2011 Code identifies the fundamental Conventions, of near universal international acceptance, and their supporting instruments the implementation of which shall be subject to audit. These include SOLAS Convention 1974 (as amended by the 1978 and 1988 Protocols), MARPOL Convention 1973 (as amended by the 1978 and 1997 Protocols), STCW Convention 1978, Load Lines Convention 1966 (as amended by the 1988 Protocol), Tonnage Convention 1969 and the Collision Regulations Convention 1972. In order to give mandatory domestic effect to the audit requirement, consequential amendments to each of these treaties were required to be prepared and approved and duly ratified by IMO Member States.[8]

2.9 The FSI Sub-Committee was renamed in 2013 as the Sub-Committee on Implementation of IMO Instruments (known as 'III') with new terms of reference including a "comprehensive review of the rights and obligations of States emanating from the IMO treaty instruments". The language describing obligation of States and mandatory compliance makes clear that, having ratified certain treaties, participants are expected proactively and themselves to ensure that those promises are then fulfilled in domestic law and in practice.[9] At this time the 2011 Code was revoked, revised and re-issued under the new title 'IMO Instruments Implementation Code'.[10] This recommends that each State:

(1) develop an overall strategy to ensure that its international obligations and responsibilities as a flag, port and coastal State are met;
(2) establish a methodology to monitor and assess that the strategy ensures effective implementation and enforcement of relevant international mandatory instruments; and
(3) continuously review the strategy to achieve, maintain and improve the overall organisational performance and capability as a flag, port and coastal State.

2.10 With effect from 1 January 2016, the audit of compliance with these key instruments became compulsory for all IMO Member States, with the aim of determining the

---

6 A.975 (24).

7 A.1054(27).

8 Effected by resolutions adopted by the IMO Assembly in December 2013 and May 2014.

9 In this way sovereignty is preserved. The recitals here too are instructive – "RECOGNIZING that parties to the relevant international Conventions have, as part of the ratification process, accepted to fully meet their responsibilities and to discharge their obligations under the Conventions and other instruments to which they are party" – that is, measures are not forced upon States but accepted by them. Adopting the language of the precursor Voluntary Member State Audit Scheme, one is here concerned with voluntary participation rather than external interference.

10 A.1070(28).

extent to which they in practice give full and complete effect to their commitments and responsibilities contained in these fundamental treaties. To the original list have since been added instruments including the Casualty Investigation Code,[11] the Recognised Organisation Code[12] and relating to Ballast Water Management.[13]

2.11 The extent to which flag States may delegate their responsibilities – for example to a classification society or similar certification body commonly referred to in this context as a recognised organisation (RO) – and be considered to fulfil their treaty obligations in so doing, can be a matter of some concern. On one view, such delegation avoids rather than assumes responsibility for the performance of such critical and practical roles as the inspection of vessels and the issuance of documentation. In circumstances where the flag State may have an insufficiency of resources, of global coverage, or of specific technical expertise the outsourcing model appears sensible. Indeed, for even the largest and most rigorous and sophisticated of registries the ability to offer a worldwide service to their owners can be seen to demand some network of authorised representation in the ports of every nation. For this reason, delegation of certain surveys and certification tasks for example to members of the International Association of Classification Societies (IACS)[14] is commonplace. The concern arises if the delegate in fact, for whatever reason, does not meet or enforce the applicable standards to the expected degree.

2.12 Chapter I, Regulation 6 of SOLAS 1974 provided that the inspection and survey of vessels

> shall be carried out by officers of the country in which the ship is registered, provided that the Government of each country may entrust the inspection and survey either to surveyors nominated for the purpose or to organizations recognised by it.[15]

That regulation continued furthermore that the flag State "fully guarantees the completeness and efficiency of the inspection and survey". Notably, the 1988 Protocol to SOLAS adds that flag States "shall undertake to ensure the necessary arrangements to satisfy this obligation", that is, the mere delegation does not fulfil the obligation and a residual and continuing responsibility remains.

---

11 Code of International Standards and Recommended Practices for a Safety Investigation into a Marine Casualty or Marine Incident, entered into force on 1 January 2010.

12 Code for Recognized Organizations adopted by resolutions MEPC.237(65) and MSC.349(92), entered into force on 1 January 2015.

13 International Convention for the Control and Management of Ships' Ballast Water and Sediments, entered into force on 8 September 2017.

14 IACS members at the time of writing are: American Bureau of Shipping (ABS), Bureau Veritas (BV), China Classification Society (CCS), Croatian Register of Shipping (CRS), Det Norske Veritas – Germanischer Lloyd (DNV GL), Indian Register of Shipping (IRS), Korean Register of Shipping (KR), Lloyd's Register of Shipping (LR), Nippon Kaiji Kyokai (NK), Polish Register of Shipping (PRS), Registro Italiano Navale (RINA) and Russian Maritime Register of Shipping (RS).

15 Similar language can be found in reg. 4 of Annex I and reg. 10 of Annex II of MARPOL 73/78; Art. 7 of the International Convention on Tonnage Measurement for Ships 1969 provides that certificates "shall be issued by the Administration or by any person or organization duly authorized by it. In every case, the Administration shall assume full responsibility for the certificate"; similarly, Art. 13 of the International Convention on Load Lines 1966 as amended by the Protocol of 1988 provides that contracting States may "entrust the surveys and marking either to surveyors nominated for the purpose or to organizations recognized by it. In every case the Administration concerned fully guarantees the completeness and efficiency of the surveys and marking."

2.13 Seeking a consistency of application and to establish a basic level of competencies for those entrusted with 'hands-on' survey and certification duties, in November 1993 the IMO adopted guidelines upon the conditions of the authority that may be delegated to nominated surveyors or recognised organisations.[16] These guidelines aimed to develop uniform procedures and a mechanism for such delegation of authority to, and the minimum standards for, those organisations acting on behalf of the flag State. The overarching goal is that, given the stated primary significance of safety of life at sea and protection of the marine environment contained within the myriad international Conventions, the supervision and verification of technical and documentary requirements on behalf of flag States may only be performed by organisations with adequate resources in terms of technical, managerial and research capabilities to accomplish the tasks being assigned.

2.14 In particular, the guidelines require the flag State to demonstrate the relative size, structure, experience and capability of the RO as being commensurate with the type and degree of authority intended to be delegated. The organisation should be able to document "extensive experience in assessing the design, construction and equipment of merchant ships and, as applicable, their safety-management system" together with minimum ISO 9000 equivalent quality system of internal verification and controls.[17]

2.15 The development from these numerous guidelines and specifications to mandatory rules upon this subject-matter reached fruition with the adoption of the Code for Recognised Organisations[18] in June 2013. Entering into force on 1 January 2015, this Code is itself one of the instruments capable of audit pursuant to the III Code. The RO Code, parts 1 and 2 of which are mandatory, provides a consolidated instrument containing criteria against which any RO shall be recognised by a flag State, and gives guidance for their ongoing monitoring. By making compulsory the rigour and discipline which a flag State is expected to undertake and demonstrate before delegation to an external provider, it is hoped to prevent avoidance or evasion of responsibility through the appointment of an organisation without verifiable appropriate competences. In this way, the effective implementation of IMO Conventions – the performance of treaty obligations – by governments is capable of appraisal by the combined approach of audit of the flag State together with a detailed assessment also of their chosen delegates.

Port State control

2.16 Disquiet among the international community at the unwillingness or inability of certain flag States (both flags of convenience and flags of economies in transition) to exercise proper control over vessels within their registered fleets has led in recent years to increasing reliance on port States to monitor compliance with international standards. Intervention by port States is sanctioned by the 1982 Convention on the Law of the Sea

---

16 A.739(18).

17 A.739(18) Appendix 1, para. 2. Further detailed treatment of specific competencies required of any RO were adopted by Resolution A.788(19) in November 1995 "Specifications on the Survey and Certification Functions of Recognized Organizations Acting on Behalf of the Administration" such as management functions and technical appraisal in disciplines including hull structures, machinery systems, subdivision and stability, structural fire protection, safety equipment and pollution prevention.

18 MEPC.237(65) and MSC.349(92).

(Articles 25 and 218) and numerous other international Conventions, which are discussed later in this chapter in the context of flag State obligations. The effectiveness of control by port States in policing compliance with international standards depends upon co-ordination between maritime authorities on a regional basis; otherwise owners and charterers might simply avoid ports where sub-standard ships are more likely to be subject to inspection and detention. This would lead to a distortion of competition between ports in the same region, that is, 'ports of convenience' to some.

2.17 The Paris Memorandum of Understanding (MOU) of 1982 represented the first step towards establishing uniformity of port State control endeavours on a regional basis. The maritime authorities of 27 States, primarily European nations together with Iceland and Canada, have now adhered to this MOU.[19] The MOU requires each authority to maintain an effective system of port State control in order to ensure that, without discrimination as to flag, foreign merchant ships visiting its ports comply with the standards laid down in the 'relevant instruments', namely international Conventions relating to safety of life at sea, prevention of pollution and working conditions on board.[20] Under the MOU, each authority must inspect all vessels evaluated as 'Priority I' high-risk according to specific historic performance criteria and an average annual inspection commitment of 'Priority II' lower-risk vessels proportionate to the number of visiting ships from those calling in the region as a whole.

2.18 In fulfilling their commitments under the MOU, maritime authorities carry out inspections which consist in the first instance of a physical inspection on board the ship in order to ensure that she is in possession of the necessary certificates and documents relevant for the purposes of the MOU. In the absence of valid certificates or if there are clear grounds for believing that the condition of a ship or her equipment and crew do not meet international standards, a more detailed inspection may be carried out. Authorities must endeavour to secure the rectification of deficiencies detected and, in the case of those that are clearly hazardous to safety, health or the environment, may refuse to allow the ship to proceed to sea. The sanction of detention is intended to act as a powerful economic disincentive to the operation of sub-standard vessels. Because merchant ships rely on their movement for their earning ability, their owners have a considerable imperative to operate such as to satisfy the basic MOU requirements. The availability of real-time and readily accessible data concerning vessels detained across the world provides an equally powerful stimulus to flag States and to owners themselves to improve their own control procedures. Advances in satellite tracking and internet-based data sources indicate that technology and information unavailable in the 1960s and 1970s may be the greatest motivation for owners who are, as a result, the subject of ever more consistent, detailed and accurate scrutiny.

2.19 The Paris MOU specifies certain criteria to be adopted by maritime authorities in selecting vessels for inspection and, in accordance with those criteria, to establish a risk profile for each which is recalculated daily. In broad terms, the risk profile established in this way determines the priority level for the inspection commitment by the port State.

---

19 Paris Memorandum of Understanding on Port State Control, 40th Amendment, adopted 26 May 2017, effective 1 July 2017.

20 The seventeen enumerated relevant instruments include the SOLAS, MARPOL, COLREGS, STCW, MLC, Tonnage, Loadlines, Bunkers and Ballast Water regimes.

The criteria include the type and age of vessel, the flag State performance (Black, Grey and White Lists), the relative performance of the recognised organisation in question, the compliance performance of the fleet of the operating company, and the vessel's historic inspection and detention record for the previous three years. In their focus on a registry's previous performance within the criteria, together with the technological ability to update and share such information effectively in real time, the port State control system might be considered a constant and inescapable oversight of flag States.

2.20 The MOU requires each authority to consult, co-operate and exchange information with other authorities in order to further the aims of the memorandum. The secretariat of the Paris MOU publishes a ranking of flag States according to the number of vessels detained during the preceding three years. The results published in 2008 ranked France first and the UK fifth, ranked according to the lowest number of vessels detained following inspection. Of the two largest fleets in the world, Panama and Liberia, these registries were ranked 65 and 20 respectively. By 2017 the statistics showed the Cayman Islands in first place and France in second; as a measure of the true progress of the much-maligned flags of convenience model on compliance grounds, the largest open registries of Panama, Liberia and the Marshall Islands are ranked 37, 24 and 8 respectively.[21]

2.21 The success of the Paris MOU has led to the establishment of regional port State control measures beyond Europe into other parts of the world. These alliances include the 1992 Viña del Mar Agreement between the maritime authorities of 15 Latin American countries; the 1993 Tokyo MOU between 21 countries in the Asia/Pacific region; the 1996 MOU between 14 countries in the Caribbean Region; the 1997 Mediterranean MOU comprising ten north African and Mediterranean littoral States; the 1999 Abjua MOU among 14 west and central African governments; the 2000 Black Sea MOU signed by six States in that region; and the Riyadh MOU signed in 2006 among the GCC States. The significant breadth of coverage of these networks of supranational scrutiny and enforcement against sub-standard tonnage is an essential element of raising operating standards.

2.22 At a mandatory European Union level, the publication by the European Commission in 1993, *A Common Policy on Safe Seas*, urged the strengthening of the level of intervention of port and coastal States in order to reduce sub-standard shipping in EU waters and approved in principle the establishment of a supranational committee to be responsible for maritime safety and pollution issues.[22] Council Directive 95/21/EC established common criteria for control of ships by port States and harmonising procedures on inspection and detention throughout the EU.[23] The Directive built upon the experience gained through the operation of the Paris MOU and sought to develop a better targeting system. In common with the Paris MOU requirements prevailing at that time, the Directive required each Member State to carry out inspections corresponding to at least 25% of the number of individual ships entering its ports annually; but in carrying out those inspections priority is to be given to the categories of ships listed in Annex I to

---

21 Paris MOU Annual Report, 2017. See Appendix III for the full White–Grey–Black listings.

22 COM (93) 66 final, 24 February 1993; Resolution of 8 June 1993 (OJ C 271, 7.10.1993 p. 11).

23 Subsequently amended by Directive 2001/106/E (OJ L 19, 22.1.2002 p. 17); The principles of this Directive were first implemented in the UK by the Merchant Shipping (Port State Control) Regulations 1995; see now the Merchant Shipping (Port State Control) Regulations 2011, SI 2011/2601 giving effect to later developments of the system discussed *infra*.

the Directive. These include ships visiting a port of a Member State for the first time or after an absence of 12 months; ships flying the flag of a State appearing in the three-year rolling average of above-average detentions and delays published in the annual report of the MOU; and ships which have been reported by pilots and port authorities as having deficiencies which may prejudice safe navigation. Certain categories of ships, including passenger ships, older tankers and bulk carriers are also subject to more comprehensive inspections.

2.23 The maritime authority in each EU Member State is required to publish quarterly information concerning ships detained during the previous three-month period and which have been detained more than once during the past 24 months; this information must include the flag States of the vessels concerned. In this way, the commercial incentive for compliance is intended to be reinforced by the knowledge that a vessel, once detained, shall be the subject of closer observance thereafter at every port she calls.

2.24 A major catalyst for these changes, and a raft of subsequent legislative measures, was the *Erika* incident in 1999. The resulting pollution affected over 400 km of the French Atlantic coast. The environmental damage caused public outrage in Europe and the widely published photograph of the sinking stern was viewed by many in the EU as a symbol of the failure of the port State control regime. The vessel had been inspected numerous times by port State control inspectors, she was classed with an IACS-member Classification Society at the time of her sinking, she had recently completed a five-year survey and all her statutory certificates were up to date – yet she is viewed with hindsight as a sub-standard ship which had 'slipped through the net'.

2.25 In response, the European Commission proposed various amendments to Council Directive 95/21/EC, the most controversial at the time being the accelerated phase-out of single-hull tankers.[24] This was prompted by the fear that vessels banned from US waters by the Oil Pollution Act 1990,[25] as a result of America's own accelerated phase-out programme for single-hulls, would end up in European waters. However, there was concern within the industry that if the EU were to take this step it might prompt unilateral action by other littoral States, rather than a measured reaction co-ordinated through the IMO. The IMO responded when its Maritime Environment Protection Committee (MEPC) proposed an acceleration of the phase-out of single-hull tankers under the 1973 MARPOL Convention as amended in 1978 – a proposal adopted by MEPC at its April 2001 session.[26] In November 2002 the European Parliament and Council established the body first proposed in principle in 1993, founding the Committee on Safe Seas and the Prevention of Pollution from Ships (COSS). This legislation tasked COSS with ensuring conformity between the maritime legislation of the European Union and international treaty law concerning, *inter alia* port State control, SOLAS and MARPOL as implemented by its Member States.

2.26 The effect of the EU legislation known as the *Erika* packages was not felt soon enough to prevent the sinking of the *Prestige* off the coast of Spain in November 2002 with the loss of some 63,000 tonnes of heavy fuel oil. The latter casualty did however emphasise the continuing necessity of regional co-operation and maintained the political

---

24 Regulation (EC) No. 417/2002, 18 February 2002 (OJ L 64, 7.3.2002); the incident also directly influenced Directive 2005/35/EC on Ship Source Pollution, 7 September 2005 (OJ L 255/11, 30.9.2005).

25 Public Law 101–380 (33 USC 2701; 104 Stat. 484) enacted in direct response to the *Exxon Valdez* incident.

26 Resolution MEPC 95(46) which entered into force on 1 September 2002.

profile for the development of the European Maritime Safety Agency (EMSA) that was approved pursuant to the *Erika* measures by the European Parliament in June 2002 and which began its work in 2003.[27] For present purposes, one key role of EMSA is the analytical and statistical task of monitoring of port State control and its outputs at an EU level. These studies, from the assessment of the inspection performance of Member States to producing vessel-specific data, creates a considerable volume of intelligence, which is then used to develop objectives and procedures for the further improvement of the system.

2.27 Directive 95/21/EC was replaced with effect from January 2011 by Directive 2009/16/EC by way of four implementing enactments.[28] At this time EMSA assumed a specific mandate for the development and implementation of a vessel inspection database "building upon the expertise and experience under the Paris MOU".[29] Coupled with advances in mobile technology and working complementary to the voluntary Paris MOU structures it can be seen that such ingathering, sharing and publicity of such information is a meaningful motivation for flag States and ship-owners alike to ensure regulatory compliance. The online database, known as THETIS, is a remarkable achievement.[30] Publicly available and fully searchable against ship names and types, owner entities, IMO numbers, flag States, classification societies, inspecting ports, dates and outcomes – THETIS records and reports the findings of approximately 18,000 inspections per year and over 3,000 daily arrivals by vessels at ports in the region.

2.28 In this light, it might be said that there is a degree of naïvety in the now rather outdated view held by those who crusade against flags of convenience that the abolition of the international or open registries would lead to the elimination of sub-standard ships. The gradual raising of safety standards and their stricter international enforcement through the networks of MOU affiliated States worldwide may have more adverse effect on the fleets of developing or transitional countries than on the flags of convenience. The major international registries are no longer dependent on smaller non-mainstream operators for their revenues and now boast some of the largest, most technologically advanced and valuable vessels in existence. Any evangelical and objectively unsupported campaign against flags of convenience based on historical issues of safety might prevent efforts to improve by many developing States aiming in time to attain a more sophisticated compliance regime based on comprehensive international standards as described in the III Code.[31]

The international safety management code

2.29 On 4 November 1993, the Assembly of the IMO adopted the International Management Code for the Safe Operation of Ships and for Pollution Prevention (ISM Code).[32] The main purposes of the ISM Code are to ensure safety at sea, prevention of human

---

27 Regulation (EC) No. 1406/2002.

28 Directive 99/35/EC in relation to ro-ro ferries and high-speed passenger crafts; Directive 2009/17/EC in relation to vessel traffic monitoring; Directive 2009/15/EC in relation to Recognised Organisations; and, from July 2013, Directive 2009/20/EC in relation to insurance for maritime claims.

29 Directive 2009/16/EC of the European Parliament and of the Council on port State control, of 23 April 2009, Art. 24.

30 https://portal.emsa.europa.eu/web/thetis.

31 See *infra*, para. 2.9.

32 Resolution A.741(18).

injury and loss of life, and avoidance of damage to the marine environment. Under the ISM Code, ship operators are required to develop, implement and maintain a safety management system (SMS) covering the following functional requirements:

(1) a safety and environmental protection policy;
(2) instructions and procedures to ensure safe operation of ships and protection of the environment in compliance with relevant international and flag State legislation;
(3) defined levels of authority and lines of communication between, and amongst, shore and shipboard personnel;
(4) procedures for reporting accidents and non-conformities with the provisions of the Code;
(5) procedures to prepare for and respond to emergency situations; and
(6) procedures for internal audits and management reviews.

The safety management objectives of the ship operator must include, *inter alia*:

(1) provision for safe practices in ship operation and a safe working environment;
(2) the establishment of safeguards against all identified risks; and
(3) the continuous improvement of safety-management skills of personnel ashore and aboard ships, including preparing for emergencies related both to safety and environmental protection.

The SMS must ensure:

(1) compliance with mandatory rules and regulations; and
(2) that applicable codes, guidelines and standards recommended by the IMO, flag States, classification societies and maritime industry organisations are taken into account.

2.30 The compliance by a ship operator with the ISM Code is evidenced by a document of compliance (DOC) relevant to the owner, operator or manager of the ship issued by the government of the flag State, by an organisation recognised by that State (such as an approved classification society) or by another government acting on behalf of the flag State. The ship itself is issued with a safety management certificate (SMC) verifying that the ship operator and its shipboard management operate in accordance with the approved safety management scheme.

2.31 Through a phased implementation between 1998 and 2002, the ISM Code has by periodic increments in its scope and application formalised and harmonised at a basic level the aspirations of the international shipping community. Whether the vessel is registered in an open registry or a closed domestic registry is now irrelevant to the mandatory requirement of demonstrable and auditable minimum safety standards that are subject to scrutiny both by the flag State and at any port of call in a MOU region. Rather than separate and possibly inconsistent national attempts to introduce a greater sense of responsibility on the part of operators, the ISM Code provides a compulsory and readily identifiable structure of minimum compliance, documented with the DOC and SMC of a vessel. Through the frequent supervision of these certificates by port State control authorities, the prioritisation of safety is no longer aspirational, but is compulsory regardless of the flag State in which vessels are registered.

2.32 Although, in accordance with traditional principles of maritime and international law discussed in Chapter 1, it is the duty of the flag State to ensure the application of the ISM Code to its vessels, much of the policing of basic compliance with its requirements inevitably falls to port State inspectors. Flag States which are found to be lax in implementing the ISM Code or permitting the issue of documents of compliance without putting proper controls in place will find their ships penalised in foreign ports. An additional requirement of the Code is that where the entity responsible for the operation of the ship is other than the owner, the full details of that entity must be disclosed to the flag State administration. Coupled with the obligation in all cases to designate a person or persons ashore having direct access to the highest level of management of the operator, and together with the Continuous Synopsis Record held on board and the compulsory IMO company number scheme,[33] this enables far easier identification of the principals involved and result in greater transparency among the maritime community.

2.33 In sum, it is clear that such supranational and harmonising documentation – implemented regardless of flag State of a vessel – defeats in many respects the complaint hitherto frequently made against open registries that their level of regulations of safety of life, property, or the environment were either missing altogether or lacking in some respects. The ISM Code, through periodic audits and the issuance of internationally recognised certification, provides a minimum level of good practice which is compulsory and no longer the sole preserve of national registers compared to those assumed by some to be safe harbours for those seeking secrecy and the avoidance of responsibility. Similarly, a report by the UK Department of Transport in 2015 described flags of convenience as "now a somewhat outdated term".[34] For the reasons to be discussed in Chapter 3, this represents well the twenty-first century recognition of the legitimacy of flag States which do not insist on national ownership.

International Ship and Port Facility Security Code

2.34 In December 2002 a diplomatic conference held at the headquarters of the International Maritime Organisation in London and attended by delegates from governments of 108 States adopted a series of amendments to the 1974 Safety of Life at Sea Convention (SOLAS) intended to strengthen maritime security and to prevent international terrorism in ports and at sea. The conference resolved to adopt a new Chapter XI-2 of SOLAS, containing the International Ship and Port Facility Security Code (ISPS Code). The ISPS Code is intended to provide a framework for the management of the security risks presented by the operation of ships and port facilities handling international trade.

2.35 These amendments to SOLAS came into force in 2004 and institute mandatory port facility security assessments by contracting States. For ship-owners, the minimum requirements include the appointment of a company security officer and a ship security officer to each vessel. The ship security officer is responsible for the application of the ship security plan approved by the flag State of each vessel subject to the Code. The Code is compulsory for all passenger ships on international trade, all cargo ships of over

---

33 See further para. 4.28 *et seq.*
34 *Maritime Growth Study: keeping the UK competitive in a global market*, September 2015.

500 gross tons, and for mobile offshore drilling units. The certification of the satisfaction of these requirements is achieved through the issuance of an international ship security certificate (ISSC) by or on behalf of the flag State. As with the ISM Code, the practical supervision and enforcement of these requirements in the first instance is achieved through port State control inspection of the ISSC of a vessel in this context as part of the security measures adopted by the port facility at which the vessel calls.

2.36 Through the adoption of counter-terrorism measures – and the additional compulsory reporting of ownership, registration and movements of ships by SOLAS signatory States – the ISPS Code adds a layer of compliance supervision both for flag States over the vessels registered under their jurisdiction, and for every port State which receives vessels on international voyages. In this way, obligations of compliance in matters of security and safety management no longer extend simply to ship-owners and their flag States – each of which may hitherto have, for the sake of convenience or competitive advantage, avoided scrutiny prior to the implementation of these international harmonising measures – but the observance of which is now also incumbent upon the States of all ports where ships involved in international trade are received.

The International Convention on Standards of Training, Certification and Watchkeeping for Seafarers

2.37 The International Convention on Standards of Training, Certification and Watchkeeping for Seafarers (STCW) 1978[35] as its name implies established basic requirements for training, certification and watchkeeping for seafarers on an international level, rules which hitherto had been administered independently by flag States. This Convention has received widespread acceptance and, by February 2018, has been adopted by 162 State Parties, representing over 99% of world shipping tonnage. Important amendments to STCW 1978 were adopted in 1995[36] which include enhanced procedures for the exercise of port State control, and which also provide greater uniformity of application among flag States. The 1995 amendments impose strict obligations regarding implementation of the Convention's provisions with a view to ensuring that certificates of competency of individual seafarers issued by national administrations meet the requirements of the Convention. In particular, participating flag States are required to provide detailed information to the IMO concerning administrative measures taken to ensure compliance with the Convention by establishing that they have the administrative, training and certification resources necessary for its implementation, and thus enabling one flag State to place reliance on certificates of competency of seafarers issued by another.

2.38 The 1978 Convention was further modernised in 2010, by what are known as the Manila amendments, which seek to keep pace with developments in practice since the 1995 revision.[37] The updating includes treatment of training requirements in evolving technologies and approaches such as electronic charts, dynamic positioning and distance learning. The Manila amendments also focus on the monitoring of compliance with the STCW requirements by flag States.

---

35 Adopted 7 July 1978, entered into force 28 April 1984.
36 Adopted 7 July 1995, entered into force 1 February 1997.
37 Adopted 25 June 2010, entered into force on 1 January 2012.

2.39 The IMO has also introduced a White List of those countries deemed to have given "full and complete effect" to the STCW Convention. The increasing global application of the STCW standards is demonstrated by the growth of the White List. When it was first published in December 2000, it contained 71 countries. The White List published in May 2016 counts 130 States as having achieved this badge for the mutual international recognition of the certification of their seafarers.[38] Flag States which have failed to demonstrate to the IMO Maritime Safety Committee that they have the resources necessary to implement the Convention and who are as a result excluded from the White List will find that their certificates of competency will not be accepted by other administrations and their vessels will be liable to detention by port States. This effectively limits the trading area of those vessels and acts as a powerful incentive to flag States to ensure that their seafarer certification procedures, as well as their vessel documentation, meet IMO standards.

---

38 MSC.1/Circ.1163/Rev.10. See Appendix IV.

CHAPTER 3

The legal requirements of ship registration

Freedom of States to fix conditions for registration

3.1 On 1 December 1873, President Ulysses S. Grant, in his fifth annual message to the Senate and House of Representatives, considered the appropriate treatment of vessels registered by a flag State while on the high seas. He described the steamer *Virginius* that in September 1870 had been duly registered at the port of New York as a part of the commercial marine of the United States and received the certificate of her register in the usual legal form. In October 1873, while sailing under the flag of the United States on the high seas, she was forcibly seized by a Spanish gunboat and was carried into the port of Santiago de Cuba where 53 of her passengers and crew – consisting of US, British and Cuban nationals – were summarily tried by court-martial for piracy and executed by firing squad. He stated:

> It is a well-established principle, asserted by the United States from the beginning of their national independence, recognized by Great Britain and other maritime powers, and stated by the Senate in a resolution passed unanimously on the 16th of June, 1858, that – American vessels on the high seas in time of peace, bearing the American flag, remain under the jurisdiction of the country to which they belong, and therefore any visitation, molestation, or detention of such vessel by force, or by the exhibition of force, on the part of a foreign power is in derogation of the sovereignty of the United States.

The government of Spain believed that the vessel and her crew were aiding insurgents on the island of Cuba, then part of the Spanish empire. The Spanish contention was that, since the vessel was in fact Cuban owned, she must have obtained her American papers by fraud and was not entitled to the protection of the American flag. The US Attorney-General Williams accepted that because of the concealment of the Cuban-national beneficial ownership at the time of registration – the oath and declaration upon registration that there was "no subject or citizen of any foreign prince or state, directly or indirectly, by way of trust, confidence, or otherwise, interested in such ship or vessel" was false – there was no right, as between her true owners and the United States, to carry the American flag. The US response was rather that the question of whether or not the ship was entitled to fly the American flag was a matter purely for US jurisdiction.[1] The proposition that

---

1 17 December 1873: "Spain no doubt has a right to capture a vessel with an American register and carrying the American flag, found in her own waters, assisting, or endeavouring to assist the insurrection in Cuba, but she has no right to capture such a vessel on the high seas upon an apprehension that, in violation of the neutrality or navigation laws of the United States, she was on her way to assist said rebellion. Spain may defend her territory and people from the hostile attack of what is, or appears to be, an American vessel, but she has no jurisdiction whatever over the question as to whether or not such vessel is on the high seas in violation of any law of the United States." Moore, *A Digest of International Law* (Government Printing Office 1906), vol. II, 895 at 899.

the courts of the flag State alone are competent to determine the right to fly a national flag appears to have been accepted by Spain, which restored the vessel to the control of the US government and paid the sum of $80,000 by way of reparation and also certain compensation to the families of the deceased British seamen.[2]

3.2 In essence, this is a question of sovereignty.[3] As discussed in Chapter 1, States have for hundreds of years and for many different reasons set conditions on who may and who may not own or register a vessel subject to their jurisdiction. Memorably considered in the context of the sovereignty of the UK Parliament as an unfettered ability even to legislate against smoking on the streets of Paris,[4] it can be seen for ordinary and arbitrary questions such as the speed limit for road traffic or the threshold ages to vote in an election, to become married, or for the purchase of alcohol, each State has an absolute discretion to decide the answers. The principle of Parliamentary sovereignty was described by A.V. Dicey as "neither more nor less than this, namely, that Parliament thus defined has, under the English constitution, the right to make or unmake any law whatever".[5] For present purposes such discretion may include whether one may register hovercraft or oil rigs or merchant vessels under 24 metres in length – and like the propriety of the registration and ownership of *Virginius* another State may not, beyond its own boundaries, complain that such policy is unlawful or take matters into its own hands because to do so would interfere with the sovereignty of the other.

3.3 A classic statement of the right of individual States unilaterally to fix the conditions for the grant of nationality to merchant vessels was made by the Permanent Court of Arbitration in 1905 in the *Case of the Muscat Dhows* between Great Britain and France: "Generally speaking it belongs to every sovereign to decide to whom he will accord the right to fly his flag and to prescribe the rules governing such grants."[6] The case concerned the legality of the grant of the right to fly the French flag to dhows owned by subjects of the Sultan of Muscat, the complaint being that such grant infringed treaty obligations and was used as a cover to enable the owners of the vessels to engage in slave-trading. Although the Court found that France's right to confer its nationality on the dhows had in fact been restricted by a treaty of 1892, it held that prior to that date: "France was

---

2 See also *The Virginius Case* (1874) 76 Parliamentary Papers (Spain No.3) 299 at 391.

3 As the etymology suggests, historically associated with the absolute or higher power of a monarch. In *R (on the application of Miller) v Secretary of State for Exiting the European Union* [2017] UKSC 5 the UK Supreme Court affirms "Originally, sovereignty was concentrated in the Crown, subject to limitations which were ill-defined and which changed with practical exigencies. Accordingly, the Crown largely exercised all the powers of the state (although it appears that even in the 11th century the King rarely attended meetings of his Council, albeit that its membership was at his discretion). However, over the centuries, those prerogative powers, collectively known as the Royal prerogative, were progressively reduced as Parliamentary democracy and the rule of law developed."

4 W. Ivor Jennings, *The Law and the Constitution* (University of London Press, 1943) preferred 'supremacy' to 'sovereignty' ("not associated with politico-theological dogmas") but recognised the terms as interchangeable. At 149: "Parliamentary supremacy means, secondly, that Parliament can legislate for all persons and all places. If in enacts that smoking on the streets of Paris is an offence, then it *is* an offence. Naturally, it is an offence by English law and not by French law, and therefore it would be regarded as an offence only by those who paid attention to English law. The Paris police would not at once begin arresting all smokers, nor would French criminal courts begin inflicting punishments upon them. But if any Frenchman came into any place where attention was paid to English law, proceedings might be taken against him."

5 *Introduction to the Study of the Law of the Constitution* (8th edn, Macmillan 1915) at 3

6 Award dated 8 August 1905, Hague Court Reports 1916, 93 at 96.

entitled to authorise vessels belonging to subjects of His Highness the Sultan of Muscat to fly the French flag, only bound by her own legislation and administrative rules."

3.4 The principle enunciated in the *Muscat Dhows* case was upheld by the US Supreme Court in the 1953 case of *Lauritzen* v. *Larsen*:[7]

> Perhaps the most venerable and universal rule of maritime law relevant to our problem is that which gives cardinal importance to the law of the flag. Each State under international law may determine for itself the conditions on which it will grant its nationality to a merchant ship, thereby accepting responsibility for it and acquiring authority over it. Nationality is evidenced to the world by the ship's papers and its flag. The United States has firmly and successfully maintained that the regularity and validity of a registration can be questioned only by the registering State.

Here can be seen the dual roles accepted by any flag State, that is, of acquiring authority over the asset and also – as discussed in Chapter 2 – the concomitant supervisory duties and responsibilities arising under international Conventions.

3.5 For a modern context, the US Supreme Court again reviewed the authorities in the 2005 case of *Spector* v. *Norwegian Cruise Line Ltd*.[8] In *Spector* the issue before the Court was whether US legislation concerned with the rights of persons with disabilities applied on board foreign-flag cruise ships operating in US waters. The cruise ships in question were registered in the Bahamas and their operator was pursued in a class action seeking that the vessels should be modified, such as by the removal of physical barriers, that would allow the "full and equal enjoyment of public accommodations and public transportation services" that the Americans with Disabilities Act of 1990 requires. By a majority decision it was held that a clear statement of congressional intent is necessary before a general statutory requirement can interfere with matters that concern a foreign-flag vessel's internal affairs and operations, as contrasted with statutory requirements that concern the security and well-being of United States citizens. The judgement canvasses historic case-law that finds

> all matters of discipline and all things done on board which affec[t] only the vessel or those belonging to her, and [do] not involve the peace or dignity of the country, or the tranquility of the port, should be left by the local government to be dealt with by the authorities of the nation to which the vessel belonged[9]

and in which light concludes:

> It is reasonable to presume Congress intends no interference with matters that are primarily of concern only to the ship and the foreign state in which it is registered. It is also reasonable, however, to presume Congress does intend its statutes to apply to entities in United States territory that serve, employ, or otherwise affect American citizens, or that affect the peace and tranquility of the United States, even if those entities happen to be foreign-flag ships.

---

7 345 US 571 (1953).

8 545 US 119 (2005).

9 *Wildenhus's Case*, 120 US 1, 12 (1887). See also *Cunard SS Co v Mellon*, 262 US 123 (1923) concerning the application of the National Prohibition Act to foreign-owned and foreign-flagged passenger vessels operating to and from US ports; and two cases concerning the application of the National Labor Relations Act to crews on board foreign-flag vessels, *McCulloch v Sociedad Nacional de Marineros de Honduras*, 372 US 10 (1963) and *Longshoremen v Ariadne Shipping Co*, 397 US 195 (1970).

3.6 In finding that the legislation of the United States for these reasons does apply to foreign-flagged vessels (described by the justices as 'flags of convenience') the court is careful nonetheless expressly to preserve rather than to tread on the principle of the sovereignty of the flag State. Drawing from the authorities, as a matter of principle and international comity, the overriding responsibility for ship-board aspects of the flag State is duly acknowledged while in practice the domestic legislation of the visited port State is applied for the simple expedient that the vessel owners have purposefully chosen to call there and to operate in US territorial waters.

3.7 In sum, the grant by a sovereign State to a ship-owner and to a vessel of the right to fly its national flag involves two determinations in each case:

(1) (a) the determination of the categories of ship-owners entitled to be entered in the national register;
   (b) the determination of whether or not a specific applicant ship-owner falls within one of these categories; and
(2) (a) the determination of the categories of vessels entitled to be entered in the national register;
   (b) the determination of whether or not a specific vessel falls within one of these categories.

Permitted categories of owner

3.8 We have seen in earlier chapters examples of flag States in the exercise of their sovereign prerogative restricting the categories of permitted owners according to their nationality, either by domicile or place of incorporation. Historically, the traditional maritime nations (e.g., Great Britain, France, and the Netherlands) have also sought to limit the categories of vessels entitled to fly their flags. The purpose of the seventeenth and eighteenth century Navigation Acts in the UK were to restrict the exploitation of the imperial trade routes to vessels not only owned by British subjects but also those built within the British Dominions. The French Navigation Act of 1793 provided that after 1 January 1794:

> Aucun bâtiment ne sera réputé français, n'aura droit aux privilèges des bâtiments français, s'il n'a pas été construit en France ou dans les colonies ou autres possessions françaises . . ., s'il n'appartient pas entièrement . . . des Français, et si les officiers et trois quarts de l'équipage ne sont pas Français.[10]

3.9 Insistence on crewing by nationals of the flag State was another method of ensuring a close nexus between the vessel and the country of her registration. In these circumstances, there was little need to examine the extent to which international law required a genuine, meaningful or substantive link between a vessel and her flag State. As demonstrated in the judgement of the US Court of Appeals in the case of *The Chiquita*[11] it appears that,

---

10 "No ship will be deemed to be French, nor will have the right to the privileges of French ships, if it has not been constructed in France or in the colonies or other lands in French possession . . ., if it does not belong entirely to French subjects, and if the officers and three quarters of the crew are not French." Decree of 21 September 1793; see Rodiere, *Droit Maritime* (Paris, 1980) Vol. 2, p. 48 *et seq.*

11 *Hartwig v United States* 19 F 2d 417 (1927).

as late as 1927, the possibility of the nationality of the ship-owner being different from the flag State was not contemplated. The vessel in question was at the relevant time provisionally registered in Honduras and in court was revealed a colourful history of previous registration in the United States, the Bahamas and the UK. She was seized on the high seas in the Gulf of Mexico by the US customs department with a cargo of liquor that was presumed to be intended for import contrary to the National Prohibition Law.[12] The court ruled that "the flag under which a merchant ship sails is *prima facie* proof of her nationality. If she is not properly registered her nationality is still that of her owner."

3.10 All this changed, however, with the flight from national flags which began slowly in the years preceding the World War II and gathered impetus in the 1950s. The traditional maritime nations saw their fleets vastly reduced in number as ship-owners sought to take advantage of the liberal conditions prevailing under the flags of, for example, Liberia and Panama. The phenomenon of what were then known as 'flags of convenience' but are now properly and less emotively described as international, or open registries, will be examined in more detail in Chapter 4. For present purposes it is necessary to examine the effect that this flight from national flags had upon the continuing belief in the precept that the grant of the right to fly a flag is an unassailable sovereign prerogative, and whether there should instead require some mandatory connection – generally ownership and control – with the flag State. Opposition to 'flags of convenience' came mainly from labour interests, since the abandonment by ship-owners of the traditional maritime nations inevitably meant a decline in the need for crews from the countries where the vessels had previously been registered. By establishing the principle of the so-called 'genuine link', it was expected that the haemorrhage of tonnage to the open registries could be stemmed.

3.11 The legal basis for the assault on the sovereign prerogative to determine the conditions of the right to fly a national flag was the decision of the International Court of Justice in *The Nottebohm Case* in April 1955.[13] This judgment did not concern the nationality of a ship, but the nationality of an individual. The case arose from the expropriation by Guatemala during World War II of coffee plantations which were the property of Friedrich Nottebohm, formerly a German national, who had acquired Liechtenstein nationality on the eve of the outbreak of war. The question at issue was whether Liechtenstein, as a result of its unilateral grant of naturalisation to Mr. Nottebohm, was entitled to exercise protection over his business interests against another State, or whether the nationality of an individual presupposed the existence of a substantive connection between the individual and the State whose nationality he claimed. This substantive connection was described as "a legal bond having as its basis a social fact of attachment, a genuine connection of existence, interests and sentiments, together with the existence of reciprocal rights and duties".[14] In this case, the International Court found, by 11 votes to 3, that no

---

12 "Of course, it may be inferred that the cargo of intoxicating liquor was intended for ultimate consumption in the United States but at the time and place of the seizure the vessel was not violating any law of the United States . . . The frequent changes of name and ownership may give rise to the suspicion that the ship's true ownership was sought to be concealed, but property may not be declared forfeit on mere suspicion. It was incumbent on the government to show with reasonable certainty that the Chiquita was an American vessel when proceeded against. That burden has not been sustained." *Ibid.*, at 418.

13 *Liechtenstein v Guatemala (Second Phase)* [1955] ICJ Rep 4.

14 *Ibid.*, p. 23.

such connection existed, and that Mr. Nottebohm had adopted Liechtenstein nationality simply to "substitute for his status as a national of a belligerent State that of a national of a neutral State".[15] In these circumstances, there was no obligation upon Guatemala to recognise Mr. Nottebohm's purported Liechtenstein nationality so as to enable him to invoke Liechtenstein diplomatic protection.

3.12 The "over-extrapolation"[16] of the *Nottebohm* decision to the question of the nationality of merchant vessels has led to much confusion. Indeed, there is a degree of illogicality in seeking to extend considerations relevant to the determination of an individual's nationality such as social attachment and sentiment to the question of State jurisdiction over a naturally itinerant chattel. Nonetheless, the concept of the 'genuine link' as applied to the nationality of merchant ships is now long enshrined in international treaty law, but as a largely undefined term. Indeed, so nebulous does the test remain that the "genuine link" had little apparent practical effect in reducing the late 20th century migration of ships from traditional national registers to open registries. As we have seen, by 2017 the proportion of open registry tonnage of the global merchant fleet exceeded 70%.[17]

Genuine link in international Conventions

3.13 The 1958 Convention on the High Seas saw the first express introduction of the concept of 'genuine link' into treaty law, three years following the publication of the *Nottebohm* judgement. Article 5 of this Convention provides:

> 1. Each State shall fix the conditions for the grant of its nationality to ships, for the registration of ships in its territory, and for the right to fly its flag. Ships have the nationality of the State whose flag they are entitled to fly. There must exist a genuine link between the State and the ship; in particular, the State must effectively exercise its jurisdiction and control in administrative, technical and social matters over ships flying its flag.

3.14 Nowhere does the Convention attempt to describe what is meant by the 'genuine link' in terms of preconditions for the grant of nationality; nor are there any sanctions indicated in cases where nationality is granted in the absence of a 'genuine link', whatever that expression may mean. Rather, the link seems to arise *ex post facto*, being expressed in terms of the jurisdiction and control exercised by the flag State over the ship after the grant of registration. Patently, such jurisdiction and control can only arise after the ship has been registered in that State. If the genuine link is seen in these terms, there seems no reason to deny the existence of such a link in the case of ships entered in a properly administered open registry. Such registration may be regarded as a mere documentary

---

15 The judgment of the Court continues: "These facts clearly establish, on the one hand, the absence of any bond of attachment between Nottebohm and Liechtenstein and, on the other hand the existence of a long-standing and close connection between him and Guatemala, a link which his naturalisation in no way weakened. That naturalisation was not based on any real prior connection with Liechtenstein, nor did it in any way alter the manner of life of the person upon whom it was conferred in exceptional circumstances of speed and accommodation. In both respects, it was lacking in the genuineness requisite to an act of such importance, if it is to be entitled to be respected by a state in the position of Guatemala. It was granted without regard to the concept of nationality adopted in international relations." *Ibid*, p. 26.

16 See McDougal and Burke, *The Public Order of the Oceans, A Contemporary International Law of the Sea* (Newhaven/Dordrecht 1962) 1029 *et seq*.

17 Chapter 1, para. 1.19.

formality, a rubber-stamp by a secretariat or civil servant, but is nonetheless genuine in its procedure and outcome. The stated socio-economic and political aims behind the introduction of the requirement of the connecting factor are, however, thereby defeated because the true nexus between owner and flag State is created by an administrative decision rather than a positive motivation and bond of attachment.

3.15 The importance of the concept of the 'genuine link' was further weakened in 1960 when the International Court of Justice was requested to deliver an advisory opinion in connection with the constitution of the predecessor to the IMO.[18] The Convention establishing the organisation provided for the appointment of a Maritime Safety Committee having certain duties with regard to – among other matters – aids for navigation, construction and equipment of vessels, manning and safety procedures. The composition of the committee was governed by Article 28(a) of the Convention, which provided:

> The Maritime Safety Committee shall consist of fourteen Members, elected by the Assembly from the Members, governments of those nations having an important interest in maritime safety of which not less than eight shall be the largest shipowning nations and the remainder shall be elected so as to ensure adequate representation of Members, governments of other nations with an important interest in maritime safety, such as nations interested in the supply of large numbers of crews or in the carriage of large numbers of berthed and unberthed passengers, and of major geographical areas.

3.16 The issue before the court was in effect the meaning of the phrase "largest shipowning nations". Did this mean simply those States with the largest gross registered tonnage of shipping registered under their flags, or did the words imply that the tonnage had to be beneficially owned by nationals of the flag States, so that the States concerned could "properly be regarded as the 'largest shipowning nations' in a real and substantial sense"?[19] The determination of the meaning of the words was significant, because if the first interpretation was adopted, Liberia and Panama, whose gross registered tonnage then ranked third and eighth respectively in world terms, would automatically become members of the committee. This was a solution unacceptable to many Member States among the traditional ship-owning nations. The Netherlands, for example, contended that:

> the concept of the largest shipowning nations was not necessarily identical with that of the nations having the largest registered tonnage; on the contrary, a country's registered tonnage might in no way reflect its actual importance as a shipowning nation.[20]

3.17 In the event, the court reached the conclusion "that the determination of the largest shipowning nations depends solely upon the tonnage registered in the countries in question".[21] While doubtless expedient, based on simple arithmetic rather than investigating the nationality of true beneficial ownership, this approach avoids any requirement to assess the quality of the connection or the effectiveness of supervision that Article 5 of the 1958 Convention describes. Any further examination of the question of "genuine link" was determined irrelevant for the purpose of the opinion and which can be considered

---

18 'Constitution of the Maritime Safety Committee of the Inter-governmental Maritime Consultative Organization' Advisory Opinion of 8 June 1960: ICJ Reports 1960, 150.
19 *Ibid.*, 166.
20 *Ibid.*, 157.
21 *Ibid.*, 171.

a missed opportunity to emphasise the necessity of meaningful attachment as contrasted with an the bare fact of having fulfilled modest administrative steps.

3.18 The United Nations Convention on the Law of the Sea (UNCLOS), signed at Montego Bay on 10 December 1982, fared no better in defining *a priori* criteria for establishing the existence of a 'genuine link'. The opening words of Article 91 of this Convention is substantially in similar terms to Article 5 of the 1958 High Seas Convention, but in which, as we have seen in Chapter 1, the latter describes at that juncture an outline of the obligations of the flag State in the effective exercise of its jurisdiction and control.[22] The duties of the flag State are treated in far greater detail by UNCLOS in the separate provision of Article 94.

3.19 It was not until the 1986 United Nations Convention on Conditions for Registration of Ships[23] that we see any attempt in international treaty law to determine precisely what is meant by the 'genuine link' when applied to merchant ships. One of the objectives of this 1986 Convention is expressed to be that of "ensuring or, as the case may be, strengthening the genuine link between a State and ships flying its flag". Whilst the earlier Conventions envisaged the 'genuine link', as we have seen, in terms of jurisdiction and control, the 1986 Convention introduces the concept of the economic link, providing for the practical participation by nationals of the flag State in the ownership, manning and management of ships. The relevant provisions for this purpose are contained in Articles 7, 8, 9 and 10.

3.20 Article 7 grants States an option: as a minimum either they may comply with the ownership requirements in Article 8 or the manning requirements in Article 9 – they may, in fact, elect to comply with both. Article 8 requires the flag State to make provision in its laws and regulations for participation "by that State or its nationals as owners of ships flying its flag or in the ownership of such ships and for the level of such participation". Article 9 requires the State of registration to "observe the principle that a satisfactory part of the complement consisting of officers and crew of ships flying its flag be nationals or persons domiciled or lawfully in permanent residence in that State". What can be seen is a diplomatic and international legislative effort better to describe and so give substance to the ideal of attachment and connection between a State and a revenue-generating asset as compared to the genesis of the concept based on a human bond of affection or loyalty.

3.21 Article 10 sets out the role of the flag State in respect of the management of shipowning companies and ships on its register. Before entering a ship in its register, the State of registration "shall ensure that the shipowning company or a subsidiary shipowning company is established and/or has its principal place of business within its territory in accordance with its laws and regulations". However, where these circumstances do not exist, the requirement may be satisfied by the appointment of a "representative or management person who shall be a national of the flag State or be domiciled therein". The

---

22 These obligations are discussed further in Chapter 2.

23 UN Doc. No. TD/RS/CONF/23 adopted by the United Nations Conference on Conditions for Registration of Ships on 7 February 1986; on the background and effects of the Convention, see McConnell, 'Business as Usual: An Evaluation of the 1986 United Nations Convention on Conditions for Registration of Ships', 18 J Mar L & Comm 435 (1987) and Wefers Bettink, 'Open Registry, the Genuine Link and the 1986 Convention on Registration Conditions for Ships', Netherlands Yearbook of International Law 1987, pp. 70–119.

appointment of such representatives is now commonplace in practice for many owners and registries, but can be seen as a step removed from the primary aim of the exercise.

3.22 Although expressed in mandatory terms, the articles relating to ownership, manning and management leave so much of their detailed implementation and interpretation to the flag State that their effect may largely be negated. Viewed in this light, the provisions can be seen as little more than statements of principle. For example, Article 8 leaves the decision as to the level of national participation in the ownership of a vessel to the flag State. The only requirement is that the relevant laws and regulations "be sufficient to permit the flag State to exercise effectively its jurisdiction and control over ships flying its flag", echoing in effect the provisions of the 1958 High Seas and 1982 Law of the Sea Conventions. With regard to manning, the determination of what is a "satisfactory" level of crewing by nationals is again left to the flag State. In making such determination, the factors which the flag State may take into account include the following:

(a)   the availability of qualified seafarers within the State of registration; . . .

(c)   the sound and economically viable operation of its ships.[24]

3.23 Presumably, therefore, if the flag State determines, for example, that the high level of its national wages precludes the economically viable operation of its ships, the Convention would not prevent the whole of the complement of officers and crew being non-nationals. Likewise, the procedure in Article 10, allowing for the appointment of a representative or manager as an alternative to national management, largely negates the object of the provision; ship-owners seeking to register their ships under flags of convenience would have little difficulty in locating suitable nominees in the flag State.

3.24 Perhaps because of these weaknesses, the diplomatic effort and to some degree the clearer articulation in treaty form of the undefined concept found in Article 5 of the 1958 High Seas Convention and Article 91 of UNCLOS has not borne fruit because the 1986 Convention on Conditions for Registration of Ships has never been widely embraced. Indeed, it now appears a relic. The Convention will only enter into force 12 months after the date on which not less than 40 States, the combined tonnage of which amounts to at least 25% of world tonnage, have become contracting parties. As of 7 February 2018, on the 32nd anniversary of its adoption in conference at Geneva, only 15 States had ratified or acceded to the Convention (Albania, Bulgaria, Côte d'Ivoire, Egypt, Georgia, Ghana, Haiti, Hungary, Iraq, Liberia, Libya, Mexico, Morocco, Oman and the Syrian Arab Republic) and the Convention had been signed, subject to ratification, acceptance or approval, by a further nine States (Algeria, Bolivia, Cameroon, Czech Republic, Indonesia, Poland, the Russian Federation, Senegal and Slovakia). In the event, which is by no means certain, that the Convention does ultimately enter into force, the question arises whether, given its greater explicitness in seeking to address the problems of 'genuine link', one would expect then to see the abandonment of open registries and a return to the flags of the traditional maritime nations. The answer would seem to be no. More than 30 years on, that moment has passed.

3.25 In this way, over 60 years after the concept of the 'genuine link' was first put forward as a means of curbing the growth of the open registries, and notwithstanding

---

24 UN Convention on Conditions for Registration of Ships 1986, Art. 9(2).

considerable diplomatic efforts on the part of the international community, little real progress has been made in establishing that principle as an effective precept of international law. Indeed, depending as it does for the vast majority of merchant ships on a specious connection between the national affiliation of corporate entities and the attribution of jurisdiction over floating structures, many would say that the doctrine of 'genuine link' quite deserves to be restricted only to questions of private international law arising between individuals and foreign governments. Two cases in point from the International Tribunal of the Law of the Sea appear to confirm that perspective.

Genuine link at the International Tribunal of the Law of the Sea

3.26 The first case heard by the International Tribunal of the Law of the Sea, a voluntary forum established pursuant to Part XV of UNCLOS, gave the opportunity for a judicial analysis of the requirement of genuine link in modern practice. The *Saiga* was an oil tanker registered in St. Vincent and the Grenadines although the period of validity of the certificate of registry held on board had expired. The vessel was owned by a limited company incorporated in Nicosia, Cyprus and managed from Glasgow, Scotland. Her Master and crew were Ukrainian. At the material time the vessel was chartered to a shipping business based in Geneva, Switzerland. On 28 October 1997 the *Saiga* had been supplying bunker fuel to fishing vessels within the 200-mile exclusive economic zone (EEZ) of Guinea. The *Saiga* was attacked and boarded from two Guinean customs launch vessels. Shots were fired, injuring two seamen on board. The vessel was taken the port of Conakry where it was arrested. The fuel on board the vessel was removed and its Master and six crew members were detained. The Master of the *Saiga* was criminally prosecuted; the State of St. Vincent and the Grenadines was also named as civilly responsible to be summoned. On 17 December 1997 the Master was found guilty by a local court at first instance of unlawful importation of fuel oil, fraud and tax evasion and was fined over 15 billion Guinean francs. The vessel was confiscated in security for payment of the fine.

3.27 On 17 November 1997 the State of St. Vincent and the Grenadines submitted to the Tribunal a formal request for prompt release of the vessel under Article 292 of UNCLOS.[25] The first judgement of the Tribunal was issued upon that request within a matter of weeks, on 4 December 1997, ordering that Guinea promptly release the *Saiga* and its crew upon the posting of a reasonable bond or security by the flag State.[26] The authorities in Guinea did not release the vessel and, on 22 December 1997, new proceedings were commenced by the flag State against Guinea for violation of UNCLOS freedoms of navigation and internationally lawful use of the sea in its pursuit, arrest and detention of the vessel; by failing promptly to release it; and for citing St. Vincent and the Grenadines

---

25 Article 292, para. 1 provides "Where the authorities of a State Party have detained a vessel flying the flag of another State Party and it is alleged that the detaining State has not complied with the provisions of this Convention for the prompt release of the vessel or its crew upon the posting of a reasonable bond or other financial security, the question of release from detention may be submitted to any court or tribunal agreed upon by the parties or, failing such agreement within 10 days from the time of detention, to a court or tribunal accepted by the detaining State under article 287 or to the International Tribunal for the Law of the Sea, unless the parties otherwise agree."

26 *The M/V "Saiga" Case (Saint Vincent and the Grenadines v Guinea)*, 4 December 1997.

before Guinean courts.[27] St. Vincent and the Grenadines also sought provisional measures to compel the release of the vessel, Master and crew – in the event they were released by the time the pleadings in the second case had closed in February 1998, although the judicial procedure continued to argument and judgement. This afforded the tribunal at this early stage of its jurisprudence the opportunity to consider and determine certain issues of general importance arising that included, for present purposes, the question of the necessity and extent of the link required between a flag State and a ship-owner under international law.

3.28 Two of the arguments advanced by Guinea before the tribunal concerned the registration of the vessel. First, Guinea alleged that the vessel was not validly registered and was in fact unregistered because at the time of its seizure its provisional certificate of Registration had expired approximately six weeks earlier. The tribunal referred to Article 91 of UNCLOS in terms of which it is for each State to determine the conditions for the grant of nationality and for the right to fly its flag.[28] The tribunal noted that the nationality of a ship is a question of fact to be adduced by evidence from the parties. While it was accepted by the flag State that the documentation on board had expired, it was held following the hearing of evidence that as a matter of fact the *Saiga* nonetheless remained registered pursuant to the Vincentian regulations until deleted from the register.[29] On this basis, Guinea was not permitted to challenge the registration or the nationality of the vessel as a means to defeat the *locus* of the flag State to appear or the Tribunal's authority to issue judgment over the dispute. Consistent with the *Virginius* case described at the opening of this chapter, any question concerning the documentation issued by the flag State is a matter of domestic law.

3.29 The second argument considered by the tribunal was that in the circumstances of the ownership, management and chartering structure of the vessel there was no genuine link between the *Saiga* and St. Vincent and the Grenadines. Guinea contended that the absence of such a link would entitle it and any other State to refuse to recognise the nationality of that vessel because it was truly a 'stateless ship'.[30] Referring again to Article 91, paragraph 1, of UNCLOS "There must exist a genuine link between the State and the ship", the tribunal proposed to answer two questions. First, whether the absence of a genuine link entitles another State to refuse to recognise the nationality of the vessel; secondly, whether or not a genuine link existed between the *Saiga* and her flag State at the time of the incident.

3.30 In answering the first question the tribunal recognised that neither Article 91 nor Articles 92 or 94, which are concerned with the status of ships and the duties of the flag State, offer guidance. The tribunal instead looked to the *travaux preparatoires* of the 1958 High Seas Convention for which the plenipotentiaries are found to have resisted

---

27 *The M/V "Saiga" (No.2) Case (Saint Vincent and the Grenadines v Guinea)*, 1 July 1999 aptly described as the sequel in Lowe, 'The M/V Saiga: the first case in the International Tribunal for the Law of the Sea' ICLQ 1999, 48(1) 187. See also O'Keefe, 'ITLOS flags its intent' [2000] CLJ 428.

28 See Appendix VIII.

29 *The M/V "Saiga" Case (No.2) op. cit.* at para. 60 the flag State contended "just as a person would not lose nationality when his or her passport expires, a vessel would not cease to be registered merely because of the expiry of a provisional certificate".

30 See Chapter 1, para. 1.4.

insertion in the final text the preliminary words "*for the purposes of recognition of the national character of the ship by other States*, there must exist a genuine link between the State and the ship" (emphasis added). The International Law Commission in its work preparatory to the 1958 Convention, the precursor of UNCLOS, proposed the concept of a genuine link as a criterion not only for the attribution of nationality to a ship but also for the recognition by other States of such nationality.[31] The delegates at the diplomatic conference, it seems, did not agree to that dual function. The tribunal ruled:

> that the purpose of the provisions of the Convention on the need for a genuine link between a ship and its flag State is to secure more effective implementation of the duties of the flag State, and not to establish criteria by reference to which the validity of the registration of ships in a flag State may be challenged by other States . . . . there is no legal basis for the claim of Guinea that it can refuse to recognize the right of the *Saiga* to fly the flag of Saint Vincent and the Grenadines on the ground that there was no genuine link between the ship and Saint Vincent and the Grenadines.[32]

3.31 In so finding, with some albeit rather distant historical foundation, the tribunal neatly avoided the need to consider to any degree the necessary content and extent of the relationship posited in the second question. In this way, the earliest cases heard by the tribunal introduced a valuable new source of jurisprudence but advanced our understanding, for present purposes, more in relation to the obligations of mutual recognition by States of the nationality of vessels than the core issue of what makes a genuine link meaningful. The nineteenth case before the tribunal offered that prospect.

3.32 The case of the *Virginia G*[33] concerned factually similar circumstances to the events described in the *Saiga* judgements. Consensual proceedings were commenced before the tribunal in 2011 between Panama as flag State and Guinea-Bissau as the detaining coastal State. The *Virginia G* was a small oil tanker that was providing fuel to fishing vessels in the EEZ of Guinea-Bissau and which was confiscated in August 2009 by the local authorities of the coastal State on account of alleged violation of customs and fisheries regulations. In this case, no issue arose in respect of the validity of the documentation held on board. At the material time, the *Virginia G* was duly registered in the ownership of a company incorporated in Panama, beneficially owned by a Spanish company, chartered to an Irish company in the bunker trade and sailed under the command of a Master who was a Cuban national. The cargo of gas oil was unloaded by the authorities of the coastal State and was ordered to be sold by public auction. Proceedings for the return of the vessel and cargo began in the courts of Guinea-Bissau and the *Virginia G* was ultimately released in September 2010 as a gesture in recognition of the friendship between Guinea-Bissau and the Kingdom of Spain, the nationality of the true owners of the vessel.

3.33 Before the tribunal, Guinea-Bissau objected to admissibility of claims by Panama because there was no genuine link between Panama and the vessel. The coastal State, adopting similar language in its submissions as found in the *Nottebohm* judgement,

---

31 Article 29 of the Draft Articles on the Law of the Sea 1956.
32 *The M/V "Saiga" Case (No.2) op. cit.*, paras. 83, 86.
33 *The M/V "Virginia G" Case (Panama v Guinea-Bissau)*, 14 April 2014.

contended that a genuine link means more than a formal registration but requires a "real and substantial connection". It was said that in circumstances where the beneficial owner and the manning of the vessel were not of Panamanian origin, the registry was a flag of convenience only and no such connection existed. On that basis, Guinea-Bissau proposed that it was not bound to recognise the right of *Virginia G* to freedom of navigation in the EEZ. Panama contended that a genuine link indeed existed because the vessel was fully documented and certified in accordance both with domestic law and in accordance with all applicable international Conventions. Panama stated that it fulfilled the obligations of supervision in administrative, technical and social matters including by means of annual inspections and delegated the issuance of documentation to a competent recognised organisation.

3.34 The tribunal referred in detail to its judgement in the *Saiga (No.2)* case and ruled that:

> article 91, paragraph 1, third sentence, of the Convention requiring a genuine link between the flag State and the ship should not be read as establishing prerequisites or conditions to be satisfied for the exercise of the right of the flag State to grant its nationality to ships . . . . In the view of the Tribunal, once a ship is registered, the flag State is required, under article 94 of the Convention, to exercise effective jurisdiction and control over that ship in order to ensure that it operates in accordance with generally accepted international regulations, procedures and practices. This is the meaning of 'genuine link'.[34]

3.35 On the facts available – including the compliance with Panamanian domestic law concerning ownership and registration; effective supervision and control by the flag State of compliance with IMO Conventions, and the delegation of annual safety inspections and certification to a recognised organisation, the tribunal concluded that a genuine link indeed existed between Panama and the vessel in question.

3.36 The tribunal expressly reaffirmed and reiterated that the purpose of the UNCLOS Article 94 requirement of a genuine link is to secure more effective implementation of the duties of the flag State, and is not concerned with means by which the validity of the registration of ships in any flag State may be challenged by another. In so doing, it suggests that a coastal State for example may raise objection as to the lack of adequate supervision or control by the flag State but may not seek to scrutinise or criticise the subjective connection between the owner and its chosen flag. One may complain of the failure of a flag State to implement its duties under the international Conventions to which it is a signatory; that is entirely different from and now seemingly irrelevant to any necessary consideration of the adequacy of bonds of any kind between the owner and the flag State. Because the *Nottebohm* case was concerned with a natural person, attention was focused on the degrees of attachment of the individual to the countries concerned; for the registration of ships that is to approach the question from the wrong perspective. Together the *Saiga (No.2)* and the *Virginia G* cases at last make clear with considerable authority that it is supervision and control, rather than any prerequisite attachment between the owner and the flag State, that must be genuine.

---

34 *The M/V "Virginia G" Case, op. cit.*, paras. 110, 113.

Permitted categories of vessel

3.37 As different as each nation is in their local and idiosyncratic interpretation of cuisine, music or dance, having determined which category of owners are permitted, each State is entitled to prescribe which categories of vessel may be registered according to their laws. Though common denominators can be found, it is these differences in flavour and emphasis between States which require consideration and comparison by an intending ship-owner. Adopting the sub-categories used in the later chapters of this book, it is useful to consider the context and reasons for differences arising between various registries in terms of their assessment of a vessel's type, size, age and classification.

3.38 "There is no watertight definition, even of a ship."[35] The first issue for consideration by the flag State is how to define a ship or vessel which may be registered. A body of case-law has developed from different sources and contexts, but from which can be discerned some principles in practice. Issues such as the requirement for motive power, the means of any propulsion, the intended and actual use of the vessel, and its physical and geographical permanence, have all been considered by the courts. These decisions, though not immediately concerned with registration of ships, reveal the principles of what is an internationally registrable asset and what is not. This jurisprudence is relevant because the Merchant Shipping Acts of the UK, from which so many worldwide ship registration laws are derived, have rested upon the arcane construction that a ship is "a vessel used in navigation not propelled by oars".[36] The reference to propulsion by means other than muscle power was repealed in the UK in 1994,[37] but remains the applicable test in numerous national and international registries.

3.39 Absent the anachronistic reference to oars, the courts have still to grapple with the concept of being "used in navigation" as it may relate to floating property as varied as jet skis and semi-submersible drilling platforms.[38] The answer is important because in addition to the question of whether an asset is registrable, the classification of property as a ship has significant legal consequences as to the applicable time limit for the commencement of proceedings,[39] whether the vessel may be the subject of arrestment to secure a claim or salvage,[40] the imposition of compulsory international safety requirements, and the ability of the owner to limit their liability for oil pollution and property damage claims.[41] As a result, the principles applied by the courts to vessels of different

---

35 Myers, *The Nationality of Ships* (1967), p. 15.

36 Merchant Shipping Act 1894, s.742.

37 Merchant Shipping (Salvage and Pollution) Act 1994, Sch. 4, para. 2.

38 For a UK judicial perspective, see generally the decisions of the House of Lords in *Wells v The Owners of the Gas Float Whitton (No. 2)* [1897] AC 337; the Scottish Court of Session in *The St Machar* (1939) 65 Ll L Rep 119; the Irish Supreme Court in *The Von Rocks* [1998] 2 Lloyd's Rep 198; and the Court of Appeal in an appeal from the Tax Commissioners in *Perks v Clark* [2001] 2 Lloyd's Rep 431. For an admirable review of the jurisprudence see Osborne, Bowtle and Buss, *The Law of Ship Mortgages* (Informa Law from Routledge, 2017) at para. 2.10.

39 *Curtis v Wild* [1991] 4 All ER 172; *The Sea Eagle* [2012] 2 Lloyd's Rep 37.

40 The 1957 International Convention relating to the Limitation of Liability of Owners of Sea-going Ships, as its full title betrays, refers only to whether property is sea-going, and does not define what constitutes a ship.

41 The 1989 International Convention on Salvage defines the vessel as "any ship or craft, or any structure capable of navigation" (Art. 1(b)); the 1952 International Convention Relating to the Arrest of Sea-going Ships does not define 'ship', leaving the question to be determined by the applicable domestic law in each case.

types may understandably not be consistent in such a variety of contexts themselves as different as personal injury, income tax or ship arrest.[42]

3.40 It is useful to consider two relevant examples of assets that may or may not be considered appropriate or applicable for registration as ships. At one extreme, in terms of their massive physical presence and significant financial value, the legal status and the ability to register offshore platforms have received relatively little specific judicial attention. At the other extreme, the categorisation of the jet-ski, an asset no more valuable than a small motor car, has been the subject of some detailed analyses by the English appellate courts.

3.41 Offshore drilling platforms, though patently satisfying the test of not being propelled by oars, may be thought to resist classification as ships because, although seagoing, they are not commonly used in navigation. In the case of *The Boss Prithvi* in 1993, the Dubai Court of Cassation ruled that a semi-submersible oil rig was not a vessel under a UAE law, and so was not capable of arrest.[43] In *The Sovereign Explorer* in 1999, the Scottish Court of Session considered the status of a semi-submersible rig as a ship and as the subject of an arrest to found jurisdiction in security for a London arbitration. The court held, approving the Irish Supreme Court review of case-law in a dispute concerning an unpowered dredger,[44] that "the preponderance of authority is against the view that either self propulsion or ability to steer is regarded as essential to the concept of a vessel".[45] In *Perks* v. *Clark*, a tax case, Longmore LJ notices a certain inconsistency in treating all types of rigs equally as ships where a jack-up cannot perform any useful function afloat.[46]

3.42 Jet-skis, 'wet bikes', and similar small powered leisure craft have received judicial attention concerning their legal status particularly because of the effect that categorisation as a ship has upon the time limit for commencement of proceedings. In *R* v. *Goodwin*[47] the English Court of Appeal was required to rule upon whether a jet-ski was "seagoing" or a "vessel used in navigation" and considered whether such craft were able to be registered as one factor in their analysis. Approving an earlier judgment by Sheen J upon the issue of the time limit applicable to a claimant injured in a jet-ski accident,[48]

---

42 Osborne, Bowtle and Buss suggest "it is difficult to discern any consistent approach by the courts to the question from an analysis of these cases – or, at least, the cases illustrate the wide range of objects that are potentially ships and the impossibility of having a test that can be applied in all cases and in different legal contexts", *op. cit.* at para. 2.10.8.

43 *Industrial Investment Corp of India Ltd v Bombay Offshore Supplies & Services Ltd* (20 February 1993) Dubai Court of Cassation No. 331/1992. The relevant definition was "a vessel shall mean any structure normally operating, or made for the purpose of operating, in navigation by sea, without regard to its power, tonnage or the purpose for which it sails". The UAE is not a signatory to the 1952 Arrest Convention. See also, Ahmed, 'Dubai: Oil Rig not a Vessel' [1993] LMCLQ 482.

44 *The Von Rocks, op. cit.*

45 *Global Marine Drilling Co v Triton Holdings Ltd*, Lord Marnoch, Outer House, Court of Session, 23 November 1999 (unreported). See also, Watt, 'From Noah's Ark to mobile drilling units' [2000] LMCLQ 299; Watt, 'Jurisprudence on Maritime Law Conventions' 2002 *Il Diritto Marittimo*, Fasc.1, p. 180.

46 "Drilling ships and drilling barges must be ships. Semi-submersible oil rigs in which drilling operations are carried out while the rig is in a floating condition, submersible oil rigs in which drilling is carried out when the rig is resting on the sea bed, and jack-up drilling rigs which, when drilling, have legs resting on the sea bed (and are thus not subject to the heaving motion of the sea, in the same way as semi-submersible oil rigs and drilling ships) are all different forms of structure; it could be said that since the jack-up rigs cannot perform their main function without their legs being on the sea bed, they should be singled out and should not be regarded as ships. It would, however, be unsatisfactory if some forms of oil rigs were ships and others were not." *Perks v Clark op. cit.* at para. 59.

47 [2006] 1 WLR 546.

48 *Steedman v Scofield* [1992] 2 Lloyd's Rep 163.

the Court of Appeal held that, although the vehicle in question was unregistered, it was capable of registration. Nonetheless, the court determined that the fact of being capable of registration was not conclusive of their inclusion in the category of 'ship'; and that the words 'used in navigation' exclude from the definition of 'ship' craft that are simply used for having fun on the water.[49]

3.43 In practice the ability to register vessels of all shapes and sizes is determined by the domestic legislation of each individual flag State. Leisure craft are commonly the subject of a separate register from merchant ships or commercial fishing vessels. Some flag States have clear and express legislative provision for the registration of vessels as diverse as submarines,[50] hovercraft[51] and offshore drilling platforms,[52] or provide for the express exclusion from registration of floating docks.[53] The jurisprudence concerning the precise legal status of floating property of any kind is relevant because the international Conventions largely do not in themselves provide guidance on what is to be included in the essential qualifying terms 'ship', 'sea-going', and 'used in navigation'.

3.44 The broadest principles to be understood from the case-law are first, that in order to be registered as a "ship" and thus become subject to the international Conventions which govern traditional modes of transport by sea and are defined by that term, motive power of any kind is not required; secondly, that where the relevant domestic legislation refers in addition to vessels requiring to be 'used in navigation' or 'sea-going' in order to satisfy that status, the concept is likely to be narrowly interpreted by the court where the craft in question does not serve a useful commercial purpose of any kind. Once satisfied under domestic law of the basic legal requirements of a vessel in this way, the registry of a flag State will consider the further factors of size, age, and classification.

Permitted size, age and classification of vessels

3.45 In terms of acceptability to a flag State, the extremes of size and age of a vessel are likely to be relevant only to those at either end of the range, that is, the smaller and the older. To the ship-owner, however, these can cause difficulties where seemingly arbitrary thresholds may serve to prohibit registration of a vessel marginally on the wrong side of either test, and so may drastically narrow the choice of States in which an owner may record his title and lenders their security interest over such assets.

3.46 The traditional threshold minimum size of a ship beyond which international Conventions generally begin to apply, and beneath which such vessels are frequently categorised as "small ships", is 24 metres in length. The historical reason for this measurement is unclear, but it is now enshrined and adopted internationally as a result of

---

49 *R. v Goodwin, op. cit.*, p. 551, 557. This approach follows *European and Australian Royal Mail Company Ltd* v. *Peninsular and Oriental Steam Navigation Com* (1866) 14 LT 704 which held that the treatment by the seller and the purchaser of a vessel, whose masts had been removed, for all purposes as a coal hulk for storage rather than movement, determined its status as a matter of fact not to be a ship in terms of the Merchant Shipping Act.

50 New Zealand, Ship Registration Act 1992, as amended, s.2(1).

51 In Hong Kong, the Merchant Shipping (Registration) Ordinance, Cap. 415, s.2; in the Isle of Man, the Hovercraft Act 1968 (Application) Order 1986 (GC 263/86).

52 Act of 12 June 1987, No. 48 relating to a Norwegian International Ship Register, s.1.

53 Norwegian Maritime Code of 24 June 1994, No.39, s.33.

the 1969 International Convention on Tonnage Measurement of Ships.[54] Certain States choose tonnage rather than length as their determining criterion as to whether a vessel is compulsory to be registered, or in a separate category or register for small ships. Many flag States offer a dedicated register specifically catering for smaller sizes, intended to facilitate registration of craft less than 24 metres in length and so to permit the registration of mortgages required by financiers lending for the acquisition of such smaller but nonetheless valuable vessels. Other flag administrations, such as in the UK, may establish a simplified model of ship register in which mortgage interests may not be recorded.

3.47 The age of a ship permitted to be registered by a State is one of the most popular and frequent grounds of criticism of flag administrations generally and flags of convenience in particular. It is difficult to draw firm conclusions as to the regulatory compliance of a flag State by this factor alone, although it can serve to identify which registers have a higher than average age of tonnage subject to their authority. Analysis by UNCTAD in 2013 suggested that the youngest fleets were those of the Marshall Islands, Hong Kong and Singapore while the oldest fleets were those of Greece, Panama and China.[55] With open registries appearing in both lists, no obvious conclusion can be drawn from that data alone. The average age of the world's merchant tonnage at January 2017 was 9.9 years.[56] More instructive is the UNCTAD analysis of the age of merchant fleet by country groupings, which demonstrates the average age of vessels registered in developed countries is 9.15 years; developing countries 16.72 years; and economies in transition 15.59 years. Vessels registered in this latter grouping of States are among those making the most frequent appearances on port State control blacklists. Among the worst performers described in the statistics published by the Paris MOU for 2016, the flag States with greater than 20% detention rate were Palau, DR Congo, Cambodia, Tanzania, Togo, Ukraine, Sierra Leone, Comoros and Moldova as opposed to the largest and well-established open registers of nations such as Panama, Liberia and the Marshall Islands which each appear on the Paris MOU White List.[57]

3.48 Very few flag States, whether national or open registers, specify a maximum permitted age of a vessel as an absolute barrier to her registration. Instead many require a pre-registration acceptance survey of vessels over 20 years, others stipulate for more exacting documentary compliance requirements depending upon the age of the vessel at the time of first registration. Close scrutiny may also be expected where a vessel with a historic keel-laying date has more recently undergone a conversion and renewal project or similar, in which event the age attributed may become to some degree subjective.

3.49 The survey and certification of a vessel by an international classification society is, in practice, the most reliable independent source of information available to a flag State at the point of the application by a ship-owner to register, whether a newbuilding or second-hand tonnage. The classification society history of a vessel should contain at

---

54 The precise formula provided by the 1969 Convention is the measurement calculated as 96% of the total length of the vessel afloat on a waterline "at 85% of the least moulded depth measured from the top of the keel, or the length from the fore side of the stem to the axis of the rudder stock on that waterline, if that be greater".

55 UNCTAD, *Review of Maritime Transport* (2013) (UNCTAD/RMT/2013), Chapter 2.

56 Propelled seagoing vessels of 100 GT and above. UNCTAD, *Review of Maritime Transport* (2017) (UNCTAD/RMT/2017), Table 2.2.

57 Paris MOU Annual Report, 2016

a minimum the basic record of its construction, and its maintenance and dry-docking cycles throughout the working life of the ship. These records, together with Port State Control data,[58] represent the best opportunity for the flag State to make an objective desktop evaluation of the acceptability or otherwise of older vessels in particular. In practice, vessels giving rise to concerns as to their acceptability for any reason should be the subject of a detailed physical inspection either by a flag State surveyor or delegated to a recognised organisation.

3.50 The classification societies which are members of the International Association of Classification Societies (IACS) are very widely but not universally accepted by all flag States. At those margins, certain traditional affiliation or recognition by certain flag States of different classification societies to the exclusion of others is a significant factor of which intending ship-owners should be aware. Such discrimination is entirely at the discretion of each flag State, and represents the degree to which the national administration is willing to delegate and entrust surveys and the issuance of documentation expressly on their behalf and in their name, to third-party organisations of differing approach and methodology. As considered in Chapter 2, the RO Code now articulates the fundamental requirements and minimum competencies of those to whom responsibility may be delegated by flag States, seeking a threshold uniformity and consistency of approach. In theory this should in time make less significant some vagaries in quality and the flexibility of interpretation among less reputable or inadequately-resourced organisations that may hitherto have permitted sub-standard vessels to receive clean bills of health.[59]

---

58 Such as published by online databases such as THETIS, Equasis and GISIS. Port State control is considered further in Chapter 2.

59 See para. 2.15.

CHAPTER 4

International registers

Meaning and use

4.1 The term 'flag of convenience' has for a long time been as widely used in the popular media as in the shipping industry. The phrase has come to signify the evils of rampant capitalism and the disregard of labour rights, safety standards and environmental protection in the pursuit of profit by anonymous offshore corporations. The phrase has developed a wide currency and emotive force, particularly following the significant oil pollution suffered as a result of the sinking of the tankers *Exxon Valdez, Braer, Erika*, and *Prestige*. Although a significant majority of the world's merchant tonnage now operates using this model of registration and with the leading open registries consistently appearing in the White Lists of port State control statistics, the phrase retains a harsh pejorative tone. Now a historic reputation without foundation, based on prejudice rather than fact, without question it can no longer be seriously maintained that open registries or flags of convenience – *per se* – harbour sub-standard vessels or are unscrupulous in their compliance with international Conventions.

4.2 There is no standard legal definition of the term 'flag of convenience', known in less emotive parlance as an 'open registry'. For the purpose of this chapter, we shall adopt the neutral and factual categorisation of 'international' or 'open" registers, signifying the ability of a ship-owner to register a vessel in a particular flag State regardless of his own nationality as a determining factor in the grounds of his qualification or entitlement to do so. These flag States permit registration for reasons of commercial expediency rather than any prerequisite sentimental, patriotic or naturally domiciled allegiance. As the *Virginia G* case confirms, the UNCLOS requirement of a genuine link existing between the flag State and the ship is concerned with supervision of the vessel by the flag administration and not conditional upon attachment or affiliation of any kind by the owner towards the country.[1]

4.3 A definition adopted by the Maritime Transport Committee of the Organisation for European Economic Co-operation in the year of the 1958 High Seas Convention referred to:

> such countries as Panama, Liberia, Honduras and Costa Rica whose laws allow – and, indeed, make it easy for – ships owned by foreign nationals or companies to fly these flags. This is in contrast to the practice in the maritime countries (and in many others) where the right to fly the national flag is subject to stringent conditions and involves far-reaching obligations.[2]

---

1 See Chapter 3, para. 3.13 *et seq.*
2 *Study of the Expansion of the Flags of Convenience and of Various Aspects Thereof* (1958).

At that time, one may reasonably conclude that the obligations referred to intended to describe the duties of the owner to the flag State, rather than incumbent upon the flag State towards the owner. According to Boczek, also writing at the time of the emergence of the practice:

> Functionally, a 'flag of convenience' can be defined as the flag of any country allowing the registration of foreign-owned and foreign-controlled vessels under conditions which, for whatever the reasons, are convenient and opportune for the persons who are registering the vessels.[3]

4.4 The report of Lord Donaldson's inquiry into the prevention of pollution from merchant shipping following the grounding of the tanker *Braer* in Shetland in 1993 noted "this expression is always used in a derogatory sense, but it is not always applied to the same flags".[4] The report recognised that "it by no means follows that ships flying flags of convenience as so defined are substandard" and, astutely focusing on the issue of supervision rather than attachment, adopted the following definition for its purposes: "A register where the State does not have the capability of supervising the safety of its ships or does not do so effectively."[5]

4.5 The fact of foreign control, if not foreign ownership, is a feature that occurs in most international registers. However, even in the case of some countries – for example the UK – which are not commonly considered to be flags of convenience, the element of foreign control may still be present. Even prior to the amendments brought about by the Merchant Shipping Act 1988,[6] a British ship could in effect be wholly controlled by non-UK interests simply through the mechanism of incorporating a ship-owning company in the UK. Provided that such a company was "established under and subject to the laws of some part of Her Majesty's dominions, and [had its] principal place of business in those dominions", the ownership requirement was satisfied, irrespective of the nationality of the shareholders. Further, the requirement to permit nationals domiciled in, or limited companies incorporated in, the European Union[7] to register vessels in the UK demonstrates the breadth of territory from which many – those who hitherto would have been considered entirely foreign – beneficial owners could, as of right, become owners of vessels under the UK flag. At least for the remaining duration of the membership of the UK in the EU, this amply demonstrates the prejudice against open registries as such to be quite baseless in circumstances where foreign nationals were permitted freely to register vessels under the red ensign without apparent dilution of the reputation of the UK in being perceived as a flag of convenience.

4.6 Likewise, the element of convenience, economic or otherwise, is not the exclusive preserve of the flags bearing that popular designation. Resort may be had to the traditional maritime registries for a variety of reasons which have nothing to do with national affinity – for example, to take advantage of government subsidies or incentives to the

---

3 *Flags of Convenience – An International Legal Study* (Harvard University Press 1962) 2.

4 *Safer Ships, Cleaner Seas* (Cm. 2560) HMSO, May 1994, para. 6.22.

5 *Ibid.*, para. 6.25.

6 See now Merchant Shipping (Registration of Ships) Regulations 1993, of which extracts are included at Appendix VI.

7 *Ibid.*, Part III, reg. 7(1)(a), (f).

shipping sector or the protection offered by the naval forces of the State concerned. The transfer of ships to the British and US flags during the Iran/Iraq conflict between 1980 and 1988 in order to take advantage of naval protection afforded by those States in the Persian Gulf is a prime example. Indeed, in the case of the British flag, there would seemingly have been nothing to prevent nationals of either of the belligerent States from taking advantage of such protection through the simple expedient of incorporating a company in the UK, transferring their vessels to that company and registering them under the British flag.[8]

4.7 Concerns relating to the "flag of convenience" model began to surface in the 1960s. A report upon the organisation and structure of the UK shipping industry by the UK Government in 1970, known as the Rochdale Report,[9] isolated six features common to flags of convenience:

(1) the country of registry allows ownership and/or control of its merchant vessels by non-citizens;

(2) access to the registry is easy. A ship may usually be registered at a consul's office abroad. Equally important, transfer from the registry at the owner's option is not restricted;

(3) taxes on the income from the ships are not levied locally or are low. A registry fee and an annual fee, based on tonnage, are normally the only charges made. A guarantee or acceptable understanding regarding future freedom from taxation may also be given;

(4) the country of registry is a small power with no national requirement under any foreseeable circumstances for all the shipping registered, but receipts from very small charges on a large tonnage may produce a substantial effect on its national income and balance of payments;

(5) manning of ships by non-nationals is freely permitted; and

(6) the country of registry has neither the power nor the administrative machinery effectively to impose any government or international regulations; nor has the country the wish or the power to control the companies themselves.

One might notice that safety concerns are not mentioned. In fact, the Report fairly acknowledges

> while at one time the ships on their registers had a low reputation for safety and there is still no formal protection for the interests of their crews, most of the ships operated today are modern and well maintained in order to meet safety requirements set by insurers.[10]

---

8 Protection was provided by the Royal Navy to any vessel registered in the UK or Dependent Territories and also to vessels registered under other flags where there was a clear British majority interest in the ownership of such vessels.

9 *Committee of Inquiry into Shipping – Report*, Cmnd. 4337, HMSO, May 1970. This seminal document is still used by the International Transport Workers' Federation (ITF) as a basis for determining whether or not a particular registry is a flag of convenience.

10 *Ibid.*, para. 70; further, "while flags of convenience certainly make possible the running of cut-price, low-standard, 'shoestring' fleets, by far the greater part of the ships on these registers is composed of modern vessels which bear full comparison with those of other registers and which are far too valuable to put at risk unnecessarily", para. 192; and concludes "we do not believe . . . that any part of them is now composed of vessels operated on sub-standard lines" para. 198.

The primary concern was economic distortion – the comparative disadvantage of ship-owners resident in high-tax countries.[11]

4.8 To this day, these features can be present to a greater or lesser degree in some open registries. Certainly, criteria (1) and (5) are the key ingredients. With regard to (2), many flag States now impose age limits on vessels entering their registry for the first time, and surveys are insisted upon in a number of cases prior to issuance of the permanent certificate of registry. Feature (6) is becoming less and less prevalent and now appears the most anachronistic – most of the major flags of convenience have gone to considerable lengths to ensure their compliance with international regulations, particularly in matters of safety and security where port State control[12] now acts as a major disincentive to the retention by open registers of sub-standard tonnage under their flags. By 2017, the Paris MOU statistics showed the four largest open registers of Liberia, Panama, the Marshall Islands and Hong Kong (together comprising over 51% of the global merchant fleet)[13] on the White List of above-average comparative regulatory performance.

4.9 It is possible also to define international registers or flags of convenience by reference to the existence or otherwise of a genuine economic link between a vessel and its country of registration. The *ad hoc* Intergovernmental Working Group, established under the auspices of UNCTAD, on the Economic Consequences of the Existence or Lack of a Genuine Link between Vessel and Flag of Registry concluded in its Report that:

> The following elements are normally relevant when establishing whether a genuine link exists between a vessel and its country of registry:
>
> (i)   the merchant fleet contributes to the national economy of the country;
> (ii) revenues and expenditure of shipping, as well as purchases and sales of vessels, are treated in the national balance-of-payments accounts;
> (iii) the employment of nationals on vessels;
> (iv) the beneficial ownership of the vessel.[14]

4.10 In sum, flags of convenience are easier to recognise than to define. From the ship-owner's point of view, the characteristics of an open register would be seen as follows:

(1)   the avoidance of tax in the country in which he is established;

(2)   lower crewing costs, since (a) registration in an international registry generally means an unrestricted choice of crew in the international market; and (b) he is not subject to onerous national wage scales;

(3)   the avoidance of publicity: the capital of the ship-owning company, which may possess no asset other than the ship, may be disguised to some degree in flag States with fewer public filing requirements or where previously bearer

---

11 The Rochdale Report acknowledges that "one or more of these features may be observable in the policies or circumstances of many maritime countries; it is only for flags of convenience countries that all apply and it is only they which effectively have no possibility of imposing taxation on shipping in the future", *ibid.*, para. 184.

12 See para. 2.16 *et seq.*

13 Propelled seagoing vessels >100GT (UNCTAD, *Review of Maritime Transport* (2017), *Table* 2.6).

14 TD/B/C.4/177 – TD/B/C.4/AC.1/3 annex.

shares may have been permitted;[15] the directors and officers may be nominees, having no say in the running of the company or the operation of the vessel. Though that practice is now rare, due to anti-money laundering regulations, ascertaining the true ownership of the vessel in those circumstances was virtually impossible; and

(4) ease of use: prompt and efficient processing of applications and the issuance of documents using modern methods such as electronic certificates and online filing. In an increasingly competitive global market, the ship-owner has the widest choice such that if criteria (1)–(3) above are satisfied equally by many flag States, customer service and speed of turnaround can be a deciding factor.[16]

4.11 The economic advantages to the flag State can be considerable and the number of smaller countries providing offshore registration facilities continues to grow. The Pacific State of Vanuatu, for example, entered the scene in the early 1980s. By 2002 the Vanuatu register, administered from the United States, had registered some 321 vessels of over 100 gross tons and by 2007, some 433 vessels of this size were entered with this flag. The size of a national fleet fluctuates from year to year – in the case of Vanuatu, the number of vessels registered appears to have reached a plateau at this level in the years since 2012. Great success has been enjoyed by the Marshall Islands, which since the introduction of its 1990 Maritime Act has seen its fleet of vessels greater than 100 gross tons increase from 302 vessels in 2000 to 1,099 in 2007.[17] From these beginnings, by January 2018 the Marshall Islands enjoyed a fleet of 4,327 vessels in total, a tonnage growth of over 12% against the prior year and is now considered the second largest of all.[18]

4.12 The International Transport Workers' Federation (ITF) which has spearheaded the opposition to the open registry system, classifies as a flag of convenience any country which allows on its register ships which are beneficially owned and/or controlled by companies incorporated elsewhere.[19] By February 2018 the ITF has designated the following countries and territories as flags of convenience: Antigua and Barbuda, Bahamas, Barbados, Belize, Bermuda, Bolivia, Cambodia, Cayman Islands, Comoros, Cyprus, Equatorial Guinea, Georgia, Gibraltar, Honduras, Jamaica, Lebanon, Liberia, Malta, Marshall Islands, Mauritius, Moldova, Mongolia, Myanmar, Netherlands Antilles, North Korea, Panama, Sao Tome and Principe, St Vincent and the Grenadines, Sri Lanka, Tonga and Vanuatu.

4.13 In addition, ships entered on certain 'second' registers[20] may be considered as flying under flags of convenience; their status as such depends upon whether or not they

---

15 International anti-money laundering regulations require a clear identification of the ultimate beneficial owners of an incorporated company when it is to any degree to become involved in any financial transaction involving the banking system. Among the 35 members of the inter-governmental Financial Action Task Force established in 1989 to counter money laundering and more recently terrorist financing, however, by 2017 of the ten largest registers in the world only Hong Kong, Singapore, China and Greece were represented.

16 Factors influencing choice of registry are considered in Chapter 6. For present purposes, the flag of convenience represents the ability of a ship-owner to choose any other flag State than his own nationality or its place of incorporation.

17 Source: Lloyd's Register – Fairplay Ltd, *World Fleet Statistics*, 2007; http://unctadstat.unctad.org.

18 Propelled seagoing vessels >100GT (UNCTAD, *Review of Maritime Transport* (2017)).

19 "A flag of convenience ship is one that flies the flag of a country other than the country of ownership" (ITF publication *What are Flags of Convenience*).

20 See further, para. 4.37 *et seq.*

are owned by nationals of the flag country and whether or not crew wage agreements acceptable to that country's unions have been entered into. These include the Norwegian International Ship Register, the Danish International Ship Register, the Isle of Man and Madeira. The second registers of Germany, France and the Faroe Islands are considered to be flags of convenience in their own right by the ITF and, as such, all ships registered there are treated as flag of convenience vessels. The ITF may also designate on an individual basis as flag of convenience vessels registered in Hong Kong, the Philippines (foreign-owned ships bareboat chartered-in) and Singapore (foreign-owned ships without approved crew agreements). Equally, ships flying the flag of countries not mentioned above will be treated as flag of convenience ships if the ITF receives information that they are beneficially owned in another country. The ITF historically compiled and published a blacklist of ship-owners, operators, managers and crewing agencies which it considers to have violated seafarers' rights. Vessels owned, operated, managed or crewed by such companies are specifically targeted by ITF inspectors and sanctions applied by means of industrial action at the visited port.

Development of international registers

4.14 The use of international registries is generally traced back to the use of the Spanish flag by English merchants to avoid Spanish monopoly restrictions on trade with the West Indies.[21] In the seventeenth century the French flag was adopted by English fishermen off Newfoundland in order to avoid fishing restrictions imposed by Great Britain. Similar use was made of the Norwegian flag by British fishermen in the nineteenth century. An early popular travel writer, A. W. Kinglake, journeying across Greece and the Levant in the 1830s, mentions that the first concern of the Greek seafarers when they undertook a shipping enterprise was:

> to procure for their vessel the protection of some European power; this is easily managed by a little intriguing with the Dragoman of one of the Embassies at Constantinople, and the craft soon glories in the ensign of Russia, or the dazzling Tricolour, or the Union Jack; thus, to the great delight of her crew, she enters upon the ocean world with a flaring lie at her peak, but the appearance of the vessel does no discredit to the borrowed flag . . . The privileges attached to the vessel and her crew, by virtue of the borrowed flag, are so great as to imply a liberty wider even than that which is often enjoyed in our more strictly civilized countries.[22]

4.15 From such beginnings, the widespread international use of flags of convenience is a twentieth-century phenomenon and seems to have had its origin in August 1919 when, with the assistance of an enterprising consul in Vancouver, a small cargo vessel, the *Belen Quezada*, was transferred from the Canadian to the Panamanian flag and thereafter engaged in rum-running in an effort to avoid American prohibition laws.[23] In 1922, two cruise

---

21 Boczek, *op. cit.*, p. 6.

22 *Eothen* (John Ollivier, 1847) p. 63. An anecdote later in the volume, concerning a different vessel to that earlier described and owned by Greeks, mentions the practice of holding on board both the Russian standard and the Union Jack, to be used interchangeably as most suitable to the port visited.

23 192 See generally on the history of flags of convenience, Carlisle, *Sovereignty for Sale: the origin and evolution of the Panamanian and Liberian flags of convenience* (Naval Institute Press 1981) and B.N. Metaxas, *Flags of Convenience* (Gower Publishing Co Ltd 1985).

liners, the *Reliance* and the *Resolute*, were transferred from the US flag to the Panamanian to avoid prohibition regulations preventing the sale of liquor on board American vessels. Prohibition, in fact, provided a considerable boost to the Panamanian flag in the 1920s. In 1925 Panama enacted a liberally drafted maritime law specifically intended to attract foreign tonnage. The early success of the Panamanian flag can be attributed in part to the assistance of the US consular service, which represented the interests of Panamanian nationals in ports where there was no Panamanian consul. In this way, it seems that many early patentes de navegacion were issued by consuls of the United States.[24] During the same period, the United Fruit Company's fleet of banana vessels was transferred from the US flag to that of Honduras.

4.16 The worsening political situation in Europe in the 1930s provided considerable opportunity and impetus to the flags of convenience model of operating registries and their fleets. In 1935, the 25 vessels forming the Esso Baltic fleet were transferred from the flag of the Free City of Danzig to that of Panama. During the Spanish Civil War, a number of Spanish vessels made use of the Panamanian flag and many Greek owners reflagged their ships in Panama to avoid the non-intervention blockade imposed by Great Britain and other powers. High crewing costs under the Greek flag in the pre-war years also led to growing use of the Panamanian flag by Greek operators. In 1932, Manuel Kulukundis registered the *Mount Athos* under the Panamanian flag; this was followed by a number of vessels in the Onassis fleet.

4.17 Following the outbreak of war between the European powers in 1939, the Panamanian flag saw a further influx of US tonnage seeking to avoid the provisions of the US Neutrality Act which prevented the carriage in American ships of cargoes destined for belligerents on either side. The transfers to the Panamanian flag were in many cases made with the knowledge of the US Government which saw to the arming of American-owned Panamanian flag vessels and the extension of war risk cover to such vessels. There seems also to have been some Axis use of the Panamanian flag during the hostilities – Carlisle[25] mentions extensive deliveries by Panamanian flag vessels of naval-grade fuel oil to Spanish installations on Tenerife, presumably destined for use by German U-boats.

4.18 The immediate post-war years saw growing dissatisfaction with some aspects of the Panamanian flag; in particular, there was concern for the stability of the Panamanian Government and criticism of excessive consular fees. A former US Secretary of State, Edward R. Stettinius, Jr, who had been cultivating business opportunities with Liberia, particularly the exploitation of iron deposits in the Bomi Hills, saw the development of an offshore shipping register as a useful adjunct to his other activities. In 1948, the Liberian Government promulgated the Liberian Maritime Law and the Liberian Corporation Law, each containing provisions culled from a variety of US legislation. Stettinius Associates, which had a profit-sharing arrangement with the Liberian Government, based the ship registry in New York and were able to offer the efficiency of a well-run business organisation in contrast to the perceived unreliability of the Panamanian consular network. The first ship entered in the new Liberian register was the Niarchos-owned *World Peace*

---

24 Carlisle, *op. cit.*, p. 32.
25 *Op. cit.*, p. 77.

in 1948. By 1950 the Liberian flag had 22 merchant vessels; by 1960 this figure rose to 977; and by 1970 some 1,869 foreign vessels had adopted this register.

4.19 It is a testimony to the resilience of the Liberian and Panamanian flags that notwithstanding fragile national governments, coups d'état, embargoes and invasion, at the beginning of 2017 they accounted between them for 11,348 ships of over 100 gross tons, over 30% of world tonnage.[26] Indeed, the Liberian system has provided the operating model for shipping registers of a number of other countries such as Vanuatu and the Marshall Islands which are also run on a corporate basis from the United States and whose maritime legislation possesses many similarities with that of Liberia.

Opposition to international registers

4.20 The widespread pejorative usage both in popular culture and to a lesser extent within the shipping industry arises because the flag of convenience system had been seen in many quarters as liberalism too far, overdue for eradication. The opponents of the system commonly focus their criticism on three aspects – safety, transparency, and labour rights – each of which are said to be detrimentally influenced by the absence of any substantive national attachment between the ship-owner and the flag State. Concerns have been expressed that this lack of national attachment and regulatory supervision by certain flag States also creates international security and terrorist risks.[27]

Safety

4.21 It is a fact that many of the most famous and widely publicised maritime disasters of the late twentieth century have involved vessels registered under flags of convenience – the *Torrey Canyon* in 1967, the *Amoco Cadiz* in 1978, the *Odyssey* in 1988, the *Haven* in 1991, the *Braer* in 1993, the *Sea Empress* in 1996 and the *Erika* in 1999. Five of those infamous vessels were registered in Liberia, but it may equally be said that the growth and early dominance of that flag State in the tanker market could also explain such apparent over-representation. The *Exxon Valdez* was registered in the United States, considered to be a closed register. Such bald comparisons are not instructive and miss the necessary analysis of the many causes of casualties in a marine adventure including mechanical failure and human elements which may yet affect the most stringently maintained vessels and the most highly qualified complements.

4.22 It is nonetheless also a fact that for some years – but no longer the case – the casualty records of open or international registry fleets revealed a considerably higher rate of losses than in the traditional maritime countries which maintained the requirement of genuine link between the ship-owner and the flag State. A report by the UNCTAD Secretariat in 1981[28] identified ten reasons why non-observance of safety standards was

---

26 UNCTAD, *Review of Maritime Transport* (2017), *op. cit.*, Table 2.6.

27 International Transport Workers' Federation/World Wide Fund for Nature publication *Real and Present Danger: Flag State Failure and Maritime Safety and Security* (2008).

28 *Action on the Question of Open Registries*, TD/B/C.4/220.

likely to be greater under open-registry flags than under the flags of States having genuine economic links with vessels:

(1) Real owners are not readily identifiable (partly because of difficulties in identifying, partly because of lack of incentive to identify) and are therefore in a good position to take risks by comparison with owners in normal registries who are living under the eyes of a maritime administration.

(2) Real owners can change their identities by manipulating brass-plate companies and consequently avoid being identified as repeated sub-standard operators or risk-takers.

(3) Since the Master and other key shipboard personnel are not nationals of the flag State, they have no need or incentive to visit the flag State and can avoid legal action.

(4) Owners who reside outside the jurisdiction of the flag State can defy the flag State by refusing to testify at an inquiry by the flag State and avoid prosecution.

(5) Since open-registry owners do not have the same interest in preserving good relations with the flag State, they do not feel the need to co-operate with inspectors of the flag State.

(6) Open-registry shipping lacks the union structure which is so essential to the application of safety and social standards in countries of normal registry: namely, a national trade union of the flag State representing basically the interests of national seamen on board vessels owned by owners who have economic links with the flag State.

(7) Open-registry owners are in a better position to put pressure on Masters and officers to take risks, since there is no really appropriate government to which shipboard personnel can complain.

(8) Port State Control is weaker because the port State can only report sub-standard vessels and practice to a flag State which has no real control over the owner.

(9) Owners can suppress any signs of militancy among crews by virtue of their freedom to change nationalities of crews at whim.

(10) Enforcement of standards is basically inconsistent with the operation of a registry with the sole aim of making a profit.

As a historical perspective, describing genuine public and intergovernmental concerns arising from significant and high-profile pollution events, this list is instructive. As a barometer of twenty-first century practices and attitudes, it is an anachronism largely superseded by better technology, communications and a new rigour of international co-operation.

4.23 Those closer to the reality of the shipping industry than the popular media may consider that much of the criticism against international registers *per se* on safety grounds is unjustified. In common with the flags of all nations, the registries of the flags of convenience contain a wide variety of tonnage, of different ages and construction; some vessels are operated by large multinational corporations, such as the major oil companies, others by enterprises of a much smaller scale. The potent combination of publicity and pollution following any oil spill results in a widespread assumption of guilt by the operator of an open register vessel, a prejudice not based in objective analysis. Some of the most modern ships are operated under open registers and a number of registers have taken steps to exclude very old tonnage. Liberia, for example, stipulates that vessels seeking registration (or re-registration) must not be more than 20 years old, although subject to certain conditions vessels exceeding that age limit may be accepted for re-registration. Panama prescribes no age limitation, but vessels over 20 years of age are subject to a special inspection before the permanent certificate of registry can be issued. Bahamas generally applies a 12-year age limit, whilst Vanuatu follows the 20-year rule. Cyprus has a basic 15-year age limit, but older vessels may be registered subject to a number of conditions, including the existence of a real and effective ownership or management link between the vessel and the island.[29]

4.24 All the principal international registers are parties to the major international safety Conventions and strive to ensure compliance through a network of worldwide inspectors. Liberia has led the field in this respect. Flag States including Liberia, Vanuatu and Panama make annual levies on ships in their registers (based on net tonnage) for casualty investigation and international participation. Liberia and the Marshall Islands both require the appointment of a 'decision maker', contactable on a 24-hour basis in the event of any incident affecting the vessel as a condition for the issuance of a permanent certificate of registry. Notably, in contrast to the findings of the UNCTAD Secretariat in 1981 referred to at the outset of this section, the UNCTAD annual statistical publication *Review of Maritime Transport* issued in December 2007 reported that no general conclusions can be drawn as regards the safety of foreign-flagged versus nationally flagged vessels.[30]

Transparency

4.25 After the Maltese registered tanker *Erika* broke in two in the Bay of Biscay in December 1999 and spilled her cargo of 31,000 tonnes of heavy fuel oil, the coastal authorities could not identify her true owner. It is said that there were 12 corporate entities between the registered owner of the vessel and its ultimate beneficial owner. The shareholders of the registered owner were two companies incorporated in Liberia. In the event, the beneficial owner stepped forward as the French government investigation had been unable to trace ownership beyond, or behind, a web of businesses concerned with the operation of the vessel which were variously operating or established in the Bahamas, India, Italy, Liberia, Malta and Switzerland.

4.26 The ability of the ultimate beneficial and controlling interests of a business to shelter or indeed to hide behind a corporate veil in a remote jurisdiction has long aroused suspicion. The means to make ownership details effectively secret, private and inaccessible – such as through bearer shares, trust structures, corporate directors or a register of companies that permits non-disclosure of shareholders and office-bearers – gives rise for many to an inference of evasion at best or illegality at worst. The Report of the UN Consultative Group on Flag State Implementation published in 2004[31] refers at length to the findings of the Maritime Transport Committee (MTC) of OECD relating to the problem of sub-standard shipping operated by certain open registers. The MTC

---

29 See *infra*, Chapter 3, para. 3.47 *et seq.*
30 Chapter 2, p. 35.
31 General Assembly, 59th session, A/59/63.

describe "effectively cloaking beneficial ownership" with "a complex web of corporate entities" but accepts:

> While some ship registers actively facilitate and promote anonymity for reluctant owners, the principal mechanisms are not the registers themselves, but the corporate mechanisms that are available to owners to cloak their identity . . . From the perspective of the ship-registering process, the most important single feature that facilitates anonymity of individuals is the ability (quite sensible from a commercial perspective) of corporations to be registered as owners of vessels. The most common and effective mechanisms that can provide anonymity for beneficial owners include bearer shares, nominee shareholders, nominee directors, the use of intermediaries to act on owners' behalf and the failure of jurisdictions to provide for effective reporting requirements . . . Open registers, which by definition do not have any nationality requirements, are the easiest jurisdictions in which to register vessels that are covered by complex legal and corporate arrangements. The arrangements will almost certainly cover a number of international jurisdictions which would be much more difficult to untangle.[32]

4.27 It is important to recognise, then, first the obvious and *prima facie* legality of the quite universal practice of permitting ownership of vessels by corporations; secondly, that the entitlement of a corporation to conceal its ultimate beneficial owners is a question of domestic company law rather than a contrivance of the ship registry itself or indeed open registers as such. The massive unauthorised release of confidential files in 2016 known as the Panama Papers was not concerned primarily with shipping, nor with Panama, but significantly raised global awareness of the use of offshore structures to conceal wealth, avoid tax and – it is insinuated – in some cases engage in criminality.[33] In the shipping context, following the *Erika* experience, concerns properly remain focused on the perceived ability of anonymous owners to evade responsibility for safety standards and pollution incidents.

4.28 Significant progress has been made in this area through amendments to SOLAS that compel greater disclosure of details of the ownership and management of vessels. In 2003 the IMO resolved to adopt the format and guidelines for a Continuous Synopsis Record (CSR) applicable to all passenger and cargo vessels over 500 gross tonnes, in implementation of SOLAS regulation XI-1/5.[34] Issued by the flag State, the CSR is a

---

32 *Ibid.*, para. 188.

33 In direct response to the Panama Papers outcry, following discussions between the leaders of the G20 countries concerning the promotion of strong and transparent corporate governance, Mr David Cameron, the then UK Prime Minister, wrote to the governments of each of the UK Overseas Territories and Crown Dependencies in 2014 recommending the establishment of a central register of company beneficial ownership information as a key step necessary to improve financial transparency. By the end of 2016 each of the Crown Dependencies (Alderney, Jersey, Guernsey and the Isle of Man) and most of the Overseas Territories (Anguilla, Bermuda, Gibraltar, the British Virgin Islands, the Cayman Islands and the Turks and Caicos Islands) had exchanged notes with the UK Government agreeing to the timely introduction of beneficial ownership registers with a means by which such information can be made available to tax and law enforcement agencies. The Cayman Islands government was one of the first countries to implement the relevant exchange of notes in the form of legislation requiring certain Cayman Islands companies and limited liability companies to maintain a beneficial ownership register. These registers will not be accessible to the public but only to the competent authority in the Cayman Islands which may disclose the information to certain Cayman Islands regulatory bodies and the law enforcement authorities of countries that have entered into an agreement with the Cayman Islands in respect of such matters. See generally, the following Cayman Islands enactments: the Companies (Amendment) Law, 2017; the Limited Liability Companies (Amendment) Law, 2017; the Beneficial Ownership (Companies) Regulations, 2017; and the Beneficial Ownership (Limited Liability Companies) Regulations, 2017.

34 A 23/Res. 959.

sequentially numbered and evolving file of relevant details including contact names and addresses of owners and operators. The introduction of this document, compulsorily to be held on board for port State inspection, provides a through-life history of the vessel including details of its flag, owner, operator, charterer, classification society, safety management, and security activities.

4.29 In 2005 the form of CSR was enhanced to require inclusion of IMO company numbers for registered owners and the ISM managers of vessel.[35] Becoming mandatory for SOLAS vessels in January 2009, this is a system similar to the long-established IMO vessel numbering regime and considerably simplifies the identification of corporations concerned with ship operation. The IMO company number, like the vessel IMO number, remains the same although its name may change. Identified in this way, companies with the same or similar names (or the unscrupulous frequently changing their names in the hope of confusion) can be readily distinguished in the records of port State inspections. These measures do not alone defeat or disentangle the perceived mischief of the corporate veil used nefariously, but they compel a record to be retained for inspection at any time that expressly identifies those responsible for the safe management and operation of the vessel. With that greater transparency, it is hoped to achieve greater accountability.

Labour rights

4.30 Organised labour opposition to open registers under the 'flags of convenience' banner began in the 1930s in the United States as a consequence of the transfer of American ships to the Panamanian and Honduran flags. The movement gathered momentum after World War II and, in 1948, the International Transport Workers' Federation (ITF) – which now unites some 700 trade unions in more than 150 countries, representing over four million transport workers including around 300,000 seafarers – adopted a resolution threatening the boycott of ships transferred to the Panamanian flag. The ITF Congress of July 1958 resolved upon a worldwide boycott of open registry ships. The main objectives of the ITF campaign were:

(1) to establish by international governmental agreement a genuine link between the flag that a ship flies and the nationality or residence of its owners, managers and seafarers, and so to eliminate the flag of convenience system entirely; and

(2) to ensure that seafarers who serve on flag of convenience ships, whatever their nationality, are protected from exploitation by shipowners.

4.31 The ITF implements its campaign by, among other strategies, urging its affiliated dockers and stevedores unions to refuse to load or discharge flag of convenience ships. The campaign has been most enthusiastically pursued in Australia and Scandinavia. Although the campaign is expressed to be directed against allegedly sub-standard labour conditions on board flag of convenience ships, the motivation was originally to prevent loss of work opportunities for seafarers in the traditional European maritime countries where spiralling wage costs have rendered the operation of ships increasingly uneconomic.

---

35 MSC 80/24/Add.1.

4.32 One tactic in the ITF campaign has been to insist that ship-owners operating vessels under flags of convenience employ their crews under the ITF Collective Agreement which contains terms and conditions for the employment of seafarers unilaterally determined by the Federation. Signature of the agreement is evidenced by the issuance of a "blue certificate" by the ITF Secretariat, which signifies acceptance by the ITF of the wages and working conditions on board the vessel in question. Failure to produce such a certificate to an ITF inspector can lead to industrial action being taken against the vessel.

4.33 It seems that the number of ships registered under flags of convenience covered by ITF agreements had for a time declined after a peak of 2,000 in 1982. In 1989 only 20% of the world's open registry fleet was covered by agreements acceptable to the ITF.[36] Academic studies have identified two reasons for this:

(1) the decreasing size of merchant fleets in the traditional maritime countries was affecting ITF membership and consequently its ability to organise effective action; and

(2) the division between affiliates in developed and developing countries – in the latter, seamen were content to work for wages below the ITF rates and Asian unions were found to acquiesce in the evasion of ITF policy by issuing blue cards even where crews were engaged below ITF wage rates.[37]

By June 2001 however the figure had recovered and by 2004 had risen to nearly 6,000 ships, and some 8,100 vessels. By 2008, approximately one-third of the world's open register fleet was said by the ITF to be subject to satisfactory working conditions. Equivalent progress can be seen in the number of seafarers working under ITF agreements, rising from almost 233,000 in 2008 to over 309,000 by 2016.[38]

4.34 The entry into force in August 2013 of the ILO Maritime Labour Convention (MLC) 2006[39] represents a meaningful step towards a global standardisation of minimum terms and conditions of employment for seafarers. A major diplomatic achievement, effectively consolidating over 35 prior ILO Conventions in relation to their particular subject matter, the MLC is considered to be the 'fourth pillar' of international maritime regulatory regimes (together with SOLAS, MARPOL and STCW). By February 2018, the Convention has been ratified by 84 States responsible for the living and working conditions for seafarers on more than 80% of the world's gross tonnage – including the largest open registries of Panama, Liberia and the Marshall Islands.

4.35 The MLC requires commercial vessels of 500 gross tonnage or more operating international voyages to obtain from the flag State two additional documents relating to crew welfare and conditions, available for inspection by port State control. These are

---

36 ITF *Seafarers' Bulletin* No. 4, 1989.

37 Bettink, 'Open Registry, the Genuine Link and the 1986 Convention on Registration Conditions for Ships' (Netherlands Yearbook of International Law, 1987) 91.

38 ITF *Seafarers' Bulletin* No. 23, 2009; ITF *Seafarers' Bulletin* No. 31, 2017.

39 Adopted by the International Labour Organisation at Geneva on 23 February 2006, the enumerated basic rights for all seafarers include the effective recognition of the right to collective bargaining; the elimination of all forms of forced or compulsory labour; the effective abolition of child labour; the elimination of discrimination in respect of employment and occupation; the right to a safe and secure workplace that complies with safety standards; the right to fair terms of employment; the right to decent working and living conditions on board ship; and the right to health protection, medical care, welfare measures and other forms of social protection.

a maritime labour certificate and a declaration of maritime labour compliance, which together evidence that the employment conditions, and the vessel in question, are operated in compliance with the requirements of the Convention. The Convention is particularly far-reaching because in addition to its application to vessels flying the flag of a ratifying State, vessels of a non-ratifying State are also subject to inspection for compliance with respect to conditions for seafarers when they enter the ports of countries in which it is in force.

4.36 As ratifications of the 2006 Convention (and amendments thereto agreed in 2014 and 2016) continue, in this new landscape – a least in the field of labour relations – the focus of the ITF and other detractors of flags of convenience may become the role of encouraging full and proper implementation of MLC requirements and making sure seafarers know their rights under the MLC, rather than policing by way of industrial action or lobbying for abandonment of the open registry concept itself.

Response of traditional maritime nations to open registers – 'second' registers

4.37 The traditional maritime States – particularly those in western Europe – have recognised that any attempt to abolish the flags of convenience altogether would be doomed to fail. For any such attempt could only succeed by placing severe limitations on national sovereignty which, if applied universally, would be less acceptable to the countries in the developed world than the prejudice suffered to their merchant marines by the existence of the open registries. The moribund state of the 1986 Convention on Conditions for Registration of Ships, a perceived champion for the notion of the prerequisite genuine economic linkage between owner and flag State, speaks to the likelihood of any significant political or policy reversal of the right of a nation to legislate as it chooses upon whom may enter its ship register. In addition to the traditional tax and other financial incentives available to the shipping sector, the response of a number of the traditional maritime nations has been either to enable the bareboat charter out of vessels under their flag, or to establish 'second' or international registries which offer many of the advantages of an open register, but nonetheless retain a link of sorts between beneficial ownership or management and the national flag.

4.38 A fear of flight from Europe has led to the establishment of new registries, a selection of which are described below, which seek to halt the decline of the merchant fleets of the traditional maritime countries by allowing ship-owners to operate in a lower-cost registry environment whilst retaining the respectability of and an affiliation to a European flag State. This model also aims to preserve the economic and cultural advantages of supporting historic and skilled domestic industries including services to the marine sector and the related supply chain – in addition to promoting seafaring as an attractive modern profession and for indigenous ship-building and repair businesses. The retention of the link with the national flag preserves the jurisdiction of the individual State over vessels owned by its nationals – important for regulatory, fiscal and strategic reasons – and may ultimately obviate the need for the subsidies and other forms of financial assistance to shipping which have characterised maritime policy in many developed nations.

4.39 In 1986, the French Government responded to ship-owners' demands to register their ships in a lower-cost jurisdiction by allowing French-owned vessels to register in the

Kerguelen Islands, part of the French Southern and Antarctic Territories. This concession enabled owners to operate their vessels with only 25% of the crew consisting of French nationals, although at least four of the officers must be French. By the end of 1996 there were 102 ships in the Kerguelen Register. In May 2005 this register was replaced by the French International Register (Registre International Français, known as RIF) which allows fiscal benefits to commercial ship-owners while subject to French law, EU regulations, and French international treaty obligations. At least 25% of the crew of vessels registered in the RIF, based on the minimum safe manning document, must be EU or EEA nationals and the permanent establishment of the owning company must be domiciled in France. By 2007 RIF had registered some 164 vessels and by 2016 some 543 vessels.[40]

4.40 In 1978, 96% of Norwegian-owned tonnage was registered under the Norwegian flag. By 1987, this had declined to just 38%, despite generous government subsidies to the shipping sector.[41] This decline was largely attributable to the high crewing costs of operating vessels on the Norwegian national register. Such registration involved negotiating wage levels with the Norwegian trade unions; the levels sought by the unions in many cases rendered the operation of vessels uneconomic in contrast to the costs of crewing with nationals from developing economies as permitted by open registers. The Norwegian Government's response was to establish the Norwegian International Ship Register (NIS), based at Bergen.

4.41 Unlike the French International Register, which excludes passenger ships, the NIS is open to all self-propelled passenger and cargo ships and hovercraft, as well as drilling platforms and other moveable installations whether Norwegian or foreign-owned, provided they meet minimum technical standards. Both FIS and NIS exclude commercial fishing vessels from their fleets. Registration in the NIS is not open to ships which are transporting cargo or passengers between Norwegian ports, nor to ships transporting passengers on a regular service between a Norwegian port and a foreign port. In the case of foreign-owned ships, not only must an agent for service of process be appointed in Norway, but a substantial part of the technical or commercial management of the vessel must be delegated to a ship management company established in Norway. The legislation therefore seeks to benefit the local onshore maritime sector in addition to increasing the size of the Norwegian fleet.

4.42 From the Norwegian ship-owner's point of view, the most important benefit of the NIS is his freedom to appoint foreign nationals to all positions on board, with the exception of the Master, who must be a Norwegian citizen. In the latter case, a waiver may be granted by the Norwegian Maritime Directorate. Both the Norwegian Seamen's Act and the Norwegian Act re Working Hours on Ships apply to vessels entered in the NIS, and the NIS Act itself lays down maximum working hours. However, certain provisions in these Acts, including those relating to hours of work, may be departed from via collective bargaining agreements. The NIS Act enables collective bargaining agreements to be concluded with Norwegian or foreign trade unions. In respect of NIS

---

40 *Lloyd's Register World Fleet Statistics*, December 2000; *Lloyd's Register – Fairplay Ltd, World Fleet Statistics 2007;* UNCTAD, *Review of Maritime Transport* (2016).

41 Kappel, *The Norwegian International Ship Register – A New Approach of a Traditional Shipping Nation* (Bremen 1988).

vessels a number of collective agreements have been concluded between the Norwegian Shipowners' Association and trade unions in Norway and abroad concerning wages and other conditions of employment on board NIS vessels.

4.43 By 2007, there were some 598 vessels of 14,708,133 gross tons registered in NIS. In comparison, tonnage on the Norwegian Ordinary Register (NOR) in 2007 amounted to nearly three times as many ships in total with 1,490 vessels registered locally, but the majority being smaller craft and fishing vessels, as demonstrated by the total gross tonnage of NOR of 3,447,874 during the same period.[42] Ten years later, by 2017, although the number of vessels registered with NIS remained approximately static, the gross tonnage entered in this register had risen considerably to 19,281,158 and the total for NOR showing a modest rise to 3,978,854.[43] Notwithstanding the existence of NIS, many vessels beneficially owned by Norwegians continue to be registered under overseas flags (the most popular being the Isle of Man, the Marshall Islands and the Bahamas).[44]

4.44 The Danish International Ship Register (DIS) was established in August 1988. By 2000 it had attracted some 524 ships totalling over 6,357,000 gross tons.[45] DIS is not an open registry – in order for a ship to qualify for registration, her owner must be a Danish individual, partnership or body corporate, a foreign body corporate in which Danish undertakings have a substantial direct or indirect interest, and the ship must be effectively administered, controlled and operated from Denmark. Bareboat registration both 'in' and 'out' of DIS is permitted. The decline of the Danish register has been halted by measures including the introduction of a tonnage tax and greater flexibility in crewing. By 2007, DIS had become one of the 20 largest fleets of the world, with some 435 vessels of some 8,967,115 gross tons subject to this jurisdiction. Ten years later, the growth trend continues; by 2017 DIS was the register of 674 vessels of some 15,148,936 gross tons.[46]

4.45 The Portuguese second register in Madeira (Registo Internacional de Navios da Madeira, known as MAR) was inaugurated in 1989 within the context of the International Business Centre established on the island. It is open to ship-owners of all nationalities and accepts vessels of any tonnage or type save for fishing vessels. There are no age restrictions, although the MAR technical commission will decide, on a case-by-case basis, the vessels that shall be accepted. Vessels registered on MAR fly the Portuguese flag. Although since 2015 the basic requirement is that 30% of the crew be EU citizens, exemptions may be granted. The earnings of crew members are exempt from Portuguese taxation; likewise, neither crew members nor their employers are liable for Portuguese social security contributions. Provision is made for the temporary registration on MAR for an initial period not exceeding five years of vessels entered in a foreign registry which are subject to a bareboat charterparty. Likewise, vessels registered in MAR which are subject to a bareboat charterparty may be temporarily entered in a foreign registry

---

42 *Lloyd's Register – Fairplay Ltd, World Fleet Statistics 2007.*

43 Data courtesy NIS/NOR, as at 24 March 2017.

44 At 1 January 2008, some 14.7% of vessels beneficially owned by Norwegian interests were registered in the Isle of Man, 11.8% in the Bahamas, and 11.4% were registered in the Marshall Islands. National preference as an influence in the choice of flag States for an owner shall be discussed further in Chapter 6.

45 *Lloyd's Register World Fleet Statistics*, December 2000; *Lloyd's Register – Fairplay Ltd, World Fleet Statistics 2007.*

46 Data courtesy DIS, as at 3 April 2017.

provided the necessary consent is obtained from the MAR administration. Initial registration fees and annual fees are levied on a sliding scale depending upon the tonnage of the vessel concerned. A wide range of tax and financial incentives are available for shipping companies incorporated and licensed to operate in Madeira within the framework of the International Business Centre.

4.46 The ITF reaction to the second registers has been less than enthusiastic. Although they do not classify second registers as such to be flags of convenience within their organisation, the German International Register, the French International Register and Madeira are so categorised. Individual vessels on other secondary registers whose beneficial ownership bears no relationship with the flag State may individually be designated as flag of convenience vessels. The general view, however, is that the transfer of ships to the international registers (where they remain subject to national controls on matters such as safety) is preferable to allowing an increasing number of vessels to abandon the traditional maritime countries altogether for international registries with no required nexus between owner and flag.

CHAPTER 5

Bareboat charter registration

Development of the system

5.1 It may seem counterintuitive that, amid fierce competition among flag States for the business of owners to register their vessels in a marketplace effectively unrestrained by nationality requirements, one register might permit and actively promote the subsequent registration of a vessel elsewhere. One of the noteworthy developments in ship registration practice in recent years has been the continued and increasingly widespread use of such a structure – whereby a vessel registered in one State is permitted to fly the flag of a second State for a determinate period under certain conditions. Legitimate objections to such a system include the risk of confusion or legal ambiguity as to the rights of the owner and the charterer at any given time; the possibility of an overlapping jurisdiction by two States; or the risk that registration of the vessel may lapse altogether as a result of the particular rules of one flag State or the other.[1] These issues are most stark at the commencement and termination of the arrangement, a moment which is determined by a private contract. This situation generally arises as a result of a bareboat charterparty in terms of which a vessel registered in State A is leased for a fixed period to nationals or corporations of State B who, during the charter period, re-register and operate the vessel under the flag of the latter State.

5.2 The essential characteristic of a bareboat charterparty in this context is that it is a contract which entirely divests the operation and maintenance of the vessel into the charge of the charterer. The vessel is leased by the owner 'bare', that is, without a Master or crew to sail her. The St Vincent and the Grenadines legislation states simply: 'bareboat' means a ship without a crew.[2] The Master and crew, the repair and maintenance, and the commercial performance of the vessel are the sole preserve of the charterer. This form of leasing can be used as a financing technique, for example as method of hire-purchase when combined with a purchase obligation at the expiry of the hire period; or with which to structure a sale and lease-back commitment.

5.3 A judicial definition is "that the legal owner gives the charterer sufficient of the rights of possession and control which enable the transaction to be regarded as a letting – a lease or demise, in real property terms".[3] Statutory descriptions of this concept refer

---

1 The possibilities for confusion or error – including among legal advisors – arising as a result of the bareboat charter of a vessel are demonstrated in *The Stolt Loyalty* [1995] 1 Lloyd's Rep 598 and *The Chevron North America* [2002] 1 Lloyd's Rep 77.
2 Shipping Act 2004, s.5A(1).
3 *The Giuseppe di Vittorio* [1998] 1 Lloyd's Rep 136 at 156.

to the lease or hire of the ship for a stipulated period of time on terms which give the charterer the whole possession and control of the ship, involving the right to appoint the Master and crew.[4] The Cyprus legislation provides a comprehensive explanation:

'Bareboat chartering' is a chartering by virtue of which the charterer for the agreed period of time, acquires full control and possession of the ship, has the nautical control and management of the ship, appoints and dismisses the master and the crew of the ship, is responsible towards third parties as if he was the shipowner and, generally, so long as the chartering continues, substitutes in all respects the shipowner, save that he has no right to sell or mortgage the ship.[5]

During the period of the bareboat charter the primary registration in State A is cancelled or suspended – at least for certain purposes – but becomes fully effective once again upon termination of the charterparty.

5.4 This method of registration of the bareboat charter of a vessel in a second State can be the subject of potentially misleading description, such as 'parallel' or 'dual' registration. Both terms demonstrate the risk of legal uncertainty as to the precedence or continuing responsibility *vis-a-vis* the other State, the applicable governing law and the respective entitlement of the owner and the charterer and any mortgagee that may arise at any time during this process. For the purpose of this chapter, we shall use the terms 'bareboat charter registration'[6] and 'primary flag' respectively to describe the procedure itself and the State in which the vessel was originally registered before the charterparty came into existence.[7]

5.5 At present, this situation is not expressly regulated by bilateral or multilateral Conventions and is entirely dependent on the compatibility of the legal systems of State A – the 'primary flag' or 'flagging-out' State – and State B to which the vessel is 'flagged-in'. Certain aspects of bareboat charter registration are addressed in Articles 11 and 12 of the 1986 United Nations Convention on Conditions for Registration of Ships. However, as we have seen in Chapter 3, this Convention is not yet in force pending adherence by not less than 40 States, the combined tonnage of which amounts to at least 25% of world tonnage. As a result of this high threshold of acceptance, the prospects of the widespread effective use of this Convention appear remote at best. More significantly, the 1993 United Nations International Convention on Maritime Liens and Mortgages entered force in 2004, requiring ratification by only ten States to do so and which contains detailed provisions concerning 'temporary change of flag' intended primarily to protect the position of mortgagees in these circumstances.[8]

5.6 The bareboat charter registration system has been adopted with enthusiasm, both by the ship-owning community and by the governments of the increasing number of emergent

---

4 For example, UK Merchant Shipping Act 1995, s.17(11); Australia Shipping Registration Act 1981, s.3; Bahamas Merchant Shipping Act, s.2; Malta Merchant Shipping Act, s.84A; New Zealand Ship Registration Act 1992, s.2. For a detailed analysis of the legal effect of one of the most commonly used standard form of bareboat charter, the BIMCO "Barecon" template, see Davis, *Bareboat Charters* (Informa 2005).

5 Merchant Shipping (Registration of Ships, Sales and Mortgages) Law, s.23B.

6 The more arcane term 'charter by demise' is also accurate, and remains in use in certain jurisdictions.

7 The UK Merchant Shipping (Registration of Ships) Regulations 1993, SI 1993/3138, uses this language at s.1(2): "primary register" means the register on which the ship is registered at the time the application is made to register the ship as a bareboat charter ship. The term "underlying registry" is also seen.

8 See further para. 5.32 *et seq.*

maritime nations which permit the 'flagging-in' of vessels, thereby ensuring training and employment for local seafarers, receipt of foreign exchange, acquisition of technology and know-how and expansion of the national fleet, without the drain on financial resources which would be consequent upon the outright purchase of the corresponding tonnage.

5.7 States whose legislation permits bareboat registration, whether involving 'flagging-out' or 'flagging-in' include Antigua and Barbuda, Australia, Azerbaijan, the Bahamas, Belize, Cambodia, the Cayman Islands, Cyprus, Denmark, France, Germany, Gibraltar, Jamaica, Kazakhstan, Liberia, Malta, the Marshall Islands, New Zealand, Panama, Poland, Russia, St Vincent and the Grenadines, Spain, Sri Lanka and Vanuatu. The UK Merchant Shipping Act 1995 and regulations made thereunder allow vessels chartered on bareboat terms to persons qualified to own British ships to be registered in a special part of the UK register for the duration of the charter period and during that period to fly the British flag.[9] The Act makes no provision for the 'flagging-out' of British ships to foreign registries.

5.8 Initially, one of the features most attractive to ship-owners of the bareboat charter registration system was that by 'flagging-in' to a country with a low-wage economy, such as the Philippines, they were able to employ as crew members nationals of the 'flagging-in' State at local rates of pay, thus escaping the perceived stigma of operating under a flag of convenience and avoiding the possibility of action by the International Transport Workers' Federation (ITF). In April 1988, however, the ITF Maritime Policy Committee agreed to treat all former open registry vessels with temporary Philippine registration as flag-of-convenience ships.[10] The ITF definition of a flag of convenience as being where the ownership and control of a vessel is found elsewhere than in the country of the flag the vessel is flying, will in most instances capture bareboat charter registered tonnage.

5.9 In certain States, bareboat charter-in of a foreign-owned vessel is not optional but compulsory. In particular, the Caspian Sea littoral States of Azerbaijan and Kazakhstan require all vessels not owned by nationals or by a locally incorporated entity to be registered in the national bareboat charter registry as a precondition of permission to operate in their domestic waters. For example, the Commercial Shipping Code of the Republic of Azerbaijan describes a "provisional right to navigate" granted to foreign-registered tonnage registered in accordance with the requirements of the local legislation.[11] Similarly, the certificate issued by the authorities in Kazakhstan at the conclusion of this procedure is entitled "Certificate of Temporary Granting the Right of Foreign Vessel Navigation".

5.10 The bareboat charter registration system demands a close nexus of interest and intent between owner and charterer and many such arrangements do contain an element of artificiality. In many cases, the arrangements are entered into to enable savings in crewing costs or to allow the owner to take advantage of subsidies or cargo reservations in favour of national carriers in the flag State. Accordingly, in many cases, notwithstanding the bareboat charter arrangements, the vessel remains subject to the practical control of the registered owner; this control may be secured by a time-charter or bareboat sub-charter back from the disponent owner to a related subsidiary. Similarly, for this purpose the owner and the bareboat charterer of the vessel may be affiliate companies established in

---

9 Part IV of the Register; Part X of the Merchant Shipping (Registration of Ships) Regulations 1993, *op. cit.*
10 *ITF Seafarers' Bulletin* No. 3, 1988.
11 Article 8.

jurisdictions acceptable to the 'flagging-in' registry in question and the contract is not entered into at arm's length. Italian legislation on bareboat registration[12] was conceived with the implicit object of enabling Italian operators to incorporate companies overseas in order to bareboat charter-in vessels and thus continue to operate them to all intents and purposes as before, but under a foreign flag. It is acknowledged[13] that the numerous obligations placed by that legislation on the bareboat charterer (particularly with regard to crew recruitment and composition) would be unacceptable to a genuine foreign charterer and would lead to irreconcilable conflicts between Italian law and that of the flag State.

5.11 The appetite of ship-owners and countries with developing economies for the bareboat registration system has, however, been tempered by reservations on the part of the financial community, which has felt that the registration of a vessel in more than one State may detract from the security afforded by a registered mortgage duly recorded in the register of the primary flag State, while the vessel flies the flag and operates subject to the laws of a second sovereign State. This is particularly so in view of the fact that under many international Conventions, mortgages and liens are governed by the law of a vessel's country of registry and no account is taken of a situation where a vessel may effectively be subject to the jurisdiction of a second State.[14] Article 6 of the 1958 Convention on the High Seas provides that:

> a ship which sails under the flags of two or more States, using them according to convenience, may not claim any of the nationalities in question with respect to any other State and may be assimilated to a ship without nationality.

5.12 The nationality of a vessel, as discussed in Chapter 1, is one of the guarantees offered by international law to ensure freedom of navigation and provides the basis for State jurisdiction, protection and intervention; furthermore, it provides the legal basis and foundation for the effective constitution of mortgages and other rights *in rem* over the vessel. The absence of a single nationality leads to the obvious danger that – standing the stark terms of Article 6 of the High Seas Convention referred to above – a port State might ignore a vessel's ostensible nationality and apply its own laws to any dispute submitted to its jurisdiction. Mortgagees are understandably hesitant in allowing the enforcement of their security to be left entirely to the *lex fori* at a port where the vessel may happen to be, instead of the vessel's national law being applied to determine the existence, nature and extent of the mortgagee's rights over the vessel.

5.13 Importantly, the mortgagee is in effect accepting a sacrifice to some degree of the certainty in their fixed security granted in the primary flag State, the continued effectiveness of which depends upon a private bargain between the owner and the bareboat charterer; and trusting the compatibility of two different legal systems. Recognising this tension, the 1986 United Nations Convention on Conditions for Registration of Ships represented the first recognition in international treaty law of this structure and introduced new definitions of the 'State of Registration', meaning the State in whose register of ships a ship

---

12 Law No. 234 of 14 June 1989.

13 Caliendo, 'Osservazioni in tema di "bareboat charter registration", nazionalit'a e bandiera della nave nella legge 14 giugno 1989', n. 234, *Il Diritto Marittimo*, 1989, Fasc. 2.

14 See, however, the discussion on the UN International Convention on Maritime Liens and Mortgages 1993, *infra*, para. 5.32 *et seq.*

has been entered; and the 'Flag State', meaning the State whose flag a ship flies and is entitled to fly. However, this Convention does not then seek to address the question of how mortgages and liens are affected by bareboat charter registration.[15]

5.14 More constructively, the 1993 United Nations Convention on Maritime Liens and Mortgages deals in some detail with this question. This Convention entered into force in September 2004 and provides that the "law of the State of registration shall be determinative for the purpose of recognition of registered mortgages, 'hypotheques' and charges".[16] Further, it is provided that no State party to the Convention shall permit a vessel registered in that State to fly temporarily the flag of another State unless all registered mortgages, 'hypotheques' and charges have been previously satisfied or the written consent of the holders of all such mortgages, 'hypotheques' or charges has been obtained.[17] In practice, the formal written consent of the mortgagee is an essential prerequisite to the grant by the primary flag State of their permission to suspend their registration of the vessel for the duration of the charterparty.

5.15 Bareboat charter registration tends to create greater conceptual problems for the common law practitioner than for his counterparts in the civil law jurisdictions of Continental Europe and Latin America. Civil law systems have always distinguished between the public law and private law functions of vessel registration. By public law in this context, we mean the rules of law governing such matters as the jurisdiction of the State over a vessel, safety of navigation, pollution of the environment, crewing, minimum accommodation requirements, labour relations and matters affecting the operation of the vessel. The private law function of registration concerns such matters as the ownership of a vessel, the recording of mortgages and the nature and extent of the security thereby provided. Bareboat charter registration effectively splits the private law and the public law functions of registration between the State of primary registry and the bareboat flag State.

5.16 This dichotomy has always existed in the civil law, although the public law and private law functions of registration have generally gone hand in hand. The distinction between public law and private law as it affects the registration of ships is in fact now enshrined in UK statute law – the first schedule to the Merchant Shipping Act 1995 is entitled "Private law provisions for registered ships" and deals with transfers and mortgages of registered vessels The relevant legislation in Malta draws the distinction succinctly: "Notwithstanding that a Maltese ship may be bareboat charter registered in a foreign registry, all matters with respect to title over the ship, mortgages and encumbrances shall continue to be governed by Maltese law."[18]

5.17 Practitioners who have acted in the purchase of Spanish vessels will be well aware of the need to investigate title and record encumbrances in two registers – that is, not only at the Maritime Registry (the Registro de la Comandancia de Marina, maintained at the vessel's port of registry) but also at the Commercial Registry (the Registro Mercantil, which may well be kept in another town or province). Although the Maritime Registry does in fact detail ownership and encumbrances, it is essentially concerned with the

---

15 This Convention is not yet in force. See further para. 5.24 below.
16 Article 16.
17 The text of the UN Convention on Maritime Liens and Mortgages 1993 is set out in Appendix X.
18 Merchant Shipping Act, s.84W(1).

public law function of registration, namely the conferment of nationality on a vessel and hence the right to fly the Spanish flag. The Commercial Registry is concerned with the private law function of recording ownership, mortgages and other charges. Thus, where a Spanish vessel is 'flagged-out', she is temporarily deleted from the Maritime Registry but remains fully entered in the Commercial Registry. In this manner, at least under Spanish law, the interests of the mortgagee remain protected in much the same way as if the 'flagging-out' had not taken place.

5.18 This is similar to the system in force in Germany which has permitted bareboat charter-in and charter-out since 1951 when the Law of the Flag Act (Flaggenrechtgesetz) was passed to enable the reconstitution of the post-war German fleet by allowing the chartering back from abroad of vessels that had previously been expropriated. Such vessels were not entered in the ship registers maintained by the German courts, but only in a special list of vessels maintained by the Federal Waterways Administration. Bareboat charter into Germany is now a relatively rare phenomenon, but 'flagging-out' by German ship-owners into countries such as Panama and Cyprus has become increasingly popular – in these cases the registration in the German court remains unaffected; the obligation on the owner to have his vessel fly the German flag is simply suspended for the charter period.

Bareboat charter registration in practice

5.19 It is useful to consider the steps of documentation required for this procedure both from a practical perspective and for an understanding of the necessary interaction between the parties and the two flag States involved. To be sure, while a considerable variety can be found and each flag State will determine its own rules, the following essential elements are commonly seen:

(1) The owner and charterer enter into bareboat charterparty agreement.
(2) The owner issues a letter of consent to the registry of the primary flag State A.
(3) Any mortgagee issues a letter of consent to the registry of the primary flag State A.
(4) The owner exhibits a copy of the charterparty to the primary flag State A, together with application forms and the payment of relevant fees.
(5) The registry of the primary flag State A issues a letter of consent to the owner.
(6) Any mortgagee issues a letter of consent to the bareboat charter registry flag State B.
(7) The charterer exhibits a copy of the charterparty to the bareboat charter registry in flag State B, together with the consent of the primary flag State A and application forms and the payment of relevant fees.
(8) The registry of the bareboat charter flag State B issues new certificates and documentation for the vessel.
(9) The owner exhibits new bareboat Registry documents of flag State B to the primary Flag State A.
(10) The charterer alters the home port shown on the stern of the vessel.

5.20 It can be seen that the parties are providing similar evidence to the appropriate registries in turn. The key document for the bareboat charter registry flag State is the official letter of consent granted by the primary flag State, that confirms the approval of the suspension of the jurisdiction by the latter for the duration of the charterparty. A transcript of registry is usually obtained to evidence the ownership and encumbrances over the vessel immediately prior to the charter-out taking effect. Certain written undertakings are also commonly sought, such as to confirm that the colours of the primary flag State shall not be flown during the bareboat charter period. The change of flag is complete when the documentation issued by the bareboat charter registry includes the compulsory amendment of the port shown on the stern of the vessel from its former home port to a port in the flagging-in State. For completeness, it can be noted that the IMO number of the vessel remains consistent and unaffected throughout this procedure.

5.21 The conceptual approach to bareboat charter registration is, however, by no means uniform among the various States which permit the practice.[19] For example, some jurisdictions take the view that a bareboat registration is in effect a registration *de novo* and insist that the vessel's underlying registration be cancelled, if only for a limited period. Other States permit bareboat registration even though the primary registration remains operative for certain purposes. With particular reference to mortgages, hypothecations and other registrable liens some 'flagging-in' States require that such instruments be re-recorded or noted in some way in their registers. In certain cases, such re-recording or noting may be purely permissive or upon request; in other cases it may simply not be possible under the applicable domestic legislation.[20] However, whatever the rules operated by individual States, it is clear that a bareboat registration can only take place if the laws of the two States involved, that is to say the State of primary, or underlying, registry and the 'flagging-in' State do not conflict. For example, section 84B of the Malta Merchant Shipping Act[21] only permits 'flagging-in' and 'flagging-out' from and to States whose laws with regard to bareboat charter registration are compatible with the provisions of the Act. In Denmark, a list of the States that are considered acceptable for a change of flag procedure in this way shall be maintained and published on the website of the Danish Maritime Authority.[22]

5.22 As previously mentioned, Italy is one of the States to have introduced legislation enabling the bareboat charter-in and bareboat charter-out of vessels.[23] Article 156 of the Navigation Code, as amended, provides for the suspension of the vessel's abilitazione alla navigazione, that is to say, her navigation licence which constitutes the owner's right to fly the Italian flag, in cases where the vessel is entered in the registers of a State which permits the temporary registration of foreign vessels for a period limited to that of the bareboat charterparty. It is clear, however, that the vessel's underlying Italian registry, including property rights and rights *in rem*, remain unaffected.

---

19 See the report on bareboat registration (JIGE (IV)/2 – TD/B/C.4/AC.8/12 of 25 March 1988) prepared by the Secretariats of UNCTAD and IMO for the Joint Intergovernmental Group of Experts on Maritime Liens and Mortgages and Related Subjects.

20 See further s.425 *et seq.*

21 Inserted by the Merchant Shipping (Amendment) Act 1990, which provides "Whenever it appears to the Minister that the provisions of the law of a State with regards to bareboat charter registration are compatible with the provisions of this Act, he may declare the ship registry of that State to be a compatible registry for the purposes of this Part of this Act."

22 Order no.1053 of 26 August 2013.

23 Law No. 234 of 14 June 1989. For a discussion of the background and effects of the legislation, see Caliendo, *op. cit.*

5.23 In the case of a bareboat charter-in to Panama, in common with most jurisdictions, the consent of the primary flag State is required.[24] There is no requirement, however, for evidence of suspension of the foreign registration during the charter period. The applicable legislation of Liberia considers this procedure in detail.[25] In the case of bareboat charter-out of Liberia, the primary flag registry issues a formal certificate of permission and the Liberian permanent certificate of registry must be surrendered in exchange for a restricted Liberian provisional certificate of registry "boldly endorsed to show that the right to fly the Liberian Flag has been withdrawn".[26] The legislation and procedures of the Marshall Islands are in strikingly similar terms.[27]

Bareboat charter registration in the 1986 Convention on Conditions for Registration of Ships

5.24 As previously indicated, the 1986 Convention introduces for the first time in international treaty law a distinction between the 'Flag State', meaning "a State whose flag a ship flies and is entitled to fly", and the 'State of Registration', meaning "the State in whose register of ships a ship has been entered".[28] 'Bareboat charter' is defined in the Convention as:

> a contract for the lease of a ship, for a stipulated period of time, by virtue of which the lessee has complete possession and control of the ship, including the right to appoint the master and crew of the ship, for the duration of the lease.

5.25 The Convention, as discussed in Chapter 3, has not entered into force. The provisions enabling bareboat registration are nonetheless instructive as a paradigm and are contained in Articles 11 and 12.[29] The following points should be noted:

(1) These articles presuppose not merely the grant of the right to fly the flag of the State where the vessel is bareboat chartered-in, but a grant of registration complying fully with the conditions of registration contained in the Convention (Art. 12(1), (2)). Accordingly, particulars of any mortgages or other similar charges upon the ship should be recorded (Art. 11(2)(i)) in both the primary flag State and the bareboat charter registry flag State.

(2) Ships may be entered in the register of the 'flagging-in' State either in the name of the owner or, where national laws and regulations so provide, the bareboat charterer. In any event, the name, address and nationality of the bareboat charterer must be recorded (Art. 11(1), (2)(h)).

(3) In the case of a ship bareboat chartered-in, a State should assure itself that the right to fly the flag of the primary flag State is suspended (Art. 11(5)).

(4) A State should ensure that a ship bareboat chartered-in and flying its flag will be subject to its full jurisdiction and control (Art. 12(4)).

---

24 Law No. 57 of 6 August 2008 of The General Merchant Marine, art. 70.
25 Liberian Maritime Law, s.85 *et seq.*
26 Liberian Maritime Law, s.94.
27 Maritime Act 1990, s.272.
28 Article 2.
29 See Appendix IX.

(5) For the purposes of applying the requirements of the Convention in the case of a ship bareboat chartered-in, the charterer will be considered to be the owner for this purpose.[30] The convention does not have the effect of providing for any ownership rights in the chartered ship other than those stipulated in the particular bareboat charter contract (Art. 12(3)).

Protection of mortgagees

5.26 The protection of the mortgagee's interest in a bareboat registry situation depends primarily on ensuring that, in the event of the mortgagee wishing to enforce his security or protect the preferred status of his lien against competing creditors, the law applied by the court in the jurisdiction where the action is heard will be the law of primary flag State rather than the law of the flag for the time being. Second, there is the need to ensure that, where the vessel is documented in a State other than that where title to and encumbrances against the vessel are recorded, third parties dealing with the vessel have notice of the legal ownership of the vessel and the existence of registered encumbrances such as mortgages. Situations do arise where a bareboat charter registered vessel is documented in the flag State under a different or local name from that recorded in the primary flag State.

5.27 As regards the law applicable to the determination of title to a vessel and the existence, nature and extent of creditors' liens, it is clearly desirable that the law of the bareboat flag State should refer such matters to the laws of the State of primary registration. Indeed, this would accord with the analysis in earlier chapters concerning the public and private law functions of registration. To this end a number of jurisdictions permitting bareboat charter-in have adopted so-called *renvoi* provisions in their maritime laws, clearly indicating that the applicable law with respect to the creation, validity and enforceability of mortgages is that of the State of underlying registry.[31] For example, under the Cyprus bareboat charter registration rules it is provided, in the case of a vessel temporarily entered in the Cyprus Ship Register on the basis of a bareboat charter, that the registration in the primary flag State shall be suspended, save as regards transfers of ownership and the creation and registration of mortgages or other encumbrances on the ship. During the period of bareboat charter registration, mortgages or other encumbrances must be created only by the owner of the vessel and in accordance with the law of the country of foreign registry in which they must be recorded.[32] Likewise, under Panamanian law, mortgages are subject to the law of the country of primary registration of the vessel. This approach is now embodied in international treaty law by Article 16 of the United Nations International Convention on Maritime Liens and Mortgages 1993, discussed further below.

---

30 The English terminology frequently used to describe the bareboat charterer being treated as the *de facto* owner by virtue of the charterparty is to refer to the charterer in possession of the vessel as the "disponent owner". The courts have also described this status as owner *pro hac vice* ("for this occasion", or "for this time"). See *Il Congreso del Partido* [1978] QB 500 at 539; *The Chevron North America* [2002] 1 Lloyd's Rep 77 at 89.

31 The legislation of St Vincent and the Grenadines states "the Commissioner and Registrar shall refuse to register any such mortgages and encumbrances; such power of registration shall remain vested in the underlying registry" – Shipping Act 2004, s.5B(1); similar prohibitions apply in the Bahamas – Shipping Act s.33(4); in Malta – Merchant Shipping Act, s.84M; and in Vanuatu – Maritime Act, s.31(2A).

32 Merchant Shipping (Registration of Ships, Sales and Mortgages) Law, s.23J.

5.28 As regards the question of notice, it is very much in the mortgagee's interests that procedures should exist for the vessel's documents issued by the bareboat registry State to be endorsed with at least a notation setting out details of registered ownership and registered security in the primary flag State. In the absence of international treaty regulation, it had been left to individual States to determine, in the case of the State of primary registration, the extent that it will require the notation of such information by the State of bareboat registry as a precondition for its granting permission for the 'flagging-out'; and in the case of the 'flagging-in' State, the extent to which it will permit or enable the official notation of such particulars. As previously mentioned, many jurisdictions will require the express written permission from the mortgagee as a precondition of the issuance of the letter of consent by the primary flag State to the procedure.[33]

5.29 As an example of the practical difficulties which may arise in the interaction of two legal systems, we may cite the experience of the Vanuatu Registry prior to the amendments to its maritime law. The Vanuatu Maritime Act originally stipulated that permission for 'flagging-out' could not be granted unless the Deputy Commissioner was satisfied that mortgages existing on the Vanuatu register would be endorsed on the vessel's foreign document. The owner of a Vanuatu vessel wishing for example to bareboat charter-in to the Philippines was faced with the problem that, although Philippine law enabled a mortgage to be registered in the disponent ownership of a Philippine company and endorsed on the vessel's Philippine document, the registration fees involved amounted to 3% of the amount secured, plus a substantial stamp tax. As a result of this the Vanuatu Maritime Act was liberalised and no annotation in the foreign register is now required.

5.30 Indeed, this liberalisation of Vanuatu law accords with the laws of most other major maritime jurisdictions as far as concerns the bareboat charter-out of vessels registered there – for example Panama and Liberia require no annotation in the foreign register. In the case of bareboat charter into Vanuatu and Liberia the maritime law of these countries requires (in the case of Vanuatu)[34] and enables (in the case of Liberia) the recording or notation of existing ship mortgages in the registers of the bareboat flag State and, in such cases, the foreign mortgage will constitute a preferred mortgage under Vanuatu or Liberian law. The Italian legislation enabling the flagging-out of vessels entered in the Italian registry contains no requirement for the recording of mortgages in the bareboat flag State or their endorsement on the vessel's documents. The provisions of the Cyprus Merchant Shipping (Registration of Ships, Sales and Mortgages) Law concerning bareboat charter registration[35] do not allow registration of foreign mortgages in the Cyprus register, but do provide for the notification of such mortgages and other encumbrances to the Registrar of Cyprus Ships for entry in a special book of parallel registration, maintained for information purposes only.

5.31 Vessels bareboat chartered-in to Panama may not have title, mortgages and other encumbrances recorded in the Panamanian public registry, although particulars of

---

33 Bahamas Shipping Act, s.33(3); Liberian Maritime Law, s.91; Marshall Islands Maritime Act 1990, s.271; Panama Law No. 57 of 2008, art. 70; Vanuatu Maritime Act, s.31(1)(d).

34 However, this requirement may be waived upon obtaining the written consent of the registered owner and the bareboat charterer of the vessel and of the holders of all the mortgages, hypothecations or similar charges against the vessel (Vanuatu Maritime Act 1981, Cap. 131 as amended in 1998, s.31(3)).

35 Section 23J(3).

encumbrances may be endorsed on the two-year special navigation licence issued to vessels so registered.[36] On the other hand, the merchant shipping legislation of St Vincent and the Grenadines requires mortgages, hypotheques or similar charges recorded in a foreign registry to be recorded in the office of the Registrar and Commissioner (in the same order as registered in the primary flag State) throughout the period of temporary registration on the basis of a bareboat charter.[37] The relevant information is also endorsed upon the vessel's bareboat charter certificate of registry and a certified copy of the instrument of charge so recorded is furnished to the bareboat charterer to be placed on board the vessel. Many primary flag States will also at the time of the commencement of the bareboat charter issue a formal letter of consent or certificate of permission signifying to third parties the temporary suspension of their jurisdiction, based on certain stated conditions to be satisfied by the owner for the duration of the charter and which may include a prohibition of the recording of any security or competing proprietary interests on the bareboat charter registry.

Bareboat charter registration in the 1993 Convention on Maritime Liens and Mortgages

5.32 It will be clear from the foregoing that by enacting appropriate national laws individual States, in their desire to promote the expansion of their shipping industries, have taken considerable steps towards ensuring the continued enforceability of the security granted to mortgagees notwithstanding the fact that a vessel is subject for certain purposes to two separate jurisdictions. However, it was considered in the interests of everyone in the shipping community that some harmonisation of these diverse and conceivably competing provisions should be sought.

5.33 The International Convention on Maritime Liens and Mortgages 1993 arose from a resolution of the General Assembly of the United Nations in December 1991, based on preparatory work by IMO and UNCTAD, "emphasizing the need for international uniformity and for the establishment of a widely acceptable international legal instrument governing the subject of maritime liens and mortgages".[38] The 1993 Convention makes explicit that the law of the primary State shall be determinative for the purpose of recognition of registered mortgages and requires a cross-reference of entries between the register of the primary State of registration of the vessel and the records of the State whose flag she is temporarily permitted to fly.[39] The entries will, however, be limited to specifying the primary flag State in the first case and the State of bareboat registration in each case. There is no requirement that mortgages and other charges registered in the State of bareboat registration be entered in the records of the flag State, although the Convention does require that the holders of all registered mortgages and charges issue their written consent to the flagging-out. As at February 2018, this Convention had been signed or ratified by 28 flag States.[40]

---

36 Law No. 57 of 2008, art. 78.

37 Shipping Act 2004, s.5B(2).

38 46/213, 20 December 1991.

39 Article 16, entitled "Temporary change of flag", reproduced in Appendix X.

40 Albania, Benin, Brazil, China, Congo, Denmark, Ecuador, Estonia, Finland, Germany, Guinea, Lithuania, Monaco, Morocco, Nigeria, Norway, Paraguay, Peru, Russian Federation, Serbia, Spain, St Kitts and Nevis, St Vincent and the Grenadines, Sweden, Syrian Arab Republic, Tunisia, Ukraine and Vanuatu.

5.34 In allocating the State that shall determine questions arising in relation to the rights of mortgagees in a bareboat registry structure, if not by prescribing the extent of recording and publicity of the mortgage itself in such circumstances, the 1993 Convention represents a significant step towards resolving the legal uncertainties surrounding the registration of charges on vessels subject to the laws of more than one jurisdiction. In this way, albeit at a high level, the uniformity sought by the initiating UN resolution has been achieved, thereby promoting the interests of ship-owners in securing reduced operating costs and potential new markets for their vessels, while protecting the security of lending banks and assisting emerging economies to obtain the benefits that a thriving maritime community can provide.

CHAPTER 6

Factors influencing choice of flag

Introduction

6.1 In a modern context where, for the reasons discussed in earlier chapters, the 'flag of convenience' label no longer carries a stigma on safety and compliance grounds; and where the vast majority of commercial tonnage is now operated from open registries – one challenge for the owner of any newbuilding or vessel purchased on the secondary market may rather be the burden of choice. Competition for business among the leading open registers is significant and often based on non-price considerations in circumstances where the available tax advantages between flag States may be broadly comparable.

6.2 A commercial ship-owner, when making the decision where to flag his vessel, must yet still initially make the important choice in principle between (1) registering the vessel in a country with which he has some genuine connection by way of national or economic ties; or (2) entering her in an open registry which will accept the vessel regardless of the nationality of the persons beneficially interested in her or the country from which the vessel is effectively controlled. Alternatively, the ship-owner may seek to enjoy certain of the benefits of the open registry system whilst retaining links with a traditional maritime nation by entering the vessel in its second register, or through the mechanism of bareboat charter registration. Considerations local to a proposed specific employment in a certain region can also play a part. The factors influencing the choice of flag for merchant ships intending a global trade, after a decision in principle has been reached, will be predominantly economic and political. The factors influencing the choice of flag of vessels intended primarily for other uses – such as fishing or yachts – will be subject to different considerations, to be discussed in turn.

Economic factors

6.3 The registration of a vessel under the flag of one of the traditional maritime nations (for example, the UK, Japan, Norway, Spain or Sweden) generally implies subjecting the operation of the vessel to the fiscal regime in force in that country. In principle, no distinction is made in developed market economies between the taxation of shipping operations and that of other commercial undertakings.[1] The countries which operate open

---

1 See the Report by the UNCTAD Secretariat, *Action on the Question of Open Registries* (3 March 1981) TD/B/ C.4/220.

74

registries in general levy no taxes on the profits arising from the operation of vessels under their flags, although they do require payment of initial registration fees and annual taxes thereafter based in each case on the tonnage of the vessel involved. Registration in an open registry does not, of course, *ipso facto* exempt an owner from taxation in the country in which he is domiciled for fiscal purposes. However, the use of certain offshore corporate or trust ownership structures permitted by an international register which is not based on any notion of 'genuine link' may make it virtually impossible to identify the true beneficiaries of the profits arising from the vessel's operation or the capital gain, if any, on her sale.[2]

6.4 The theme has been taken up, in a more general context, by the OECD. This resulted in the setting up in 1998 of a Forum on Harmful Tax Practices, intended to support fair competition and to minimise tax-induced distortion of financial and investment flows among OECD member countries. In 2000, the OECD Council identified a number of potentially harmful preferential tax regimes which included the shipping registries and related practices of seven countries.[3] An ambitious timetable of measures was proposed, starting with a plan to achieve international standards and moving on to compulsory disclosure of beneficial interests and to the exchange of tax information within the OECD. The criteria adopted for determining whether a tax regime is potentially harmful include:

(1)   a regime imposing low or no taxes on relevant income;
(2)   a regime which is ring-fenced from its domestic economy; and
(3)   a regime lacking transparency, or with inadequate regulatory supervision or disclosure.

Significantly, none of the fiscal regimes investigated by the OECD Forum in connection with this mandate were determined to be harmful "in the context of the particularities of the shipping industry".[4] The concluding report of this project, published in 2006, identified the regimes in seven further flag States as potentially harmful and which were also determined not to be actually harmful upon further investigation.[5]

6.5 Typically, a vessel registered in an open registry is owned by a corporation specially formed for that purpose and having no assets other than the vessel itself. If an owner operates more than one vessel, he will generally establish a separate corporate entity[6] as the registered owner in respect of each vessel. In this way, the beneficial owner of the vessel can effectively ring-fence or isolate financial risks arising from the operation of the ship in question. Some open registries stipulate as a general principle that vessels under their flag be owned by a company incorporated in the flag State. Liberia operates such a rule, although waiver of the ownership requirement may in special circumstances be granted; in these cases, the owning corporation must register as a foreign maritime entity under the Business Corporation Act.[7] Cyprus requires as a general rule that more

---

2 See further Chapter 4, para. 4.25 *et seq.*

3 The regimes identified were in Canada, Germany, Greece, Italy, the Netherlands, Norway and Portugal.

4 OECD, *The OECD's Project on Harmful Tax Practices: The 2004 Progress Report* (February 2004), para. 14.

5 The further regimes investigated were in Belgium, Denmark, Finland, France, Ireland, Spain and the UK: OECD, *The OECD's Project on Harmful Tax Practices: 2006 Update on Progress in Member Countries.*

6 Such corporations are known variously as SPV (special purpose vehicle), SPE (special purpose entity) or SPC (single purpose company).

7 Maritime Act, s.51.

than half the shares in the ship be owned by a Cypriot national or a citizen of another EU Member State or by a corporation established and having its registered office in the Republic, or another Member State but with an authorised representative and ship manager in Cyprus.[8] In other countries (e.g. Panama and the Bahamas) the operator has complete freedom as to the place of incorporation of the ownership vehicle. None of the open registries is concerned with the underlying beneficial interests, whether or not the owning company is incorporated in the flag State.

6.6 Until recently, in some cases the share capital of the vessel-owning company may have been represented by bearer shares which, because of their ease of transferability, render the identification of the shareholders effectively impossible. In countries which do not permit the share capital of companies to be represented by bearer shares (for example, Cyprus) the same result can be achieved by the simple expedient of registering the shares in the name of an offshore company, whose capital is itself represented by bearer shares. Profits arising from the operation of vessels may in their turn be deposited in bank accounts opened in the name of the owning company or in that of another bearer-share company incorporated for the purpose. The increased transparency demanded by international anti-money laundering regulations has led to a significant reduction in the number of jurisdictions whose law permits the use of bearer shares. Nevertheless, even in many offshore jurisdictions in which registered shares are the norm, beneficial ownership details are often not required to be disclosed as a matter of public record.[9]

6.7 The offshore ship-owning company in those circumstances is thus rendered effectively opaque as far as concerns the underlying ultimate beneficial interests. The true seat of management and control can be similarly disguised. In the case of Liberian corporations, for example, there is no compulsory or public register of directors or officers; accordingly, a third party has no means of ascertaining the identity of those persons except by inspection of the corporate books of the company to which he will have no access. Other countries (e.g. Panama and Cyprus) do require that the names of directors and officers be recorded; however, a ship-owner wishing to conceal the true management of the company will generally have little difficulty in appointing nominees.[10]

6.8 The type of corporate structure outlined above although not illegal can produce important advantages for the unscrupulous ship-owner:

(1) beneficial ownership is capable of being concealed: this may enable him to escape tax liabilities in the country of his establishment;
(2) the anonymity secured has the effect in the past not only of facilitating tax avoidance, but also of escaping accountability in other respects, for example, responsibility for failure to observe laws relating to safety, environmental protection and labour conditions.

---

8 Merchant Shipping (Registration of Ships, Sales and Mortgages) Laws of 1963 to 2005, s.5(1)(a).

9 For companies incorporated in countries whose shipping registers are members of the Red Ensign Group of registers (REG) (Anguilla, Bermuda, British Virgin Islands, Cayman Islands, Falkland Islands, Guernsey, Gibraltar, Isle of Man, Jersey, Montserrat, St Helena, the Turks & Caicos Islands and the UK) see further in this context Chapter 4, footnote 34.

10 But see the discussion concerning the disclosure requirements of a continuous synopsis record and in terms of the ISM and ISPS Codes *supra*, para. 4.28 *et seq*.

6.9 On the other hand, the traditional maritime nations have in many cases sought to soften the impact of their fiscal regimes on the shipping sector by offering owners a package of incentives, such as tax rebates or deferrals, investment grants, accelerated writing-off of assets on account of depreciation and the use of tonnage tax systems. In the words of the UNCTAD Secretariat Report "Action on the Question of Open Registries":[11]

> most of the [traditional maritime countries] allow shipowners various concessions . . . to defer or eliminate tax liability, which reduce the effective tax level below the statutory rate level, and in many cases are reported to result in an effective rate of zero . . .
> . . . in Western Europe the concessions are believed to be particularly liberal, and shipowners who not only operate ships, but also buy and sell on a large scale do not appear to have any difficulty in minimising their taxes to a low level or even avoiding taxes altogether.

The Report accordingly concluded that: "The effects of fiscal regimes in influencing ship-owners to operate under open registry flags appear to be relatively minor."[12]

6.10 In July 1997 the European Commission introduced new Community Guidelines on State Aid to Maritime Transport, intended to encourage the reflagging of vessels in EU Member States in the light of competition from the open registers.[13] Since the aim of the Commission was to promote the European shipping industry, State aid may generally only be granted in respect of vessels entered in Member States' registers governed by the law of a Member State applying to their territories which form part of the European Union.[14] The 1997 EU Guidelines identify fiscal costs (corporate taxation and wage-related liabilities in respect of seafarers) as being the critical factor affecting the competitiveness of flag States. Permitted measures cited as examples of State aid include replacing the normal corporate tax system by a tonnage tax, a typical feature of an open register.

6.11 Tonnage tax is recognised as one of the key elements which grant international or open registers their competitive advantage over traditional national flag States applying traditional fiscal methods. Under this system, the ship-owner pays an amount of tax linked directly to the tonnage of his operated fleet, without reference to the company's profits or losses. In Greece, for example, the package of benefits provided to ship-owners under Law 2687/53 for the Protection of Foreign Capital and the ministerial decisions issued pursuant to that law approving the registration of individual vessels effectively removed the shipping sector from the Greek fiscal system. Tonnage tax systems have been successfully adopted, following the example of Greece, by many jurisdictions including the Netherlands and Norway in 1996; Germany in 1999; the UK in 2000; and Denmark, Finland, Ireland and Spain in 2002.[15] In 2004, the European Commission introduced further Guidelines on State Aid to Maritime Transport, which recognised the modest

---

11 *Op. cit.*, para. 26.

12 *Op. cit.*, para. 38.

13 97/C 205/05. (OJ C 205, 5.7.1997).

14 Member States' registers defined in this way included, in addition to the ordinary national registers, the Danish International Register, the German International Register, the Italian International Shipping Register, the Madeira International Register, the Canary Islands Register and the Gibraltar Register. The Netherlands Antilles, Isle of Man, Bermuda and Cayman Islands registers are not considered to be Member States' registers because they are located beyond Europe or are subject to the law of territories where the Treaty of Rome does not apply.

15 A report by Maritime UK, *The Success of the Tonnage Tax* published in 2012 describes tonnage tax regimes to apply also in Belgium, Bulgaria, Cyprus, France, India, Italy, Japan, Malta, Poland, South Africa, South Korea, Spain, Sweden and the USA.

success of such measures and proclaimed a reversal in the trend identified to 1997 of owners abandoning Community flags for open registers.[16]

Operating costs

6.12 The freedom to avoid the high labour costs prevailing in the traditional maritime nations provided the greatest stimulus for a ship-owner to register his vessel in an open registry as compared to one that compels the appointment of the Master and crew according to their nationality. Manning represents by far the largest item in the direct operating costs of a vessel registered in an economically developed country. As a historical perspective taken at the time of rapid growth in the use of open registries, a report by the UK Government in 1990 considered comparative costs of manning by various nationalities.[17] Annual crewing costs for a UK-registered tanker with a British crew were estimated at US$908,000. In the case of a Hong Kong-registered ship with Hong Kong crew the figure could be reduced to US$396,000. The Report calculated the annual crew costs of a 30,000-ton deadweight bulk carrier crewed by UK officers and ratings paid at UK rates at that time, at £635,362. If the vessel were crewed by Filipino officers and ratings, paid at ITF approved rates, the annual cost would be reduced by more than half, to £279,841. It is self-evident that ship-owners paying their Masters and crew less than the ITF approved rates would stand to save yet more in comparison to their competitors operating from a closed registry flag State.

6.13 Registration of a vessel in one of the traditional maritime nations generally restricted the owner to employing a certain number of crew members who are nationals of the country concerned and involves negotiation with local trades unions on rates of pay, manning levels, conditions and benefits. Unlike the practice in States operating closed or national registers, where legislation compels to a greater or lesser degree the nationality of the crew on board their vessels, registration in an open registry will in principle normally give the ship-owner complete freedom in determining the nationality of his crew and agreeing rates of pay. As discussed in Chapter 4, the entry into force in 2013 of the Maritime Labour Convention moves significantly towards a global standard for minimum terms and conditions of employment for seafarers, if not rates of pay.[18]

6.14 A number of countries have established themselves as crew-supplying nations. These countries include India, Korea, Pakistan, the Philippines, Poland and Sri Lanka. Indeed, notwithstanding the low rates of pay by Western standards, there is no doubt that the employment of seafarers from developing countries on board open registry vessels represents a substantial advantage – not only to the seafarers themselves, but also to the labour-supplying nations, since the remittances from the seafarers ensure a steady receipt of foreign exchange. The reverse of the coin is that, in a number of cases, unscrupulous operators have taken advantage of crews from the developing countries, leading to reports of non-payment of wages, failure to repatriate and other instances of exploitation. In such cases, the seafarers may have great difficulty in obtaining redress against the owner or

---

16 2004/C 13/03. (OJ C 13, 17.1.2004).
17 *British Shipping: Challenges and Opportunities* (HMSO 1990).
18 Para. 4.34 *et seq.*

employer, for the reasons of the fleet and corporate structure, and disguised beneficial ownership, indicated earlier in this chapter.

Access to capital markets

6.15 Commercial vessels are rarely acquired without secured finance of some kind. The ship, as a moveable asset, presents both the borrower and the lender with a number of questions. One of these is certainly where the vessel is, or shall be, flagged. In times where certain institutions may be seeking to distance themselves from the shipping sector after suffering losses during the global financial crisis, the question is ever more relevant because a key consideration in the bank's lending decision will include the mechanisms to enforce their security in the event of a significant payment default or other breach of the loan facility. The lender's knowledge of the applicable procedures and the law of the Flag State, which govern the fixed security to be provided by their customer, is a major factor. The international promotion of the registries in well-established onshore or offshore financial centres – such as the Cayman Islands, Hong Kong and Singapore – as being attractive to lending institutions is based on their greater degree of familiarity and hence comfort to banks due to the presence of a mature, sophisticated and trusted legal system.

6.16 Registration of a vessel in an open register has the effect of distancing the ship-owner from the economic and political situation of his country and so can enable a financing institution to take greater comfort in the enforceability of their debts. Institutions specialising in advances to the shipping sector may proceed with a transaction in the knowledge that they are dealing with a legal system with which they are familiar – and distinct from the domicile of their customer – and that in the worst-case scenario their security will be enforceable in a predictable jurisdiction. These factors led to a significant transfer of tonnage from Russia and other States of the former Soviet Union to Cyprus and other open registries.

Political factors

6.17 Among the political factors which have to be taken into account when choosing between a national flag and an international registry, we may mention:

(1) the ability to trade worldwide without any restrictions imposed by the flag State with regard to the carrying of cargoes to certain countries against whom sanctions, embargoes or boycotts have been applied – examples include the Russian Federation, Israel and Iran;

(2) the avoidance of discrimination against vessels trading under certain flags; for example, Taiwanese operators invariably flag their ships in open registries since Taiwan is recognised as a State by only a small number of nations;

(3) freedom from requisition in time of conflict;

(4) the possible sacrifice of naval protection offered by the traditional maritime nations in time of conflict as, for example, during the Iran/Iraq conflict, which resulted in substantial loss of shipping in the Persian Gulf. The situation gave considerable impetus to the registration of vessels under the flag of the nations participating in the Armilla naval protection force. During that period, a large

number of Kuwaiti-owned tankers were reflagged in the United States and numerous vessels were registered in UK dependencies, such as Bermuda and the Cayman Islands, thus securing British naval protection without sacrificing the low-cost advantages of an open registry;

(5) loss of access to cabotage trade and other cargo reservations exclusively in favour of national carriers.

Choosing between international registries

6.18 Once the ship-owner has elected to register his vessel in an international register as compared to the flag of his legal domicile, place of business, chosen allegiance or other reason based upon substantive connection of some kind rather than none, he is then faced with the task of choosing between the plethora of open registries seeking his custom. If one starts from the basic premise that a broadly comparable low-tax or tax-free regime is available in all the open registries, what other factors should the owner take into account in reaching the important flagging decision?

Vessel eligibility

6.19 As discussed in Chapter 3, the major registers place some restriction on the type, size and age of vessels which they will accept under their flag. Most open registries will accept any type of self-propelled vessel. In the case of vessels lacking any means of propulsion, such as oil rigs, or barges, the choice may be more restricted. A number of registries impose a minimum limit on the size of vessels which they will accept under their flag. Since the fees earned by open registers are based on tonnage, the rationale of this restriction is obvious. Liberia stipulates a minimum size of 500 net tons for foreign-going vessels. Panama does not impose any minimum size limits, except in the case of pleasure yachts which must be over 50 net tons. Vessels of any tonnage may be registered under the Cyprus or the Marshall Islands or the Vanuatu flag. In some instances, the length of a vessel less than 24 metres may become a significant factor and prevent registration in a particular flag State. For example, certain States, while they may permit registration of merchant vessels of this size, their legislation may prohibit the owner's ability to bareboat charter-out small ships.

6.20 As we have seen, age restrictions vary considerably. The Bahamas have a 12-year age limit, although a procedure exists for registering older vessels provided special ministerial permission is obtained. Panama has no age restrictions, but requires a special inspection for vessels over 20 years of age. Liberia and Vanuatu each has a 20-year limit, although in certain circumstances older vessels may be accepted for re-registration or waivers granted. The Cayman Islands authorities subject older tonnage to a calculation matrix against which applicant vessels are scored according to criteria such as their classification and survey history, in order to determine eligibility for acceptance.

Ownership restrictions

6.21 Although no international register imposes restrictions as to ultimate or true beneficial ownership, a number of such registers require, as we have seen, that the owning company be incorporated under the laws of the jurisdiction concerned. Countries imposing such a requirement include Liberia, Singapore and Vanuatu. In the case of Liberia, waiver of the ownership requirement may be granted where valid reasons are advanced and the owning company registers as a foreign maritime entity under the Liberian Business Corporation Act. Vanuatu adopts a liberal policy with regard to ownership waiver upon application. The Cayman Islands, an offshore British register, permits registration by ship-owning companies incorporated in the EU, the EEA or a long list of approved foreign countries. Panama, Bahamas and Barbados impose no ownership restrictions.

Government stability

6.22 This factor seems to be less important in influencing flagging decisions than one might imagine. The turbulent internal political histories of Liberia and Panama seem to have had little effect on the number of vessels entering their registers in the late twentieth century. Undoubtedly, there is a tacit assumption that no government, whatever its political complexion, would wish to jeopardise the valuable earnings in foreign currency generated by its open registry operations. In the case of Liberia, confidence in the registry has undoubtedly been bolstered by the fact that the effective administrative seat of the flag is located in the United States. In this way, the registry was able to conduct its business uninterrupted after the overthrow of the Liberian Government in 1980. The effects of the subsequent civil war which followed in 1989 caused a number of commentators to express doubts as to whether, in view of the *de facto* suspension of the Liberian Constitution during this time, Liberian laws adopted thereunder continue to be effective. In the event, the confidence of ship-owners and lending institutions providing finance for vessels operating under the Liberian flag seems to have been surprisingly little affected.

Labour relations

6.23 The International Transport Workers' Federation (ITF) campaign against open registry fleets affects all registries which have been classified by that organisation as flags of convenience. The classification does not, however, include all registers possessing flag of convenience characteristics – a number of second registers, for example the Isle of Man and the Norwegian International Ship Register, have so far escaped being designated as flags of convenience by the ITF. If a vessel is trading in areas where the ITF boycott campaign has been most vigorously pursued – for example Scandinavia and Australia – the possibility of the vessel encountering problems at a loading or discharging port must be taken into account, although the effects of the broad raising of living and working standards for seafarers brought about by the Maritime Labour Convention may now dilute that risk to some degree.[19]

Manning and certification

6.24 Not all open registries impose the same requirements with regard to manning levels and the degree of recognition accorded to foreign certificates of competency. For

---

19 See further, para. 4.34 *et seq.*

example, Bermuda, an offshore British registry, initially saw its expansion as a flag of convenience hampered by the UK requirement that Masters, mates and chief engineers hold British or Commonwealth certification of competency. Those requirements have now been relaxed. As discussed in Chapter 2, the 1995 and 2010 amendments to the International Convention on Standards of Training, Certification and Watchkeeping for Seafarers have led to enhanced standards of competence among seafarers, and for their mutual recognition between jurisdictions. Any flag States which issue certificates of competency without ensuring that proper training procedures exist or recognise certificates of other flag States which have not put such procedures in place will find their vessels subject to detention.[20]

Costs

6.25 In view of the fact that all open registries offer broadly similar advantages, competition in terms of initial registration fees and annual costs has become intense. Liberia, for example, announced a wholesale waiver of initial registration fees irrespective of the size of vessel. For large vessels, in comparison with registers charging initial fees according to tonnage of the ship, the potential savings are considerable. Annual tax charges, however, are still widely based on tonnage and represent the primary source of revenue for the flag State. Many registries now make available online fee calculator tools, making the comparison of tonnage taxes and recurring charges immediately possible. Owners who are anxious to save costs should look beyond published figures, for many other cost factors have to be taken into account in the flagging decision. Consuls of certain flag States have enjoyed a reputation for levying excessive fees against shipowners on registration of a ship or mortgage.

6.26 Ancillary fees for incidental business and the issuance of routine documentation can on occasion appear to be an additional but relatively hidden source of revenue for the flag State. To these elements one may also add the annual fees of corporate maintenance for a special purpose company, local representatives or foreign maritime entity status, as may be required by the flag State in question. Translation fees may have to be taken into account and higher legal fees when dealing with unfamiliar jurisdictions, particularly where bank security documentation is involved. For example, in the case of Panama, title documents are required to be translated into Spanish, if not already in that language, before a vessel can be permanently registered.

National preference

6.27 The ship-owner may be influenced by the choice of flag adopted by other shipping businesses of the same nationality or market sector. Historical, geographical and cultural affiliations can give rise to the beneficial owners of certain nationalities establishing a popular or conventional flag of choice in respect of certain types of vessel. Combined with these factors, flag States may choose to market themselves as specialist in particular categories of tonnage. For these reasons, certain types of vessel and the nationalities of their beneficial owners are statistically over-represented in particular flag States. Recent

---

20 See further, para. 2.37 *et seq.*

examples based on an analysis of underlying beneficial ownership by UNCTAD include the ownership of over 46% of the Panama registered fleet by Japanese; over 31% of tonnage registered in Liberia is owned by German interests; and over 44% of vessels registered in the Bahamas are owned by Greek owners.[21]

Technical expertise

6.28 Certain registers can boast an in-house technical support capability, as compared to the outsourcing of routine technical requirements to a classification society. This aspect is most relevant to newbuild or conversion projects and specialist ships and is a true differentiator. In such circumstances on occasion the registry itself must be capable of evaluating proposed structural and design features of a vessel, for compliance with its own domestic regulations in addition to international safety requirements and the rules of the classification society chosen by the owner. Such a situation arises because of the distinction between the respective roles of the flag State and class – one is the principal, the other the agent – the latter can only act within the scope of its authority as a recognised organisation and not as a decision-maker in questions of statutory acceptability or otherwise. Such technical support and expertise is a noticeable layer of expense to the registry of a flag State offering this comprehensive support to their owners. Certain administrations may simply not be able to afford a global coverage of highly qualified and experienced surveyors, naval architects and engineers as their own employees.

Accessibility

6.29 Not all international registers offer registration facilities in all the major maritime centres. It is in practice easier to deal with a registry official face to face, rather than relying on email and couriers; at the completion of a sale and purchase matters may be further complicated by time-zone differences. Certain registries will make it their business to open around the clock as required in order to facilitate simultaneous registration of a vessel and her mortgage with a documentary closing taking place in another part of the world. In a sale and purchase transaction, particularly where the ship has a tight sailing deadline or where the registration of a lender's security is involved, the ability to register the vessel immediately upon delivery being taken is of crucial importance.

6.30 The ability and willingness of a flag State registrar to accept documents out of hours and by email or fax copies of certain prerequisites, such as a bill of sale or builder's certificate, is a key practical consideration. Many flag States now have legislative provision or delegated rules expressly permitting the receipt of particular documentary deliverables by email attachment; some that yet insist on receipt of all applications and supporting documents in hard copy only may find themselves left behind.

---

21 Cargo-carrying merchant ships of greater than 1,000 gross tons, as at 1 January 2012 – UNCTAD, *Review of Maritime Transport* (2012), Figure 2.7.

Electronic certificates

6.31 Distinct from the receipt of documents from an applicant electronically, the ability of some but not all registries to issue electronic certification is for the time being a key differentiator. Liberia has been at the vanguard of this movement. Since October 2006 Liberia has authorised the formal issuance of certificates of registry and SOLAS and MARPOL certification to be treated as 'original' or 'authentic' although provided only electronically. Such e-certificates are protected from alteration and since 2007 bear a unique tracking identification number that can be verified online for their genuineness and current status – for example by port State control – in real time. In 2014 the IMO issued guidelines on the use of e-certificates, seeking consistency in the development of this practice such as in relation to the security of information provided, protection from editing and consistency of unique tracking number systems.[22]

Fishing vessels

6.32 Where a fishing vessel is intended to be used for commercial fishing operations, such use will invariably require the owner to obtain a licence or quota to undertake such activity. This may be either by means of an application to the appropriate government department, or as happens in the UK, by purchasing a licence entitlement from the owner of an existing UK registered fishing vessel. While the licensing of fishing vessels falls outside the scope of this work, it should be borne in mind that fishing licences may require the vessel concerned to be registered in the country issuing the relevant licence. That is certainly the case in the UK. The UK Ship Register has a separate section for fishing vessels, namely Part II, for which the entitlement to register differs from that which applies to commercial vessels registered on Part I.[23]

Pleasure yachts

6.33 The owner of a pleasure yacht has perhaps the widest range of flagging options. In the UK and in certain other countries an owner is not obliged to register a small craft at all. Alternatively, an owner who does not wish to register a vessel on a title register may, in the UK, register a vessel of less than 24 metres in length on the Small Ships Register which provides a simple registration document for a modest charge with the minimum of formalities. Similar registers are offered in many other countries for small boat users. The State of Delaware in the United States offers a similar service not only to individuals, but also to corporations.

6.34 Pleasure yachts may be registered with full registration on a title register which will be necessary if the owner wishes to borrow money secured by means of a mortgage registered over the yacht. Certain international registers do not accept small yachts. Others, like Gibraltar, provide a separate yacht registry. Because the sale or importation of a yacht may result in a liability to pay value added tax or equivalent, and in a few

---

22 FAL.5/Circ.39/Rev.1, 7 October 2014; replaced by FAL.5/Circ.39/Rev.2, 20 April 2016.

23 See UK Merchant Shipping (Registration of Ships) Regulations 1993, SI 1993/3138, regs. 12–16, extracts of which are reproduced in Appendix VI.

other countries such as Spain, an additional "matriculation tax", or luxury goods tax, any choice of flag and ownership structure should take into account the tax status of both the yacht and its owner.

Commercial yachts

6.35 The steady growth in the size of yachts and the increasing number of them being operated for charter on a commercial basis over the past 35 years highlighted the fact that several key international shipping Conventions[24] did not apply to or were unsuited to large yachts, even though such vessels were often manned by professional crews and chartered out on a commercial basis on a regular basis for large sums of money. These concerns within the industry resulted in consultation between representatives of the Red Ensign Group of registries ('REG') and key yachting industry representatives. This resulted in the publication of the Maritime and Coastguard Agency ('MCA') Code of Practice for Safety of Large Commercial Sailing and Motor Vessels in 1998.[25] The code comprised a detailed set of alternative rules for the safety, construction and manning of large yachts which were notified to the International Maritime Organisation by the UK as an equivalent arrangement[26] under the provisions of each of the three Conventions.

6.36 The Code was intended to be revised on a periodic basis after public consultation, and the most recent version known as the Large Yacht Code or LY3 was published by the MCA in 2012. It lays down the safety requirements for large yachts over 24 metres in length that are used commercially for sport or pleasure and do not carry more than 12 passengers. LY3 also sets out the qualifications that are mandatory for crew members, depending upon the size of vessel, engine power and cruising range. It applies to all such vessels registered in the Red Ensign Group of registries, among which the Cayman Islands has attracted the largest number of vessels coded under LY3 and the previous editions of the Code.[27] The success of LY3 has to a large extent resulted in the Code becoming an industry standard within the large yacht and 'megayacht' industries. Similar provisions have since been introduced in other flag States including Malta and the Marshall Islands in particular.

6.37 Anyone considering the choice of flag for a commercial charter yacht should first ascertain whether the vessel has a current LY3 compliance certificate, or equivalent in another jurisdiction. If not, a professional survey or visit from a flag State surveyor will establish if the yacht is likely to comply with LY3 or the commercial coding require-ments in another jurisdiction. In the case of a new construction the yacht builder and the owner's technical advisors will liaise closely with the flag State surveyors department to ensure that the technical design of a future vessel will comply with LY3 and the relevant

---

24 The International Convention on Load Lines, 1966 (ICLL), the International Convention on the Safety of Life at Sea, 1974/1978 (SOLAS), and the International Convention on Standards of Training, Certification and Watchkeeping for Seafarers, 1978/1995, as amended (STCW).

25 SI 1998/2771.

26 See Art. 8 of the ICLL, regs. 1–5 of the SOLAS Convention and Art. 9 of the STCW Convention.

27 LY1 in 1998, LY2 Edition 1 in 2005 and LY2 Edition 2 in 2007. A new edition of LY3 was published by the Red Ensign Group in November 2017 as part of the new REG Yacht Code (REG-YC). The new REG-YC combines the existing LY3 and the Passenger Yacht Code into one document. See, further, para. 6.39 below.

classification society's rules for commercial yachts. The proposed crew should also hold the prescribed qualifications. The ability of a vessel and crew to comply with LY3 or equivalent will determine whether it will be possible to register the yacht for commercial use under the chosen flag.

Passenger yachts

6.38 If before 2010 an owner of a yacht wished to carry more than 12 passengers, whether they were private guests or commercial charterers, the then LY2 Large Yacht Code would not apply. The owner's only option would be to operate the vessel as a passenger ship fully compliant with the SOLAS Convention which would, for example, necessitate the use of commercial life-boats that would be inappropriate on a large yacht. Because of the demand for increasingly large, innovative yachts and the use of advanced production materials, the Red Ensign Group supported the Cayman Islands Shipping Registry ('CISR') in developing a new code that would enable a yacht of any size[28] to carry up to 36 passengers. The Code of Practice for Yachts Carrying 13–36 Passengers, generally known as the Passenger Yacht Code, or 'PYC', was first published in November 2010 and was duly tabled at the IMO by the UK Government as the State party to the relevant IMO Conventions referred to above. To keep abreast of the steady flow of resolutions updating IMO Conventions, new editions of the PYC were issued each year until 2016.

6.39 Because of the frequency of updates necessary to update the LY3 and the PYC, and certain other reasons, it was felt by the Red Ensign Group desirable to bring together both codes into a new REG Yacht Code with annexes containing material common to both types of yacht, for example relating to helicopter landing areas. Technical working groups from across the large yacht industry met between September 2016 and May 2017, with the aim of launching the REG Yacht Code in November 2017. The new code will come into force on 1 January 2019, thereby giving the industry ample time to take on board the changes relevant to both predecessor codes.

Reputation

6.40 Many open registers have sought to remedy the perceived disrepute of the flag of convenience label by reinforcing their administration systems and thereby ensuring even better compliance with international standards in respect of vessels under their flag, as compared to their competitors. Liberia has for many years been considered the leader in this field. There is evidence that major charterers, in particular the large oil companies who may incur massive liabilities for environmental damage, view the flag of a vessel as one of the most important factors in considering the suitability of vessels tendered to them for charter. Furthermore, as we have seen, due to developments in technology and with port State control as a mechanism both (1) for ensuring the compliance of ships and flag States with international standards (regarding not least safety at sea, pollution prevention, on-board working conditions and international security requirements); and (2) for the wide and near-immediate publication of the results of such independent eyewitness

---

28 At that time the application of LY2 was restricted to vessels of less than 3,000 gross tons.

scrutiny – has enabled the ready identification of flags where vessels are more likely than others to be sub-standard. The vast network of memorandum of understanding participant States[29] presents a substantial disincentive to ship-owners whose vessels are the subject of supervision measures if registered with flag States with a poor overall safety and compliance record. Without adequate documentation verifying their attainment of minimum international standards upon such inspection, the reputation of such flag States is soon reflected by their detention rate under the MOU. The intended purpose of such targeting and publicity is to induce operators to register their ships under flags whose ships have a low detention rate because their governments have taken proper measures to ensure the attainment of their basic treaty obligations.

---

29 See *supra*, para. 2.16 *et seq.*

CHAPTER 7

Bahamas

7.1 The Bahamas is a group of islands situated in the Atlantic Ocean extending from the east coast of Florida in the north-west towards Haiti in the south-east. The Commonwealth of the Bahamas is an independent nation within the British Commonwealth. The head of State is HM Queen Elizabeth II who is represented in the Bahamas by the Governor General. The government is comprised of a lower house known as the House of Assembly and an upper house known as the Senate. The head of government is the Prime Minister. The local currency is the Bahamian dollar (B$).

7.2 The shipping register is administered by a government agency, the Bahamas Maritime Authority (BMA), which operates offices in a number of major international shipping centres. In terms of dead-weight tonnage, the Bahamian flagged fleet was the seventh largest in the world and ranked third by value in 2017.[1] In relation to the flag State performance in port State control inspections, the Bahamas appears fifth on the White List of the Paris MOU statistics published in 2017.[2]

Sources of law

7.3 The registration of vessels under the Bahamas flag is governed by the Merchant Shipping Act 1976,[3] as amended ('the Act'). Provisions of the Act are derived from the UK Merchant Shipping Acts 1894–1975. The Act is supplemented by regulations, rules and orders. The Act includes a legislative device enabling UK statutory instruments to be incorporated into Bahamian subordinate legislation, where the Bahamian Government considers it appropriate. Bahamian regulations may also reflect practice in other common law jurisdictions.

Vessel eligibility

Vessel type

7.4 Any ship may be registered as a Bahamian ship if it is wholly owned by citizens of the Bahamas or by a Bahamian company which has its principal place of business in the Bahamas, or is beneficially owned in its entirety by Bahamian citizens. Subject to

---

1 See UNCTAD, *Review of Maritime Transport* (2017), Tables 2.6 and 2.7.
2 See Appendix III.
3 Chapter 268 of the Statute Laws of the Bahamas.

the age limit referred to below, any ship may, regardless of the nationality of its owner, register as a Bahamian ship if it is a seagoing vessel of 1,600 net registered tons or more and is engaged in foreign-going trade. A 'foreign-going ship' is defined as a ship employed on voyages beyond the limits of a 'home-trade voyage', namely the carriage of goods or passengers solely within the Bahamas or between the Bahamas and the coast of east Florida between Jupiter in the north and Key West in the south. It will be apparent from these definitions that fishing vessels may not be registered on the Bahamas Register. A ship that is less than 1,600 net register tons may be registered with the express permission of the minister responsible for Maritime Affairs. The eligibility of yachts for registration in the Bahamas will be discussed in paragraph 7.23.

Age limits

7.5 A ship must be less than 20 years old at the time of first registration as a Bahamian ship. This age limit is calculated from the date of completion of first construction to the commencement of the year in which the registration application is made. Where an older ship has been maintained to an exceptionally high standard, such a vessel may be registered with the permission of the minister, subject to certain additional acceptance criteria being satisfied.

Bareboat charter registration

7.6 Section 3(4) of the Act provides that a foreign-registered ship which is bareboat chartered to any citizen of the Bahamas or to a Bahamian company, in addition to being registered under the law of that foreign country, may upon application be registered as a Bahamian ship for the duration of the bareboat charter and the Registrar shall notify the proper officer of that foreign country of such registration as a Bahamian ship.

7.7 The Act also provides that a Bahamian ship which is bareboat chartered to a citizen of a foreign country, or to a foreign company, may upon application to the proper officer of that foreign country, be 'flagged-out' to the foreign register. Upon receiving notification of bareboat registration from the foreign registry, the Bahamian Registrar shall for the period of such registration suspend the certificate of Bahamian registry and notify the foreign registry of that suspension and of any mortgage instrument which is recorded on the Bahamian Register in respect of that ship.

Trading limits

7.8 There are no trading limits other than those imposed on Bahamian home-trade ships.

Manning requirements

7.9 Manning levels and crew certification requirements for Bahamian ships can be found in Part III of the Act, the Regulations[4] made thereunder, and the International

---

4 See, in particular, the Bahamas Merchant Shipping (Training, Certification, Manning and Watchkeeping) Regulations 2011 and the Bahamas Merchant Shipping (MLC) Regulations 2012.

Convention on Standards of Training, Certification and Watchkeeping for Seafarers 1978, as amended in 1995 (STCW); the 2010 amendments to STCW, the associated code; and the Maritime Labour Convention 2006.[5]

Certificates of competency for officers and ratings

7.10 Ratings on Bahamian-registered ships are required to hold appropriate certificates and complete the training required by the STCW Convention. Training approved by another STCW party is accepted by the Bahamas. Officers serving on board Bahamian ships are required to hold Bahamian certificates of competency or endorsements for the rank to which they serve. Certificates of competency issued by a number of foreign governments are currently recognised by the Bahamas for the issue of Bahamian endorsements of equivalent grade. Endorsements issued by the Bahamian authorities will bear the same validity and last for the same duration as the foreign certificate of competency on which the endorsement is based. The countries whose certificates are currently recognised are to a large extent signatories of the STCW Convention, but do not include Honduras and St Vincent and the Grenadines. Those which are considered acceptable include the majority of those countries on the IMO STCW 'White List',[6] but is subject to periodic review. To facilitate the issue of flag State endorsements and certification the Bahamas Maritime Authority has developed a web-based system known as BORIS (Bahamas On-line Registration Information System), which enables registered users to submit seafarers' documents for processing and to check the validity of existing Bahamian certificates.

Nationality of crew

7.11 There are no nationality restrictions.

Document of safe manning

7.12 Every Bahamian foreign-going ship must have a minimum safe manning document issued by the Bahamas Maritime Authority. In order to obtain such a certificate, the owner or an authorised representative is required to complete an application form setting out details of the ship, her machinery and other characteristics. It will also set out the proposed manning scales, broken down by deck officers, engineers and ratings. The application and the appropriate fee must be submitted to the Bahamas Maritime Authority which will consider the owner's application on behalf of the Government of the Bahamas. A minimum safe manning document will reflect the statutory manning scales and international guidelines. However, it should be noted that the 2000 amendments give the administration a general power to grant exemptions.

---

5 For a detailed analysis, see J. Lavelle (ed.), *The Maritime Labour Convention 2006* (Informa Law from Routledge 2014).

6 See Appendix IV.

Approved classification societies

7.13 Since December 2014 the following classification societies have been recognised[7] by the Bahamas Registry for the purpose of carrying out statutory surveys, the audit and certification of Bahamian ships and the audit and certification of companies operating them.

American Bureau of Shipping (ABS)
Bureau Veritas (BV)
China Classification Society (CCS)
Croatian Register of Shipping (CRS)
DNV GL
Indian Register of Shipping (IRS)
Korean Register of Shipping (KR)
Lloyd's Register (LR)
Nippon Kaiji Kyokai (Class NK-NKK)
Polski Rejestr Statkow (Polish Register of Shipping-PRS)
Registro Italiano Navale (RINA)
Russian Maritime Register of Shipping (RS)

Radio traffic accounting authorities

7.14 The Utilities Regulation and Competition Authority (URCA), the telecommunications authority in the Bahamas at the time of writing, is likely to approve any radio accounting authority listed and accepted by the International Telecommunications Union (ITU). In the first instance, an applicant may approach the BMA to ascertain whether a chosen accounting authority is already used by other Bahamian-registered vessels. If not, it may be necessary for the preferred accounting authority to apply for formal approval by the URCA.

Procedure for registration

Provisional registration

7.15 If an owner of a ship intends to apply for registration under the Bahamas flag, but the ship is at a foreign port, or there are outstanding surveys or other formalities, it is possible to apply for provisional registration (s.26). Provisional registration entitles a ship to all the privileges of a Bahamian ship. A ship under construction may be registered in the Bahamas as "a ship being built" (s.3(5)).

Validity of the provisional registration and extension

7.16 A provisional certificate of registry is valid, in the first instance, for six months from the date of issue and may be extended or renewed at the discretion of the registrar

---

7 Recognised organisations ('ROs') that meet the standards required by IMO Resolution A.739(18), many of whom are members of IACS. The BMA's current list of ROs is taken from Information Bulletin No.03 Revision 05 dated 9 December 2014.

or the Director. A mortgage may be registered against a provisionally registered ship and provisional registration will not affect the validity of a registered mortgage. Provisional registration may be extended or renewed at the discretion of the Registrar.

Permanent registration

7.17 Registration applications and permanent registration of Bahamian ships may take place in Nassau, London, New York, Hong Kong or Piraeus at any offices of the Bahamas Maritime Authority located worldwide. Registration applications may also be processed in Tokyo by local BMA authorised representatives. The Registrar who undertakes the registration becomes the 'original registrar' and thereafter administers the ship, although the owner may subsequently request the transfer of the administration of the ship to another registrar. The owner must submit a written application (Form R102) accompanied by the following documents or items, using the prescribed Bahamian forms where appropriate:

(1) in the case of a company, an appointment of authorised officer(s) (Form R103);
(2) evidence of ownership in the form of a builder's certificate or bill of sale, or where no transfer of ownership is concerned, a transcript of the previous registry setting out the name of the owner;
(3) a declaration of ownership (Form R105);
(4) in the case of a company, a certified true copy of the certificate of incorporation and an original certificate of good standing;
(5) a memorandum as to the registration of managing owners, etc. (Form R104);
(6) official permission from a proper officer in the country of previous registry for the transfer of registration or a statement that such permission is not required by the law of that country;
(7) a recent certificate from a proper officer in the country of previous registry of any mortgages or liens recorded on the register of ships of that country;
(8) an international tonnage certificate and a certificate of survey (or certificate of registry);
(9) copies of valid SOLAS, Load Line, MARPOL and all other necessary statutory certificates issued by the former flag State administration or the ship's classification society;
(10) a current class certificate and class status report issued by the vessel's classification society;
(11) a Bahamas ISM DOC;
(12) an URCA[8] ship radiocommunications licence application (Form R108);
(13) application for a MLC 2006 DMLC Part I (Form R109);
(14) a radio accounting authority identity code;
(15) an application for a minimum safe manning certificate (Form R106);
(16) an application for a continuous synopsis record (CSR);
(17) copies of previously issued CSRs;
(18) blue cards for wreck removal, bunkers and oil;

---

8 Utilities Regulation & Competition Authority.

(19) a certificate of insurance of ship-owner's liability under regulation 4.2;
(20) a certificate of insurance of seafarer repatriation costs and liabilities under regulation 2.5.2;
(21) payment of annual and other fees.

7.18 A list of the above requirements may be found in Forms R101a, R101b and R101c. Specimen forms are provided within Appendix XI(a). It should also be noted that under s.13 of the Act, the Registrar may be permitted to waive certain statutory registration requirements, in particular, with regard to the documents mentioned under (7) and (8) above, if it is shown to the satisfaction of the minister that the owner has attempted to obtain such documents, but owing to wholly exceptional and abnormal circumstances prevailing in the country of previous registry inordinate delay has occurred for reasons beyond the control of the owner. Any such waiver will be subject to any direction as to the production of such documents as may be made by the minister.

7.19 Where the ship is over 12 years of age at the time of first registration as a Bahamian ship, a pre-registration inspection must first be carried out by a Bahamas-approved nautical inspector. On completion of registration the registrar will enter particulars of the ship and her owner(s) in the register and forward a copy of the entry to the Director as well as the original survey certificate, builder's certificate, any previous bills of sale or condemnation by a competent court and all declarations of ownership.

Registration of mortgages and security interests

7.20 A ship that has been registered with provisional or permanent registration may be made security for a loan or other valuable consideration by means of a prescribed statutory form of mortgage. On production of such a mortgage executed by the owner, the administering Registrar will enter it on the register against the ship, subject to payment of a registration fee. Mortgages are recorded in the order in time in which they are produced to the administering Registrar and in the case of more than one mortgage over the same ship, rank in priority between each other in the order in which they are recorded.

Surveys

7.21 Bahamian ships must be inspected for safety:

(1) before the ship is put into service with permanent registration;
(2) thereafter annually;
(3) whenever an accident occurs or a defect is discovered which affects the safety of the ship; or
(4) whenever important repairs or renewals are made.

Inspections are carried out by one of the many inspectors in ports around the world who are appointed to carry out inspections on behalf of the BMA. Inspections cover hull, machinery, boiler, engines and other main propulsion gear, auxiliary engines, electrical installations, radio installations in the ship and her lifeboats, life-saving equipment, fire detection and extinguishing apparatus, crew accommodation and the cleanliness of the engine room and other areas. Important information bulletins issued by the Inspections and Surveys Department provide guidance and advice. These may be found on the BMA website.[9]

Deregistration procedure

7.22 In the event of a ship being lost or ceasing to be a Bahamian ship, the owner must give notice to the original registrar who will close the register. If there are any outstanding registered mortgages, they will be shown as being outstanding at the date of closure. If an owner of a Bahamian ship wishes to transfer the ship to a foreign registry, this may be done provided that there are no outstanding fees due to the Bahamian Government or any outstanding mortgages, in which case the following documents or information should be submitted to the original registrar:

(1) a written application specifying the name of the ship;
(2) the reason for the proposed transfer;
(3) the name and nationality of the proposed new owner;
(4) the name of the country to whose registry transfer is desired and the address of the new registry;
(5) the original certificates of Bahamian registry.

Yachts

7.23 Although the Bahamas flag is primarily associated with merchant shipping, the BMA has in recent years taken steps to encourage the registration of both commercial and non-commercial yachts on the register. In April 2008 the BMA first published a guide to the registration and technical requirements of yachts which can be found in Information Bulletin B102.[10] The procedure for registering yachts is generally the same as applies to other types of vessels. However, the following should be noted:

(1) yachts that are more than 20 years old will not normally be eligible for registration in the Bahamas;
(2) yachts of less than 12 metres load line[11] length will not be eligible for registration;
(3) all yachts will require a review by the BMA Technical Department of their technical standards prior to provisional or permanent registration, irrespective of age;
(4) all commercial yachts over 300 gross tons will be required to be in class with one of the classification societies listed in paragraph 7.11 above;
(5) in addition to the classification requirements, all new and existing commercial and non-commercial yachts over 24 metres in length must, in addition, comply with the Bahamas Yacht Code (BYC), a safety code introduced by the Bahamas

---

9 www.bahamasmaritime.com.

10 The most recent edition, B102 Revision 6, was issued on 20 December 2011 and can be downloaded from the BMA Website.

11 Calculated in accordance with reg. 3 of the International Convention on Load Lines, 1966 as amended.

Maritime Authority in March 2011, based very closely on the Large Commercial Yacht Code (LY2) of the UK Maritime and Coastguard Agency;

(6) all new yachts constructed on or after 1 January 2011, commercial and non-commercial, of less than 24 metres in length are required to be built and maintained in accordance with the UK Small Commercial Vessels & Pilot Boat Code of Practice (SCV Code)[12] of the UK Maritime and Coastguard Agency, or a similar code of practice agreed by the Bahamas Maritime Authority. Non-commercial vessels are not required to comply with those sections of the code that relate only to commercial operation, but the Bahamas Maritime Authority recommends that pleasure yachts at least comply with the life-saving, survival craft and fire-fighting requirements provisions of the SCV Code.

Contact addresses

7.24

London office

120 Old Broad Street
London EC2N 1AR
Tel: (44) (0)20 7562 1300
Fax: (44) (0)20 7256 5619
Email: CMoree@bahamasmaritime.com
Website: www.bahamasmaritime.com

Nassau office

Shirlaw House
226 Shirlaw Street
PO Box N – 4679
Nassau, Bahamas
Tel: (1 242) 356 5772
Fax: (1 242) 356 5889
Email: Nassau@bahamasmaritime.com

New York office

Bahamas House
231 East 46th Street
New York, NY – 10017
USA
Telephone: (1) 212 829 0221
Fax: (1) 212 829 0356
Email: newyork@bahamasmaritime.com

---

12 MGN 280.

Hong Kong office

Room 2019–2020
20th Floor
Hutchison House
10 Harcourt Road, Central
Hong Kong
Telephone: (852) 2522 0095
Fax: (852) 2522 0094
Email: hongkong@bahamasmaritime.com

Piraeus office

10 Antoniou
Ampatielou Str.
185 36 Piraeus
Greece
Telephone: (30) 210 429 3802–4
Fax: (30) 211 198 3175
Email: greece@bahamasmaritime.com

Tokyo Agency office

Mr Hiroyuki Miike (Registrar)
Mitsui Soko C. Ltd., Ship Registration Team
3–20–1 Nishi-Shimbashi
Minato-Ku, Tokyo 105–0003
Japan
Telephone: (81) 3 6400 8306
Fax: (81) 3 6880 9936
Email: miike@mitsui-soko.co.jp
Web: www.bahamasmaritime.jp

CHAPTER 8

Barbados

8.1 The most easterly of the Windward Islands in the Caribbean, the island of Barbados became an independent State in 1966, having been a British colony since 1627. Despite its independence, Barbados remains an active member of the Commonwealth and continues to have strong links with Britain through the office of the Governor General who is appointed by the Crown. The links with Britain are evident in the parliamentary and legal system, which are based largely on the British model. The Privy Council still remains the highest court of appeal. English is the official language. The official unit of currency is the Barbados dollar, which has been linked to the US dollar since 1975.

8.2 The registry function is administered by Barbados Maritime Ship Registry ('the Barbados Register') which has a head office in London and a network of registrars worldwide. Barbados appears on the White List of the Paris MOU of port State control compliance.[1] In January 2018 there were 141 vessels over 100 gross tons, totaling 1,112,542 gross tons, on the Barbados Register.[2]

Sources of law

8.3 Registration of ships and mortgages on the Barbados Register is now governed by the Shipping Act 1994, Cap. 296 of the Laws of Barbados, as amended ('the Act'). References to sections in this chapter are to sections of the Act. The Act governs the eligibility of vessels and their owners, the terms and conditions of service of the officers and crew and the safety of passengers, crew and cargo in conformity with the international Conventions to which Barbados is a party. The Act distinguishes between ships owned by and trading within the Caribbean community and foreign-going ships. The Act is supplemented from time to time by the Shipping Regulations, which lay down the prescribed fees for initial registration, annual fees and fees for the issuance of various documents. They also set out the prescribed format for various registration documents and application forms.

---

1 See Appendix III.
2 Statistics provided by Capt. Peter Green, Principal Registrar, Barbados Maritime Ship Registry on 22 January 2018.

Vessel eligibility

Vessel type

8.4 Section 8 of the Act permits the registration of the following vessels on the Barbados Register:

(1) pleasure yachts;
(2) local fishing vessel registered under the Fishing Acts;
(3) any ship where at least 44 of its 64 shares are owned by persons singly or in association, who are either qualified persons or Caricom persons;[3]
(4) a foreign-owned ship engaged in foreign-going trade only. Foreign-going trade is defined in section 8(11) as trade to and from, but not within, the states of the Caribbean community or trade between ports outside the Caribbean community.

In the case of near coastal trade ships (ships that trade within 500 miles of Barbados) or Caribbean trade ships of 150 gross tons or over, the provisions of (3) above are relaxed and registration will be permitted regardless of whether less than 44 of the 64 shares are in Barbadian ownership, provided the ship is owned by a Caricom person and will operate generally as a near coastal vessel or Caribbean trade ship (s.10).

8.5 Any type of vessel of 150 tons or over may be registered on the Barbados Register, subject to the age limits and ownership qualifications referred to below.

Age limits

8.6 The Act imposes a 20-year age limit on first registration. The Registrar has discretion to extend the limit provided that, upon survey, the condition of the ship warrants the exercise of such discretion. The age of the ship will be calculated from the date that construction was actually completed and not the laying of the keel.

Ownership

8.7 Vessels registered on the Barbados Register may be owned by:

(1) any individual who is resident, or a company that is incorporated, outside Barbados;
(2) a Barbados company incorporated under the Shipping Corporation Act;
(3) an international business company incorporated in Barbados under the International Business Companies Act 1991.

---

3 The Caribbean Community and Common Market, of which the following States are members: Antigua and Barbuda, Bahamas, Barbados, Belize, Dominica, Grenada, Guyana, Haiti, Jamaica, Montserrat, St Lucia, Trinidad and Tobago, St Vincent and the Grenadines, Suriname and St Kitts and Nevis.

8.8 All other Barbados-registered vessels (other than pleasure yachts and local fishing vessels) must be owned by qualified persons or Caricom persons as outlined in paragraph 8.4. The Act defines a qualified person as:

(1) an individual who is either a citizen of Barbados, resident in Barbados, or a permanent resident in Barbados within the meaning the Immigration Acts; or

(2) a Barbadian shipping company.

A Caricom person is defined as:

(1) an individual who is a citizen of a State of the Caribbean Community and a resident in a State of the Community; or

(2) a Caricom shipping company, being a shipping company incorporated under the laws of a State of the Caribbean Community and whose principal place of business is within a State of the Caribbean Community or its stocks and shares are beneficially owned by Caricom persons or by another Caricom shipping company.

Bareboat charter registration

8.9 The Act permits Barbadian ships to be both bareboat-chartered into and out of the Register.

Bareboat charter into the Register

8.10 Section 9(2) of the Act permits a vessel registered in a foreign country which has been bareboat-chartered to a Barbadian citizen or body corporate to be registered on the Barbados Register for the duration of the charter. Registration will only be approved if the ship is less than 20 years old at the time of the charter, the approval of the owners has been obtained and the vessel is able to produce a valid certificate of class. During the time of such registration no mortgages may be recorded against the vessel on the Barbados Register (s.47(4)). For the period that the vessel is registered on the Barbados Register the vessel must only fly the Barbados flag.

Bareboat charter out to a foreign register

8.11 Section 38 permits a Barbadian ship chartered to a foreign national or body corporate to be registered under the law of that foreign country. On production of a copy of the bareboat charter and notification from the proper officer of the foreign registry, the vessel's Barbados certificate of registry will be suspended for the period of the charter. The Registrar is obliged under the Act to notify the foreign register of all mortgages registered against the vessel in Barbados. The Act also provides that no mortgage may be registered in the foreign register against the vessel whose registry has been so suspended (s.47(5)).

Trading limits

8.12 There are no trading limits on ships registered under the Barbados flag.

Manning requirements

Certificates of competency for officers and ratings

8.13 Barbados is a party to the International Convention on Standards of Training, Certification and Watchkeeping 1978, including the 1995 Protocol and the 2010 Manila Amendments ('the STCW Convention').[4] The Barbados Registry does not issue certificates of competency (CoCs). However, all officers serving on board Barbadian ships must be qualified and hold CoCs issued by a foreign administration acceptable to the Barbados administration and issued in accordance with the requirements laid down the STCW Convention. Where a foreign-trained officer holds a certificate of competency issued by another flag State administration with whom Barbados has an agreement under STCW Regulation 1/10,[5] an application for an officer's endorsement document should be submitted to the Barbados Registry in London on Form 19 with supporting documents and payment of the appropriate fee. Upon receipt of a correctly completed application the Registry will issue a certificate of receipt of application (CRA). Once in possession of a CRA the holder will be permitted to serve on board a Barbados-registered ship for a maximum of three months pending the issue of a full endorsement. On completion of the application, the Registry will issue a Barbados officer's endorsement document in the grade equivalent to the foreign certificate of competency with any additional STCW endorsements such as a GMDSS[6] or radio electronic operator.

8.14 The Barbados Registry does not issue endorsements to ratings, but all ratings must hold STCW deck or engine room rating certificates appropriate to their duties, issued by flag State administrations in countries that are parties to the STCW Convention.[7]

Nationality of crew

8.15 There are no nationality restrictions on officers or crew serving on board Barbadian ships, provided they are in possession of seafarers' certification issued by flag States with whom Barbados have mutual agreements under STCW Regulation 1/10.[8]

Document of safe manning

8.16 All Barbadian ships are required to carry on board a minimum safe manning document, which can be obtained on application to the Registry. The manning levels

---

4 See generally, Barbados Maritime Ship Registry (BMSR) Information Bulletin No.262 – Guidance on the Implementation of the Manila Amendments to the STCW Convention, published 26 September 2016.

5 See BMSR Information Bulletin No.231, List of Administrations with agreement with Barbados under STCW Reg. 1/10, published 8 December 2014.

6 Global Maritime Distress and Safety System.

7 See generally, the BMSR Ship-Master's Guide, version 3 March 2017, chapter 1 at http://barbadosmaritime. org/ship-masters-guide-3.pdf.

8 See para. 8.13.

for Barbadian vessels are laid down in a statutory instrument made pursuant to the Act (s.86(1)). A vessel proceeding to sea that is not manned in accordance with her minimum safe manning document will be liable to detention, fines and suspension of her certificate of registry.

Approved classification societies

8.17 The following classification societies are recognised by the Barbados authorities:

American Bureau of Shipping (ABS)
Bureau Veritas (BV)
China Classification Society (CCS)
DNV GL
Indian Register of Shipping (IRS)International Naval Surveys Bureau (INS)
Korea Register of Shipping (KR)
Lloyd's Register (LR)
Nippon Kaiji Kyokai (Class NK)
Overseas Marine Certification Services (OMC)
Polski Rejestr Statkow (Polish Register of Shipping) (PRS)
Registro Italiano Navale (RINA)
Register of Russian Shipping (RS)

Procedure for registration

Provisional registration

8.18 The provisional registration of a vessel on the Barbados Register can be undertaken either through the Central Registry office in London or through one of the Registrars who have been appointed elsewhere in the world to issue provisional registration documents. The current details of Barbados Registrars can be found at the end of this chapter. Vessels can also be provisionally registered through the Deputy Principal Registrar in Bridgetown, Barbados.

8.19 The first stage in the registration procedure is for the owner or his agent to submit a notice of name proposed on Form 04[9] either directly to the Central Registry in London or to one of the other Registrars. Approval for the registration of the vessel, the use of the name and the issuance of the official number, call sign and maritime mobile service identity (MMSI) number is in all cases given by the Central Registry office. Once initial approval has been obtained and the owner approval for registration has been given, the owner should then submit the following documents to the Registrar:

(1) original notice of name proposed – (Form 04);
(2) survey certificate information (descriptive particulars of ship) – (Form 05);
(3) notarised appointment of authorised officer – (Form 06);

---

9 This form and the other forms referred to in this paragraph can be downloaded from the BMSR website, http://barbadosmaritime.org/forms/.

(4) declaration of ownership on behalf of a body corporate – (Form 07);

(5) appointment of managing owner, manager or ship's husband – (Form 08);

(6) particulars of radio equipment installed – (Form 16);

(7) statement as to radio accounting authority;

(8) minimum safe manning certificate application – (Form 12);

(9) EPIRBS information application – (Form 13);

(10) copy of the bill of sale or builder's certificate (original later);

(11) evidence of protection and indemnity insurance (all vessels);

(12) blue card (tankers only);

(13) official permission to transfer registration from the foreign register or evidence that the original registry does not require such permission;

(14) declaration that no liens are recorded on the former register;

(15) copy of the former tonnage certificate (with English translation where necessary);

(16) copy of the certificate of incorporation of owning company;

(17) copies of all statutory certificates issued by former registry, including safety certificate, load line certificate, MARPOL certificate, safety equipment certificate, safety construction certificate and safety radio certificate where applicable; and

(18) application for issue of DMLC Part 1, accompanied by copy of certificates of insurance issued under ILO Standard A2.5.2 and A4.2.

The initial registration fees, annual fees and miscellaneous fees are also payable at the time of provisional registration.

8.20 If a vessel is transferring to the Barbados Register from a port of registry within a Commonwealth country, provided that the transferring Registrar agrees and there is no change of ownership involved, the transfer can be completed through the Central Registry without the need for submission of the survey information, declaration of ownership, or certificate of incorporation of the owning company. The transcript of the register from the former port of registry will be sufficient, as this will show the ownership of the vessel and any registered encumbrances. The vessel will be entered on the Barbados Register and, provided that all the registered mortgagees agree to the transfer in writing, any mortgages registered against the vessel on the former register will be noted on the Barbados Register in the same order of precedence.

Validity of the provisional registration and extension

8.21 When all the documents have been submitted in the correct form, the Registrar will issue the provisional certificate of registry valid for six months to the owners. Provisional registration can be extended for a further six months at the discretion of the Registrar.

Permanent registration

8.22 Permanent registration will be effected once the ship has been permanently marked in accordance with the carving note and on submission of the original documents not submitted at the time of provisional registration. These should include the bill of sale or builder's certificate, original or notarised appointment of authorised officer, original notarised declaration of ownership, and original declaration of owner/manager. When these documents have been received, the permanent certificate of registry is issued. Under section 27(2) of the Act, the Principal Registrar has power to waive the requirement to produce documents from a foreign registry where the owner has attempted to obtain such documents but, because of exceptional and abnormal circumstances prevailing in that foreign country, has been unable to do so.

Registration of mortgages and security interests

8.23 A mortgage on the prescribed form (Form 01) can be registered against a provisionally or permanently registered Barbados vessel. Where more than one mortgage is registered against a vessel, or shares in a vessel, mortgagees are entered in order of priority between each other according to the date and time at which each mortgage is recorded in the Register and not according to the date of the mortgages (s.49).

Surveys

8.24 All ships registered in Barbados are subject to pre-registration surveys. Barbadian ships are also required to renew all safety certification annually and, to this end, the Registry has an extensive network of nautical inspectors worldwide who carry out annual crew and safety surveys of all ships registered under the Barbados flag.

Deregistration procedure

8.25 A deletion certificate will be issued on request, provided the consent of all mortgagees have been obtained and on payment of all outstanding fees owed to the Registry, plus the return of the Barbados certificate of registry.

Yachts

8.26 The Barbados Registry does not publish its own code of practice to regulate the construction and operation of large yachts registered in Barbados. However, large commercial yachts that are over 24 metres in load line length and under 3,000 gross registered tons are required to comply with the UK Maritime and Coastguard Agency Large Yacht Code (LY2), published in 2007.[10] Yachts not yet built are required to comply with LY3, the more recent edition of the code published in 2012. LY3 includes equivalent arrangements to the crew accommodation requirements of the Maritime Labour Convention 2006 that apply to vessels built after the date of entry into force of the Convention. Private pleasure yachts of any size that do not undertake any commercial charter activity are not required to comply with the Large Yacht Code, but voluntary compliance is recommended for safety reasons.[11]

---

10 MSN 1792.
11 See generally, Information Bulletin No. 209 – Large Commercial Yacht Standards 'LY2' Code, published 4 September 2013.

Contact addresses

8.27

Central Ship Registry

Barbados Maritime Ship Registry
c/o Barbados High Commission
1 Great Russell Street
London
WC1B 3ND
Tel: (44) (0)20 7 636 5739
Fax: (44) (0)20 7 636 5745
Email: pg@barbadosmaritime.org
Contact: Captain P.J. Green (Principal Registrar)

Other Registrars

Barbados

Captain G.N. Fergusson
Barbados Port Authority
University Row
Bridgetown
Barbados
Tel: (1) 245 434 6100
Email: gfergusson@caribsurf.com

China

Mr. Juan Jose Moron
OMCS Class
Overseas Marine Certification Services, Inc.
Room 1506
Suncome Liauw's Plaza
No. 738 Shangcheng Road
Pu-Dong, new Area
Shanghai
China
Tel: (86) 21 5836 0772
Fax: (86) 21 5836 0773
Email: china@omcsclass.org

Germany

Mr. Gunter Metzger
IMCS Germany Partnerschaft
Rasch Metzger Borsbach

Sachverstandige, Segelmacherstrasse 1
D-28777 Bremen, Germany
Tel: 0049 421 38927–20 (24/7)
Fax: 0049421 38927–11
Email: office at imcsgermany.de

Greece

Mr. Steve Eustathiou
Navegadora Transpacifica S.A.
65 Akti Miaouli
185 36 Piraeus
Greece
Tel: (30) 210 4294620

Hong Kong

Captain Q. Lloyd
c/o Carmichael & Clarke *Co* Ltd
17F Jade Centre
98 Wellington Street
Central
Hong Kong
Tel: (852) 2581 2678
Fax: (852) 2581 2722
Email: carmi@hkstar.com

India

Captain B.C. Modi
UK Marine (India)
Plot 114, GIDC Sector 10A near Oslo Cinema
Gandhiham 370201
Gujarat
India
Tel: (91) 2836 231 385
Email: india@uk-marine.com/
bcm@uk-marine.com

Indonesia

Mr. A. Junus
PT. Belvamas Maritim Indontama
Jakarta
Indonesia
Tel: (62) 21 475 7860
Fax: (62) 21 475 7947
Email: ayub@belvamas.com

Iran

Captain Mohammed Reza Dodangeh
Safe Sea Group, No.2 Nili Building
North Sohrevardi St.
Tehran
Iran
Tel: (982) 1887 34638/9
Email: dodangeh@safeseagroup.com

Lebanon

Captain Haytham Chaaban
Bshara El Khory Blvd.
Adonis Bldg., 5th Floor
Beirut
Lebanon
Tel: (961) 3 894098
Fax: (961) 7 623269
Email: capt.chaaban@gmail.com

Malta

Dr. M. Sammut
West End Buildings 215
Suite 3A
Triq il-Fran
Valletta VLT 15
Malta
Tel: (356) 21 24 61 62
Fax: (356) 21 46 24 36
Email: sammar@onvol.net

Pakistan

Captain Khahil Ur Rahman Khan
Oceanic Surveyors Ltd
Oceanic House
58 Timber Pond Keamari
Karachi-75620
Tel: (92) 21 285 1548
Fax: (92) 21 285 1231
Email: oceanic@fascom.com

Panama

Mr. Rogelio Barsallo F
Apdo 0830–1438

Panama City
Panama
Tel: (507) 203 8259
Fax: (507) 393 0475
Email: rbarsallof@cableonda.net

Russia

Mrs. Ekaterina Fetisova
Office 507
Pogranichnaya Street 15-B
Vladivostok 690091
Russia
Tel: (7) 908 4487 180
Fax: (7) 423 2404 934
Email: v.strokach@inbox.ru

Singapore

Captain V. Swamynathan
Ritchie and Bisset (Far East) Pte Ltd
Blk 209
03–01 Henderson Road
Henderson Industrial Park
Singapore 159551
Tel: (65) 6271 8700
Fax: (65) 6271 3263
Email: singapore@ritchie-and-bisset.com

Sweden

Captain Eric Carlen
Eric Carlen AB
Storangsvagen 25
115 41 Stockholm
Sweden
Tel: (46) 8 775 1749
Fax: (46) 8 6622 6899
Email: eric@ecarlen.se

Turkey

Dr. Ersin Ahmet Ozturker
Astra Marine Survey Ltd.
Acibadem 34660
Alsancak Sitesi E15
Uskudar Istanbul
Turkey

Tel: (90) 533 276 7381
Email astra@astra-marine.com

USA

Captain James F. Gavin
4830 Line Ave., Suite 168
Shreveport
LA 71106
USA
Tel: (1) 318 470 5459
Email: jamesgavin68@gmail.com

United Arab Emirates

Captain A Srivastava
Penta Ocean Ship Management & Operations LLC
PO Box 9614
Dubai
UAE
Tel: (971) 4 386 2678
Fax: (971) 4 386 2679
Email: operations@pentaoceanship.com/ info@pentaoceanship.com
Website: www.barbadosmaritime.org

CHAPTER 9

Bermuda

9.1 Bermuda is a British Overseas Territory,[1] in which the Crown is represented by the Governor and Commander-in-Chief. It is also the oldest self-governing former UK colony, representative government having been first introduced in 1620 and internal self-government in 1968. A referendum was held in 1995 in which the electorate voted to retain Bermuda's links with the UK. The legislature comprises two Houses of Parliament, similar to the British model. The lower house, the House of Assembly, consists of 36 elected members. The upper house, known as the Senate, has 11 members. The Crown remains responsible for the administration of justice, external affairs, internal security and defence. Geographically, Bermuda is located in the western Atlantic Ocean approximately 570 miles to the east of the North Carolina coast. Bermuda comprises a chain of 150 islands, although only about half are inhabited. The resident population is approximately 65,500. English is the national language. The current unit of currency is the Bermudan dollar, which is linked to and is equivalent in value to the US dollar.

9.2 Since 1 October 2016, a new quango,[2] the Bermuda Shipping and Maritime Authority ('the Bermuda Authority') has taken over from the Department of Maritime Administration all responsibilities relating to the registration of ships in Bermuda.[3] Bermuda is ranked as the 21st largest register in the world by dead-weight tonnage[4] and also appears 21st in the Paris MOU White List of port State control compliance performance published in July 2017.[5] With an average of 69,795 dwt per vessel, Bermuda has the highest such figure in the leading 35 flag States.

Sources of law

9.3 The registration of Bermuda ships is governed by the Merchant Shipping Act 2002 (as amended) ('the Act') and the Merchant Shipping (Registration of Ships) Regulations 2003 (as amended) ('the Regulations'). Unless otherwise stated, references to sections and regulations in this chapter are references to sections and regulations in the Act and the Regulations, respectively.

---

1 British Overseas Territories Act 2002, s.1.
2 A quasi-autonomous non-governmental organisation.
3 Bermuda Shipping and Maritime Authority Act 2016.
4 UNCTAD, *Review of Maritime Transport* (2017), Table 2.6.
5 See Appendix III.

Vessel eligibility

Vessel type

9.4 The Register maintained by the Registrar in accordance with section 23 is divided into two parts:

Part I for ships owned by persons qualified in accordance with the Regulations;
Part II for ships which are registered under section 31 (ships on charter by demise).

As a Category 1 British Register, there are no restrictions on the type of vessel or tonnage that may be registered in Bermuda.[6]

Age limits

9.5 Provided the vessel meets all safety requirements, there are no restrictions on the age of a ship applying for registration.

Ownership

9.6 Any vessel may be registered in Bermuda if the majority interest (i.e. 33 of the 64 shares) is legally and beneficially owned by a qualified person, individual or body corporate. For the purposes of the Act, the following categories of person are designated as 'qualified' to own a Bermuda Ship (reg. 5(1)):

(1) British citizens;
(2) non-UK nationals exercising their right of freedom of movement of workers or right of establishment;
(3) British Overseas Territories citizens;
(4) British Overseas citizens;
(5) persons who under the British Nationality Act 1981 of the UK are British subjects;
(6) persons who under the Hong Kong (British Nationality) Order 1986 of the UK are British Nationals (Overseas);
(7) bodies corporate incorporated in a EEA State;
(8) bodies corporate incorporated in the UK or in any relevant British possession;
(9) bodies corporate incorporated in Bermuda; and
(10) European Economic Interest Groupings being groupings formed in pursuance of Article 1 of Council Regulation (EEC) No. 2137/85 (set out in the Schedule to UK Statutory Instrument 1989/638) and registered in the UK.

9.7 If the majority of the shares in the vessel are owned by non-residents or entities incorporated outside Bermuda, a Bermuda resident must be appointed as a representative person for the majority ownership. The representative person may be an individual or a

---

6 See Merchant Shipping Act 1995, s.18 and the Merchant Shipping (Categorization of Relevant British Possessions) Order 2003, SI 2003/1248.

body corporate. Furthermore, regulation 5(2) provides that a person who is not qualified to be an owner of a Bermuda ship may nevertheless be one of the owners of such a ship if:

(1) a majority interest in the ship is owned by persons who are qualified to be owners of Bermuda ships; and

(2) the ship is registered on Part 1 of the Register.

Bareboat charter registration

9.8 Section 31 permits bareboat charter registration or 'flagging-in' from 'compatible' foreign registries, subject to the consent of the Bermuda Authority. Section 32 also permits ships on the principal Register to be 'flagged-out' to compatible registries for the duration of a bareboat charter.

Flagging-in to the bareboat (Demise) Charter Register

9.9 For a ship to be eligible to be entered on the Demise Charter Register she must not be a fishing vessel or a ship of less than 24 metres in length, she must be eligible to be entered in a 'compatible' register and the demise charterer must be qualified to be the owner of a ship registered in Bermuda. If the charterer is not a resident of Bermuda, the charterer must appoint an individual or body corporate that is a resident in Bermuda to be the representative person in relation to the ship. Application for registration on the Demise Charter Register should be made to the Registrar of Shipping on form DCR 3. If the charterer is a body corporate, an authorised officer should be appointed to make the application. The following documents should be submitted to the Registrar in support of the application:

(1) a certified copy of the charterparty;

(2) a certified transcript of the underlying registry of owners, which should include both details of ownership and any mortgages, charges or liens registered against the ship;

(3) the written consent of the appropriate maritime authorities of the country of underlying registration;

(4) a current international tonnage certificate and certificate of survey;

(5) the written consent of the mortgagees, if any, on Form DCR5;

(6) the written consent of the owners or, if more than one, each owner on Form DCR4;

(7) the name and address of the individual or body corporate appointed as the demise charterers' representative person in Bermuda on Form DCR14;

(8) a manager to be appointed by the charterers on Form DCR3;

(9) such supplementary information and evidence relating to the ship as the Registrar may require in order to determine whether the ship may be properly registered.

The ship will usually retain her original name unless this clashes with an existing ship's name on the Register, or a demise charterer wishes to change the name to one that fits with his fleet's nomenclature, in which case a change of name form will also need to be submitted at the time of application.

9.10 On satisfactory completion of the registration, a certificate of demise charter registration will be issued to the applicants (Form DCR 1). This is similar in format to the certificate of British registry under Part I of the principal Act and is enclosed in a red cover. The certificate is to be produced on demand to designated officials and if lost or damaged may be replaced by submission of a completed Form DCR 8. The certificate of demise charter must be delivered up to the Registrar on termination of the charter or on deletion of the ship from the underlying registry of owners. Upon the issue of the certificate, the charterer is required to surrender to the underlying register all certificates previously issued by them and to make a declaration to that effect to the Registrar on Form DCR 11.

9.11 All ships bareboat-chartered into the Registry will have the port of HAMILTON marked on their stern. The ship will be assigned a registration number and the charterer issued with a carving and marking note (Form DCR 6). The carving and marking note will need to be certified by a marine surveyor of the Bermuda Authority to the effect that the ship has been correctly marked prior to being entered on the Register. The entry on the Register is effective for the period of the charter or five years, whichever is the longer. Applications for renewal of registration for a further period of five years can be made by the charterer using Form DCR 10.

Flagging-out from the bareboat Charter Register

9.12 The Bermuda Authority may grant dispensation for a Bermudian ship of 24 metres or above in length to be registered on the Demise Charter Register of a foreign country subject to receiving the written consent of the registered owners and mortgagees. This should be supplied on Forms DCR 15 and DCR 16, along with a copy of the demise charterparty. Thereafter, the Bermuda Authority will provide consent on Form DCR 18.

9.13 Upon registration in a foreign registry, the registered owner is required to provide the Bermuda Authority with a certified transcript/extract of registration, together with an English translation where appropriate, and an undertaking to notify the Registry in the event of the closure or lapse of the foreign demise charter registration. Owners are also required to surrender the Bermuda certificate of registry, and other statutory certificates issued by the Registry. The foreign registry will thereafter issue its own Convention certificates. The charterers will be required to give an undertaking not to fly the Red Ensign (except as a courtesy flag) during the period in which the ship is registered on the foreign register (Form DCR 17). The ship's home port will be that of the foreign registry and the registered owners are required to provide confirmation to the Bermuda Administration within 15 days of registration that the foreign port of registry has been marked in place of HAMILTON.

9.14 For the duration of the foreign registration, the Bermuda registration will be considered suspended except in respect of matters relating to title. Usually the ship will retain her original name unless the Bermuda Registry gives permission for it to be changed. For the duration of the registration on the foreign register, the owner will remain liable for payment of the annual tonnage fee in Bermuda, plus any transactional fees. Dispensation for the registration on a foreign demise charter register will automatically cease when either the charterparty comes to an end, or after five years, whichever is the longer, or if the ship fails to maintain internationally agreed safety standards as a result of which the Bermuda Registry revokes its consent.

Trading limits

9.15 Bermuda ships are not subject to any trading restrictions.

Manning requirements

Certificates of competency for officers and ratings

9.16 Bermuda is a party to the International Convention on Standards of Training, Certification and Watchkeeping for Seafarers 1978 (STCW 78) and its relevant amendments. Subject to verification, Bermuda recognises the qualification of other STCW white listed countries accepted by the UK & REG Members for the purposes of issuing STCW endorsements to existing certificates without examination.[7] Bermuda STCW endorsements are valid for a period of five years, subject to the validity of the underlying certificate. New officers without certificate endorsements who are scheduled to join Bermuda vessels can be issued with an STCW valid for a period of three months pending the issue of the full-term Bermuda endorsement.

Nationality of crew

9.17 There are no restrictions on crew nationality.

Document of safe manning

9.18 All Bermuda-registered ships are required to hold a safe manning document setting out the minimum number of officers and ratings considered to be the minimum safe level for the operation of the ship. Each ship is considered on an individual basis by the Bermuda Authority prior to the issue of a safe manning document. The manning levels set out in a safe manning document will reflect the IMO guidelines in respect of watchkeeping duties, dealing with emergencies and the routine operations of the ship.[8]

Approved classification societies

9.19 The following recognised organisations have been approved by the Bermuda Authority for the purposes of issuing tonnage, safety and classification certificates and for carrying out surveys on ship entered on the Bermuda Register:

American Bureau of Shipping (ABS)
Bureau Veritas (BV)
DNV GL
Lloyd's Register of Shipping (LR)
Nippon Kaiji Kyokai (NKK)
Registro Italiano Navale (RINA)

---

7 See, Bermuda Shipping Notice 2016–015, Officer Certification and Issue of Endorsements.

8 See IMO Resolution A.1047(27) on the Principles of Minimum Safe Manning dated 20 December 2011, at Annex 2 at www.imo.org/en/KnowledgeCentre/IndexofIMOResolutions/Documents/A%20-%20Assembly/1047(27) (accessed 20 January 2018).

Procedure for registration

Provisional registration

9.20 Where it is impossible for the Registrar to issue a full registration certificate, pending receipt of full documentation, or the return of the carving and marking note, a provisional certificate of registration can be issued. This permits the ship to fly the Red Ensign for three months or until the ship's arrival in Bermuda or a port specified in the certificate of provisional registration, whichever occurs first. (reg. 55). Until full registration has been effected and the ship is entered in the principal Register, no mortgages can be registered against the ship.

Permanent registration

9.21 Upon submitting an application to register on Form ROSF C190, along with an application for approval of the ship's proposed name on Form ROSF C215, the ship will be surveyed by a surveyor of the Bermuda Authority or the UK Maritime and Coastguard Agency to assess the vessel's compliance with international and national merchant shipping legislation, following which a letter of compliance will be issued by the Registry. A carving and marking note will also be issued. Thereafter, the owners should submit the following documentation to the Registrar along with the appropriate fee:

(1) declaration of eligibility (includes appointment of representative person, managing owner or ship's manager person on Form ROSF C196);
(2) builder's certificate or original bill of sale;
(3) tonnage certificate;
(4) if the ship is owned by a body corporate:
   (a) a copy of the company's memorandum and articles of association (or memorandum of association and bye-laws if a Bermuda exempted company); and
   (b) the appointment of an authorised officer (Form ROSF C193).

The marking of the ship's name, IMO number, official number, port of registry and tonnage will then be verified by the Registry, following which a certificate of registry and the tonnage certificate will be issued to the owners.

9.22 Where the vessel is simply transferring from the UK Register or another Category 1 British register, the application process is simplified and an application to transfer, along with the declaration of eligibility and payment of the applicable fee,[9] is all that is required. Thereafter, the vessel will be issued with a new carving and marking note and a new certificate of registry will be granted in exchange for the surrender of the old one.

---

9 For the registration and tonnage fees payable in Bermuda see the Merchant Shipping (Fees) Regulations 2012 BR18/2012 which can be downloaded from the Bermuda Shipping and Maritime Authority website, www.bermudashipping.bm/.

Registration of mortgages

9.23 A mortgage can only be registered against a permanently registered Bermudan vessel using a statutory form of mortgage, similar in layout and content to those forms prescribed by the UK Ship Register.[10] For this reason, it will not be necessary to register with the Registrar of Ships the collateral deed of covenant that will normally set out in more the obligations of both parties to the mortgage.[11] It is not possible to register a mortgage over a ship that is only provisionally registered. Where more than one mortgage is registered against a vessel or shares in a vessel, mortgages are entered in priority between each other according to the date and time at which each mortgage is recorded in the Register and not according to the date of the mortgages.

9.24 Where a lender intends to take a mortgage over a Bermuda-registered vessel it is possible for the lender to obtain priority for the mortgage by delivering to the Registrar an executed notice of mortgage intent.[12] Upon receipt of such notice and payment of the prescribed fee, the Registrar will record the relevant details, giving priority for the intended notice for up to 30 days. On the expiry of such notice the lender will be entitled to renew the priority notice for a further period, or periods, of 30 days upon written request.

Surveys

9.25 All new ships flagging into the Register, with the exception of vessels previously registered under the UK flag or under a Category 1 Red Ensign Register, are required to undergo a flagging-in survey by a surveyor from the Bermuda Authority or a surveyor from the UK Maritime and Coastguard Agency, acting on behalf of the Bermuda Authority. Following satisfactory completion of the survey, a letter of compliance is issued accepting the ship for registration. Every Bermuda-registered ship will also be subject to a mandatory five-yearly general inspection in conjunction with the Bermuda flag State inspection. The Bermuda Authority has delegated all survey, audit and certification functions to the six recognised organisations,[13] apart from the following functions:

(1) passenger ship survey;
(2) ISM code certificate;
(3) ISPS code certificate; and
(4) MLC 2006 certificate.

Deregistration procedure

9.26 A Bermuda-registered ship may be deregistered on the written request of the owner in the event of a change of status in the registered owner or where the vessel is sold to a person that is not qualified to own a Bermuda-registered ship, provided

---

10 See the UK account current mortgage form MSF 4736 at Appendix XI(k).

11 For a detailed analysis of the English law relating to ship mortgages see D. Osborne, G. Bowtle and C. Buss, *The Law of Ship Mortgages* (2nd edn, Informa Law from Routledge, 2017)

12 Regulation 47 is identical to the equivalent UK provision, the Merchant Shipping (Registration of Ships) Regulations 1993 at reg. 59.

13 See para. 9.19 above.

there are no outstanding monies owed to the Bermuda Authority and the consent of all registered mortgagees has been obtained. On closure a closed transcript of the Register will be issued to the owner and all mortgagees having the benefit of an undischarged mortgage.

Yachts

9.27 The registration and survey requirements for yachts will depend on whether the yachts are owned by individuals or corporations and upon the size and mode of operation. Registration fees vary according to the same factors. Commercial yachts over 24 metres in length are required to comply with the UK Maritime and Coastguard Agency Large Commercial Yacht Code ('LY3') or, where permissible, earlier editions of that code. Passenger yachts carrying between 13 and 36 passengers are required to comply with the Passenger Yacht Code ('PYC') whether operated as private pleasure yachts or on a commercial basis.[14] It should be noted that undated versions of LY3 and the PYC were incorporated into the Red Ensign Group Yacht Code published in November 2017 ('REG-YC'), which is expected to come into force on 1 January 2019 in Bermuda and all other flag States within the Red Ensign Group of registries.

Contact addresses

9.28

Registrar of Shipping
Bermuda Shipping and Maritime Authority
PO Box HM 1628,
Hamilton HMGX
Bermuda
Tel: (1 441) 295 7251
Fax: (1 441) 295 3718
Email: registry@bermudashipping.bm
Website: www.bermudashipping.bm

---

14 See generally Chapter 6, para. 6.35 *et seq.*

CHAPTER 10

British Virgin Islands

10.1 The British Virgin Islands ('the BVI') consists of a group of islands and islets in the easternmost part of the Virgin Islands archipelago in the Caribbean Sea, situated to the east of St John and St Thomas and to the north of St Croix, all part of the US Virgin Islands. The largest island in the BVI is Tortola where the capital, Road Town, is situated. The population is approximately 35,000. Originally a Dutch colony, the BVI was annexed by the British in 1672 and was part of the Leeward Islands colony between 1872 and 1960. A period of direct rule followed, after which self-government was first introduced in 1977. The BVI is now a British Overseas Territory. Under the 2007 Constitution, which replaced an earlier one dating from 1976, the Governor, who is appointed by the Crown, has reserved powers on matters such as defence, security and external affairs.[1] There is a House of Assembly consisting of a Speaker, one ex-officio member (the Attorney-General), and 13 members who are each elected for a four-year term. There is an Executive Council comprised of the Premier, four other Assembly members and the Attorney-General, who has no vote. The country's main industries are tourism and offshore financial services. Rum is a major export. The legal tender is the US dollar.

10.2 The Virgin Islands Shipping Registry ('VISR') is a government department. The registry has been classified under the UK Merchant Shipping Act 1995 as a Category 1 registry (unlimited tonnage and type) since June 2008 and is the most recent Red Ensign Group registry to be advanced from Category 2 to Category 1 status.[2]

Sources of law

10.3 BVI law is based on English law. Some Westminster statutes and subordinate legislation apply in the BVI, while local legislation often adopts English legal principles. The registration of ships under the BVI flag is governed by the Merchant Shipping Act 2001, as amended ('the Law') which consolidated and replaced the previous BVI statutes dealing with ship registration and other merchant shipping matters. The Law applies much of the UK provisions of law relating to registration and safety. Unless otherwise stated, references in this chapter to sections are references to sections of the Law. In the Law, the BVI are referred to as the Virgin Islands and a ship that is registered in the Virgin Islands is defined as a Virgin Islands ship.[3]

---

1 Virgin Islands Constitution Order 2007, SI 2007/1678.
2 The Merchant Shipping (Categorisation of Registries of Overseas Territories) Order 2008, SI 2008/1243.
3 Section 3(1), Merchant Shipping Act 2001.

Vessel eligibility

Vessel type

10.4 Since 2014, any type of vessel may be registered as a Virgin Islands ship, provided it meets the required internationally recognised safety standards and is owned by persons qualified to be the owners of BVI ships. The popularity of the BVI as a destination for cruising yachts is said to have contributed to VISR's success in attracting foreign-owned yachts to the BVI flag, Yachts will be considered separately in paragraph 10.32 below. Part VIII of the Law also provides for the registration of submersible craft, the details of which are recorded in a separate part of the register in accordance with section 11(3) of the Law.

Age limits

10.5 Whilst there are no mandatory age limits for Virgin Islands ships, age is a factor that is taken into account when assessing the acceptability of a ship for registration under section 7 (refusal of registration).

Ownership

10.6 Section 4(1) provides that the following categories of persons are qualified to be the owners of Virgin Islands ships:

(1) Virgin Islands citizens;
(2) British citizens;
(3) British Dependent Territories[4] citizens;
(4) British Overseas citizens;
(5) British subjects;
(6) persons who under the Hong Kong (British Nationality) Order 1986 are British Nationals (Overseas);
(7) persons, other than those referred to in paragraphs (1)–(6), who are nationals or citizens of a Member State of the European Union or European Economic Area including the overseas territories of such Member State;
(8) bodies corporate, incorporated in any Member State of the European Union or European Economic Area, including the UK, and having a place of business in any such Member State;
(9) bodies corporate incorporated in any relevant British possession, other than the Virgin Islands or in any overseas territory of a Member State of the European Union or the European Economic Area and having a place of business in any such possession or overseas territory; and

---

4 Now, British Overseas Territories, see s.1, British Overseas Territories Act 2002.

(10) bodies corporate incorporated in the Virgin Islands or incorporated in a Member State of the Caribbean Community[5] or the Organisation of Eastern Caribbean States[6] and registered in the Virgin Islands.

10.7 Furthermore, section 4(2) provides that a person who is not qualified under subsection (1) to be an owner of a Virgin Islands ship may nevertheless be one of the owners of such a ship if:

(1) a majority interest in the ship, within the meaning of section 5, is owned by persons who are qualified to be owners of Virgin Islands ships; and

(2) the ship is registered in accordance with the provisions of section 5.

Finally, sections 5 and 6 provide that where the majority interest in the ship is owned by persons who are not resident in the Virgin Islands, the ship shall only be entitled to be registered if a 'representative person' is appointed in relation to the ship. A representative person is either an individual resident in the Virgin Islands, or a body corporate incorporated in the Virgin Islands with a place of business there. Intended owning entities that are not BVI incorporated or registered will usually appoint a professional BVI service provider approved by the VISR as a local representative person. The local representative has certain responsibilities under BVI anti-money laundering rules and in relation to vessel emergencies.

Bareboat charter registration

10.8 The Law permits bareboat chartered vessels to be 'flagged in' to the Virgin Islands register and Virgin Islands vessels to be 'flagged out' to foreign registers, subject to the requirements set out in sections 28–35. Section 28 provides that ships of 1,500 gross tonnage and above may be 'flagged in' to the Virgin Islands on the Demise Charter Register if:

(1) the ship is operated under a bareboat charter that meets the requirements referred to below;

(2) the charterer is qualified to be the owner of a Virgin Islands ship;

(3) the charterer appoints a representative person (if not resident in the Virgin Islands);

(4) the ship is registered on a register outside the Virgin Islands for the purpose of property rights;

(5) the primary flag State or 'home' register is prepared to grant dispensation permitting dual registration.

---

5 The Caribbean Community and Common Market ('CARICOM') was established in 1973 by the Treaty of Chaguaramas and currently has 15 member States and five associate members, comprising the BVI and four other British Overseas Territories. A full list of the Member States and further information about CARICOM can be found on the CARICOM website www.caricom.org (accessed 8 February 2018).

6 The Organisation of Eastern Caribbean States ('OECS') was created in 1981 by the Treaty of Basseterre. There are now ten Member States: Antigua and Barbuda, Dominica, Grenada, Montserrat, St Kitts and Nevis, St Lucia, and St Vincent and the Grenadines. There are three associate members, Anguilla, the BVI and Martinique. For further information about OECS see www.oecs.org (accessed 8 February 2018).

In order to satisfy the statutory requirements:

(1) the charter must be in writing;

(2) the demise effected by the charter must be made by the owner of the ship to a charterer with a single legal personality for a fixed term of two or more years, or for such lesser period as may be allowed by the Director of the VISR;

(3) the terms of the charter must vest in the charterer the operation, management and control of the ship, including responsibility for the engagement or employment of her Master and crew.

Even if a bareboat chartered vessel is entitled to be 'flagged in' to the VISR under section 28(1), the Registrar of Shipping has an overriding power to refuse registration on a number of grounds listed in section 28(3). These include the right to refuse to register a vessel if "it is not in the interests of the Islands that the ship should be registered".

10.9 The Director may grant dispensation to permit a Virgin Islands ship of 1,500 gross tonnage and above to be registered on a bareboat register of a foreign country (s.33). Such dispensation will not be granted until the Director is satisfied that:

(1) the ship is subject to a demise charter under which the owner is not responsible for the management, operation or control of the ship for the period of the charter;

(2) any mortgagee has consented to the flagging out;

(3) the ship is intended to be registered under the law of a country outside the Islands;

(4) upon registration outside the Islands, the ship will be subject to laws which implement the Collisions Conventions, the Load Line, Marine Pollution, Safety and STCW Conventions and the ILO Maritime Labour Convention[7] to the same extent as they apply to the ship in the Virgin Islands.

When a dispensation has taken effect, the ship will be entitled to fly only the flag of the country named in the owner's application and not the Virgin Islands flag. A dispensation granted by the Director under section 33 will terminate automatically if the ship ceases to be registered in the country named in the owner's declaration in support of the application. It will also terminate when the demise charter comes to an end, for whatever reason.

Trading limits

10.10 While foreign-going Virgin Islands ships are not subject to trading restrictions, they are, as with any other flag, subject to any international (i.e. United Nations) embargoes in force, or any unilateral, bilateral or multilateral sanctions. In practice, trading limits will also be impacted by the insurance provisions of the relevant ship.

Manning requirements

10.11 Section 111 permits the Governor in Council to make safe manning regulations dealing with required numbers of officers and seamen for individual vessels, standards of competence and medical fitness requirements for seafarers. In making such regulations the Cabinet is required to give due regard to the STCW Convention.

---

7 Maritime Labour Convention 2006. See generally, J. Lavelle (ed.), *The Maritime Labour Convention 2006, International Labour Law Redefined* (Informa Law from Routledge 2014).

Certificates of competency for officers and ratings

10.12 The VISR issues STCW endorsements to seafarers in accordance with the provisions of the STCW Convention in recognition of acceptable certificates of competency held by them which have been issued by other STCW States, to allow such seafarers to serve on those Virgin Islands ships that are required to be manned by STCW certificated officers. The State issuing the certificate of competency will itself need to meet applicable STCW/IMO criteria, including, but not limited to, that State being on the IMO White List as an issuing State.[8] However, every application for a Virgin Islands STCW endorsement is also assessed on its merits. Dispensations for an officer to serve, for a limited period, in the rank next above that for which an acceptable certificate of competency is held, may also be issued, in exceptional circumstances, on a case-by-case basis.

Nationality of crew

10.13 As a general rule there are no restrictions on the nationality of officers or crew.

Document of safe manning

10.14 All Virgin Islands ships of 500 gross tonnage or more which are in commercial use and engaged in international voyages are required to carry a minimum safe manning document issued by the VISR.[9] In order to obtain this document application should be made to the VISR supported by proposals for the minimum safe manning of the ship concerned. Each application is assessed on an individual basis, based on type, size and complexity of the vessel and its trading pattern.

Approved classification societies

10.15 The following six classification societies are currently listed by the VISR as recognised organisations:

American Bureau of Shipping (ABS)
Bureau Veritas (BV)
DNV GL
Lloyd's Register (LR)
Nippon Kaiji Kyokai (Class NK)
Registro Italiano Navale (RINA)

Radio ship station licensing

10.16 Ship radio station licences are issued by the BVI Government Telecommunications Unit, The RG Hodge Plaza, Road Town, Tortola, British Virgin Islands. The Telecommunications

---

8 See Appendix IV.
9 VISR Guidance Note No. 1/2009 may be of assistance to the reader.

Regulatory Commission is the regulator that has oversight of the grant of such licences.[10] For further contact details see paragraph 10.34 below.

Procedure for registration

Permanent registration

10.17 An application for permanent registration may be made to the Registrar of Shipping, nominating one of three alternative ports of registry in the BVI: namely, Road Harbour, Gorda Sound or White Bay, the last two ports having been added by the Governor in 2012.[11] Road Town remains the most popular home port. The procedure for permanent registration is very similar to that which prevails in the UK, except that in the BVI permanent registration is often preceded by provisional registration by virtue of the fact that the VISR requires all original documents to be presented before a ship can be permanently registered.

10.18 An owner is required to produce original documents of title in the form of a bill or bills of sale, or in the case of a new vessel, a builder's certificate. In the case of a ship previously registered on a register other than the VISR, a closed transcript (or equivalent document) of the previous register is generally required, although it is not a prerequisite for proceeding with registration. At the time of registration, an application to delete from the previous register will suffice, on the understanding that the closed transcript will follow in due course. The title documents must be accompanied by a declaration of ownership and eligibility signed by a person entitled to be registered as owner of the ship, or a share therein, or in the case of a body corporate, by a person authorised by the company to make such declarations, containing the following information:

(1) a statement of his qualifications to own a Virgin Islands ship or, in the case of a body corporate, proof of incorporation and good standing;
(2) in the case of a foreign ship, a statement of its foreign name;
(3) a statement of the number of shares in the ship the legal title in which is vested in him, or the body corporate whether alone or jointly;
(4) a declaration that to the best of his knowledge and belief, a majority interest in the ship is owned by persons qualified to be the owners of Virgin Islands ships, and the ship is otherwise entitled to be so registered.

10.19 Prior to registration, every ship is required to be surveyed by a surveyor appointed under section 414 who will issue a tonnage certificate. This must be delivered to the Registrar (in practice the VISR) at the time of registration (s.13). Upon receipt of a tonnage certificate, together with the other application documents, the VISR will issue a carving and marking note. This document confirms the name, port of registry, official number, net tonnage and draught markings which are required to be permanently marked on every ship, other than a pleasure yacht which is under 24 metres in length, in the manner and position stipulated (s.14(1)).

---

10 See the Telecommunications Act 2006 as amended.
11 See s.20(2).

10.20 On completion of the necessary marking, an approved surveyor is required to inspect the vessel to satisfy himself that the work has been carried out and sign a certificate to that effect on the carving and marking note. The signed note must be returned to the Registrar before permanent registration can be completed. It should be borne in mind that a vessel should not proceed to sea until carving and marking is complete. When all of the preliminary registration requirements have been complied with, the Registrar will register the ship by entering its particulars in the Register and issue a certificate of British registry to the owner, subject to the requirements for the ship to comply with safety and pollution prevention standards, as may be applicable.

Interim registration

10.21 Section 36 of the Law permits a vessel to be registered on an interim basis during the course of a transfer of ownership prior to the transfer of title by a bill of sale. Interim registration may only take place where:

(1) there is in existence a written contract for the transfer of a ship or a share in a ship;

(2) under the terms of the contract the owner has agreed:

    (a) to transfer the ship, or a share in the ship, to a person qualified to own a Virgin Islands ship who intends to register it in the Virgin Islands; and

    (b) to provide the buyer with a bill of sale and a certificate stating that the ship is free of registered mortgages; and

(3) upon the issue of a bill of sale the buyer will be entitled to register the ship in the Virgin Islands.

A certificate of interim registration will be valid for a period of 21 days only. Prior to the expiry of that period the buyer is required to deliver to the Registrar of Shipping the original bill of sale and a completed declaration of eligibility. If those documents are not delivered within the time limit, the interim registration will lapse and the interim certificate of registry and any other documents issued by the VISR shall be returned to the Registrar of Shipping (s.36(6)).

Provisional registration

10.22 An application for provisional registration may be made if a vessel becomes entitled to be registered while at a port outside the Virgin Islands. As has already been mentioned in paragraph 10.17, provisional registration will be necessary when permanent registration cannot be completed because of a delay in delivering all necessary original documents to the VISR. The 'proper officer', usually a British consul, may, on application and by prior arrangement with the Registrar of Shipping, grant a provisional certificate stating:

(1) the name of the ship;

(2) the time and place of purchase of the ship and the names of the purchasers;

(3) the best particulars of the tonnage, build and description of the ship which the person granting the certificate is able to obtain

and shall forward a copy of the certificate to the Registrar of Shipping at the first convenient opportunity (s.27(1) and (2)).

Validity of the provisional registration and extension

10.23 A provisional certificate of registry shall be valid for a period of three months, or until the ship's arrival at the port of Road Harbour, or another Virgin Islands port of registry, if earlier. No further provisional certificate may be granted within one year of the date of the original, except with the consent of the Director of Shipping.

Registration of ships under construction

10.24 The Law at present makes no provision for the registration of ships under construction, as is possible in the Cayman Islands.[12]

Registration of mortgages and security interests

10.25 When a vessel is registered under the BVI flag, a loan or other financial obligation can be secured over the ship by delivering to the Registrar for registration an executed mortgage using a statutory form of mortgage. The Registrar will record details of the mortgage on the Register and endorse on the mortgage itself the date and time of registration. Mortgages rank for priority in order of registration. There is also provision to record 'priority notices'. This device enables the mortgagee who issues a priority notice to maintain priority as of the date of execution of the mortgage and to release funds even though the mortgage is registered at a later date. It prevents a subsequent mortgagee from gaining priority by registering his interest before the prior mortgagee who has issued a priority notice is able to register his mortgage. This device may be particularly useful in cases where mortgage transactions take place outside the Virgin Islands by adding another layer of mortgage protection. In practice, the process is seldom used.

10.26 Where a mortgage instrument contains a prohibition against a transfer of ownership, a transfer of flag or the creation of further mortgages without the prior written consent of the mortgagee, the Registrar will note such restriction on the Register and will not deal with a subsequent transfer or accept a further mortgage for registration unless the mortgagee's written consent is produced to him. Interim registration in the course of a transfer of ownership allows 21 days to deliver all requisite registration documents. A mortgage may be recorded at the time of interim registration and will continue to be protected by virtue of such registration pursuant to section 83, even if the vessel fails to meet the 21-day requirement and interim registration is thus terminated.

10.27 Where a ship is provisionally registered through a British consular office and a mortgage is also recorded pursuant to section 83, that mortgage will continue to be a registered mortgage until it is discharged, even if the provisional registration ceases or lapses after the statutory three months without full registration. A vessel may transfer registration from one British port to another and record the same ownership and mortgage

---

12 See Chapter 11.

details at the registry of the new port. Thus, on a transfer, say, from the Registry of Shipping and Seamen at Cardiff to VISR at Road Harbour, the owner and mortgage details would be recorded in the Virgin Islands before the registry of the vessel in Cardiff was closed, thus maintaining a continuous mortgagee protection.

10.28 Where a BVI company grants a mortgage over a Virgin Islands ship there will arise an obligation to comply with Part VII of the BVI Business Companies Act 2004, as amended by a series of amending Acts and Orders, the most recent of which came into force on 1 January 2018.[13] The regime contained in Part VII requires every BVI company to record details of every written form of security interest created over its property in a private register that is required to be kept at its registered office or the office of its BVI registered agent.[14] This obligation will extend not only a statutory ship mortgage but also to any collateral deed of covenant or other security document creating a charge over other assets provided as security for the loan. In addition to the compulsory private registration of the mortgage, a BVI company or a mortgagee may apply to the Registrar of Corporate Affairs to register the security interest in the Register of Registered Charges maintained under the BVI Business Companies Act.[15] Section 166 of that Act provides that once a security interest has been registered it will have priority over a security interest that is subsequently registered under the Act or one that has not been so registered.

Surveys

10.29 A tonnage measurement survey is always required before registration, though this can be based on an existing tonnage certificate. A compliance survey is required for merchant ships, commercial ships and yachts to which the International Convention on Tonnage Measurement of Ships 1969 as amended ('the Tonnage Convention') requirements apply, and this is usually done in parallel with the registration processes, though in appropriate circumstances the registration process may be completed before the statutory surveys for Tonnage Convention compliance are complete. A vessel that is subject to statutory Tonnage Convention requirements cannot, however, operate until it has complied with the relevant requirements and has been issued with the necessary certificates.

Deregistration procedure

10.30 A Virgin Islands ship must be deleted from the Register when it is sold to an owner who is not qualified to be the owner. No export licence is necessary to sell a ship to an unqualified owner, or to delete a ship from the Register. The Registrar will issue a closed transcript of the Register when any registered mortgages are discharged and any outstanding Registry fees paid. A qualified closed transcript may be issued in the event of closure with an undischarged mortgage (known as a 'qualified closure').

---

13 The BVI Business Companies Act (Amendment of Schedules) Order 2017, SI 2017/17.
14 Section 162, The BVI Business Companies Act, 2004, as amended.
15 See, ss.163–168, The BVI Business Companies Act. 2004, as amended

Yachts

10.31 Yachts may be registered in the Virgin Islands in the same manner as merchant ships, but the level of application of the various safety and pollution prevention Conventions will vary according to the size and operation of the vessel. The COLREG Convention will always apply, to the relevant extent depending on the length of the ship. MARPOL certification may be required, depending on the ship's tonnage, though some level of compliance with the pollution prevention annexes to MARPOL would apply in all cases. The application of SOLAS requirements will depend on the size and use of the yacht (i.e. private or engaged in trade). In the case of pleasure yachts in private use, there are minimum Convention and statutory requirements under the SOLAS, MARPOL and COLREG Conventions.

10.32 Pleasure yachts not engaged in charter work may comply voluntarily with the Large Yacht Code ('LY3'),[16] in which case such a vessel will be surveyed by a VISR surveyor and, if found to comply with the code, the relevant certificates will be issued. Compliance with LY3 will be essential for any Virgin Islands registered pleasure yacht of over 300 gross tons operating in US navigable waters in order to satisfy the US Coast Guard ('USCG') minimum standards required of foreign-flagged pleasure yachts.[17] Compliance with LY3 or, where applicable, earlier editions of LY3, is mandatory for all large yachts over 24 metres in length that undertake commercial charter work.[18] As well as imposing annual statutory inspections, LY3 also stipulates the required crew qualifications and manning scales, depending on the gross tonnage, engine power output and cruising range from a safe haven. Yachts of over 3,000 gross tons are required to be manned to the same levels as cargo vessels of the same size.

10.33 Where a private pleasure or commercial yacht is required to carry between 13 and 36 passengers, VISR will require the yacht to comply with the Passenger Yacht Code ('PYC')[19] as an alternative to full passenger ship certification under the SOLAS Convention that would otherwise be mandatory. As mentioned in Chapter 6, updated versions of LY3 and PYC were published in November 2017 by the Red Ensign Group of Registries in the consolidated REG Yacht Code ('REG-YC') which will come into force after the UK Government has tabled REG-YC with the International Maritime Organisation under the equivalence provisions in the relevant IMO Conventions. It is expected that REG-YC will come into force on 1 January 2019. In the meantime, LY3 and PYC will apply.

Contact addresses

10.34 The VISR no longer has a representative office in the UK but does have approved surveyors in ports around the world.

---

16 See further Chapter 6, para. 6.36 *et seq.*

17 The United States Coast Guard Code of Federal Regulations 46 Sub-Chapter T (certification of small passenger yachts).

18 Where a yacht is less than 24 metres in length such a vessel is required to comply with the UK Merchant Shipping (Safety of Commercial Sailing and Motor Vessels) Regulations, 2004, SI 2004/6 and the UK Blue and Yellow Codes of Practice published thereunder; see also VISR Guidance Note No.1/2009.

19 See Chapter 6, para. 6.38.

Head office – Tortola, British Virgin Islands

Virgin Islands Shipping Registry
2nd Floor, RG Hodge Plaza) (Old Traffic Building)
Road Town, Tortola
British Virgin Islands, VG1110
Attention: Captain Raman Bala, Director
Tel: (1 284) 468 9499
For Survey issues: Mr. Frank Akoto, Senior Surveyor
Tel: (44) 7904 343452
Email: bvishipregister@gmail.com
Website: www.bvi.gov.vg/departments/visr

Government of the Virgin Islands Telecommunications Unit

Telecommunications Unit
(Upstairs Vehicle Licensing Dept.)
RG Hodge Plaza
Road Town, Tortola
British Virgin Islands, VG1110
Tel: (1 284) 468 3603, (1 284) 494 3701
Email: gnelson@gov.vg

CHAPTER 11

Cayman Islands

11.1 The Cayman Islands consists of a group of three islands, Grand Cayman, Cayman Brac and Little Cayman, situated about 150 miles south of Cuba, the largest island being Grand Cayman. The population is approximately 58,500. Formerly linked politically to Jamaica, the Cayman Islands opted to remain a British Overseas Territory when Jamaica gained its independence in 1962. As with all British Overseas Territories, Parliament at Westminster retains the right to legislate. The Governor, who is appointed by the Crown, has reserved powers on matters such as defence and external affairs. There is a Legislative Assembly whose 19 members are elected every four years and a Cabinet comprising the Governor, the Premier, the Deputy Premier, five ministers elected by, and from, the Legislative Assembly and two ex-officio members, the Deputy Governor and the Attorney-General. The country is a major offshore financial centre, as well as a popular destination for tourists. The legal tender is the Cayman Islands dollar (CI$1 = US$1.219).

11.2 The Cayman Islands Shipping Registry ('CISR') is a division of the Maritime Authority of the Cayman Islands ('MACI'), a governmental authority. The Cayman Islands registry is part of the Red Ensign Group and is classified under the UK Merchant Shipping Act 1995 as a Category 1 registry (unlimited tonnage and type). The Cayman Islands appears as one of the largest 35 flag States for merchant vessels as at 1 January 2017 and is first ranked in the Paris MOU White List of port State control inspections for the reporting period 2014–2016, published in July 2017.[1]

Sources of law

11.3 Cayman Islands law is based on English law. Some Westminster statutes apply in the Cayman Islands, while local legislation often adopts English legal principles. The registration of ships under the Cayman Islands flag is now governed by the Merchant Shipping Law (2016 Revision) ('the Law') which has consolidated and replaced a large number of earlier Cayman statutes dealing with ship registration and other merchant shipping matters. The Law applies much of the UK provisions of law relating to registration and safety. Unless otherwise stated, references in this chapter to sections are references to sections of the Law.

---

1 UNCTAD, *Review of Maritime Transport* (2017), Table 2.6; See Appendix III.

Vessel eligibility

Vessel type

11.4 Any type of vessel may be registered as a Cayman Islands ship, provided it meets the required internationally recognised safety standards and is owned by persons qualified to be the owners of Cayman Islands ships. The Cayman Islands flag has been particularly successful in attracting a significant number of luxury yachts.[2] Yachts will be considered separately in paragraphs 11.30 onwards. Part VIII of the Law provides for the registration of submersible craft, the details of which are recorded in a separate part of the Register in accordance with section 11(2) of the Law.

Age limits

11.5 Whilst there are no mandatory age limits for Cayman Islands ships, age is a factor that is taken into account when assessing the acceptability of a ship for registration under section 7.

Ownership

11.6 Section 4(1) provides that the following categories of persons are qualified to be the owners of Cayman Islands ships:

(1)   British citizens;
(2)   British Overseas Territories and Crown Dependencies citizens;
(3)   British Overseas citizens;
(4)   British subjects;
(5)   persons who under the Hong Kong (British Nationality) Order 1986 are British Nationals (Overseas);
(6)   Cayman Islands citizens;
(7)   persons, other than those referred to in paragraphs (1)–(6), who are nationals or citizens of a Member State of the European Union, European Economic Area or an approved country, including the overseas countries, territories or dependencies of such Member State or country;
(8)   bodies corporate, shipping entities or foreign companies incorporated, established or registered in and having a place of business in:
   (a)   the UK or any of its Overseas Territories or Crown Dependencies;
   (b)   a Member State of the European Union or European Economic Area, including any overseas country, territory or dependency of such Member State; or
   (c)   an approved country[3] or any overseas country, territory or dependency of such approved country; and

---

2 The number of vessels on the Register on 31 December 2017 included 1,018 yachts of 24 metres and above in length (including pleasure, commercial and passenger yachts) and 210 merchant vessels (excluding fishing vessels) with a gross tonnage of 100 tons and above. Source: Mr. John-Kaare Aune, Deputy Director (GT), CISR, 2 February 2018.

3 For a list of these the reader should refer to the list of countries and territories deemed to have equivalent anti-money laundering and counter-terrorist financing legislation to the Cayman Islands issued by the Cayman Islands Anti-Money Laundering Steering Group ('AMLSG') available at the Cayman Islands Monetary Authority website, www.cima.ky/ pursuant to Shipping Notice 04/2010, Rev 4, dated 16 November 2017, which can be found on the CISR website.

(9) foreign companies as defined in section 183 of the Companies Law (2016 Revision) carrying on business within the Islands which comply with all the requirements of foreign companies under that Law.

Furthermore, section 4(2) provides that a person who is not qualified under subsection (1) to be an owner of a Cayman Islands ship may nevertheless be one of the owners of such a ship if:

(1) a majority interest in the ship, within the meaning of section 5, is owned by persons who are qualified to be owners of Cayman Islands ships; and

(2) the ship is registered in accordance with the provisions of that section.

11.7 Sections 5 and 6 provide that where the majority interest in the ship is owned by persons who are not resident in the Islands, the ship shall only be entitled to be registered if a 'representative person' is appointed in relation to the ship. A representative person is either an individual resident in the Islands, or a body corporate incorporated in the Islands with a place of business there. Intended owning entities that are not Cayman incorporated or registered will usually appoint a professional Cayman service provider approved by the Registrar as a local representative person. The local representative has certain responsibilities under Cayman anti-money laundering rules and in relation to vessel emergencies.

Bareboat charter registration

11.8 The Law permits bareboat chartered vessels to be 'flagged in' to the Cayman register and Cayman vessels to be 'flagged out' to foreign registers, subject to the requirements set out in sections 28–35. Section 28 provides that foreign-registered ships of 24 metres or above in length may be 'flagged in' to the Cayman Islands on the Demise Charter Register if:

(1) the ship is operated under a demise (bareboat) charter that meets the requirements referred to below;

(2) the charterer is qualified to be the owner of a Cayman Islands ship;

(3) the charterer appoints a representative person (if not resident in the Cayman Islands);

(4) the ship is registered on a register outside the Cayman Islands for the purpose of property rights;

(5) the primary flag State or 'home' register is prepared to grant dispensation permitting dual registration.

In order to satisfy the statutory requirements:

(1) the charter must be in writing;

(2) the demise effected by the charter must be made by the owner of the ship to a charterer with a single legal personality for a fixed term of two or more years, or for such lesser period as may be allowed by the Director of the Cayman Islands Shipping Registry;

(3) the terms of the charter must vest in the charterer the operation, management and control of the ship, including responsibility for the engagement or employment of her Master and crew.

Even if a bareboat chartered vessel is entitled to be 'flagged in' to the Cayman register under section 28(1), the Registrar of Shipping has an overriding power to refuse registration on a number of grounds listed in section 28(3). These include the right to refuse to register a vessel if "it is not in the interests of the Islands that the ship should be registered".

11.9 The Director may grant dispensation to permit a Cayman Islands ship of 24 metres or above in length to be registered on a bareboat register of a foreign country (s.33). Such dispensation will not be granted until the Director is satisfied that:

(1) the ship is subject to a demise charter under which the owner is not responsible for the management, operation or control of the ship for the period of the charter;

(2) any mortgagee has consented to the flagging out;

(3) the ship is intended to be registered under the law of a country outside the Islands;

(4) upon registration outside the Islands, the ship will be subject to laws which implement the Collisions Conventions, the Load Line, Marine Pollution, Safety and STCW Conventions and the Maritime Labour Convention to the same extent as they apply to the ship in the Cayman Islands.

When a dispensation has taken effect, the ship will be entitled to fly only the flag of the country named in the owner's application and not the Cayman Islands flag. A dispensation granted by the Director under section 33 will terminate automatically if the ship ceases to be registered in the country named in the owner's declaration in support of the application. It will also terminate when the demise charter comes to an end, for whatever reason.

Trading limits

11.10 While foreign-going Cayman Islands ships are not subject to trading restrictions, they are, as with any other flag, subject to any international (i.e. UN) embargoes in force, or any unilateral, bilateral or multilateral sanctions.

Manning requirements

11.11 Section 110 permits the Cabinet to make safe manning regulations dealing with required numbers of officers and seamen for individual vessels, standards of competence and medical fitness requirements for seafarers. In making such regulations the Cabinet is required to give due regard to the STCW Convention. Manning Regulations were passed in 2002 with amendments in 2003 and 2004.[4] A series of further regulations were introduced in 2014 as a result of the coming into force of the Maritime Labour Convention in the Cayman Islands.[5]

---

4 Merchant Shipping (Certification, Safe Manning, Hours of Work and Watchkeeping) Regulations (2004 Revision).

5 For example, the Merchant Shipping (Maritime Labour Convention) (Medical Certification) Regulations 2014.

Certificates of competency for officers and ratings

11.12 The Cayman Islands issues STCW endorsements to seafarers in recognition of acceptable certificates of competency held by them which have been issued by other STCW States, to allow such seafarers to serve in Cayman Islands ships which require STCW certificated officers. The State issuing the certificate of competency will itself need to meet applicable STCW/IMO criteria, including, but not limited to, that State being on the IMO White List as an issuing State.[6] However, every application for a Cayman Islands STCW endorsement is also assessed on its merits. Dispensations for an officer to serve, for a limited period, in the rank next above that for which an acceptable certificate of competency is held, may also be issued, in exceptional circumstances, on a case-by-case basis. Provisions also exist for a non-STCW licence to be issued to a seafarer holding a non-STCW qualification for service in a Cayman Islands ship which is not required to comply with STCW manning requirements.

Nationality of crew

11.13 As a general rule there are no restrictions on the nationality of officers or crew.

Document of safe manning

11.14 All Cayman Islands ships of 500 gross tonnage or more which are in commercial use and engaged in international voyages are required to carry a minimum safe manning document issued by the Cayman Islands Maritime Administration. In order to obtain this certificate application should be made to the Cayman Islands authorities supported by proposals for the minimum safe manning of the ship concerned. Each application is assessed on an individual basis, based on type, size and complexity of the vessel and its trading pattern.

Approved classification societies

11.15 The following classification societies are currently appointed as recognised organisations by the Cayman Islands Shipping Registry for the survey and classification of vessels:

American Bureau of Shipping (ABS)
Bureau Veritas (BV)
DNV GL
Lloyd's Register (LR)
Nippon Kaiji Kyokai (Class NK)
Registro Italiano Navale (RINA)

Radio ship station licensing

11.16 Since October 2017, ship radio station licences have been issued in the Cayman Islands by the Utility Regulation and Competition Office ('Ofreg'), an independent

---

6 See Appendix IV.

multi-sector regulatory body, following the amalgamation of the previous licensing authority, the Information and Communications Technology Authority ('ICTA') with two other public utility bodies.[7] Applications should be sent direct to Ofreg, rather than CISR. Upon approval, licences are issued only in digital form and will be sent to applicants by the same means. Further information can be obtained from the Ofreg website.[8]

Procedure for registration

Permanent registration

11.17 An application for permanent registration may be made to the Registrar of Shipping, nominating one of three alternative ports of registry in the Cayman Islands; namely, George Town, The Creek or Bloody Bay. The procedure is very similar to that which prevails in the UK. Specimen forms are provided within Appendix XI. An owner is required to produce original documents of title in the form of a bill or bills of sale or, in the case of a new vessel, a builder's certificate. In the case of a ship previously registered on a register other than the Cayman Islands, a closed transcript (or equivalent document) of the previous register is generally required, although it is not a prerequisite for proceeding with registration. At the time of registration, an application to delete from the previous register will suffice, on the understanding that the closed transcript will follow in due course. The title documents must be accompanied by a declaration of ownership and eligibility signed by a person entitled to be registered as owner of the ship, or a share therein or, in the case of a body corporate, by a person authorised by the company to make such declarations, containing the following information:

(1) a statement of his qualifications to own a Cayman Islands ship, or in the case of a body corporate proof of incorporation and good standing;

(2) in the case of a foreign ship, a statement of its foreign name;

(3) a statement of the number of shares in the ship the legal title in which is vested in him, or the body corporate whether alone or jointly;

(4) a declaration that to the best of his knowledge and belief, a majority interest in the ship is owned by persons qualified to be the owners of Cayman Islands ships, and the ship is otherwise entitled to be so registered.

11.18 Prior to registration, every ship is required to be surveyed by a surveyor appointed under section 419 including the approved classification societies listed in paragraph 11.12 above who will issue a tonnage certificate and a certificate of survey. These must be delivered to the Registrar at registration (s.13). Upon receipt of a tonnage certificate, together with the other application documents, the Registrar will issue a carving and marking note. This document confirms the name, port of registry, official number, net tonnage and draught markings which are required to be permanently marked on the ship in the manner and position stipulated (s.14(1)).

---

7 Utility Regulation and Competition Law 2016.
8 www.ofreg.ky

11.19 On completion of the necessary marking, an approved surveyor[9] is required to inspect the vessel to satisfy himself that the work has been carried out and sign a certificate to that effect on the carving and marking note. In the case of a vessel that is already recorded on the Register, which is being transferred and re-registered on the Register in the name of another person, the signed note must be returned to the Registrar before permanent registration can be completed. However, in the case of a vessel that is not already on the Register, CISR will allow the vessel and, if necessary, a mortgage to be registered, provided that an undertaking is given to deliver up the signed carving and marking note within 21 days and will issue a certificate of British registry based on such undertaking prior to the signed note being returned to the Registrar. A vessel should not proceed to sea until carving and marking is complete. When all of the preliminary registration requirements have been complied with, the Registrar will register the ship by entering its particulars in the Register and issue a certificate of British registry to the owner, subject to the requirements for the ship to comply with safety and pollution prevention standards, as may be applicable.

Interim registration

11.20 Section 36 of the Law permits a vessel to be registered on an interim basis during the course of a transfer of ownership prior to the transfer of title by a bill of sale. Interim registration may only take place where the Registrar of Shipping is satisfied that it is proper and:

(1) there is in existence a written contract for the transfer of a ship or a share in a ship;

(2) under the terms of the contract the owner has agreed:
  (a) to transfer the ship, or a share in the ship, to a person qualified to own a Cayman Islands ship who intends to register it in the Cayman Islands; and
  (b) to provide the buyer with a bill of sale and a certificate stating that the ship is free of registered mortgages; and

(3) upon the execution of a bill of sale the buyer will be entitled to register the ship in the Cayman Islands, provided the buyer is qualified to be the owner of a Cayman Islands vessel in accordance with paragraph 11.6 above.

A certificate of interim registration will be valid for a period of 21 days only. Prior to the expiry of that period the buyer is required to deliver to the Registrar of Shipping the original bill of sale and a completed declaration of eligibility. If those documents are not delivered within the time limit, the interim registration will lapse and the interim certificate of registry and any other documents issued by CISR shall be returned to the Registrar of Shipping (s.36(6)).

Provisional registration

11.21 Seldom used, particularly since the introduction of interim registration, an application for provisional registration may be made if a ship becomes entitled to be registered

---

9 In the case of a pleasure vessel under 24 metres in length, an owner can certify completion of such work.

while at a port outside the Cayman Islands. The 'proper officer',[10] usually a British consul, may, on application and by prior arrangement with the Registrar of Shipping, grant a provisional certificate stating:

(1)   the name of the ship;
(2)   the time and place of purchase of the ship and the names of the purchasers;
(3)   the best particulars of the tonnage, build and description of the ship which the person granting the certificate is able to obtain,

and shall forward a copy of the certificate to the Registrar of Shipping at the first convenient opportunity (s.27(1), (2)).

Validity of the provisional registration and extension

11.22   A provisional certificate of registry shall be valid for a period of three months, or until the ship's arrival at the port of George Town, if earlier. No further provisional certificate may be granted within one year of the date of the original, except with the consent of the Director of Shipping.

Registration of ships under construction

11.23   Ships under construction may be registered and mortgaged. The point at which a ship may be so registered is when the keel is laid. Documentation for registration will be the same as for traditional registration, except that, in lieu of the builder's certificate, documentary evidence of the ship under construction must be supplied together with an agreement signed by the owner and builder assenting to registration. The Registrar will issue a certificate of registry under construction. This is a form of provisional registration maintained on a separate part of the Register. When satisfactory evidence is provided to CISR that construction is complete the vessel, and any mortgage recorded on the Register, will automatically be transferred to another part of the Register appropriate for a completed vessel. Such evidence will usually take the form of a builder's certificate or a bill of sale.

Registration of mortgages and security interests

11.24   When a ship is registered under the Cayman Islands flag, a loan or other financial obligation can be secured over the ship by delivering to the Registrar for registration an executed mortgage using a statutory form of mortgage. The Registrar will record details of the mortgage on the Register and endorse on the mortgage itself the date and time of registration. Mortgages rank for priority in order of registration. There is also provision to record 'priority notices'. This device enables the mortgagee who issues a priority notice to maintain priority as of the date of execution of the mortgage and to release funds even though the mortgage is registered at a later date. It prevents a subsequent mortgagee from gaining priority by registering his interest before the prior mortgagee who has issued a priority notice is able to register his mortgage. This device may be particularly useful

---

10 A term defined in s.2.

in cases where mortgage transactions take place outside the Cayman Islands by adding another layer of mortgage protection. Where a mortgage instrument contains a prohibition against a transfer of ownership, a transfer of flag or the creation of further mortgages without the prior written consent of the mortgagee, the Registrar will note such restriction on the Register and will not deal with a subsequent transfer or accept a further mortgage for registration unless the mortgagee's written consent is produced to him.

11.25 A mortgage on a ship under construction is treated as a registered ship mortgage. It will have the same priority as a registered ship mortgage and will continue to be treated as such until it is discharged, even if the ship under construction ceases to be registered. A ship under construction is treated as property for the purposes of a mortgage. This treatment is expressed in the Law so as to apply under the Law, or any other law. There is no express provision in the Law that will enable a ship mortgage to be registered over a vessel that has only interim registration, but it is possible for an intending mortgagee to obtain priority for a future mortgage by means of a notice of mortgage intent, or priority notice, referred to above. Where a ship is provisionally registered through a proper officer and a mortgage is also recorded, that mortgage will continue to be a registered mortgage until it is discharged, even if the provisional registration ceases or lapses after the statutory three months without full registration.

11.26 A ship may transfer registration from one British port to another and record the same ownership and mortgage details at the registry of the new port. Thus, on a transfer, say, from the Registry of Shipping and Seamen at Cardiff to CISR at George Town, the owner and mortgage details would be recorded in the Cayman Islands before the registry of the vessel in Cardiff was closed, thus maintaining a continuous mortgagee protection.

11.27 There is no requirement or facility to register a ship mortgage in the Cayman Islands Companies Registry.

Surveys

11.28 A tonnage measurement survey is always required before registration, though this can be based on an existing tonnage certificate.[11] A compliance survey is required for merchant ships, commercial ships and yachts to which Convention requirements apply, and this is usually done in parallel with the registration processes, though in appropriate circumstances the registration process may be completed before the statutory surveys for Convention compliance are complete. A ship that is subject to statutory Convention requirements cannot, however, operate until it has complied with the relevant requirements and has been issued with the necessary certificates.

Deregistration procedure

11.29 A Cayman Islands ship must be deleted from the Register when it is sold to an owner who is not qualified to be the owner. No export licence is necessary to sell a ship to an unqualified owner, or to delete a ship from the Register. The Registrar will issue a

---

11 A tonnage measurement survey will usually be carried out by a classification society to enable it to issue on behalf of the Cayman Islands as the flag State two separate documents, a certificate of survey and an international tonnage certificate (ITC 1969).

closed transcript of the Register when any registered mortgages are discharged and any outstanding Registry fees paid. A qualified closed transcript may be issued in the event of closure with an undischarged mortgage (known as a 'qualified closure').

Yachts

11.30 Yachts may be registered in the Cayman Islands in the same manner as merchant ships, but the level of application of the various safety and pollution prevention Conventions will vary according to the size and operation of the vessel. The COLREG Convention will always apply, to the relevant extent depending on the length of the ship. MARPOL certification may be required, depending on the ship's tonnage, though some level of compliance with the pollution prevention annexes to MARPOL would apply in all cases. The application of SOLAS requirements will depend on the size and use of the yacht (i.e. private or engaged in trade). In the case of pleasure yachts in private use, there are minimum Convention and statutory requirements under the SOLAS, MARPOL and COLREG Conventions. Pleasure yachts not engaged in charter work may comply voluntarily with the Large Commercial Yacht Code ('LY3'),[12] in which case such a vessel will be surveyed by a CISR surveyor and if found to comply with the code, the relevant certificates will be issued.

11.31 The US Coast Guard ('USCG') requires that all yachts over 300 gross tons are certificated, regardless of registration type, and yachts registered as a 'pleasure yacht' are no longer exempt from this requirement. Yachts that are registered as a 'commercial vessel' or voluntarily hold certification demonstrating compliance with SOLAS or LY3 can use their existing certificates to comply with this requirement. Pursuant to Shipping Notice 02/2016 Rev 2[13] for yachts that do not already hold the required certification to meet this USCG requirement, the CISR will issue a Cayman Islands national certificate ('CINC-PY') to eligible yachts which will be valid for five years. To be eligible for a CINC-PY:

(1) the yacht must be registered as a 'pleasure yacht' of any tonnage, carrying 12 or fewer passengers;

(2) prior to the required survey, a minimum safe manning document must be obtained;

(3) the yacht must be surveyed and certified by CISR in accordance with the shipping notice, in particular to confirm that:

    (a) a record of safety equipment on the yacht accurately describes the yacht and its equipment is developed and is on board; and

    (b) the applicable safety equipment and pollution prevention requirements set out in Annex 2 of the Shipping Notice have been complied with;

(4) as a minimum, the yacht must meet the requirements of LY3 as set out in Annex 1 of the Shipping Notice, and;

(5) The yacht must undergo annual surveys and a renewal survey every five years.

---

12 See Chapter 6, para. 6.36.

13 Shipping Notice 02/2016 Rev 2, Certification of Pleasure Yachts Operating in US Navigable Waters and Certification of Pleasure Yachts in Limited Commercial Use in the 'Caribbean Cruising Area' dated 24 August 2016 ('the shipping notice').

11.32 Compliance with LY3 or, where applicable, earlier editions of the code, is mandatory for all large yachts over 24 metres in length that undertake commercial charter work, excepting those less than 500 gross tons in limited commercial use in the 'Caribbean Cruising Area', discussed below. As well as imposing annual statutory inspections, LY3 also stipulates the required crew qualifications and manning scales, depending on the gross tonnage, engine power output and cruising range from a safe haven. Yachts of over 3,000 gross tons are required to be manned to the same levels as cargo vessels of the same size.

11.33 Since June 2016, CISR has introduced two separate provisions that will in two important geographical areas give yacht-owners greater flexibility in the manner in which their yachts are certificated. Shipping Notice 02/2016, referred to in footnote 12, allows pleasure yachts of less than 500 gross tons to engage in limited commercial charter activity with a maximum of 12 passengers or guests within the Caribbean Cruising Area[14] for a maximum of 120 days in any 365-day period, subject to certain conditions. Shipping Notice 03/2017[15] sets out a procedure that will, on certain conditions, allow a Cayman Islands registered pleasure yacht to be issued with a certificate of compliance and a temporary certificate of British registry for a yacht engaged in trade ('YET') enabling the yacht to undertake occasional charter work in EU waters for a period of up to 84 days a year. To qualify as a YET, the yacht must have EU VAT paid status, or operate under the EU Temporary Admission regime and be fully compliant with LY3 and all other requirements set out in the Shipping Notice.[16] Finally, it should be noted that at the current time charters under the YET programme are only permitted in French and Monegasque waters. While a detailed analysis of the YET programme is beyond the scope of this chapter, it is nevertheless clear that for yachts and their beneficial owners who meet the necessary conditions, the programme will give yacht-owners the means of having the private use of their yachts with a limited ability to charter them out without switching from pleasure to commercial registration. It will also avoid the need for the beneficial owners of commercially registered yachts to enter into formal charters of their 'own' yachts and to pay VAT on the charter fees.

11.34 Where a private pleasure or commercial yacht is required to carry between 13 and 36 passengers, CISR will require the yacht to comply with the Passenger Yacht Code ('PYC')[17] as an alternative to full passenger ship certification under the SOLAS Convention that would be otherwise be mandatory. As mentioned in Chapter 6, updated versions of LY3 and PYC were published in November 2017 by the Red Ensign Group of Registries in the consolidated REG Yacht Code ('REG-YC') which will come into force after the UK Government has tabled REG-YC with the International Maritime Organisation under

---

14 Defined as up to 60 nautical miles from a safe haven in a list of countries and territories in the Wider Caribbean Region, including the littoral countries around the Caribbean Sea, apart from the USA; see Shipping Notice 02/2016, Part B, part 1.3.

15 Shipping Notice 03/2017 Rev 1, Cayman Islands Shipping Registry Engaged in Trade dated 19 December 2017.

16 For the VAT treatment of yachts within the EU and the circumstances in which a foreign-owned yacht may obtain temporary admission, see generally Chapter 3, F. Lorenzon and R. Coles, *The Law of Yachts and Yachting* (2nd edn, Informa Law from Routledge, 2018).

17 See para. 6.37 above.

the equivalence provisions in the relevant IMO Conventions. It is expected that REG-YC will come into force on 1 January 2019. In the meantime, LY3 and PYC will apply.

Contact addresses

11.35 Because of the number of Cayman-registered vessels operating worldwide, CISR have their own surveyors based in Southampton, Cannes, Athens, and Singapore, as well as in George Town and Fort Lauderdale.

Head office – Grand Cayman

Cayman Island Shipping Registry
PO Box 2256
133 Elgin Street
Grand Cayman KY1–1107
Cayman Islands
Tel: (1 345) 949 8831
Fax: (1 345) 949 8849
Email:[18] The reader should use the appropriate group e-mail addresses below:
   Accounts: accounts@cishipping.com
   Convention Insurance Certificates: bunkers@cishipping.com
   Client Relationships: client.relationships@cishipping.com
   Crew Documentation and Queries: crew@cishipping.com
   Freedom of Information Requests: foi@cishipping.com
   Registration Services: registration@cishipping.com
   Reporting Incidents and Other Occurences: reporting@cishipping.com
   Crew Welfare: shipping.master@cishipping.com
   Ship Security Alerts: ssas@cishipping.com
   Technical Enquiries: technical@cishipping.com
To request a survey or audit in the Americas or the Caribbean: Survey.ky@cishipping.com
To request a survey or audit in the Far East: Survey.asia@cishipping.com
To request a survey or audit in Europe or the rest of the World: Survey.uk@cishipping.com

European Regional Office – UK

1st Floor, Vanburgh House
Grange Drive
Southampton, SO30 2AF
England
Tel: (44) (0)1489 799203
Fax: (44) (0)1489 799204
Email: cisruk@cishipping.com

---

18 See Guidance Note 04/2017 (Rev 1.0), Contacting the Maritime Authority of the Cayman Islands and the Cayman Islands Shipping Registry.

Asian regional office – Singapore

8 Marina View
Asia Square Tower 1
Level 07–04
Singapore, 108960
Tel: (65) 9760 4026
Email: cisrsg@cishipping.com

Representative office – London

Dover House
34 Dover Street
London W1S 4NG
England
Tel: (44) (0)20 7491 5050
Fax: (44) (0)20 7491 7944
Email: cisrlondon@cishipping.com

Representative office – France

6 Rue Joseph Bermond
06560 Valbonne
France
Tel: (33) 4 89 02 76 09
Mob: (33) 0 62 01 26 35 7
Email: cisrfr@cishipping.com

Representative office – Greece

107–109 Vasileos Pavlou Street
Voula, GR166 73
Athens
Greece
Tel: (30) 210 965 9700
Fax: (30) 210 899 6040
Email: cisrgr@cishipping.com

Representative office – Japan

1-20-21-1003,
Chuo-ko, Chuo-ku
Chiba 260–0024
Tokyo
Japan
Tel/Fax: (81) 43 247 8441
Email: cisrjp@cishipping.com

Representative office – Panama

Plaza Obarrio Building
Suite 205
Samuel Lewis Avenue
PO Box 0830–00913
Panama City
Republic of Panama
Tel: (507) 6305 4361
Email: cisrpan@cishipping.com

Representative office – United States

750 West Sunrise Boulevard
Suite 201
Ft. Lauderdale, FL 33311
United States
Toll Free: (1) 844 239 4482
Tel: (1) 954 332 9786
Fax: (1) 954 256 5062
Email: cisrfl@cishipping.com

Out of office hours and emergencies

UK Duty Surveyor: +44 7824 302 502
George Town Duty Surveyor: +1 345 815 1666.
Website:www.cishipping.com

CHAPTER 12

Cyprus

12.1 Cyprus is an island situated in the eastern Mediterranean with a population of about 1,170,000. A British Crown Colony from 1925, it achieved independence in 1960. Following an invasion in 1974, approximately one-third of the island remains under Turkish occupation. The Republic is a multi-party democracy with an electoral system based on proportional representation. Under its constitution, the President of the Republic is the head of State and is elected every five years. He appoints the Council of Ministers which is the main executive body of the Republic. The legislative body is the House of Representatives. The Republic became a member of the European Union on 1 May 2004 and adopted the Euro as legal tender on 1 January 2008.

12.2 Cyprus is ranked as the 12th largest register in the world by dead-weight tonnage[1] and appears 19th in the Paris MOU White List of port State control compliance performance published in July 2017.[2]

Sources of law

12.3 The registration of ships under the Cyprus flag is governed by the Merchant Shipping (Registration of Ships, Sales and Mortgages) Laws of 1963 to 2005 as amended by Circular No. 14/2009. Unless otherwise stated, references to sections in this chapter are references to sections of these Laws, as so consolidated. Current registration fees and related matters are detailed in the Merchant Shipping (Fees and Taxing Provisions) Laws of 1992–2007. In connection with Tonnage Tax, the fees are detailed in the Merchant Shipping (Fees and Taxing Provisions) Law of 2010. It should be noted that as Greek and Turkish are the official languages in Cyprus, the published English translations of these enactments are not the authentic versions of the texts.

Vessel eligibility

Vessel type

12.4 Subject to the age limits and ownership qualifications mentioned below, any type of ship may be registered as a Cyprus ship apart from:

---

1 UNCTAD, *Review of Maritime Transport* (2017), Table 2.6.
2 See Appendix III.

(1) ships with an overall length of less than 13 metres employed solely in coastal navigation along the coast of the Republic of Cyprus or the British Sovereign Base Areas of Cyprus;

(2) ships not having a whole or fixed deck employed solely in fishing, lightering or coastal trading on the shore of the Republic, or of the Sovereign Base Areas or within a radius of such shore as may be prescribed from time to time.

Age limits

12.5 A variety of age limits is applied, according to the type of ship and her intended trade. Approval for the registration of all ships of not more than 15 years old is given as a matter of course provided:

(1) the ship's classification society provides the Registrar of Cyprus Ships with a confirmation of class by email or (or a statement attesting to the class position of the ship). This must be sent by the head office of the ship's classification society and must include:

    (a) a statement that the society is willing to proceed with the survey and certification of the ship on behalf of the Government of Cyprus in accordance with the applicable provisions of SOLAS 74 (as amended), LOADLINES 66 and MARPOL 73/78 (as amended) as well as in accordance with any other IMO codes and/or resolutions on safety and marine environment pollution prevention which may be applicable to the ship; and

    (b) advice of the dates of validity of all statutory certificates currently held by the ship; and

    (c) confirmation that the ship complies with the GMDSS Rules;

(2) a recognised radio accounting authority confirms to the Registrar that it will enter into a contract with the new owner or manager of the ship for the clearance of radio accounts; and

(3) if the ship falls within the scope of the ISM regulations, the notification procedure for the issue of a Cyprus document of compliance and/or safety management certificate in accordance with the International Safety Management Code 1994 ('the ISM Code') is complied with, by the production to the Registrar of the relevant form ISM 01 duly completed and signed by both the new owner and the manager.

12.6 In the case of cargo ships and tug boats with an engine power equal to, or greater, than 1,500kW, or with a certified bollard pull of 20 tons or more and which are more than 15 years of age, registration will be approved subject to the conditions set out in (1) above, and to the following additional conditions:

(1) Ships of more than 15, but not more than 20, years of age:
the ship undergoes a one-off entry inspection which must be completed with satisfactory results. This inspection is carried out by a surveyor of the Cyprus Department of Merchant Shipping, at the expense of the owner, either before the provisional registration of the ship, or within three months thereafter.

(2) Ships of more than 20, but not more than 23, years of age:
   (a) as in (1) above; and
   (b) the ship is operated by a Cyprus or other EU ship management company having its place of business in Cyprus staffed with sufficient numbers of qualified personnel and certified for compliance with the ISM Code.

12.7 Any such ships of more than 23 years of age will not be accepted for registration as Cyprus ships, except in special cases, namely:

(1) Where a ship of over 20 years of age is owned by a company which belongs to a group of companies having, at the time of its registration, at least five vessels registered under the Cyprus flag aged up to 12 years of age, provided that the ship:
   (a) has not been detained by port State control more than once in the preceding 12 months on grounds of safety or pollution prevention; and
   (b) has undergone an entry inspection which has been completed with satisfactory results; or
(2) Where a ship over 23 years of age:
   (a) will serve the Cyprus trade and will call at Cyprus ports at least twice per month or at least 24 times in any one year; and
   (b) has not been detained by port State control more than once in the preceding 12 months; and
   (c) undergoes an entry inspection which has been completed with satisfactory results; and
   (d) is operated by a Cyprus or other EU ship management company having its place of business in Cyprus staffed with sufficient qualified personnel and certificated for compliance with the ISM Code.

12.8 Cargo ships with a gross tonnage of less than 1,000 tons and not more than 20 years of age may be registered without any additional conditions. Ships that are over 20 years of age will be approved subject to the conditions set out in paragraph 12.5 above, as well as the following additional conditions:

(1) the ship may not be more than 23 years of age;
(2) the ship will be required to undergo a one-off entry inspection which must be completed with satisfactory results.

12.9 Any such ships more than 23 years of age will not be accepted for registration as Cyprus ships, except in exceptional circumstances, namely:

(1) where the ship will serve the Cyprus trade and will call at Cyprus ports at least twice per month or at least 24 times in any one year; and
(2) where the ship has not been detained by port State control more than once in the preceding 12 months on grounds of safety or pollution prevention; and
(3) the ship has undergone an entry inspection which has been completed with satisfactory results; and
(4) the ship is operated by a Cyprus or other EU ship management company having its place of business in Cyprus staffed by a sufficient number of qualified personnel and certificated for compliance with the ISM Code.

12.10 In the case of passenger ships registration will be approved subject to the conditions set out in paragraph 12.5 above and the following additional conditions if the ship is not more than 30 years of age:

(1) the ship undergoes an entry inspection which is completed with satisfactory results; and

(2) the ship is subject to annual special inspections; and

(3) if the ship is engaged in service which includes at least two calls per month at a Cypriot port for a period of at least six months, at least two cadets who are Cypriot citizens and/or citizens of the EU who are resident in Cyprus for the last six months, if available, are engaged for sea-going training for a period up to six months.

12.11 Registration of passenger ships more than 40 years of age will not normally be approved. However, in exceptional circumstances registration may be permitted, provided:

(1) the ship will serve the Cyprus trade and will call at Cyprus ports at least twice per month or at least 24 times in any one year; and

(2) the ship has not been detained by port State control more than once in the preceding 12 months on grounds of safety or pollution prevention; and

(3) it undergoes an entry inspection which is completed with satisfactory results before commencing trading as a passenger vessel and annual inspections are subsequently carried out; and

(4) the ship is operated by a Cyprus or other EU ship management company having its place of business in Cyprus with sufficient qualified staff and certificated for compliance under the ISM code.

12.12 Coastal passenger vessels and small passenger vessels have an age limit of 23 years in the case of motor vessels, but no age limit at all for sailing vessels including those with auxiliary engines.

12.13 Fishing vessels may not be registered provisionally, permanently or in parallel on the Register of Cyprus Ships without the prior written consent of the Director of Fisheries and Marine Research. Fishing vessels up to 25 years of age also need an entry inspection and other requirements specific to fishing operations prior to registration. Fishing vessels over 25 years of age will not be accepted for registration.

12.14 Pleasure yachts, auxiliary vessels, offshore support vessels, research ships and mobile offshore drilling units are subject to a 25-year age limit. Any such vessels over that age may be accepted subject to a requirement for an entry survey and the appointment of a Cyprus-based manager certificated under the ISM Code.

Ownership

12.15 A ship may not be registered on the Cyprus Register unless:[3]

---

3 Ships registered as Cyprus ships prior to that date are not affected by the current legislation. The present requirements as to ownership were introduced in 2004 and 2005 by s.4 of the Amendment Law 169(I)/2004 following the accession of the Republic of Cyprus to the EU, and by s.3(a) of Amendment Law 108(I)/2005. The current requirements apply only to applications submitted on or after 1 May 2004. Ships registered as Cyprus ships prior to that date are not affected by the current legislation.

(1) more than 50% of the 100 shares in the ship are owned:
  (a) by Cypriot citizens; or
  (b) by citizens of other Member States of the EU who if not permanent residents of the Republic of Cyprus have appointed an authorised representative in Cyprus in accordance with section 5A; or
(2) 100% of the shares in the ship are owned by one or more corporations established and operating:
  (a) in accordance with Cyprus law with their registered office in Cyprus; or
  (b) in accordance with the law of any other Member State and having their registered office, central administration or principal place of business within the EEA and which will either appoint during the whole period of registration an authorised representative in Cyprus, or entrust the management of the ship to a Cypriot or Community ship management company with its place of business in Cyprus; or
  (c) in accordance with the law of any other country, which are controlled by Cypriot citizens or natural persons who are citizens of any other Member State, and which will either appoint during the whole period of registration an authorised representative in Cyprus, or entrust the management of the ship to a Cypriot or Community ship management company with its place of business in Cyprus. For this sub-paragraph, the word 'controlled' means either more than 50% of the shares of the foreign corporation are owned by citizens of Cyprus or of a Member State, or the majority of the directors are citizens of Cyprus or of a Member State.

Bareboat charter registration

12.16 The Cyprus merchant shipping legislation permits the 'flagging-in' of foreign-flag vessels and the 'flagging-out' of Cyprus-registered vessels to foreign registries. This procedure is known in Cyprus as 'parallel registration'. A ship registered in a foreign registry may be registered in parallel in Cyprus and fly the Cyprus flag if she is bareboat chartered to a Cypriot citizen or another person entitled to own a share in a Cyprus ship (s.23C) (see para. 11.5), provided the law of the country of foreign registry permits such parallel registration and the maritime authorities of that country, the ship-owner and registered mortgagees, if any, consent (s.23D). During the period of parallel registration in Cyprus, the registration in the foreign register must be suspended, except in so far as relates to ownership, mortgages and other encumbrances.

12.17 Likewise, a Cyprus ship may, on application of the ship-owner and with the approval of the Minister of Communications and Works, be registered in parallel in a foreign registry and fly the flag of the country of such foreign registry if she is bareboat chartered to a foreign person or corporation, provided that the law of such country permits the parallel registration and the maritime authorities of that country, the charterer and mortgagees, if any, consent (s.23N). The owners and charterers must also undertake to produce to the Cyprus Registrar within one month a certified copy of the foreign certificate of parallel registration and to notify every alteration which takes place regarding the name or other particulars of the ship during the period in which the status of parallel registration of the ship in the foreign register is in force.

Trading limits

12.18 Cyprus flag vessels may be unable to enter ports in Turkey due to the embargo Turkey applies to Cyprus flag ships.

Manning requirements

12.19 The manning of Cyprus flag ships is regulated mainly by the following:

(1) the Merchant Shipping (Masters and Seamen) Laws 1963 to 2002;
(2) the International Convention on the Standards of Training, Certification and Watchkeeping for Seafarers 1978 and 1995 (ratification) and Connected Matters Laws 1985 to 1998;
(3) the Merchant Shipping (Safe Manning, Hours of Work and Watchkeeping) Law of 2000 (Law 105(I)/2000) as amended; and
(4) the Merchant Shipping (Issue and Recognition of Certificates and Marine Training) Law of 2000, as amended.

The regulations are in line with those of the traditional maritime countries.

Certificates of competency for officers and ratings

12.20 Officers and ratings serving on board Cyprus flag vessels are not required to hold certificates of competency issued by the Government of the Republic of Cyprus. However, they must hold valid and recognised certificates of competency or training documentary evidence for the post they hold on board. Officers serving on board Cyprus flag vessels are required to hold, in addition to their non-Cyprus certificate of competency, a Cyprus endorsement attesting the recognition of their certificate in accordance with the STCW 1978 Convention as amended, which is issued by the Cyprus Maritime Administration. All registered seamen serving on board Cyprus ships are required to apply for a seafarer's identification and sea-service record book (SISR) which is issued by the Cyprus Maritime Administration or a relevant exemption within 30 days of the engagement of the seafarer onboard the Cyprus-flagged ship. The seafarer's identification and sea-service record booklet is valid for a period of ten years from the date of its issue, after which a new one is issued by the Cyprus Maritime Administration.

Nationality of crew

12.21 Crew members may be of any nationality. In order to facilitate the manning of ships flying its flag, the Cypriot government has concluded a number of bilateral agreements in the field of merchant shipping with labour-supplying countries. A list of such agreements is set out below. Most of these agreements contain provisions for the employment on Cypriot ships of properly qualified seamen from these countries. The terms of employment of these seamen are those approved by the competent authorities and/or seafarers' unions of their country. The aim of these agreements is to promote friendly relations between Cyprus and other countries, explore areas of co-operation related to shipping which could benefit the economic development of both countries, and facilitate seaborne trade and employment of seamen.[4]

Document of safe manning

12.22 Every Cypriot ship should be in possession of a valid document of safe manning (form MS.38A, MS.38B, MS.38C, MS.38D or MS.39) specifying the number and composition of her complement. Owners of Cypriot ships should apply to the Cyprus Maritime Administration requesting the issue of a document of safe manning. If the vessel is designed and constructed with unattended machinery spaces, or is provided with any other automated machinery or remote controls entitling the owner to seek reduced manning, then the owner should indicate these in his application and request the vessel's classification society to advise the Department accordingly and include in such advice the corresponding class notation and confirmation of the class position of the vessel as far as this notation is concerned.

12.23 If the vessel is to be engaged exclusively in trading in a particular geographical area and the owner seeks reduced manning on this account, he should state in his application the names of the ports from which the vessel will be plying or provide the geographical coordinates (latitude and longitude) and other appropriate information defining the area in which the vessel will be sailing or submit an appropriately marked chart. It should be noted that, on application to the Minister of Communications and Works, dispensation from the requirements of the relevant laws relating to safe manning may be obtained if special circumstances apply.

Approved classification societies

12.24 The following classification societies are recognised by the Government of the Republic of Cyprus:

American Bureau of Shipping (ABS)
Bureau Veritas (BV)
China Classification Society (CCS)
DNV GL
Korean Register of Shipping (KRS)
Lloyd's Register of Shipping (LRS)
Nippon Kaiji Kyokai (NKK)
Polski Rejestr Statkow (PRS)
Registro Italiano Navale (RINA)
Russian Maritime Register of Shipping (RS)
Cyprus Bureau of Shipping (CBS) is only recognised for non-Convention ships.

Classification societies authorised to carry out assessment, auditing, verification and certification of safety management systems and ISPS Code, on behalf of the Government of the Republic of Cyprus are as follows:

American Bureau of Shipping (ABS)
Bureau Veritas (BV)

---

4 Agreements are in force with Algeria, Bulgaria, China, Cuba, Egypt, Georgia, India, Iran, Israel, Italy, Jordan, Korea, Latvia, Lithuania, Malta, Mauritius, Philippines, Poland, Romania, Russia, Sri Lanka, Syria, and Ukraine. Agreements with Belgium and Luxembourg, Greece, Pakistan, and Antigua & Barbuda have been signed and will enter into force in due course.

China Classification Society (CCS)
DNV GL
Korean Register of Shipping (KRS)
Lloyd's Register of Shipping (LRS)
Nippon Kaiji Kyokai (NKK)
Polski Rejestr Statkow (PRS)
Registro Italiano Navale (RINA)
Russian Maritime Register of Shipping (RS)

Procedure for registration

Provisional registration

12.25 The application for the approval of the registration of the ship under the Cyprus flag must be made by a Cypriot lawyer on behalf of the prospective owner to the Minister of Communications and Works through the Registrar of Cyprus Ships. The initial registration will be provisional unless the ship is at a Cyprus port at the time of registration. Provisional registration can be effected either at a Cyprus consulate abroad, or with the Registrar of Cyprus Ships in Limassol. Provided the ship complies with the applicable conditions relating to eligibility, the Registrar will authorise the registration to proceed against production of the following documents:

(1) a certificate of deletion of the ship from her previous registry or in lieu of the certificate, a certificate of ownership and freedom of encumbrance from the ship's previous registry which is not dated more than three days prior from the date of provisional registration to the Cyprus Flag;

(2) the bill of sale under which the ship is sold to the company, duly executed by her registered owners, notarially attested and either legalised by a consul of the country of the current registry of the ship, or by a Cyprus consul, or apostilled in accordance with the Hague Convention 1961;

(3) resolutions of the board of directors of the owning company resolving to acquire the vessel and register her in the Register of Cyprus Ships and of the appointment of one or more several attorneys, who will attend to the registration of the ship at the relevant Cyprus consulate and will sign on behalf of the company the Form M.S.3 referred to in (5) below;

(4) power of attorney executed pursuant to the above resolutions, under the common seal of the company which must certified if executed inside Cyprus and notarially attested or legalised if executed outside Cyprus;

(5) declaration of ownership (Form M.S.3). This form is available at all Cyprus consulates abroad and must be signed by an attorney of the company, in the presence of the consul or the Registrar who effects the registration of the ship;

(6) application for radio licence (Form M.S.34), the IMS01 notification form relating to the ISM Code, and the ISPS 1 form relating to the ISPS Code. These forms are also available at all Cyprus consulates or at the Register and must be completed with all relevant details and be signed accordingly;

(7) registration of search and rescue (SAR) particulars (Form M.S.45). This form is again available at all Cypriot consulates or at the Registry and must be completed and signed on behalf of the company in accordance with IMO Resolutions A.229(vii) and A.387(x);

(8) a copy of the current tonnage certificate of the ship, which the consul will use in order to transcribe the relevant information into the provisional certificate of Cyprus registry;

(9) confirmation of ship's classification society where applicable;

(10) Continuous Synopsis Record (CSR) where applicable;

(11) certificate evidencing insurance pursuant to the international Convention on Civil Liability for Bunker Oil Pollution Damage (blue card) where applicable;

(12) memorandum and articles of association/byelaws of the company or ID/passport in case of an individual.

12.26 Lastly, it should be noted that once a ship has been provisionally registered under the Cyprus flag, all statutory certificates (i.e. SOLAS, load line, IOPP and other certificates as applicable to the size and type of the ship) with which she was furnished under her previous registry must be reissued on behalf of the Cyprus Government. The Registrar will request the ship's classification society to liaise with the Cyprus consul effecting registration of the ship in order that such certificates may be reissued upon completion of registration. The Registrar will also request the port authorities of the port where the ship is lying not to allow her to sail after hoisting the Cyprus flag until all statutory certificates issued on behalf of the Government of Cyprus have been placed on board.

Validity of the provisional registration and extension

12.27 The provisional certificate of Cyprus registry is valid for six months or until the ship comes to a Cyprus port, whichever occurs earlier (s.23(2)). Its validity may be extended for a further period of three months if an application for extension is made and official extension fees are paid on or before the date on which the first six months' period of provisional registration expires.

Permanent registration

12.28 The permanent registration of a provisionally registered ship is to be completed on M.S.4 or M.S.4B within six months from the date that it was provisionally registered or within nine to 12 months if an extension has been granted. The additional formalities required for the permanent registration of a ship are:

(1) an international tonnage certificate (1969) on the Cyprus form (Form M.S.12, M.S.12A or M.S.12B) and a certificate of survey (Form M.S.1) must be issued by a recognised classification society and submitted to the Registry. These forms are available at the offices of all classification societies and must be completed, signed and sealed by a surveyor representing the ship's classification society;

(2) after submission of the above forms to the Registrar in Cyprus, the ship's carving and marking note shall be issued (M.S. 32). This note contains all particulars which must be marked and carved on the ship, i.e. the name of the ship, her port of registry (in all cases Limassol), her registered tonnage and IMO number.

The marking and carving of the above particulars are carried out by the crew, whereafter a surveyor from the ship's classification society should attend on board in order to verify that the marking and carving has been done. The surveyor then signs the marking and carving note which is returned to the Registrar;

(3) production of the certificate of deletion of the ship from her previous registry, unless this was submitted at the time of provisional registration;

(4) the furnishing to the Registrar of official copies of all statutory certificates issued on behalf of the Cyprus Government by the ship's classification society, valid and in full force and without recommendations at the time of the completion of the permanent registration;

(5) submission to the Registrar of a copy of the shore-based maintenance agreement or certificate of the ships GMDSS station;

(6) submission of the safety management certificate (SMC) where applicable.

After the requirements referred to in (1)–(5) above have been met, the ship is permanently registered and the Registrar issues the permanent certificate of Cyprus registry. No other registration fees are payable for the permanent registration, provided it is effected within the period of the validity of the provisional certificate of Cyprus registry or during the three-month extension thereof, if granted.

Registration of mortgages and security interests

12.29 Once a ship has been registered (even provisionally) under the Cyprus flag, a mortgage can be created thereby securing a loan or other financial obligations on conditions agreed to by the parties. A mortgage once created must be deposited with the Registrar of Cyprus Ships or with a consular officer acting on the authority of the Registrar. Whether deposited with the Registrar or with a consular officer, the mortgage is recorded in the Register as from the date and hour of its deposit and remains an encumbrance on the vessel until discharged by the mortgagees. If the ship on which a mortgage was created belongs to a Cypriot company, the mortgage will also have to be registered with the Registrar of Companies in Cyprus within a maximum period of 42 days after its creation. The mortgagee's security is thus protected in the case of liquidation of the ship-owning company.

Surveys

12.30 Reference should be made above to the special inspections and subsequent annual inspections required in the case of registration of ships over 15 years old.

Deregistration procedure

12.31 A Cypriot ship has to be deleted from the Register of Cyprus Ships as soon as ownership is transferred to a person (legal or natural) not qualified to own a Cyprus ship under the merchant shipping legislation. A Cypriot ship may also be deleted from the Register of Cyprus Ships upon application of the ship-owner while continuing in the same ownership. This is useful when a ship-owner wishes to change flag to his ship. No export licence is required for the deletion of a vessel from the Register of Cyprus Ships.

A deletion certificate or a closed transcript of registry is issued as soon as the registered mortgages and other encumbrances are discharged and all matters pending with the Registry, including financial obligations, are settled.

Contact addresses

12.32

Vessel registration

Director of Merchant Shipping
Ministry of Communications and Works
Kyllinis Street
Mesa Geitonia
CY 4007 Limassol
Postal Address:
PO Box 56193
CY 3305
Cyprus
Tel: (357) 25 848100
Fax: (357) 5 848 200
Email: maritimeadmin@dms.mcw.gov.cy
Website: www.shipping.gov.cy

Company formation

The Department of the Official Receiver and Registrar
c/o Ministry of Commerce and Industry
Xenios Building
Cnr Archip. Makarios Avenue & Karpenisiou Street
Nicosia
Cyprus
Tel: (357) 22404302
Fax: (357) 2 304887

Cyprus Shipping Chamber

General Secretary
6 Regas Feros Street
City Chambers, 1st floor
PO Box 56607
3309 Limassol
Cyprus
Tel: (357) 253 60717
Fax: (357) 253 58642
Email: csc@csc-cy.org
Website: www.csc-cy.org

CHAPTER 13

Gibraltar

13.1 Gibraltar is a British Overseas Territory and the Crown is represented by the Governor and Commander in Chief. It has a population of some 29,500. As a British Overseas Territory, Gibraltar has been part of the European Union since Britain joined in 1973, although membership is subject to a number of important derogations, the most notable of which is that Gibraltar is excluded from the Common Agricultural Policy and the European VAT regime. It seems likely that Gibraltar will leave the EU simultaneously with Britain. Until then, ships registered in Gibraltar are entitled to EU cabotage privileges. While Britain retains responsibility for defence and foreign affairs, domestic affairs are regulated by the Gibraltar Parliament. Geographically, Gibraltar is a promontory 5 km long and situated close to the western entrance to the Mediterranean with Spain to the north and Morocco to the south across the Straits of Gibraltar. English remains the official language although Spanish is widely spoken. The official unit of currency is the Gibraltar pound (GB£) at par with the pound sterling though English, most other UK currency and the Euro is generally accepted.

13.2 Vessels registered in Gibraltar are British ships, but are subject to the control of the Gibraltar Maritime Administration (GMA). The GMA was established in its present form in 1997 and has grown considerably in registered tonnage in that time. With an enduring maritime heritage and a Category 1 member of the Red Ensign Group, the group of British registries collectively promoting their quality brand and reputation, Gibraltar appears among the top 25 in the list of best-performing flag States in the 2017 Paris MOU White List.[1] Vessels registered in Gibraltar fly the Red Ensign defaced with the Gibraltar arms, the Castle and Key.

Sources of law

13.3 The registration of vessels in Gibraltar is governed by the Gibraltar Merchant Shipping (Registration) Act 1995, as amended, and is originally based on the merchant shipping legislation of the UK. Registration is performed by a government official known as the Maritime Administrator. In this chapter, references to 'the Act' are references to the Gibraltar Merchant Shipping (Registration) Act 1995 and references to 'a section' or to 'a schedule' are to a section or schedule of this Act. Safety and crewing requirements on

---

1 See Appendix III.

153

board Gibraltar ships are set out in the Gibraltar Merchant Shipping (Manning, Training and Certification for Seafarers) Regulations 2006, as amended.

Vessel eligibility

Vessel type

13.4 With the exception of fishing vessels and nuclear-powered craft, the Registry accepts all types of vessels provided they are classed by a recognised classification society. The Registry operates a separate register for yachts and pleasure craft.[2]

Age limits

13.5 Ships of 20 years or more from the date of construction are subject to a pre-registration survey and are only registrable at the discretion of the Maritime Administrator.

Ownership

13.6 The following categories of persons are qualified under section 7(3)(a) and (b) of the Act to be the owners of ships registered in Gibraltar:

(1)   British citizens;
(2)   British Dependent Territory citizens;
(3)   British Overseas citizens;
(4)   persons who under the British Nationality Act 1981 (an Act of the UK Parliament) are British subjects;
(5)   persons who under the Hong Kong (British Nationality) Order 1986 are British Nationals (Overseas);
(6)   citizens of the Republic of Ireland and such other relevant countries as may be prescribed, which includes the Channel Islands and colonies of the UK;
(7)   nationals of any Member State of the European Union or other State which is a party to the European Economic Area Agreement and thereby enjoys the right of establishment in Gibraltar;
(8)   bodies corporate incorporated under the laws of Gibraltar or under the laws of a Member State of the European Union or a country which is a party to the European Economic Area Agreement and has a place of business, or a representative person within Gibraltar;
(9)   a foreign maritime entity.[3]

The application for registration of a ship should be made in the prescribed form in writing from the entity to make the application or on its behalf and should be accompanied

---

2 See further, para. 13.28 below.

3 Schedule 2 permits any foreign entity whose instrument of trust, charter, articles of incorporation or partnership agreement is recognised by the foreign State or by force of law as providing the power to own or operate ships and confers or recognises the capacity under the law of that State to sue and be sued in the name of the entity to apply to the Maritime Administrator to be recognised as a foreign maritime entity.

by the certificate of incorporation and a certificate of good standing of the entity, together with the address of the principal place of business and the name and address of a representative person within Gibraltar.

Company formation

13.7 Gibraltar companies are registered under the provisions of the Companies Act 1930, as amended. Formation is in all cases processed by a Gibraltarian lawyer or company formation agent. Incorporation is usually possible within two working days of delivery of the relevant documents to the Registrar of Companies, although same-day registration is possible on payment of an additional fee. In practice, professional firms that handle company formation work usually hold ready-made 'shelf' companies available for immediate use.

Resident status and registered office

13.8 It is not necessary to incorporate a limited company within Gibraltar to own or manage ships registered under the flag, although some owners may prefer to do so. The Companies Ordinance provides for international companies incorporated elsewhere to register with the Companies Registrar. All companies registered or incorporated in Gibraltar are required to have a registered office in the territory.

Directors and secretary

13.9 There must be at least one director who may be an individual or body corporate. The director need not hold a qualifying share under the company's articles, unless the articles provide otherwise. A secretary must also be appointed.

Bareboat charter registration

13.10 The Act provides for both the bareboat charter registration of foreign ships on to the Gibraltar Register ('bareboat charter-in') and also for the bareboat charter registration of Gibraltar ships in a foreign State ('bareboat charter-out') provided in either case that the law of the State of the foreign registry is compatible with the provisions of the Act.

Bareboat charter-in

13.11 The requirements for the bareboat registration of a foreign vessel on to the Gibraltar register are set out in section 32 and this permits bareboat registration if:

(1) the applicant is in possession of the ship under a bareboat charter;
(2) the bareboat charterer is a qualified person as set out in section 7(1)(b);
(3) the applicant has appointed a registered agent in Gibraltar; and
(4) the charterer has provided an undertaking in a form approved by the Maritime Administrator that the ship will only fly the Gibraltar flag and only show Gibraltar as the home port for the duration of the charter.

13.12 An application to register the ship under a bareboat charter should be made on the Registry's standard form (RA-09-F003) with a notice of proposed name of the vessel and be accompanied by:

(1) a declaration of eligibility made by the charterer accompanied by a copy of the bareboat charter agreement (such charter agreement will not be available for public inspection);
(2) a letter of consent from the primary register;
(3) the consent in writing of the owners and any mortgagees;
(4) official authorised transcript of underlying registry;
(5) application for allotment of signal letters;
(6) appointment of representative person on the standard form;
(7) appointment of registered agent on the standard form;
(8) certificate of incorporation of the charterer, if a body corporate;
(9) certificate of good standing of the charterer;
(10) memorandum and articles of association of the charterer;
(11) certificate of class;
(12) international tonnage certificate;
(13) certificates of insurances (P&I; hull & machinery; CLC, Bunker Convention, Wreck Removal and MLC as applicable);
(14) application for survey and inspection; and
(15) application for safe manning document.

13.13 The charterer is required to pay the necessary registration fees before the Registrar will issue a certificate of bareboat registry. The certificate is valid for a period not exceeding two years, which may on application be extended for further periods, each of which may not exceed two years. For the period that the ship is registered under the Gibraltar flag she will also be required to comply with the international maritime Conventions to which Gibraltar is a party. If additional certificates are required, these will usually be issued by the Gibraltar Registry, although the Maritime Administrator may accept certificates issued by the registry of the underlying flag State.

Bareboat charter-out

13.14 The Maritime Administrator will only give consent to a Gibraltar ship being registered under a foreign flag for the duration of a bareboat charter if the requirements of section 33(1) have been complied with. The application should be made on the Registry's standard form (RA-09-F004) and accompanied by the following:

(1) the written permission of all mortgagees;
(2) written undertaking by the charterer that the Gibraltar flag shall not be hoisted during the period of bareboat charter registration; and
(3) a copy of the bareboat charter.

13.15 The Maritime Administrator will issue a certificate of permission once the certificate of registry or certificate of provisional registry has been surrendered along with all other documents and certificates issued by the Registry. Thereafter, the Maritime Administrator will issue a new certificate recording the changed nature of the vessel's registration on the

Gibraltar Register. During the time a Gibraltar ship is registered in a foreign registry, she may not hoist the Gibraltar flag or claim Gibraltar as her home port. All matters with respect to the title over the ship, mortgages and encumbrances continue to be governed by Gibraltar law.

Trading limits

13.16 There are no trading limits on ships registered in Gibraltar.

Manning requirements

Certificates of competency for officers and ratings

13.17 Masters and other officers are required to hold either a valid UK certificate of competency, certificate of equivalent competency or a certificate issued by an acceptable country and accompanied by an endorsement issued by Gibraltar. The UK certificate of competency will only be acceptable if it has a clearly stated STCW endorsement and not more than five years have passed since the last revalidation date. A certificate holder will only be permitted to serve in the capacity or capacities stated in the STCW endorsement. Gibraltar currently recognises certificates of competency issued by States on the IMO STCW White List.[4] An officer holding an acceptable non-UK certificate will be issued with an endorsement document by the Maritime Administration to accompany the certificate of competency.

13.18 Ratings who form part of a watch (bridge or engine room) must hold an appropriate watch-rating certificate. These can be issued by the Marine Administration for ratings who do not hold a certificate issued by another country. Every Gibraltar-registered ship must have at least one crew member who holds a global maritime distress and safety system general operations certificate (GMDSS-GOC). All deck officers keeping navigational watch must be in possession of at least a restricted operators certificate (GMDSS-ROC) to enable them to use GMDSS emergency radio equipment.

Nationality of crew

13.19 There are no restrictions on the nationality of officers or ratings who serve on Gibraltar ships.

Document of safe manning

13.20 The SOLAS Convention requires that ships engaged in international trade must carry, at all times, a valid minimum safe manning certificate. Accordingly, the Gibraltar Maritime Administrator issues at the time of registration of a ship and upon application by the owner or representative in Gibraltar, a minimum safe manning certificate. The certificate ceases to be valid upon closure of the Gibraltar registry of the ship, or in the event of any change in the equipment or construction, which affects the stipulated manning. The safe manning certificate is issued in compliance with Chapter V, regulation 14

---

4 See Appendix IV.

of SOLAS 74, in accordance with the principles and guidelines set out in IMO Resolution A.890 (21), and may be revised subject to a practical demonstration of the crew's ability and at the discretion of the Maritime Administrator.

Approved classification societies

13.21 The Maritime Administration currently approve the following list of classification societies as recognised organisations for the purpose of survey and the issue of safety documentation for vessels:

American Bureau of Shipping (ABS)
Bureau Veritas (BV)
DNV GL
Lloyd's Register (LR)
Nippon Kaiji Kyokai (NKK)
Registro Italiano Navale (RINA)

Procedure for registration

Provisional registration

13.22 Where the owner of a ship intends to register a ship under the Gibraltar flag the Maritime Administrator may issue a provisional certificate of registry for a limited period, pending the completion of the requirements for full registration. Provisional registration entitles the ship to all the privileges of permanent registration including the right to fly the Gibraltar flag. Provisional registration is valid for a period of three months, but may be extended by a further three months.

Permanent registration

13.23 An application for permanent registration requires to be made in the prescribed form by a qualified person or their representative to the Maritime Administration in Gibraltar. The Maritime Administrator may, at his discretion, accept an application in electronic form. The application should be submitted in the Registry's standard form (RA-09-F005) with a notice of proposed name of the vessel and in all cases should be supported by the following documentation:

(1) a completed declaration of ownership on behalf of a body corporate or individual in the prescribed form;
(2) a completed appointment of a representative person officer in the prescribed form;
(3) a completed appointment of a registered agent in the prescribed form;
(4) evidence of title, such as a builder's certificate or bill of sale and protocol of delivery;
(5) a declaration that the ship is free of maritime liens;
(6) confirmation that an application for the allotment of signal letters has been made to Gibraltar Regulatory Authority;

(7) evidence of previous registration such as a closed transcript of register or deletion certificate;

(8) a certificate of class;

(9) an international tonnage certificate;

(10) a certificate of survey;

(11) evidence of insurance (P&I; hull & machinery; CLC, Bunker Convention, Wreck Removal and MLC as applicable);

(12) in the case of a body corporate, a certificate of incorporation and any certificate of change of company name, the memorandum and articles of association and a certificate of good standing;

(13) application for survey and inspection;

(14) application for safe manning document; and

(15) completed Form 2 amendments to Continuous Synopsis Record.

Thereafter, the ship will be issued with a carving and marking note indicating the name approved by the Maritime Administrator, her official registration number and Gibraltar as her home port, all of which must be conspicuously marked on the vessel prior to registration. On completion of registration, and upon payment of the prescribed fees, the Maritime Administrator will issue a certificate of registry which will include the particulars of the ship entered on the Register.

Registration of mortgages and security interests

13.24 The Act permits any registered vessel or a share in a registered vessel to be made security for the repayment of a loan, debt or the discharge of any other obligation. The instrument creating such security shall be one of the standard printed forms of mortgage approved by the Maritime Administrator that are similar to the statutory forms of mortgage used for British vessels registered in the UK. In order to register a mortgage, the original document shall be delivered to the Maritime Administrator or to an official outside Gibraltar appointed by the Maritime Administrator who will cause the relevant details to be recorded in the Register. He will then endorse on the mortgage deed the date and time of recording. If the mortgage is received in an office other than the office in Gibraltar of the Maritime Administrator, such mortgage shall not be deemed as recorded until particulars have been received and duly recorded in Gibraltar. Where there is more than one mortgage against a single vessel, mortgages will be registered in the order in which they are produced to the Maritime Administrator for registration purposes, and will rank between each other for priority in order of such registration.

13.25 If a ship has previously been registered in a foreign registry, and mortgages or related instruments were registered in respect of the ship, the Maritime Administrator will at his discretion record such mortgages or instruments in the Gibraltar Register in the same priority as in the original register, provided the mortgage instruments or true copies of same are submitted at the time of the application for registration in Gibraltar, together with the written consent of any mortgagees. If, within 30 days of the expiration of a certificate of provisional registry, the applicant ship-owner has not fulfilled the requirements for full registration, the mortgagee shall have power absolutely to dispose of the ship or share in respect of which his interest is recorded in the Register, notwithstanding that the mortgagor may have complied fully with all the other requirements of the mortgage instrument.

Surveys

13.26 All ships are required to undergo a pre-registration survey prior to being accepted by the Registry. In addition, a certificate of survey and tonnage measurement is required.

Deregistration procedure

13.27 The Act allows a ship to be deregistered at the written request of the owner in the event of a change of eligibility status in the registered owner or where the vessel is a total loss or is sold to a person who is not qualified to own a Gibraltar ship, provided there are no outstanding monies owed to the government and the consent of all registered mortgagees has been obtained.

Yacht registration

13.28 Yachts over 24 metres in length and those used commercially may be registered with GMA in the register of ships. Those over 24 metres and carrying up to 12 passengers require to be classed with one of the recognised classification societies and certificated under the UK Large Yacht Code (LY2). Yachts operating commercially intended to carry more than 12 passengers must comply with the Passenger Yacht Code. Pleasure yachts, those which are not used commercially, may be registered in a separate register established for this category of vessel.

Contact addresses

13.29

Ship Registry

Gibraltar Ship Registry
Watergate House
2/8 Casemates Square
Gibraltar
Tel: (+350) 200 46 861
Fax: (+350) 200 47 770
Email: maritime.registry@gibraltar.gov.gi
Website: www.gibraltarship.com

Yacht Registry

Gibraltar Yacht Registry Limited
Watergate House
2/8 Casemates Square
PO Box 71
Gibraltar
Tel: (+350) 200 78 343
Fax: (+350) 200 77 044
Email: maritime.yachts@gibraltar.gov.gi
Website: www.gibraltaryacht.com

CHAPTER 14

Hong Kong

14.1 Hong Kong is arguably the financial and commercial centre of south-east Asia. A British colony from 1841, it returned to Chinese rule on 1 July 1997 and is now known as the Hong Kong Special Administrative Region (HKSAR). Geographically, Hong Kong is located to the south-east of mainland China and consists of a large number of islands and a peninsula which are now largely interconnected through a number of sophisticated underground road links and bridges. The main areas are Hong Kong Island itself, Kowloon and New Territories. They total some 412 square miles. With a population of some 7.3 million it is one of the most densely populated areas in the world and maintains one of the world's busiest container ports. English and Chinese remain the official languages of the HKSAR. The currency is the Hong Kong dollar (HK$), and it is linked to US$ at the rate of HK$7.80 to US$1.

14.2 Under the principle of 'one country, two systems', the Basic Law of the HKSAR, based on the common law system, is in force until at least 2047. Articles 124–127 of the Basic Law provide the constitutional rights and legal basis for the HKSAR to continue to maintain an autonomous shipping register. The port of registry of every registered ship is Hong Kong. The Hong Kong Shipping Register was established in 1990 and is centralised, administered by the Government of HKSAR through the offices of the Marine Department. By January 2017 it was the fourth largest registry in the world by dead-weight tonnage with over 9% of the global merchant fleet.[1] Hong Kong appears in the top ten best-performing flag States in the Paris MOU and Tokyo MOU White Lists of Port State Control regulatory compliance.[2]

Sources of law

14.3 The registration of ships in Hong Kong is governed by the Merchant Shipping (Registration) Ordinance (Cap. 415, 'the Ordinance') and supplementary legislation in the form of the Merchant Shipping (Registration) (Tonnage) Regulations, Merchant Shipping (Registration) (Fees and Charges) Regulations and the Merchant Shipping (Registration) (Ship's Names) Regulations, hereafter collectively referred to as the 'Regulations'.

---

1 UNCTAD, *Review of Maritime Transport* (2017), Table 2.6.
2 See Appendix III; Tokyo MOU Annual Report 2016.

161

Vessel eligibility

Vessel type

14.4 A ship is a defined as a vessel capable of navigating in water not propelled by oars, including air-cushion vehicle. Any vessel may be registered under the Hong Kong flag, except for the following:

(1) non-self-propelled barges carrying petroleum products or dangerous goods;
(2) accommodation barges;
(3) fishing vessels;
(4) ships engaged in processing living resources of the sea, including whale or fish factory ships;
(5) specialised ships engaged in research, expeditions or survey work;
(6) non-Convention ships serving exclusively within the domestic waters of a country (other than Hong Kong or Chinese Mainland waters) and not proceeding to sea;
(7) nuclear-propelled vessels; and
(8) mobile offshore drilling units.

The Ordinance allows that the Director of Marine may by notice published in the *Gazette* provide that a thing designed or adapted for use at sea and described in the notice is or is not to be treated as a ship for the purpose of any provision of the Ordinance as specified in the notice, and any such notice may make different provision in relation to different occasions.[3]

Age limits

14.5 There are no age or tonnage restrictions for Hong Kong ships as such but, as part of its pre-registration quality control (PRQC) procedures, vessels of significant age are subject to satisfactory survey reports. The PRQC system is to ensure a ship applying for Hong Kong registration meets all safety and pollution prevention standards promulgated by IMO at the time of entry. Upon receiving application for registration in Hong Kong, the Marine Department will assess the ship's condition to consider whether the vessel requires a PRQC inspection. If a PRQC inspection is deemed necessary, a fee will be chargeable to the ship-owner for such inspection by the Marine Department's surveyors.

Ownership

14.6 Section 11(4) of the Ordinance provides that the following categories of person are qualified to be the owners of Hong Kong ships:

(1) an individual who holds a valid Hong Kong identity card and is ordinarily resident in Hong Kong;
(2) a body corporate incorporated in Hong Kong; or

---

3 Section 3.

(3) an overseas company registered in the Hong Kong Companies Registry under Part XI of the Hong Kong Companies Ordinance (Cap. 32) or Part 16 of the Hong Kong Companies Ordinance (Cap. 622).

In all cases, a Hong Kong representative must also be appointed (s.68). The representative person shall be itself a qualified person and the owner or part owner of the ship, or a body corporate incorporated in Hong Kong which is engaged in the business of managing, or acting as agent for, ships.

Bareboat charter registration

14.7 Section 11(1)(b) of the Ordinance allows the registration of a bareboat chartered vessel in the Register, provided the charterer is a qualified person (see above). An application for bareboat charter registration should be accompanied by the following, in addition to the documents submitted for registration in the name of owner:

(1) a form of authority for making and signing application and declaration by the demise charterer (Form M.O. 812);
(2) the original or certified true copy of certificate of incorporation or registration of the demise charterer in Hong Kong;
(3) a certified true and complete copy of the demise charterparty made between the owner and demise charterer:
(4) a declaration of entitlement (Form RS/D6) by both the owner and demise charterer:
 (a) that the demise charterer is a qualified person;
 (b) that the owner's consent to the ship's registration in Hong Kong is obtained;
 (c) that the demise charterer will under the demise charter have possession of the ship and sole control of all matters relating to navigation and operation including the employment of the Master and the crew; and
 (d) that the ship will not be registered elsewhere so long as it is registered in Hong Kong (s.19(5)(b)).

14.8 Under section 84 of the Ordinance, all declarations made by a body corporate must be made by either the company secretary or authorised officer and any declaration made outside Hong Kong must be notarised by a notary public. A body corporate must also include a declaration under section 20(2) as follows:

(1) a statement that the declarant is authorised to make the declaration on behalf of the company;
(2) a statement of the circumstances of incorporation of the body corporate in Hong Kong, or of registration under Part XI of the Companies Ordinance (Cap. 32) as in force before 3 March 2014 or under Part 16 of the Companies Ordinance (Cap. 622), as the case may be;
(3) a statement that the body corporate has entered into a demise charterparty in respect of the ship with the owner of the ship;
(4) a statement that pursuant to the terms of the demise charterparty the body corporate is able to register the ship in its name as the demise charterer;

(5) a statement that a general description of the ship contained in the application is correct;

(6) a statement that the ship is not registered outside Hong Kong or, if it is so registered, that the declarant will secure deletion of the ship from the register in such place;

(7) a statement that a true, correct and complete copy of the demise charterparty is attached to the application; and

(8) a statement that the consent of the owner of the ship to registration is attached to the declaration.

Trading limits

14.9 There are no trading limits on Hong Kong ships.

Manning requirements

14.10 There are no nationality or residential requirements for officers and crew serving on Hong Kong ships. Crew size depends on the size and type of ship, and is set out in the minimum safe manning certificate required by the SOLAS Convention. Officers as listed in the minimum safe manning certificate are required to hold respective classes of certificates of competency issued by Hong Kong, or Hong Kong licences issued in recognition of certificates of competency issued by other maritime authorities in accordance with the STCW 95 Convention, regulation 1/10. Ratings engaged on watchkeeping duties should hold STCW watchkeeping certificates issued in accordance with the STCW 95 Convention. Enquiries concerning the recognition of foreign certificates should be forwarded to the Senior Surveyor of the Seafarers' Certification Section, whose details appear at the end of this chapter.

Approved classification societies

14.11 The classification societies listed below have been authorised by the Marine Department to undertake survey and certification works on Hong Kong registered ships:

American Bureau of Shipping (ABS)
Bureau Veritas (BV)
China Classification Society (CCS)
DNV GL
Korean Register of Shipping (KR)
Lloyd's Register of Shipping (LR)
Nippon Kaiji Kyokai (NKK)
Registro Italiano Navale (RINA)

Taxation

14.12 The profits of an overseas company registered in Hong Kong under Part XI of the Companies Ordinance (Cap. 32) or Part 16 of the Companies Ordinance (Cap. 622)

but made outside Hong Kong are not subject to Hong Kong corporation tax. Income derived solely from the international operation of Hong Kong registered ships is exempt from profits tax under the Inland Revenue Ordinance (Cap. 112). The exemption applies to the income derived from the international carriage of passengers and goods (including livestock and mail) shipped aboard Hong Kong ships from any location within Hong Kong waters. Hong Kong has also entered into bilateral agreements on double taxation reliefs with 40 major trading partners for income derived from the international operation of ships. Hong Kong registered ships are also entitled to up to a preferential 29% discount from port dues in Mainland China ports.

Procedure for registration

Provisional registration

14.13 Provisional registration is not a prerequisite for permanent registration. However, provisional registry should be appropriate when the original title documents cannot be produced at the time of registration. Provisional registration is valid for one month. In special circumstances, it may be extended for a further period of one month maximum, upon application by the owner with acceptable justification. The following documents are required for provisional registration:

(1) an application form (Form RS/A1);
(2) a form of authority for making and signing the application and declaration, where necessary (Form M.O. 812);
(3) a declaration of entitlement to own a ship registered in Hong Kong. Each owner must make a separate declaration when there is more than one owner to a ship;
(4) a copy of the title document (builder's certificate or bill of sale plus certificate of ownership free from encumbrances) as required for permanent registration;
(5) a copy of the ship's current international tonnage certificate certified by any one of the following:
   (a) the issuing authority of that certificate;
   (b) the ship-owner; or
   (c) the representative person appointed in relation to the ship;

(6) a certificate of incorporation or registration in Hong Kong of the owner or the Hong Kong identity card of the owner;
(7) a certificate of incorporation and articles of association of the representative person appointed in relation to the ship, where applicable;
(8) a certificate or declaration of marking of ship (Form No. RS/S1), after the ship has been marked as directed by the Registrar. A marking note completed by the Master of the ship or an authorised surveyor is acceptable;
(9) a certificate or evidence of deletion from the previous registry.

Permanent registration

14.14 For permanent registration, the following documents will need to be submitted. These must be originals, unless otherwise specified:

(1) an application form (Form RS/A1);
(2) a form of authority for making and signing applications and declarations, where necessary (Form M.O. 812);
(3) a declaration of entitlement to own a ship registered in Hong Kong. (Where a ship has more than one owner, a separate declaration of entitlement must be made by each owner.);
(4) the title documents (i.e. a builder's certificate for a new ship; or a duly executed bill of sale plus a copy of the certificate of ownership free of encumbrance where there has been a sale of the ship in favour of the owner; or a certificate of ownership, free of encumbrance where there has not been a sale of the ship which is not a new ship, i.e. a change of flag application);
(5) a certificate or evidence of deletion from a previous registry if it is not a new ship. The evidence can be in any one of the following forms:
   (a) a certificate of deletion from the last registry where the ship was registered;
   (b) a letter or fax from the ship's last registry informing the Hong Kong Shipping Registry that it has consented to close the ship and that steps are being taken to effect the closure;
   (c) a certified true copy of the application made by the owner or the representative person of the ship to the registry where the ship was last registered to close the registration of the ship.
   (Where the certificate(s) of deletion cannot be produced at the time of registration, it/they must be presented to the Registrar within 30 days from date of registration. If the ship is concurrently registered in more than one register, such as a bareboat charter registry situation, evidence of deletion from each of the registers is required.);
(6) a certificate of incorporation or registration in Hong Kong of the owner or Hong Kong identity card of the owner, as appropriate. A certified true copy of the company certificate or Hong Kong identity card is also accepted;
(7) originals or certified true copies of the certificate of incorporation and memorandum of association of the representative person appointed in relation to the ship, where applicable;
(8) a certificate of survey (Form SUR59E) giving the principal particulars of the ship, international tonnage measurement, etc.;
(9) a certificate or declaration of marking of ship (Form No. RS/S1), after the ship has been marked as directed by the Registrar. This marking note may be completed by the Master of the ship or an authorised surveyor.

Registration of mortgages and security interests

14.15 A mortgage is an instrument created to secure any obligation on the owner of a ship. Once a ship is registered, whether provisionally or permanently, a mortgage may be created. The registration of a mortgage must be in the specified form (Form No. RS/M1). Mortgages rank in priority according to the date and time when they are presented and accepted for registration, and not according to the date of the mortgage instrument. When a ship is provisionally registered, the mortgagee is also required to produce a 'confirmation by mortgagee' to the Registrar. The confirmation, in specified form, is to confirm that the mortgagee has sighted the original title document and knows that the original title document will not be produced to the Registrar at the time of registration. An individual, joint mortgagees or bodies corporate may be entered in the Register as mortgagees. Mortgagees need not be 'qualified persons' – foreign bodies corporate can be registered as mortgagees.

14.16 A mortgage is executed under seal or power of attorney (original or certified true copy) and witnessed. In the case of a body corporate, a mortgage should also be executed in accordance with its articles of association. A mortgage will remain on the Register until the Registry has been informed that it has been discharged, notwithstanding any sale of the ship to a third party or the loan being repaid. A mortgagee should submit a memorandum of discharge of mortgage in the specified form (Form No. RS/M2) together with the original mortgage instrument. A memorandum of discharge by a body corporate must be given under its seal. The date and time of the discharge will then be entered on the Register.

Flag State quality control system

14.17 Hong Kong has adopted most of the international Conventions in relation to safety and marine pollution prevention. Under these Conventions, Hong Kong has an obligation to ensure that ships registered in Hong Kong meet the standards and requirements specified in these Conventions with respect to safety, protection of marine environment, health and welfare of the crew. A flag State quality control (FSQC) system has been introduced to monitor the quality of ships entered in the Register and the performance of the recognised organisations carrying out the survey and certification work on behalf of the Hong Kong Administration.

14.18 The FSQC system operates by maintaining a database of Hong Kong registered ships obtained from various sources, including inspection records of recognised organisations and Port State Control memoranda of understanding. The emphasis of the FSQC system is to find out those ships whose quality is declining and to bring them up to standard. The collected information is analysed. Ships will be identified and selected by the system for inspection or audit by the Marine Department surveyors prior to the development of solutions with the appropriate parties to arrest the decline in quality of a ship. The cost of these inspections/audits are borne by the Register. Only when a ship is detained for serious deficiencies found by Port State Control inspecting authorities will the Marine Department charge for the costs of carrying out the FSQC vessel inspections and management or operating company audit.

Surveys

14.19 Under the FSQC system, the Marine Department is not directly involved in the surveys and issue of relevant certificates to Hong Kong registered cargo ships, except when requested by the ship-owners. The classification societies shown in paragraph 14.11 are specifically authorised to carry out statutory surveys and issue related certificates on behalf of the flag administration. For passenger ships registered in Hong Kong, all surveys and issue of relevant certificates must be carried out by the Marine Department.

Deregistration procedure

14.20 If the ship-owner wishes to close the registration of a Hong Kong vessel, the following procedures are required to be fulfilled:

(1) The owner should complete the 'notice of intention to close a ship's registration by owner' (Form No. RS/N1).
(2) If there are registered mortgages on the ship, such mortgages should be discharged. Otherwise, the express consent of every registered mortgagee to close the ship's registration is required (Form No. RS/C4).
(3) The owner should also notify the demise charterer (if any) of the intention to close the register.

Contact addresses

14.21

For ship registration

The Registrar of Ships
Hong Kong Shipping Registry
Marine Department
3/F, Harbour Building
38 Pier Road, Central
Hong Kong
Tel: (852) 2852 4421
Fax: (852) 2541 8842
Email: hksr@mardep.gov.hk
Website: www.mardep.gov.hk

Manning information

For Cargo Ships:
Senior Surveyor/Cargo Ships Safety Section
Tel: (852) 2852 4510
Fax: (852) 2545 0556
Email: ssb@mardep.gov.hk
For Passenger Ships:
Senior Surveyor/Passenger Ships Safety Section
Tel: (852) 2852 4500
Fax: (852) 2545 0556
Email: sspax@mardep.gov.hk

Certification and licences

Senior Surveyor/Seafarers' Certification Section
Tel: (852) 2852 4368
Fax: (852) 2541 6754
Email: sscrt@mardep.gov.hk

CHAPTER 15

Isle of Man

15.1 The Isle of Man is an island situated in the Irish Sea with a population of approximately 85,000. Part of a Norse kingdom until the thirteenth century, the Lordship of Man was purchased by the English Crown in 1765. It is an internally self-governing Crown Dependency forming part of the British Isles, but not the UK. It has its own parliamentary and legal systems, while the Crown remains responsible for international relations and defence issues. The Queen's representative on the Island is known as the Lieutenant-Governor. The Isle of Man is outside the European Union, but enjoys a special relationship under Protocol 3 of the Treaty of Accession, enabling the inhabitants to enjoy freedom of trade with EU countries. The legislature, the Tynwald, is made up of two parts: the Legislative Council and the House of Keys, the latter body having 24 elected members. The legal tender is the Manx pound, equivalent to the pound sterling.

15.2 Vessels registered in the Isle of Man are British ships, but are subject to the control of the Isle of Man Ship Registry. Part of the Red Ensign Group, the group of British registries collectively promoting their quality brand and reputation, the Isle of Man is a popular choice for tankers, bulk carriers and offshore support vessels as well as for large commercial yachts, and appears as 11th in the list of best-performing flag States in the 2017 Paris MOU White List.[1] In July 2017 the website of the registry was fully modernised and re-launched with online services now available. Vessels registered in the Isle of Man fly the Red Ensign, defaced with the 'triskelion' symbol of three conjoined legs.

Sources of law

15.3 Registration of ships in the Isle of Man is regulated by an Act of Tynwald, the Merchant Shipping Registration Act 1991 ('the Act'), as amended. Unless otherwise stated, references to sections in this chapter are references to sections of the Act. The Isle of Man is classified under the UK Merchant Shipping Act 1995 as a Category 1 registry (unlimited tonnage and type).

---

1 See Appendix III.

Vessel eligibility

Vessel type

15.4 Most of the more common types of vessel may be registered in the Isle of Man. However, the following categories of vessel will not be accepted for registration:[2]

(1) ships and commercial yachts that are not classed by approved classification societies;

(2) ships of less than 500 gross tons, unless operating locally in and around the Isle of Man;

(3) single hull oil tankers;

(4) high speed craft and passenger ships operating outside the Irish Sea area;

(5) floating dry docks;

(6) harbour and estuarial craft operating outside Isle of Man waters;

(7) pilgrim ships;

(8) ships engaged in the carriage of irradiated nuclear fuel.

Age limits

15.5 There are no defined age limits in legislation which would prevent a ship from being registered under the Isle of Man flag. However, the Registry will not normally accept ships over 20 years old. Merchant vessels intended to be registered require an initial general inspection (IGI) by an Isle of Man surveyor either prior to registration or within six months of registration as follows, according to the life-cycle of the vessel concerned. For existing ships, the timing of the IGI is dependent upon the age of the vessel and its Port State Control (PSC) history. Generally, existing vessels of less than ten years old, which maintain an acceptable PSC inspection history, will not require an IGI prior to registration. Such vessels will however need to be attended for an IGI within six months of registration. Vessels more than ten years old will require a satisfactory IGI attended by an Isle of Man surveyor prior to registration. For new ships, a vessel built at a shipyard which has delivered IoM-registered ships previously to an owner or manager that has vessels currently registered with the Isle of Man administration will not normally be subject to an IGI prior to registration. The IGI will however be required to be carried out within six months of registration. Vessels delivered from shipyards that have not previously built ships to the Isle of Man flag, and ships owned or managed by companies previously unknown to the Isle of Man Ship Registry, will normally be subject to an IGI prior to registration.

Ownership

15.6 The following categories of persons are qualified to be the owners of ships registered in the Isle of Man:

(1) British citizens;

(2) British Dependent Territory citizens;

---

2 See further, www.iomshipregistry.com/merchant-ships/.

(3) British Overseas citizens;

(4) persons who under the British Nationality Act 1981 (an Act of the UK Parliament) are British subjects;

(5) persons who under the Hong Kong (British Nationality) Order 1986 are British Nationals (Overseas);

(6) bodies corporate incorporated in the Island or in any relevant country and having their principal place of business in the Island or in any such country;

(7) citizens of the Republic of Ireland and such other relevant countries as may be prescribed under section 45; and

(8) limited partnerships having their principal place of business in the Island or a prescribed relevant country.

15.7 The following countries are currently prescribed as additional relevant countries under section 45 and the Merchant Shipping (Qualified Owners of Manx Ships) (Relevant Countries) Regulations 2007, as amended:

(1) the UK;

(2) any of the Channel Islands;

(3) any British Dependent Territory;[3]

(4) any Member State of the European Union or other State which is a party to the European Economic Area Agreement;

(5) Australia; the Bahamas; Canada; China; Hong Kong; India; Japan; Liberia; Malta; Marshall Islands; Monaco; New Zealand; Pakistan; Panama; Russia; Singapore; South Africa; South Korea; Switzerland; United Arab Emirates; and the USA.

Bareboat charter registration

15.8 The Act introduced into the Isle of Man a demise (bareboat) charter register that enables ships registered in a compatible foreign register to be demise charter registered in the Isle of Man, provided that the charterer is a person or corporation qualified to be the owner of a Manx ship. Such ships fly the Red Ensign and are subject to Manx regulations concerning safety, prevention of pollution and manning, but retain their status on the foreign underlying register in respect of ownership and mortgages.

15.9 Ships registered in the main Part I Register in the Isle of Man and demise chartered to foreign interests may be demise charter registered 'out' to a compatible foreign registry. Such ships operate and trade as ships of that foreign country and are not entitled to fly the Red Ensign; they are subject to the foreign country's statutory regulations concerning safety, prevention of pollution and manning, but retain their status on the Isle of Man in respect of ownership and mortgages.

Trading limits

15.10 There are no limitations on trading, subject to any prevailing EU or UN sanctions.

---

3 British Dependent Territories include Anguilla, Bermuda, British Antarctic Territory, British Indian Ocean Territory, Cayman Islands, Falkland Islands, Gibraltar, Montserrat, Pitcairn Islands, St Helena and Dependencies, Turks and Caicos Islands, British Virgin Islands.

Manning requirements

15.11 The Isle of Man has adopted the International Convention on Standards of Training, Certification and Watchkeeping for Seafarers 1978, including its Annex and the STCW Code, and all amendments made to that Convention up to and including those amendments made by resolutions 1 and 2 of the 2010 STCW Conference (the Manila Amendments). The detailed requirements of this Convention are introduced by the Merchant Shipping (Manning and STCW) Regulations 2014.

Certificates of competency for officers and ratings

15.12 Masters and other officers are required to hold either a valid UK certificate of competency or a national certificate of competency issued by an acceptable country accompanied by an Isle of Man endorsement. Since 1 February 1997 a UK certificate of competency will only be acceptable if it has a clearly stated STCW endorsement and not more than five years have passed since the last revalidation date. A certificate holder will only be permitted to sail in the capacity stated in the STCW endorsement. The 2014 Regulations permit the Ship Registry to recognise certificates of competency obtained after examination and issued by other countries that have ratified and implemented the STCW Convention. Ratings who form part of a watch (bridge or engine room) must hold an appropriate watch rating certificate. These can be issued by the Isle of Man Ship Registry for ratings who do not hold a certificate issued by another country. Each application to the Manx authorities for approval of non-UK certificates will be considered on its individual merits. The process for application of STCW endorsement is now available online, with electronic certificates issued to operators using the system.[4]

Nationality of crew

15.13 There are no restrictions on the nationality of officers or ratings, recognition is based upon the issuing country of the candidate's certificate of competency. The Isle of Man Ship Registry maintains a current list of acceptable countries whose standards of crew training and certification are accepted by the Isle of Man Ship Registry and a signed undertaking is in place between the two countries.[5]

Document of safe manning

15.14 All Manx ships, apart from vessels on the small ships register (Part II), pleasure craft of under 24 metres load line length, and fishing vessels, are required to hold a safe manning certificate setting out the minimum number of officers and ratings considered to be the minimum safe level for the operation of the ship. Each ship is considered on an individual basis by the Isle of Man Ship Registry prior to the issue of a certificate. The manning levels set out in a safe manning certificate will reflect the IMO guidelines,

---

4 Instructions can be found at: www.iomshipregistry.com/media/1794/msn-051-iom-endorsement-application-process-revised-feb-18.pdf.

5 This list can be found at: www.iomshipregistry.com/crew/recognised-countries/.

having regard to watchkeeping, dealing with emergencies and routine operations. The new format certificates issued under recent legislation make it clear when a ship is permitted to sail with fewer crew than specified in the safe manning certificate.

Approved classification societies

15.15 The following classification societies are approved by the Isle of Man Government to act as recognised organisations:

American Bureau of Shipping (ABS)
Bureau Veritas (BV)
DNV GL
Korean Register of Shipping (KRS)
Lloyd's Register of Shipping (LR)
Nippon Kaiji Kyokai (NKK)
Registro Italiano Navale (RINA)

Taxation

15.16 Since 6 April 2006, the standard rate of corporate income tax for resident and non-resident companies has been 0%. Companies receiving income from banking or from land and property in the Isle of Man are subject to income tax at the rate of 10%. No withholding taxes are payable on dividends or interest paid by resident companies to foreign companies. There are no taxes on capital gains, no inheritance tax or stamp duties in the Isle of Man. The country has a customs union with the UK.

Procedure for registration

Provisional registration

15.17 There is no provisional registration in the Isle of Man. Full registration can be achieved to suit ship delivery times wherever they may be.

Permanent registration

15.18 An application for registration shall be made by contacting the Ship Registry using the contact details shown at the end of this chapter. There are four possible ports of registry: Castletown, Douglas, Peel, and Ramsey. In the case of merchant ships and large yachts the Registry should be consulted to confirm whether an initial general inspection (IGI) by an Isle of Man surveyor is required before registration. Specimen forms are provided in Appendix XI. In the case of an application by a body corporate the following documents will need to be submitted:

(1) a completed application form to register an Isle of Man ship (Form REG 1);
(2) a completed appointment of authorised officer (Form REG 3);
(3) a completed declaration of ownership on behalf of a body corporate, an individual or LLP (Form REG 4, REG 5, or REG 14 respectively);

(4) a copy certificate of incorporation and any certificate of change of company name;

(5) a completed appointment of a representative person in the Isle of Man;

(6) evidence of ownership title: in the case of a new ship, a builder's certificate acceptable form and all subsequent documents of sale (if any) prior to registration in the applicant's name; in the case of a ship that is not new and previously foreign registered, a bill of sale from the last foreign owner to the applicant;

(7) for a pleasure vessel, complete form REG 15 declaring that the vessel is to be used for pleasure;

(8) a certificate of survey, normally prepared by an approved classification society, detailing the parameters of the vessel;[6]

(9) tonnage certificate;

(10) a deletion certificate or evidence that the previous registry of the vessel has closed, in the case of transfer from a foreign flag;

(11) evidence of liability insurance – CLC blue card (oil tankers only), bunker oil blue card (if vessel over 1000 GT), and Nairobi wreck removal certificate (if vessel over 300 GT) as applicable; and

(12) a new call sign and MMSI number.[7]

Registration of mortgages and security interests

15.19 Any registered vessel or a share in a registered vessel may be made a security for the repayment of a loan or the discharge of any other obligation. The instrument creating such security shall be on one of the standard printed forms of mortgage approved by the Department and similar to the statutory forms of mortgage used for British vessels registered in the UK. In order to register a mortgage, the original document shall be delivered to the Registrar who will cause the relevant details to be recorded in the Register. He or she will then endorse on the mortgage deed the date and time of recording. Where there is more than one mortgage against a single vessel, mortgages will be registered in the order in which they are produced to the Ship Registry for registration purposes, and will rank between each other for priority in order of such registration. In such cases the later mortgage will receive a subsequent identifying priority letter.

15.20 Where a party intends to take a mortgage over a vessel or a share in a registered vessel, advance priority may be obtained by delivering a 'notice of mortgage intent' (MORT 1) to the Ship Registry. Once delivered to the Registry with the appropriate fee, such a notice will give priority to the intended mortgagee for a period of 30 days from the time on which the notice was recorded on the register. If the mortgagee is unable to register a mortgage within 30 days, the notice of mortgage intent may be extended for a further 30-day period.

Surveys

15.21 In view of the availability of improved ship performance data, the Isle of Man Ship Registry may waive the requirement for an IGI of any vessel under ten years old.

---

6 See further Registry Advice Notes RAN 3 in respect of pleasure yachts and RAN 4 in respect of other ships.

7 The Isle of Man Ship Registry has no responsibility for the issue of the call sign, MMSI number or ship station licences, which may be obtained from Spectrum Licensing.

Whether or not an IGI is necessary, a tonnage measurement survey by a classification society surveyor will normally be required to enable the issue of a certificate of survey and international tonnage certificate on behalf of the Isle of Man Government.

Deregistration procedure

15.22 A ship may be deregistered on the written request of the owner in the event of a sale to an unqualified owner, or the scrapping or total loss of the vessel. The owner is required to surrender to the Ship Registry the original certificate of registry, if available. Following the closure of the register, the Registry will issue a closed transcript as official evidence of the closure.

Yachts

15.23 Pleasure yachts have been registered in the Isle of Man for many years. The ownership qualification requirements and registration procedures are largely the same as those applied to commercial vessels. Because of the favourable tax regime in the Isle of Man and the growth of indigenous yacht management, professional and financial expertise, the Isle of Man has become a centre for the management of yachts whether used for pleasure purposes or commercial charter.

15.24 The Isle of Man applies the UK's Large Commercial Yacht Code (LY3) to all commercially-operated yachts over 24 metres in length constructed on or after 20 August 2013. Such vessels are subject to inspection by Isle of Man Ship Registry surveyors and are issued with certificates of compliance (with LY3), equivalent to the 'MCA Code' compliance certificates issued to commercial yachts registered with the UK and with other Red Ensign Group registries.

Contact addresses

15.25

Isle of Man Ship Registry
St. Georges Court
Upper Church Street
Douglas
Isle of Man IM1 1EX
British Isles
Tel: +44 1624 688 500
Email:
shipping@gov.im (general enquiries)
registry.marine@gov.im (registry enquiries)
marine.survey@gov.im (survey enquiries)
marinemlc.ded@gov.im (MLC enquiries)
Website: www.iomshipregistry.com

CHAPTER 16

Jamaica

16.1 The island of Jamaica is situated in the Caribbean Sea to the south-east of Cuba and has a population of approximately three million. The capital is Kingston where the main port is located. A former British colony, the country gained its independence on 6 August 1962 and is now an independent parliamentary democracy within the Commonwealth. The head of State is Queen Elizabeth II who is represented in Jamaica by the Governor-General. The legal system is based on English common law and the organs of government are the legislature (consisting of the Senate and the House of Representatives), the executive (the Cabinet headed by the Prime Minister) and the judiciary which is independent of both the legislature and the executive. The Prime Minister is the leader of the party having a majority of the 63 seats in the House of Representatives and is responsible for forming the government. The legal tender is the Jamaican dollar (JMD or J$).

Sources of law

16.2 The Jamaica Ship Registry was first established in 1921. Registration of ships in Jamaica is now primarily governed by the Shipping Act 1998. The Shipping Act established the Maritime Authority of Jamaica (MAJ) as the body that administers the Registry and is responsible for the training and certification of seafarers, safety and pollution issues, and the development of shipping generally. The Shipping Act came into force in January 1999 and is closely modelled on UK legislation and practice. The port of Montego Bay has been declared the national port of registry pursuant to section 32 of the Act. Unless otherwise stated, references to sections in this chapter are references to sections in the Shipping Act 1998.

Vessel eligibility

Vessel type

16.3 All vessels used in navigation in Jamaican waters must be registered, licensed (an option for vessels under 24 metres) or exempt by reasons of their size, as described below. Separate registers are maintained for:

(1) ships;
(2) ships under construction;
(3) provisionally registered ships;

176

(4) bareboat chartered ships;
(5) pleasure craft; and
(6) fishing vessels.

Vessels below 24 metres in length, wholly owned by persons qualified to own Jamaican ships and operating in or from Jamaican waters, have the option of being licensed. Licensing is a simple form of registration. Pleasure craft of less than 5 metres in length not equipped with propulsion machinery or pleasure craft of less than 3 metres in length equipped with propulsion machinery of less than 5 horsepower, are exempt.

Age limits

16.4 There are no specific age restrictions on the registration of Jamaican ships. Vessels in excess of ten years may be required to meet more stringent survey requirements prior to registration than younger vessels, depending on the type of vessel, her condition and maintenance history. The Registrar may refuse to register a ship where, having regard to the condition of the ship so far as is relevant to safety or any risk of marine pollution, it would be detrimental to the interest of Jamaica for the vessel to be registered.

Ownership

16.5 There are no restrictions on the nationality of corporations which may become the owner of a Jamaican ship. In accordance with section 20 the following persons are entitled to own Jamaican ships:

(1) citizens of Jamaica;
(2) persons who, pursuant to the Immigration Restriction (Commonwealth Citizens) Act, are deemed to belong to Jamaica (Commonwealth Citizens);
(3) bodies corporate or partnerships established under and subject to the law of Jamaica, or having a place of business or a managing owner or agent in Jamaica;
(4) business entities established under and subject to the laws of a State other than Jamaica, which pursuant to that law are entitled to own and operate the ship ('a foreign maritime entity'). A foreign maritime entity may include partnerships and limited partnerships established in a jurisdiction other than Jamaica; and
(5) such other persons as the minister may specify by order, subject to affirmative resolution of the House of Representatives.

Only bodies corporate, partnerships and other business entities established in a jurisdiction outside of Jamaica are required to appoint a managing owner or agent in Jamaica. A managing owner or agent is entitled to accept proceedings in Jamaica on behalf of the ship-owner. He must satisfy the requirements of section 20(2) where:

(1) in the case of an individual, he is resident in Jamaica;
(2) in the case of a body corporate, it is incorporated under the laws of Jamaica and has a place of business in Jamaica; and
(3) he possesses such other qualifications as may be prescribed.

Company formation

16.6 If a ship-owner wishes to incorporate a company in Jamaica for the purpose of registering a vessel as a Jamaican ship, it will be possible for a limited liability company to be registered in Jamaica under the Companies Act 2004. Single purpose companies may be acquired 'off the shelf' from the offices of the major law firms in Jamaica. Alternatively, companies may be incorporated within 24 hours. The information filed at the Registrar of Companies is available to the general public.

Registering an overseas company

16.7 Registration of an overseas company is a simple process facilitated under the Companies Act. The following documents are required for registration:

(1) a certified copy of the memorandum, articles or instruments incorporating the overseas company;

(2) a list of directors of the overseas company; and

(3) the names and addresses of one or more persons resident in Jamaica authorised to accept service and any notices to be served on the overseas company.

The overseas company is required to file accounts and a declaration of assets in accordance with the Jamaican Companies Act 2004.

Non-resident status

16.8 All companies incorporated in Jamaica are deemed to be resident for tax purposes. As a result, there is no distinction in this regard between a resident and a non-resident company. Companies which are approved shipping entities are exempted from taxation.

Registered office

16.9 A company's memorandum of association must specify that the registered office of the company is situated in Jamaica.

Shareholders, directors and secretary

16.10 A company may have one or more shareholders. The nationality or place of residence of shareholders is irrelevant. A private company registered in Jamaica must have at least one director. Their nationality or place of residence is irrelevant. A company secretary must also be appointed. The sole director of a company cannot also be appointed as the company secretary.

Returns

16.11 Annual returns must be filed each year with the Registrar of Companies. The appropriate accounts and particulars of directors must be annexed to this return. The names and addresses of the members of the company and the particulars of the directors must be submitted with the returns.

Bareboat charter registration

16.12 Section 18 of the Act permits a foreign registered ship to be bareboat chartered into the Jamaican Register. Such registration shall remain in force for the period of the bareboat charter and the validity of the underlying registration and for that time the ship is entitled to the privileges of a registered Jamaican ship. The provisions of the Act relating to title and mortgages do not, however, apply to foreign ships which are registered as Jamaican ships by virtue of a bareboat charter. An application for bareboat charter registration should be made in the prescribed form and is required to be supported by the following:

(1) the written consent of the owners as registered on the primary register;
(2) the written consent of the primary registry for the bareboat charter of the ship into Jamaica;
(3) the written consent of all registered mortgagees of the vessel;
(4) a statutory declaration by the bareboat charterer (in lieu of a declaration of ownership); and
(5) a certified copy of the bareboat charterparty.

A ship that is bareboat chartered into the Jamaican Registry shall retain the name it is registered under on the owner's primary flag State register, provided that name is not already the name of an existing Jamaican ship. If a change of name is necessary, then the consent of owners, mortgagee and the primary flag State registry is also required.

16.13 The Act also permits, under section 19, a Jamaican ship to be bareboat chartered out to a foreign registry, provided that the owners and any mortgagees consent in writing, upon submission of a certified copy of the bareboat charterparty. The entry on the Jamaican Register will be suspended for the duration of the bareboat charter and, with the exception of the provisions relating to title, mortgages and other matters relating to proprietary interests in a Jamaican ship, the provisions of the Act will cease to apply.

Trading limits

16.14 There are no international trading limits on Jamaican ships.

Manning requirements

16.15 Jamaica is party to the STCW Convention and Code. Manning levels and certification requirements for Masters and seamen employed on Jamaican ships are set out in the Shipping (Training Certification, Safe Manning, Hours of Work and Watchkeeping) Regulations 1998 as amended, which incorporate the STCW Convention of 1978 as amended in 1995 and the 2010 Manila amendments.

Certificates of competency for officers and ratings

16.16 The 1998 Regulations referred to above require Masters and officers serving on board Jamaican ships to hold a Jamaican certificate of competency or a Jamaican endorsed certificate of competency issued by a STCW State party. Jamaica has made the

'White List' of countries with approved maritime administrations. There is a reciprocal recognition of certificates between Jamaica and the UK.

Nationality of crew

16.17 There are no nationality restrictions on crews of Jamaican registered ships. However, incentives are offered to ship-owners who employ Jamaican crew.

Document of safe manning

16.18 The STCW Convention requires all vessels to hold and carry on board at all times a safe manning certificate. Owners' manning proposals are considered and approved by MAJ on a case-by-case basis and details of such proposals should be submitted at the time of application for registration.

Approved classification societies

16.19 The Jamaican Registry recognises the following classification societies:

American Bureau of Shipping (ABS)
Bureau Veritas (BV)
China Classification Society (CCS) for Chinese-owned tonnage only
Det Norske Veritas Germanischer Lloyd (DNV GL)
International Naval Surveys Bureau
Isthmus Bureau of Shipping
Korean Register of Shipping (KRS)
Lloyd's Register (LR)
Nippon Kaiji Kyokai (NKK)
Polish Register of Shipping (PRS)
Registro Italiano Navale
Russian Maritime Register of Shipping (RMRS)

Taxation

16.20 Shipping entities which intend to own or operate exempted ships may apply for tax exemptions. Approval for the status as an exempted ship is simple and based on an application being made to MAJ at the time of registration of a vessel. Approval is given to ships which are engaged in foreign-going trade and in the carriage of goods or passengers and which have paid the relevant fees for registration. Special provisions for exemption exist for vessels under 24 metres. The initial term of exemption is ten years with automatic annual renewals thereafter.

16.21 Under the Act, no tax shall be charged or payable on the capital gains or income of an approved shipping entity for profits derived from the ownership or operation of an exempted ship. Similarly, any dividend paid to the shareholders of such companies or, in the case of a partnership, profits paid to the partners are exempt from income tax. The Act also exempts from income tax any interest or other income payable to a person by an approved shipping entity in respect of any loan raised or other debt due by such shipping entity for the purpose of acquiring the ownership of an exempted ship or the operation of an exempted ship. An approved shipping entity is exempt from the payment of transfer tax and stamp duty. Seafarers working on board Jamaican ships are not required to pay tax on the income derived from such employment.

Procedure for registration

Provisional registration

16.22 A person shall not be registered as the owner of a Jamaican ship until they have made and signed a declaration of ownership. The declaration should be made on the prescribed form JSR02 and should contain the following:

(1) full name and address of the owner;
(2) year and place where the vessel was first built or, if the ship was built outside Jamaica and the year and place is not known, a statement to that effect;
(3) the owner's citizenship or national status or, in the case of a body corporate or other entity, the place of incorporation or formation;
(4) in the case of a ship previously registered outside Jamaica, the name under which it was previously registered; and
(5) the number of shares in the ship in respect of which the person is entitled to be registered as owner.

The declaration should be accompanied by an application for registration form JSR01, notice of the appointment of a ship's manager or agent each in the prescribed form supported by:

(1) confirmation from one of the approved classification societies that the ship is in class as well as the validity and expiration dates of certificates. The confirmation should indicate exemptions and conditions pertaining to the certificates;
(2) certified copy of international tonnage certificate from the previous registry;
(3) deletion certificate from the previous registry or evidence of permission to transfer;
(4) consent of mortgagees to the ship's registration on the Jamaican Register;
(5) builder's certificate and/or bill of sale or condemnation order;
(6) written application for MMSI number, radio licence and radio call sign;
(7) application for minimum safe manning certificate and crew endorsements;
(8) declaration for Continuous Synopsis Record and CSR from any previous flag;
(9) declaration of company security officer;
(10) application for certificate of insurance;
(11) certificate of incorporation, notice of directors and a certificate of good standing of the ship-owning company; and
(12) LRIT conformance test report.

Provisional registration may be effected using faxed or email copies of documents, with original documents to be provided to MAJ within 30 days. The statutory certificates of any previous registry are not required to be submitted in original.

Validity of the provisional registration and extension

16.23 Provisional registration is limited to six months, allowing an owner to undertake necessary surveys and comply with the documentary formalities of full registration. The provisional registration of a Jamaican ship remains valid until the ship arrives in port in Jamaica, six months have expired since the date of issue of the provisional certificate, or the conditions warranting provisional registration no longer exist, whichever occurs first.

Permanent registration

16.24 In addition to the documents required for provisional registration, the following will need to be submitted to the Registrar:

(1) deletion, cancellation or de-registration certificate from any previous registry, if not already provided;

(2) original safety certificates issued by or under the authority of the Maritime Authority of Jamaica (where applicable):
    (a) certificate of hull and machinery
    (b) international tonnage certificate
    (c) international load lines certificate
    (d) cargo ship safety construction certificate
    (e) cargo ship safety radio telegraphy certificate
    (f) cargo ship safety equipment certificate
    (g) certificate of financial responsibility
    (h) IOPP certificate
    (i) passenger ship safety certificate.

(3) safe manning certificate, crew documents and/applications;

(4) certificate of survey; and

(5) carving and marking note.

Registration of mortgages and security interests

16.25 The registration of mortgages is dealt with in section 69 of the Act which provides that:

(1) a Jamaican ship, may be made a security for a loan or other valuable consideration, provided that the instrument of the mortgage creating such security is completed in the prescribed form;

(2) mortgages rank in priority according to the date and time they are presented and accepted for registration, and not according to the date of the mortgage instrument; and

(3) where a mortgage instrument prohibits the creation of further mortgages without consent of every mortgagee, an entry to this effect shall be entered into the register to protect the mortgagee.

The Act permits a mortgage to be registered as soon as the ship is provisionally registered and/or where the ship is still under construction. Mortgages so registered shall, for the purposes of determining priority under the Act, be treated as a registered ship mortgage. The claims of holders of registered ship mortgages take priority over the maritime liens recognised in section 80 of the Act, except in respect of wages and other sums due to ship's crew and Master's disbursements.

Surveys

16.26 Section 43 of the Act requires every ship to be surveyed prior to registration as a matter of course and re-measured for the purposes of ascertaining a ship's tonnage. Vessels over ten years old may be subject to more stringent survey requirements. Jamaica is a party to the International Convention on the Tonnage Measurement of Ships 1969 and, where it appears to the Registrar that the existing ITC has been issued in accordance with the Convention, the requirements for the vessel to be re-measured may be waived.

Deregistration procedure

16.27 A registered Jamaican ship may be deregistered upon completion of an application to deregister the ship made under section 29 of the Act. The registration of a Jamaican ship may otherwise be cancelled:

(1) if the annual fees of the vessel remains unpaid for a stipulated period;
(2) where the ship becomes a total loss or is otherwise destroyed such as by ship-wreck, demolition, fire or sinking;
(3) where the Director is satisfied that it would be detrimental to the interest of Jamaica or of international shipping; and
(4) if the ship is no longer entitled to remain on the Register.

Contact addresses

16.28

The Maritime Authority of Jamaica
12 Ocean Boulevard
Kingston 2
Jamaica
Tel: (1 876) 967 1060 5 ext. 128
Fax: (1 876) 922 5766
Email: registrar@jamaicaships.com
Website: www.jamaicaships.com

CHAPTER 17

Liberia

17.1 Liberia is an independent democratic republic situated on the coast of west Africa between Sierra Leone and the Côte d'Ivoire, with a population of approximately 4.7 million. It was founded in 1822 as a colony for freed American slaves and subsequently gained its independence in 1847. It was the first democratic republic on the African continent. The Republic's historical origins explain the country's close links with the USA. Seven years of civil war ended in 1995, followed by a further period of instability and another civil war followed. In 2003, following an internationally recognised peace agreement, a National Transitional Government took control of the running of the country with the support of a UN International Stabilisation Force. In 2006 Ellen Johnson Sirleaf became Africa's first elected female head of State and was re-elected in 2011. In 2018, George Weah took office following democratic elections. The President, who is elected for a six-year term, is chief of State and head of government. The legislative branch of government consists of the Senate and the House of Representatives, members of which are elected by popular vote. Following an Ebola epidemic, originated in Guinea, which began in March 2014 and ended in May 2015, Liberia continues to receive significant levels of international aid and material inward investment from, among others, the USA, the EU and China. Such inward investment includes several multi-billion dollar concession agreements in the iron ore and palm oil industries with numerous multinational corporations. The Liberian dollar (L$) and the US dollar are the two legal currencies. English is the official language.

17.2 Liberia has provided an open shipping register since 1948 and the Liberian fleet was in January 2017 the second largest in the world by dead-weight tonnage with over 11% of the global merchant fleet.[1] In 1949 Liberia was a founding member of the International Maritime Organisation and remains active in this intergovernmental body. In 2017 it was re-elected as a member of the IMO Council. Since its inception, the administration and operation of both the maritime and corporate registries has been delegated by the Liberian Government to commercial entities based in the USA, acting as an exclusive agent. The Registry managed to operate continuously and successfully, even throughout the difficult years or war and epidemic. Led from central offices in Virginia and New York, Liberian International Ship and Corporate Registry LLC ('LISCR') assumed these responsibilities in 2000 and developed a global network of regional offices. The Liberia flag is now at the forefront of international practice including technological developments

---

1 UNCTAD, Review of Maritime Transport (2017), Table 2.7.

such as online registry services and mobile applications. For example, Liberia has pioneered the use of a self-service electronic application platform for sea-farer documents by manning agents (known as the SEA System) and since 2006 the adoption of electronic vessel certificates using a unique tracking identification number for each document or certificate, verifiable online in real time by Port State Control inspectors. The flag State of Liberia appears on the White Lists of all MOUs, including the Paris and Tokyo and USGC, of Port State Control regulatory compliance[2] and was the first State to accede to the Maritime Labour Convention.

Sources of law

17.3 The registration of vessels under the Liberian flag is governed by the Liberian Maritime Law, being Title 21 of the Liberian Code of Laws of 1956, as amended. Unless otherwise stated, all references to sections in this chapter are references to sections of the Liberian Maritime Law. Legislative changes introduced in 2002 incorporated, among other things, improved ship mortgage financing laws and provided for the formation of new types of corporate vehicles. The Maritime Program of the Republic of Liberia established by the provisions of Title 21 and of Regulations and Rules made by the Commissioner pursuant to the provisions of section 11 shall be administered by an agent of the Liberian Government, designated and appointed by the Government of the Republic of Liberia for the purpose of aiding the Commissioner in the effective administration of the provisions of the Maritime Law.

Vessel eligibility

Vessel size and type

17.4 Any sea-going vessel of more than 500 net tons engaged in the foreign trade, wherever built, owned by a citizen or national of Liberia. (s.51(2)) may be registered in the registry administered by LISCR. Self-propelled or sailing vessels of 20 net tons and over engaged in trade exclusively between ports of Liberia and pleasure boats of 24 metres or over may be registered (s.51(1), (3)) with the Liberian Small and Pleasure Watercraft Registry. An application for waiver of tonnage is required for consideration by the Commissioner or Deputy Commissioner to register a sea-going vessel of less than 500 net tons. A waiver can be granted if applicable conditions and all other requirements for registration in accordance with section 51(2)(a), (6) and (7) are fulfilled.

Age limits

17.5 Sea-going vessels or pleasure yachts will not be eligible for initial registration if they are more than 20 years old from the date of first construction on 1 January in the year when registration is sought. However, the Commissioner or Deputy Commissioner has a discretion to waive the age limit if a vessel can be shown to meet all other

---

2 See Appendix III.

applicable requirements and it can be shown that there is a genuine need for such a waiver (s.51(6)). An application for waiver should be accompanied by written confirmation from the vessel's classification society that the vessel is in class and that the society is willing to issue all necessary statutory certificates. Stringent safety conditions may be imposed upon the vessel if a waiver is granted. Applications for vessels which are 15 years old or more must be accompanied by the most recent classification society narrative reports from the last drydock for review by the Liberian Marine Safety Division.

Ownership

17.6 A registered Liberian vessel is required to be owned by a Liberian citizen or national, although a waiver may be given to permit registration by a foreign corporate body that has been registered in Liberia as a foreign maritime entity (FME). The expression 'citizen or national' includes corporations, registered business companies, partnerships, limited partnerships, limited liability companies, FMEs and associations of individuals. Payments can be made by wire transfer, check and credit card. The Liberian Corporate Registry offers also electronic self-service online platform, eCORP, to its corporate clients.

Company formation

17.7 Incorporation of corporations, limited partnerships, limited liability companies (LLCs) and registered business companies in Liberia is regulated by two separate pieces of legislation, depending on the type of corporate vehicle:

(1) the Business Corporation Act (as amended), which forms part of the Associations Law, Title 5 of the Liberian Code of Laws Revised, 1977. The Business Corporation Act, which is modelled on the equivalent statute in the State of Delaware, applies to every resident and non-resident domestic corporation, limited partnership and LLC (as well as foreign corporations authorised to do business in Liberia), other than registered Business companies (see below);

(2) the Registered Business Company Act came into effect in 2002. This Act was introduced in response to a demand for an alternative type of company, which is required to file annual returns and other information in much the same way as in the UK. Indeed, the legislation has much in common with the UK Companies Act 1929. Registered business companies offer a greater degree of public transparency than Liberian business corporations.

Liberian business entities may be incorporated to order, or purchased off the shelf through the global offices network of LISCR. Corporations and companies can be incorporated by LISCR within one working day.

Registered agent and registered office

17.8 Liberian ship-owning companies registered by LISCR have to be non-domestic offshore entities. The principal place of business has to be outside of Liberia. Every Liberian corporation and company not having a place of business in Liberia is required to have its registered office at the Monrovia address of the LISCR Trust Company, which acts as exclusive registered agent for all such Liberian corporations, companies, limited partnerships, LLCs, partnerships and registered FMEs.

Bareboat charter registration

17.9 Liberian law permits the 'flagging-in' and 'flagging-out' of bareboat chartered vessels to and from the Liberian flag if the law of both States concerned permit bareboat charter registration in this way according to their respective legislation.

Flagging-in

17.10 If a vessel is 'flagged-in' to the Liberian Register, Liberian law will apply to the vessel's operation, navigation and management. For the duration of the bareboat charter, registration the vessel is not permitted to fly its original national flag and must show Monrovia as its port of registry. The law of the underlying register will apply to any registered mortgages; however the Liberian maritime law allows recording a notice of such foreign mortgages in accordance with section 89. An application to 'flag-in' a vessel can be submitted to any LISCR office, which will require the following documents:

(1) an application for official number, call sign and registration (Form RLM – 101A);
(2) a written letter of request from the Liberian bareboat charterer;
(3) an oath or affirmation from the charterer containing various undertakings;
(4) an original or certified true copy of the bareboat charterparty, with proof of execution in the form of a legal certificate from a special agent of the Liberian Deputy Commissioner of Maritime Affairs, a notary public or other person authorised to take acknowledgements;
(5) an original transcript of the underlying register with details of any registered mortgages;
(6) the written consents of the ship-owner and any mortgagees to the Liberian registration;
(7) evidence that the underlying flag State will withdraw the right or obligation to fly its flag for the duration of the Liberian bareboat charter;
(8) status of classification – such a statement or affidavit issued by the classification society confirming the vessel has a valid classification certificate and the vessel type/classification notations issued;
(9) proof of liability insurance, such as a certificate of entry from a P&I club;
(10) application for minimum safe manning certificate;
(11) ISM Code declarations;
(12) evidence of authority of the applicant, such as a corporate resolution and power of attorney in favour of the signatory.

Flagging-out

17.11 An application to 'flag-out' a Liberian-registered vessel to a foreign bareboat register is referred to as foreign bareboat charter registration (FBCR). The FBCR application procedure will require different documents (see para 17.9), together with a letter of request from the owner for permission to bareboat charter-out, namely:

(1) an original application from the charterer;
(2) the written consent of any mortgagees on record in Liberia;
(3) the owner's undertaking to surrender the Liberian certificate of registry and notify LISCR of the termination of the charter;
(4) an agreement between the owner and charterer acknowledging the waiver of the right to fly the Liberian flag for the duration of the charter and the obligation to maintain and operate the vessel to no less than the standards required under Liberian law during the same period;
(5) evidence that the foreign flag State consents to bareboat registration-in of a Liberian vessel and that the law of Liberia as the underlying register will apply to any registered mortgages;
(6) an original or certified true copy of the charterparty with any amendments and proof of execution.

Once the Republic of Liberia has consented to foreign bareboat charter registration, the existing Liberian certificate of registry must be surrendered to any LISCR office and a new provisional FBCR certificate of registry will be issued, but retained by the Office of the Deputy Commissioner of Maritime Affairs for the duration of the foreign bareboat charter registration. The vessel will receive a certified copy of the certificate of registry along with the certificate of permission to FBCR which should be kept on board.

Trading limits

17.12 There are no trading restrictions for Liberian flag vessels.

Manning requirements

17.13 Manning requirements are set out in Chapter X of the Liberian Maritime Regulations and are in compliance with the STCW Conventions. No Liberian-registered vessel may navigate without a duly licensed Master and, in the case of vessels over 375 kw/500 hp, a duly licensed chief engineer.

Certificates of competency for officers and ratings

17.14 Officers must possess a Liberian licence, valid for five years, which may be issued against a foreign licence recognised to be equivalent by the Liberian authorities, subject to proof of experience. A Liberian licence may also be issued to candidates who have taken and successfully passed a Liberian examination. Seafarers must hold a valid Liberian seaman's identification and record book.

Nationality of crew

17.15 There are no nationality restrictions.

Document of safe manning

17.16 The minimum number of deck officers and engineers, and deck and engine rating as deemed necessary for the safe manning and operation of the ship is prescribed in respect of each manned vessel by the Commissioner or Deputy Commissioner. The manning scales depend on the size of the vessel, engines propelling power, class of automation of the machinery space and type of trade.

Approved classification societies

17.17 The Republic of Liberia recognises only International Association of Classification Societies (IACS) members as recognised organisations (RO) for the purpose of surveys and the issue of statutory certificates on behalf of the Liberian Government:

American Bureau of Shipping (ABS)
Bureau Veritas (BV)
China Classification Society (CCS)
Croatian Register of Shipping (CRS)
DNV GL
Indian Register of Shipping (IRS)
Korean Register of Shipping (KRS)
Lloyd's Register of Shipping (LR)
Nippon Kaiji Kyokai (NKK)
Polish Register of Shipping (PRS)
Registro Italiano Navale (RINA)
Russian Maritime Register of Shipping (RS)

Taxation

17.18 The income of a corporation or company incorporated under the Business Corporation Act or the Registered Business Company Act and not having a place of business in Liberia is exempt from tax in Liberia, unless the income is generated in or remitted to Liberia or more than 25% of the shares are owned by Liberian residents. Registered owners of vessels registered in Liberia are subject to an annual tonnage tax.

Procedure for registration

17.19 Applications for registration under the Liberian flag should be made to LISCR's vessel registration and recordation division at its offices in New York or one of the regional offices in Dubai, Hamburg, Hong Kong, Houston, Istanbul, London, Panama City, Piraeus, Rio de Janeiro, Seoul, Shanghai, Singapore, Tokyo, Vienna (VA) and Zurich which are also authorised to accept applications for and to issue certificates of registry and associated documentation. The registration process in Liberia does not require an appointment of a Liberian attorney. Registration documents required in original, or mortgage and conveyance instruments submitted for recordation, must be acknowledged before a notary public or a Liberian special agent or a Deputy Commissioner of Maritime. Documents do

Provisional registration

17.20 An application for provisional registration must be made on the prescribed form RLM – 101A, which can be submitted to one of the LISCR offices. For re-registration of second-hand Liberian-flagged vessels, a letter of request for permission for sale is required to be issued by the current Liberian owner. The application should be accompanied by the following documents:

(1) proof of ownership in the form of a bill of sale transferring title to the present owner or, in the case of a newbuilding, a builder's certificate;

(2) an authority of agent or officer in the form of a power of attorney or certified copy of a corporate resolution authorising the individual in question to apply for registration;

(3) confirmation of class in the form of a statement or affidavit issued by the classification society confirming the vessel has a valid classification certificate and the vessel type/classification notations issued or an interim certificate of class in the case of a newbuilding;

(4) survey reports, if applicable. Where a vessel is 15 years of age or older, recent copies of the following reports must be submitted for review by the flag administration's head of maritime operations and standards prior to registration (a pre-registration physical inspection may be not required upon review of such survey reports):
classification special survey, hull;
classification special survey, machinery and electrical equipment;
drydocking (bottom) survey, if conducted since last special survey;
loadline survey;
safety construction survey;
safety radio survey;
safety equipment survey; and
international oil pollution prevention (IOPP) survey;

(5) proof of liability insurance in the form of a certificate of entry, cover note or similar document from a member of the International Group of P & I Clubs confirming the existence of liability insurance cover;

(6) blue cards in relation to insurance for Bunker Pollution, Wreck Removal, Civil Liability Convention and Maritime Labour Convention obligations, as applicable;

(7) consent to transfer from the vessel's previous registration authority, if a closed transcript or other evidence of deletion from the previous registry is not produced. If the previous registration authority does not issue such letters, evidence of that fact may be required in the form of an affirmation from a lawyer practising in the jurisdiction concerned. Evidence from the previous registry that the vessel is free from recorded liens, if proof of such is not already contained in the consent to transfer or cancellation certificate referred to above;

(8) International Safety Management (ISM) Code declaration forms (RLM – 297) (designated person and company); and

(9) application for minimum safe manning certificate (MSD 336RL).

Unusually, the Liberian Maritime Regulations permit the provisional (and permanent) registration of vessels with laid-up status. In such cases, the list of supporting documents is simplified.

A provisional certificate of registry will be issued on acceptance of the application form, the appropriate supporting documents and payment of the registration fees, plus the first year's tonnage tax and annual fees.

Validity of the provisional registration and extension

17.21 The certificate of registry – whether permanent, provisional or extension of provisional certificate of registry, restricted, navigational or non-navigational, is *prima facie* evidence of the Liberian nationality of a vessel. A provisional certificate of registry is valid for a period of six months. The provisional certificate may be extended upon approval by the Registrar if a vessel does not qualify for a permanent certificate, with payment of a fee. A vessel registered with laid-up status may be issued both the provisional certificate of registry and its extension for a period of up to 12 months. An extension is issued upon written request and payment of a fee. A provisional certificate of bareboat charter registry (in and out) can be issued for periods up to two years.

Permanent registration

17.22 An application for a permanent certificate of registry can be submitted to any LISCR office. For this, the vessel is required to have verified by the Registrar:

(1) a report of satisfactory completion of an initial Liberian safety inspection;

(2) a current full-term classification certificate showing the present name of the vessel and the home port of Monrovia, Liberia;

(3) full-term Liberian statutory certificates issued by the vessel's classification society (as recognised organisation authorised to issue such certificates on behalf of the Government of Liberia) including:

    (a) an international tonnage certificate;

    (b) an international load line certificate;

    (c) an international oil pollution prevention (IOPP) certificate and/or noxious liquid substances (NLS) certificate;

    (d) SOLAS certificates relating to safety construction, safety equipment, safety radio, and where applicable, carriage of grain, bulk chemicals, safety management etc.;

    (e) Liberian ship station radio licence;

    (f) minimum safe manning certificate;

    (g) Liberian national or IMO code or resolution certificates. These certificates may be required for vessels under 500 gross tons, non-propelled vessels, fishing vessels, mobile offshore drilling units or other vessels not covered by (c) above; and

    (h) certificate of cancellation of vessel's former registry (if not already produced at the time of provisional registration).

Registration of preferred mortgages and security interest

17.23 The Liberian Maritime Law contains detailed provisions relating to the registration of security instruments over vessels. Chapter 3 of the Law deals with the concept of the preferred mortgage, which gives a lender priority ahead of certain other lien holders. A preferred mortgage over a Liberian ship must be prepared in a prescribed form and recorded at the Central Office of the Deputy Commissioner of Maritime Affairs in New York or any other location authorised by the Commissioner or Deputy Commissioner. A preferred mortgage must also be acknowledged before a notary public or a special agent or a Deputy Commissioner of Maritime Affairs. A preferred mortgage must be executed with four original counterparts together with a memorandum of particulars, all of which must be executed by or on behalf of the ship-owner. Applications for mortgage recordation can be made at any of the LISCR regional offices.

17.24 Mortgages are recorded on a public register to show the time and date of registration, the name of the vessel, the names of the parties and the amount secured by the mortgage instrument. Once a mortgage is recorded, evidence of recordation will be provided in the form of a certificate of ownership and encumbrances and a certified extract of the preferred mortgage index. Three certified counterparts of the recorded mortgage instruments are returned to the recording party for the lender/mortgagee, owner/mortgagor and the vessel's records.

Surveys

17.25 An initial safety inspection is required before a permanent certificate of registry is issued.

Deregistration procedure

17.26 If the owner of a Liberian vessel wishes to transfer it to another register, sell it for scrap or to a buyer who intends to register the vessel on a register other than Liberia, the owner of the vessel must submit an application in writing for permission to transfer. The application must contain the name and domicile of the buyer (unless change of flag is without change of ownership) and the intended new flag of registry. Upon receipt of such application, and the appropriate fee, LISCR will issue a certificate of permission to transfer, valid for 180 days. A certificate of cancellation of registry will be issued upon completion of the following requirements:

(1) a certificate of permission to transfer must have been issued;
(2) an instrument of satisfaction, release or discharge must have been recorded at a LISCR office in respect of any preferred mortgage or preferred lien;
(3) the following documents must be delivered to the LISCR Vessel Registration Department in New York or any regional LISCR office:
    (a) the current Liberian certificate of registry (if not in electronic format);
    (b) a copy of the relevant bill of sale transferring title to the purchaser in the event of a change of ownership;
(4) payment in full of any outstanding fees or penalties due in respect of the vessel or her owner.

Contact addresses

17.27

Head office

LISCR LLC
22980 Indian Creek Drive, Suite 200
Dulles,
Virginia 20166
USA
Tel: (1) 703 790 3434
Fax: (1) 703 790 5655
Email: info@liscr.com
Website: www.liscr.com

Vessel registration

LISCR LLC
99 Park Avenue, Suite 1830
New York, New York 10016–1601 USA
Tel: (1) 212 697 3434
Fax: (1) 212 697 5655
Email: registration@liscr.com

Regional offices

Dubai

LISCR
Al Mina Road
PO Box 50350
Dubai
United Arab Emirates
Tel: (971) 4 3452 541
Fax: (971) 4 3453 340
Email: infodubai@liscr.com

Hamburg

LISCR (Deutschland) GmbH
Hohe Bleichen 11
20354 Hamburg
Germany
Tel: (49) 40 3500 4660
Fax: (49) 40 3500 4670
Email: info@liscr.de

Hong Kong

LISCR (Far East) Limited
Jubilee Centre
42–46 Gloucester Road
Wan Chai
Hong Kong
Tel: (852) 2810 1068
Fax: (852) 2810 0023
Email: liscrfe@liscr.com.hk

Houston

LISCR LLC
PO Box 131285
Spring,
Texas 77393
USA
Tel: (1) 281 796 8085
Fax: (1) 936 231 8623
Email: info@liscr.com

Istanbul

LISCR Istanbul
The Maritime House
Ağaoğlu MyOffice
Barbaros Mah. Lale sok
No: 1 Kat: 13 Daire: 54
Atasehir 34746
Istanbul
Turkey
Tel: (90) 216 688 37 56
Fax: (90) 216 688 00 37
Email: infoturkey@liscr.com

London

LISCR (UK) Ltd
3rd floor
107 Fenchurch Street
London, EC3M 5JP
England
Tel: (44) (0)207 799 3434
Fax: (44) (0)207 799 3456
Email: info@liscr.co.uk

Panama City

LISCR
Hi Tech Plaza
Floor #8, Office 8a
53 Street East and San Jose Street
Obarrio Bella Vista
Panama City
Republic of Panama
Tel: (507) 263 2199
Email: rcigarruista@liscr.com

Piraeus

LISCR (Hellas) S.A.
2 Efplias Street
185 37 Piraeus
Greece
Tel: (30) 210 452 9670
Fax; (30) 210 452 9673
Email: info@liscr.gr

Monrovia

LISCR
80 Broad Street
Monrovia 10
Liberia
Tel: (231) 77 000 400
Fax: (231) 77 000 422
Email: info@liscr.com

Rio de Janeiro

Seoul

LISCR-Korea
602 Greenville
237 Dangsan-R, Yeongdeungpo-Gu
Seoul 07222
South Korea
Tel: (82) 70 7518 9139
Fax: (82) 70 7548 9139
Email: info@liscr.kr

Shanghai

LISCR (Shanghai) Co Ltd
Room 625–626
Summit Center
No. 1088 West Yan'an Road
Changning District
Shanghai 200052
PR China
Tel: (86) 21 5258 8082
Fax: (86) 21 5258 8083
Email: infoshanghai@liscr.com

Singapore

LISCR (Singapore)
36 Eng Hoon Street
Singapore 169782
Tel: (65) 6323 1048
Fax: (65) 6323 1049
Email: info@liscr.sg

Tokyo

LISCR Japan K.K.
Shibakoen Plaza Building 4F
3–6–9 Shiba
Minato-Ku, Tokyo 105–0014
Japan
Tel: (81) 3 5419 7001
Fax: (81) 3 5419 7002
Email: info@liscr.jp

Zurich

LISCR, SA
Stauffacherstrasse 26
8004 Zurich
Switzerland
Tel: (41) 44 250 8650
Fax: (41) 44 250 8655
Email: info@liscr.ch

CHAPTER 18

Malta

18.1 Situated in the centre of the Mediterranean some 58 miles to the south of Sicily, Malta is made up of a number of islands, namely Gozo and Comino as well as Malta itself, on which the capital Valletta is located. Malta gained its independence from Britain in 1964, became a republic ten years later and is a member of the Commonwealth. Malta joined the European Union in 2004 and has a population of some 415,000. Malta is a parliamentary democracy with members of the House of Representatives elected for a five-year term by proportional representation. The official languages are Maltese and English. The official unit of currency is the Euro.

18.2 Malta has a long maritime tradition and, since independence, the Maltese Register has established itself as a major open and international ship register. The register is administered by the Merchant Shipping Directorate, a department of the Authority for Transport in Malta. Malta appears within the top 25 best-performing flag States in the 2017 Paris MOU White List and as at 1 January 2017 was the sixth largest registry, with over 5% of the world merchant fleet under its flag.[1]

Sources of law

18.3 The registration of vessels under the Maltese flag is governed by the Merchant Shipping Act 1973 (as amended), a statute based originally on the merchant shipping legislation of the UK. In this chapter, references to 'the Act' are references to the Merchant Shipping Act, 1973 as subsequently amended, and references to an 'article' are to an article of the Act.

Vessel eligibility

Vessel type

18.4 Any vessel over six metres in length and used in navigation (including pleasure yachts and oil rigs) is eligible for registration.

Age limits

18.5 Merchant ships of 15 years and over are subject to the outcome of a priori registration inspection by an authorised flag State inspector. Ships of ten0 years and over

---

1 See Appendix III; UNCTAD, *Review of Maritime Transport* (2017), Table 2.6.

197

but less than 15 years shall also be presented for an inspection, by an authorised flag State inspector, within one month of provisional registration. As a rule, trading ships of 25 years and over may not be registered.

Bareboat charter registration

18.6 Part IIA of the Act, inserted by the Merchant Shipping (Amendment) Act 1990, provides for both bareboat charter registration of foreign ships on to the Malta flag and also for the bareboat charter registration of Maltese ships on to a foreign flag, provided that in either case the provisions of the law of the State of the foreign registry are compatible with the provisions of the Act.

Bareboat chartering in

18.7 The duration of the bareboat charter registration of a foreign vessel under the Malta flag is determined by the duration of the bareboat charter or until the expiry date of the underlying registration, whichever is the shorter, but in no case for a period exceeding two years (art. 84G). The period of registration may be extended and further extended at the request of the charterer or his authorised representative (art. 84H). The requirements for the bareboat registration of a foreign vessel on the Maltese flag are set out in article 84C and permits bareboat registration if:

(1) the ship is bareboat chartered to Maltese citizens, bodies corporate or other persons qualified to own a Maltese ship in accordance with article 4;

(2) the ship is not a Maltese ship, and she is registered in a compatible registry;

(3) the ship is not registered in another bareboat registry; and

(4) provided the following documents are submitted to the Registrar:
    (a) application for registration;
    (b) a declaration of bareboat charter made by the charterer accompanied by a copy of the charter agreement (such charter agreement will not be available for public inspection);
    (c) a transcript or an extract of the underlying registration of the vessel which must include a description of the vessel, her owners and, where applicable, details of all registered mortgages and encumbrances on the vessel (which document is available for public inspection); and
    (d) the consent in writing for the ship to be bareboat charter registered in Malta of:
        (i) the underlying registry, who may be further required by the Registrar to declare that during the period of bareboat charter registration the ship will not be entitled to fly their flag;
        (ii) the owners of the ship;
        (iii) all registered mortgagees;
    (e) evidence of seaworthiness of the vessel (in the case of a trading vessel, confirmation of class);
    (f) tonnage certificate; and
    (g) evidence of payment of all registration fees.

For the period that the ship is registered under the Maltese flag she will be required to comply with the international Conventions to which Malta is a party. If additional certificates are required, these will usually be issued by the Maltese Registry, although the Registrar may accept certificates issued by the underlying registry (art. 84-I). During the period of the bareboat registration in Malta, the vessel may only hoist the Maltese flag and her home port must be shown as Valletta. Mortgages and encumbrances may not be registered on the Maltese Register (art. 84M).

Bareboat chartering out

18.8 A Maltese ship may be bareboat charter registered in a foreign registry if the Registrar General gives his consent in writing thereto. The Registrar General will only give consent to a Maltese ship being registered under a foreign flag for the duration of the bareboat charter or for a period not exceeding two years, whichever is the shorter period, if the requirements of article 84P have been complied with. These are as follows:

(1) the ship must be registered as a Maltese ship under Part II of the Act;
(2) the bareboat charter registry where the ship is to be registered is a compatible registry; and
(3) the following documents have been submitted to the Registrar General:
   (a) an application for bareboat charter registration in a foreign registry made by the owners containing such information as may be required by the Registrar General;
   (b) the consent in writing to such registration of all registered mortgagees, if any;
   (c) a written undertaking by the owners to surrender the Certificate of Registry issued under the Act within 30 days from entry into the bareboat charter registry;
   (d) a written undertaking by the charterer that the Maltese flag shall not be hoisted during the period of bareboat charter registration; and
   (e) a copy of the bareboat charter.

Immediately upon such registration taking place, the owners must notify the Registrar, and within 30 days surrender to the Registrar the certificate of Maltese registry and deliver to him a transcript or an extract of the foreign bareboat charter registration. The Registrar, if satisfied that such registration has been effected in accordance with the provisions of the Act, makes an entry to that effect in the register of the vessel. During the time a Maltese ship is registered in a foreign registry, she shall not hoist the Maltese flag and her home port is that of the foreign registry (art. 84T). All matters with respect to the title over the ship, mortgages and encumbrances continue to be governed by Maltese law (art. 84W). At the request of the owner or his authorised representative, the Registrar-General may extend and further extend his consent for the remaining period of the charter or until the expiry of the registration of the ship under Part II of the Act, whichever is the shorter period, but in no case for periods exceeding two years at a time.

Trading limits

18.9 Provided that they comply with the respective rules and regulations, there are no trading restrictions to Maltese registered ships.

Manning requirements

Certificates of competency for officers and ratings

18.10 The issuance of certificates of competency and other seafarer certificates is regulated by the Merchant Shipping (Training and Certification) Regulations which give effect to the provisions found in the International Convention on Standards of Training, Certification and Watchkeeping for Seafarers 1978 (STCW 78), as amended, to which Malta is party.

Nationality of crew

18.11 There are no restrictions on the nationality of the Master, officers and crew engaged on Maltese ships. Foreign certificates issued in terms of STCW 78, require an endorsement issued by the Maltese Administration attesting their recognition.

Document of safe manning

18.12 The SOLAS Convention requires that trading ships of 500 gross tonnage (in accordance with the International Tonnage Convention 1969) and over must carry, at all times, a valid minimum safe manning certificate. Accordingly, the Maltese administration issues upon registration of a ship, against application by the owner, a minimum safe manning certificate valid for a period of five years from the date of provisional registration, renewable for a further period of five years prior to its expiration. The certificate ceases to be valid upon closure of the Maltese registry of the ship or in the event of any change in the equipment, construction or use of the ship which affects the stipulated manning. The safe manning certificate is issued in compliance with Chapter V, regulation 13(b) of SOLAS 74 in accordance with the principles and guidelines set out in IMO Resolution A.1047(27) and may be revised subject to a practical demonstration of the crew's ability. As an example, the minimum safe manning guidelines for cargo ships are set out in the tables below:

Deck department

Gross tonnage	Under 500	500 to 999	1,000 to 1,599	1,600 to 2,999	3,000 to 4,999	5,000 to 14,999	15,000 & over
Master	1	1	1	1	1	1	1
Chief officer	1	1	1	1	1	1	1
Deck officer	–	1^2	1^2	1	1	2	2
Deck rating	2	2	3	3	4	5	6

At least two deck officers must be holders of a recognised GMDSS general operator's certificate (GOC), or otherwise the vessel must carry a dedicated radio officer, holder of at least a recognised GMDSS general operator's certificate.

2 In restricted trading one deck officer may be omitted.

Engine department

Kilowatts	350 to 750	751 to 1,500	1,501 to 3,000	3,001 to 7,450	7,451 to 11,200	11,201 & Over
Chief engineer	1	1	1	1	1	1
Second engineer	1[3]	1[3]	1	1	1	1
Officer in charge of an engineering watch	–	–	1[4]	1[4]	1[4]	2[4]
Engine rating	1	1	2[5]	3[5]	3[5]	3[5]

On tankers of 1,000 GT and over, an extra engine rating is required.

Approved classification societies

18.13 At the time it is being registered as a Maltese ship and during the period of its registration under the Maltese flag, a merchant vessel must be classed with a classification society authorised to issue statutory certificates on behalf of the Government of Malta. A ship-by-ship authorisation to the classification society is required in order to issue statutory certificates on behalf of the Government of Malta. The survey, tonnage and safety certification of a ship or any other related matter may be dealt with on behalf of the Maltese Government by any of the following recognised classification societies:

American Bureau of Shipping (ABS)
Bureau Veritas (BV)
China Classification Society (CCS)
Class NK (NK)
Croatian Register of Shipping (CRS)
DNV GL
Indian Register of Shipping (IRS)
Korean Register of Shipping (KR)
Lloyd's Register (LR)
Polish Register of Shipping (PRS)
Registro Italiano Navale (RINA)
Russian Maritime Register of Shipping (RS)

Procedure for registration

18.14 An application for registration of a vessel is made by or on behalf of the owners or prospective owners to the Registrar of Maltese Ships at the Merchant Shipping Directorate within the Authority for Transport in Malta, the address of which can be found at the end of this chapter. The registration of a ship will be provisional in the first instance.

---

3 On ships with UMS documentary evidence, second engineer may be omitted.
4 On ships with UMS documentary evidence, one engineer officer may be omitted.
5 On ships with UMS documentary evidence, one engine rating may be omitted.

Provisional registration

18.15 An application to provisionally register a ship should be made on Form MS (R) 21 A and supported by the following documents:

(1) application for change of name where applicable;

(2) proof of the prospective owner's qualification to own a Maltese ship, such as a Maltese passport or identity card in the case of individuals or certificate of incorporation, memorandum and articles of association in the case of a body corporate;

(3) copy of the builder's certificate or if there has been any sale or transfer, the bill of sale or the other document under which the ship or share therein was transferred to the applicant for registry;

(4) declaration of ownership made before the Registrar by the owner or his authorised representative;

(5) written authority of the owner in favour of any representative who may submit the application on behalf of the owner;

(6) evidence of seaworthiness of the vessel, such as confirmation that she is classed with a recognised classification society (not applicable to pleasure craft);

(7) application for a safe manning certificate;

(8) copy of international tonnage certificate issued by previous registry;

(9) application for ship radio station licence; and

(10) payment of initial and annual registration fees.

18.16 On completion of the provisional registry of a ship, the Registrar shall, subject to such conditions as he may deem proper, issue a provisional certificate of registry. Provided that, unless exempted, if the ship is not in possession of valid certificates required by international Conventions, ratified or acceded to or accepted by the Government of Malta, the Registrar shall issue a non-operational provisional certificate of registry. Within one month of provisional registry, which period may for good reason be extended for a further period of two months, the owner must, unless the vessel is otherwise exempted, produce to the Registrar the following documents and evidence (art. 13(1)):

(1) a builder's certificate (in the case of a newbuilding); or, if a sale has taken place, the bill of sale or other document by which the vessel or a share therein was transferred to the applicant for registry.

(2) a deletion certificate or closed transcript of register from the previous country of registry (to be accompanied by a translation if not in the English language).[6]

18.17 Within six months of provisional registry, which may be extendable for good reason for a further period up to and not exceeding six months, the owner shall, unless the ship is otherwise exempted, produce to the Registrar the following documents and evidence:

(1) proof that the ship has been issued with such valid certificates required by international Conventions, ratified or acceded to or accepted by the Government of Malta;

---

6 The deletion certificate must be issued by the Registrar of Ships in the previous country of registry. Certificates issued by a consular or high commission official are not acceptable.

MALTA

(2) certificate of survey issued in terms of article 14 and a copy of the tonnage measurement certificate, as issued on behalf of the Government of Malta. Provided that the Registrar-General may, subject to such conditions as he may deem proper, in case of a ship which is being built, rebuilt or equipped, exempt such ship from the requirements of this paragraph for a period of one year extendable for good reason for another period of one year; and

(3) a carving and marking note issued in accordance with article 15 or evidence satisfactory to the Registrar that the vessel has been marked in accordance with the Act.

Permanent registration

18.18 When all the above items have been submitted and subject to:

(1) payment of any additional registration fees as adjusted in accordance with the tonnages established by the certificate of survey, and

(2) submission of an undertaking to return the provisional certificate of registry originally issued to the ship,

the Registrar will issue a permanent certificate of registry. If issued within the first 12 months following provisional registration, the certificate will only be valid for the remaining period of the said 12 months. As in the case of the provisional certificate of registry, a non-operational certificate of registry shall be issued by the Registrar if the vessel is not in possession of valid certificates required by international Conventions. All subsequent certificates of registry are issued for a period of 12 months provided that, within a period of three months prior to the expiry of the certificate, the Registrar shall issue a renewal certificate upon payment of the annual registration fee. For ships of 500 gross tonnage and over, certificates of registry or the respective renewal certificates of registry may be valid for a maximum period of five years.

Validity of the provisional registration and extension

18.19 Provisional registration (subject to such conditions as the Registrar may deem proper) is valid for a period of six months, provided that the Registrar may, on good cause being shown, renew the provisional registration for a further period or periods not exceeding in the aggregate six months. The Registrar may refuse to provisionally register a ship more than three times in succession in the names of different owners, and shall automatically refuse to consecutively register a ship provisionally more than twice in the name of the same owner (art. 16(5)). Prior to provisional registration of a ship, the Registrar may require such ship to be inspected by an appropriate inspector or a surveyor of ships (art. 12). The home port of every registered ship is Valletta (art. 5).

Certificate of registry in the name of the charterer or lessee

18.20 Where a ship registered under Part II of the Act is being operated under charter or is leased in any year in respect of which the charterer or the lessee shall have paid to the Registrar an amount equal to the annual registration fee for that year in addition to that paid by the owner, and such ship is not bareboat charter registered in a foreign registry, the Registrar-General, on submission of an application made by such charterer or the lessee accompanied by a copy of the charter agreement or the lease agreement and the consent in writing of the owners of the ship and all registered mortgagees may, subject to conditions, authorise the issue of a certificate of Malta registry in terms of article 19A, whether provisional or otherwise, in the name of such charterer or lessee instead of in the name of the registered owner. The copy of the charter or the lease agreement presented with the application shall not be available for public inspection.

Ship's radio licence

18.21 A provisional ship station licence will be issued with a validity period of six months from the date of issue on receipt of the relative application form for the issue of the provisional licence. A permanent GMDSS ship radio station licence will be issued with a validity period of not more than 36 calendar months on receipt of the following:

(1) the appropriate application form for the issue of the radio licence duly completed by the owner or his agent and

(2) either a copy of a valid ship safety radio certificate (including Form R) and/or a copy of a recent record of approved GMDSS radio installation issued by the ship's classification society;

(3) a copy of a valid shore-based maintenance agreement certificate in respect of GMDSS equipment on board the vessel;

(4) EPIRB test report and/or programming certificate; and

(5) LRIT conformance test report

Registration of mortgages and security interests

18.22 Mortgages shall be recorded in the Register in the order in time in which they are produced to the Registrar. Where it is stated in the mortgage instrument that it is prohibited to create further mortgages over a vessel without the prior written consent of the mortgagee, a note in the register shall be made and the Registrar shall not record further mortgages unless the consent in writing of the holder of the prior mortgage has been obtained. Where the mortgage instrument states that it is prohibited to effect the transfer of the ship, or a share therein, without the written consent of the mortgagee, a record of such condition shall be made in the ship's registry, and the Registrar will not record any transfer in the ship or allow deregistration unless such consent is produced or the transfer is made pursuant to a court order or sale by auction (art. 39). The Act specifically provides that the mortgage will attach to any proceeds from an indemnity arising from collisions and other mishaps as well as insurance proceeds (art. 38(3)).

Deregistration procedure

18.23 The registry of a Maltese ship may be closed at the request of the owner provided that all liabilities and obligations in respect of the ship towards the State of Malta have been paid and the written consent of all registered mortgagees is produced. A deletion certificate of Malta registry is issued upon surrender of the certificate of Malta registry (art. 28(2)).

Contact addresses

18.24

Merchant shipping matters and vessel registration

Registrar General of Shipping and Seamen
Merchant Shipping Directorate
Authority for Transport in Malta
Malta Transport Centre
Hal Lija LJA 2021
Malta
Tel: (356) 21250360
Fax: (356) 21241460
Email: mershipmalta.tm@transport.gov.mt
Website: www.transport.gov.mt/ship-registration

CHAPTER 19

Marshall Islands

19.1 The Republic of the Marshall Islands consists of two parallel chains of islands and atolls, roughly 800 miles long, between Hawaii and Guam in the central Pacific Ocean, with a total population of some 74,000. A former UN Trust Territory that was administered by the USA until 1986, the country is now an independent democracy with a constitution based on British and US concepts. The legislature consists of the Council of Iroij of 12 members and the Nitijela, the law-making chamber which has 33 members. The head of State is the President who is elected every four years by the Nitijela. The legal tender is the US dollar (US$).

19.2 The registry model adopted by the Marshall Islands government is outsourced and decentralised. International Registries Inc. and its affiliates, which provides administrative and technical support to the Republic of the Marshall Islands Maritime and Corporate registries is headquartered in Virginia, USA and maintains a global network of 28 worldwide offices and local representatives. The evident success of the Marshall Islands as a leading flag State suggests that such an operating model brings advantages – by 2017 the Marshall Islands had become the third largest register in the world by dead-weight tonnage with over 11% of the global merchant fleet sailing under its flag.[1] In a challenging market environment, the pace of growth of this flag State is also remarkable. Between 2016 and 2017 the registered tonnage increased by over 12%; between 2015 and 2016 by some 9%; and between 2014 and 2015 by over 11%. In June 2017, it was reported that the Marshall Islands had overtaken Liberia as the second-largest register in the world, measured by gross tonnage and by dead-weight tonnage. As of 31 January 2018, the Marshall Islands-registered fleet stood at 4,327 vessels and over 158 million gross tons. The Marshall Islands appears within the top ten best-performing flag States in both the 2017 Paris MOU and Tokyo MOU White Lists and is listed as a quality flag administration by the US Coast Guard, appearing for 13 consecutive years on the US Qualship 21 list.[2] Since June 2017, the Marshall Islands has issued certain documents and certificates in electronic format, which can be verified online using their quick response code and unique tracking number.[3]

---

1 UNCTAD, *Review of Maritime Transport* (2017), Table 2.6 – as at 1 January 2017.
2 See Appendix III.
3 See further, Marine Notice No. 1–109–1. and the authentication facility: https://verify.register-iri.com.

Sources of law

19.3 Registration of ships in the Marshall Islands is governed by the Republic of the Marshall Islands Maritime Act 1990, as amended ('the Act'). Section 103 of the Act provides for the appointment of the Republic of the Marshall Islands Maritime Administrator to administer all matters relating to vessels of the Republic engaged in foreign trade, including the promulgation of rules and regulations. The Maritime Administrator has promulgated the Republic of the Marshall Islands Maritime Regulations ('the Regulations') to expand upon the requirements of the Act. Unless otherwise stated, references in this chapter to sections and regulations are references to sections and regulations in the Act and the Regulations, respectively.

Vessel eligibility

Vessel type

19.4 Subject to the age limits mentioned below, any seagoing vessel engaged in foreign trade is eligible for registration under the Act (s.203). A vessel 'engaged in foreign trade' means any vessel not exclusively engaged in coastwise trade or transportation between atolls, islands and/or ports of the Marshall Islands. Private yachts (including private yachts limited charter and yachts engaged in trade), passenger yachts, and commercial yachts may also be registered in the Marshall Islands. Fishing vessels may only be considered for registration if operated by an entity resident in the Marshall Islands and if the vessel regularly lands its catches solely in the Republic or aboard Marshall Islands-registered processing vessels. In 2012, the Marshall Islands adopted legislation to allow for the registration of vessels under construction.

Age limits

19.5 In order to be eligible for registration, a vessel must be less than 20 years old on 1 January in the year when registration is sought. Notwithstanding the 20-year maximum age, the Maritime Administrator has the discretion to waive the age requirement when:

(1)   the vessel meets all other applicable requirements; and
(2)   it has been satisfactorily demonstrated that there is a genuine need for a waiver.

In practice, a pre-registration inspection of any vessel over 20 years of age is required before the Maritime Administrator will issue a waiver of the age limit. Additionally, a waiver will only be granted if an approved classification society has issued a certificate of confirmation of class and confirmed that it is prepared to issue all necessary statutory certificates to the vessel.

Ownership

19.6 In order to be eligible to register a vessel under the Marshall Islands flag, an owner must be either a citizen or national of the Republic, a Marshall Islands corporation, partnership, limited partnership or limited liability company, or a foreign maritime entity. A foreign maritime entity is a foreign entity such as a corporation, partnership or trust, that is registered in the Marshall Islands as such an entity (s.203). The fee for an application to register a foreign maritime entity is currently US$1,300 with an additional US$900 payable each year to maintain that status.

Company formation

19.7 If a foreign owner wishes to use a Marshall Islands corporation to acquire a vessel to be registered under the Marshall Islands flag, such a corporation will be incorporated under the Business Corporations Act. This statute is largely based on US corporation law principles, but utilises a number of features of English law such as the ability to appoint a managing director and the requirement to appoint a company secretary. Marshall Islands corporations are incorporated by the Registrar of Non-resident Domestic Corporations, the Trust Company of the Marshall Islands, Inc.

Non-resident status

19.8 A Marshall Islands non-resident domestic corporation is exempt from any taxation or exchange control in the Marshall Islands.

Registered agent

19.9 A Marshall Islands corporation, partnership, limited partnership, LLC or foreign maritime entity must maintain a registered agent in the Marshall Islands. In the case of a non-resident domestic entity or foreign maritime entity, the registered agent is statutorily mandated to be the Trust Company of the Marshall Islands, Inc.

Shareholders

19.10 A minimum of one shareholder is required. The maximum number and class of shares is determined by the articles of incorporation.

Directors and Secretary

19.11 One or more directors may be appointed. Unless the articles of incorporation provide otherwise, directors may be of any nationality and need not be resident in the Marshall Islands. Non-resident domestic corporations may elect or appoint corporations as directors. Every corporation shall have a secretary who may be a corporate entity.

Bareboat charter registration

19.12 The Act permits vessels to be 'flagged in' under a bareboat charter to the Marshall Islands. It also allows vessels already registered in the Marshall Islands to be 'flagged out' under a foreign bareboat charter to foreign registers that permit bareboat registration. Section 260 provides that a Marshall Islands corporation or a foreign maritime entity may register provisionally a vessel which it has taken on bareboat charter, provided that the following documents are filed with the Maritime Administrator:

(1) a certified copy of the bareboat charter. Any subsequent amendments or addenda shall also be submitted for recording within 30 days of execution;

(2) an official certificate from the foreign State of registration giving details of the ownership of the vessel and any registered encumbrances;

(3) the written consents of the ship-owner and any mortgagees to provisional registration in the Marshall Islands;

(4) satisfactory evidence that the foreign State of registration will withdraw from the vessel the right to fly its flag during the period of bareboat registration;

(5) an undertaking that while the vessel is granted the right to fly the Marshall Islands flag it will fly no other flag nor show any home port other than Majuro, and that the bareboat charterer will notify the Maritime Administrator if the charter is terminated or if any foreign State shall grant the vessel the right to fly its flag.

Once a bareboat charter is registered the following information will be recorded with the Maritime Administrator:

(1) the name of the vessel;

(2) the names of the bareboat charterer, ship-owner and holders of any registered mortgages, hypothecations or similar charges;

(3) the time and date of recording of the charterparty;

(4) the duration of the charterparty; and

(5) the foreign State of registration of the vessel.

When a charterparty has been recorded, an application to register has been filed and all fees and taxes paid, a certificate of provisional registration will be issued for a period of up to two years, or until the date of termination of the charterparty, if earlier. It is possible for a certificate of provisional registration to be renewed subject to the payment of the required fee plus necessary documentation for a further period of up to two years, subject to the termination date of the bareboat charter.

19.13 Section 270 provides that a vessel registered in the Marshall Islands may not be 'flagged out' to the bareboat register of a foreign State unless its owner first applies for, and receives, the permission of the Maritime Administrator. Prior to requesting such permission, an owner must file the written consent of each mortgagee to the proposed foreign bareboat charter registration. If the request is granted, the Maritime Administrator will issue a certificate of permission stating that the right to fly the Marshall Islands flag and to display Majuro as the home port has been withdrawn, and that the named foreign State is recognised as having exclusive jurisdiction and control over the vessel. Any outstanding mortgages will, however, remain in full force and effect and be governed by Marshall Islands law. The owner is required to surrender the original certificate of registry, and a new provisional certificate of registry is issued, endorsed to show that the right to fly the Marshall Islands flag has been withdrawn. An endorsed provisional certificate of registry may be reissued for a further period of up to two years, subject to the termination date of the bareboat charter, if application is made before the expiry of the previous certificate.

Trading limits

19.14 Seagoing Marshall Islands vessels that are engaged in foreign trade are not subject to any trading restrictions.

Manning requirements

19.15 Manning requirements are described in detail in Chapter 7 of the Regulations and Marine Notice No. 7–038–2 (Rev. Oct/2017) promulgated by the Maritime Administrator. The Regulations and the Marine Notice give effect to the International Convention on Standards of Training, Certification and Watchkeeping for Seafarers (STCW). The Convention was amended in 1991, 1994, 1995 (STCW 95), 1997, 2006, 2010 (Manila Amendments), 2014, 2015 and 2016. The STCW 95 amendments have been fully implemented in the Marshall Islands since 1 February 2002. The Manila Amendments came into force in the Marshall Islands on 1 January 2012, with a five-year transitional period until 1 January 2017.

Certificates of competency for officers and ratings

19.16 Officers and ratings serving on Marshall Islands-registered vessels must hold an appropriate certificate of competence issued by the Commissioner, or a Deputy Commissioner, of Maritime Affairs on behalf of the Maritime Administrator. Alternatively, a Marshall Islands endorsement certificate may be issued to an applicant who holds a certificate issued by a foreign government that complies with STCW, as amended and is approved by the Marshall Islands Government for certification purposes.

Nationality of crew

19.17 There are no nationality restrictions.

Document of safe manning (minimum safe manning certificate)

19.18 Every Marshall Islands vessel subject to the International Convention for the Safety of Life at Sea, 1974 (SOLAS) is required to have a valid minimum safe manning certificate issued by the Maritime Administrator setting forth the minimum number of officers and crew required for the safe navigation and operation of the vessel. The Maritime Administrator will conduct a review of each vessel's needs consistent with IMO Resolution A.1047(27), Principles of Safe Manning. Each vessel is considered individually, bearing in mind the size, trade, type of vessel and automation. The Maritime Administrator will only issue a minimum safe manning certificate in accordance with IMO Resolution A.1047(27) and Marshall Islands law and regulation. The minimum safe manning certificate may be withdrawn if the owner persistently fails to comply with manning requirements, including rest periods, or fails to submit new safe manning proposals when there are changes in trading area, construction, machinery or other factors that affect safe manning.

Approved classification societies

19.19 The following members of the International Association of Classification Societies are authorised agents for the purpose of issuing international Convention statutory certificates on behalf of the Republic of the Marshall Islands Maritime Administrator:

American Bureau of Shipping (ABS)
Bureau Veritas (BV)
China Classification Society (CCS)
Class NK (NK)
Croatian Register of Shipping (CRS)
DNV GL
Hellenic Register of Shipping – non-IACS member, authorized for yachts only
Indian Register of Shipping (IRS)
Korean Register (KR)
Lloyd's Register of Shipping (LR)
Polski Rejestr Statkow (PRS)
Registro Italiano Navale (RINA)
Russian Maritime Register of Shipping (RS)

Taxation

19.20 No tax is payable in the Marshall Islands upon income earned by Marshall Islands non-resident domestic entities. The Republic of the Marshall Islands is not a party to any double tax treaties.

Procedure for registration

Provisional registration

19.21 An application for registration of a ship under the Marshall Islands flag must be made by written application to the office of Maritime Administrator via one of the 28 worldwide offices of International Registries Inc. Specimen forms are provided within Appendix XI. Initial registration will normally be provisional if the ship is a newbuilding or is being transferred from another registry. The Maritime Administrator will authorise the issue of a provisional certificate of registry provided the officer receiving the application is satisfied:

(1) as to the ownership of the ship evidenced by a bill of sale or builders certificate, submitted in triplicate;

(2) that if the ship has been registered on a foreign register the government concerned has consented to the surrender of the foreign registration document, the owner has instructed the Master to surrender the foreign registration document for cancellation on receipt of the Republic of the Marshall Islands provisional certificate of registry on board, or that the foreign registration document has been legally cancelled;

(3) that the vessel is in seaworthy condition. Evidence of such condition shall be in the form of a certificate of confirmation of class, a certificate of seaworthiness or an interim certificate of class and a class statement or affidavit issued by a Maritime Administrator approved IACS approved classification society not more than ten days prior to registration. If the ship is more than 15 years old, a status report of the vessel's statutory certification and a copy of its latest intermediate or special survey must be submitted;

(4) that the initial registration fee and tonnage tax have been paid;

(5) that the ship has been marked with her name, official number, home port and draft or that instructions have been given by the owner for the Master to have such markings made on receipt of the provisional certificate of registry;

(6) that a power of attorney or corporate resolutions have given authority to the officer or agent to make the application and perform all acts necessary to complete the registration;

(7) that an oath has been sworn by the owner, managing owner, part owner, or his agent or authorised officer, in a prescribed form, giving details of the ship and its owner;

(8) that the owner has provided proof of liability insurance including for oil pollution, bunker pollution, wreck removal and for the repatriation of the crew, usually in the form of a cover note or P&I certificate of entry and individual subject-matter certificates for each relevant Convention;

(9) that an application for a minimum safe manning certificate has been made;

(10) that ISM and ISPS Code declarations have been provided relative to the company, designated person and company security officer;

(11) that the Continuous Synopsis Record amendments form and index have been provided;

(12) that the MARPOL Annex I Condition Assessment Scheme (CAS) statement of compliance and supporting documentation have been provided, as applicable;

(13) that a permission to transfer or cancellation certificate has been issued by the previous registry, as applicable;

(14) that the long-range identification and tracking (LRIT) conformance test reports have been provided; and

(15) that the vessel is free of encumbrances.

Within 90 days of registration, an application for ship radio station licence must also be submitted. For registration of second-hand tonnage, if the name of the vessel is to be changed at the time of reflagging to the Marshall Islands, then all applications should be filed using the intended new name of the vessel, and should also mention the vessel's former name in the space provided.

Validity of the provisional registration and extension

19.22 A provisional certificate of registry has the same validity and standing as a permanent certificate of registry. A Marshall Islands provisional certificate of registry is valid for a period of not more than one year, or until earlier revocation or suspension. Its validity may be extended for a further period of not more than one year if good reason is shown for an extension.

Permanent registration

19.23 The additional formalities for the permanent registration of a ship are:

(1)   a report of satisfactory completion of a Marshall Islands safety inspection;

(2)   a permanent classification certificate;

(3)   permanent international Convention certificates;

(4)   a radio station licence;

(5)   a certificate of cancellation from the previous registry (if not previously submitted); and

(6)   the completion or submission of any outstanding documentation or surveys.

Registration of mortgages and security interests

19.24 Once a ship has been registered in the Marshall Islands a valid mortgage or mortgage assignment may only be created if it is recorded with the Maritime Administrator or one of his duly appointed representatives. The record of the mortgage will include the name of the ship, the name of the parties, the time and date of receipt of the mortgage, the interest in the ship transferred or affected and the amount of the contingent obligations that are or may be secured by the mortgage. Since 2000, Marshall Islands law has permitted an outstanding previously recorded foreign mortgage to be 'tacked' on to the Marshall Islands registration, which continues the preferred status of the existing mortgage with priority ranking from the date of registration on the foreign register. To enable such a mortgage to be recorded, the original mortgage must be produced and an additional mortgage instrument signed, changing the governing law to that of the Marshall Islands. In 2013, the Act was amended to permit the recordation of a financing charter, in the form of a demise or bareboat charter, with the same priority and status as a preferred mortgage.

Surveys

19.25 There is normally no requirement for physical inspection of a ship by the Marshall Islands Maritime Administrator prior to registration; however, a physical inspection must be carried out prior to the issuance of a permanent certificate of registry. Bulk carriers of 15 years of age or more and all other vessels of 20 years of age and more are required to undergo a pre-registration inspection prior to registration.

Deregistration procedure

19.26 The owner of a Marshall Islands vessel must apply for 'permission to transfer' in order to start the procedure for transferring its registration out of the Marshall Islands. Prior to being issued with a cancellation certificate, the owner must surrender the certificate of registry and radio station licence, CSR amendment forms, and minimum safe manning certificate issued to the vessel, submit one copy of the bill of sale, confirm the satisfaction, release or discharge of any recorded mortgage, and pay any outstanding fees due to the Maritime Administrator.

Yachts

19.27 In 2001, in response to international demand, the Marshall Islands Government expanded the Registry to allow the registration of private, passenger and commercial yachts in the Marshall Islands. At the end of January 2018 there were a total of 536 yachts registered in the Marshall Islands, amounting to 12% of the Marshall Islands flagged fleet by number of vessels.

19.28 Commercial yachts are registered in generally the same way as merchant vessels. The Marshall Islands Yacht Code (MI-103) sets out the conditions for registration and outlines the requirements for the construction, equipment, machinery, and stability of commercial yachts, passenger yachts, private yachts limited charter, and yachts engaged in trade (a type of private yacht registration). Yacht owners may select Jaluit or Bikini, Marshall Islands as the home port for registration purposes.

19.29 Private yachts of 12 metres or more in length are eligible to be registered in the Marshall Islands. A unique feature of the Marshall Islands regulations is that a private yacht (registered as a private yacht limited charter) may be chartered out on a commercial basis for up to 84 days each year without the need to be registered as a commercial yacht, subject to certain additional safety requirements that do not apply to yachts solely used for private purposes. Additionally, a private yacht (registered as eligible to be a yacht engaged in trade) which meets all commercial yacht requirements, may charter in certain EU waters without registering as a commercial yacht. Private yachts flagged in the Marshall Islands are eligible to obtain a US cruising licence permitting such vessels to cruise in US coastal waters without the need for formal entry and customs clearance at each port of call in the USA. A US cruising licence can be obtained from US Customs at the first port of entry in the USA and will normally be valid for one year.

Contact addresses

19.30
Republic of the Marshall Islands Maritime Administrator
c/o Marshall Islands Maritime and Corporate Administrators, Inc.
11495 Commerce Park Drive
Reston, Virginia 20191–1507
USA
Tel: +1 703 620 4880
Fax: +1 703 476 8522
Email: info@register-iri.com

New York

Republic of the Marshall Islands Maritime Administrator
c/o International Registries, Inc.
1500 Broadway, 20th Floor
New York, New York 10036437 USA
Tel: +1 212 486 0042
Fax: +1 212 486 5313
Email: newyork@register-iri.com

London

Republic of the Marshall Islands Maritime Administrator
c/o International Registries (U.K.) Limited
3rd Floor
42 Moorgate
London EC2R 6EL
UK
Tel: +44 (0)20 7638 4748
Fax: +44 (0)20 7382 7820
Email: london@register-iri.com]

Piraeus

Republic of the Marshall Islands Maritime Administrator
c/o International Registries, Inc.
47–49 Akti Miaouli Street
Livanos Building, 8th Floor
Tel: +30 210 4293 223
Fax: +30 210 4293 228
Email: piraeus@register-iri.com

Hong Kong

Republic of the Marshall Islands Maritime Administrator
c/o International Registries (Far East) Limited
2210 Harbour Centre
25 Harbour Road
Wanchai, Hong Kong
Tel: +852 2526 6641
Fax: +852 2845 0172
Email: hongkong@register-iri.com

Other offices are maintained in Baltimore, Busan, Dalian, Dubai, Ft. Lauderdale, Geneva, Hamburg, Hong Kong (Gloucester Road), Houston, Imabari, Istanbul, Long Beach, Manila, Mumbai, New York (Downtown), Rio de Janeiro, Roosendaal, Seoul, Shanghai, Singapore, Taipei, Tokyo, and Zurich. To reach most of these offices by email the reader should insert the name of the city followed by @register-iri.com or go to www.register-iri.com for the most up-to-date contact information.

CHAPTER 20

Norway

20.1 The Kingdom of Norway has one of the longest coastlines in the world, facing the North Sea from the Skagerrak in the south and extending north beyond the Arctic Circle. A glaciated, mountainous territory, its recent economic history owes much to the rich oil and gas reserves within its sphere of influence. The country has a constitutional monarchy and the legal system is a blend of customary law, civil and common law traditions. The national currency of Norway is the Krone (NOK).

20.2 Norway has a long-established maritime heritage, and is also one of the foremost remaining shipbuilding nations in western Europe. The Norwegian International Ship Register (NIS) is the country's second register, launched in 1987, and the NIS fleet is now the 13th largest in the world by dead-weight tonnage.[1] References to the Register throughout this chapter refer to NIS, not the domestic Norwegian ordinary register known as NOR. Since 2012, both the Norwegian ship registers (NIS and NOR) are administered by the Norwegian Maritime Authority's Department of Ship Registration in Bergen. The NMA's headquarters is located in Haugesund. In April 2017, the Norwegian Maritime Authority signed a joint memorandum of understanding with the Danish Maritime Authority and the Maritime and Port Authority of Singapore promoting the mutual recognition of electronic certificates under their respective flags for port entry and Port State Control inspections, as well as the sharing of information and experiences relating to issuance, use and acceptance of such certificates. The NIS appears within the top ten best-performing flag States in the 2017 Paris MOU White List.[2]

Sources of law

20.3 The registration of vessels in NIS is governed by the Act of 12 June 1987 No.48 establishing a Norwegian International Ship Register as amended up to the Act of 9 May 2014 No. 16 ('the NIS Act') and by the Norwegian Maritime Code of 24 June 1994 No.39 as amended up to the Act of 17 June 2016 No.71. Unless otherwise stated, all references to sections in this chapter are references to sections of the NIS Act. Ships registered in NIS fly the Norwegian flag and are subject to Norwegian jurisdiction (s.3).

---

1 UNCTAD, *Review of Maritime Transport* (2017), Table 2.6. The concept and practice of second registers is discussed fully in Chapter 4.

2 See Appendix III.

216

Vessel eligibility

Vessel type

20.4 Self-propelled passenger and cargo ships, hovercraft, drilling platforms and other moveable installations may be registered (s.1).

Age limits

20.5 Neither the Norwegian Maritime Code nor the NIS Act specify a maximum age of vessels which are permitted to be registered. Rather, the NIS requires a SOLAS certificate issued by an approved classification society or by the Norwegian Maritime Authority to be submitted with all applications for registration. This requirement establishes a basic minimum threshold of suitability and necessitates an independent assessment of a vessel's construction, intended to deter the very oldest tonnage.

Ownership

20.6 A vessel registered in NIS may be owned by Norwegian or non-Norwegian persons or companies. Section 1 of the NIS Act permits registration of vessels by non-Norwegian owners who have appointed a representative who satisfies the nationality requirements of the Maritime Code, and who is authorised to accept service of writs on behalf of the owner. The technical or commercial management must also be carried out by a Norwegian shipping company with its head office in Norway or by one of its management offices abroad. Non-Norwegian owners must submit a notarised and legalised certificate of registration, secretary's certificate, or certificate of good standing which contains details of the name and type of company, registered office, share capital and appointed directors.

Bareboat charter registration

20.7 The NIS Act does not currently permit the 'flagging-in' or the 'flagging-out' of bareboat chartered vessels to or from the Norwegian flag.

Trading limits

20.8 Traditionally, vessels registered in NIS have not been permitted to carry cargo or passengers between Norwegian ports, which for this purpose include oil and gas installations on the Norwegian continental shelf (s.4). Separate regulations govern offshore vessels serving such installations. Nor have vessels registered in NIS been able to engage in regular scheduled passenger transport between Norwegian and foreign ports. At the beginning of 2016, these restrictions were relaxed to the following extent:

(1) Cargo ships are now permitted to carry cargo between ports on Svalbard and between Svalbard and the mainland.
(2) Cargo ships where a significant part of the ship's activities takes place outside of Norwegian waters are permitted to carry cargo between Norwegian ports as

a part of a regular route between a Norwegian and a foreign port or as carriage of petroleum in bulk from a unit on the Norwegian continental shelf or occasionally for up to three months. The Norwegian Maritime Authority controls that the conditions are satisfied.

(3) Extension of trade area for special cargo ships: In addition to the trade area extension above, cargo ships constructed or equipped to carry special types of cargo are permitted to carry such cargo between Norwegian ports when the ship is en route to or from a foreign port and the carriage does not form part of a regular scheduled service. The Master must be a Norwegian national or a national of an EEA country. It is a condition that such carriage leads to a rational utilisation of the tonnage available, and does not involve undesirable consequences for ships registered in the Norwegian Ordinary Ship Register.

(4) Construction vessels are permitted to trade between Norwegian ports, including on the Norwegian continental shelf.

In this context, a construction vessel means any vessel engaged in construction activities, subsea operations, pipe laying or maintenance of units. The changes in trade areas for vessels in the NIS are connected to the strengthening of the current subsidy for employment of seafarers both for NIS and NOR ships in that, according to various models, the company will receive grants for payment of advanced tax deduction, social security contributions and payroll taxes.

Manning requirements

20.9 The statutory manning requirements of NIS are determined by the Norwegian Maritime Authority. The legislative source of these requirements is the Norwegian Regulation of 18 June 2009 No. 666 which in turn is based on IMO Resolution A.890(21) 'Principles of Safe Manning'. The NMA is determined to support tripartite co-operation and therefore requires that employee representatives are involved in the application process. The proposed safe manning shall cover all relevant operations, tasks and functions required to safely operate the ship. In the application, the ship-owner must substantiate that the crew members proposed for safe manning are capable of carrying out these responsibilities. Safe manning is the minimum manning level a ship may have in order to operate – the NMA regulation must not be understood to be a regulation determining the correct manning in all situations.

Certificates of competency for officers and ratings

20.10 Details of the officers and crew serving on board NIS vessels must be recorded in the State Register of Employers and Employees (Aa-registeret). The Norwegian-issued certificate of competency is granted based on education in terms of STCW 1995 at a maritime academy in Norway approved by the Maritime Authority. The Maritime Authority may endorse certificates of competency issued by foreign flag States with whom the Norwegian Government has a reciprocal agreement. Applications for endorsements may now be submitted online.

Nationality of crew

20.11 There are no nationality restrictions concerning the employment of non-Norwegian seafarers on board NIS-registered vessels, with the exception of the Master, who should hold Norwegian citizenship. Applications for a dispensation from this requirement may, however, be directed to the Norwegian Maritime Authority.

Document of safe manning

20.12 The number of deck officers and engineers deemed necessary for the safe manning and operation of an NIS-registered vessel is prescribed in respect of each ship individually by the Norwegian Maritime Authority.

Approved classification societies

20.13 The following six classification societies are approved by the Norwegian Maritime Directorate for the purpose of surveys and the issue of statutory certificates:

American Bureau of Shipping (ABS)
Bureau Veritas (BV)
DNV GL
Lloyd's Register of Shipping (LR)
Nippon Kaiji Kyokai (Class NK)
RINA

Taxation

20.14 Since the 2007 tax year, the profits of ship-owners whose vessels are registered in NIS have been exempt from taxation. A tonnage tax system is instead applied to the income from ownership, leasing and operations of qualifying vessels.

Procedure for registration

20.15 Specimen forms are provided within Appendix XI. Applications for registration in NIS should be made to the Department of Ship Registration in Bergen by the submission of the following forms and documents:

(1) application to reserve the name of the vessel;
(2) notification form stating nationality of intended owner;
(3) international tonnage certificate issued by an approved classification society or the Maritime Authority;
(4) SOLAS confirmation or confirmation of survey issued by an approved classification society or the Maritime Authority;
(5) bill of sale or builder's certificate, together with the original documents evidencing the progress of title to the vessel since last registration;
(6) certificate of deletion from prior registry;

(7) application for Continuous Synopsis Record;
(8) for newbuild vessels, the protocol of delivery and acceptance between the builder and the owner;
(9) for foreign owners, appointment of a norwegian representative;
(10) declaration of nationality for the Norwegian owner or, for foreign owners, their Norwegian representative;
(11) company documentation for non-Norwegian owners, notarised and apostilled or legalised;
(12) certified true copy of the management agreement (the greater part of the technical or commercial management must be done by a Norwegian management company) between the owner and a Norwegian management company; and
(13) notification of assignment or responsibilities imposed by the ISM Code.

20.16 Title documents, company certificates and powers of attorney must be notarised to verify the identity and authority of the signatory and thereafter legalised by a Norwegian consulate or by the attachment of an apostille. Company certificates (such as secretary's certificates) must also be notarised with regards to the given information. Deletion certificates from foreign flag States must be also legalised with an apostille. All foreign-language documents must be issued in English, a Scandinavian language, or translated by an official translator.

20.17 Registration may take place upon submission of PDF copies of the documents provided by email. Final registration will depend on receipt of the originals within three weeks of annotation. Ship mortgages must, however, be submitted in original before they can be entered into the journal of the Norwegian ship registers.

Registration of preferred mortgages and security interests

20.18 The Norwegian Maritime Act permits the registration of encumbrances over a ship registered in NIS, described as "documents concerning the creation, amendment to, transfer, mortgaging, acknowledgement or setting aside of a right, the object of which is a registered vessel". The original mortgage deed, the signature of which must be authenticated by two Norwegian-resident witnesses or a notary public, must be submitted to NIS for registration. The signature of the notary public must be legalised by a Norwegian consulate or by the attachment of an apostille. Any subsequent encumbrances must be submitted endorsed with the consent of the prior mortgagee.

Deregistration procedure

20.19 A vessel registered with NIS may be deleted from the Register by written application signed by the owner of the vessel stating the reasons for deletion. Deletion is compulsory where the vessel is re-registered in a foreign flag State; or where the vessel is lost, broken up, or sold for breaking up to a foreign owner. If the vessel is being sold to be registered in a foreign flag State, the applicant owner must also submit an original or notarised true copy of the bill of sale. Deletion from NIS requires the written consent of any mortgagee.

Contact addresses

20.20

The Department of Ship Registration (NIS & NOR)

Street address

Nygårdstangen 114
5008 Bergen
Norway

Postal address

PO Box 73 Nygårdstangen
N-5838 Bergen
Norway
Phone: + 47 55 54 12 50
Website: www.sjofartsdir.no
Email: post@nis-nor.no

Norwegian Maritime Authority

Street address

Smedasundet 50 A
5528 Haugesund
Norway

Postal address

PO Box 2222
N-5509
Haugesund
Norway
Phone: + 47 52 74 50 00
Fax: + 47 52 74 50 01
Website: www.sjofartsdir.no
Email: postmottak@sjofartsdir.no

CHAPTER 21

Panama

21.1 Panama is situated on the isthmus connecting the continents of North and South America, the Panama Canal linking the Caribbean Sea with the Pacific Ocean. The country has a population of 3.7 million, more than 1.6 million of whom live in the capital, Panama City. Panama gained its independence from Colombia in 1903 and is now a republic. A number of US military bases near the Panama Canal, and the canal itself, was transferred to Panama in December 1999. Between 2007 and 2016 the canal was widened to double the transit capacity, creating a new 'post-Panamax' category of vessel. The government of the Republic of Panama consists of a legislative assembly, an executive branch with executive power vested in the President, assisted by a Vice-President and an appointed cabinet, and a judicial branch. The legal tender is the Balboa, but following a treaty of 1904 US currency is used. Balboa paper currency is not printed, only coins.

21.2 Panama is the largest register in the world by dead-weight tonnage with over 18% of the global merchant fleet sailing under its flag.[1] The flag State appears within the Paris MOU White List published in July 2017.[2] Since October 2017, the Panama flag administration has agreed to the issuance of certain documents and certificates in electronic format, which can be verified online using an online resource and unique QR codes shown on each electronic certificate.[3]

Sources of law

21.3 Law No. 8 of 1925 of the Republic of Panama created the National Merchant Marine which is the foundation of Panama's open registry system. The 'dual registry system' was introduced as a result of Law No. 11 of 1973, as amended by Law No. 83 of 1973. The law relating to the registration and validity of ship mortgages was changed by Law No. 14 of 1980 and Law No. 43 of 1984. All these statutes have now been incorporated into Law No. 57 of 2008 on the National Merchant Marine and Law No. 55 of 2008 which replaces the whole of Book II of the Code of Commerce of Panama, now known as the Law on Maritime Commerce.

---

1 UNCTAD, *Review of Maritime Transport* (2017), Table 2.6.
2 See Appendix III.
3 Merchant Marine Circulars MMC-347 and MMC-355.

Vessel eligibility

Vessel type

21.4 Vessels and floating structures of any size, age or type may be enrolled on the Panamanian flag.

Age limits

21.5 Vessels engaged in commercial trade that are over 20 years old on first registration are subject to a safety inspection by the Directorate of Safety at Sea of the Panama Maritime Authority ('SEGUMAR') as a precondition of issue of a certificate of permanent registry. Thereafter an inspection is required on an annual basis.

Ownership

21.6 A Panamanian-registered vessel may either be owned by a Panamanian or foreign national who may be an individual, a corporation or other legal entity.

Company formation

21.7 If a foreign ship-owner wishes to use a Panamanian company as the owner of a vessel to be registered in Panama, a company can be incorporated within 2–4 days or can be purchased from a local law firm or company registration agent. The relevant law is set out in Law No. 32 of 1927.

Registered office and non-resident status

21.8 A company must have a lawyer or law firm actung as registered agent of the company. A registered office is not required, other than to verify that the company's domicile is Panama, and service of notice should be made personally on the president of the company or whoever in the board is designated as legal representative. A company which does not conduct business in the Republic of Panama will be treated as non-resident in Panama.

Shareholders

21.9 A Panamanian company requires two subscribers on incorporation, but may subsequently have only one shareholder. Shares may be issued to named shareholders, or as bearer shares. The issuance of bearer shares is now subject to a custody regime, as created by Law No. 47 of 2013, as modified by Law No. 18 of 2015, and if the company chooses to issue bearer shares, these must be placed with a custodian (which can be duly authorised lawyer, law firm or bank) together with a sworn document confirming the name of the ultimate beneficial owner. There is no restriction on the nationality of shareholders.

Directors and secretary

21.10 A minimum of three directors and three officers are required (president, treasurer and secretary). The minimum three officer positions may be held by one person and the officers may also be directors. Their nationality or place of residence is irrelevant. A corporation may now act as a director and officer of a Panamanian company (Law No. 5 of 1997). No secretary is required to be appointed.

Bareboat charter registration

21.11 Panama was among the first maritime nations to permit the 'flagging-in' of vessels, sometimes known in Panama as the 'dual registry system'. The original system under Law No. 11 of 1973 was repealed by Law No. 57 of 2008, under which now a foreign flag vessel that is subject to a bareboat charter may be registered in Panama for renewable periods without abandoning the primary registration. In such cases the vessel is entered in a Special Register in the joint names of the owner and charterer and is issued with a special navigation licence. The licence will refer to the port of registry in the State of primary registration and will also include details of any mortgages or other encumbrances recorded on the primary register.

21.12 In order to register a vessel on the Special Register, a certified copy of the original bareboat charterparty, the consent of the ship-owner, the primary flag State authority and any mortgagees must be filed with the Directorate General of Merchant Marine ('DIGEMAR') in Panama City, together with a certificate showing the registration in the primary register. During the period of such registration, ownership title may not be recorded, nor any mortgages or encumbrances. Mortgages recorded in the State of primary registration remain subject to the law of that State.

21.13 By virtue of Law No. 83 of 1973, as repealed by Law No. 57 of 2008, a vessel registered in the ordinary way in Panama and subject to a bareboat charterparty may be flagged out to a foreign registry without losing its underlying Panamanian registration, provided the government of the State of secondary registration permits dual registration. The permission of DIGEMAR must also be obtained. A vessel which is 'flagged out' from Panama remains subject to Panamanian fiscal and legal obligations. Ownership title or mortgages may not be recorded on the foreign register on penalty of annulment of the Panamanian primary registration.

Special registration

21.14 The facility of short (three months) or 'single voyage' registration is available in Panama, which can be extremely effective for a ship-owner requiring short-term solutions for a particular project. Special (lower) fees and requirements are applicable for this type of registration.

Trading limits

21.15 Vessels registered in Panama are not subject to any trading limits.

Manning requirements

21.16 The interpretation and implementation of manning requirements is the responsibility of SEGUMAR. Panama has instituted a number of innovative standards in safe manning that have become widely emanated and accepted. Panama was one of the first administrations to accept the use of general purpose ratings, bringing down the total manning on some large container ships to 12 crew; to adopt the reduction of one engineering officer and one motorman for vessels designated for unmanned machinery space operations and to exempt vessels over 1,600 GRT from carrying a radio telegraph operator if the vessel's operations are always carried on within 200 miles of land.

Certificates of competency for officers and ratings

21.17 Every officer serving on board Panamanian registered ships of over 200 gross tons is required to hold a certificate of competency issued by the DIGEMAR permitting the holder to perform the duties corresponding with the position described in such certificate. Alternatively, DIGEMAR will issue endorsement certificates to holders of certificates of competency issued by the national maritime organisations of countries that are included in the International Maritime Organisation STCW White List.[4] Distinct from the White/Grey/Black lists published by Port State Control organisations, this White List is a list of IMO Member States which are considered, for the purpose of mutual recognition by other flag States, to comply by giving 'full and complete effect' to the minimum competency requirements laid down by the 1995 Amendments to the International Convention on Standards of Training, Certification and Watchkeeping for Seafarers.[5]

Nationality of crew

21.18 According to Article 266 of the Panamanian Labour Code, at least 10% of a vessel's crew must be Panamanians. However, owing to the difficulty of recruiting a sufficient number of Panamanian seafarers, this is not insisted upon.

Document of safe manning

21.19 Every passenger and cargo vessel of more than 500 GRT registered under the Panamanian flag is required to have on board a minimum safe manning certificate. Such certificates can be obtained on application to SEGUMAR and accompanied by the applicable payment of their fees. An application must include the proposed manning of the vessel in the deck and engine departments, both officers and ratings, showing numbers and grades. It must also contain full particulars of the vessel, its propulsion system and power output, the nature of service and the trading area that might affect the normal

---

4 Merchant Marine Circular MMC-343.
5 See Appendix IV.

manning requirements. Once issued, a certificate is valid indefinitely, unless a change of equipment or trading circumstances occurs. It is the responsibility of the ship-owner to notify DIGEMAR if a change of circumstances occurs which might affect the safe manning of a vessel.

Approved classification societies

21.20 The following organisations are recognised by the Panama flag State as approved for the issuance of certificates to Panamanian vessels:[6]

American Bureau of Shipping (ABS)
Bureau Veritas (BV)
China Classification Society (CCS)
CR Classification Society
Croatian Register of Shipping
DNV GL
Dromon Bureau of Shipping
Hellenic Register of Shipping (HRS)
Indian Register of Shipping
Intermaritime Certification Services, S.A.
International Naval Survey Bureau
International Register of Shipping (Panama) Inc.
Isthmus Bureau of Shipping, S.A.
Korean Register of Shipping (KRS)
Lloyd's Register of Shipping (LR)
Macosnar Corporation
National Shipping Adjuster Inc.
Nippon Kaiji Kyokai (NKK)
Overseas Marine Certification Services, Inc.
Panama Maritime Documentation Services, Inc.
Panama Shipping Registrar Inc.
Phoenix Register of Shipping
Polski Rejestr Statkow (PRS)
Qualitas Register of Shipping
Registro Italiano Navale (RINA Services S.p.A)
Russian Maritime Register of Shipping
Türk Loydu

Taxation

21.21 A non-resident Panamanian company is not liable to pay any income or other taxes in Panama, apart from the annual government corporate tax.

---

6 Merchant Marine Circular MMC-284.

Double tax treaties

21.22 The Republic of Panama has signed treaties to prevent double taxation with: Barbados, Czech Republic, France, Ireland, Israel, Italy, Luxemburg, Mexico, Netherlands, Portugal, Qatar, Singapore, South Korea, Spain, United Arab Emirates and the UK; as well as tax information exchange treaties with Canada, Denmark, Faroe Islands, Finland, Greenland, Iceland, Japan, Norway, Sweden and the USA.

Procedure for registration

Provisional registration

21.23 An application for a provisional navigation licence (patente provisional de navegación) can be made to DIGEMAR through a Panamanian law firm, to be issued either at a Panamanian consulate or in Panama. It must contain particulars of the vessel, her owners, former registry, her IMO number, classification society, the name of the law firm in Panama appointed as legal representative of the vessel and the authority responsible for radio accounts. Specimen forms are provided within Appendix XI. The application must be accompanied by the following documents:

(1) notice of the name proposed for the vessel;
(2) a power of attorney from the owner in favour of the law firm handling the registration and being appointed as legal representative for the vessel;
(3) a deletion or cancellation certificate from any previous registry;
(4) evidence of title in the form of a builder's certificate in the case of a newbuilding, or a bill of sale in other cases. In either case, an original and two certified copies are required, all of which should be notarially attested and legalised. The builder's certificate or bill of sale must either be endorsed with the new owner's acceptance, or a separate document prepared containing such acceptance. Where no change of ownership has occurred prior to provisional registration under the Panamanian flag, a certified true copy of the previous certificate of registry will suffice; and
(5) safety certificates carried by the vessel in order to comply with the relevant international Conventions;

21.24 On receipt of the required information and payment of the prescribed fees, DIGEMAR will authorise the issue of a provisional patente entitling the vessel to fly the Panamanian flag. The provisional patente may be issued by DIGEMAR to the vessel's lawyers in Panama or through a Panamanian consulate. It should be noted that a provisional patente is not a document of title, as title is only capable of registration when the relevant documents are recorded in the Public Registry in Panama City. As a result, no mortgages may be registered until an owner's title has been recorded. To overcome this problem, Law No. 14 of 1980, as amended by Law No. 43 of 1984 and by Law No. 55 of 2008, introduced a system whereby title documents and mortgages can be preliminarily recorded in Panama or through one of the principal Panamanian consulates abroad. A preliminary recording by a consul has the same validity as a final recording in the Public Registry, except that the registration is valid for only six months. This period gives an owner sufficient time to complete protocolisation and registration in Panama.

Validity of the provisional registration and extension

21.25 A provisional patente is valid for six months. If an owner is unable to deliver to DIGEMAR within the six months all necessary documents leading to permanent registration, a three-month extension may be granted on payment of a fixed penalty and a monthly fee.

Permanent registration

21.26 The issue of a permanent patente will be authorised by DIGEMAR when the following documents are delivered to the Bureau:

(1) the original builder's certificate, bill of sale or other document of title, having been received in Panama by the lawyers acting as resident agent for the vessel and translated into Spanish (if necessary), protocolised before a Panamanian notary and registered in the Public Registry in Panama City;

(2) a deletion or cancellation certificate from the vessel's former registry, notarially attested and legalised;

(3) a power of attorney in favour of lawyers in Panama City appointing them as resident agents in respect of the vessel, notarially attested and legalised;

(4) a tonnage measurement certificate issued by an approved classification society on behalf of the Panamanian Government;

(5) safety certificate issued by an approved classification society on behalf of the Panamanian Government and submitted to the Shipping Bureau;

(6) an application for a permanent radio licence.

A permanent patente is valid for four years in the case of a merchant vessel and two years in the case of a yacht.

Registration of mortgages and security interests

21.27 It has been already mentioned that the issue of a provisional patente does not amount to registration of title and that a ship-owner's title is not complete until the bill of sale or other document of title has been recorded in the Public Registry in Panama City. In the past, difficulties arose because mortgages could not be registered until completion of registration of the ship-owner's title. However, Law No. 14 of 1980, as amended by Law No. 43 of 1984 and Law No. 55 of 2008, permits the preliminary registration of a ship mortgage through one of the principal Panamanian consulates outside Panama or by the attorney in Panama. Such preliminary recordings are valid for a period of six months and give the same priority as a final recording of a mortgage in the Public Registry. Once a mortgage has been preliminarily registered it must be sent to Panama to be protocolised and registered in the Public Registry to achieve final registration. If final registration has not taken place within six months, the preliminary registration will be cancelled. Documents creating, amending, assigning and releasing mortgages may be preliminarily registered through a Panamanian consulate or in Panama in a similar manner.

Surveys

21.28 A vessel over 20 years old is required to pass a special safety inspection by an authorised Panamanian inspector before a permanent patente is issued. Thereafter, such an inspection must be carried out annually. Inspections are carried out by the Department of Maritime Safety (SEGUMAR), which has offices in New York, Panama and Tokyo and a network of authorised inspectors worldwide.

Deregistration procedure

21.29 A ship-owner can apply for deregistration in Panama through a law firm, subject to discharge of any outstanding mortgage and providing information on the vessel's buyer and new registry or confirmation that the vessel is to be scrapped and payment of a fee for deletion from the register.

Contact addresses

21.30

Directorate General of Merchant Marine (DIGEMAR)
Head Office
PO Box 0843–0533 Balboa, Ancon
Republic of Panama
Tel: +507 501 5006
Fax: +507 501 5007
Email: dgmercante@amp.gob.pa

Directorate of Safety at Sea (SEGUMAR)
Head Office
PO Box 0843–0533 Balboa, Ancon
Republic of Panama
Tel: +507 501 5361/62/50
Fax: +507 501 5363/64
Email: msm@segumar.com
Web: www.segumar.com

Consulate General of Panama
Panama House
40 Hertford Street
London
W1J 7SH
Tel: +44 20 7409 2255
Fax: +44 20 7493 4499

Dubai

SEGUMAR
PO Box 2121, Kanoo Group Building
Office 204, 2nd Floor
Trade Center Road
Burjuman

Dubai
UAE
Tel: +971 43 37 25 38
Email: segumar.dubai@segumar.com

London

SEGUMAR
40 Hertford Street
W1J 7SH
London
Tel: +44 207 629 3650
Email: segumar.uk@segumar.com

Manila

SEGUMAR
Suite 11B, 11th floor, National Life Insurance Company Bldg.
6762 Ayala Avenue
Makati City 1200
PO Box 1072, Makati CPO
Philippines
Tel: +63 2 834 2391
Email: segumar.manila@segumar.com

Miami

SEGUMAR
One Biscayne Tower, Suite 2410
Two South Biscayne Boulevard
Miami
Florida 33131
USA
Tel: +1 212 869 6440
Email: segumar.miami@segumar.com

Singapore

SEGUMAR
41–06 Hong Leong Building
16 Raffles Quay
Singapore
048581
Tel: +65 62 21 86 77
Email: segumar.sg@segumar.com

Tokyo

SEGUMAR
Kowa Building No.38, Room 805
Nishi-Azabu 4–12–24
Minato-ku
Tokyo 106–0031
Japan
Tel: +81 03 35 85–3661
Email: sguevara@panaconsul-tokyo.com

CHAPTER 22

Singapore

22.1 The Republic of Singapore is an island city State located between Malaysia and Indonesia. Founded by Sir Stamford Raffles as a British trading colony in 1819, it has long been the focal point of south-east Asian sea routes. Singapore achieved independence from the Malaysian Federation in 1965 and has a written constitution and a legal system based on English common law. English is the official administrative language of the country. With a population of around six million, it is a prosperous and successful financial services and transportation hub. The free market economy depends heavily on exports, and the port of Singapore is one of the busiest in the world in terms of tonnage handled. The local currency is the Singapore Dollar (SGD).

22.2 The Singapore Registry of Ships was established in 1966 and is operated as a division of the Maritime and Port Authority (MPA) of Singapore, a statutory board created by the Maritime and Port Authority of Singapore Act 1996. The Singapore flag State is not an open registry because it restricts ownership to Singapore nationals or companies. With certain exceptions, the Singapore-incorporated company may, however, have foreign ownership or control but the management of the vessel must be Singapore-resident. In this way it is a leading example of a closed register and has been successful in this model. By 2017, it was the fifth largest register in the world by dead-weight tonnage with over 6% of the global merchant fleet.[1] In April 2017, MPA signed a joint memorandum of understanding with the Danish Maritime Authority and the Norwegian Maritime Authority promoting the mutual recognition of electronic certificates under their respective flags for port entry and Port State Control inspections, as well as the sharing of information and experiences relating to issuance, use and acceptance of such certificates.

Sources of law

22.3 The registration of vessels under the Singapore flag is governed by the Merchant Shipping Act 1996 (Act 7 of 1996, Cap. 179) as amended. Unless otherwise stated, all references to sections in this chapter are references to sections of the Merchant Shipping Act.

---

1 UNCTAD, *Review of Maritime Transport* (2017), Table 2.6.

Vessel eligibility

Vessel type

22.4 The statutory definition of a ship is "any kind of vessel used in navigation by water, however propelled or moved" and includes barges, lighters, air-cushion vehicles and mobile offshore drilling units.

Age limits

22.5 Vessels will not generally be eligible for registration in Singapore if they are more than 17 years old.

Ownership

22.6 A Singapore-registered vessel must be owned by a citizen or permanent resident of Singapore, or a company incorporated in Singapore with a minimum paid-up share capital of SGD 50,000. A Singapore incorporated company in which more than 50% of its equity is owned by non-citizens of Singapore, is described as a 'foreign owned company'. Such companies are permitted to register any self-propelled vessels of not less than 1,600 GT. Applications by a foreign-owned company to allow registration of a vessel which is not self-propelled or which is of less than 1,600 GT may be requested from the MPA if the vessel is proved to be operated from or based in Singapore.

Company formation

22.7 The formation and operation of Singapore companies is governed by the Companies Act (2006, Revised Edition, Cap. 50). Every Singaporean company is required to have a registered office in Singapore.

Shareholders

22.8 As described above, a distinction is drawn between locally owned and foreign-owned Singapore incorporated companies. A Singapore company need only have one shareholder. There is no restriction on a shareholder's nationality. The shareholder can be a natural person or a company. However, if the Singapore company intends to register any vessel with the MPA, it must have a minimum paid-up capital of SGD 50,000. Further, in the event that the Singapore company intends to register a vessel with tonnage of less than 1,600 GT or a vessel which is not self-propelled, such as a dumb barge, then the majority of the issued share capital of the company must be owned by Singapore citizens, Singapore permanent residents, or by Singapore companies whose majority shareholding is held by Singaporeans or Singapore permanent residents, unless a specific waiver to this requirement is obtained from the MPA.

Directors

22.9 A Singapore company must have a minimum of one director who must be ordinarily resident in Singapore. Corporate directors are not allowed in Singapore.

Secretary

22.10 Every Singapore company must have a company secretary. If the Singapore company has only one director, this sole director cannot also perform the role of the company secretary. The nationality of a company secretary is immaterial, save that he or she must be ordinarily resident in Singapore and save that the directors of the company have to take all reasonable steps to ensure that the company secretary has the requisite knowledge and experience to discharge his duties.

Returns and accounts

22.11 Singapore companies are required to file an annual return each year with the Accounting and Corporate Regulatory Authority of Singapore (ACRA), showing, *inter alia*, the summary of the share capital and shares and the company's financial highlights. The company's audited accounts (where the company's revenue exceeds SGD 10 million) or unaudited accounts (where the company's revenue does not exceed SGD 10 million) must also be filed at ACRA, together with the annual return.

Bareboat charter registration

22.12 Singapore law permits the 'flagging-out' of bareboat chartered vessels from the Singapore flag on satisfying the documentary requirements and procedures described below and upon payment of the appropriate fee. The Registrar of Singapore Ships has the discretion to allow 'flagging-in' of vessels which are primary registered in another State on a case-by-case basis.

Flagging-out

22.13 An application to 'flag-out' a Singapore-registered vessel to a foreign bareboat charter registry will require the owner to submit documents to the MPA, namely:

(1) a completed application form;
(2) the return of the certificate of Singapore registry;
(3) a certified transcript of registry or similar document evidencing the bareboat registration in the vessel in the secondary flag State; and
(4) a certified true copy of the bareboat charterparty.

Provisional suspension of the Singapore registration of the vessel may be granted upon payment of the requisite fee in circumstances where these documents may be unavailable at the time of the bareboat charter-out application, upon the condition that such documents are provided within 60 days. During the period of suspension of the Singapore registration of the vessel, the Merchant Shipping Act ceases to apply, save for provision relating to the property of the vessel and any registered mortgages. In this way both proprietary and security interests are maintained intact and subject to Singapore law throughout the period of bareboat charter-out. During the period of suspension, annual tonnage tax continues to be payable in respect of the vessel to the Singapore Registry.

Trading limits

22.14 There are no trading restrictions for Singapore flag vessels.

Manning requirements

22.15 Manning requirements are set out in the Merchant Shipping (Training, Certification and Manning) Regulations 1998. For vessels above 3,000 GT the minimum number of certificated deck officers is three (Master, chief officer, second officer) and for vessels above 3,000 KW, the minimum number of certificated engineers on board is three.

Certificates of competency for officers and ratings

22.16 The MPA recognises valid foreign certificates of competency (COC) provided that they are issued in accordance with STCW 1978 as amended in 1995, and issued by a flag State administration which is recognised by the MPA. Officers serving on board a Singapore vessel who hold a foreign COC must also obtain a certificate of endorsement evidencing the recognition of their certificates by the MPA, valid for a maximum period of five years from the date of issue.

Nationality of crew

22.17 There are no nationality restrictions, as long as the crew hold current STCW certification.

Document of safe manning

22.18 The number of deck officers and engineers deemed necessary for the safe manning and operation of a Singapore vessel is prescribed by the compulsory safe manning document, approved by and issued on behalf of the MPA.

Approved classification societies

22.19 The following classification societies are approved by the MPA for the purpose of surveys and the issue of statutory certificates on behalf of the Singapore Government:

American Bureau of Shipping (ABS)
Bureau Veritas (BV)
China Classification Society (CCS)
DNV GL
Korean Register of Shipping (KRS)
Lloyd's Register of Shipping (LR)
Nippon Kaiji Kyokai (NKK)
Registro Italiano Navale (RINA)

Taxation

22.20 Profits derived from the operation of a Singapore registered ship are exempt from Singapore income tax.

Procedure for registration

22.21 Applications for registration under the Singapore flag should be made to the MPA at its offices in the city. There are no foreign offices of the MPA. Specimen forms are provided at Appendix X(l). The first step in any vessel registration in Singapore is the application for reservation of the vessel's name and application for the allocation of an official number and call sign (if applicable). The name reservation is valid for one year. Once the name has been reserved and the official number has been allocated, the party seeking to register may, upon the submission of a copy of the existing tonnage certificate of the vessel, apply for the issue of a carving and marking note.

Provisional registration

22.22 An application for provisional registration must be made in the prescribed form which includes a formal declaration which must be made before the Director of Marine, a surveyor of ships, a commissioner for oaths, or a notary public. The application should be accompanied by the following documents:

(1) a business profile report from the Accounting and Corporate Regulatory Authority, which includes certified copy of the certificate of incorporation of the owning company, together with details of its directors, secretaries and shareholders;

(2) proof of ownership in the form of a copy bill of sale transferring title in the vessel to the present owner, or in the case of a newbuilding, a copy builder's certificate. Where there have been successive changes in ownership, continuity of title must be demonstrated;

(3) an appointment of a local agent authorising the individual in question to apply for registration;

(4) appointment of a manager resident in Singapore, who shall be the Singapore Registry's contact person for issues related to the operation of the vessel, her crew, her safety and prevention of pollution;

(5) evidence of the value of the vessel in the form of a letter from the owning company, if such value is not shown on the builder's certificate or bill of sale;

(6) a copy of the tonnage certificate for the vessel, calculated in accordance with the International Convention on Tonnage Measurement of Ships 1969;

(7) a copy of the vessel's certificate of class issued by an approved classification society, together with a statement of class maintained in respect of second-hand tonnage or evidence that the vessels latest class survey has been completed; and

(8) for second-hand tonnage, a copy of the free from encumbrances certificate for the vessel, issued by the vessel's then existing registry.

A provisional certificate of registry and carving and marking note will be issued on acceptance of the application form and supporting documents and upon receipt of the registration fee and annual tonnage tax. If the bill of sale or builder's certificate is executed outside Singapore, this is required to be notarised and legalised by the Singapore consulate if there exists a Singapore consulate at the place of execution of the document. In the event that the bill of sale or builder's certificate is signed by an attorney-in-fact of the seller or shipbuilder then the power of attorney must also be duly notarised and legalised by the local Singapore consulate in this way and must also be submitted to the MPA at the time of application. If there is no Singapore consulate in the city of execution of the documents, then the MPA will require a written confirmation in this regard from a lawyer practising in that city.

Validity of the provisional registration and extension

22.23 A provisional certificate of registry is valid for one year; this period cannot be extended.

Permanent registration

22.24 A vessel may be permanently registered in Singapore by submitting to the MPA those documents required for provisional registration described above, and also the following documents:

(1) the original builder's certificate, the original bill of sale or other original evidence of title. For existing vessels, continuity of title must be demonstrated by the production of intervening bills of sale. Any builder's certificates or bills of sale which have been executed outside Singapore must be notarised and legalised. As described above, the original notarised and legalised power of attorney in favour of the signatory of any documents, is also required;

(2) a current copy of the vessel's full-term classification certificate;

(3) copies of full term statutory certificates issued by the MPA or an approved classification society for the vessel under Singapore Registry including:

(a) SOLAS certificates relating to safety construction, safety equipment, safety radio, and where applicable, passenger ship safety.;

(b) an international load line certificate;

(c) an international oil pollution prevention (IOPP) certificate and/or noxious liquid substances (NLS) certificate;

(d) an international air pollution prevention (IAPP) certificate;

(e) a safety management certificate (if the vessel is covered by ISM regulations);

(f) an international ship security certificate (if the vessel is covered by ISM regulations);

(g) a document of compliance issued to the owner or operator of the vessel (if the vessel is covered by ISM regulations);

(4) an official document such as closed transcript or certificate of deletion evidencing cancellation of vessel's former registry free of registered encumbrances; and

(5) a carving and marking note certified by an MPA Surveyor or an authorised classification society, within 30 days from the date of issue.

Registration of mortgages

22.25 The Merchant Shipping Act contains detailed provisions relating to the registration of mortgages over Singapore vessels. A mortgage over a Singaporean ship must be prepared in the prescribed form and submitted to the MPA, where it will be recorded on a public register to show the date and time of such registration. Where the mortgage instrument has been signed by an attorney-in-fact, the original power of attorney must also be provided.

Deregistration procedure

22.26 The owner of a Singaporean vessel may, by written application to the MPA, request the closure of the register of such vessel. The application must state the intended new port and flag of registry, or other reason for closure (such as sale for scrap). Upon receipt of the application, one original bill of sale of the vessel, the return of the original certificate of Singapore registry by the owner, and payment of the appropriate fee, the MPA will issue a deletion certificate. The closure of registry for any vessel shall only be granted where the MPA accepts that there is no unsatisfied mortgage; no statutory prohibition on any dealing with the vessel; no unpaid MPA fees; and no outstanding claims of the Master or any seamen for wages which have been notified to the MPA.

Contact addresses

22.27

Maritime and Port Authority of Singapore
Singapore Registry of Ships
460 Alexandra Road
#19–00 PSA Building
Singapore
119963
Tel: (65) 63 75 1932
Email: marine@mpa.gov.sg
Website: www.mpa.gov.sg

CHAPTER 23

St Vincent and the Grenadines

23.1 The State of St Vincent and the Grenadines consists of a chain of 32 small islands in the Caribbean Sea between St Vincent in the north and Grenada in the south. The main island is St Vincent, the capital of which is Kingstown. The current population is approximately 110,000. A British Crown Colony until 1979, the country is now fully independent and a member of the Commonwealth. The head of State is Queen Elizabeth II whose representative is the Governor-General. The government consists of the House of Assembly, made up of 15 elected members and four senators. Kingstown is the home port of registry for all vessels registered under the flag of St Vincent and the Grenadines. The Cabinet has appointed a Commissioner for Maritime Affairs to supervise all matters relating to merchant shipping and to perform the duties of a registrar outside the country. The legal tender is the East Caribbean dollar (EC$).

23.2 The Commissioner for Maritime Affairs maintains offices in Geneva and Monaco, at which registry business is conducted, supported by regional offices in Dubai, Hong Kong, London and Piraeus. In addition, offices serving the registration of yachts are established in Fort Lauderdale and Luxembourg. The flag State appears within the Paris MOU Grey List published in July 2017.[1]

Sources of law

23.3 The registration of vessels under the flag of St Vincent and the Grenadines is governed by the Shipping Act 2004, as amended by the Shipping (Amendment) Act 2007. References in this chapter to 'the Act' are references to the Shipping Act 2004 as amended, and references to a section are to a section of the Act. The Act consolidated the law relating to shipping and for that reason repealed the Merchant Shipping Act 1982, the earlier statute which dealt with ship registration and related matters.

Vessel eligibility

Vessel type

23.4 Any type of ship may be registered (except fishing vessels, for which registration has been suspended), subject to the age and ownership requirements referred to below.

---

1 See Appendix III.

Age limits

23.5 A ship under construction may be registered. A ship must not be older than 18 years (15 years for tankers) at the time of registration, unless special permission is granted. This condition does not apply to ships that are to be registered for one last voyage to a scrap yard.

Ownership

23.6 In order to be eligible for registration under the St Vincent and the Grenadines flag a vessel must be owned by either:

(1) a body corporate, partnership or other association of individuals registered in any foreign country or whose main office is situated outside St Vincent and the Grenadines which has appointed a registered agent in St Vincent and the Grenadines;

(2) an individual who is a citizen of St Vincent and the Grenadines domiciled in St Vincent and the Grenadines;

(3) a body corporate, partnership or other association of individuals registered in accordance with the laws of St Vincent and the Grenadines and having its main office in St Vincent and the Grenadines.

Company formation

23.7 The main company law statutes in St Vincent and the Grenadines consist of the Companies Act 1994 and the more recent International Business Companies (Amendment and Consolidation) Act, Chapter 149 of the Revised Laws of St Vincent and the Grenadines, 2009 ('the 2009 Act'). The 2009 Act consolidated and amended an earlier statute in 1996 that introduced into St Vincent law the concept of the international business company ('IBC'). An IBC is not permitted to engage in certain types of activity, for example the provision of goods or services in the ordinary course of business to persons resident in St Vincent and the Grenadines. Since most potential users of the Register are unlikely to trade with St Vincent and the Grenadines, the fiscal advantages of using an IBC will make it a more appropriate type of ship-owning vehicle than a domestic company. Although an IBC will continue in existence until dissolved, section 6 of the 2009 Act permits an IBC to be registered as a limited duration company for a fixed period of up to 30 years if such a facility is particularly required. An IBC is deemed to be non-resident.

Registered office

23.8 An IBC is required to have a registered office in St Vincent and the Grenadines which may be the office of its registered agent (s.67 of the 2009 Act).

Shareholders

23.9 An IBC may have only one shareholder. There are no nationality restrictions.

Directors and secretary

23.10 The number of directors of an IBC is fixed by its articles or bylaws. There must be at least one director. Directors may be individuals or corporations. There are no nationality restrictions. There is no requirement for an IBC to have a company secretary. However, if the directors wish to appoint a traditional UK-style company secretary, section 108 of the 2009 Act permits them to appoint by resolution an officer or agent of the company who may be authorised to affix the common seal of the company.

Bareboat charter registration

23.11 Section 5A gives a discretion to the Commissioner for Maritime Affairs to allow the registration in the St Vincent and the Grenadines Registry of vessels registered in a foreign registry which have been bareboat chartered to persons otherwise qualified to own a registered St Vincent and the Grenadines vessel. This may be effected for the duration of the bareboat charter or the expiry date of the underlying charter if sooner, but not, as a general rule, for more than four years. Should a charterer wish to extend registration beyond the maximum of four years, then an application can be made by either the charterer or its authorised agent, for extensions of up to two years at a time, subject to the written consent of the underlying registry, the owner of the vessel and any registered mortgagees. Such consent must be provided within seven days of the Commissioner informing those parties of the request for an extension. Before a vessel can be registered on the Bareboat Charter Register, the Commissioner for Maritime Affairs must receive the following:

(1) a written application from the charterer or his registered agent;

(2) a declaration of bareboat charter accompanied by a copy of the bareboat charter agreement (which will not be available for public inspection);

(3) a copy of the existing tonnage certificate;

(4) payment of the relevant fees and taxes;

(5) a certificate of good standing of the bareboat charterer (if foreign);

(6) true copies of any mortgages, with authenticated translations if not in English, indicating the name of the vessel, the names of the parties, the total amount originally secured, the amount required to discharge the mortgage and the maturity date;

(7) confirmation from the relevant classification society that the vessel is in class and is in possession of valid statutory certificates;

(8) a transcript or an extract of the underlying registration of the vessel that shall include a description of the vessel, the owners and, where applicable, all registered mortgages and encumbrances of the vessel (which will be available for public inspection);

(9) the written consent for the vessel to be bareboat charter registered in St Vincent and the Grenadines of the appropriate authorities of the underlying registry who may be required by the Commissioner to declare that during the period of bareboat charter registration the vessel will not be entitled to fly their flag; the owners of the vessel and all holders of registered mortgages, hypotheques and charges;

(10) proof of liability insurance, such as P&I certificates for third party, crew, pollution and wreck removal;

(11) ISM Code and ISPS Code declarations of company, designated persons and officers;

(12) confirmation from an authorised organisation that the interim SMC, ISSC and MLC/MLC inspection reports are being issued;

(13) Continuous Synopsis Records file and application for amendment to CSR;

(14) application for Maritime Labour Convention declaration Part I; and

(15) LRIT conformance test report.

Any mortgages or other charges entered in the foreign register are recorded, during the period of bareboat charter registration, in a bareboat charter registry book maintained by the Registrar of Ships and the Commissioner for Maritime Affairs. No mortgages or encumbrances may be registered against a bareboat charter registered vessel, such power remaining vested in the underlying registry (s.5B(1)).

23.12 Section 5D(1) enables the bareboat charterer of a permanently registered St Vincent and the Grenadines vessel to register her on a foreign register upon obtaining the written consent of the Registrar of Ships or the Commissioner for Maritime Affairs, which may be granted upon presentation of the following:

(1) a written application from the owner containing such information as the Commissioner may require;

(2) the written consent to such registration from all registered mortgagees, if any;

(3) a written undertaking by the owners to surrender the certificate of registry within 15 days of the vessel being entered in the bareboat charter registry;

(4) a written undertaking by the charterer that the St Vincent and the Grenadines flag shall not be hoisted during the period of bareboat charter registration;

(5) a copy of the bareboat charter;

(6) the return of the original St. Vincent and the Grenadines registration certificates; and

(7) a copy of the foreign bareboat certificate of registry, evidencing a record of the mortgages (if applicable).

Trading limits

23.13 There are no restrictions on trading.

Manning requirements

23.14 Manning levels and certification requirements are laid down in sections 99–103 of the Act and in the 1995 amendments to the International Convention on Standards of Training, Certification and Watchkeeping for Seafarers. St Vincent and the Grenadines ratified the MLC 2006 Convention on 9 November 2010. In accordance with Standard A4.5 (2) and (10), the Government has specified the following branches of social security: sickness benefit; unemployment benefit; maternity benefit and survivors' benefit.[2]

---

2 National requirements with respect to MLC 2006 can be found on www.svg-marad.com.

Certificates of competency for officers and ratings

23.15 All seafarers serving on board St Vincent and the Grenadines flagged vessels must be trained in compliance with STCW standards and must hold the STCW certificates appropriate to their position and function on board. The St Vincent Maritime Administration recognises all national endorsements issued by the countries listed in the current IMO White List.[3] After a duly completed application form with the supporting documents is processed, the Maritime Administration will issue a certificate known as an 'Endorsement Attesting the Recognition of a Certificate under the Provisions of the Regulation 1/10 of the STCW 1995' for Masters, deck and engineer officers. Upon receipt of an application, the Administration will issue a letter of confirmation of receipt enabling the applicant to carry out his or her duties on board for up to three months. The Administration will check the authenticity of copy documents with the issuing administration. After doing so, it will post the St Vincent and the Grenadines STCW endorsement to the applicant. The Maritime Administration recognises yacht crew certificates issued by the UK Maritime and Coastguard Agency and the US Coast Guard for the purpose of St Vincent and Grenadines flagged yachts.

Nationality of crew

23.16 There are no nationality requirements for officers and crew, although priority is expected to be given to Vincentian nationals.

Document of safe manning

23.17 Safe manning certificates are issued by the Maritime Administration for every vessel, taking into consideration her size, power and intended trade, setting out the required level of manning in accordance with international standards.

Approved classification societies

23.18 The following classification societies are recognised by the St Vincent and the Grenadines Government:

American Bureau of Shipping (ABS)
Bureau Veritas (BV)
China Classification Society (CCS)
Croatian Register of Shipping (CR)
DNV GL
Hellenic Register of Shipping (HRS)
Indian Register of Shipping (IRS)
International Naval Surveys Bureau (INBS)
Korean Register of Shipping (KRS)
Lloyd's Register of Shipping (LR)

---

3 See Appendix IV.

Nippon Kaiji Kyokai (NKK)
Polish Register of Shipping (PRS)
Registro Italiano Navale (RINA)
Russian Maritime Register of Shipping (RS)

Taxation

23.19 Foreign owners of St Vincent and the Grenadines flagged ships and their crews are exempt from tax on income or capital unless they are domiciled in St Vincent and the Grenadines. Section 180 of the 2009 Act provides that IBCs are not subject to corporate tax, income tax, withholding tax, capital gains tax or any other taxes in St Vincent and the Grenadines if the company satisfies the requirements of the 2009 Act.

Procedure for registration

Provisional registration

23.20 In order to obtain provisional registration of a vessel (and a provisional radio licence), an application must be submitted to the Registrar of Ships in Kingstown, St Vincent and the Grenadines or to the Geneva or Monaco offices of the Commissioner for Maritime Affairs. The documents may be submitted by email in the first instance, with the originals to follow in hard copy:

(1) completed application forms for registration and a safe manning certificate;
(2) a certificate of good standing of the owning company or a recent certificate of registration;
(3) a copy of an international tonnage certificate (ITC 1969) for vessels of 24 metres and over or copy of a tonnage certificate issued by the recognised organisation on behalf of SVG for vessels of less than 24 metres;
(4) confirmation from the ship's classification society that the ship is in class and has valid statutory certificates. The classification society must confirm that the ship's class will be retained under her new ownership and flag and that new statutory certificates will be issued after completion of the necessary surveys;
(5) permission for transfer, or a transcript of register or certificate of ownership and non-encumbrance, or a certificate of deletion from the present registry;
(6) evidence of title in the form of a copy of a legalised and/or apostilled bill of sale or, in the case of a new vessel, a builder's certificate;
(7) a copy of an ISM document of compliance of the vessel's operator and a copy of the short-term (or interim) safety management certificate or confirmation from the authorised organisation that the same is being issued (if applicable);
(8) ISM Code declaration of company (if applicable);
(9) when the ISPS Code is applicable:
    (a) all Continuous Synopsis Records;
    (b) a company security officer declaration;
    (c) confirmation from an authorised organisation that the interim ISSC is being issued;

(10) particulars of the radio accounting authority identification code (AAIC) and confirmation from the accounting authority that it will handle the clearance of radio traffic accounts;

(11) proof of liability insurance, such as P&I certificates for third party, crew, pollution and wreck removal;

(12) application for Maritime Labour Convention declaration Part I;

(13) LRIT conformance test report; and

(14) payment of initial registration and annual fees.

Upon their issue, registry certificates are provided electronically with the release of the originals thereafter.

Validity of the provisional registration and extension

23.21 A provisional registration certificate is issued for six months and can be extended, under certain circumstances, for a further period of six months.

Full-term registration

23.22 To obtain a full-term registration certificate (and ship station licence) the following documents should be submitted:

(1) a completed application form;

(2) the original or a certified true copy of a legalised and/or apostilled bill of sale or builder's certificate;

(3) original ship's carving and marking note (supplied with provisional registration documents), completed and stamped by a classification society surveyor;

(4) certificate of deletion from the previous registry (original or certified copy), except in the case of a new vessel;

(5) cover note and/or certificate of entry in respect of protection and indemnity insurance (third party liability, cargo and crew cover);

(6) copies of class and statutory certificates, including ISM Code safety management certificate, if applicable;

(7) original radio installations survey report (supplied with provisional registration documents), completed and stamped by a classification society surveyor;

(8) Continuous Synopsis Record showing the date of deletion from the former flag (when the ISPS Code is applicable);

(9) evidence of payment of any additional fees due.

Registration of mortgages and security interests

23.23 Once a ship has been registered under the St Vincent and the Grenadines flag, a mortgage can be created to secure a loan or other financial obligations of the owner. No exchange control permission is needed to create a ship mortgage. To register a mortgage over the vessel, the following documents must be delivered to the original registrar:

(1) the original mortgage deed, stating the date and amount of the mortgage, the discharge amount and the maturity date. The mortgage deed should be executed

by both the mortgagor and the mortgagee and be notarially attested and provided in duplicate;

(2) an affidavit of good faith;

(3) a recent certificate of good standing of the mortgagee if not a bank;

(4) payment for the registration fees and transcript of the register showing the recorded mortgage.

If more than one mortgage is registered against a vessel, they will rank for priority in order of registration. The mortgage can be registered upon receipt of the fax or email copies of the document. The original transcript of register will be released upon receipt of the two original mortgage deeds.

Surveys

23.24 A pre-registration survey is not normally required prior to registration unless a vessel is older than 18 years of age.

Deregistration procedure

23.25 To delete a ship from the Register the following documents must be submitted:

(1) a written request by the registered owner or its manager requesting deletion of the vessel from the Register stating the reason for deletion and the new port of registry if applicable;

(2) a photocopy of the bill of sale if the deletion is required as a result of a transfer of ownership, the scrap certificate if sold for scrap or the foreign certificate of registry if transferred to a foreign registry;

(3) the original St Vincent and the Grenadines certificate of registry;

(4) the original radio licence;

(5) a certificate of discharge of any registered mortgage or other encumbrance;

(6) payment for all outstanding fees due to the Maritime Administration including the issue of the CSR for deletion (if applicable);

(7) the original deletion certificate from the previous flag and copies of all CSRs, if not already received (if applicable).

Yachts

23.26 The Maritime Administration encourages the registration of pleasure yachts, both private and commercial, on the Register, provided such vessels meet certain specified standards of safety and pollution prevention. To that end, the Administration published two codes of practice in July 2008, the Safety Code of Practice for Pleasure Yachts Engaged in Commercial Trade and the Safety Code of Practice for Pleasure Yachts. The Commercial Code applies to yachts of 10 metres and over in length, but less than 500 gross tonnage. The Pleasure Code applies to yachts of 10 metres and over in length, but less than 3,000 gross tonnage. Pleasure yachts over 500 gross tonnage are required to carry a minimum safe manning document as well as a classification certificate.

23.27 The Commercial Code sets out detailed safety and manning requirements for St Vincent and the Grenadines registered yachts which are engaged in commercial trade, carry no cargo and take up to 12 charter guests. Such vessels are required to undergo an annual inspection and to carry a valid document of compliance issued on behalf of the Government of St Vincent and the Grenadines. The Pleasure Yacht Code applies only to yachts used for private purposes, not carrying passengers for reward or remuneration. A pleasure yacht is required to have an initial survey and renewal surveys carried out at intervals of up to five years, rather than annually.

23.28 A pleasure yacht of less than 24 metres is required to have an initial survey and document of compliance. For these yachts, renewal surveys are at the owner's discretion. Pleasure yachts of 18 metres up to 500 gross tonnage may be chartered out under certain conditions for 12 weeks or 84 days in a calendar year, with a maximum of 12 passengers. Pleasure yachts up to 24 metres which use this limited charter allowance privilege should be inspected every five years by an authorized surveyor or recognised organisation while yachts over 24 metres should be inspected every year. The latter are required to carry a minimum safe manning document on board.

Contact addresses

23.29

For locally registered vessels

The Registrar of Ships
Cruise Ship Berth
Kingstown
St Vincent and the Grenadines
West Indies
Tel: (1784) 456 1378
Fax: (1784) 451 2445
Email: svgmarad@gmail.com

Head offices of the St Vincent and the Grenadines Maritime Administration

Geneva

8 Avenue Frontenex
Ch – 1207 Geneva
Switzerland
Tel: (41) 22 707 63 00
Fax: (41) 22 707 63 48
Email: geneva@svg-marad.com

Monaco

74, Bd. d'Italie E/F
MC 98000
Monaco
Tel: (377) 93 10 44 50

Fax: (377) 93 10 44 99
Email: monaco@svg-marad.com

Genoa (quality and technical division)

Mr. Armando Capurro
Via delle Eriche 63/8
I-16148 Genoa
Italy
Tel: (39) 010 839 6314
Fax: (39) 010 831 3514
Email: qualtech@svg-marad.com

CHAPTER 24

United Kingdom

24.1 The United Kingdom of Great Britain and Northern Ireland is situated in the British Isles, to the north-west of continental Europe. The UK is a constitutional monarchy whose head of State is Her Majesty Queen Elizabeth II. The organs of government comprise the legislature (Parliament), the executive (Her Majesty's Government) and the judiciary, which is independent of both the legislature and the executive. The UK has been a member of the European Union since 1972 and in 2016 voted by referendum to leave. The legal tender is the pound sterling (£ or GBP).

24.2 The UK Ship Register ('UKSR') is part of the Maritime and Coastguard Agency, an executive agency of the UK Government Department for Transport. Following an extensive consultation process, UKSR was modernised and re-launched in September 2017. The 'Maritime Growth Study', published in September 2015, contained proposals that aimed to enable UKSR to compete internationally following a period of some decline.[1] It was reported that the registered merchant fleet of the UK had diminished by 17% between 2013 and 2014, to 19th in the world by dead-weight tonnage. By November 2017 it was announced that the UK had reached 14th place on world fleet tonnage statistics, the highest since 2013.[2] The UK appears ninth in the Paris MOU White List of Port State Control compliance published in July 2017[3] and is a member of the US Coast Guard QUALSHIP 21 program.

Sources of law

24.3 Registration of British ships in the UK is governed primarily by the Merchant Shipping Act 1995, as amended ('the Act') and the Merchant Shipping (Registration of Ships) Regulations 1993, as amended ('the Regulations'). Extracts from the Act and the Regulations are provided in Appendix V and Appendix VI. Unless otherwise stated, references to sections and regulations in this chapter are references to sections and regulations in the Act and the Regulations respectively. Section 18 enables the UK Government to

---

1 Department for Transport, 'Maritime Growth Study: keeping the UK competitive in a global market', September 2015. The proposals included in particular the perceived need to improve customer service and for a more commercial focus and culture within UKSR. The implementation of these proposals can be seen in the significantly enhanced UKSR website, although it was resolved to retain the administration of the register within a government agency rather than to create a new Government corporation or entity for this purpose.

2 UKSR Press Release, 15 November 2017.

3 See Appendix III.

249

establish different categories of registries[4] in those Overseas Possessions that maintain shipping registers. In the Overseas Possessions[5] the UK's legislation is supplemented by local legislation and regulations.

Vessel eligibility

Vessel type

24.4 The Register maintained by the Registrar under section 8 is divided into four parts:

Part I for ships, owned by qualified persons, which are not fishing vessels or 'small ships';
Part II for fishing vessels;
Part III for small ships under 24 metres in length owned by individuals who require simple registration which is not a registration of title; and
Part IV for bareboat chartered vessels.

Subject to a vessel satisfying the requirements for the relevant part of the Register, any vessel used in navigation (other than a Government ship referred to in s.308) may be registered without restriction as to size.

Age limits

24.5 There are no age restrictions for vessels joining or remaining on the Register. However, it should be noted that the Registrar may refuse to register a ship if he considers it inappropriate to do so, having regard to the condition of the vessel or its equipment, the safety, health and welfare of its crew and any risk of pollution.

Ownership

24.6 The following categories of persons are qualified to be the owners of ships registered in the UK:[6]

(1) British citizens or non-UK exercising their right of freedom of movement of workers or right of establishment;
(2) British overseas territories citizens;
(3) British Overseas citizens;
(4) persons who under the British Nationality Act 1981 are British subjects;

---

4 *Category 1*: unlimited tonnage and type: Bermuda, British Virgin Islands, Cayman Islands, Gibraltar and Isle of Man. *Category 2*: limited tonnage and type: Anguilla, Falkland Islands, Guernsey, Jersey, Monserrat, St Helena and the Turks and Caicos Islands. To date, no Order in Council has been made establishing either category of register in the British Antarctic Territory, British Indian Ocean Territory, Pitcairn Island or the Sovereign Base Areas of Akrotiri and Dhekelia (in Cyprus).

5 This term includes the British Overseas Territories and Crown Dependencies (Isle of Man and the Channel Islands).

6 Regulation 7

(5) persons who under the Hong Kong (British Nationality) Order 1986 are British Nationals (Overseas);

(6) bodies corporate incorporated in an EEA State;[7]

(7) bodies corporate incorporated in any relevant British possession and having their principal place of business in the UK or in any such possession;

(8) European Economic Interest Groupings, being groupings formed in pursuance of Article 1 of Council Regulation (EEC) No. 2137/85 and registered in the UK.

A person not falling within one of the above categories may nevertheless be entitled to be registered as an owner of a vessel on Part I of the Register if a majority interest (within the meaning of reg. 8) is owned by persons who are entitled to be so registered. There are additional requirements that apply to fishing vessels registered on Part II of the Register.

Company formation

24.7 If a ship-owner wishes to incorporate a company in the UK for the purpose of acquiring a vessel to be registered on the UK Register, it will be possible for a limited liability company to be registered in England and Wales, or in Scotland, in both cases under the Companies Act 2006 or in Northern Ireland under the equivalent Northern Ireland legislation. Ready-made companies can be acquired 'off the shelf' from company registration agents. Alternatively, companies can be incorporated to order in England and Wales or Scotland in as little as 24 hours.

Non-resident status

24.8 All companies that are incorporated in the UK are deemed to be resident for tax purposes. As a result, there is no distinction between a resident and non-resident company.

Bareboat charter registration

24.9 Section 17 permits the registration of a foreign-flag vessel that is chartered on bareboat charter terms by a charterer who is qualified to own a British ship. A bareboat chartered ship which is 'flagged-in' to the UK Register will be registered in Part IV of the Register. The vessel is required to be surveyed[8] and the applicant is required to submit documents including the following:

(1) a completed application to register a bareboat charter ship (Form MSF 4738);

(2) a completed declaration of eligibility for a bareboat charter ship (Form MSF 4735);

(3) a copy certificate of incorporation, or equivalent document (if a company);

(4) a copy of the charter party agreement;

(5) a copy of the registration document from the primary (underlying) flag State;

---

7 The European Economic Area comprises Member States of the EU, plus Iceland, Liechtenstein and Norway.

8 See further para. 24.30.

(6) a certificate of survey for tonnage and measurement;
(7) an international tonnage certificate (ITC69);
(8) a copy of the vessel's current Continuous Synopsis Record;
(9) application for a safe manning document, for vessels >500 GT;
(10) an electronic application for compulsory insurance certificates (bunker Convention, civil liability Convention, passengers and luggage, wreck removal) as applicable;[9]
(11) ISM and ISPS certification and application for audit; and
(12) information about Maritime Labour Convention compliance and seafarer employment agreements.

24.10 On completion of registration the Registrar will notify the responsible authority in the country of primary registration that the ship has been registered as a bareboat chartered ship on the British Register. Registration of such a vessel shall expire on the expiry of the charter, or at the end of a period of five years from the date of registration, whichever is the earlier. Registration may be renewed on presentation of a fresh declaration of eligibility and a certificate of bareboat charter.

24.11 There is no corresponding provision that allows a UK registered vessel to be 'flagged-out' to a foreign register while retaining UK registration.

Trading limits

24.12 There are no trading limits that affect UK registered vessels on a permanent basis. However, from time to time UK vessels may be subject to trading restrictions or sanctions imposed by resolutions of the United Nations.

Manning requirements

24.13 Manning levels and certification requirements for Masters and seamen employed on sea-going ships registered in the UK are set out in Merchant Shipping (Standards of Training, Certification and Watch-keeping) Regulations 2015,[10] which incorporate the provisions of the International Convention and Code on Standards of Training, Certification and Watchkeeping for Seafarers 1978, as amended and 2010 Code and gives effect to the International Maritime Organisation Resolution A1047(27) on the Principles of Safe Manning.[11] As far as officers qualified in other EU countries are concerned, these Regulations give effect to a general system of recognition of higher education diplomas and qualifications. The Regulations set out the certification structure for officers reflecting the requirements of the STCW Convention and enabling the Secretary of State for Transport to recognise certificates issued by the authorities of other EEA countries which are party to the Convention, provided he is satisfied that such authorities comply fully with the standards of competency required.

---

9 MSF 3241, latest revision (currently REV 0917).
10 SI 2015/782.
11 See further, Merchant Shipping Notice MSN 1868 (M) UK requirements for safe manning and watchkeeping, published 12 June 2015.

Certificates of competency for officers

24.14 Masters and officers serving on board UK registered ships are required to hold either a UK certificate of competency ('CoC') or a UK certificate of equivalent competency ('CEC') issued by the Maritime and Coastguard Agency ('MCA'). A CEC will be issued if an applicant holds a valid certificate of competency issued by another STCW Convention government which is recognised by the MCA as complying with Convention requirements. The CEC process also requires the applicant to demonstrate a satisfactory knowledge of the English language. In addition, a Master will be required to pass the UK legal and administrative processes ('UKLAP') grade 1 test.[12]

Nationality of crew

24.15 The Aliens Restriction (Amendment) Act 1919, section 5, which restricted the posts of Master, first officer and chief engineer to persons of certain nationalities, has long since been repealed.[13] However, in the case of 'strategic ships', defined as:

(1) British registered fishing vessels of 24 metres in length;
(2) UK ships (as defined in s.85(2) of the 1995 Act) of 500 gross tons or more which are class 1 passenger ships, product tankers, i.e. oil or chemical tankers, or ro-ro ships,

the Master is required to be a British, Commonwealth, EU, EEA or NATO national.[14] There are no nationality requirements for other officers or seamen serving on strategic ships, so long as the seafarers concerned have a sufficient understanding of the English language.

Document of safe manning

24.16 All UK ships of over 500 gross tons are required to carry a valid safe manning certificate. The manning requirements for UK ships were revised by the Merchant Shipping (Standards of Training, Certification and Watch-keeping) Regulations 2015. These regulations impose on the owners or operators of UK-registered seagoing ships an obligation to ensure that their vessels are manned by crew of appropriate grades who are properly trained and hold the appropriate certificates. Incidentally, this obligation also extends to the owners of non-UK registered ships while in UK national waters. General guidelines as to the numbers and qualifications of officers can be found in MSN 1868 (M). An application for a safe manning certificate should be made to the MCA, Seafarers' Training and Certification Branch in Southampton on Form MSF 4227.

---

12 See further, Merchant Shipping Notice MSN 1867 Recognition of non-UK certification for issue of a CEC, published 12 June 2015.

13 Merchant Shipping Act 1970 (Commencement No. 12) Order 1995, SI 1995/1426.

14 Merchant Shipping (Officer Nationality) Regulations 1995, SI 1995/1427.

Approved classification societies/authorised surveyors and inspectors of marks

24.17 The following classification societies are approved by the UK Government to act as recognised organisations (ROs) for the survey and inspection of merchant ships:

American Bureau of Shipping (ABS)
Bureau Veritas (BV)
Class NK (NK)
DNV GL
Lloyd's Register of Shipping (LR)
Registro Italiano Navale (RINA)

Taxation

24.18 A company incorporated in the UK is liable to pay corporation tax on its profits, wherever arising. A foreign company that carries on business in the UK through a branch or agency is liable to pay corporation tax on the trading income arising directly or indirectly from the branch or agency. In 1999, the UK Government introduced an alternative system of taxation known as tonnage tax. This regime gives UK-based shipping companies the option to pay corporation tax calculated by reference to the net tonnage of the ships operated, rather than by reference to actual business results. Under Schedule 22 of the Finance Act 2000 (as amended), a company may elect to pay tonnage tax, for a ten-year period if:

(1) it operates 'qualifying ships'; and those ships are strategically and commercially managed from the UK;
(2) not more than 75% of a company's fleet is chartered-in otherwise than on bareboat charter terms;
(3) it enters into a commitment with the Department for Transport (DfT) to train a specified number of new seafarers each year or makes a payment in lieu of training (PILOT) to the Maritime Training Trust with the agreement of DfT. In the case of officers, the commitment is to recruit and train one UK-resident British or EEA national per annum for every 15 officer posts entered on the safe manning certificates of all vessels entered in the tonnage tax regime, with adjustments for back-up crew.[15]

24.19 For tonnage tax purposes, a 'qualifying ship' means a sea-going ship of 100 GRT or more used for:

(1) the carriage by sea of passengers;
(2) the carriage by sea of cargo;
(3) towage, salvage or other marine assistance carried out at sea or;
(4) transport by sea in connection with other services of a kind necessarily provided at sea.

---

15 See further, the Tonnage Tax (Training Requirement) Regulations 2000, SI 2129/2000, as amended by the Tonnage Tax (Training Requirement) (Amendment) Regulations 2017, SI 2017/882, which increases the value of the PILOT in line with inflation.

However, the legislation specifically excludes the following types[16] of vessel from this definition:

(1) fishing vessels or factory ships (meaning vessels providing processing services to the fishing industry);
(2) pleasure craft (meaning vessels whose primary use is for the purposes of sport or recreation);
(3) harbour or river ferries;
(4) offshore installations;
(5) tankers dedicated to a particular oil field;
(6) dredgers, other than 'qualifying dredgers'.[17]

Also excluded are ships chartered out on bareboat charter terms, unless such bareboat charter is to a charterer in the same group of companies, or for a period not exceeding three years when the ship is temporarily surplus to requirements.

Procedure for registration

Provisional registration

24.20 An application for provisional registration may be made to the Registrar where a ship to be registered on Part I or Part II is outside the British Isles at the time of the application. Alternatively, the owner may apply to a British consul in or near the port where the ship is situated. The application shall be in a form approved by the Secretary of State for Transport and must be accompanied by, if the owner is:

(1) a company registered in the UK, a copy of the certificate of incorporation and of any change of name, or
(2) a company incorporated in another EEA State or a relevant British possession, proof of incorporation in the country concerned, or
(3) a company incorporated outside the UK, but with a place of business in the UK, a certificate from the relevant Registrar of Companies that the company is registered as an overseas company.[18]

The Registrar will check the documents to satisfy himself that the ship is eligible for registration, and where the documents have been submitted by a consul he will notify the consul that it is permissible for him to proceed with registration. Although the Regulations make provision for provisional registration, the ease of modern communications is such that provisional registration is seldom used in practice as most applicants prefer to apply for permanent registration from the outset.

---

16 See para. 19 of Sch. 22 to the Finance Act 2000, as amended by s.93 Finance Act 2005.

17 Paragraph 20(7) of Sch. 22 to the Finance Act 2000 defines 'qualifying dredger' as a self-propelled dredger constructed for the carriage of cargo.

18 Regulation 24.

Validity of the provisional registration and extension

24.21 A certificate of provisional registration is valid for three months from date of issue or until the ship's arrival in the UK or termination by the Registrar on request from the owner, whichever happens earlier (reg. 68). Once a ship has been provisionally registered, it may not be provisionally registered again within one year of the date of issue of the certificate of provisional registration, except with the consent of the Registrar (reg. 69).

Permanent registration

24.22 An application for permanent registration shall be made to the UKSR in Cardiff. First, a summary of the proposed registration is required to be provided on form MSF 5547, which includes the information necessary to check if the vessel and owner are eligible for UK registration. Following a successful check, the applicant is assigned a customer account manager (CAM) as a dedicated point of contact for administration and general policy matters, and for guidance through the procedure; and a customer service manager (CSM) who will support with technical issues regarding the survey and inspection of the vessel during the 'flag-in' process. The applicant will need to submit the following documents:

(1) a completed application to register a British ship (Form MSF 4740A);
(2) a completed declaration of eligibility[19] (Form MSF 4727);
(3) a copy certificate of incorporation, or equivalent document (if a company);
(4) in the case of a new ship, a builder's certificate using either the builder's own form or Form MSF 4743;[20]
(5) in the case of a ship which is not new, a bill or bills of sale showing the ownership of the ship for at least five years before the application is made. If the ship has been registered with full registration within the last five years, bills of sale must be produced covering all transfers since the date of such registration. In the case of full registration of a fishing vessel the relevant period is reduced to three years;[21]
(6) for fishing vessels the maximum continuous engine power must be declared and, if the vessel is 12 metres in length or over, a UK fishing vessel safety certificate must be produced;
(7) a certificate of survey for tonnage and measurement;
(8) an international tonnage certificate (ITC69) for vessels >500 GT;
(9) an application for a safe manning document, for vessels >500 GT;
(10) an electronic application for compulsory insurance certificates (Bunker Convention, Civil Liability Convention, passengers and luggage, wreck removal) as applicable;[22] and
(11) information about Maritime Labour Convention compliance and seafarer employment agreements.

---

19 Regulation 22.
20 Regulation 28(1)(a).
21 Regulation 28(1)(b).
22 MSF 3241, latest revision (currently REV 0917)

If the ship is currently registered on another Register the following additional documents must also be submitted:

(12) an official extract or transcript from the current Register;
(13) a written undertaking to provide a deletion certificate or closed transcript from the current register within six weeks after registration on the UK Register;
(14) a copy of the ship's current Continuous Synopsis Record; and
(15) a copy of the relevant bareboat charter if the ship is bareboat chartered.

24.23 The application Form MSF 4740A will include the name(s) chosen for the ship, if more than one in order of preference. Once a ship has been registered as a UK vessel, any request for a change of name must be made using a form designated for that purpose (Form MSF 4741).

24.24 Every ship, other than a fishing vessel less than 15 metres in length, shall before registration be surveyed by an approved surveyor and her tonnage ascertained in accordance with the tonnage regulations made under the Merchant Shipping Act 1995. For all other ships an authorised measurer completes the appropriate form. On completion of the survey, the surveyor issues a certificate specifying the ship's tonnage, build and other required particulars. The certificate is then sent direct to the Registrar, who will, on receipt of the other documents referred to above, and payment of the registration fee, issue a carving and marking note stating the name approved for the ship, the official number allocated to the ship and the port of choice chosen by the owner. A fishing vessel will also be allocated a port number.

24.25 The owner is responsible for arranging for the name, port of choice, official number and tonnage details to be marked and carved on the ship in the manner required in the tonnage regulations. When the work is completed a classification society surveyor (where applicable) must inspect the ship, sign the carving and marking note and return it direct to the Registrar.[23] In the case of a pleasure yacht under 24 metres in length, the owner is permitted to sign the certificate himself and, in the case of fishing vessels' certification, the certificate may be made by the authorised person. When the Registrar is satisfied that:

(1) the ship has been duly carved and marked and the appropriate survey and measuring certificate provided, and
(2) the particulars of the ship are correct, and
(3) title has been adequately proved (where necessary), and the Regulations have been complied with,

he will register the ship and issue a certificate of British registry to the owner.[24] However, it should be noted that the Registrar has a discretion to refuse to register where in his opinion the condition of a ship or its equipment constitutes a safety or pollution risk (reg. 36(5)).

24.26 In October 2017, UKSR took a meaningful step towards the modernisation and ease of use for customers that the Maritime Growth Study had sought, in the acceptance

---

23 Regulation 33.
24 Regulation 36(1).

of certain application documents electronically. By this amendment to the Regulations, the submission of documentation by email is sufficient to enable registration to proceed, while original documents such as mortgage deeds can be provided subsequently if the applicant requires them to be endorsed by the Registrar.[25]

Registration of mortgages and security interests

24.27 A mortgage may be created over a ship using one of the printed forms of ship mortgage supplied by the Registry.[26] There are two types of mortgage: principal and interest (Form MSF 4736) and account current (Form MSF 4737). An executed mortgage must be delivered or posted to the Registrar for registration. Mortgages rank for priority in order of registration. An account current mortgage will normally be regulated by a separate deed of covenant which will often include an assignment of earnings and insurance, as well as setting out in detail the rights and obligations of both parties to the mortgage. The Registrar does not require any deed of covenant to be produced when dealing with the registration of a mortgage.[27]

24.28 A party intending to take a mortgage over a ship may obtain priority by delivering to the Registrar an executed notice of mortgage intent (Form MSF 4739). The Registrar will record details of the notice on the Register for a period of up to 30 days. A notice may be renewed for a further 30 days on written request.[28]

24.29 If a mortgagor is a company incorporated in Great Britain, or a non-resident company with a registered branch or agency, a ship mortgage and any collateral deed of covenant must also be registered at Companies House within 21 days of creation (s.859A Companies Act 2006, as amended).

Surveys

24.30 Except in the case of pleasure craft and small ships, all newbuildings or ships transferring from another flag are required to be surveyed before being registered on the UK Register. In the case of merchant ships the UKSR-appointed customer service manager for the applicant will assist the ship-owner in dealing with the necessary surveys. These will usually be undertaken by MCA surveyors, although it may be possible for this work to be delegated to a classification society surveyor where a vessel is entered with the voluntary Alternative Compliance Scheme. If a ship has been registered under another flag copies of the existing statutory certificates should be forwarded to the UKSR prior to survey to assist the MCA with the preparation of new statutory certificates. In the case of fishing vessels, a condition survey will be required prior to the issue of a mandatory UK safety certificate.

---

25 Merchant Shipping (Registration of Ships)(Amendment) Regulations 2017, SI 2017/879.
26 Regulation 57.
27 For the law relating to ship mortgages generally see Osborne, Bowtle and Buss, *The Law of Ship Mortgages* (Informa Law from Routledge, 2017).
28 Regulation 59.

Deregistration procedure

24.31 A ship may be deregistered on the written request of the owner if registration is no longer required, for example in the event of sale to a foreign buyer, or if the ship has been lost or scrapped. Where the Registrar terminates registration, a closed transcript of the Register is issued to the owner and any mortgagee is notified of the closure. The termination of registration of a ship does not affect any undischarged registered mortgage over that vessel or any share in it.[29] The owner is required to submit an application to remove the vessel from the Register (Form MSF 4744) together with a CSR amendment form and also surrender the ship's certificate of registry for cancellation.

Yachts

24.32 Yachts may be registered on Part I or Part III of the Register (if eligible for registration as a small ship). While small pleasure yachts are subject to minimal regulation, the growth of the commercial yachting industry prompted the Maritime and Coastguard Agency to consult with yachting industry professionals as well as representatives of other Red Ensign Group registers with a view to establishing an acceptable set of safety standards for large yachts. These consultations resulted in the publication in 1997 of *The Code of Practice for the Safety of Large Commercial and Sailing Yachts*, commonly known as the 'MCA Code' or 'LY1'. The Code set out standards for safety, pollution control and the levels of manning and crew qualifications, based on the size of vessel, engine power and the intended cruising range.

24.33 Ongoing consultations between the MCA and international yacht industry experts gave rise to an amended Code in 2004. Known simply as *The Large Commercial Yacht Code or* 'LY2', it replaced the original Code. LY2 applies to all motor or sailing vessels with a load line length of 24 metres or over, engaged in chartering activities and carrying no more than 12 passengers. The current version of the Code, known as LY3, came into effect in 2013.[30] It introduced equivalent requirements for large yachts to the requirements of the Maritime Labour Convention (MLC) as well as updating for advantages in technology and communications since LY2.

24.34 Where a private pleasure or commercial yacht is capable of carrying between 13 and 36 passengers, UKSR require that the yacht comply with the Passenger Yacht Code ('PYC') as an alternative to full passenger ship certification under the SOLAS Convention that would be otherwise be mandatory.[31] As mentioned in Chapter 6, updated versions of LY3 and PYC were published in November 2017 by the Red Ensign Group of Registries in the consolidated REG Yacht Code ('REG-YC') which will come into force after the UK Government has tabled REG-YC with the International Maritime Organisation under the equivalence provisions in the relevant IMO Conventions. It is expected that REG-YC will come into force on 1 January 2019. In the meantime, LY3 and PYC will apply.

---

29 Regulation 63.

30 See MSN 1851 (M) published 20 August 2013.

31 A code of practice for yachts carrying 13 to 36 passengers: the passenger yacht code, 4th edn, January 2014 (REG 13–36).

Contact addresses

24.35

Registry of Shipping and seamen

UK Ship Register
Anchor Court
Keen Road
Cardiff
CF24 5JW
Tel: +44 (0)29 2044 8800
Fax: +44 (0)29 2044 8820
For registration enquiries email: cam@mcga.gov.uk
For technical enquiries email: ctm@mcga.gov.uk
For general enquiries email: ukshipregister@mcga.gov.uk
Website: www.ukshipregister.co.uk

For seafarer certification

Seafarer Training and Certification
Maritime and Coastguard Agency
Bay 2/11
Spring Place
105 Commercial Road
Southampton
SO15 1EG
Phone: +44 (0)203 817 2200
Select Option 1 for Revalidation
Select Option 2 for Deck
Select Option 3 for Engineering
Email:
Deck team: deck@mcga.gov.uk
Engineering team: engineering@mcga.gov.uk
Revalidation team: revalidation@mcga.gov.uk

Large Yacht Unit (yachts over 24 metres)

ENSIGN, Maritime and Coastguard Agency
c/o South Tyneside College
St George's Avenue
South Shields
NE34 6ET
Tel: +44 (0)20 381 72014
Email: large.yachts@mcga.gov.uk

CHAPTER 25

Vanuatu

25.1 Vanuatu consists of a group of islands in the South Pacific, situated approximately 1,500 miles north-east of Sydney, Australia and 500 miles due west of Fiji. Captain Cook sailed through the islands in 1774, naming them the New Hebrides, after the group of islands off the north-west coast of Scotland. There is a population of some 283,000. From 1906 onwards, the islands were administered jointly by Britain and France as a condominium, the only one of its kind in the world. In 1980 the country became an independent republic and a member of the Commonwealth. The legislature consists of a single chamber of 50 elected members, with a general election being held every four years. Executive power is vested in the Prime Minister and a Council of Ministers who are responsible to Parliament. The head of State is the President who is elected for a term of five years. The capital is Port Vila on the island of Efate. Agriculture is the principal economic activity, followed by tourism.

25.2 Since gaining independence, Vanuatu has established itself as an offshore financial and shipping centre. The model of registry structure and organisation which has been adopted is outsourced and decentralised – similar to that of Liberia and the Marshall Islands. Vanuatu Maritime Services Ltd ('VMSL') is a privately owned Vanuatu company, which acts as Maritime Administrator on behalf of the Vanuatu Government and operates the Vanuatu Ship Registry from its operational office in New York. The functions of VMSL are supported by a global network of appointed Deputy Commissioners and special agents in major ports and cities. The legal tender in Vanuatu is the Vatu (VUV), but all fees payable to VMSL are payable in US dollars. By 2017, Vanuatu was estimated to be within the top 25 registries in the world by value, if not by dead-weight tonnage.[1]

Sources of law

25.3 Vanuatu's former condominium status has resulted in a legal system containing elements of both common law and the French Napoleonic Code. Registration of ships under the Vanuatu flag is governed by the Maritime Act (Cap. 131) which was introduced in 1981. This statute, and its subordinate Maritime Regulations, are based on US maritime law and will be familiar to legal practitioners used to US and Liberian legislation. The Maritime Act (Cap. 131) (as amended) and the Maritime Regulations Order No. 25 of 1990 (as amended) will in this chapter be referred to as 'the Act' and 'the Regulations',

---

1 UNCTAD, *Review of Maritime Transport* (2017), Table 2.7.

respectively. Unless otherwise stated, references in this chapter to sections are references to sections of the Act.

Vessel eligibility

Vessel type

25.4 Any sea-going vessel engaged in foreign trade and any yacht or other vessel used exclusively for pleasure of 50 net tons or over may be registered as a Vanuatu vessel, subject to the age limits, ownership and condition of the vessel as referred to below (s.17(1)).

Age limits

25.5 As a general rule, a vessel will not be eligible to be registered under the Vanuatu flag if it is more than 20 years old on 1 January in the year in which registration is sought, the 20-year period being computed from completion of first construction. However, the 20-year age limit may be waived by the Commissioner or Deputy Commissioner of Maritime Affairs and the vessel registered in exceptional cases where it is demonstrated to the satisfaction of the Commissioner or Deputy Commissioner that:

(1) the vessel meets all other requirements for registration; and
(2) the vessel meets the highest classification requirements of one of the classification societies authorised by the Act or any order made thereunder.

An application form for a waiver of the age requirement may be made on Form A20.

Ownership

25.6 In order to be eligible for registration, a vessel must be owned by a Vanuatu citizen or national, which terms include Vanuatu corporations, partnerships and associations of individuals. However, the Commissioner or Deputy Commissioner may, in exceptional cases, waive the Vanuatu nationality requirement where:

(1) the vessel meets all other requirements for registration; and
(2) it has been satisfactorily demonstrated that there is an absolute and genuine need for such waiver.

An application for a waiver may be made on Form A21.

Company formation

25.7 There are two separate pieces of legislation in Vanuatu regulating the formation of companies, the Companies Act (Cap. 191), which was modelled on the British Companies Acts 1948 and 1967, and the more recent International Companies Act (No. 32 of 1992), as amended. The International Companies Act was modelled on the British Virgin Islands International Business Companies Ordinance and to some extent the New Zealand Companies Act. For tax reasons, it is likely that ship-owners who carry on business outside Vanuatu will prefer to incorporate international companies under the International Companies Act.

Bareboat charter registration

25.8 Section 31 of the Act provides that a bareboat charterer of a vessel which is registered on a foreign register may obtain a Vanuatu bareboat charter certificate of registry for a period of up to five years, on payment of the prescribed fee and presentation of the following documents:

(1) a written application;

(2) a copy of the charterparty in a form satisfactory to the Commissioner or Deputy Commissioner and certified by an approved person;

(3) proof of ownership, and consent of the registered owner;

(4) consent from the holders of all mortgages, hypothecations or similar charges against the vessel in the foreign registry;

(5) written consent of the country of registry, or presentation of satisfactory evidence that such consent is not required;

(6) a certificate of ownership and encumbrance, transcript of registry, or other such document from the foreign registry showing all recorded liens and encumbrances.

Where permitted by the underlying foreign register, a bareboat charter certificate of registry may be extended for a period of five years by filing an application to that effect together with copies of the relevant bareboat charter, a certificate of ownership and encumbrance or transcript of the register, the written consent of all mortgages and payment of the prescribed fees and taxes (s.31(4)). A bareboat charter certificate of registry may be cancelled prior to the date of expiry on presentation of the written consent of all relevant parties and the surrender of the bareboat charter certificate of registry and the Vanuatu radio licence (s.31(5)).

25.9 A Vanuatu flag vessel which is the subject of a bareboat charter may be 'flagged out' to a foreign registry that permits the 'flagging in' of bareboat chartered vessels, provided that written consent is obtained from the Commissioner or Deputy Commissioner. Such consent may be granted on presentation of the following documents:

(1) written consent of the owner;

(2) written consent of all holders of record of any mortgage, hypothecation or other charges recorded in the offices of the Commissioner and Deputy Commissioner;

(3) a copy of the foreign document, certified as true and correct, submitted by the bareboat charterer within 30 days following registration in the foreign jurisdiction (s.31(6)).

Trading limits

25.10 Vanuatu flag vessels are not subject to any trading limits.

Manning requirements

25.11 Manning levels for officers and ratings are set out in section 40 of the Regulations, which were substantially amended in 1998 in order to reflect the changes required by STCW 1995. The requirements may be summarised as follows:

(1) no vessel shall be navigated unless she has on board, and in her service, a licensed Master;

(2) every vessel, other than a passenger vessel, of between 100 and 499 gross tons shall also have on board and in her service at least one additional deck officer;

(3) the number and grades of deck officers required on passenger vessels shall be prescribed for such vessels from time to time by the Commissioner or Deputy Commissioner;

(4) the number and grades of deck officers on vessels of 500 gross tons or more shall be determined by the Commissioner or Deputy Commissioner from time to time by reference to the gross tonnage specified in Chapter II of STCW 1995, length of voyage, type, service and particular characteristics and equipment of such vessels;

(5) no motor vessel of less than 750 kW (1,005 hp) shall be navigated unless she has on board and in her service an engineer holding a licence issued in compliance with criteria specified by the Commissioner or Deputy Commissioner;

(6) the number and grades of engineer officers required on vessels propelled by engines of 750 kW or more shall be determined by the Commissioner or Deputy Commissioner according to the propulsion power specified in Chapter III of STCW 1995, having regard to length of voyage, type of machinery, degree of automation and whether the vessel is equipped for manned or periodically unmanned machinery space operation;

(7) the number of navigational and engineering ratings shall be determined by the Commissioner or Deputy Commissioner by reference to length of voyage, type, service, size, propulsion power and type of machinery and any particular characteristics and equipment of the vessel;

(8) in cases of exceptional necessity, the Commissioner or Deputy Commissioner may grant dispensation for a post to be filled by a person licensed to fill the post immediately below the post in question, subject to compliance with all the provisions of Article VIII of STCW 1995.

Certificates of competency for officers and ratings

25.12 Every Master and officer serving on board a Vanuatu vessel is required to hold an appropriate certificate of competency issued or endorsed by the Commissioner or Deputy Commissioner. Certificates will only be issued if the officer in question is able to satisfy the regulations contained in STCW 1995. Where a Master, officer or radio operator holds a certificate of competency issued by another party to STCW 1995, the holder will be entitled to apply for endorsement of such certificate, or the issue of an equivalent Vanuatu licence, subject to the provisions of Regulation I/10 of STCW 1995. An endorsement is valid only when accompanied by the holder's licence.

An application for recognition of a foreign certificate of a deck officer, engineer officer or radio operator must be made immediately the individual is assigned to a Vanuatu vessel. However, an officer, other than a radio operator, holding an appropriate licence may serve on board a Vanuatu vessel for a period of up to three months without a Vanuatu endorsement, provided he or she can provide proof on board ship that an application for an endorsement has been submitted, notwithstanding that any officer found without a Vanuatu licence is subject to an immediate fine under section 8 of the Act. This fine may be waived if the application is submitted within 30 days of the finding.

Ratings forming part of a navigational watch on vessels in excess of 500 gross tons and certain engineer ratings are also required to be certificated under STCW 1995.

Crew certification and licensing is also handled by VMSL on behalf of the Vanuatu government.

Nationality of crew

25.13 There are no restrictions on crew nationality.

Document of safe manning

25.14 Every vessel is required to be manned in accordance with IMO principles of safe manning and to the satisfaction of the Commissioner and Deputy Commissioner, and shall carry a safe manning certificate. The manning of a vessel is required to be maintained at all times to at least the levels stipulated in the safe manning certificate. An application for a safe manning certificate is required to include the proposed numbers and grade of personnel that the owners consider appropriate for the voyages intended to be undertaken by the vessel.

Approved classification societies

25.15 The following IACS member classification societies are approved by VMSL as recognised organisations for the purpose of issuance of certification on behalf of the Vanuatu flag State:

American Bureau of Shipping (ABS)
Bureau Veritas (BV)
China Classification Society (CCS)
Croatian Register of Shipping (CRS)
DNV GL
Indian Register of Shipping (IRS)
Korean Register of Shipping (KR)
Lloyd's Register of Shipping (LR)
Nippon Kaiji Kyokai (NKK)
Polski Rejestr Statkow (PRS)
Registro Italiano Navale (RINA)
Russian Maritime Register of Shipping (RS)

Non-IACS member classification societies may issue ISM, ISPS and MLC certification on a case-by-case basis as may be authorised by the Commissioner or a Deputy Commissioner with reference to the size and type of vessel in question.

Taxation

25.16 No personal income or corporation tax is payable in Vanuatu, neither are there any withholding taxes, capital gains tax, capital transfer taxes or estate duty. Stamp duty is payable on certain documents, but not if the company concerned is an international company incorporated under the International Companies Act. International companies also benefit from a 20-year guarantee against all other taxes, duties and exchange control restrictions.

Procedure for registration

Provisional registration

25.17 An application for registration of a vessel under the Vanuatu flag must be made in writing to the Office of the Deputy Commissioner for Maritime Affairs in New York, in the prescribed form A01, together with payment of the appropriate fee. A certificate of provisional registry will be issued, provided that the owner furnishes satisfactory proof:

(1) as to his or its ownership of the vessel;

(2) that if there is an outstanding foreign registration document in existence, such document has been surrendered or the Master has been instructed to do so on receipt of the Vanuatu provisional certificate of registry, or the document has been legally cancelled;

(3) that the vessel is in a seaworthy condition;

(4) that the initial registration fees have been paid;

(5) that the markings of name, official number, net tonnage or tonnages, home port and draught have been made, or that the owner has issued orders to the Master to have such markings made on receipt of the Vanuatu provisional certificate of registry on board the vessel.

Validity of the provisional registration and extension

25.18 A provisional certificate of registry is valid for 30 days, but may be extended for up to a year if good reason is shown to the Commissioner or Deputy Commissioner.

Permanent registration

25.19 A certificate of permanent registration may be issued by the Commissioner or Deputy Commissioner upon receipt of an application and declaration on the prescribed form, payment of the appropriate fee and presentation of satisfactory proof:

(1) as to his ownership of the vessel;

(2) that any foreign registration document for the vessel has been surrendered with the consent of the government that issued it; or has been legally cancelled;

(3) that the vessel is in a seaworthy condition;

(4) that the owner has paid the registration fees due in respect of the vessel;

(5) that the markings of name, official net tonnage or tonnages, home port and draft have actually been made;

(6) that a certificate of measurement has been issued;

(7) that applicable statutory certificates have reissued;

(8) of correct EPIRB encoding and LRIT verification; and

(9) of oil pollution coverage (Bunker and/or Civil Liability Convention, as applicable).

Registration of mortgages and security interests

25.20 A mortgage or assignment of a mortgage of a Vanuatu vessel will not be valid until the instrument evidencing such transaction is recorded in the office of the Commissioner or Deputy Commissioner. Before a mortgage can be recorded it must be acknowledged before the Commissioner or Deputy Commissioner, a Vanuatu consul or consular agent or a notary public or other officer authorised to take acknowledgement of deeds in the place where the acknowledgement is made. Such instruments will be recorded in the order in which they are received in books kept for the purpose and indexed to show:

(1) the name of the vessel;

(2) the name of the parties;

(3) the time and date of reception of the instrument;

(4) the interest in the vessel transferred or affected; and

(5) the amount and date of maturity of any instrument.

A valid mortgage which, when created, covers the whole of a vessel will be deemed to be a preferred mortgage once it is recorded, unless the mortgage document waives its preferred status. A preferred mortgage constitutes a maritime lien under Vanuatu law in the amount of the mortgage indebtedness secured on the vessel.

Surveys

25.21 As a general rule, it is not necessary for a vessel to be surveyed prior to registration under the Vanuatu flag. However, if an owner requests a waiver of the 20-year age rule and/or the vessel is a small non-Convention sized, non-classed vessel regardless of age, then a general condition survey must be completed prior to registration.

Deregistration procedure

25.22 If the registered owner of a vessel wishes to deregister, a written application must be submitted to the Commissioner or Deputy Commissioner specifying the name of the vessel, the reasons for the proposed surrender of registration documents, the name and nationality of the new owner, if any, and, if a transfer to a foreign registry is contemplated, the name of the country to whose registry transfer is desired. All outstanding obligations to the Republic of Vanuatu must be paid prior to deletion. If a vessel is subject to a preferred mortgage, a vessel may not be deregistered without the consent of the mortgagee.

Contact addresses

25.23

Vanuatu Maritime Services Ltd
Suite 2020
39 Broadway
New York
NY 10006, USA
Tel: (1) 212 425 9600
Fax: (1) 212 425 9652
Email: email@vanuatuships.com
Website: www.vanuatumaritimeships.com

APPENDICES

Statistics

     I   Leading flags of registration by tonnage
    II   Ownership of the world fleet, 2017
   III   Paris MOU – White/Grey/Black Lists
   IV   STCW White List

Legislation and Conventions

     V   Extracts from UK Merchant Shipping Act 1995
   VI   Extracts from UK Merchant Shipping (Registration of Ships) Regulations 1993
  VII   Geneva Convention on the High Seas
 VIII   Extract from UN Convention on the Law of the Sea 1982
   IX   UN Convention on Conditions for Registration of Ships 1986
    X   International Convention on Maritime Liens and Mortgages 1993

Forms

 XI(a)   Bahamas forms
 XI(b)   Cayman Islands forms
 XI(c)   Gibraltar forms
 XI(d)   Isle of Man forms
 XI(e)   Liberia forms
 XI(f)   Malta forms
 XI(g)   Marshall Islands forms
 XI(h)   Norway forms
 XI(i)   Singapore forms
 XI(j)   UK forms

STATISTICS

APPENDIX I

Leading flags of registration by tonnage

Flag State	Number of vessels	Vessel share of world total (%)	Dead-weight tonnage	Share of world total dead-weight tonnage (%)	Cumulated share of dead-weight tonnage (%)	Dead-weight tonnage growth, 2016–2017 (%)
Panama	8,052	8.64	343,397,556	18.44	18.44	2.75
Liberia	3,296	3.54	219,397,222	11.78	30.23	5.66
Marshall Islands	3,199	3.43	216,616,351	11.63	41.86	7.76
Hong Kong (China)	2,576	2.77	173,318,337	9.31	51.17	6.23
Singapore	3,558	3.82	124,237,959	6.67	57.84	0.21
Malta	2,170	2.33	99,216,415	5.53	63.17	5.14
Bahamas	1,440	1.55	79,842,485	4.29	67.46	0.79
China	4,287	4.60	78,400,273	4.21	71.67	2.12
Greece	1,364	1.46	74,637,988	4.01	75.68	1.60
UK	1,551	1.66	40,985,692	2.20	77.88	10.42
Japan	5,289	5.68	34,529,405	1.85	79.74	6.60
Cyprus	1,022	1.10	33,764,669	1.81	81.55	1.82
Norway	1,585	1.70	21,900,458	1.18	82.73	6.89
Indonesia	8,782	9.43	20,143,854	1.08	83.81	7.58
India	1,674	1.80	17,253,564	0.93	84.74	5.34
Denmark	654	0.70	16,893,333	0.91	85.64	−1.73
Italy	1,430	1.53	15,944,268	0.86	86.50	−2.32
Republic of Korea	1,907	2.05	15,171,035	0.81	87.31	−10.80
Portugal	466	0.50	13,752,758	0.74	88.05	54.97
United States	3,611	3.88	11,798,309	0.63	88.69	0.75
Bermuda	160	0.17	10,957,895	0.59	89.27	2.44
Germany	614	0.66	10,443,669	0.56	89.84	−6.15
Antigua and Barbuda	964	1.03	10,153,044	0.55	90.38	−9.68
Malaysia	1,690	1.81	10,058,653	0.54	90.92	4.70
Russian Federation	2,572	2.76	8,277,175	0.44	91.37	−2.95

(*Continued*)

APPENDIX I

(Continued)

Flag State	Number of vessels	Vessel share of world total (%)	Dead-weight tonnage	Share of world total dead-weight tonnage (%)	Cumulated share of dead-weight tonnage (%)	Dead-weight tonnage growth, 2016–2017 (%)
Turkey	1,285	1.38	8,200,982	0.44	91.81	−3.83
Belgium	185	0.20	8,039,665	0.43	92.24	−3.57
Vietnam	1,818	1.95	7,991,039	0.43	92.67	2.96
Netherlands	1,244	1.34	7,619,143	0.41	93.08	−5.31
France	547	0.59	6,966,582	0.37	93.45	0.90
Islamic Republic of Iran	739	0.79	6,583,064	0.35	93.80	34.49
Philippines	1,508	1.62	6,135,144	0.33	94.13	−3.63
Cayman Islands	161	0.17	5,549,056	0.30	94.43	28.52
Thailand	781	0.84	5,374,875	0.29	94.72	0.13
Kuwait	161	0.17	5,155,256	0.28	95.00	−3.85
Top 35 total	**72,342**	**77.65**	**1,768,707,283**	**95.00**	**95.00**	**4.02**
Rest of world	**20,819**	**22.35**	**94,530,523**	**5.07**	**5.07**	**−12.80**
World total	**93,161**	**100.00**	**1,861,851,750**	**100.00**	**100.00**	**2.94**

Source: Review of Maritime Transport (2017) (UNCTAD/RMT/2017) Table 2.6
Adopting UNCTAD secretariat calculations, based on data from Clarksons Research.

Notes: Propelled seagoing merchant vessels of 100 gross tons and above, ranked by dead-weight tonnage; beginning-of-year figures.
For a complete list of all countries, see http://stats.unctad.org/fleet (accessed 9 September 2017)

APPENDIX II

Ownership of the world fleet, 2017

Rank (dead-weight tonnage)	Country or territory	Number of vessels	Dead-weight tonnage	Foreign flag as a percentage of total (dwt)	Rank (dollars)	Total Value (million dollars)
1	Greece	4,199	308,836,933	78.76	3	72,538
2	Japan	3,901	223,855,788	85.89	2	77,898
3	China	5,206	165,429,859	53.97	4	65,044
4	Germany	3,090	112,028,306	90.77	8	38,412
5	Singapore	2,599	104,414,424	38.02	7	39,193
6	Hong Kong (China)	1,532	93,629,750	23.98	9	25,769
7	Republic of Korea	1,656	80,976,874	81.98	11	20,928
8	USA	2,104	67,100,538	85.73	1	96,182
9	Norway	1,842	51,824,489	64.622	5	58,455
10	UK	1,360	51,150,767	80.55	6	40,671
11	Bermuda	440	48,059,392	98.93	13	19,691
12	Taiwan Province of China	926	46,864,949	90.62	17	10,857
13	Denmark	920	36,355,509	56.00	15	18,694
14	Monaco	338	31,629,834	100.00	23	7,903
15	Turkey	1,563	27,732,948	71.57	20	9,055
16	Switzerland	405	23,688,303	92.58	22	8,458
17	Belgium	263	23,550,024	67.81	27	6,505
18	India	986	22,665,452	27.35	25	6,938
19	Russian Federation	1,707	22,050,283	67.38	19	9,081
20	Italy	768	20,609,725	29.36	10	23,184
21	Islamic Republic of Iran	238	18,838,747	68.80	32	2,799
22	Indonesia	1,840	18,793,019	7.96	26	6,613
23	Malaysia	644	18,351,283	51.07	16	14,641

(*Continued*)

APPENDIX II

(Continued)

Rank (dead-weight tonnage)	Country or territory	Number of vessels	Dead-weight tonnage	Foreign flag as a percentage of total (dwt)	Rank (dollars)	Total Value (million dollars)
24	Netherlands	1,256	18,033,334	64.72	12	19,970
25	United Arab Emirates	883	17,876,272	97.30	24	7,406
26	Saudi Arabia	283	15,659,518	77.97	30	4,101
27	Brazil	394	14,189,164	72.25	14	19,676
28	France	452	11,931,397	69.93	18	10,616
29	Canada	376	10,235,954	75.48	28	5,231
30	Kuwait	86	10,208,147	49.92	31	3,749
31	Cyprus	277	9,257,094	63.95	33	2,711
32	Vietnam	943	8,801,765	17.84	29	4,161
33	Oman	49	7,490,956	99.92	34	2,215
34	Thailand	393	7,022,484	27.84	35	1,949
35	Qatar	117	6,640,467	87.56	21	8,827
Subtotal, top 35		**44,036**	**1,755,783,748**	**70.30**		**770,109**
Rest of world and unknown		*6,119*	*91,847,146*	*64.30*		*58,509*
World total		**50,155**	**1,847,630,894**	**70.01**		**828,618**

Source: Review of Maritime Transport (2017) (UNCTAD/RMT/2017) Table 2.3
Adopting UNCTAD secretariat calculations, based on data from Clarksons Research.

Notes: Propelled seagoing merchant vessels of 1,000 gross tons and above, ranked by dead-weight tonnage; beginning-of-year figures.
For a complete list of all countries, see http://stats.unctad.org/fleetownership (accessed 9 September 2017)

APPENDIX III

Paris MOU – White/Grey/Black Lists[1]

White List

Rank	Flag	Inspections 2014–2016	Detentions 2014–2016	Black to Grey Limit	Grey to White Limit	Excess Factor
1	Cayman Islands	393	1	36	19	−1,91
2	France	266	0	26	11	−1.91
3	Denmark	1201	9	99	69	−1,90
4	Netherlands	3103	35	241	193	−1,84
5	Bahamas	2291	27	181	140	−1,80
6	Italy	1164	13	96	67	−1,75
7	Hong Kong, China	1921	25	153	116	−1,73
8	Marshall Islands	3704	54	285	233	−1,73
9	UK	1260	15	104	73	−1,73
10	Norway	1450	18	118	85	−1,73
11	Isle of Man	747	8	64	40	−1,70
12	Sweden	331	2	31	15	−1,69
13	Singapore	1816	26	146	109	−1,68
14	Belgium	219	1	22	9	−1,59
15	Germany	629	8	55	33	−1,58
16	Ireland	124	0	14	4	−1,45
17	Greece	917	18	77	51	−1,37
18	Finland	407	6	37	20	−1,36
19	Cyprus	1965	47	157	118	−1,32
20	Luxembourg	213	2	22	8	−1,32
21	Bermuda	241	3	24	10	−1,24
22	Gibraltar	770	17	66	42	−1,23
23	Malta	4586	135	350	292	−1,21

(*Continued*)

1 Courtesy Paris MOU secretariat, as at 1 July 2017

APPENDIX III

(Continued)

Rank	Flag	Inspections 2014–2016	Detentions 2014–2016	Black to Grey Limit	Grey to White Limit	Excess Factor
24	Liberia	4170	128	320	264	−1,15
25	China	207	3	21	8	−1,04
26	Latvia	85	0	10	2	−0,96
27	Philippines	151	2	16	5	−0,87
28	Estonia	79	0	10	1	−0,86
29	Barbados	325	8	31	15	−0,84
30	Portugal	582	18	51	30	−0,80
31	Faroe Islands	256	6	25	11	−0,77
32	Antigua and Barbuda	3160	129	245	197	−0,76
33	Saudi Arabia	73	0	9	1	−0,75
34	Kazakhstan	72	0	9	1	−0,73
35	Japan	94	1	11	2	−0,54
36	USA	194	5	20	7	−0,50
37	Panama	6082	313	459	393	−0,45
38	Islamic Republic of Iran	89	1	11	2	−0,44
39	Russian Federation	1258	61	103	73	−0,34
40	Croatia	108	2	12	3	−0,31
41	Spain	173	5	18	6	−0,28
42	Turkey	1237	65	102	71	−0,19

Grey List

Rank	Flag	Inspections 2014–2016	Detentions 2014–2016	Black to Grey Limit	Grey to White Limit	Excess Factor
43	Republic of Korea	90	2	11	2	0,02
44	Poland	123	4	14	3	0,05
45	Kuwait	36	0	6	0	0,08
46	Lithuania	137	6	15	4	0,17
47	Switzerland	126	6	14	4	0,23
48	Libya	33	1	5	0	0,27
49	Morocco	43	2	6	0	0,34
50	Algeria	74	4	9	1	0,36
51	Thailand	72	4	9	1	0,37
52	India	71	4	9	1	0,38

Rank	Flag	Inspections 2014–2016	Detentions 2014–2016	Black to Grey Limit	Grey to White Limit	Excess Factor
53	Azerbaijan	31	2	5	0	0,47
54	Egypt	52	4	7	0	0,55
55	Bulgaria	38	3	6	0	0,56
56	Curacao	149	12	16	5	0,64
57	Albania	68	6	9	1	0,66
58	St Vincent & the Grenadines	647	50	56	34	0,71
59	Tunisia	41	5	6	0	0,83
60	Lebanon	74	8	9	1	0,84
61	Ukraine	129	14	14	4	0,97

Black List

Rank	Flag	Inspections 2014–2016	Detentions 2014–2016	Black to Grey Limit	Grey to White Limit	Excess Factor
62	Belize	488	47	44	Medium Risk	1,19
63	Cook Islands	404	40	37	Medium Risk	1,20
64	Vanuatu	277	31	27	Medium Risk	1,43
65	Saint Kitts and Nevis	299	34	29	Medium Risk	1,52
66	Cambodia	293	36	28	Medium Risk	1,78
67	Sierra Leone	260	39	25	Medium to High Risk	2,52
68	Palau	123	23	14	High Risk	3,09
69	Comoros	228	40	23	High Risk	3,20
70	Moldova, Republic of	515	85	46	High Risk	3,30
71	Togo	399	70	37	High Risk	3,51
72	Tanzania United Rep.	211	40	21	High Risk	3,57
73	Congo, Republic of the	86	24	10	Very High Risk	5,40

APPENDIX IV

STCW White List[1]

Parties to the International Convention on Standards of Training, Certification and Watchkeeping for Seafarers (STCW) 1978, as amended, confirmed by the Maritime Safety Committee to have communicated information which demonstrates that full and complete effect is given to the relevant provisions of the Convention:

Albania	Republic of Korea	Kenya
Algeria	Denmark**	Kiribati
Antigua and Barbuda	Dominica	Kuwait
Argentina	Ecuador	Latvia
Australia	Egypt	Lebanon
Azerbaijan	El Salvador	Liberia
Bahamas (the)	Eritrea	Lithuania
Bahrain	Estonia	Luxembourg
Bangladesh	Ethiopia	Libya
Barbados	Fiji	Madagascar
Belgium	Finland	Malaysia
Belize	France	Malawi
Brazil	Georgia	Maldives
Brunei Darussalam	Germany	Malta
Bulgaria	Ghana	Marshall Islands
Cambodia	Guatemala	Mauritania
Canada	Greece	Mauritius
Cabo Verde	Honduras	Mexico
Chile	Hungary	Micronesia (Federated
China*	Iceland	States of)
Colombia	India	Montenegro*****
Comoros	Indonesia	Morocco
Cook Islands (the)	Iran (Islamic Republic of)	Mozambique
Côte d'Ivoire	Ireland	Myanmar
Croatia	Italy	Netherlands***
Cuba	Israel	New Zealand
Cyprus	Jamaica	Nigeria
Czech Republic	Japan	Norway
Democratic People's	Jordan	Oman

---

1 *Source*: MSC.1/Circ.1163/Rev. 10, 23 May 2016

APPENDIX IV

Pakistan
Panama
Papua New Guinea
Peru
Philippines
Poland
Portugal
Qatar
Republic of Korea
Romania
Russian Federation
St Vincent and the Grenadines
Samoa
Saudi Arabia
Senegal

Serbia*****
Seychelles
Singapore
Slovak Republic
Slovenia
Solomon Islands
South Africa
Spain
Sri Lanka
Sweden
Switzerland
Syrian Arab Republic
Thailand
Togo
Tonga

Trinidad and Tobago
Tunisia
Turkey
Tuvalu
Ukraine
United Arab Emirates
UK****
United Republic of
Tanzania
USA
Uruguay
Vanuatu
Venezuela (Bolivarian
Republic of)
Viet Nam

* Includes: Hong Kong, China (Associate Member to the IMO).
** Includes: Faroe Islands (Associate Member to the IMO).
*** Includes: Aruba, Curacao and St Maarten.
**** Includes: Bermuda, British Virgin Islands, Cayman Islands, Gibraltar, Isle of Man.
***** Part of ex Yugoslavia. As from 4 February 2003, the name of the State of the Federal Republic of Yugoslavia was changed to Serbia and Montenegro. Following the dissolution of the State of Serbia and Montenegro on 3 June 2006, all treaty actions relating to the provisions of the STCW Convention undertaken by Serbia and Montenegro continue to be in force with respect to the Republic of Serbia and the Republic of Montenegro with effect from the same date, i.e. 3 June 2006.

LEGISLATION AND CONVENTIONS

APPENDIX V

Extracts from UK Merchant Shipping Act 1995[1]

An Act to consolidate the Merchant Shipping Acts 1894–1994 and other enactments relating to merchant shipping.

Part I British ships

British ships and United Kingdom ships

1. – (1) A ship is a British ship if –
   (a) the ship is registered in the United Kingdom under Part II; or
   (b) the ship is, as a Government ship, registered in the United Kingdom in pursuance of an Order in Council under section 308; or
   (c) the ship is registered under the law of a relevant British possession; or
   (d) the ship is a small ship other than a fishing vessel and –
        (i)   is not registered under Part II, but
        (ii) is wholly owned by qualified owners, and
        (iii) is not registered under the law of a country outside the United Kingdom.
   (2) For the purposes of subsection (1)(d) above –
        "qualified owners" means persons of such description qualified to own British ships as is prescribed by regulations made by the Secretary of State for the purposes of that paragraph; and
        "small ship" means a ship less than 24 metres in length ("length" having the same meaning as in the tonnage regulations).
   (3) A ship is a "United Kingdom ship" for the purposes of this Act (except section 85 and 144(3)) if the ship is registered in the United Kingdom under Part II (and in Part V "United Kingdom fishing vessel" has a corresponding meaning).

British flag

2. – (1) The flag which every British ship is entitled to fly is the red ensign (without any defacement or modification) and, subject to subsections (2) and (3) below, no other colours.
   (2) Subsection (1) above does not apply to Government ships.

---

1 As amended, at 1 March 2018 by (1) the Ministry of Agriculture, Fisheries and Food (Dissolution) Order 2002, SI 2002/794 and (2) the Legal Aid, Sentencing and Punishment of Offenders Act 2012 (Fines on Summary Conviction) Regulations 2015, SI 2015/664.

Source: Contains public sector information licensed under the open Government License v3.0.

APPENDIX V

(3) The following are also proper national colours, that is to say –
  (a) any colours allowed to be worn in pursuance of a warrant from Her Majesty or from the Secretary of State;
  (b) in the case of British ships registered in a relevant British possession, any colours consisting of the red ensign defaced or modified whose adoption for ships registered in that possession is authorised or confirmed by Her Majesty by Order in Council.
(4) Any Order under subsection (3)(b) above shall be laid before Parliament after being made.

Offences relating to British character of ship

3. – (1) If the master or owner of a ship which is not a British ship does anything, or permits anything to be done, for the purpose of causing the ship to appear to be a British ship then, except as provided by subsections (2) and (3) below, the ship shall be liable to forfeiture and the master, the owner and any charterer shall each be guilty of an offence.
(2) No liability arises under subsection (1) above where the assumption of British nationality has been made for the purpose of escaping capture by an enemy or by a foreign ship of war in the exercise of some belligerent right.
(3) Where the registration of any ship has terminated by virtue of any provision of registration regulations, any marks prescribed by registration regulations displayed on the ship within the period of 14 days beginning with the date of termination of that registration shall be disregarded for the purposes of subsection (1) above.
(4) If the master or owner of a British ship does anything, or permits anything to be done, for the purpose of concealing the nationality of the ship, the ship shall be liable to forfeiture and the master, the owner and any charterer of the ship shall each be guilty of an offence.
(5) Without prejudice to the generality of subsections (1) and (4) above, those subsections apply in particular to acts or deliberate omissions as respects –
  (a) the flying of a national flag;
  (b) the carrying or production of certificates of registration or other documents relating to the nationality of the ship; and
  (c) the display of marks required by the law of any country.
(6) Any person guilty of an offence under this section shall be liable –
  (a) on summary conviction, to a fine;
  (b) on conviction on indictment, to imprisonment for a term not exceeding two years or a fine, or both.
(7) This section applies to things done outside, as well as to things done within, the United Kingdom.

Penalty for carrying improper colours

4. – (1) If any of the following colours, namely –
  (a) any distinctive national colours except –
    (i) the red ensign,
    (ii) the Union flag (commonly known as the Union Jack) with a white border, or
    (iii) any colours authorised or confirmed under section 2(3)(b); or
  (b) any colours usually worn by Her Majesty's ships or resembling those of Her Majesty, or

APPENDIX V

 (c) the pendant usually carried by Her Majesty's ships or any pendant resembling that pendant,

are hoisted on board any British ship without warrant from Her Majesty or from the Secretary of State, the master of the ship, or the owner of the ship (if on board), and every other person hoisting them shall be guilty of an offence.

(2) A person guilty of an offence under subsection (1) above shall be liable –

 (a) on summary conviction, to a fine not exceeding the statutory maximum;

 (b) on conviction on indictment, to a fine.

(3) If any colours are hoisted on board a ship in contravention of subsection (1) above, any of the following, namely –

 (a) any commissioned naval or military officer,

 (b) any officer of customs and excise, and

 (c) any British consular officer,

may board the ship and seize and take away the colours.

(4) Any colours seized under subsection (3) above shall be forfeited to Her Majesty.

(5) In this section "colours" includes any pendant.

Duty to show British flag

5. – (1) Subject to subsection (2) below, a British ship, other than a fishing vessel, shall hoist the red ensign or other proper national colours –

 (a) on a signal being made to the ship by one of Her Majesty's ships (including any ship under the command of a commissioned naval officer); and

 (b) on entering or leaving any foreign port; and

 (c) in the case of ships of 50 or more tons gross tonnage, on entering or leaving any British port.

(2) Subsection (1)(c) above does not apply to a small ship (as defined in section 1(2)) registered under Part II.

Duty to declare national character of ship

6. – (1) An officer of customs and excise shall not grant a clearance or transire for any ship until the master of such ship has declared to that officer the name of the nation to which he claims that the ship belongs, and that officer shall thereupon enter that name on the clearance or transire.

(2) If a ship attempts to proceed to sea without such clearance or transire, the ship may be detained until the declaration is made.

Proceedings on forfeiture of a ship

7. – (1) Where any ship has either wholly or as to any share in it become liable to forfeiture under this Part –

 (a) any commissioned naval or military officer, or

 (b) any person appointed by the Secretary of State for the purposes of this section;

may seize and detain the ship and bring the ship for adjudication before the court.

(2) Where a ship is subject to adjudication under this section the court may –

 (a) adjudge the ship and her equipment to be forfeited to Her Majesty; and

 (b) make such order in the case as seems just.

(3) No officer or person bringing proceedings under this section shall be liable in damages in respect of the seizure or detention of the ship, notwithstanding that the ship

APPENDIX V

has not been proceeded against or, if proceeded against, adjudicated not liable to forfeiture, if the court is satisfied that there were reasonable grounds for the seizure or detention.

(4) If the court is not so satisfied the court may award costs (or in Scotland expenses) and damages to the party aggrieved and make such other order as the court thinks just.

(5) In this section "the court" means the High Court or, in Scotland, the Court of Session.

Part II registration

General

Central register of British ships

8. – (1) There shall continue to be a register of British ships for all registrations of ships in the United Kingdom.

(2) The register shall be maintained by the Registrar General of Shipping and Seamen as registrar.

(3) The Secretary of State may designate any person to discharge, on behalf of the registrar, all his functions or such of them as the Secretary of State may direct.

(4) The Secretary of State may give to the registrar directions of a general nature as to the discharge of any of his functions.

(5) The register shall be so constituted as to distinguish, in a separate part, registrations of fishing vessels and may be otherwise divided into parts so as to distinguish between classes or descriptions of ships.

(6) The register shall be maintained in accordance with registration regulations and the private law provisions for registered ships and any directions given by the Secretary of State under subsection (4) above.

(7) The register shall be available for public inspection.

Registration of ships: basic provisions

9. – (1) A ship is entitled to be registered if –

(a) it is owned, to the prescribed extent, by persons qualified to own British ships; and

(b) such other conditions are satisfied as are prescribed under subsection (2)(b) below; (and any application for registration is duly made).

(2) It shall be for registration regulations –

(a) to determine the persons who are qualified to be owners of British ships, or British ships of any class or description, and to prescribe the extent of the ownership required for compliance with subsection (1)(a) above;

(b) to prescribe other requirements designed to secure that, taken in conjunction with the requisite ownership, only ships having a British connection are registered.

(3) The registrar may, nevertheless, if registration regulations so provide, refuse to register or terminate the registration of a ship if, having regard to any relevant requirements of this Act, he considers it would be inappropriate for the ship to be or, as the case may be, to remain registered.

(4) The registrar may, if registration regulations so provide, register a fishing vessel notwithstanding that the requirement of subsection (1)(a) above is not satisfied in relation to a particular owner of a share in the vessel if the vessel otherwise has a British connection.

APPENDIX V

(5) Where a ship becomes registered at a time when it is already registered under the law of a country other than the United Kingdom, the owner of the ship shall take all reasonable steps to secure the termination of the ship's registration under the law of that country.

(6) Subsection (5) above does not apply to a ship which becomes registered on a transfer of registration to the register from a relevant British possession.

(7) Any person who contravenes subsection (5) above shall be liable on summary conviction to a fine not exceeding level 3 on the standard scale.

(8) In this section "the relevant requirements of this Act" means the requirements of this Act (including requirements falling to be complied with after registration) relating to –

(a) the condition of ships or their equipment so far as relevant to their safety or any risk of pollution; and

(b) the safety, health and welfare of persons employed or engaged in them.

(9) In this Part references to a ship's having a British connection are references to compliance with the conditions of entitlement imposed by subsection (1)(a) and (b) above and "declaration of British connection" is to be construed accordingly.

Registration regulations

10. – (1) The Secretary of State shall by regulations (to be known as registration regulations) make provision for and in connection with the registration of ships as British ships.

(2) Without prejudice to the generality of subsection (1) above, registration regulations may, in particular, make provision with respect to any of the following matters –

(a) the persons by whom and the manner in which applications in connection with registration are to be made;

(b) the information and evidence (including declarations of British connection) to be provided in connection with such applications and such supplementary information or evidence as may be required by any specified authority;

(c) the shares in the property in, and the numbers of owners (including joint owners) of, a ship permitted for the purposes of registration and the persons required or permitted to be registered in respect of a ship or to be so registered in specified circumstances;

(d) the issue of certificates (including provisional certificates) of registration, their production and surrender;

(e) restricting and regulating the names of ships registered or to be registered;

(f) the marking of ships registered or to be registered, including marks for identifying the port to which a ship is to be treated as belonging;

(g) the period for which registration is to remain effective without renewal;

(h) the production to the registrar of declarations of British connection or other information relating thereto, as respects registered ships, at specified intervals or at his request;

(i) the survey and inspection of ships registered or to be registered and the recording of their tonnage as ascertained (or re-ascertained) under the tonnage regulations;

(j) the refusal, suspension and termination of registration in specified circumstances;

(k) matters arising out of the expiration, suspension or termination of registration (including the removal of marks and the cancellation of certificates);

(l) the charging of fees in connection with registration or registered ships;

(m) the transfer of the registration of ships to and from the register from and to registers or corresponding records in countries other than the United Kingdom;

APPENDIX V

(n)   inspection of the register;

(o)   any other matter which is authorised or required by this Part to be prescribed in registration regulations;

but no provision determining, or providing for determining, the fees to be charged or prescribing any arrangements for their determination by other persons shall be made without the approval of the Treasury.

(3)   Registration regulations may –

(a)   make different provision for different classes or descriptions of ships and for different circumstances;

(b)   without prejudice to paragraph (a) above, make provision for the granting of exemptions or dispensations by the Secretary of State from specified requirements of the regulations, subject to such conditions (if any) as he thinks fit to impose; and

(c)   make such transitional, incidental or supplementary provision as appears to the Secretary of State to be necessary or expedient, including provision authorising investigations and conferring powers of inspection for verifying the British connection of a ship.

(4)   Registration regulations –

(a)   may make provision for the registration of any class or description of ships to be such as to exclude the application of the private law provisions for registered ships and, if they do, may regulate the transfer, transmission or mortgaging of ships of the class or description so excluded;

(b)   may make provision for any matter which is authorised or required by those provisions to be prescribed by registration regulations; and

(c)   shall make provision precluding notice of any trust being entered in the register or being receivable by the registrar except as respects specified classes or descriptions of ships or in specified circumstances.

(5)   Registration regulations may create offences subject to the limitation that no offence shall be punishable with imprisonment or punishable on summary conviction with a fine exceeding level 5 on the standard scale.

(6)   Registration regulations may provide for –

(a)   the approval of forms by the Secretary of State; and

(b)   the discharge of specified functions by specified authorities or persons.

(7)   Registration regulations may provide for any of their provisions to extend to places outside the United Kingdom.

(8)   Any document purporting to be a copy of any information contained in an entry in the register and to be certified as a true copy by the registrar shall be evidence (and, in Scotland, sufficient evidence) of the matters stated in the document.

(9)   Registration regulations may provide that any reference in any other Act or in any instrument made under any other Act to the port of registry or the port to which a ship belongs shall be construed as a reference to the port identified by the marks required for the purpose by registration regulations.

Tonnage ascertained for registration to be tonnage of ship

11.   When the tonnage of any ship has been ascertained and registered in accordance with the tonnage regulations that tonnage shall be treated as the tonnage of the ship except so far as registration regulations provide, in specified circumstances, for the ship to be re-measured and the register amended accordingly.

APPENDIX V

Tonnage of ships of foreign countries adopting tonnage regulations

12. – (1) Her Majesty may by Order in Council make such provision in relation to the ships of a foreign country as is authorised by this section where it appears to Her that the tonnage regulations have been adopted by the foreign country and are in force there.

(2) An Order under this section may order that the ships of the foreign country shall, without being re-measured in the United Kingdom, be treated as being of the tonnage denoted by their certificates of registration or other national papers, to the same extent, and for the same purposes as the tonnage denoted in the certificate of registration of a United Kingdom ship is treated as being the tonnage of that ship.

(3) Where an Order under this section is in force in relation to the ships of any country any space shown in the ship's certificate of registration or other national papers as deducted from the tonnage shall, if a similar deduction in the case of a United Kingdom ship depends on compliance with any conditions or on the compliance being evidenced in any manner, be treated as complying with those conditions and as being so evidenced, unless a surveyor of ships certifies to the Secretary of State that the construction and equipment of the ship as respects that space do not come up to the standard which would be required if the ship were a United Kingdom ship.

(4) Any such Order may –
(a) operate for a limited time; and
(b) be subject to such conditions and qualifications (if any) as Her Majesty may consider expedient.

(5) If it appears to Her Majesty that the tonnage of any foreign ship, as measured by the rules of the country to which the ship belongs, materially differs from what it would be under the tonnage regulations, Her Majesty may by Order in Council order that, notwithstanding any Order in Council in force under this section, any of the ships of that country may, for all or any of the purposes of this Act, be re-measured in accordance with the tonnage regulations.

Status of certificate of registration

13. The certificate of registration of a British ship shall be used only for the lawful navigation of the ship, and shall not be subject to detention to secure any private right or claim.

Offences relating to a ship's British connection

14. – (1) Any person who, in relation to any matter relevant to the British connection of a ship –
(a) makes to the registrar a statement which he knows to be false or recklessly makes a statement which is false; or
(b) furnishes to the registrar information which is false, shall be guilty of an offence.

(2) If at any time there occurs, in relation to a registered ship, any change affecting the British connection of the ship the owner of the ship shall, as soon as practicable after the change occurs, notify the registrar of that change; and if he fails to do so he shall be guilty of an offence.

(3) Any person who intentionally alters, suppresses, conceals or destroys a document which contains information relating to the British connection of the ship and which he has been required to produce to the registrar in pursuance of registration regulations shall be guilty of an offence.

APPENDIX V

(4) A person guilty of an offence under this section shall be liable –
  (a) on summary conviction, to a fine not exceeding the statutory maximum;
  (b) on conviction on indictment, to imprisonment for a term not exceeding two years or a fine, or both.

(5) This section applies to things done outside, as well as to things done within, the United Kingdom.

Supplementary provisions as respects fishing vessels

15. – (1) Subject to subsection (2) below, if a fishing vessel which –
  (a) is either –
    (i) entitled to be registered, or
    (ii) wholly owned by persons qualified to be owners of British ships, but
  (b) is registered neither under this Act in the part of the register relating to fishing vessels nor under the law of any country outside the United Kingdom,
  fishes for profit the vessel shall be liable to forfeiture and the skipper, the owner and the charterer of the vessel shall each be guilty of an offence.

(2) Subsection (1) above does not apply to fishing vessels of such classes or descriptions or in such circumstances as may be specified in regulations made by the Secretary of State.

(3) If the skipper or owner of a fishing vessel which is not registered in the United Kingdom does anything, or permits anything to be done, for the purpose of causing the vessel to appear to be a vessel registered in the United Kingdom, then, subject to subsection (4) below, the vessel shall be liable to forfeiture and the skipper, the owner and any charterer of the vessel shall each be guilty of an offence.

(4) Where the registration of a fishing vessel has terminated by virtue of any provision of registration regulations, any marks prescribed by registration regulations displayed on the fishing vessel within the period of 14 days beginning with the date of termination of that registration shall be disregarded for the purposes of subsection (3) above.

(5) Any person guilty of an offence under this section shall be liable –
  (a) on summary conviction, to a fine;
  (b) on conviction on indictment, to imprisonment for a term not exceeding two years or a fine, or both.

(6) Proceedings for an offence under this section shall not be instituted –
  (a) in England and Wales, except by or with the consent of the Attorney General or the Secretary of State; or
  (b) in Northern Ireland, except by or with the consent of the Attorney General for Northern Ireland, the Secretary of State or the Minister.

(7) In subsection (6) above "the Minister" –
  (a) [repealed]
  (b) in relation to Northern Ireland, means the Secretary of State concerned with sea fishing in Northern Ireland.

(8) This section applies to things done outside, as well as to things done within, the United Kingdom.

(9) Sections 8 and 9 of the Sea Fisheries Act 1968 (general powers of British sea-fishery officers and powers of sea-fishery officers to enforce Conventions) shall apply in relation to any provision of this section or of registration regulations in their application to fishing vessels or fishing vessels of any class or description as they apply in relation to any order mentioned in section 8 of that Act and in relation to any Convention

APPENDIX V

mentioned in section 9 of that Act respectively; and sections 10 to 12 and 14 of that Act (offences and supplemental proceedings as to legal proceedings) shall apply accordingly.

Private law provisions for registered ships and liability as owner

16. – (1) Schedule 1 (which makes provision relating to the title to, and the registration of mortgages over, ships) shall have effect.

(2) Schedule 1 does not apply in relation to ships which are excluded from its application by registration regulations under section 10(4)(a).

(3) Where any person is beneficially interested, otherwise than as mortgagee, in any ship or share in a ship registered in the name of some other person as owner, the person so interested shall, as well as the registered owner, be liable to any pecuniary penalties imposed by or under this Act or any other Act on the owners of registered ships.

(4) Where the registration of any ship terminates by virtue of any provision of registration regulations, the termination of that registration shall not affect any entry made in the register so far as relating to any undischarged registered mortgage of that ship or of any share in it.

(5) In subsection (4) above "registered mortgage" has the same meaning as in that Schedule.

(6) In this Part "the private law provisions for registered ships" means the provisions of Schedule 1 and registration regulations made for the purposes of that Schedule or the provisions of registration regulations made under section 10(4)(a).

Ships on bareboat charter

Ships bareboat chartered-in by British charterers

17. – (1) This section applies to any ship which –

(a) is registered under the law of a country other than the United Kingdom ("the country of original registration"),

(b) is chartered on bareboat charter terms to a charterer who is a person qualified to own British ships, and

(c) is so chartered in circumstances where the conditions of entitlement to registration prescribed under section 9(2)(b), read with the requisite modifications, are satisfied as respects the charterer and the ship.

(2) The "requisite modifications" of those conditions are the substitution for any requirement to be satisfied by or as respects the owner of a ship of a corresponding requirement to be satisfied by or as respects the charterer of the ship.

(3) A ship to which this section applies is entitled to be registered if an application for registration is duly made, but section 9(3) applies also in relation to registration by virtue of this section.

(4) The registration of a ship registered by virtue of this section shall remain in force (unless terminated earlier by virtue of registration regulations and subject to any suspension thereunder) until the end of the charter period and shall then terminate by virtue of this subsection.

(5) Section 9(5) does not apply to a ship registered by virtue of this section but registration regulations shall include provision for securing that the authority responsible for the registration of ships in the country of original registration is notified of the

registration of the ship and of the termination of its registration whether by virtue of subsection (4) above or registration regulations.

(6) Accordingly, throughout the period for which a ship is registered by virtue of this section –

(a) the ship shall, as a British ship, be entitled to fly the British flag;

(b) this Act shall, subject to subsections (7) and (8) below, apply to the ship as a British ship or as a registered ship as it applies to other British ships and to registered ships; and

(c) any other enactment applicable to British ships or ships registered under this Act shall, subject to subsection (8) below, apply to the ship as a British ship or as a registered ship.

(7) The private law provisions for registered ships shall not apply to a ship registered by virtue of this section and any matters or questions corresponding to those for which the private law provisions for registered ships make provision shall be determined by reference to the law of the country of original registration.

(8) Her Majesty may, subject to subsection (9) below, by Order in Council, provide that any enactment falling within subsection (6)(b) or (c) above –

(a) shall not have effect in accordance with that subsection in relation to a ship registered by virtue of this section, or

(b) shall so have effect subject to such modifications (if any) as may be specified in the Order.

(9) No provision shall be made by an Order in Council under subsection (8) above which would have the effect of relaxing the relevant requirements of this Act (as defined in section 9(8)) in their application to a ship to which this section applies.

(10) An Order in Council under subsection (8) above may make such transitional, incidental or supplementary provision as appears to Her Majesty to be necessary or expedient (including provision divesting or providing for the divestment of ownership in the ship).

(11) In this section –

"bareboat charter terms", in relation to a ship, means the hiring of the ship for a stipulated period on terms which give the charterer possession and control of the ship, including the right to appoint the master and crew; and

"the charter period" means the period during which the ship is chartered on bareboat charter terms.

Supplemental

Regulation of registration in British possessions by reference to categories of registries

18. – (1) Her Majesty may by Order in Council make provision for regulating the registration in relevant British possessions of ships other than small ships and fishing vessels by reference to categories of registries established by the Order.

(2) Any such Order may –

(a) establish different categories of registries to which different restrictions on the registrations of ships in such possessions apply, being restrictions framed by reference to –

(i) ships' tonnages, or

(ii) types of ships, or

(iii) any other specified matter, or

APPENDIX V

      (iv) any combination of matters falling within one or more of the preceding sub-paragraphs, as well as a category of registries to which no such restriction applies;

  (b) assign any relevant British possession to such one of the categories so established as appears to Her Majesty to be appropriate;

  (c) provide that, where a relevant British possession has been assigned to a category to which any such restriction on registration as is mentioned in paragraph (a) applies, no ship covered by that restriction shall be registered under the law of that possession;

  (d) specify circumstances in which ships may be exempted from any provision made by virtue of paragraph (c) above.

(3) Any provision made by virtue of subsection (2)(c) above shall be expressed to be without prejudice to the operation of any provision for the time being in force under the law of any such possession as is mentioned in subsection (2)(c) above by virtue of which the registration of ships in that possession is, or may be, further restricted.

(4) An Order in Council under this section may make such transitional, incidental or supplementary provision as appears to Her Majesty to be necessary or expedient.

(5) In this section "small ship" has the meaning given by section 1(2).

Tonnage regulations

19. – (1) The tonnage of any ship to be registered under this Part shall be ascertained in accordance with regulations made by the Secretary of State ("tonnage regulations").

(2) Tonnage regulations –

  (a) may make different provisions for different descriptions of ships or for the same description of ships in different circumstances;

  (b) may make any regulation dependent on compliance with such conditions, to be evidenced in such manner, as may be specified in the regulations;

  (c) may prohibit or restrict the carriage of goods or stores in spaces not included in the registered tonnage and may provide for making the master and the owner each liable to a fine not exceeding level 3 on the standard scale where such a prohibition or restriction is contravened.

(3) Tonnage regulations may make provision –

  (a) for assigning to a ship, either instead of or as an alternative to the tonnage ascertained in accordance with the other provisions of the regulations, a lower tonnage applicable where the ship is not loaded to the full depth to which it can safely be loaded;

  (b) for indicating on the ship, by such mark as may be specified in the regulations, that such a lower tonnage has been assigned to it; and

  (c) where the lower tonnage has been assigned to it as an alternative, for indicating on the ship the depth to which the ship may be loaded for the lower tonnage to be applicable.

(4) Tonnage regulations may provide for the measurement and survey of ships to be undertaken, in such circumstances as may be specified in the regulations by persons appointed by such organisations as may be authorised for the purpose by the Secretary of State.

(5) Tonnage regulations may provide for the issue, by the Secretary of State or by persons appointed by such organisations as may be authorised for the purpose by the Secretary of State, of certificates of the registered tonnage of any ship or of the tonnage which is to be taken for any purpose specified in the regulations as the tonnage of a ship not registered in the United Kingdom, and for the

APPENDIX V

cancellation and delivery up of such certificates in such circumstances as may be prescribed by the regulations.

(6) Regulations requiring the delivery up of any certificate may make a failure to comply with the requirement an offence punishable on summary conviction with a fine not exceeding level 3 on the standard scale.

Proceedings on forfeiture of ship

20. Section 7 applies in relation to ships or shares in ships which become liable to forfeiture under this Part as it applies in relation to ships or shares in ships which become liable to forfeiture under Part I.

Disclosure of information relating to registration by other government departments

21. – (1) No obligation as to secrecy or other restriction on the disclosure of information (whether imposed by statute or otherwise) shall preclude any of the persons mentioned in subsection (2) below from disclosing –
(a) to the Secretary of State, or
(b) to the registrar, or
(c) to an authorised officer of the Secretary of State,
information for the purpose of assisting the Secretary of State in the performance of his functions under this Part.

(2) The persons referred to in subsection (1) above are –
(a) the Minister of Agriculture, Fisheries and Food,
(b) the Secretaries of State respectively concerned with sea fishing in Scotland, Wales and Northern Ireland,
(c) the Department of Agriculture for Northern Ireland,
(d) the Commissioners of Customs and Excise, and
(e) an authorised officer of any of the persons falling within paragraphs (a) to (d) above.

(3) Information obtained by any person in pursuance of subsection (1) above shall not be disclosed by him to any other person except where the disclosure is made –
(a) to a person to whom the information could have been disclosed by any of the persons mentioned in subsection (2) above in accordance with subsection (1) above, or
(b) for the purposes of any legal proceedings arising out of this Part.

Forgery of documents: Scotland

22. – (1) In Scotland, if any person forges or fraudulently alters –
(a) any entry or endorsement in the register; or
(b) subject to subsection (2) below, any other document as respects which provision is made by, under or by virtue of this Part (or any entry or endorsement in or on such other document and as respects which provision is so made),
he shall be liable –
(i) on summary conviction, to a fine not exceeding the statutory maximum or to imprisonment for a term not exceeding six months or to both; or
(ii) on conviction on indictment, to a fine or to imprisonment or to both.

(2) Subsection (1)(b) does not apply in respect of actings which constitute an offence under section 288(6) or 300(8).

296

APPENDIX V

Interpretation

23. – (1)   In this Part –
"British connection" and "declaration of British connection" have the meaning given in section 9(9);
"the private law provisions for registered ships" has the meaning given in section 16;
"the register" means the register of British ships maintained for the United Kingdom under section 8 and "registered" (except with reference to the law of another country) is to be construed accordingly; and
"the registrar" means the Registrar General of Shipping and Seamen in his capacity as registrar or, as respects functions of his being discharged by another authority or person, that authority or person.

(2)   Where, for the purposes of any enactment the question arises whether a ship is owned by persons qualified to own British ships, the question shall be determined by reference to registration regulations made under section 9(2)(a).

Schedule 1. Private law provisions for registered ships

(Section 16)

General

1. – (1)   Subject to any rights and powers appearing from the register to be vested in any other person, the registered owner of a ship or of a share in a ship shall have power absolutely to dispose of it provided the disposal is made in accordance with this Schedule and registration regulations.

(2)   Sub-paragraph (1) above does not imply that interests arising under contract or other equitable interests cannot subsist in relation to a ship or a share in a ship; and such interests may be enforced by or against owners and mortgagees of ships in respect of their interest in the ship or share in the same manner as in respect of any other personal property.

(3)   The registered owner of a ship or of a share in a ship shall have power to give effectual receipts for any money paid or advanced by way of consideration on any disposal of the ship or share.

Transfers etc of registered ships

2. – (1)   Any transfer of a registered ship, or a share in such a ship, shall be effected by a bill of sale satisfying the prescribed requirements, unless the transfer will result in the ship ceasing to have a British connection.

(2)   Where any such ship or share has been transferred in accordance with sub-paragraph (1) above, the transferee shall not be registered as owner of the ship or share unless –
(a)   he has made the prescribed application to the registrar; and
(b)   the registrar is satisfied that the ship retains a British connection and that he would not refuse to register the ship.

(3)   If an application under sub-paragraph (2) above is granted by the registrar, the registrar shall register the bill of sale in the prescribed manner.

(4)   Bills of sale shall be registered in the order in which they are produced to the registrar for the purposes of registration.

APPENDIX V

3. – (1) Where a registered ship, or a share in a registered ship, is transmitted to any person by any lawful means other than a transfer under paragraph 2 above and the ship continues to have a British connection, that person shall not be registered as owner of the ship or share unless –

(a) he has made the prescribed application to the registrar; and

(b) the registrar is satisfied that the ship retains a British connection and that he would not refuse to register the ship.

(2) If an application under sub-paragraph (1) is granted by the registrar, the registrar shall cause the applicant's name to be registered as owner of the ship or share.

4. – (1) Where the property in a registered ship or share in a registered ship is transmitted to any person by any lawful means other than a transfer under paragraph 2 above, but as a result the ship no longer has a British connection, the High Court or in Scotland the Court of Session may, on application by or on behalf of that person, order a sale of the property so transmitted and direct that the proceeds of sale, after deducting the expenses of the sale, shall be paid to that person or otherwise as the court direct.

(2) The court may require any evidence in support of the application they think requisite, and may make the order on any terms and conditions they think just, or may refuse to make the order, and generally may act in the case as the justice of the case requires.

(3) Every such application must be made within the period of 28 days beginning with the date of the occurrence of the event on which the transmission has taken place, or within such further time (not exceeding one year) as the court may allow.

(4) If –

(a) such an application is not made within the time allowed by or under sub-paragraph (3) above; or

(b) the court refuse an order for sale,

the ship or share transmitted shall be liable to forfeiture.

5. – (1) Where any court (whether under paragraph 4 above or otherwise) order the sale of any registered ship or share in a registered ship, the order of the court shall contain a declaration vesting in some named person the right to transfer the ship or share.

(2) The person so named shall be entitled to transfer the ship or share in the same manner and to the same extent as if he were the registered owner of the ship or share.

(3) The registrar shall deal with any application relating to the transfer of the ship or share made by the person so named as if that person were the registered owner.

6. – (1) The High Court or in Scotland the Court of Session may, if they think fit (without prejudice to the exercise of any other power), on the application of any interested person, make an order prohibiting for a specified time any dealing with a registered ship or share in a registered ship.

(2) The court may make the order on any terms or conditions they think just, or may refuse to make the order, or may discharge the order when made (with or without costs or, in Scotland, expenses) and generally may act in the case as the justice of the case requires.

(3) The order, when a copy is served on the registrar, shall be binding on him whether or not he was made a party to the proceedings.

298

APPENDIX V

Mortgages of registered ships

7. – (1)   A registered ship, or share in a registered ship, may be made a security for the repayment of a loan or the discharge of any other obligation.

(2)   The instrument creating any such security (referred to in the following provisions of this Schedule as a "mortgage") shall be in the form prescribed by or approved under registration regulations.

(3)   Where a mortgage executed in accordance with sub-paragraph (2) above is produced to the registrar, he shall register the mortgage in the prescribed manner.

(4)   Mortgages shall be registered in the order in which they are produced to the registrar for the purposes of registration.

Priority of registered mortgages

8. – (1)   Where two or more mortgages are registered in respect of the same ship or share, the priority of the mortgagees between themselves shall, subject to sub-paragraph (2) below, be determined by the order in which the mortgages were registered (and not by reference to any other matter).

(2)   Registration regulations may provide for the giving to the registrar by intending mortgagees of "priority notices" in a form prescribed by or approved under the regulations which, when recorded in the register, determine the priority of the interest to which the notice relates.

Registered mortgagee's power of sale

9. – (1)   Subject to sub-paragraph (2) below, every registered mortgagee shall have power, if the mortgage money or any part of it is due, to sell the ship or share in respect of which he is registered, and to give effectual receipts for the purchase money.

(2)   Where two or more mortgagees are registered in respect of the same ship or share, a subsequent mortgagee shall not, except under an order of a court of competent jurisdiction, sell the ship or share without the concurrence of every prior mortgagee.

Protection of registered mortgagees

10.   Where a ship or share is subject to a registered mortgage then –

(a)   except so far as may be necessary for making the ship or share available as a security for the mortgage debt, the mortgagee shall not by reason of the mortgage be treated as owner of the ship or share; and

(b)   the mortgagor shall be treated as not having ceased to be owner of the ship or share.

Transfer of registered mortgage

11. – (1)   A registered mortgage may be transferred by an instrument made in the form prescribed by or approved under registration regulations.

(2)   Where any such instrument is produced to the registrar, the registrar shall register the transferee in the prescribed manner.

APPENDIX V

Transmission of registered mortgage by operation of law

12. Where the interest of a mortgagee in a registered mortgage is transmitted to any person by any lawful means other than by a transfer under paragraph 11 above, the registrar shall, on production of the prescribed evidence, cause the name of that person to be entered in the register as mortgagee of the ship or share in question.

Discharge of registered mortgage

13. Where a registered mortgage has been discharged, the registrar shall, on production of the mortgage deed and such evidence of the discharge of the mortgage as may be prescribed, cause an entry to be made in the register to the effect that the mortgage has been discharged.

Definitions

14. In this Schedule –
"mortgage" shall be construed in accordance with paragraph 7(2) above;
"prescribed" means prescribed in registration regulations; and
"registered mortgage" means a mortgage registered under paragraph 7(3) above

APPENDIX VI

Extracts from UK Merchant Shipping (Registration of Ships) Regulations 1993[1]

(SI 1993/3138)

Part I general

Citation, commencement and interpretation

1. – (1)   These Regulations may be cited as the Merchant Shipping (Registration of Ships) Regulations 1993 and shall come into force on 21st March 1994.

   (2)   In these Regulations unless the context otherwise requires:

   "the Act" means the Merchant Shipping (Registration, etc) Act 1993;

   "application for registration" includes, except where otherwise stated, application for registration of a ship or share in a ship; application for registration of a small ship; application for re-registration of the same; and application for the registration of a transfer or transmission of a ship or a share in a ship; but not application for the renewal of registration;

   "appropriate person" means in relation to a port in a country outside the British Islands:

   (a)   any British consular officer within whose consular district the port lies; or

   (b)   where Her Majesty's Government in the United Kingdom is represented in that country by a High Commissioner, any member of the High Commissioner's official staff nominated by him for the purposes of these Regulations; or

   (c)   where that country is a colony, the Governor of the colony or any person appointed by him for those purposes;

   and in this definition "High Commissioner" includes an acting High Commissioner and "Governor" includes an acting Governor;

   "appropriate attestation" means attestation in a form approved by the Secretary of State;

   "authorised measurer" means the Secretary of State or any person authorised under the Merchant Shipping (Tonnage) Regulations 1982 the Merchant Shipping (Fishing Vessels-Tonnage) Regulations 1988 to carry out the measurement of ships for the purposes of those Regulations;

   "bareboat charter ship" means a ship registered under section 7 of that Act;

---

1 As amended, to 1 March 2018
Source: Contains public sector information licensed under the open Government License v3.0.

301

APPENDIX VI

"beneficial ownership" shall be determined by reference to every beneficial interest in that vessel, however arising (whether held by trustee or nominee or arising under a contract or otherwise), other than an interest held by any person as mortgagee;

"builders certificate" means a certificate signed by the builder of the ship and containing a true account of the proper denomination and of the tonnage of the ship, as estimated by him, and of the date and place where it was built, and of the name of the person, if any, for whom the ship was built, or the name of the person to whom it was delivered;

"certificate of registry" means a certificate of registration which is issued to a ship which is registered under the Act and includes a certificate of bareboat charter unless the context otherwise requires;

"certificate of bareboat charter" means a certificate of registration issued to a ship which is registered under section 7 of the Act;

"classification society" means a person authorised to act as a "Certifying Authority" for the purposes of the Merchant Shipping (Tonnage) Regulations 1982;

"closure transcript" means a certified extract from the register showing that the entry in the register in respect of a ship has been closed, the date of its closure, and the details about the ship and its ownership at the time of closure;

"declaration of eligibility" means a declaration which complies with the provisions of regulation 22(1);

"EEA Agreement" means the Agreement on the European Economic Area signed at Oporto on 2nd May 1992 as adjusted by the Protocol signed at Brussels on 17th March 1993;

"EEA State" means a State which is a contracting party to the EEA Agreement;

"fishing vessel" means a vessel within the meaning of paragraph 2(1)(c) of Schedule 4 to the Act;

"fishing vessel certificate" means a certificate of that name specified in section 123 of the Merchant Shipping Act 1995;

"freeze" means to prevent any entry (which includes a deletion of an entry) being made in the Register;

"identifying number" means:

(a) where the Registrar has allocated a bareboat charter ship a number under regulation 79(2)(b) or (3), that number, or

(b) in any other case, the unique number allocated to a bareboat charter ship for identification purposes by its primary register;

"inspector of marks" means an authorised measurer or any person authorised by the Secretary of State to verify the carving and marking of a ship under these Regulations;

"length" in regulations 29, 42 and 56 (except in regulation 56(4)(b)) has the same meaning as in the Tonnage Regulations;

"local office" means an office of the Ministry of Agriculture, Fisheries and Food, The Scottish Office Agriculture and Fisheries Department or the Department of Agriculture for Northern Ireland, listed in the list published by the Department of the Environment, Transport and the Regions and entitled "List of Local Offices for Fishing Vessel Registration";

"maximum continuous engine power" has the same meaning as "engine power" in Article 5.1 of Council Regulation (EEC) No 2930/86 (defining characteristics for fishing vessels);

302

APPENDIX VI

"modification explanation" means the clear explanation, referred to in Article 3.3 of Commission Regulation (EEC) No 1381/87 (establishing detailed rules concerning the marking and documentation of fishing vessels), of the method by which any modification of engine power has been carried out;

"non-United Kingdom nationals exercising their right of freedom of movement of workers or right of establishment" means persons who are either –

(a) nationals of a member State other than the United Kingdom exercising in the United Kingdom their rights under Article 45 or 49 of the Treaty on the functioning of the European Union, as the case may be, or

(b) nationals of a State, other than a member State, which is a Contracting Party to the EEA Agreement exercising in the United Kingdom their rights under Article 28 or 31 of the EEA Agreement;

"overall length" has the same meaning as "length overall" in the Tonnage Regulations; "owner" means, in relation to a ship or share in a ship, the person owning the ship, or as the case may be, a share in the ship, whether or not registered as owner;

"permanently de-rated engine power" means a modification of the maximum continuous engine power referred to in Article 3.3 of Commission Regulation (EEC) No 1381/87;

"pleasure vessel" means a pleasure vessel as defined in regulation 2 of the Merchant Shipping (Vessels in Commercial Use for Sport or Pleasure) Regulations 1998;

"port letters" means the letters for the port of choice;

"port number" means the number allocated for a fishing vessel within its port of choice under regulation 31(2)(b), 53(2) or 79(2)(a);

"port of choice" means a port listed in Schedule 2 which an applicant chooses as a port to be marked on his ship;

"primary register" means the register on which the ship is registered at the time the application is made to register the ship as a bareboat charter ship;

"the Register" means the Register of British ships established under section 1 of the Act;

"the Registrar" means the person described as "the registrar" in section 9(2) of the Act;

"representation" means probate, administration, confirmation, or other instrument constituting a person the executor, administrator or other legal representative of a deceased person, including a certificate of confirmation relating to a vessel;

"salmon coble" means a vessel under 10 metres in overall length used for fishing for profit only in connection with the private rights of fishing for salmon or migratory trout;

"ship" includes a fishing vessel but does not include a small ship or a bareboat charter ship except for the purposes of Part XII (Miscellaneous) and Part XIII (Offences);

"small ship" means a ship which is less than 24 metres in overall length and is, or is applying to be, registered under Part XI;

"submersible vessel" means any vessel used or designed to be used under the surface of any waters;

"surveyor of ships" means a marine surveyor nominated by the Secretary of State to undertake the surveys required by these Regulations and includes any marine surveyor of the Department of the Environment, Transport and the Regions;

"Tonnage Regulations" means the Merchant Shipping (Tonnage) Regulations 1997;

"transfer of a ship" includes, except where the context otherwise requires, transfer of a share in a ship.

APPENDIX VI

Part II the register of British ships in the United Kingdom

The register

2. – (1) The Register maintained by the Registrar in accordance with section 1(1) and (2) of the Act shall be divided into the following parts:

   (a) Part I for ships, owned by persons qualified in accordance with these regulations, which are not:

     (i) fishing vessels, or

     (ii) registered on that Part which is restricted to small ships,

   (b) Part II for fishing vessels,

   (c) Part III for small ships, and

   (d) Part IV for ships which are registered under section 7 of the Act ("bareboat charter ships").

(2) The Register may consist of both paper and computerised records and such other records as the Secretary of State may consider to be expedient.

(3) Any person shall be entitled on application to the Registrar to obtain a transcript, certified by an authorised officer, of the entries in the Register.

(4) During the official opening hours of the General Registry of Shipping and Seamen any person shall be entitled on request to inspect the entries in the Register.

(5) Entries in the Register shall be made in accordance with the following provisions:

   (a) the property in a ship shall be divided into sixty-four shares;

   (b) subject to the provisions of the Act and these Regulations with respect to joint owners or owners by transmission, not more than sixty-four persons shall be entitled to be registered at the same time as owners of any one ship. This rule shall not affect the beneficial title of any persons represented by or claiming under or through any registered owner or joint owner;

   (c) a person shall not be entitled to be registered as owner of a part of a share; but any number of persons not exceeding five may be registered as joint owners of a ship or of any share or shares in a ship;

   (d) joint owners shall be considered as constituting one person only as regards the persons entitled to be registered, and shall not be entitled to dispose in severalty of any interest in a ship, or in any share in a ship in respect of which they are registered.

(6) The Registrar shall be entitled to amend the Register where:

   (a) a clerical error has occurred, or

   (b) sufficient evidence is produced to satisfy him that the entry is incorrect, and on making the amendment he shall issue a new certificate of registry if necessary.

Registration of fishing vessels to be of two kinds

3. Registration on Part II of the Register shall be of two kinds:

   (a) registration of vessels to which the provisions of Schedule 1 to the Act relating to transfers by bill of sale and the registration of mortgages do not apply (hereinafter called "simple registration"), and

   (b) registration of vessels to which those provisions do apply (hereinafter called "full registration").

APPENDIX VI

Fishing vessels changing from full registration to simple registration subject to conditions

    4.   A fishing vessel which has once been registered with full registration shall not thereafter be registered with simple registration unless:

        (a)   it is not subject to a registered mortgage, and

        (b)   the vessel has in the meantime been registered outside the United Kingdom, and

        (c)   the Registrar consents.

Registration on only one Part of the Register

    5.   No ship, including a small ship, may be registered on more than one part of the Register at any one time.

Trusts not to be entered

    6. – (1)   Subject to paragraph (2) no trust, express, implied or constructive may be registered by the Registrar.

        (2)   Where, on the bankruptcy (or in Scotland, sequestration) of a registered owner or mortgagee his title is transmitted to his trustee in bankruptcy (or in Scotland his permanent trustee), that person, if a qualified person, may be registered as the owner or mortgagee of a British ship or share in a ship.

    . . .

Part VI registration

Form of application

    20. – (1)   Every application made under these Regulations shall be made to the Registrar at the General Registry of Shipping and Seamen. Applications in respect of fishing vessels may also be made through a local office.

        (2)   The application shall be made in a form approved by the Secretary of State and shall contain the name and address of the applicant and sufficient information to enable the ship to be identified.

The applicant

    21. – (1)   Every application made under these Regulations shall be made:

        (a)   in the case of individuals, by some one or more of the individuals registered or requiring to be registered as owners or by his or their agent, or

        (b)   in the case of a body corporate, by a duly authorised officer of that body corporate, or by its agent, or

        (c)   in the case of an European Economic Interest Group, by a duly authorised officer of that Group, or by its agent.

Applications for registration

    22. – (1)   Subject to regulation 25 every application for registration must be supported by a declaration of eligibility which shall be in a form approved by the Secretary of State and shall include:

        (a)   a declaration of British connection;

APPENDIX VI

(b) a declaration of ownership by every owner setting out his qualification to own a British ship;

(c) a statement of the number of shares in the ship the legal title of which is vested in each owner whether alone or jointly with any other person or persons; and

(d) in respect of an application to register a fishing vessel, a statement of the beneficial ownership of any share which is not beneficially owned by its legal owner.

(2) Every application for registration of a ship which has, immediately prior to the application, been registered on any other register shall be accompanied by a certified extract from that register in respect of that ship.

(3) Every application for registration of a fishing vessel on Part II of the Register shall state whether the application is for full or simple registration.

Appointment of managing owner

23. – (1) Where application is made in respect of a ship which has more than one owner, or whose shares are owned by more than one owner, and no representative person has been appointed under Part V, one of those owners who is resident in the United Kingdom shall be nominated as the managing owner, and the Register shall be marked accordingly and all correspondence shall be sent to that person at the address recorded in the Register in respect of that owner.

(2) Where the owners determine that a different managing owner should be appointed, the Registrar shall be notified in writing and the Register noted accordingly.

(3) Any document required or authorised to be served, by or under the Merchant Shipping Acts or required or authorised, by virtue of any statutory provision, to be served for the purpose of the institution of, or otherwise in connection with, proceedings for an offence under the Merchant Shipping Acts, or under any instrument in force under those Acts, on the owner of a ship shall be treated as duly served on him if:

(a) delivered to the managing owner, or

(b) sent to the managing owner by post at the address notified (or, as the case may be, last notified) to the Registrar under paragraph (1) or (2) above in relation to that person, or

(c) left for the managing owner at that address.

Applications by bodies corporate

24. Where application is made on behalf of a body corporate, the application must be accompanied by:

(a) if it is a company registered in the United Kingdom, a copy of its certificate of incorporation, and, in the case of a company which has changed its name since incorporation, its certificates of change of name, or

(b) if it is:

(i) a company incorporated in a member State other than the United Kingdom, or

(ii) a company incorporated in any relevant British possession,

proof in accordance with the laws of the country of its incorporation that the company is an incorporated company,

(c) if it is a company, other than a company incorporated in the United Kingdom, with a place of business in the United Kingdom, a certificate from the Registrar of Companies in England and Wales, the Registrar of Scottish Companies or the Registrar of Northern Ireland Companies that the company is registered with

APPENDIX VI

him as an overseas company, and

(d) if it is a body corporate incorporated by virtue of an Act of Parliament, a Charter granted by Her Majesty, or an Act or Ordinance of a relevant British possession, proof, sufficient to satisfy the Registrar, of its incorporation.

Declaration of intent

25. Where, at the time when the application for registration is made, the ownership of a ship has not yet passed (or fully passed) to the persons who are to be its owners when it is registered, the application shall be accompanied by a declaration of intent instead of a declaration of eligibility.

Form of declaration of intent

26. The declaration of intent shall consist of:

(a) a draft declaration of eligibility setting out particulars of ownership of the ship as they are intended to be when the ship is registered; and

(b) a declaration that the ownership of the ship will, at the time when registration occurs, be as stated in the draft declaration of eligibility.

Declaration of eligibility to be submitted before registration

27. Where an application for registration is accompanied by a declaration of intent and not by a declaration of eligibility, a duly completed declaration of eligibility shall be submitted to the Registrar prior to registration.

Evidence of title on . . . registration

28. – (1) An application to register a ship . . . , other than an application in respect of a fishing vessel requiring simple registration, must be supported by the following evidence of title:

(a) in the case of a new ship, the builder's certificate;

(b) in the case of a ship which is not new,

(i) in respect of a pleasure vessel,

(a) a previous bill or bills of sale showing the ownership of the ship for at least 5 years before the application is made, or

(b) if the ship has been registered with a full registration at any time within the last 5 years, a bill or bills of sale evidencing all transfers of ownership during the period since it was so registered, . . .

(ii) in respect of a fishing vessel,

(a) a previous bill or bills of sale showing the ownership of the vessel for at least 3 years before the application is made, or

(b) if the ship has been registered with full registration at any time within the last 3 years, a bill or bills of sale evidencing all transfers of ownership during the period since it was so registered, or

(c) evidence that the vessel has been for at least 3 years continuously registered as a British fishing vessel with simple registration in the names of the owners applying to be registered and remains so registered; or

(iii) in respect of a ship other than a pleasure vessel or a fishing vessel, one bill of sale showing the most recent transfer of ownership;

307

APPENDIX VI

(c)   where the evidence required by sub-paragraph (a) or (b) above is not available, other evidence of title satisfactory to the Registrar.

(2)   Where a ship has entered the Register by virtue of paragraph (1)(b)(iii) and subsequently becomes a pleasure vessel or a fishing vessel, the owner shall then provide the title evidence required under paragraph (1)(b)(i) or (ii) respectively or under paragraph (1)(c) for the ship to remain eligible to be registered.

Survey and measurement of ship

29. – (1)   Subject to regulation 29A every ship, other than a fishing vessel less than 24 metres in length to which Part IIA of Merchant Shipping Tonnage Regulations 1997 does not apply, shall before registration be surveyed by a surveyor of ships and her tonnage ascertained in accordance with the Tonnage Regulations.

(2)   Subject to regulation 29A a fishing vessel of less than 24 metres other than a fishing vessel to which Part IIA of the Tonnage Regulations applies shall before registration be measured by an authorised measurer and her tonnage calculated in accordance with the tonnage regulations made under the Merchant Shipping Act 1965.

(3)   After survey or measurement, the surveyor or measurer shall issue a certificate specifying the ship's tonnage and build and such other particulars describing the identity of the ship as may be required by the Secretary of State. The certificate shall be delivered to the Registrar before the ship may be registered.

(4)   Subject to paragraph (5) below, a ship which is being:
(a)   registered for the first time which has been surveyed or measured and its tonnage ascertained within the previous 12 months; or
(b)   re-registered within 12 months of its registration on the Register ceasing,
shall not be required to be surveyed or measured, or its tonnage ascertained, again in accordance with paragraphs (1) or (2) above, if a declaration is made by the owners confirming that the survey or measurement and tonnage details have not changed from those previously provided to the Registrar.

(5)   The Registrar may direct, if he thinks it appropriate, that such declaration be provided by an authorised measurer or surveyor.

. . .

Registration and refusal of registration of a ship

36. – (1)   Where a Registrar is satisfied in respect of an application that:
(a)   the ship is eligible to be registered as a British ship; and
(b)   the ship has been duly carved and marked and that the appropriate survey or measuring certificate has been provided, and
(c)   the particulars of the ship furnished to him are correct, and
(d)   title to the ship has been adequately proved (where necessary), and
(e)   the relevant requirements of these Regulations have been complied with,
he shall, subject to paragraphs (2), (3) and (4) register the ship by entering in the Register the particulars of the ship and its owners specified in Schedule 4.

(2)   The Registrar may refuse to register any fishing vessel if he is not satisfied that there is in force in respect of the vessel any certificate required to be so in force by virtue of section 4 of the Fishing Vessels (Safety Provisions) Act 1970.

(3)   The Registrar shall refuse to register any vessel intending to fish in Community waters if that vessel has received a de-commissioning grant or any other financial

308

APPENDIX VI

assistance from the European Commission or a member State on condition that it refrains from fishing in those waters or has been withdrawn from fishing as a condition of an award of a construction grant to another boat.

(4) If the Registrar is not satisfied as mentioned in paragraph (1) he shall, subject to regulation 106 (Requirement for supplementary information), refuse the application.

(5) Notwithstanding that a ship is otherwise entitled to be registered, the Registrar may refuse to register it if, taking into account any requirement of the Merchant Shipping Acts (including any instrument made under them) relating to the condition of the ship or its equipment so far as it is relevant to its safety or to any risk of pollution or to the safety, health and welfare of persons employed or engaged in any capacity on board the ship, he considers that it would be inappropriate for the ship to be registered.

Issue of certificate of registry

37. Upon registering a ship the Registrar shall issue and send to the owner a certificate of registry containing the particulars set out in Schedule 5.
. . .

Evidence of title on registration of transfer of ship

43. – (1) On application for registration under paragraph 2(1) of Schedule 1 to the Act of a transfer of a registered ship or a share in a registered ship, other than a fishing vessel registered with simple registration, the bill of sale shall be produced to the Registrar.

(2) When an application is made for the registration of a transfer of a fishing vessel which is registered with simple registration evidence of the transfer satisfactory to the Registrar shall be produced to him.

Form of bill of sale

44. Every bill of sale effecting a transfer of a registered ship or a share in a ship under the Act and these Regulations shall be in the form approved by the Secretary of State with appropriate attestation and shall contain a description of the ship sufficient to identify it.

Registration of transfer of a ship

45. – (1) If the application under paragraph 2(2) of Schedule 1 to the Act (Transfer of ship or shares in a ship) is granted by the Registrar, he shall:

(a) register the bill of sale by entering the name of the new owner in the Register as owner of the ship or share in question, and

(b) where an original is provided, endorse on the bill of sale the fact that the entry has been made, together with the date and time when it was made.

(2) If the Registrar is satisfied with the evidence under regulation 43 (Evidence of title on registration of transfer of ship) that the ship or share in a ship has been transferred, he shall enter the name of the new owner in the Register as the owner of the ship or share in question and issue a new certificate, which shall be valid for a period of 5 years.

APPENDIX VI

Evidence of title on transmission of a registered ship

46. – (1) An application for registration of a transmission of a registered ship or a share in a registered ship under paragraph 3(1) of Schedule 1 to the Act shall be made in the form approved by the Secretary of State.

(2) The following evidence shall be produced to the Registrar on an application for a transfer of a registered ship or share therein by way of transmission:

(a) if the transmission was consequent on death, the grant of representation or a copy thereof or of an extract therefrom,

(b) if the transmission was consequent on bankruptcy such evidence as is for the time being receivable in courts of justice as proof of title of persons claiming under bankruptcy,

(c) if the transmission was consequent on an order of a court, a copy of the order or judgment of that court.

. . .

Part VII mortgages

Form of mortgage

57. (a) A mortgage produced for registration under Schedule 1 to the Act, and

(b) a transfer of a registered mortgage, and

(c) a discharge of a registered mortgage,

shall be in a form approved by the Secretary of State, in each case with appropriate attestation.

Registration of mortgage

58. Where a mortgage executed in accordance with regulation 57 (Form of mortgage) is produced to the Registrar for registration, he shall:

(a) register the mortgage, and

(b) where an original is provided, endorse on it the date and time it was registered.

Notices by intending mortgagees: priority notices

59. – (1) Where any person who is an intending mortgagee under a proposed mortgage of:

(a) a registered ship, or

(b) a share in a registered ship,

notifies the Registrar of the interest which it is intended that he should have under the proposed mortgage, the Registrar shall record that interest.

(2) For the purpose of paragraph (1) the notice to the Registrar shall be in a form approved by the Secretary of State and shall contain the name and official number of the ship, the name address and signature of the intending mortgagor, the number of shares to be mortgaged, and the name and address of the intending mortgagee.

(3) Where any person who is an intending mortgagee under a proposed mortgage of:

(a) a ship which is not for the time being registered, or

(b) a share in any such ship,

notifies the Registrar in writing of the interest which it is intended that he should have under the proposed mortgage, the Registrar:

(i) shall record that interest in the Register, and

APPENDIX VI

(ii) if the ship is subsequently registered, shall register the ship subject to that interest or, if the mortgage has by then been executed in accordance with regulation 57 and produced to the Registrar, subject to that mortgage.

(4) For the purposes of paragraph (3) the notice shall be in a form approved by the Secretary of State and contain the following information:
 (a) the present name of the ship;
 (b) the intended name of the ship;
 (c) the approximate length of the ship;
 (d) where the ship is registered outside the United Kingdom, a copy of its certificate of registry or other document evidencing its registration and giving its port of registration;
 (e) where the ship is a new ship, the builder's certificate or if that is not available, the name and address of the builder and the ship's yard number;
 (f) where the ship is neither a new ship nor a registered ship, details of any permanent marks on the ship which enable it to be clearly identified;
 (g) the name, address and signature of the intending mortgagor, the number of shares to be mortgaged, and the name and address of the intending mortgagee.

(5) In a case where:
 (a) paragraph 8 of Schedule 1 to the Act operates to determine the priority between two or more mortgagees, and
 (b) any of those mortgages gave notification under paragraph (1) or (3) above with respect to his mortgage,
 paragraph 8 of the said Schedule shall have effect in relation to that mortgage as if it had been registered at the time when the relevant entry was made in the Register under the said paragraphs (1) or (3).

(6) Any notification given by a person under paragraphs (1) or (3) (and anything done as a result of it) shall cease to have effect:
 (a) if the notification is withdrawn, or
 (b) at the end of the period of 30 days beginning with the date of the notification, unless the notification is renewed in accordance with paragraph (7).

(7) The person by whom any such notification is given may renew or further renew the notification on each occasion for a period of 30 days, by notice in writing given to the Registrar:
 (a) before the end of the period mentioned in paragraph (6)(b), or
 (b) before the end of a period of renewal,

as the case may be.

(8) Any notice given under this regulation shall be in a form approved by the Secretary of State.

Evidence of transmission of mortgage

60. On the application for registration of a transmission of a registered mortgage as mentioned in paragraph 12 of Schedule 1 to the Act the evidence to be produced to the Registrar shall be:
 (a) a declaration of transmission of mortgage in a form approved by the Secretary of State; and
 (b) (i) if the transmission was consequent on death, the grant of representation or a copy thereof or of an extract therefrom;

311

APPENDIX VI

(ii) if the transmission was consequent on bankruptcy such evidence as is for the time being receivable in courts of justice as proof of title of persons claiming under bankruptcy;

(iii) if the transmission was consequent on an order of a court, a copy of the order of that court.

Transfer or transmission of registered mortgage

61. Where a transfer of a registered mortgage or evidence of a transmission is produced to the Registrar, he shall:

(a) enter the name of the transferee, or the name of the person to whom the mortgage has been transmitted, in the Register as mortgagee of the ship or share in question;

(b) in respect of a transfer, where an original is provided, endorse on the instrument of transfer the date and time the entry was made.

Discharge of mortgages

62. – (1) Where a registered mortgage has been discharged, the Registrar shall, on production of the mortgage deed and with such evidence of the discharge as satisfies him that the mortgage has been discharged, record in the Register that the mortgage has been discharged.

(2) If for good reason the registered mortgage cannot be produced to the Registrar, he may, on being satisfied that the mortgage has been properly discharged, record in the Register that the mortgage has been discharged.

Effect of termination of registration on registered mortgage

63. Where the registration of a ship terminates by virtue of any of these Regulations, that termination shall not affect any entry in the Register of any undischarged registered mortgage of that ship or any share in it.

. . .

Part X bareboat charter-in

Qualification and entitlement for registration of bareboat charter ships other than fishing vessels

73. The persons qualified to be the owners of British ships by virtue of regulation 7(1) who charter a ship (other than a fishing vessel) on bareboat charter terms shall be qualified to register a bareboat charter ship under section 7 of the Act.

Qualification and entitlement for registration of a fishing vessel as a bareboat charter ship

74. – (1) The persons prescribed by regulation 12 who charter a fishing vessel on bareboat charter terms shall be eligible to register it on Part IV of the Register under section 7 of the Act.

(2) A fishing vessel shall not be registered on Part IV of the Register unless it is managed, and its operations controlled and directed, from within the United Kingdom.

312

APPENDIX VI

Appointment of representative person

75.   Where the charterer is not resident in the United Kingdom he shall appoint a representative person and Part V shall apply as if the charterer were the owner.

Dispensations for the bareboat charterers of fishing vessels

76.   The charterers of fishing vessels which are, or are to be, registered as bareboat charter ships may apply for dispensation from the eligibility requirements in accordance with regulation 15 (Dispensations).

Applications

77. – (1)   Every application for registration of a bareboat charter ship shall be made to the Registrar at the General Registry of Shipping and Seamen . . . .

(2)   Regulation 21 (The applicant) shall apply to this Part as if the charterer were the owner.

(3)   Every application for registration of the ship shall be in a form approved by the Secretary of State and accompanied by:

(a)   a declaration of eligibility which shall include:

(i)   a declaration by every charterer setting out his qualification to register a bareboat charter ship, and

(ii)   in respect of fishing vessels, a declaration that the management, and direction and control, of the ship, will be carried out from within the United Kingdom,

(b)   a copy of the charter-party showing:

(i)   the name of the ship;

(ii)   the name of the charterer or charterers and the name of the owner or owners of the ship;

(iii)   the date of the charter-party;

(iv)   the duration of the charter-party;

(c)   the certificate of registry, or other document, issued by the authority responsible for the registration of ships in the country of primary registration showing the ownership of the ship; and

(d)   where the charterer is a body corporate, the document or documents required by regulation 24 (Applications by bodies corporate).

(4)   Regulation 29 (Survey and measurement) shall apply to this Part.

(5)   The Registrar may refuse to register any fishing vessel as a bareboat charter ship if he is not satisfied that there is in force in respect of the vessel any certificate required to be so in force by virtue of section 4 of the Fishing Vessels (Safety Provisions) Act 1970.

Names

78. – (1)   On making an application for registration of a bareboat charter ship the applicant shall propose a name which the ship is to be called while so registered.

(2)   If the Registrar is satisfied that the name is in compliance with the provisions of Schedule 1 he shall approve the name.

APPENDIX VI

Allocation of identifying number; port of choice and port numbers

79. – (1) On making application for registration of a bareboat charter ship the applicant shall specify one of the ports listed in part 1 or 2 of Schedule 2, as is appropriate, which it is intended shall be the port of choice.

(2) Where the application is made in respect of a fishing vessel and the Registrar is satisfied that the vessel is eligible to be registered as a bareboat charter ship, he shall:

(a) allocate a port number, and

(b) allocate an identifying number, whether or not the vessel already has a number allocated by its primary register.

(3) In the case of any other ship the Registrar may allocate an identifying number, whether or not the ship already has a number allocated by its primary register.

Marking

80. – (1) On being satisfied that the ship is eligible for registration and on production of any certificate for survey required under regulation 29 (Survey and measurement of ship) the Registrar shall issue a carving and marking note.

(2) On receipt of a carving and marking note the charterer shall:

(a) where the ship is not already so marked cause it to be marked with;

(i) its name, and

(ii) its port of choice, and

(iii) in respect of a fishing vessel, its port number, and

(b) where the ship is not already so carved, cause it to be carved with its identifying number and the number denoting its tonnage,

in accordance with Schedule 3.

Inspection of marks etc

81. Regulations 33 (Inspection of marks) and 35 (Cancellation of carving and marking note) shall apply to this Part as if any reference in them to the owner was a reference to the charterer.

Registration

82. – (1) Where the Registrar is satisfied in respect of an application:

(a) that the ship has been duly carved and marked, and

(b) that, where required, the appropriate certificate of survey has been provided, and

(c) that the other requirements preliminary to registration have been complied with, he shall enter in the Register the details prescribed in Schedule 4.

(2) Upon registering a ship the Registrar shall issue and send to the charterer a certificate of bareboat charter registry containing the particulars set out in Schedule 5.

(3) Upon registering a ship the Registrar shall retain in his possession a copy of the charter, a copy of any certificate of survey and all declarations of eligibility, and if applicable any declarations required by regulation 24 (Applications by bodies corporate).

(4) Notwithstanding that a ship is otherwise entitled to be registered, the Registrar may refuse to register it if, taking into account any requirements of the Merchant Shipping Acts (including any instrument made under them) relating to the condition of the ship or its equipment so far as relevant to its safety or to any risk of pollution or to the

APPENDIX VI

safety, health and welfare of persons employed or engaged in any capacity on board the ship, he considers that it would be inappropriate for the ship to be registered.

Period of registration

83. – (1) The registration of a bareboat charter ship shall expire:
    (a) on the expiry of the charter period, or
    (b) at the end of a period of 5 years beginning with the date of registration specified in the certificate of bareboat charter registry,
    whichever is the earlier.

(2) 3 months before the expiry of the registration period the Registrar shall issue to the charterer of the ship a renewal notice.

(3) Application for renewal of registration may be made during the last three calendar months of the current registration period.

(4) Application for renewal shall be in a form approved by the Secretary of State and shall be accompanied by a declaration of eligibility and by the certificate of bareboat charter registry.

Notification of changes

84. – (1) If at any time there occurs, in relation to a bareboat charter ship any change affecting the eligibility of the ship to be registered, the charterer of the ship shall, as soon as practicable after the change occurs, notify the Registrar.

(2) Notification made under paragraph (1) shall be made in writing, shall be signed by the charterer and shall specify the nature of the change and the name and the identifying number of the ship.

(3) Any person who contravenes paragraph (1) shall be guilty of an offence.

Application of other regulations to this Part

85. Regulations 51 (Change in registered particulars of ship), 52 (Change of name), 53 (Transfer of port of choice) and 54 (Re-marking of ship) shall apply to this Part as if any reference in them to the owner was a reference to the charterer.

Notification to foreign registries by Registrar

86. The Registrar shall notify the responsible authority for registration of ships in the country of primary registration when:
    (a) the ship has been registered as a bareboat charter ship on the British Register, or
    (b) the ship's registration has closed by reason of the expiry of the certificate of registry under regulation 83(1)(b) (Period of registration), or
    (c) the ship's registration has been closed by the Registrar by reason of regulation 87 (Closure of bareboat charter ship's registration by the Registrar).

Closure of bareboat charter ship's registration by the Registrar

87. – (1) The Registrar may, subject to regulation 101 (Service of notices), close the registration of a bareboat charter ship:
    (a) on application by the charterer;
    (b) on the ship no longer being eligible to be registered;

315

APPENDIX VI

    (c) on the ship being destroyed (which includes, but is not limited to, shipwreck, demolition, fire and sinking);

    (d) if, taking into account any requirement of the Merchant Shipping Acts (including any instrument made under them) relating to the condition of the ship or its equipment so far as it is relevant to its safety or to any risk of pollution or to the safety, health and welfare of persons employed or engaged in any capacity on board the ship, he considers that it would be inappropriate for the ship to remain registered;

    (e) if the bareboat charter ship is a fishing vessel which requires a licence to fish but at the time of registration did not have such a licence and has not acquired such a licence within 6 months of the issue of its certificate of bareboat charter registry;

    (f) where the charterer of a fishing vessel fails to respond to the Registrar within 15 days of a request from him to supply information concerning details on the Register;

    (g) where the charterer of a fishing vessel supplies information requested by the Registrar, but that information is either false or incorrect or is reasonably considered by the Registrar to be insufficient;

    (h) where under regulation 84 the charterer is required to notify the Registrar, and has not done so;

        (i) where under regulation 51 as applied by regulation 85 a person is required to make an application, and has not done so; or

        (j) where a fishing vessel certificate has expired.

(2) On closure of a ship's registration under paragraph (1) the charterer shall forthwith surrender to the Registrar the certificate of bareboat charter registry for cancellation.

    . . .

Schedule 1 Approval of names

1. Every application to the registrar to approve a name shall specify a name which is in Roman letters; any numerals shall be in Roman or Arabic numerals.

2. In respect of an application to register a ship, other than a fishing vessel, on Parts I or IV of the register, the registrar shall not approve the proposed name if it is:

    (a) already the name of a registered British ship, or

    (b) a name so similar to that of a registered British ship as to be calculated to deceive or likely to confuse;

    (c) a name which may be confused with a distress signal;

    (d) a name which is prefixed by any letters or name which could be taken to indicate a type of ship or any other word, pre-fix or suffix which might cause confusion as to the name of the ship.

3. In respect of an application to register a fishing vessel on Parts II or IV of the register, the registrar shall not approve the proposed name in it is:

    (a) already the name of a vessel in its port of choice, or

    (b) a name so similar to that of a registered British fishing vessel in its port of choice as to be calculated to deceive or likely to confuse;

    (c) a name which may be confused with a distress signal;

    (d) a name which is prefixed by any letters or name which could be taken to indicate a type of ship or any other word, pre-fix or suffix which might cause confusion as to the name of the ship.

APPENDIX VI

4. Subject to paragraph 5 below, if the registrar is satisfied that a name does not fall within 2(a) to (d) or 3(a) to (d) he shall notify the applicant in writing that the name is approved and the ship may be registered with that name.

5. Notwithstanding that the registrar is satisfied as to paragraphs 2 or 3 he may refuse to approve a name –
   (a) which might cause offence or embarrassment;
   (b) which has a clear and direct connection with the royal family.

6. Any approval given under paragraphs 2 or 3 shall be valid only for the period of 3 months beginning with the date it is notified to the applicant.

7. If the registrar is not so satisfied he shall notify the applicant accordingly.

8. Notwithstanding paragraph 6, the registrar may allow the reservation of a ship's name or designation for a period of 10 years if he is satisfied that:
   (a) the ship is intended to replace another of the same name which is to be registered within 10 years of the date of the application, and
   (b) the applicant is the owner of a registered ship with the same name as that which is to be reserved and its British registration will be closed before the registration of the new vessel, or
   (c) the applicant is the owner of a registered ship with the same name as that which is to be reserved and it will be sold before the registration of the new vessel on condition that it changes its name and that its name is so changed.

9. Applications for a reservation under paragraph 8 must be accompanied by a full statement of the circumstances of the case.

10. Where a ship having once been registered has ceased to be registered, no person (unless ignorant of the previous registration, 9 [sic] (proof whereof will lie on him) shall apply for registration of the ship other than by the name by which it was previously registered except with the written permission of the registrar.

Schedule 2

Part 1 – Ports of Choice for Ships to be Registered on Part I of the Register

Aberdeen	Fraserburgh
Aberystwyth	Glasgow
Alloa	Gloucester
Arbroath	Goole
Ardrossan	Grangemouth
Ayr	Granton
Banff	Great Yarmouth
Barnstaple	Greenock
Barrow	Grimsby
Beaumaris	Hartlepool
Belfast	Hartlepool West
Berwick-On-Tweed	Harwich
Bideford	Hull
Blyth	Invernesss
Borrowstoness	Ipswich
Boston	Irvine

APPENDIX VI

Bridgwater

Bristol

Brixham

Buckle

Burntisland

Caernarvon

Campbeltown

Cardiff

Cardigan

Chester

Colchester

Coleraine

Cowes

Dartmouth

Dover

Dumfries

Dundee

Exeter

Falmouth

Faversham

Felixstowe

Fishguard

Fleetwood

Folkestone

Fowey

Penzance

Peterhead

Plymouth

Poole

Portland

Port Talbot

Portsmouth

Preston

Ramsgate

Rochester

Runcorn

Rye

Salcombe

Scarborough

Scilly

Shoreham

South Shields

King's Lynn

Klrkcaldy

Klrkwall

LANCASTER

Leith

Lerwick

Littlehampton

Liverpool

Llanelli

London

Londonderry

Lowestoft

Maldon

Manchester

Maryport

Methil

Middlesbrough

Milford Haven

Montrose

Newcastle

Newhaven

Newport

Newry

North Shields

Padstow

Southampton

St Ives

Stockton

Stornoway

Stranraer

Sunderland

Swansea

Teignmouth

Troon

Truro

Weymouth

Whitby

Whitehaven

Wick

Wigtown

Wisbech

Workington

318

APPENDIX VI

Part 2 – Ports for Ships to be Registered on Part II of the Register (Fishing Vessels)

Port letters and Name

A	Aberdeen		CE	Coleraine
AB	Aberystwyth		CS	Cowes
AA	Alloa		DH	Dartmouth
AH	Arbroath		DR	Dover
AD	Ardrossan		DS	Dumfries
AR	Ayr		DE	Dundee
BA	Ballantrae		E	Exeter
BF	Banff		FH	Falmouth
BE	Barnstaple		F	Faversham
BW	Barrow		FD	Fleetwood
BS	Beaumaris		FE	Folkestone
B	Belfast		FY	Fowey
BK	Berwick-On-Tweed		FR	Fraserburgh
BD	Bideford		GW	Glasgow
BH	Blyth		GR	Gloucester
BO	Borrowstoness		GE	Goole
BN	Boston		GH	Grangemouth
BR	Bridgwater		GN	Granton
BL	Bristol		YH	Great Yarmouth
BM	Brixham		GK	Greenock
BRD	Broadford		GY	Grimsby
BCK	Buckle		HL	Hartlepool
BU	Burntisland		HH	Harwich
CO	Caernarvon		H	Hull
CN	Campbeltown		INS	Inverness
CF	Cardiff		IH	Ipswich
CA	Cardigan		IE	Irvine
CL	Carlisle		LN	King's Lynn
CY	Castlebay, Barra		PT	Port Talbot
CH	Chester		KY	Kirkcaldy
CK	Colchester		K	Kirkwall
LR	Lancaster		RR	Rochester
LH	Leith		RO	Rothesay
LK	Lerwick		RN	Runcorn
LI	Littlehampton		RX	Rye
LL	Liverpool		SS	St Ives
LA	Llanelli		SE	Salcombe
LO	London		SH	Scarborough
LY	Londonderry		SC	Scilly

APPENDIX VI

LT	Lowestoft	SN	Shields, North
MN	Maldon	SSS	Shields, South
MR	Manchester	SM	Shoreham
MT	Maryport	SU	Southampton
ML	Methil	ST	Stockton
MH	Middlesbrough	SY	Stornoway
M	Mllford Haven	SR	Stranraer
ME	Montrose	SD	Sunderland
NE	Newcastle	SA	Swansea
NN	Newhaven	TT	Tarbert, Loch Fyne
NT	Newport, Gwent	TH	Teignmouth
N	Newry	TN	Troon
OB	Oban	TO	Truro
PW	Padstow	UL	Ullapool
PZ	Penzance	WH	Weymouth
PD	Peterhead	WY	Whitby
PH	Plymouth	WK	Wick
PE	Poole	WN	Wigtown
PO	Portland	WA	Whitehaven
P	Portsmouth	WI	Wisbech
PN	Preston	WO	Workington
R	Ramsgate		

Schedule 3 Carving and Marking

1. Every ship is required, before it may be registered, to be marked permanently and conspicuously to the satisfaction of the Registrar in accordance with this Schedule.

2. The Secretary of State may exempt any class of ship from all or any of the requirements of this Schedule, subject to such conditions, if any, as he thinks fit.

3. Subject to any exemption in respect of that class of ship, a ship other than:
   (a) a fishing vessel,
   (b) a pleasure vessel which is under 24 metres, is to be marked as follows:

   (i) its name shall be marked on each of its bows, and its name and its port of choice must be marked on its stern;
   (ii) the marking is to be on a dark ground in white or yellow letters, or on a light ground in black letters, the letters being not less than 10 centimetres high and of proportional breadth; and
   (iii) its official number and the number denoting its registered tonnage shall be cut on its main beam or if that is not possible, marked or fixed thereon in the manner prescribed in paragraph 4(a) below.

4. A pleasure vessel which is under 24 metres in length is to be marked as follows:
   (a) the official number and registered tonnage are:
   (i) to be marked on the main beam or, if there is no main beam, on a readily accessible visible permanent part of the structure of the pleasure vessel either by cutting in, centre punching or raised lettering, or

APPENDIX VI

    (ii)   to be engraved on plates of metal, wood or plastic, secured to the main beam (or, if there is no main beam, to a readily accessible visible permanent part of the structure) with rivets, through bolts with the ends clenched), or screws with the slots removed;

(b) the name and port of choice (unless an exempted ship), are to be marked on a conspicuous and permanent part of the stern on a dark ground in white or yellow letters, or on a light ground in black letters, the letters being not less than 5 centimetres high and of proportionate breadth, or, where this is not possible by the alternative methods given below:

    (i)   by engraving on plates of metal or of plastic or by cutting in on a shaped wooden chock. Where a shaped wooden chock is used it should be secured to the hull through bolts, the ends being clenched, or

    (ii)   by individual glass reinforced plastic letters and numbers approximately 2mm in thickness. These to be fixed to the hull with epoxy adhesive, and painted with suitable paint and coated with translucent epoxy resin;

    (iii) where metal or plastic plates have been used these must be fixed by the use of epoxy adhesives. Metal or plastic plates secured by adhesives should be coated with translucent epoxy resin after they have been fixed in position.

5. A fishing vessel is to be marked as follows:

(a) The name of the vessel and the port of choice shall be painted in white on a black background or in black on a white background outside the stem of the boat in letters which shall not be less than 8 centimetres in height and 1.5 centimetres in breadth, and

(b) the port letters and the port number shall be painted or displayed on both sides of the bow and on each quarter, as high above the water as possible so as to be clearly visible from the sea and the air, in white on a black background or black on a white background;

(c) for vessels not over 17 metres in length, the height of the port letters and port number shall be at least 25 centimetres with a line thickness of at least 4 centimetres;

(d) for vessels over 17 metres in length, the height of the port letters and port number shall be at least 45 centimetres with a line thickness of at least 6 centimetres;

(e) the port letters and port number shall in addition be painted or displayed on the wheel house top or some other prominent horizontal surface;

(f) the vessel's official number shall be carved into the main beam of the vessel or, if that is not possible, marked or fixed thereon in the manner prescribed in paragraph 4(a) above.

6. A scale of decimetres, or metres and decimetres, denoting a draught of water shall be marked on a ship, other than an exempted ship, on each side of its stem and its stern post, as follows:

(a) in figures in two-decimetre intervals, if the scale is in decimetres; and

(b) in figures at each metre interval and at intervening two-decimetre intervals, if the scale is in metres and decimetres;

the capital letter "M" being placed after each metre figure; the top figure of the scale showing both the metre and (except where it marks a full metre interval) the decimetre figure; the lower line of the figures, or figures and letters (as the case may be), coinciding with the draught line denoted thereby; the figures and letters being not less than one decimetre in length and being marked by being cut in and painted white or yellow on a dark ground, or in such other way as the Secretary of State approves.

APPENDIX VI

7. The name of a ship shall be marked in Roman letters and any numerals shall be in Roman or Arabic numerals.

Schedule 4 Details to Go on Register

1. The following information is to be registered about each owner who is an individual:
    (a) surname, forename and title,
    (b) address,
    (c) nationality,
    (d) number of shares owned by him, and if held jointly, with whom the shares are held,
    (e) the name of the managing owner.
2. The following information is to be registered about each owner which is a body corporate:
    (a) name of owner,
    (b) the address of its registered office,
    (c) country of incorporation,
    (d) where it is a body corporate incorporated in the United Kingdom or in a relevant British possession, its principal place of business,
    (e) where it is a body corporate incorporated in a member State other than the United Kingdom, its place of business in the United Kingdom,
    (f) number of shares owned by the company, and if held jointly, with whom the shares are held.
3. The following information is to be registered about:
    (a) any representative person, and
    (b) in respect of fishing vessels, any charterer:
        (i) the full name of the individual or body corporate,
        (ii) the address of the individual, or the place of business in the United Kingdom of the body corporate.
4. The following information is to be registered about ships registered or to be registered on Part I of the Register:
    (a) name,
    (b) either the IMO number or the International Standards Organisation Hull Identification Number (HIN), as appropriate,
    (c) radio call sign,
    (d) port of choice,
    (e) official number,
    (f) year of build,
    (g) method of propulsion eg whether sail, steam, motor or dumb,
    (h) where built,
    (i) name and address of builders,
    (j) date keel laid/when built,
    (k) length – metric units,
    (l) breadth – metric units,
    (m) depth – metric units,
    (n) type of ship eg dry cargo, oil tanker, passenger, bulk carrier,
    (o) material used to construct hull,
    (p, q, r) such of the following tonnages as are specified in the certificate of survey: gross, net and registered,
    (s) make and model of engine(s),
    (t) total power of engines in kilowatts.

APPENDIX VI

5. The following is to be registered about fishing vessels registered or to be registered on Part II of the Register:
   (a) official number and EC Number,
   (b) IMO number,
   (c) port letters and port number,
   (d) name,
   (e) radio call sign,
   (f) whether full or simple registration,
   (g) material used to construct hull,
   (h) name of builder,
   (i) year of build,
   (j) place and country of build,
   (k) date of entry into service,
   (l) overall length – metric units,
   (m) registered length – metric units,
   (n) breadth – metric units,
   (o) depth – metric units,
   (p) gross tonnage,
   (q) net tonnage,
   (r) maximum continuous engine power in kilowatts, or, if the owner notifies the Registrar of a modification, permanently de-rated engine power in kilowatts,
   (s) make and model of engine,
   (t) number of cylinders,
   (u) number of engines,
   (v) number of revolutions per minute,
   (w) modification explanation.

6. In addition to the information in either paragraph 4 or 5 the following is to be registered in respect of bareboat charter ships:
   (a) the name and address of the owner,
   (b) the name and address of the charterer,
   (c) the name and address of any representative person,
   (d) the unique number allocated to the ship for identification purposes by its primary register,
   (e) its country of original registration,
   (f) commencement date of the charter period and its expiry date,
   (g) the name by which the ship is known on the primary register (or a translation of that name).

Schedule 5 Certificate of Registry

1. A certificate of registry for a ship registered or to be registered on Part I of the Register shall contain:
   (a) the full name and address of the owner(s),
   (b) the number of shares owned by each owner and if any are jointly owned, with whom they are owned,
   (c) the following information about the ship:
       (i) name,
       (ii) either the IMO number or HIN number, as appropriate,
       (iii) radio call sign,
       (iv) port of choice,

APPENDIX VI

    (v)   official number,
    (vi)   year of build,
    (vii) method of propulsion eg whether sail, steam, motor or dumb,
    (viii) length – metric units,
    (ix)   breadth – metric units,
    (x)   depth – metric units,
    (xi)   type of ship eg dry cargo, oil tanker, passenger, bulk carrier,
    (xii, xiii, xiv) such of the following tonnages as are specified in the certificate of survey: gross, net and registered,
    (xv)   engine make and model,
    (xvi) engine power in kilowatts,

(d)   the date of issue of the certificate,
(e)   the date the certificate expires.

2.   A certificate of registry for a fishing vessel registered or to be registered on Part II of the Register shall contain:

(a)   the name and address of each owner,
(b)   the name and address of any charterer,
(c)   the number of shares and, if any are jointly owned, with whom they are owned,
(d)   the following details about the vessel:
    (i)   name,
    (ii)   port of choice and port number,
    (iii)   official number,
    (iv)   IMO number,
    (v)   radio call sign,
    (vi)   registered length,
    (vii) overall length,
    (viii) breadth,
    (ix)   depth,
    (x)   net tonnage,
    (xi)   gross tonnage,
    (xii) engine make and model,
    (xiii) maximum continuous engine power, in kilowatts, or if the owner notifies the Registrar of a modification, permanently de-rated engine power in kilowatts,
    (xiv) year of build,
    (xv) date of entry into service,
    (xvi) modification explanation,
(e)   the date and time of the issue of the certificate,
(f)   the date of expiry of the certificate,
(g)   the kind of registration (i.e. whether it is full or simple registration).

3.   Bareboat Charter Ships

A certificate of bareboat charter registry for ships registered or to be registered on Part IV of the Register shall contain the details prescribed by either paragraph 1(a), (c), (d) and (e) (for ships other than fishing vessels) or paragraph 2(a), (b), (d), (e) and (f) (for fishing vessels) and the following:

(a)   the name and address of the charterer,
(b)   the unique number allocated to the ship for identification purposes by its primary register,
(c)   country of primary registration,
(d)   original name (or a translation thereof) if different from its registered name.

APPENDIX VII

Geneva Convention on the High Seas[1]

The States Parties to this Convention,

Desiring to codify the rules of international law relating to the high seas,

Recognising that the United Nations Conference on the Law of the Sea, held at Geneva from 24 February to 27 April, 1958, adopted the following provisions as generally declaratory of established principles of international law,

Have agreed as follows:

Article 1

The term "high seas" means all parts of the sea that are not included in the territorial sea or in the internal waters of a State.

Article 2

The high seas being open to all nations, no State may validly purport to subject any part of them to its sovereignty. Freedom of the high seas is exercised under the conditions laid down by these articles and by the other rules of international law. It comprises, *inter alia*, both for coastal and non-coastal States:

(1) Freedom of navigation;

(2) Freedom of fishing;

(3) Freedom to lay submarine cables and pipelines;

(4) Freedom to fly over the high seas.

These freedoms, and others which are recognised by the general principles of international law, shall be exercised by all States with reasonable regard to the interests of other States in their exercise of the freedom of the high seas.

Article 3

1. In order to enjoy the freedom of the seas on equal terms with coastal States, States having no seacoast should have free access to the sea. To this end States situated between the sea and a State having no sea-coast shall by common agreement with the latter and in conformity with existing international conventions accord;

(a) To the State having no sea-coast, on a basis of reciprocity, free transit through their territory; and

---

[1] Courtesy UN Treaty Collection.

APPENDIX VII

(b) To ships flying the flag of that State treatment equal to that accorded to their own ships, or to the ships of any other States, as regards access to seaports and the use of such ports.

2. States situated between the sea and a State having no sea-coast shall settle, by mutual agreement with the latter, and taking into account the rights of the coastal State or State of transit and the special conditions of the State having no sea-coast, all matters relating to freedom of transit and equal treatment in ports, in case such States are not already parties to existing international conventions.

Article 4

Every State, whether coastal or not, has the right to sail ships under its flag on the high seas.

Article 5

1. Each State shall fix the conditions for the grant of its nationality to ships, for the registration of ships in its territory, and for the right to fly its flag. Ships have the nationality of the State whose flag they are entitled to fly. There must exist a genuine link between the State and the ship; in particular, the State must effectively exercise its jurisdiction and control in administrative, technical and social matters over ships flying its flag.

2. Each State shall issue to ships to which it has granted the right to fly its flag documents to that effect.

Article 6

1. Ships shall sail under the flag of one State only and, save in exceptional cases expressly provided for in international treaties or in these articles, shall be subject to its exclusive jurisdiction on the high seas. A ship may not change its flag during a voyage or while in a port of call, save in the case of a real transfer of ownership or change of registry.

2. A ship which sails under the flags of two or more States, using them according to convenience, may not claim any of the nationalities in question with respect to any other State, and may be assimilated to a ship without nationality.

Article 7

The provisions of the preceding articles do not prejudice the question of ships employed on the official service of an inter-governmental organisation flying the flag of the organisation.

Article 8

1. Warships on the high seas have complete immunity from the jurisdiction of any State other than the flag State.

2. For the purposes of these articles, the term "warship" means a ship belonging to the naval forces of a State and bearing the external marks distinguishing warships of its nationality, under the command of an officer duly commissioned by the government and whose name appears in the Navy List, and manned by a crew who are under regular naval discipline.

Article 9

Ships owned or operated by a State and used only on government non-commercial service shall, on the high seas, have complete immunity from the jurisdiction of any State other than the flag State.

Article 10

1. Every State shall take such measures for ships under its flag as are necessary to ensure safety at sea with regard *inter alia* to:
  (a) The use of signals, the maintenance of communications and the prevention of collisions;
  (b) The manning of ships and labour conditions for crews taking into account the applicable international labour instruments;
  (c) The construction, equipment and sea-worthiness of ships.

2. In taking such measures each State is required to conform to generally accepted international standards and to take any steps which may be necessary to ensure their observance.

Article 11

1. In the event of a collision or of any other incident of navigation concerning a ship on the high seas, involving the penal or disciplinary responsibility of the master or of any other person in the service of the ship no penal or disciplinary proceedings may be instituted against such persons except before the judicial or administrative authorities either of the flag State or of the State of which such person is a national.

2. In disciplinary matters, the State which has issued a master's certificate or a certificate of competence or licence shall alone be competent, after due legal process, to pronounce the withdrawal of such certificates, even if the holder is not a national of the State which issued them.

3. No arrest or detention of the ship, even as a measure of investigation, shall be ordered by any authorities other than those of the flag State.

Article 12

1. Every State shall require the master of a ship sailing under its flag, in so far he can do so without serious danger to the ship, the crew or the passengers,
  (a) To render assistance to any person found at sea in danger of being lost;
  (b) To proceed with all possible speed to the rescue of persons in distress if informed of their need of assistance, in so far as such action may reasonably be expected of him;
  (c) After a collision, to render assistance to the other ship, her crew and her passengers and, where possible, to inform the other ship of the name of his own ship, her port of registry and the nearest port at which she will call.

2. Every coastal State shall promote the establishment and maintenance of an adequate and effective search and rescue service regarding safety on and over the sea and – where circumstances so require – by way of mutual regional arrangements co-operate with neighbouring States for this purpose.

Article 13

Every State shall adopt effective measures to prevent and punish the transport of slaves in ships authorised to fly its flag, and to prevent the unlawful use of its flag for that purpose. Any slave taking refuge on board any ship, whatever its flag, shall *ipso facto* be free.

Article 14

All States shall co-operate to the fullest possible extent in the repression of piracy on the high seas or in any other place outside the jurisdiction of any State.

Article 15

Piracy consists of any of the following acts:
(1)   Any illegal acts of violence, detention or any act of depredation, committed for private ends by the crew or the passengers of a private ship or a private aircraft, and directed:
    (a)   On the high seas, against another ship or aircraft, or against persons or property on board such ship or aircraft;
    (b)   Against a ship, aircraft, persons or property in a place outside the jurisdiction of any State;
(2)   Any act of voluntary participation in the operation of a ship or of an aircraft with knowledge of facts making it a pirate ship or aircraft;
(3)   Any act of inciting or of intentionally facilitating an act described in sub-paragraph 1 or subparagraph 2 of this article.

Article 16

The acts of piracy, as defined in Article 15, committed by a warship, government ship or government aircraft whose crew has mutinied and taken control of the ship or aircraft are assimilated to acts committed by a private ship.

Article 17

A ship or aircraft is considered a pirate ship or aircraft if it is intended by the persons in dominant control to be used for the purpose of committing one of the acts referred to in Article 15. The same applies if the ship or aircraft has been used to commit any such act, so long as it remains under the control of the persons guilty of that act.

Article 18

A ship or aircraft may retain its nationality although it has become a pirate ship or aircraft. The retention or loss of nationality is determined by the law of the State from which such nationality was derived.

Article 19

On the high seas, or in any other place outside the jurisdiction of any State, every State may seize a pirate ship or aircraft, or a ship taken by piracy and under the control of pirates, and arrest the persons and seize the property on board. The courts of the State which carried out the seizure may decide upon the penalties to be imposed, and may also determine the action to be taken with regard to the ships, aircraft or property, subject to the rights of third parties acting in good faith.

Article 20

Where the seizure of a ship or aircraft on suspicion of piracy has been effected without adequate grounds, the State making the seizure shall be liable to the State the nationality of which is possessed by the ship or aircraft, for any loss or damage caused by the seizure.

Article 21

A seizure on account of piracy may only be carried out by warships or military aircraft, or other ships or aircraft on government service authorised to that effect.

Article 22

1. Except where acts of interference derive from powers conferred by treaty, a warship which encounters a foreign merchant ship on the high seas is not justified in boarding her unless there is reasonable ground for suspecting:

(a) That the ship is engaged in piracy; or
(b) That the ship is engaged in the slave trade; or
(c) That, though flying a foreign flag or refusing to show its flag, the ship is, in reality, of the same nationality as the warship.

2. In the cases provided for in sub-paragraphs (a), (b) and (c) above, the warship may proceed to verify the ship's right to fly its flag. To this end, it may send a boat under the command of an officer to the suspected ship. If suspicion remains after the documents have been checked, it may proceed to a further examination on board the ship, which must be carried out with all possible consideration.

3. If the suspicions prove to be unfounded, and provided that the ship boarded has not committed any act justifying them, it shall be compensated for any loss or damage that may have been sustained.

Article 23

1. The hot pursuit of a foreign ship may be undertaken when the competent authorities of the coastal State have good reason to believe that the ship has violated the laws and regulations of that State. Such pursuit must be commenced when the foreign ship or one of its boats is within the internal waters or the territorial sea or the contiguous zone of the pursuing State, and may only be continued outside the territorial sea or the contiguous zone if the pursuit has not been interrupted. It is not necessary that, at the time when the foreign ship within the territorial sea or the contiguous zone receives the order to stop, the ship giving the order should likewise be within the territorial sea or the contiguous zone. If the foreign ship is within a contiguous zone, as defined in Article 24 of the Convention on the Territorial Sea and the Contiguous Zone the pursuit may only be undertaken if there has been a violation of the rights for the protection of which the zone was established.

2. The right of hot pursuit ceases as soon as the ship pursued enters the territorial sea of its own country or of a third State.

3. Hot pursuit is not deemed to have begun unless the pursuing ship has satisfied itself by such practicable means as may be available that the ship pursued or one of its boats or other craft working as a team and using the ship pursued as a mother ship are within the limits of the territorial sea, or as the case may be within the contiguous zone. The pursuit may only be commenced after a visual or auditory signal to stop has been given at a distance which enables it to be seen or heard by the foreign ship.

4. The right of hot pursuit may be exercised only by warships or military aircraft, or other ships or aircraft on government service specially authorised to that effect.

5. Where hot pursuit is effected by an aircraft:

(a) The provisions of paragraphs 1 to 3 of this article shall apply *mutatis mutandis*;
(b) The aircraft giving the order to stop must itself actively pursue the ship until a ship or aircraft of the coastal State, summoned by the aircraft, arrives to take over the pursuit, unless the aircraft is itself able to arrest the ship. It does not suffice to justify an arrest on the high seas that the ship was merely sighted by the aircraft as an offender or suspected offender, if it was not both ordered to stop and pursued by the aircraft itself or other aircraft or ships which continue the pursuit without interruption.

6. The release of a ship arrested within the jurisdiction of a State and escorted to a port of that State for the purposes of an enquiry before the competent authorities may not be claimed solely

APPENDIX VII

on the ground that the ship, in the course of its voyage, was escorted across a portion of the high seas, if the circumstances rendered this necessary.

7. Where a ship has been stopped or arrested on the high seas in circumstances which do not justify the exercise of the right of hot pursuit, it shall be compensated for any loss or damage that may have been thereby sustained.

Article 24

Every State shall draw up regulations to prevent pollution of the seas by the discharge of oil from ships or pipelines or resulting from the exploitation and exploration of the seabed and its subsoil, taking account of existing treaty provisions on the subject.

Article 25

1. Every State shall take measures to prevent pollution of the seas from the dumping of radio-active waste, taking into account any standards and regulations which may be formulated by the competent international organisations.

2. All States shall co-operate with the competent international organisations in taking measures for the prevention of pollution of the seas or air space above, resulting from any activities with radio-active materials or other harmful agents.

Article 26

1. All States shall be entitled to lay submarine cables and pipelines on the bed of the high seas.

2. Subject to its right to take reasonable measures for the exploration of the continental shelf and the exploitation of its natural resources, the coastal State may not impede the laying or maintenance of such cables or pipelines.

3. When laying such cables or pipelines the State in question shall pay due regard to cables or pipelines already in position on the seabed. In particular, possibilities of repairing existing cables or pipelines shall not be prejudiced.

Article 27

Every State shall take the necessary legislative measures to provide that the breaking or injury by a ship flying its flag or by a person subject to its jurisdiction of a submarine cable beneath the high seas done wilfully or through culpable negligence, in such a manner as to be liable to interrupt or obstruct telegraphic or telephonic communications, and similarly the breaking or injury of a submarine pipeline or high-voltage power cable shall be a punishable offence. This provision shall not apply to any break or injury caused by persons who acted merely with the legitimate object of saving their lives or their ships, after having taken all necessary precautions to avoid such break or injury.

Article 28

Every State shall take the necessary legislative measures to provide that, if persons subject to its jurisdiction who are the owners of a cable or pipeline beneath the high seas, in laying or repairing that cable or pipeline, cause a break in or injury to another cable or pipeline, they shall bear the cost of the repairs.

APPENDIX VII

Article 29

Every State shall take the necessary legislative measures to ensure that the owners of ships who can prove that they have sacrificed an anchor, a net or any other fishing gear, in order to avoid injuring a submarine cable or pipeline, shall be indemnified by the owner of the cable or pipeline, provided that the owner of the ship has taken all reasonable precautionary measures beforehand.

Article 30

The provisions of this Convention shall not affect conventions or other international agreements already in force, as between States Parties to them.

Article 31

This Convention shall, until 31 October 1958, be open for signature by all States Members of the United Nations or of any of the specialised agencies, and by any other State invited by the General Assembly of the United Nations to become a Party to the Convention.

Article 32

This Convention is subject to ratification. The instruments of ratification shall be deposited with the Secretary-General of the United Nations.

Article 33

This Convention shall be open for accession by any states belonging to any of the categories mentioned in Article 31. The instruments of accession shall be deposited with the Secretary-General of the United Nations.

Article 34

1. This Convention shall come into force on the thirtieth day following the date of deposit of the twenty-second instrument of ratification or accession with the Secretary-General of the United Nations.

2. For each State ratifying or acceding to the Convention after the deposit of the twenty-second instrument of ratification or accession, the Convention shall enter into force on the thirtieth day after deposit by such State of its instrument of ratification or accession.

Article 35

1. After the expiration of a period of five years from the date on which this Convention shall enter into force, a request for the revision of this Convention may be made at any time by any Contracting Party by means of a notification in writing addressed to the Secretary-General of the United Nations.

2. The General Assembly of the United Nations shall decide upon the steps, if any, to be taken in respect of such request.

APPENDIX VII

Article 36

The Secretary-General of the United Nations shall inform all States Members of the United Nations and the other States referred to in Article 31:

(a) Of signatures to this Convention and of the deposit of instruments of ratification or accession, in accordance with Articles 31, 32 and 33.

(b) Of the date on which this Convention will come into force, in accordance with Article 34;

(c) Of requests for revision in accordance with Article 35.

Article 37

The original of this Convention, of which the Chinese, English, French, Russian and Spanish texts are equally authentic, shall be deposited with the Secretary-General of the United Nations, who shall send certified copies thereof to all States referred to in Article 31.

In witness whereof the undersigned Plenipotentiaries, being duly authorised thereto by their respective Governments, have signed this Convention.

APPENDIX VIII

Extract from UN Convention on the Law of the Sea 1982[1]

Part VII High seas

Section 1. General provisions

Article 86. Application of the provisions of this part

The provisions of this Part apply to all parts of the sea that are not included in the exclusive economic zone, in the territorial sea or in the internal waters of a State, or in the archipelagic waters of an archipelagic State. This article does not entail any abridgement of the freedoms enjoyed by all States in the exclusive economic zone in accordance with Article 58.

Article 87. Freedom of the high seas

1. The high seas are open to all States, whether coastal or land-locked. Freedom of the high seas is exercised under the conditions laid down by this Convention and by other rules of international law. It comprises, *inter alia*, both for coastal and land-locked States:
   - (a) freedom of navigation;
   - (b) freedom of overflight;
   - (c) freedom to lay submarine cables and pipelines, subject to Part VI;
   - (d) freedom to construct artificial islands and other installations permitted under international law, subject to Part VI;
   - (e) freedom of fishing, subject to the conditions laid down in section 2;
   - (f) freedom of scientific research, subject to Parts VI and XIII.
2. These freedoms shall be exercised by all States with due regard for the interests of other States in their exercise of the freedom of the high seas, and also with due regard for the rights under this Convention with respect to activities in the Area.

Article 88. Reservation of the high seas for peaceful purposes

The high seas shall be reserved for peaceful purposes.

Article 89. Invalidity of claims of sovereignty over the high seas

No State may validly purport to subject any part of the high seas to its sovereignty.

---

[1] Courtesy UN Treaty Collection.

APPENDIX VIII

Article 90. Right of navigation

Every State, whether coastal or land-locked, has the right to sail ships flying its flag on the high seas.

Article 91. Nationality of ships

1. Every State shall fix the conditions for the grant of its nationality to ships, for the registration of ships in its territory, and for the right to fly its flag. Ships have the nationality of the State whose flag they are entitled to fly. There must exist a genuine link between the State and the ship.

2. Every State shall issue to ships to which it has granted the right to fly its flag documents to that effect.

Article 92. Status of ships

1. Ships shall sail under the flag of one State only and, save in exceptional cases expressly provided for in international treaties or in this Convention, shall be subject to its exclusive jurisdiction on the high seas. A ship may not change its flag during a voyage or while in a port of call, save in the case of a real transfer of ownership or change of registry.

2. A ship which sails under the flags of two or more States, using them according to convenience, may not claim any of the nationalities in question with respect to any other State, and may be assimilated to a ship without nationality.

Article 93. Ships flying the flag of the United Nations, its specialised agencies and the International Atomic Energy Agency

The preceding articles do not prejudice the question of ships employed on the official service of the United Nations, its specialised agencies or the International Atomic Energy Agency, flying the flag of the organisation.

Article 94. Duties of the flag State

1. Every State shall effectively exercise its jurisdiction and control in administrative, technical and social matters over ships flying its flag.

2. In particular every State shall:
   (a) maintain a register of ships containing the names and particulars of ships flying its flag, except those which are excluded from generally accepted international regulations on account of their small size; and
   (b) assume jurisdiction under its internal law over each ship flying its flag and its master, officers and crew in respect of administrative, technical and social matters concerning the ship.

3. Every State shall take such measures for ships flying its flag as are necessary to ensure safety at sea with regard, *inter alia*, to:
   (a) the construction, equipment and seaworthiness of ships;
   (b) the manning of ships, labour conditions and the training of crews, taking into account the applicable international instruments;
   (c) the use of signals, the maintenance of communications and the prevention of collisions.

4. Such measures shall include those necessary to ensure:
   (a) that each ship, before registration and thereafter at appropriate intervals, is surveyed by a qualified surveyor of ships, and has on board such charts, nautical publications

APPENDIX VIII

and navigational equipment and instruments as are appropriate for the safe navigation of the ship;

(b) that each ship is in the charge of a master and officers who possess appropriate qualifications, in particular in seamanship, navigation, communications and marine engineering, and that the crew is appropriate in qualification and numbers for the type, size, machinery and equipment of the ship;

(c) that the master, officers and, to the extent appropriate, the crew are fully conversant with and required to observe the applicable international regulations concerning the safety of life at sea, the prevention of collisions, the prevention, reduction and control of marine pollution, and the maintenance of communications by radio.

5. In taking the measures called for in paragraphs 3 and 4 each State is required to conform to generally accepted international regulations, procedures and practices and to take any steps which may be necessary to secure their observance.

6. A State which has clear grounds to believe that proper jurisdiction and control with respect to a ship have not been exercised may report the facts to the flag State. Upon receiving such a report, the flag State shall investigate the matter and, if appropriate, take any action necessary to remedy the situation.

7. Each State shall cause an inquiry to be held by or before a suitably qualified person or persons into every marine casualty or incident of navigation on the high seas involving a ship flying its flag and causing loss of life or serious injury to nationals of another State or serious damage to ships or installations of another State or to the marine environment. The flag State and the other State shall co-operate in the conduct of any inquiry held by that other State into any such marine casualty or incident of navigation.

Article 95. Immunity of warships on the high seas

Warships on the high seas have complete immunity from the jurisdiction of any State other than the flag State.

Article 96. Immunity of ships used only on government non-commercial service

Ships owned or operated by a State and used only on government non-commercial service shall, on the high seas, have complete immunity from the jurisdiction of any State other than the flag State.

Part XII Protection of the marine environment

Section 6. Enforcement

Article 217. Enforcement by flag States

1. States shall ensure compliance by vessels flying their flag or of their registry with applicable international rules and standards, established through the competent international organisation or general diplomatic conference, and with their laws and regulations adopted in accordance with this Convention for the prevention, reduction and control of pollution of the marine environment from vessels and shall accordingly adopt laws and regulations and take other measures necessary for their implementation. Flag States shall provide for the effective enforcement of such rules, standards, laws and regulations, irrespective of where a violation occurs.

2. States shall, in particular, take appropriate measures in order to ensure that vessels flying their flag or of their registry are prohibited from sailing, until they can proceed to sea in compliance with the requirements of the international rules and standards referred to in paragraph 1, including requirements in respect of design, construction, equipment and manning of vessels.

3. States shall ensure that vessels flying their flag or of their registry carry on board certificates required by and issued pursuant to international rules and standards referred to in paragraph 1. States shall ensure that vessels flying their flag are periodically inspected in order to verify that such certificates are in conformity with the actual condition of the vessels. These certificates shall be accepted by other States as evidence of the condition of the vessels and shall be regarded as having the same force as certificates issued by them, unless there are clear grounds for believing that the condition of the vessel does not correspond substantially with the particulars of the certificates.

4. If a vessel commits a violation of rules and standards established through the competent international organisation or general diplomatic conference, the flag State, without prejudice to Articles 218, 220 and 228, shall provide for immediate investigation and where appropriate institute proceedings in respect of the alleged violation irrespective of where the violation occurred or where the pollution caused by such violation has occurred or has been spotted.

5. Flag States conducting an investigation of the violation may request the assistance of any other State whose co-operation could be useful in clarifying the circumstances of the case. States shall endeavour to meet appropriate requests of flag States.

6. States shall, at the written request of any State, investigate any violation alleged to have been committed by vessels flying their flag. If satisfied that sufficient evidence is available to enable proceedings to be brought in respect of the alleged violation, flag States shall without delay institute such proceedings in accordance with their laws.

7. Flag States shall promptly inform the requesting State and the competent international organisation of the action taken and its outcome. Such information shall be available to all States.

8. Penalties provided for by the laws and regulations of States for vessels flying their flag shall be adequate in severity to discourage violations wherever they occur.

Article 218. Enforcement by port States

1. When a vessel is voluntarily within a port or at an off-shore terminal of a State, that State may undertake investigations and, where the evidence so warrants, institute proceedings in respect of any discharge from that vessel outside the internal waters, territorial sea or exclusive economic zone of that State in violation of applicable international rules and standards established through the competent international organisation or general diplomatic conference.

2. No proceedings pursuant to paragraph 1 shall be instituted in respect of a discharge violation in the internal waters, territorial sea or exclusive economic zone of another State unless requested by that State, the flag State, or a State damaged or threatened by the discharge violation, or unless the violation has caused or is likely to cause pollution in the internal waters, territorial sea or exclusive economic zone of the State instituting the proceedings.

3. When a vessel is voluntarily within a port or at an off-shore terminal of a State, that State shall, as far as practicable, comply with requests from any State for investigation of a discharge violation referred to in paragraph 1, believed to have occurred in, caused, or threatened damage to the internal waters, territorial sea or exclusive economic zone of the requesting State. It shall likewise, as far as practicable, comply with requests from the flag State for investigation of such a violation, irrespective of where the violation occurred.

APPENDIX VIII

4. The records of the investigation carried out by a port State pursuant to this article shall be transmitted upon request to the flag State or to the coastal State. Any proceedings instituted by the port State on the basis of such an investigation may, subject to section 7, be suspended at the request of the coastal State when the violation has occurred within its internal waters, territorial sea or exclusive economic zone. The evidence and records of the case, together with any bond or other financial security posted with the authorities of the port State, shall in that event be transmitted to the coastal State. Such transmittal shall preclude the continuation of proceedings in the port State.

APPENDIX IX

UN Convention on Conditions for Registration of Ships 1986[1]

The States Parties to this Convention,

Recognising the need to promote the orderly expansion of world shipping as a whole.

Recalling General Assembly resolution 35/36 of 5 December 1980, the annex to which contains the International Development Strategy for the Third United Nations Development Decade, which called, *inter alia*, in paragraph 128, for an increase in the participation by developing countries in world transport of international trade,

Recalling also that according to the 1958 Geneva Convention on the High Seas and the 1982 United Nations Convention on the Law of the Sea there must exist a genuine link between a ship and a flag State and conscious of the duties of the flag State to exercise effectively its jurisdiction and control over the ships flying its flag in accordance with the principle of the genuine link,

Believing that to this end a flag State should have a competent and adequate national maritime administration,

Believing also that in order to exercise its control function effectively a flag State should ensure that those who are responsible for the management and operation of a ship on its register are readily identifiable and accountable,

Believing further that measures to make persons responsible for ships more readily identifiable and accountable could assist in the task of combating maritime fraud,

Reaffirming, without prejudice to this Convention, that each State shall fix the conditions for the grant of its nationality to ships, for the registration of ships in its territory and for the right to fly its flag,

Prompted by the desire among sovereign States to resolve in a spirit of mutual understanding and co-operation all issues relating to the conditions for the grant of nationality to, and for the registration of, ships,

Considering that nothing in this Convention shall be deemed to prejudice any provisions in the national laws and regulations of the Contracting Parties to this Convention, which exceed the provisions contained herein,

Recognising the competences of the specialised agencies and other institutions of the United Nations system as contained in their respective constitutional instruments, taking into account arrangements which may have been concluded between the United Nations and the agencies, and between individual agencies and institutions in specific fields,

Have agreed as follows:

---

[1] Courtesy UN Treaty Collection. Not yet in force.

APPENDIX IX

Article 1. Objectives

For the purpose of ensuring or, as the case may be, strengthening the genuine link between a State and ships flying its flag, and in order to exercise effectively its jurisdiction and control over such ships with regard to identification and accountability of ship-owners and operators as well as with regard to administrative, technical, economic and social matters, a flag State shall apply the provisions contained in this Convention.

Article 2. Definitions

For the purposes of this Convention:

> "Ship" means any self-propelled sea-going vessel used in international seaborne trade for the transport of goods, passengers, or both with the exception of vessels of less than 500 gross registered tons,
> "Flag State" means a State whose flag a ship flies and is entitled to fly,
> "Owner" or "shipowner" means, unless clearly indicated otherwise, any natural or juridical person recorded in the register of ships of the State of registration as an owner of a ship,
> "Operator" means the owner or bareboat charterer, or any other natural or juridical person to whom the responsibilities of the owner or bareboat charterer have been formally assigned,
> "State of registration" means the State in whose register of ships a ship has been entered,
> "Register of ships" means the official register or registers in which particulars referred to in Article 11 of this Convention are recorded,
> "National maritime administration" means any State authority or agency which is established by the State of registration in accordance with its legislation and which, pursuant to that legislation, is responsible, *inter alia*, for the implementation of international agreements concerning maritime transport and for the application of rules and standards concerning ships under its jurisdiction and control,
> "Bareboat charter" means a contract for the lease of a ship, for a stipulated period of time, by virtue of which the lessee has complete possession and control of the ship, including the right to appoint the master and crew of the ship, for the duration of the lease;
> "Labour-supplying country" means a country which provides seafarers for service on a ship flying the flag of another country.

Article 3. Scope of application

This Convention shall apply to all ships as defined in Article 2.

Article 4. General provisions

1. Every State, whether coastal or land-locked, has the right to sail ships flying its flag on the high seas.
2. Ships have the nationality of the State whose flag they are entitled to fly.
3. Ships shall sail under the flag of one State only.
4. No ships shall be entered in the registers of ships of two or more States at a time, subject to the provisions of paragraphs 4 and 5 of Article 11 and to Article 12.
5. A ship may not change its flag during a voyage or while in a port of call, save in the case of a real transfer of ownership or change of registry.

APPENDIX IX

Article 5. National maritime administration

1. The flag State shall have a competent and adequate national maritime administration, which shall be subject to its jurisdiction and control.

2. The flag State shall implement applicable international rules and standards concerning, in particular, the safety of persons on board and the prevention of pollution of the marine environment.

3. The maritime administration of the flag State shall ensure:

(a) That ships flying the flag of such State with its laws and regulations concerning registration of ships and with applicable international rules and standards concerning, in particular, the safety of ships and persons on board and the prevention of pollution of the marine environment;

(b) That ships flying the flag of such State are periodically surveyed by its authorised surveyors in order to ensure compliance with applicable international rules and standards;

(c) That ships flying the flag of such State carry on board documents, in particular those evidencing the right to fly its flag and other valid relevant documents, including those required by international conventions to which the State of registration is a Party;

(d) That the owners of ships flying the flag of such State comply with the principles of registration of ships in accordance with the laws and regulations of such State and the provisions of this Convention.

4. The State of registration shall require all the appropriate information necessary for full identification and accountability concerning ships flying its flag.

Article 6. Identification and accountability

1. The State of registration shall enter in its register of ships, *inter alia*, information concerning the ship and its owner or owners. Information concerning the operator, when the operator is not the owner, should be included in the register of ships or in the official record of operators to be maintained in the office of the Registrar or be readily accessible to him, in accordance with the laws and regulations of the State of registration. The State of registration shall issue documentation as evidence of the registration of the ship.

2. The State of registration shall take such measures as are necessary to ensure that the owner or owners, the operator or operators, or any other person or persons who can be held accountable for the management and operation of ships flying its flag can be easily identified by persons having a legitimate interest in obtaining such information.

3. Registers of ships should be available to those with a legitimate interest in obtaining information contained therein, in accordance with the laws and regulations of the flag State.

4. A State should ensure that ships flying its flag carry documentation including information about the identity of the owner or owners, the operator or operators or the person or persons accountable for the operation of such ships, and make available such information to port State authorities.

5. Log-books should be kept on all ships and retained for a reasonable period after the date of the last entry, notwithstanding any change in a ship's name, and should be available for inspection and copying by persons having a legitimate interest in obtaining such information, in accordance with the laws and regulations of the flag State. In the event of a ship being sold and its registration being changed to another State, log-books relating to the period before such sale should be retained and should be available for inspection and copying by persons having a legitimate interest in obtaining such information, in accordance with the laws and regulations of the former flag State.

6. A State shall take necessary measures to ensure that ships it enters in its register of ships have owners or operators who are adequately identifiable for the purpose of ensuring their full accountability.

APPENDIX IX

7. A State should ensure that direct contact between owners of ships flying its flag and its government authorities is not restricted.

Article 7. Participation by nationals in the ownership and/or manning of ships

With respect to the provisions concerning manning and ownership of ships as contained in paragraphs 1 and 2 of Article 8 and paragraphs 1 to 3 of Article 9, respectively, and without prejudice to the application of any other provisions of this Convention, a State of registration has to comply either with the provisions of paragraphs 1 and 2 of Article 8, or with the provisions of paragraphs 1 to 3 of Article 9, but may comply with both.

Article 8. Ownership of ships

1. Subject to the provisions of Article 7, the flag State shall provide in its laws and regulations for the ownership of ships flying its flag.

2. Subject to the provisions of Article 7, in such laws and regulations the flag State shall include appropriate provisions for participation by that State or its nationals as owners of ships flying its flag or in the ownership of such ships and for the level of such participation. These laws and regulations should be sufficient to permit the flag State to exercise effectively its jurisdiction and control over ships flying its flag.

Article 9. Manning of ships

1. Subject to the provisions of Article 7, a State of registration, when implementing this Convention, shall observe the principle that a satisfactory part of the complement consisting of officers and crew of ships flying its flag be nationals or persons domiciled or lawfully in permanent residence in that State.

2. Subject to the provisions of Article 7 and in pursuance of the goal set out in paragraph 1 of this article, and in taking necessary measures to this end, the State of registration shall have regard to the following:

    (a) the availability of qualified seafarers within the State of registration;

    (b) multilateral or bilateral agreements or other types of arrangements valid and enforceable pursuant to the legislation of the State of registration;

    (c) the sound and economically viable operation of its ships.

3. The State of registration should implement the provision of paragraph 1 of this article on a ship, company or fleet basis.

4. The State of registration, in accordance with its laws and regulations, may allow persons of other nationalities to serve on board ships flying its flag in accordance with the relevant provisions of this Convention.

5. In pursuance of the goal set out in paragraph 1 of this article, the State of registration should, in co-operation with shipowners, promote the education and training of its nationals or persons domiciled or lawfully in permanent residence within its territory.

6. The State of registration shall ensure:

    (a) that the manning of ships flying its flag is of such a level and competence as to ensure compliance with applicable international rules and standards, in particular those regarding safety at sea;

    (b) that the terms and conditions of employment on board ships flying its flag are in conformity with applicable international rules and standards;

APPENDIX IX

(c)   that adequate legal procedures exist for the settlement of civil disputes between seafarers employed on ships flying its flag and their employers;

(d)   that nationals and foreign seafarers have equal access to appropriate legal processes to secure their contractual rights in their relations with their employers.

Article 10. Role of flag States in respect of the management of shipowning companies and ships

1. The State of registration, before entering a ship in its register of ships, shall ensure that the shipowning company or a subsidiary shipowning company is established and/or has its principal place of business within its territory in accordance with its laws and regulations.

2. Where the shipowning company or a subsidiary shipowning company or the principal place of business of the shipowning company is not established in the flag State, the latter shall ensure, before entering a ship in its register of ships, that there is a representative or management person who will be a national of the flag State, or be domiciled therein. Such a representative or management person may be a natural or juridical person who is duly established or incorporated in the flag State, as the case may be, in accordance with its laws and regulations, and duly empowered to act on the shipowner's behalf and account. In particular, this representative or management person should be available for any legal process and to meet the shipowner's responsibilities in accordance with the laws and regulations of the State of registration.

3. The State of registration should ensure that the person or persons accountable for the management and operation of a ship flying its flag are in a position to meet the financial obligations that may arise from the operation of such a ship to cover risks which are normally insured in international maritime transportation in respect of damage to third parties. To this end the State of registration should ensure that ships flying its flag are in a position to provide at all times documents evidencing that an adequate guarantee, such as appropriate insurance or any other equivalent means, has been arranged. Furthermore, the State of registration should ensure that an appropriate mechanism, such as a maritime lien, mutual fund, wage insurance, social security scheme, or any governmental guarantee provided by an appropriate agency of the State of the accountable person, whether that person is an owner or operator, exists to cover wages and related monies owed to seafarers employed on ships flying its flag in the event of default of payment by their employers. The State of registration may also provide for any other appropriate mechanism to that effect in its laws and regulations.

Article 11. Register of ships

1. A State of registration shall establish a register of ships flying its flag, which register shall be maintained in a manner determined by that State and in conformity with the relevant provisions of this Convention. Ships entitled by the laws and regulations of a State to fly its flag shall be entered in this register in the name of the owner or owners or, where national laws and regulations so provide, the bareboat charterer.

2. Such register shall, *inter alia*, record the following:

(a)   the name of the ship and the previous name and registry if any;

(b)   the place or port of registration or home port and the official number or mark of identification of the ship;

(c)   the international call sign of the ship, if assigned;

(d)   the name of the builders, place of build and year of building of the ship;

(e)   the description of the main technical characteristics of the ship;

(f)   the name, address and, as appropriate, the nationality of the owner or of each of the owners;

and, unless recorded in another public document readily accessible to the Registrar in the flag State:

APPENDIX IX

(g)　the date of deletion or suspension of the previous registration of the ship;

(h)　the name, address and, as appropriate, the nationality of the bareboat charterer, where national laws and regulations provide for the registration of ships bareboat chartered-in;

(i)　the particulars of any mortgages or other similar charges upon the ship as stipulated by national laws and regulations.

3. Furthermore, such register should also record:

(a)　if there is more than one owner, the proportion of the ship owned by each;

(b)　the name, address and, as appropriate, the nationality of the operator, when the operator is not the owner or the bareboat charterer.

4. Before entering a ship in its register of ships a State should assure itself that the previous registration, if any, is deleted.

5. In the case of a ship bareboat chartered-in a State should assure itself that right to fly the flag of the former flag State is suspended. Such registration shall be effected on production of evidence, indicating suspension of previous registration as regards the nationality of the ship under the former flag State and indicating particulars of any registered encumbrances.

Article 12. Bareboat charter

1. Subject to the provisions of Article 11 and in accordance with its laws and regulations a State may grant registration and the right to fly its flag to a ship bareboat chartered-in by a charterer in that State, for the period of that charter.

2. When shipowners or charterers in States Parties to this Convention enter into such bareboat charter activities, the conditions of registration contained in this Convention should be fully complied with.

3. To achieve the goal of compliance and for the purpose of applying the requirements of this Convention in the case of a ship so bareboat chartered-in the charterer will be considered to be the owner. This Convention, however, does not have the effect of providing for any ownership rights in the chartered ship other than those stipulated in the particular bareboat charter contract.

4. A State should ensure that a ship bareboat chartered-in and flying its flag, pursuant to paragraphs 1 to 3 of this article, will be subject to its full jurisdiction and control.

5. The State where the bareboat chartered-in ship is registered shall ensure that the former flag State is notified of the deletion of the registration of the bareboat chartered ship.

6. All terms and conditions, other than those specified in this article, relating to the relationship of the parties to a bareboat charter are left to the contractual disposal of those parties.

Article 13. Joint ventures

1. Contracting Parties to this Convention, in conformity with their national policies, legislation and the conditions for registration of ships contained in this Convention, should promote joint ventures between shipowners of different countries, and should, to this end, adopt appropriate arrangements, *inter alia*, by safeguarding the contractual rights of the parties to joint ventures, to further the establishment of such joint ventures in order to develop the national shipping industry.

2. Regional and international financial institutions and aid agencies should be invited to contribute, as appropriate, to the establishment and/or strengthening of joint ventures in the shipping industry of developing countries, particularly in the least developed among them.

Article 14. Measures to protect the interests of labour-supplying countries

1. For the purpose of safeguarding the interests of labour-supplying countries and of minimising labour displacement and consequent economic dislocation, if any, within these countries, particularly

developing countries, as a result of the adoption of this Convention, urgency should be given to the implementation, *inter alia*, of the measures as contained in Resolution 1 annexed to this Convention.

2. In order to create favourable conditions for any contract or arrangement that may be entered into by shipowners or operators and the trade unions of seamen or other representative seamen bodies, bilateral agreements may be concluded between flag States and labour-supplying countries concerning the employment of seafarers of those labour-supplying countries.

Article 15. Measures to minimise adverse economic effects

For the purpose of minimising adverse economic effects that might occur within developing countries, in the process of adapting and implementing conditions to meet the requirements established by this Convention, urgency should be given to the implementation, *inter alia*, of the measures as contained in Resolution 2 annexed to this Convention.

Article 16. Depositary

The Secretary-General of the United Nations shall be the depositary of this Convention.

Article 17. Implementation

1. Contracting Parties shall take any legislative or other measures necessary to implement this Convention.

2. Each Contracting Party shall, at appropriate times, communicate to the depositary the texts of any legislative or other measures which it has taken in order to implement this Convention.

3. The depositary shall transmit upon request to Contracting Parties the texts of the legislative or other measures which have been communicated to him pursuant to paragraph 2 of this article.

Article 18. Signature, ratification, acceptance, approval and accession

1. All States are entitled to become Contracting Parties to this Convention by:
   (a) signature not subject to ratification, acceptance or approval; or
   (b) signature subject to and followed by ratification, acceptance or approval; or
   (c) accession.

2. This Convention shall be open for signature from 1 May 1986 to and including 30 April 1987, at the Headquarters of the United Nations in New York and shall thereafter remain open for accession.

3. Instruments of ratification, acceptance, approval or accession shall be deposited with the depositary.

Article 19. Entry into force

1. This Convention shall enter into force 12 months after the date on which not less than 40 States, the combined tonnage of which amounts to at least 25% of world tonnage, have become Contracting Parties to it in accordance with Article 18. For the purpose of this article the tonnage shall be deemed to be that contained in Annex III to this Convention.

2. For each State which becomes a Contracting Party to this Convention after the conditions for entry into force under paragraph 1 of this article have been met, the Convention shall enter into force for that State 12 months after that State has become a Contracting Party.

APPENDIX IX

Article 20. Review and amendments

1. After the expiry of a period of eight years from the date of entry into force of this Convention, a Contracting Party may, by written communication addressed to the Secretary-General of the United Nations, propose specific amendments to this Convention and request the convening of a review conference to consider such proposed amendments. The Secretary-General shall circulate such communication to all Contracting Parties. If, within 12 months from the date of the circulation of the communication, not less than two-fifths of the Contracting Parties reply favourably to the request, the Secretary-General shall convene the Review Conference.

2. The Secretary-General of the United Nation shall circulate to all Contracting Parties the texts of any proposals for, or views regarding, amendments, at least six months before the opening date of the Review Conference.

Article 21. Effect of amendments

1. The decisions of a review conference regarding amendments shall be taken by consensus or, upon request, by a vote of a two-thirds majority of the Contracting Parties present and voting. Amendments adopted by such a conference shall be communicated by the Secretary-General of the United Nations to all the Contracting Parties for ratification, acceptance, or approval and to all the States signatories of the Convention for information.

2. Ratification, acceptance or approval of amendments adopted by a review conference shall be effected by the deposit of a formal instrument to that effect with the depositary.

3. Any amendment adopted by a review conference shall enter into force only for those Contracting Parties which have ratified, accepted or approved it, on the first day of the month following one year after its ratification, acceptance or approval by two-thirds of the Contracting Parties. For any State ratifying, accepting or approving an amendment after it has been ratified, accepted or approved by two-thirds of the Contracting Parties, the amendment shall enter into force one year after its ratification, acceptance or approval by that State.

4. Any State which becomes a Contracting Party to this Convention after the entry into force of an amendment shall, failing an expression of a different intention by that State:
   (a) Be considered as a Party to this Convention as amended; and
   (b) Be considered as a Party to the unamended Convention in relation to any Contracting Party not bound by the amendment.

Article 22. Denunciation

1. Any Contracting Party may denounce this Convention at any time by means of a notification in writing to this effect addressed to the depositary.

2. Such denunciation shall take effect on the expiration of one year after the notification is received by the depositary, unless a longer period has been specified in the notification.

In witness whereof the undersigned, being duly authorised thereto, have affixed their signature hereunder on the dates indicated.

Done at Geneva on 7 February 1986 in one original in the Arabic, Chinese, English, French, Russian and Spanish languages, all texts being equally authentic.

APPENDIX X

International Convention on Maritime
Liens and Mortgages 1993[1]

The States Parties to this Convention,

Conscious of the need to improve conditions for ship financing and the development of national merchant fleets,

Recognizing the desirability of international uniformity in the field of maritime liens and mortgages, and therefore

Convinced of the necessity for an international legal instrument governing maritime liens and mortgages,

Have decided to conclude a Convention for this purpose and have therefore agreed as follows:

Article 1. Recognition and enforcement of mortgages, "hypotheques" and charges

Mortgages, "hypotheques" and registrable charges of the same nature, which registrable charges of the same nature will be referred to hereinafter as "charges", effected on seagoing vessels shall be recognized and enforceable in States Parties provided that:

  (a) such mortgages, "hypotheques" and charges have been effected and registered in accordance with the law of the State in which the vessel is registered;

  (b) the register and any instruments required to be deposited with the registrar in accordance with the law of the State in which the vessel is registered are open to public inspection, and that extracts from the register and copies of such instruments are obtainable from the registrar; and

  (c) either the register or any instruments referred to in subparagraph (b) specifies at least the name and address of the person in whose favour the mortgage, "hypotheque" or charge has been effected or that it has been issued to bearer, the maximum amount secured, if that is a requirement of the law of the State of registration or if that amount is specified in the instrument creating the mortgage, "hypotheque" or charge, and the date and other particulars which, according to the law of the State of registration, determine the ranking in relation to other registered mortgages, "hypotheques" and charges.

Article 2. Ranking and effects of mortgages, "hypotheques" and charges

The ranking of registered mortgages, "hypotheques" or charges as between themselves and, without prejudice to the provisions of this Convention, their effect in regard to third parties shall be determined by the law of the State of registration; however, without prejudice to the provisions of this

---

[1] Courtesy UN Treaty Collection.

APPENDIX X

Convention, all matters relating to the procedure of enforcement shall be regulated by the law of the State where enforcement takes place.

Article 3. Change of ownership or registration

1. With the exception of the cases provided for in articles 11 and 12, in all other cases that entail the deregistration of the vessel from the register of a State Party, such State Party shall not permit the owner to deregister the vessel unless all registered mortgages, "hypotheques" or charges are previously deleted or the written consent of all holders of such mortgages, "hypotheques" or charges is obtained. However, where the deregistration of the vessel is obligatory in accordance with the law of a State Party, otherwise than as a result of a voluntary sale, the holders of registered mortgages, "hypotheques" or charges shall be notified of the pending deregistration in order to enable such holders to take appropriate action to protect their interests; unless the holders consent, the deregistration shall not be implemented earlier than after a lapse of a reasonable period of time which shall be not less than three months after the relevant notification to such holders.

2. Without prejudice to article 12, paragraph 5, a vessel which is or has been registered in a State Party shall not be eligible for registration in another State Party unless either:

(a) a certificate has been issued by the former State to the effect that the vessel has been deregistered; or

(b) a certificate has been issued by the former State to the effect that the vessel will be deregistered with immediate effect, at such time as the new registration is effected. The date of deregistration shall be the date of the new registration of the vessel.

Article 4. Maritime liens

1. Each of the following claims against the owner, demise charterer, manager or operator of the vessel shall be secured by a maritime lien on the vessel:

(a) claims for wages and other sums due to the master, officers and other members of the vessel's complement in respect of their employment on the vessel, including costs of repatriation and social insurance contributions payable on their behalf;

(b) claims in respect of loss of life or personal injury occurring, whether on land or on water, in direct connection with the operation of the vessel;

(c) claims for reward for the salvage of the vessel;

(d) claims for port, canal, and other waterway dues and pilotage dues;

(e) claims based on tort arising out of physical loss or damage caused by the operation of the vessel other than loss of or damage to cargo, containers and passengers' effects carried on the vessel.

2. No maritime lien shall attach to a vessel to secure claims as set out in subparagraphs (b) and (e) of paragraph 1 which arise out of or result from:

(a) damage in connection with the carriage of oil or other hazardous or noxious substances by sea for which compensation is payable to the claimants pursuant to international conventions or national law providing for strict liability and compulsory insurance or other means of securing the claims; or

(b) the radioactive properties or a combination of radioactive properties with toxic, explosive or other hazardous properties of nuclear fuel or of radioactive products or waste.

Article 5. Priority of maritime liens

1. The maritime liens set out in article 4 shall take priority over registered mortgages, "hypotheques" and charges, and no other claim shall take priority over such maritime liens or over

347

APPENDIX X

such mortgages, "hypotheques" or charges which comply with the requirements of article 1, except as provided in paragraphs 3 and 4 of article 12.

2. The maritime liens set out in article 4 shall rank in the order listed, provided however that maritime liens securing claims for reward for the salvage of the vessel shall take priority over all other maritime liens which have attached to the vessel prior to the time when the operations giving rise to the said liens were performed.

3. The maritime liens set out in each of subparagraphs (a), (b), (d) and (e) of paragraph 1 of article 4 shall rank *pari passu* as between themselves.

4. The maritime liens securing claims for reward for the salvage of the vessel shall rank in the inverse order of the time when the claims secured thereby accrued. Such claims shall be deemed to have accrued on the date on which each salvage operation was terminated.

Article 6. Other maritime liens

Each State Party may, under its law, grant other maritime liens on a vessel to secure claims, other than those referred to in article 4, against the owner, demise charterer, manager or operator of the vessel, provided that such liens:

    (a)   shall be subject to the provisions of articles 8, 10 and 12;
    (b)   shall be extinguished
        (i)   after a period of 6 months, from the time when the claims secured thereby arose unless, prior to the expiry of such period, the vessel has been arrested or seized, such arrest or seizure leading to a forced sale; or
        (ii) at the end of a period of 60 days following a sale to a *bona fide* purchaser of the vessel, such period to commence on the date on which the sale is registered in accordance with the law of the State in which the vessel is registered following the sale;
        whichever period expires first; and
    (c)   shall rank after the maritime liens set out in article 4 and also after registered mortgages, "hypotheques" or charges which comply with the provisions of article 1.

Article 7. Rights of retention

1. Each State Party may grant under its law a right of retention in respect of a vessel in the possession of either:

    (a)   a shipbuilder, to secure claims for the building of the vessel; or
    (b)   a shiprepairer, to secure claims for repair, including reconstruction of the vessel, effected during such possession.

2. Such right of retention shall be extinguished when the vessel ceases to be in the possession of the shipbuilder or shiprepairer, otherwise than in consequence of an arrest or seizure.

Article 8. Characteristics of maritime liens

Subject to the provisions of article 12, the maritime liens follow the vessel, notwithstanding any change of ownership or of registration or of flag.

Article 9. Extinction of maritime liens by lapse of time

1. The maritime liens set out in article 4 shall be extinguished after a period of one year unless, prior to the expiry of such period, the vessel has been arrested or seized, such arrest or seizure leading to a forced sale.

APPENDIX X

2. The one-year period referred to in paragraph 1 shall commence:
  (a) with respect to the maritime lien set out in article 4, paragraph 1(a), upon the claimant's discharge from the vessel;
  (b) with respect to the maritime liens set out in article 4, paragraph 1 (b) to (e), when the claims secured thereby arise;
  and shall not be subject to suspension or interruption, provided, however, that time shall not run during the period that the arrest or seizure of the vessel is not permitted by law.

Article 10. Assignment and subrogation

1. The assignment of or subrogation to a claim secured by a maritime lien entails the simultaneous assignment of or subrogation to such a maritime lien.

2. Claimants holding maritime liens may not be subrogated to the compensation payable to the owner of the vessel under an insurance contract.

Article 11. Notice of forced sale

1. Prior to the forced sale of a vessel in a State Party, the competent authority in such State Party shall ensure that notice in accordance with this article is provided to:
  (a) the authority in charge of the register in the State of registration;
  (b) all holders of registered mortgages, "hypotheques" or charges which have not been issued to bearer;
  (c) all holders of registered mortgages, "hypotheques" or charges issued to bearer and all holders of the maritime liens set out in article 4, provided that the competent authority conducting the forced sale receives notice of their respective claims; and
  (d) the registered owner of the vessel.

2. Such notice shall be provided at least 30 days prior to the forced sale and shall contain either:
  (a) the time and place of the forced sale and such particulars concerning the forced sale or the proceedings leading to the forced sale as the authority in a State Party conducting the proceedings shall determine is sufficient to protect the interests of persons entitled to notice; or,
  (b) if the time and place of the forced sale cannot be determined with certainty, the approximate time and anticipated place of the forced sale and such particulars concerning the forced sale as the authority in a State Party conducting the proceedings shall determine is sufficient to protect the interests of persons entitled to notice.
  If notice is provided in accordance with subparagraph (b), additional notice of the actual time and place of the forced sale shall be provided when known but, in any event, not less than seven days prior to the forced sale.

3. The notice specified in paragraph 2 of this article shall be in writing and either given by registered mail, or given by any electronic or other appropriate means which provide confirmation of receipt, to the persons interested as specified in paragraph 1, if known. In addition, the notice shall be given by press announcement in the State where the forced sale is conducted and, if deemed appropriate by the authority conducting the forced sale, in other publications.

Article 12. Effects of forced sale

1. In the event of the forced sale of the vessel in a State Party, all registered mortgages, "hypotheques" or charges, except those assumed by the purchaser with the consent of the holders,

and all liens and other encumbrances of whatsoever nature, shall cease to attach to the vessel, provided that:

- (a) at the time of the sale, the vessel is in the area of the jurisdiction of such State; and
- (b) the sale has been effected in accordance with the law of the said State and the provisions of article 11 and this article.

2. The costs and expenses arising out of the arrest or seizure and subsequent sale of the vessel shall be paid first out of the proceeds of sale. Such costs and expenses include, inter alia, the costs for the upkeep of the vessel and the crew as well as wages, other sums and costs referred to in article 4, paragraph 1 (a), incurred from the time of arrest or seizure. The balance of the proceeds shall be distributed in accordance with the provisions of this Convention, to the extent necessary to satisfy the respective claims. Upon satisfaction of all claimants, the residue of the proceeds, if any, shall be paid to the owner and it shall be freely transferable.

3. A State Party may provide in its law that, in the event of the forced sale of a stranded or sunken vessel following its removal by a public authority in the interest of safe navigation or the protection of the marine environment, the costs of such removal shall be paid out of the proceeds of the sale, before all other claims secured by a maritime lien on the vessel.

4. If at the time of the forced sale the vessel is in the possession of a shipbuilder or of a shiprepairer who under the law of the State Party in which the sale takes place enjoys a right of retention, such shipbuilder or shiprepairer must surrender possession of the vessel to the purchaser but is entitled to obtain satisfaction of his claim out of the proceeds of sale after the satisfaction of the claims of holders of maritime liens mentioned in article 4.

5. When a vessel registered in a State Party has been the object of a forced sale in any State Party, the competent authority shall, at the request of the purchaser, issue a certificate to the effect that the vessel is sold free of all registered mortgages, "hypotheques" or charges, except those assumed by the purchaser, and of all liens and other encumbrances, provided that the requirements set out in paragraph 1 (a) and (b) have been complied with. Upon production of such certificate, the registrar shall be bound to delete all registered mortgages, "hypotheques" or charges except those assumed by the purchaser, and to register the vessel in the name of the purchaser or to issue a certificate of deregistration for the purpose of new registration, as the case may be.

6. States Parties shall ensure that any proceeds of a forced sale are actually available and freely transferable.

Article 13. Scope of application

1. Unless otherwise provided in this Convention, its provisions shall apply to all seagoing vessels registered in a State Party or in a State which is not a State Party, provided that the latter's vessels are subject to the jurisdiction of the State Party.

2. Nothing in this Convention shall create any rights in, or enable any rights to be enforced against, any vessel owned or operated by a State and used only on Government non-commercial service.

Article 14. Communication between States Parties

For the purpose of articles 3, 11 and 12, the competent authorities of the States Parties shall be authorized to correspond directly between themselves.

Article 15. Conflict of conventions

Nothing in this Convention shall affect the application of any international convention providing for limitation of liability or of national legislation giving effect thereto.

APPENDIX X

Article 16. Temporary change of flag

If a seagoing vessel registered in one State is permitted to fly temporarily the flag of another State, the following shall apply:

(a) For the purposes of this article, references in this Convention to the "State in which the vessel is registered" or to the "State of registration" shall be deemed to be references to the State in which the vessel was registered immediately prior to the change of flag, and references to "the authority in charge of the register" shall be deemed to be references to the authority in charge of the register in that State.

(b) The law of the State of registration shall be determinative for the purpose of recognition of registered mortgages, "hypotheques" and charges.

(c) The State of registration shall require a cross-reference entry in its register specifying the State whose flag the vessel is permitted to fly temporarily; likewise, the State whose flag the vessel is permitted to fly temporarily shall require that the authority in charge of the vessel's record specifies by a cross-reference in the record the State of registration.

(d) No State Party shall permit a vessel registered in that State to fly temporarily the flag of another State unless all registered mortgages, "hypotheques" or charges on that vessel have been previously satisfied or the written consent of the holders of all such mortgages, "hypotheques" or charges has been obtained.

(e) The notice referred to in article 11 shall be given also to the competent authority in charge of the vessel's record in the State whose flag the vessel is permitted to fly temporarily.

(f) Upon production of the certificate of deregistration referred to in article 12 paragraph 5, the competent authority in charge of the vessel's record in the State whose flag the vessel is permitted to fly temporarily shall, at the request of the purchaser, issue a certificate to the effect that the right to fly the flag of that State is revoked.

(g) Nothing in this Convention is to be understood to impose any obligation on States Parties to permit foreign vessels to fly temporarily their flag or national vessels to fly temporarily a foreign flag.

Article 17. Depositary

This Convention shall be deposited with the Secretary-General of the United Nations.

Article 18. Signature, ratification, acceptance, approval and accession

1. This Convention shall be open for signature by any State at the Headquarters of the United Nations, New York, from 1 September 1993 to 31 August 1994 and shall thereafter remain open for accession.

2. States may express their consent to be bound by this Convention by:
    (a) signature without reservation as to ratification, acceptance or approval; or
    (b) signature subject to ratification, acceptance or approval, followed by ratification, acceptance or approval; or
    (c) accession.

3. Ratification, acceptance, approval or accession shall be effected by the deposit of an instrument to that effect with the depositary.

Article 19. Entry into force

1. This Convention shall enter into force 6 months following the date on which 10 States have expressed their consent to be bound by it.

351

APPENDIX X

2. For a State which expresses its consent to be bound by this Convention after the conditions for entry into force thereof have been met, such consent shall take effect 3 months after the date of expression of such consent.

Article 20. Revision and amendment

1. A conference of States Parties for the purpose of revising or amending this Convention shall be convened by the Secretary-General of the United Nations at the request of one-third of the States Parties.

2. Any consent to be bound by this Convention, expressed after the date of entry into force of an amendment to this Convention, shall be deemed to apply to the Convention, as amended.

Article 21. Denunciation

1. This Convention may be denounced by any State Party at any time after the date on which this Convention enters into force for that State.

2. Denunciation shall be effected by the deposit of an instrument of denunciation with the depositary.

3. A denunciation shall take effect one year, or such longer period as may be specified in the instrument of denunciation, after the receipt of the instrument of denunciation by the depositary.

Article 22. Languages

This Convention is established in a single original in the Arabic, Chinese, English, French, Russian and Spanish languages, each text being equally authentic.

DONE AT Geneva this sixth day of May, one thousand nine hundred and ninety-three.

IN WITNESS WHEREOF the undersigned being duly authorized by their respective Governments for that purpose have signed this Convention.

FORMS

APPENDIX XI(A)

Bahamas forms

(1) Application to register a ship, form R102
(2) Appointment of authorised officer, form R103
(3) Memorandum of the registration of managing owners, form R104
(4) Declaration of ownership, form R105
(5) Application for safe manning document, form R106

Note

Reproduced courtesy of the Bahamas Maritime Authority.
For additional and updated forms see: www.bahamasmaritime.com

APPENDIX XI(A)

R102 - Application to Register a Ship -Version 1.1

THE COMMONWEALTH OF THE BAHAMAS

Application to Register a Ship or Change the name of a Bahamian Ship

Proposed Name of Ship:- a) Preferred name choice: b) Alternative name(s):	
If a new ship:- b) Name and address of builder: c) Yard number:	
If the ship has previously been on the Bahamian register: d) Last Bahamian name: e) Official number:	
If the ship last sailed under another flag state:- f) Last foreign name: g) Nationality:	
Port at which ship is now lying:	
Net tonnage and details of propulsion:	Propulsion: Gross Tonnage: Net Tonnage:
Type of Vessel:	Date of Build: Date of Rebuild:
Usage: (Tick as Appropriate)	**Commercial** **Non Commercial** **Home Trade**
Proposed trade of ship:	
Bare Boat Charter: (Tick as Appropriate)	**In** **Out** **N/A**
Classification Society Certificates Issued By:	
Proposed date of registry:	
OWNERSHIP DETAILS	
Name and Registered Office of the Owner(s)	Number of sixty-four shares
Applicant's name and address:	
Date of application:	
Applicant's signature:	
Why have you chosen to register your vessel with The Bahamas?	(i) Quality of Service : (ii) Easy Registration Procedure : (iii) Delivery of Technical Service : (iv) Top 'White Flag' Register : (v) Competitive Fees : (vi) Established relationship :(vii) Other :
For BMA office use only:	Official Number assigned:- MMSI Number assigned:- IMO Number assigned: Call sign assigned:-

Form: R102 Rev 1   Issued: 1 July 2012

APPENDIX XI(A)

R103 – Appointment of Authorised Officers – Version 1.1

Please carefully read footnotes for guidance before completing and submitting this Form

THE COMMONWEALTH OF THE BAHAMAS

Appointment of Authorised Officer

Vessel Name: Official Number: IMO Number:

To the Registrar of Bahamian Ships   Port of Nassau
(**London, Nassau, New York, Hong Kong or Piraeus** office)

(a) .... having its principal place of business at ....

hereby authorises (b) ....
of ....
to make and sign all Declarations of Ownership or otherwise for and on behalf of the said Company as required under the provisions of the Merchant Shipping Act, 1976.

In witness whereof we have affixed our common seal this .... day of ....

Seal		
	....	.(insert name of individual/corporation)
	per	(insert signature of Individual/Director/Officer/Secretary/Attorney-in-fact)
	and	(insert signature of Individual/Director/Officer/Secretary/Attorney-in-fact)
	in the presence of the witness whose attestation is given below*	

I, (c) .... of (d) ....

.... hereby testify that in my presence

(i) this Appointment of Authorised Officer was signed by (e) ....

as Individual/Director/Officer/Secretary/Attorney-in-Fact(f) and (e)..

as Individual/Director/Officer/Secretary/Attorney-in-fact(f) and ....

(ii) the seal of the corporation/individual was affixed this ....day of ....

     Signature of witness / seal ....

(a) insert name of corporation/individual, (b) insert name of individual to be appointed authorised officer
(c) insert name of witness, (d) insert address of witness, (e) insert name of official, (f) delete as applicable.
*The witness to the execution of the document must be a disinterested party, independent of the body corporate or individual executing it e.g. Notary Public, Consular Officer, Magistrate, Justice of Peace. A director officer or employee of an owner which is a body corporate should not be an attesting witness.

APPENDIX XI(A)

Form R104 – Registration of Managing Owners – Version 1.5

THE COMMONWEALTH OF THE BAHAMAS

MEMORANDUM as to the Registration of Managing Owners etc.

It is requested that the information required by Section 52 of the Merchant Shipping Act, 1976, as to the Appointment of Managing Owner / Ships Husband / Manager be supplied to the Registrar of Bahamian Ships as indicated below. (To be completed by vessel owner or owner's representative)

Name of Vessel	IMO Number	Official Number	Port of Registry
			NASSAU

Owner Details

Owner (Company Name):		Telephone:	
Company IMO No:		Fax:	
Full Address:		E-mail:	
City:			
Postal / Zip Code:			
Country:			

Acknowledged by BMA in accordance with IMO A.741(18) section 1.1.2 (ISM Code)   Date:

Managers ISM Code or Technical Contact for non-ISM ships

Company Name:		DPA Name:	
Company IMO No:		24 hour Telephone:	
Full Address:		Fax:	
City:		E-mail:	
Postal / Zip Code:			
Country:			

Acknowledged by BMA in accordance with IMO A.741(18) section 4 (ISM Code)   Date:

ISPS Code Contact (If applicable)

Company Name:		CSO Name:	
Company IMO No:		24 hour Telephone:	
Full Address:		Fax:	
City:		E-mail:	
Postal / Zip Code:			
Country:			

Acknowledged by BMA in accordance with SOLAS XI-2 & (ISPS Code 11.1)   Date:

Accounting Contact

Company Name:		Contact Name:	
Full Address:		Telephone:	
City:		Fax:	
Postal / Zip Code:		E-mail:	
Country:			

Crew Managers Contact

Company Name:		Contact Name:	
Full Address:		Telephone:	
City:		Fax:	
Postal / Zip Code:		E-mail:	
Country:			

Date: Signature of Owner:

For official use only

Date: BMA Acknowledgement:

NB: All applicable contacts, inclusive of email address and 24 hour telephone number, **must** be completed in order to register a vessel, or a change of managing company.

Issued: 26 Feb 2012

APPENDIX XI(A)

R105 – Declaration of Ownership – Version 1.1

Please carefully read footnotes for guidance before completing and submitting this Form

THE COMMONWEALTH OF THE BAHAMAS

Declaration of Ownership

Official Number	IMO Number	Name of Ship	Port of Registry

Propulsion and Engine Details	Vessel Dimensions	
Propulsion:	Length:	metres
Type of Engines:	Breadth:	metres
Total Power:	Depth:	metres

Particulars of Tonnage
GROSS TONNAGE: .... tons   NET TONNAGE: .... tons

I, the undersigned ……………………………………………………………of (a) …………………………………………………

in the country of ……………………………………………being (b) ………………………………………………………

of (c) ………declare as follows:

The said company was incorporated by virtue of (d)

……………………………………………………………………………………………

……………………………………………………………………………………………

on the …… day of ……………………………and is subject to the laws of (e) ………………………………………………

The said company has its Registered Office/principal place of business at

……………………………………………………………………………

where all the important business of the Company is, in fact, controlled and managed at meetings of Directors or Managers of the company.

The above described ship was built at ……………………………………………………in the year ………………………

The general description of the ship is correct. The said company is entitled to be registered as owner of ………………………shares in the said ship.

And I make this solemn Declaration conscientiously believing the same to be true.

In witness whereof we have affixed our common seal this ………. day of ………………………………………

Seal	Individual/Corporation	Attestation
	name of individual/corporation per………………………………………….. signature as Individual/Director/Secretary/Officer Attorney-in-fact (h) and…………………………………………… signature as Individual/Director/Secretary/Officer Attorney-in-fact (h) in the presence of the witness whose attestation is given opposite	I, (f)…………………………………………………..... of (g) ………………………………………………....... hereby testify that in my presence (i) this Declaration of Ownership was signed by …………………………………………………………… as Individual/Director/Secretary/Officer/ Attorney-in-fact (h) and ……………………………………………………. as Individual/Director/Secretary/Officer/ Attorney-in-fact (h) and …………………………………………………….. (ii) the corporate seal (h)/personal seal (h) of …………… the transferee was affixed this ………. day of ………… Signature of witness / seal …………………………………

(a) insert full address (b) insert the office of the person making the declaration (c) insert full name of the body corporate (d) insert such of the descriptions as are applicable:- "an Act or Ordinance of the Legislature of ……… (cite the year in which the Act was passed, its chapter and title)" or "The Companies Act (Chapter 184)". If incorporated prior to the Act, the Act mentioned in the certificate of incorporation should be stated.) (e) insert The Bahamas (or as the case may be). In the case of a Company incorporated by virtue of the Companies Act, insert also "and its registered office is at …………………………".
(f) insert name of witness. The witness to the execution of the document must be a disinterested party, independent of the body corporate or individual executing it e.g. Notary Public, Consular Officer, Magistrate, Justice of Peace. A director, officer or employee of an owner which is a body corporate should not be an attesting witness.
(g) address of witness (h) delete as applicable.

APPENDIX XI(A)

Official Use only

Date of receipt:

Application for Minimum Safe Manning Document (MSMD)

Any document issued will reflect the minimum manning levels approved by the Authority. The document will not include personnel carried in the ship in excess of the approved minimum scale. Reference shall be made to BMA Information Bulletins 115 and 105 which provide guidance relating to manning.

SECTION 1 MANAGERS / MANAGEMENT COMPANY'S DETAILS
(Please note all correspondence relating to the Minimum Safe Manning Document will be made through this address. Unless requested otherwise, the original copy of the MSMD will also be posted to this address.)

Name of Manager/Management Company
Mailing Address
Telephone Numbers

Email	Fax

SECTION 2 GENERAL PARTICULARS (Please put 'N/A' if any box is not applicable)

Ships name	Port of Registry
IMO Number	Official Number
Type of Ship	
Length	Breadth
Gross Tonnage	Trading Area

Numbers of Tanks	Number of Holds	Type of Hatch covers
Number of Pump rooms/space	Cargo Gear Type	Cargo Gear Numbers
Total Persons on Board	Number of Life Rafts	Number of Lifeboats
Type of Lifeboat or Liferaft Davits	Number of Marine Evacuation System (MES)	
Number of Assembly Stations	Number of Rescue Boats	Number of Muster Teams

SECTION 3 MACHINERY (Please tick the relevant box)

Type of Main Engine	Propulsion Power (KW)	Periodically unmanned E/R ◯ Yes ◯ No
Bridge Control ◯ Yes ◯ No	E/R Watch Alarm system ◯ Yes ◯ No	Number of Generators
E/R Bilge Alarm System ◯ Yes ◯ No	E/R Fire Detection System ◯ Yes ◯ No	Fire Pumps capable of remote operation ◯ Yes ◯ No

Application for Minimum Safe Manning / R106 / Rev:04 / Date: January 2014

APPENDIX XI(A)

SECTION 4 COMMUNICATIONS (Please tick the relevant box)

GMDSS	Radio Maintenance Agreement	Particulars of Internal Communications
◯A1 ◯A2 ◯A3 ◯A4	◯Onboard ◯Shorebased	

Who will be the primary GMDSS/Radio operator?

SECTION 5 MOORING ARRANGEMENTS

Number of Winches	Winch Type
Power Source of Winches	How many persons required for mooring stations?

SECTION 6 PROPOSED MANNING SCALE

CAPACITY	QUALIFICATION[1]	NUMBER[5]	NUMBER[5]		QUALIFICATION[1]	NUMBER[5]	NUMBER[5]
MASTER				CHIEF ENGINEER			
CHIEF MATE				SECOND ENGINEER			
OFFICER IN CHARGE OF NAVIGATION WATCH				OFFICER IN CHARGE OF ENGINEERING WATCH			
ABLE SEAFARER (DECK)[3]				ELECTRO TECHNICAL OFFICER			
RATING FORMING PART OF NAVIGATIONAL WATCH				ABLE SEAFARER (ENGINE)[3]			
GMDS RADIO OPERATOR[6]				RATING FORMING PART OF ENGINEERING WATCH			
OFFSHORE INSTALLATION MANAGER (OIM)				ELECTRO TECHNICAL RATING[4]			
BARGE SUPERVISOR				MAINTENANCE SUPERVISOR			
BALLAST CONTROL OPERATOR				COOK			
OTHER[2]				DOCTOR			

1) In the 'qualifications' column, please put relevant 'STCW notations' or 'IMO resolution number' as appropriate.

2) In the 'Other' category , please put the number of additional persons required to manage any operational or emergency situations taking into account 'Total Persons on Board'. These persons only need to have STCW training or instructions dependent on their assigned shipboard duties in respect of safety, security or environmental protection.

3) A STCW II/4 or III/4 certificate will continue to be accepted for existing seafarers for Able Seafarer (Deck) or Able Seafarer (Engine) positions until 31 December 2016 ; after this date a STCW II/5 or STCW III/5 qualification respectively will be required. New entrants from 01 July 2013 will need a II/5 or III/5 qualification respectively whenever they are accepted for above positions.

4) Existing Elecro-Technical Offic ers and Electro-Technical Ratings may continue to work with non-STCW national certificates until 31 December 2016; after this date a STCW III/6 or STCW III/7 qualification respectively will be required. New entrants from 01 July 2013 will need a STCW III/6 or a STCW III/7 qualification respectively whenever they are accepted for above positions.

5) There are tw o columns for putting the number for each capacity. If two different manning levels are proposed for different trading area, then the number for common trading area (e.g. Near Coastal area) should be put on the left column and number for occasional trading area (e.g. Unlimited area) should be on the right column. If two columns are used, there should be a statement in 'section 8' briefly explaining why different manning levels are required. If manning is required only for one trading area, then one column should be used and if more than 2 manning levels are required, the additional level can be inserted in 'Section 8'.

6) This row should only be c ompleted if a dedicated GMDSS Radio Operator is required and this person is separate to the navigational Officers.

Application for Minimum Safe Manning / R106 / Rev:04 / Date: January 2014

361

APPENDIX XI(A)

SECTION 7 ADDITIONAL INFORMATION

Does the Master take a navigational watch? ◯ Yes ◯ No	Does the Chief Engineer take a watch? ◯ Yes ◯ No

Who acts as the designated Security Officer, if any?

How many persons are assigned designated security?

Who is responsible for the maintenance of Fire and Life Saving appliance?

Who is designated for medical care/first aid on board?

Who is responsible for the Electrical, Electronic, Control and Computer network System and equipment?[7]

7) (If these are essential equipment which requires an onboard personnel who is not an STCW Engineer, then that person(s) should be included in 'Section 6' and must hold an appropriate STCW certificate).

How many persons required to operate the cargo handling gear(s), if applicable?	How many persons required to clean machinery space and to assist in the machinery space in the event of a breakdown?
How many persons required for hold/tank cleaning, if applicable?	

SECTION 8 ANY OTHER FACTORS

(Any issue not included in other sections but is pertinent to the Application may be mentioned. Also, please state the name of the company to be invoiced for the fees related to the Minimum Safe Manning Document.)

SECTION 9 DECLARATION

On behalf of the owners of the vessel, I hereby confirm that an assessment has been carried out taking into consideration the international and flag state requirements relating to the Minimum Safe Manning Document and the proposed manning is deemed to be the minimum for the vessel's safe operation, for its security, for protection of the marine environment, and for dealing with emergency situations.

I CERTIFY THAT TO THE BEST OF MY KNOWLEDGE THE PARTICULARS GIVEN BY ME IN THIS FORM ARE CORRECT.

Signature	Full Name
Position	Company
Date	

The application should be f orwarded to the appropriate BMA office. The addresses of BMA offices worldwide are available from the website: www.bahamasmaritime.com

Application for Minimum Safe Manning / R106 / Rev:04 / Date: January 2014

362

APPENDIX XI(B)

Cayman Islands forms

(1) Vessel name proposal and reservation, form CISR 854
(2) Appointment of an authorised person, form CISR 855
(3) Vessel registration in Cayman, form CISR 856
(4) Application for miscellaneous services, form CISR 857
(5) Application for minimum safe manning document (ships), form CISR 750
(6) Application for minimum safe manning document (yachts), form CISR 750A
(7) Declaration of maritime labour compliance – Part I

Note

Reproduced courtesy of Cayman Islands Shipping Registry.
For additional and updated forms see: www.cishipping.com

APPENDIX XI(B)

VESSEL NAME PROPOSAL AND RESERVATION

Cayman Islands Shipping Registry
HEAD OFFICE
133 Elgin Avenue P.O. Box 2256
Grand Cayman KY1-1107 Cayman Islands
Tel: +1 345 949 8831 Fax: +1 345 949 8849
Email: registration@cishipping.com
Website: www.cishipping.com

1 Proposed Name & Port of Registry

PLEASE COMPLETE IN BLOCK LETTERS

NOTE: List alternative name(s) in order of preference in case the first name cannot be approved.
Once a name has been approved it may not be possible to change to an alternative name.

1st: _____   3rd: _____

2nd: _____   4th: _____

Please select your choice of Port(s):   ☐ George Town   ☐ The Creek   ☐ Bloody Bay
NOTE: You will be charged for each Port selection

2 Vessel Status

Is the ship new?   ☐ Yes   ☐ No   (if yes, please fill in A below, only)

A: Name and Address of Builder: _____

   Yard No. allocated to this ship: _____

B: Current Flag State: _____

   Current Registered Name: _____

Proposed Registration Date (DD/MM/YYYY): _____

Method of Propulsion: ☐ Sail   ☐ Non-propelled   ☐ Steam   ☐ Motor   Total Propulsion Engine (kw): _____

Gross Tonnage (approx): _____   Type of Ship: _____

3 Client Details

Name of Owner/Demise Charterer: _____

Mailing Address: _____

Telephone: _____   Email: _____   Signature of Applicant: _____

4 Registrar Approval

The Vessel Name: _____   has been reserved for a period of twelve months from the date below.

Date (DD): _____   of (MONTH): _____   20 (YY): _____   Approved by: _____

REGISTRAR OF SHIPPING

NOTE: This form is to be filed with the Registrar of Shipping prior to the submission of the other registration forms/documents. If th vessel is not registered within twelve months of the date of the name approval, it will be considered to have lapsed. Upon a furthere request, the Registrar may renew the reservation if the name remains available.

A division of

CISR 854
REV 01/17
Page 1 of 1

APPENDIX XI(B)

APPOINTMENT OF AN AUTHORISED PERSON

Cayman Islands Shipping Registry
HEAD OFFICE
133 Elgin Avenue P.O. Box 2256
Grand Cayman KY1-1107 Cayman Islands
Tel: +1 345 949 8831 Fax: +1 345 949 8849
Email: registration@cishipping.com
Website: www.cishipping.com

Proposed Appointment

Name of Vessel: Official Number: IMO Number:

Name of Owner(s):

Place of Business:

Hereby Authorises (Name of Appointee):

to make and sign all Declarations of Ownership or Eligibility or otherwise for and behalf of the said Owner(s) as required under the relevant provisions of the Cayman Islands Merchant Shipping Law, as amended.

This appointment is valid until:

PLEASE NOTE a Power of Attorney or Board Resolution may be submitted in lieu of the CISR 855 Form.

The Common Seal of the Owning Company was affixed hereto in the presence of:

Name: Owner's/Director's Signature:

Capacity:

Date (DD/MM/YYYY):

COMPANY'S SEAL:

NOTE: Where a company seal or stamp is not used, signatures on pages 1 and 2 of this form must be made before the Registrar of Shipping or other authorised officer of the Cayman Islands Shipping Registry, a Justice of the Peace, a Commissioner for Oaths within the meaning of the Cayman Islands Oaths Law, a Notary Public, a British Consular Officer, or other persons with a professional qualification at the discretion of the Registrar. The qualification of the person acting as a witness and the place of attestation are to be added to his/her signature.

A division of

CISR 855
REV 01/17

APPENDIX XI(B)

APPOINTMENT OF AN AUTHORISED PERSON

Authorised Signatures

Authorised Signatures as at the: (DD) day of   (MM) 20   (YY)

Name of Authorised Signatory	Signature Specimen	Job Title	Company

(I/We) hereby certify:

(i) that the signatures contained on this form are authentic and are true copies of those named;

(ii) that (I/We) are authorised signatories on behalf of the Registered Owners and have the relevant authority (delegated or otherwise) to complete this form for and on behalf of the Registered Owners.

Signed in the presence of (WITNESS NAME):

Print Name

Signature

COMPANY'S SEAL:

A division of

CISR 855
REV 01/17

366

APPENDIX XI(B)

VESSEL REGISTRATION IN CAYMAN

Cayman Islands Shipping Registry
HEAD OFFICE
133 Elgin Avenue P.O. Box 2256
Grand Cayman KY1-1107 Cayman Islands
Tel: +1 345 949 8831 Fax: +1 345 949 8849
Email: registration@cishipping.com
Website: www.cishipping.com

1 Applicant Details

Name of Owner/Demise Charterer:

Physical Address:

Mailing Address:

Contact Person 1:   Contact Person 2:

Telephone: Fax: Email:

Unique Registered Owner Identification Number:

Type of Registration Service(s) Required
PLEASE CHECK ALL THAT APPLY

☐ Full Registration - Pleasure   ☐ Transfer of Port to the Port of George Town

☐ Full Registration - Commercial   ☐ Transfer of Port to the Port of The Creek

☐ Full Registration - Local Fishing Vessel   ☐ Transfer of Port to the Port of Bloody Bay

☐ Transfer of Ownership   ☐ Demise Charter-In to the Port of George Town

☐ Transmission of Ownership   ☐ Demise Charter-In to the Port of The Creek

☐ Vessel Under Construction   ☐ Demise Charter-In to the Port of Bloody Bay

☐ Interim Registration

Representative/Authorised Person:

Signature:

Capacity:

Date (DD/MM/YYYY):

A division of

CISR 856
REV 01/17
Page 1 of 7

APPENDIX XI(B)

VESSEL REGISTRATION IN CAYMAN

2a Vessel Details

Proposed Name of Vessel*:   Select Choice of Ports [2]: ☐ George Town ☐ The Creek ☐ Bloody Bay

Current Registered Name of Vessel: Current Port of Registry: ☐ George Town ☐ The Creek ☐ Bloody Bay

Official Number: IMO Number (if applicable):   Date of Construction (DD/MM/YYYY):

Method of Propulsion: ☐ Sail   ☐ Non-Propelled   ☐ Steam   ☐ Motor - Total Propulsion Engine (KW):

Type of Ship: Tonnage: GROSS   NET

Measurements (metric units, as specified in ship's Tonnage Certificate or Certificate of Survey):

Length (M):   Breadth (M):   Moulded Depth (M):

*On a separate sheet, list in order of preference any additional names.

2b Declaration of Ownership or Eligibility on Behalf of a Company/Body Corporate

NOTE: Declarations must be made before the Registrar of Shipping or other authorised officer of the Cayman Islands Shipping Registry, a Justice of the Peace, a Commissioner for Oaths within the meaning of the Cayman Islands Oaths Law, a Notary Public, a British Consular Officer, or other persons with a professional qualification at the discretion of the Registrar. The qualification of the person making the declaration and the place of attestation are to be added to his/her signature.

UPON COMPLETION OF SECTION 2B, GO TO SECTION 3

Name of Vessel: Official Number [1]:   IMO Number:

The Company/Body Corporate Declaration

I: of:

Declare as follows; The said company was incorporated by virtue of[3]:

on the (DD):   day of (MONTH):   Year (YYYY):   and is subject to the laws of[4]:

The said company has its registered office at:

and a place of business at:

where meetings of the Directors of the Company are regularly held.

The said company is registered as a foreign company in the Cayman Islands with an address at[5]:

The aforementioned general description of the ship is correct.
The said company/body corporate is eligible to be registered as Owner of   shares in the said sh ip.

APPENDIX XI(B)

VESSEL REGISTRATION IN CAYMAN

To the best of my knowledge and belief, a majority interest in the said ship will at the time of registration be owned by a body corporate who is qualified to own Cayman Islands ships under the relevant provisions of the Cayman Islands Merchant Shipping Law, as amended. I make this solemn Declaration conscientiously believing the same to be true.

Made and subscribed the (DD):	day of (MONTH):	20 (YY):
by the above named (PRINT NAME OF SIGNATORY)		(SIGNATURE)
in the presence of (PRINT NAME OF WITNESS)		(SIGNATURE)
Capacity in which Witness is acting:		

2c Declaration of Ownership or Eligibility on Behalf of an Individual

UPON COMPLETION OF SECTION 2C, GO TO SECTION 3

Name of Vessel:	Official Number [1]:	IMO Number:

Individual Declaration

I: of:

Declare as follows:

The above described ship was built at: in the year (YYYY)

The aforementioned general description of the ship is correct. I am eligible to be registered as Owner of   shares in the said ship.

To the best of my knowledge and belief, a majority interest in the said ship will at the time of registration be owned by a per son who is qualified to be the owner of a Cayman Islands ship under the relevant provisions of the Cayman Islands Merchant Shipping Law, as amended. I make this solemn Declaration conscientiously believing the same to be true.

Made and subscribed the (DD):	day of (MONTH):	20 (YY):
by the above named (PRINT NAME OF SIGNATORY):		(SIGNATURE):
in the presence of (PRINT NAME OF WITNESS):		(SIGNATURE):
Capacity in which Witness is acting:		
Declaration/Date commission expires (DD/MM/YYYY):		

A division of

CISR 856
REV 01/17

APPENDIX XI(B)

VESSEL REGISTRATION IN CAYMAN

2d Declaration of Ownership or Eligibility on Behalf of Joint Owners

UPON COMPLETION OF SECTION 2D, GO TO SECTION 3

Name of Vessel: Official Number[1]:   IMO Number:

Joint Ownership Declaration

1 Name (IN FULL)*:   Occupation:

Address:

2 Name (IN FULL)*:   Occupation:

Address:

3 Name (IN FULL)*:   Occupation:

Address:

4 Name (IN FULL)*:   Occupation:

Address:

* If Joint Owners exceed space provided, please provide additional information on another sheet.

We: of:

Declare as follows:

The above described ship was built at: in the year (YYYY)

The aforementioned general description of the ship is correct. We are eligible to be registered as Joint Owners of   shares in the said ship.

To the best of my knowledge and belief, a majority interest in the said ship will at the time of registration be owned by persons who are qualified to be the owners of a Cayman Islands ship under the relevant provisions of the Cayman Islands Merchant Shipping Law, as amended. We make this solemn Declaration conscientiously believing the same to be true.

Made and subscribed the (DD):   day of (MONTH):   20 (YY)

by the above named   (PRINT NAME OF SIGNATORY)   (SIGNATURE)

     (PRINT NAME OF SIGNATORY)   (SIGNATURE)

     (PRINT NAME OF SIGNATORY)   (SIGNATURE)

     (PRINT NAME OF SIGNATORY)   (SIGNATURE)

in the presence of   (PRINT NAME OF WITNESS)   (SIGNATURE)

Capacity in which Witness is acting:

Declaration/Date commission expires   (DD/MM/YYYY):

A division of
Cayman ★★
Maritime

CISR 856
REV 01/17

APPENDIX XI(B)

VESSEL REGISTRATION IN CAYMAN

2e Declaration of Ownership or Eligibility on Behalf of a Partnership

UPON COMPLETION OF SECTION 2E, GO TO SECTION 3

Name of Vessel: Official Number[1]:   IMO Number:

The Limited Liability/Exempted Limited Partnership Declaration

I: of:

Declare as follows; The said partnership was registered by virtue of [3]:

on the (DD):   day of (MONTH):   Year (YYYY):   and is subject to the laws of [4]:

The said partnership has its registered office at:

and a place of business at:

where meetings of the General Partners of the Partnership are regularly held.

The aforementioned general description of the ship is correct.

The said partnership is eligible to be registered as Owner of   shares in the said ship.

To the best of my knowledge and belief, a majority interest in the said ship will at the time of registration be owned by a body of persons who is qualified to be the owner of Cayman Islands ships under the relevant provisions of the Cayman Islands Merchant Shipping Law, as amended. I make this solemn Declaration conscientiously believing the same to be true.

Made and subscribed the (DD):   day of (MONTH):   20 (YY):

by the above named (PRINT NAME OF SIGNATORY):   (SIGNATURE):

in the presence of (PRINT NAME OF WITNESS):   (SIGNATURE):

Capacity in which Witness is acting:

---

[1] Insert the Official Number if allocated by the Cayman Islands or if the Vessel is currently registered with another Red Ensign flag.
[2] For merchant vessels, only the Port of George Town can be uesed.
[3] Insert the name of the statutory provision pursuant to which the company was incorporated/partnership registered (including the name of the country pursuant to whose law such statutory provisions was made).
[4] The Cayman Islands or as the case may be.
[5] If applicable.

A division of

CISR 856
REV 01/17

APPENDIX XI(B)

VESSEL REGISTRATION IN CAYMAN

3 Appointment of a Cayman Representative Person

Name of Vessel: Official Number[1]:   IMO Number:

I hereby confirm the appointment of a Cayman Representative Person for the above described vessel as follows:

Name of Individual or Body Corporate to act as a Cayman Representative Person:

Physical Address:

Mailing Address:

Telephone: Fax: Email:

Name: Owner's/Authorised Person's Signature:

Capacity: Date (DD/MM/YYYY):

4 Undertaking to Act as a Cayman Representative Person

I acknowledge that the duties of a Cayman Representative Person include:

- Knowledge of the Beneficial Owner and attaching due diligence to the same degree as though he or she were screening a client or company registered in the Cayman Islands in accordance with the Laws or codes of practice applicable to the local professional associations.
- An obligation to remain a Cayman Representative Person until such time as a replacement is appointed and accepted as prescribed under the law.
- An obligation to abide by such directives as may be prescribed from time to time by the Chief Executive Officer of the Maritime Authority of the Cayman Islands.

I hereby accept the appointment of a Cayman Representative Person for the described vessel (as per Section 3) as follows:

Name of Individual or Body Corporate to act as a Cayman Representative Person:

Physical Address:

Mailing Address:

Telephone: Fax: Email:

Name:

Representative/Authorised Signatory or Body Corporate:

Capacity:

Date (DD/MM/YYYY):

A division of

APPENDIX XI(B)

VESSEL REGISTRATION IN CAYMAN

5 Declaration and Undertakings

☐ i **Private Use**

I/We

Owner(s)/Authorised Person(s) declare that the above vessel is for private use and will not be engaged in trade. Further, it is also declared that should the vessel be chartered, this will only be for private use under a written charter party agreement. The number of persons carried onboard to sea, in addition to crew, will never exceed twelve (12).

☐ ii **Carving & Marking**

I/We

Owner(s)/Authorised Person(s) undertake to have the above named vessel marked with its Port of Registry, Official Number, Net or Registered Tonnage and IMO Number (if applicable), within 21 days in accordance with the relevant provisions of the Merchant Shipping Law, as amended, or before the vessel proceeds to sea, whichever is sooner.

☐ iii **Original Documents**

I/We

Owner(s)/Authorised Person(s) undertake to have the original title-related documents (i.e. Builder's Certificate, Bill of Sale, and Mortgage Deed) submitted to the Cayman Islands Shipping Registry for stamping within 7 days of the date of service.

☐ iv **Bill of Sale and Declaration of Ownership (Interim Registration)**

I/We

Owner(s)/Authorised Person(s) undertake to submit the original Bill of Sale and Declaration of Ownership or Eligibility for the above named vessel to the Cayman Islands Shipping Registry within 21 days of the issue date of the Interim Certificate of Registry.

6 Supporting Documents Enclosed (Registration - All Vessels)

The following documents have been included (where applicable) with this application in accordance with the prescribed requirements of the Cayman Islands Shipping Registry.

PLEASE CHECK ALL THAT HAVE BEEN INCLUDED

☐ Bill of Sale	☐ Shipyard Letter	☐ Builder's Certificate
☐ Transferee's Declaration	☐ Certificate of Good Standing	☐ Certificate of Registry
☐ Transcript of Register	☐ Certificate of Survey	☐ Deletion Certificate
☐ Tonnage Certificate	☐ Owner's/Mortgagee's Consent	☐ Charter Party Agreement
☐ Court Order	☐ Construction Contract	☐ Resolution to Sell
☐ Declaration of Transmission	☐ Other (PLEASE SPECIFY)	

A division of

APPENDIX XI(B)

APPLICATION FOR MISCELLANEOUS SERVICES

Cayman Islands Shipping Registry
HEAD OFFICE
133 Elgin Avenue P.O. Box 2256
Grand Cayman KY1-1107 Cayman Islands
Tel: +1 345 949 8831 Fax: +1 345 949 8849
Email: registration@cishipping.com
Website: www.cishipping.com

1 Applicant Details

Name of Applicant:

Physical Address:

Mailing Address:

Contact Person 1:   Contact Person 2:

Telephone: Fax: Email:

Name of Vessel: Official Number: IMO Number:

2 Type of Service(s) Required

PLEASE CHECK ALL THAT APPLY

- [ ] Registration of Mortgage   - [ ] Change of Vessel Name
- [ ] Transfer of Mortgage   - [ ] Change of Registered Owner's Name
- [ ] Change of Mortgagee's Name   - [ ] Discharge of Mortgage
- [ ] Discharge of Mortgage Without Original Deed   - [ ] Change of Vessel Type
- [ ] Recording of a Priority Notice   - [ ] Demise Charter-Out of the Port of George Town
- [ ] Transfer of Port Out of George Town   - [ ] Demise Charter-Out of the Port of The Creek
- [ ] Transfer of Port Out of The Creek   - [ ] Demise Charter-Out of the Port of Bloody Bay
- [ ] Transfer of Port Out of Bloody Bay   - [ ] Change of Registered Office's Address
- [ ] Reissue Carving & Marking Note   - [ ] Current Transcript of Register
- [ ] Duplicate Certificate   - [ ] Change of Registered Owner's Address
- [ ] Change of Mortgagee's Address   - [ ] Change of Representative Person's Address
- [ ] Change of Representative Person   - [ ] Recording of Lifeboats, Tenders & Other Appurtenances
- [ ] Deletion: [ ] Deletion Certificate [ ] Closed Transcript
  Reason for Deletion (PLEASE SPECIFY)

- [ ] Registration Anew: [ ] Change of Ownership [ ] Change of Vessel's Tonnage & Particulars
- [ ] Other (PLEASE SPECIFY)

A division of

CISR 857
REV 01/17

APPENDIX XI(B)

APPLICATION FOR MISCELLANEOUS SERVICES

3 Supporting Documents Enclosed

The following documents have been included (where applicable) with the application in accordance with CISR 840, Annex 3, Cayman Vessel Registration and Related Services matrices:

PLEASE CHECK ALL THAT HAVE BEEN INCLUDED

☐ Bill of Sale	☐ Owner's/Mortgagee's Consent
☐ Builder's Certificate	☐ Letter of Dispensation
☐ Certificate of Good Standing	☐ Letter of Request from Owner
☐ Certificate of Survey	☐ Tonnage Certificate
☐ Court Order	☐ Priority Notice
☐ Contract	☐ Mortgagee's Consent
☐ Transferee's Declaration	☐ Resolution to Sell
☐ Shipyard Letter	☐ Charter Party Agreement
☐ Power of Attorney	☐ Certificate of Registration/Transcript/Deletion Certificate
☐ Statutory Declaration given by Mortgagee If Lost Original Mortgage Document	☐ Original Mortgage Document
	☐ Original Mortgage Document with Discharge
☐ Affidavit If Lost Original Certificate of British Registry	☐ Letter or Assurance from Gaining Flag
☐ Certificate of Registry	☐ Completed Record of Lifeboats, Tenders & Other Appurtenances
☐ Letter of Confirmation from Gaining Flag	
☐ Letter of No Objection from a Cayman Representative Person	
☐ Other (PLEASE SPECIFY):	

Name of Vessel: Official Number: IMO Number:

Applicant's Signature:

Capacity:

Date (DD/MM/YYYY):

A division of

CISR 857
REV 01/17
Page 2 of 2

375

APPENDIX XI(B)

APPLICATION FOR A MINIMUM SAFE MANNING DOCUMENT
IN ACCORDANCE WITH SOLAS CHAPTER V REGULATION 14, AND TAKING INTO ACCOUNT THE "PRINCIPLES OF SAFE MANNING ADOPTED BY IMO RESOLUTION A.1047(27)

Maritime Authority of the Cayman Islands
133 Elgin Avenue P.O. Box 2256
Grand Cayman KY1-1107 Cayman Islands
Tel: +1 345 949 8831 Fax: +1 345 949 8849
Email: crew.compliance@cishipping.com
Website: www.cishipping.com

PLEASE READ THE ATTACHED IMO RESOLUTION A.1047(27) BEFORE COMPLETING THIS FORM

Please complete in ENGLISH using BLOCK CAPITALS and black ink. All sections must be completed.

1 Applicant

Entity Making the Application

Company: Name of Responsible Person:

Telephone: Email:

Relationship to vessel (Tick as appropriate):   Owner ☐   Manager ☐   Other ☐ (Specify)

2 Vessel and Voyage Details

Name of Vessel: IMO Number:

Gross Tonnage: Main Propulsion (kW):   Generating Power (kw):

Classification Society: Type of Ship:

Full Class Notations Assigned: Maximum Number of Passengers:

Trading Area: Distinctive Number or Letters:

Operating Company: Unique Company Number:

Please give a brief description of the intended nature of the vessel's operation, including any restrictions applicable to vessel or crew:

Intended voyage type: International Voyages ☐   Short International Voyages ☐   Near Coastal Voyages ☐

Where a trading area other than International is identified, a clear description should be indicated:

A division of
Cayman Maritime

FRM CIMSMDAAPP
REV 01/16
Page 1 of 6

APPENDIX XI(B)

APPLICATION FOR A MINIMUM SAFE MANNING DOCUMENT
IN ACCORDANCE WITH SOLAS CHAPTER V REGULATION 14, AND TAKING INTO ACCOUNT
THE "PRINCIPLES OF SAFE MANNING ADOPTED BY IMO RESOLUTION A.1047(27)

3 Navigational Equipment

The vessel is provided with the following navigational equipment:

Gyro Compass ☐	Auto-Pilot ☐	Radar ☐	ARPA ☐
ECDIS ☐	GPS ☐	BNWAS ☐	IBS ☐

Dynamic Positioning Systems:

Unclassified ☐	DP-1 ☐	DP-2 ☐	DP-3 ☐

Other ☐ (Specify)

4 Communication Equipment

The vessel is provided with **Internal Communication** equipment as follows:

FUNCTION	EQUIPMENT PROVIDED (Telephones, PA Systems, Intercoms, etc)
Within Accommodation:	
Bridge to Engine Room:	
Bridge to Mooring Stations:	
Bridge to Emergency Steering Position:	

The vessel is provided with **External Communication** equipment as follows:

Certified for GMDSS Sea Areas:

A1 ☐	A1 + A2 ☐	A1 + A2 + A3 ☐	A1 + A2 + A3 + A4 ☐

APPENDIX XI(B)

APPLICATION FOR A MINIMUM SAFE MANNING DOCUMENT
IN ACCORDANCE WITH SOLAS CHAPTER V REGULATION 14, AND TAKING INTO ACCOUNT
THE "PRINCIPLES OF SAFE MANNING" ADOPTED BY IMO RESOLUTION A.1047(27)

5 Machinery and Propulsion

The vessel utilises the following form of propulsion:

Diesel Direct ☐	Diesel Geared ☐	Diesel Electric ☐	Steam ☐
Gas Turbine ☐	Fixed Propellers ☐	Controllable Pitch Propellers ☐	ASD ☐
Pods ☐	Other ☐ (Specify)		

Number of Engine Rooms: Number of Main Engines: Number of Main Boilers:

Number of Auxy Boilers: Number of Auxy Engines: Max Generating Voltage:

Engine Control Room Provided ☐   Engine Control LOCAL ☐   Engine Control REMOTE ☐

UMS Certified ☐   UMS in operation ☐   Bridge Control ☐

6 Cargo Spaces and Cargo Gear

Types of Cargoes Carried:

Number of Cargo Holds: Number of Cargo Tanks: Number of RO/RO Decks:

Crude Oil Washing ☐   Inert Gas Generator ☐

Details of Cargo Gear (Cranes, Derricks, Grabs, Conveyors, etc):

7 Life Saving Appliances

Number of Lifeboats: Number of Free Fall Lifeboats: Number of Rescue Boats:

Number of Fast Rescue Boats: Number of Davit Launched Liferafts:

8 Fire Fighting Equipment

The following Fire Fighting Equipment is provided in the **Accommodation Spaces** onboard:

| Central Control Station ☐ | Fixed detection and alarm system ☐ | Fire Door Indication and Closure Panel ☐ |
| Manual Call Points ☐ | Sprinkler System ☐ | |

The following Fire Fighting Equipment is provided in the **Machinery Spaces** onboard:

| Fixed detection and alarm system ☐ | CO2 Smothering ☐ | Hi Fog Smothering ☐ |
| NOVEC / FM 200 Smothering ☐ | Manual Call Points ☐ | Foam ☐ |

APPENDIX XI(B)

APPLICATION FOR A MINIMUM SAFE MANNING DOCUMENT
IN ACCORDANCE WITH SOLAS CHAPTER V REGULATION 14, AND TAKING INTO ACCOUNT
THE "PRINCIPLES OF SAFE MANNING" ADOPTED BY IMO RESOLUTION A 1047(27)

8 Fire Fighting Equipment (contd)

The following Fire Fighting Equipment is provided in the **Cargo Spaces, Pump Rooms & RO/RO Spaces** onboard:

Fixed detection and alarm system ☐	CO2 Smothering ☐	Hi Fog Smothering ☐
NOVEC / FM 200 Smothering ☐	Water Deluge ☐	Foam ☐

9 Pilot Boarding Arrangements

Mechanical Pilot Hoist ☐	Pilot Ladder ☐	Pilot Ladder & Gangway ☐
Shell Doors for Pilot Access ☐	Helideck ☐	

10 Mooring Operations

Number of Mooring Stations: Number of Mooring Winches:

Self Tensioning Winches ☐	Bridge Control of Anchors ☐	Stern Anchor ☐

11 Pollution Prevention

SOPEP Kit Provided ☐	Sewage Incinerator ☐	Sludge Incinerator ☐
Garbage Incinerator ☐	Manual Call Points ☐	

12 Plans and Drawings Submitted

PLAN OR DRAWING	Tick (if enclosed or confirmed)	OFFICIAL USE ONLY
General Arrangement	☐	
Safety Plan	☐	
Mooring Plan	☐	
Other (Specify)	☐	
Other (Specify)	☐	
Other (Specify)	☐	

APPENDIX XI(B)

APPLICATION FOR A MINIMUM SAFE MANNING DOCUMENT
IN ACCORDANCE WITH SOLAS CHAPTER V REGULATION 14, AND TAKING INTO ACCOUNT THE "PRINCIPLES OF SAFE MANNING" ADOPTED BY IMO RESOLUTION A.1047(27)

13 Requested Minimum Manning Level

Please indicate the proposed manning scale, which may be used for the assessment of the minimum manning requirements as per Cayman Islands manning requirements. When deciding on proposed manning scales, applicants are advised to fully consider the Principles of Safe Manning contained in IMO Assembly Resolution A.1047(27).

Personnel:

CAPACITY	CERTIFICATE (STCW REG.)	NO.	WATCHKEEPER (Y)	WATCHKEEPER (N)	TB[1]	TA[2]
Master			☐	☐	☐	☐
Chief Engineering Officer			☐	☐	☐	☐
Chief Mate			☐	☐	☐	☐
Second Engineering Officer			☐	☐	☐	☐
Officer in Charge of a Navigational Watch			☐	☐	☐	☐
Officer in Charge of an Engineering Watch			☐	☐	☐	☐
Assistant Engineer Officer			☐	☐	☐	☐
Radio Operator			☐	☐	☐	☐
Cargo Engineer			☐	☐	☐	☐
Deck Rating forming part of a Navigational Watch			☐	☐	☐	☐
Deck Rating for Safe Operation of Ship			☐	☐	☐	☐
Deck Rating (Trainee)			☐	☐	☐	☐
Able Seafarer Deck			☐	☐	☐	☐
Engine Rating forming part of an Engineering Watch			☐	☐	☐	☐
Engine Rating **not** forming part of an Engineering Watch			☐	☐	☐	☐
Able Seafarer Engine			☐	☐	☐	☐
Electro-technical Officer			☐	☐	☐	☐
Electro-technical Rating			☐	☐	☐	☐
Ship's Cook			☐	☐	☐	☐
Ship's Doctor			☐	☐	☐	☐

Total number of crew to be carried onboard:

Special requirements or conditions (if any):

---

[1] TB - Tanker Familiarisation (Tanker Basic Training)
[2] TA - Tanker Specialised Training (Tanker Advanced Training)

FRM CIMSMDAAPP
REV 01/16

APPENDIX XI(B)

APPLICATION FOR A MINIMUM SAFE MANNING DOCUMENT
IN ACCORDANCE WITH SOLAS CHAPTER V REGULATION 14, AND TAKING INTO ACCOUNT
THE "PRINCIPLES OF SAFE MANNING" ADOPTED BY IMO RESOLUTION A.1047(27)

14 Declarations

Declaration by applicant

I, the undersigned, declare that the information I have given is, to the best of my knowledge, true and complete. I also declare that the copies of the documents submitted are true copies of genuine documents.

Full Name: Date (DD/MM/YYYY):

Signature

15 Guidance Notes for the Completion of this Application Form

Please ensure that you read and understand IMO Resolution A.1047(27) before completing the form.

Please complete this form in **BLOCK LETTERS** and in black ink. If a section is not relevant to your application enter NIL.

ENSURE YOU COMPLETE THIS FORM IN FULL – FAILURE TO DO SO MAY CAUSE APPLICATION PROCESSING DELAYS

Glossary of Abbreviations Used:	
AIS:	Automatic Identification System
ARPA:	Automatic Radar Plotting Aid
ASD:	Azimuth Stern Drive
BNWAS:	Bridge Navigational Watch Alarm System
ECDIS:	Electronic Chart Display and Information System
GPS:	Global Positioning System
IBS:	Integrated Bridge System
SOPEP:	Shipboard Oil Pollution Emergency Plan

381

APPENDIX XI(B)

CSR 750A Rev 02/06

CAYMAN ISLANDS SHIPPING REGISTRY

MINIMUM SAFE MANNING DOCUMENT (YACHT APPLICATION)

Please indicate below the owner's/operator's proposed manning scale, which may be used as a guide by this Administration in the assessment of the minimum manning requirements for the intended service of the vessel.

PERSONNEL:

Capacity	*GRADE OF CERTIFICATE	NO.	CAPACITY	*GRADE OF CERTIFICATE	NO.
Master			Chief Engineer		
Chief Mate			Second Engineer		
Officer of the Watch (Navigational)			Officer of the Watch (Engineering)		
Radio Operator			Assistance Engineering Officer		
Deck Rating (Navigational Watch)			Engine Rating (Engineering Watch)		
Deck Rating for Safe Operation of vessel			Engine Rating for Safe Operation of vessel		
Deck Rating (Trainee)			Engine Rating (Trainee)		
Cook			Electrician		

Total number of crew to be carried on board: * (see below for explanation on Grade of Certificate)

GRADE OF CERTIFICATE   MEANING OF GRADE

(Full STCW 78, as amended Certificates)

R.II/1	Reg. II/1, Officer in charge of a navigational watch on ships of 500 GT or more
R.II/2	Reg. II/2, Master and Chief Mate on ships of between 500 and 3,000 GT and over 3,000 GT
R.II/3	Reg. II/3, Master and Officers on ships of less than 500 GT
R.II/4	Reg. II/4, Ratings forming part of a navigational watch
R.III/1	Reg.III/1, Officer in charge of an engineering watch of ships of over 750 kW
R.III/2	Reg.III/2, Chief Engineer and Second Engineer of ships over 3,000 kW
R.III/3	Reg.III/3, Chief Engineer and Second Engineer of ships less than 3,000 kW
R.III/4	Reg.III/4, Ratings forming part of an engineering watch

(Yacht certificates system introduced by the MCA)

R.II/1	Reg.II/1, Officer of the Watch (Yacht) of vessels less than 3,000 GT (MGN 195(M))
R.II/2	Reg.II/2, Chief Mate (Yacht) of vessels less than 3,000 GT (MGN 195(M))
R.II/3	Reg.II/2, Master 500 GT (Yacht) of vessels less than 500 GT (MGN 195(M))
R.II/4	Reg.II/2, Master (Yacht) of vessels less than 3,000 GT (MGN 195(M))
R.III/3 (Y4)	Reg.III/3, Chief Engineer (Yacht 4) or (Y4) (MGN 156 (M))
R.III/2 (Y3)	Reg.III/2, Chief Engineer (Yacht 3) or (Y3) (Chief Engineer "Service Endorsement") (MGN 156 (M))
R.III/2 (Y2)	Reg.III/2, Chief Engineer (Yacht 2) or (Y2) (MGN 156 (M))
R.III/2 (Y1)	Reg.III/2, Chief Engineer (Yacht 1) or (Y1) ("Large Yacht Endorsement") (MGN 156 (M))

(Non – STCW 78, as amended certificates of competency recognized on yachts of certain size)

Coast Skipper	Coastal Skipper with Commercial Endorsement, as appropriate
YM Offshore	Yachtmaster Offshore with Commercial Endorsement, as appropriate
YM Ocean	Yachtmaster Ocean with Commercial Endorsement, as appropriate
AEC	Approved Engine Course
SMEOL	Senior Marine Engine Operator Licence
MEOL	Marine Engine Operator Licence

MINIMUM SAFE MANNING DOCUMENT (YACHT APPLICATION)   Page 3 of 3   CSR 750A Rev 02/06

APPENDIX XI(B)

CISR 750A
Rev 02/06

MINIMUM SAFE MANNING APPLICATION
(YACHT APPLICATION)

APPLICATION for obtaining a Cayman Islands Minimum Safe Manning Document for a LARGE COMMERCIAL SAILING AND MOTOR VESSEL, in compliance with the provisions of 'The Large Commercial Yacht Code (LY2)', or for a PLEASURE YACHT

GRAND CAYMAN	UNITED KINGDOM	USA	GREECE	JAPAN
3rd Floor, Kirk House	1st Floor, Vanbrugh House	110 East Broward Boulevard	107-109 Vasileos Pavlou Street	Chibaminato Park House II-804
22 Albert Panton Street	Grange Drive, Hedge End	Suite 1700	Voula, GR 166 73	8-1, Chibaminato, Chuo-ku, Chiba
P.O. Box 2256, Grand Cayman	Southampton, S030 2AF	Ft. Lauderdale, Florida 33301	Athens, Greece	260-0026
KY1-1107, Cayman Islands	England, UK	USA	Tel: +30 210 965 9700	Tokyo, Japan
Tel: +1 345 949 8831	Tel: +44 1489 799 203	Tel: +1 954 315 3820	Fax: +30 210 899 6040	Tel/Fax: +81 43 247 8441
Fax: +1 345 949 8849	Fax: +44 1489 799 204	Fax: +1 954 315 3893	Email: cisrgr@cishipping.com	Email: cisrjp@cishipping.com
Email: cisrky@cishipping.com	Email: cisruk@cishipping.com	Email: carfl@cishipping.com	athenian@atheniansa.gr	nori.uno@cishipping.com

Website: www.cishipping.com . General Email: registration@cishipping.com

SECTION 1: PARTICULARS OF SHIP: (PLEASE USE BLOCK LETTERS)

Name:	Official number:
IMO number:	Port of registry: **George Town**
Gross tonnage (ITC 1969):	Main Propulsion Power (kW):
Type of vessel:	Manning of machinery space: Periodically unattended ☐ Continuously attended ☐

Has a 'Letter' or 'Certificate of Compliance' been issued for compliance with the Mega Yacht Code?:   ☐ YES   ☐ NO
If the answer is 'YES',   Date of Issue :   Date of Expiry:

Operational mode:

Area of operation (miles from a SAFE HAVEN):   ☐ Up to 60 miles   ☐ Up to 150 miles   ☐ Over 150 miles

SECTION 2: PARTICULARS OF OWNER/APPLICANT

Name of owner:	Name of applicant (if not owner) :
Address:	Address:

SECTION 3: CONTACT DETAILS OF APPLICANT

Phone:	Fax:	E-mail:

SECTION 4: PLEASE CHECK THE FOLLOWING BOXES ACCORDINGLY USING A CHECK MARK (X)

NAVIGATION EQUIPMENT:

Magnetic Compass	☐	Gyro Compass	☐	Automatic steering	☐	Bridge control	☐
GPS/DGPS	☐	Radar	☐	ARPA	☐	ECDIS	☐
Other:							

SECTION 5: COMMUNICATION

Internal:	Telephone	☐	Cordless Telephone	☐	Pager	☐
	Intercom	☐				
Other:						
Bridge/Engine room:	Telephone	☐	Cordless Telephone	☐	Pager	☐
	Loud speaker	☐	Intercom	☐	Voice pipe	☐
Other:						
Bridge/Mooring stations:	Telephone:	☐	Cordless Telephone	☐	Loud speaker	☐
	Walkie talkie	☐	Intercom	☐		
Other:						
External: GMDSS	A1	☐	A1+A2	☐	A1+A2+A3	☐	A1+A2+A3+A4	☐
External:	Radio telephone	☐	Other:			

Page 1 of 3

APPENDIX XI(B)

CAYMAN ISLANDS SHIPPING REGISTRY

CISR 750A Rev 02/06

MINIMUM SAFE MANNING DOCUMENT (YACHT APPLICATION)

SECTION 6: MACHINERY SPACE

Engine Type:	Diesel	☐	Diesel-electric	☐	Steam	☐	Gas turbine	☐
Number of engine rooms		☐	Number of main engines		Number of auxiliary engines			
Engine control room fitted			UMS certified and operational					
Survey and inspection system (CSM, CSH, etc.):		☐						☐

SECTION 7: LIFE SAVING APPLIANCES (LSA)

Life boats:	Fitted	☐	Not fitted	☐	No. of life boats	☐	Rescue boat	☐	Fast rescue boat	☐
Launching arrangements:					Gravity	☐	Free fall			☐
Life rafts:	With launching appliances:			☐	Without	☐	Other:			

SECTION 8: FIRE FIGHTING APPLIANCES (FFA)

Accommodation:	Central control station fitted		☐	Fixed fire detection and alarm system fitted		☐
Fixed fire detection and alarm system and sprinkler system			☐	Fire door indicator panel and closures		☐
General/fire alarms	☐	Manual call points		☐	Protected means of escape provided	☐
Engine room:	Automatic fire detection fitted		☐	Type of fixed smothering system:	Gas	☐
Foam	☐	Hi fog	☐	Other:		
Quick closing valves for fuel tanks fitted		☐	Fire flaps closed:	Manually	☐ Remotely	☐
Fuel pumps shut down:	Manually		☐	Remotely		☐

SECTION 9: PILOT BOARDING ARRANGEMENTS

Mechanical pilot hoist fitted	☐	Pilot ladder	☐	Pilot ladder/gangway combination	☐

SECTION 10: MOORING OPERATIONS

Number of docking stations		Mooring ropes on winch drums	☐
Self-tensioning winches fitted	☐	Anchor control from bridge possible	☐

SECTION 11: POLLUTION PREVENTION

Oil pollution control equipment and chemicals provided	☐	Garbage compactor fitted		☐
Pumps and piping provided for pumping oily residues ashore	☐	Incinerator fitted	☐ Garbage tank fitted	☐

The following plans and drawings must be provided with this application form:
- General arrangement
- Safety plan(s) to include arrangement of life saving appliances and fire control plans
- Mooring arrangements
- Other plans as requested by the Cayman Islands Shipping Registry

Please give below a brief description of the nature of intended operation of the vessel including restrictions, if any, applicable to the vessel and/or her crew.

MINIMUM SAFE MANNING DOCUMENT (YACHT APPLICATION)

CISR 750A Rev 02/06

384

APPENDIX XI(B)

CAYMAN ISLANDS SHIPPING REGISTRY

CISR 750A Rev 02/06
MINIMUM SAFE MANNING DOCUMENT (YACHT APPLICATION)

Please indicate below the owner's/operator's proposed manning scale, which may be used as a guide by this Administration in the assessment of the minimum manning requirements for the intended service of the vessel.

PERSONNEL:

Capacity	*GRADE OF CERTIFICATE	NO.	CAPACITY	*GRADE OF CERTIFICATE	NO.
Master			Chief Engineer		
Chief Mate			Second Engineer		
Officer of the Watch (Navigational)			Officer of the Watch (Engineering)		
Radio Operator			Assistance Engineering Officer		
Deck Rating (Navigational Watch)			Engine Rating (Engineering Watch)		
Deck Rating for Safe Operation of vessel			Engine Rating for Safe Operation of vessel		
Deck Rating (Trainee)			Engine Rating (Trainee)		
Cook			Electrician		

Total number of crew to be carried on board:	* (see below for explanation on Grade of Certificate)

GRADE OF CERTIFICATE   MEANING OF GRADE

(Full STCW 78, as amended Certificates)

R.II/1	Reg. II/1, Officer in charge of a navigational watch on ships of 500 GT or more
R.II/2	Reg. II/2, Master and Chief Mate on ships of between 500 and 3,000 GT and over 3,000 GT
R.II/3	Reg. II/3, Master and Officers on ships of less than 500 GT
R.II/4	Reg. II/4, Ratings forming part of a navigational watch
R.III/1	Reg.III/1, Officer in charge of an engineering watch of ships of over 750 kW
R.III/2	Reg.III/2, Chief Engineer and Second Engineer of ships over 3,000 kW
R.III/3	Reg.III/3, Chief Engineer and Second Engineer of ships less than 3,000 kW
R.III/4	Reg.III/4, Ratings forming part of an engineering watch

(Yacht certificates system introduced by the MCA)

R.II/1	Reg.II/1, Officer of the Watch (Yacht) of vessels less than 3,000 GT (MGN 195(M))
R.II/2	Reg.II/2, Chief Mate (Yacht) of vessels less than 3,000 GT (MGN 195(M))
R.II/3	Reg.II/2, Master 500 GT (Yacht) of vessels less than 500 GT (MGN 195(M))
R.II/4	Reg.II/2, Master (Yacht) of vessels less than 3,000 GT (MGN 195(M))
R.III/3 (Y4)	Reg.III/3, Chief Engineer (Yacht 4) or (Y4) (MGN 156 (M))
R.III/2 (Y3)	Reg.III/2, Chief Engineer (Yacht 3) or (Y3) (Chief Engineer "Service Endorsement") (MGN 156 (M))
R.III/2 (Y2)	Reg.III/2, Chief Engineer (Yacht 2) or (Y2) (MGN 156 (M))
R.III/2 (Y1)	Reg.III/2, Chief Engineer (Yacht 1) or (Y1) ("Large Yacht Endorsement") (MGN 156 (M))

(Non – STCW 78, as amended certificates of competency recognized on yachts of certain size)

Coast Skipper	Coastal Skipper with Commercial Endorsement, as appropirate
YM Offshore	Yachtmaster Offshore with Commercial Endorsement, as appropriate
YM Ocean	Yachtmaster Ocean with Commercial Endorsement, as appropriate
AEC	Approved Engine Course
SMEOL	Senior Marine Engine Operator Licence
MEOL	Marine Engine Operator Licence

385

APPENDIX XI(B)

(DMLC I **400/2017**)

MARITIME LABOUR CONVENTION, 2006

DECLARATION OF MARITIME LABOUR COMPLIANCE – PART I
(Note: This Declaration must be attached to the ship's Maritime Labour Certificate)

Issued under the authority of the Government of the Cayman Islands by
THE CAYMAN ISLANDS SHIPPING REGISTRY
of
THE MARITIME AUTHORITY OF THE CAYMAN ISLANDS

With respect to the provisions of the Maritime Labour Convention, 2006, the following referenced ship:

Name of ship	IMO number	Gross tonnage

is maintained in accordance with Standard A5.1.3 of the Convention.

The undersigned declares, on behalf of the abovementioned competent authority, that:

(a) the provisions of the Maritime Labour Convention are fully embodied in the national requirements referred to below;

(b) these national requirements are contained in the national provisions referenced below; explanations concerning the content of those provisions are provided where necessary;

(c) the details of any substantial equivalencies under Article VI, paragraphs 3 and 4, are in the section provided for this purpose below;

(d) any exemptions granted by the competent authority in accordance with Title 3 are clearly indicated in the section provided for this purpose below; and

(e) any ship-type specific requirements under national legislation are also referenced under the requirements concerned.

Title	National Legislation
1. Minimum age (Regulation 1.1)	Merchant Shipping (Certification, Safe Manning, Hours of Work and Watchkeeping) Regulations, 2004, prohibits employment of persons under the age of sixteen. The Merchant Shipping (Maritime Labour Convention) (Health and Safety) Regulations, 2014 prohibit seafarers under the age of 18 from being employed for "hazardous work" which means any work undertaken on board or in relation to the ship which, by its nature or the circumstances under which it is to be carried out, is likely to harm the health or safety of the seafarer, and includes- ▪ working in enclosed spaces; ▪ working adjacent to open holds or tanks; ▪ working over the ship's side; ▪ working aloft such as on masts, mast tables, or samson posts etc.; ▪ operating machinery, winches or lifting equipment with heavy loads;

Declaration of Maritime Labour Compliance – Part I   Page 1 of 10   Cert 3903 Rev 4

APPENDIX XI(B)

Name of Ship: **DMLC 400 / 2017**

Title	National Legislation
	☒ work in the vicinity of cargo operations; ☒ mooring operations or other such similar work; and ☒ employment as a ship's cook Merchant Shipping (Maritime Labour Convention) (Health and Safety) Regulations, 2014 restricts night work for under 18s and defines "night" as a period of at least nine consecutive hours, including the period from midnight to 0500 hours. A seafarer of the age of 16 or 17 may work at night if the work forms part of an established programme of training the effectiveness of which would be impaired by the prohibition above.
2. Medical certification (Regulation 1.2)	The Merchant Shipping (Maritime Labour Convention)(Medical Certification) Regulations, 2014, require every seafarer to have a valid medical fitness certificate and prohibits the employment of a seafarer who does not hold such a certificate, except in the circumstances provided for in regulations 5(3) and (4). In urgent cases (regulation 5(4)) the seafarer's medical certificate must have expired no more than 1 month prior to joining the ship, and must have been issued for the full validity appropriate to the seafarer's age (i.e. 1 year for a seafarer under 18 years of age at the time of issue, and 2 years for other seafarers). A valid medical certificate is a Certificate issued under the authority of one of the list of countries whose medical certificates are accepted listed in Shipping Notice CISN 05/2011 (as amended). Any medical fitness certificate shall be valid for no more than two years; or no more than one year if the seafarer is under the age of 18 years. If the seafarer is employed at the time of their medical examination, the employer must bear the cost. The certificate must be in English. The Approved Doctor may issue a seafarer with a "Fit" certificate with restrictions on the geographical locations or duties in which the seafarer is fit to work – for example, the restriction "not fit for lookout duties" where the seafarer has a colour vision deficiency.
3. Qualifications of seafarers (Regulation 1.3)	Merchant Shipping (Certification, Safe Manning, Hours of Work and Watchkeeping) Regulations, 2004 set training requirements in accordance with STCW 1978 (as amended). All officers to be qualified as specified on the safe manning document (MSMD). All seafarers shall receive on board safety familiarisation training prior to commencing their duties on board the ship. More information is provided in Shipping Notice CISN 05/2011 (as amended).

Declaration of Maritime Labour Compliance – Part I   Page 2 of 10   Cert 3903 Rev 4

APPENDIX XI(B)

Name of Ship: DMLC **400 / 2017**

Title	National Legislation
4. Seafarers' employment agreements (Regulation 2.1)	The Merchant Shipping (Maritime Labour Convention)(Seafarer Employment Agreement, Shipowner's Liabilities and Wages) Regulations, 2014, requires all seafarers to have a Seafarer's Employment Agreement (SEA). If the SEA is signed by a representative of the shipowner (e.g. a manning agent or management company), that representative must be named as an authorised representative in the shipowner's DMLC Part 2. Other documents can form part of the SEA. The SEA itself and any documents forming part of the SEA, if they are not in English are to be available on board in English translation. Minimum period of notice: 7 days, except by mutual agreement. Merchant Shipping (Crew Agreements, Lists of Crew and Discharge of Seamen) Regulations 1992, Part 4 Discharge of Seamen requires that the master or authorised person shall record details of the ship and the voyage from which the seafarer is being discharged. Wages: See section 14. Annual leave: Regulation 10 of the Merchant Shipping (Maritime Labour Convention)(Seafarer Employment Agreement, Shipowner's Liabilities and Wages) Regulations, 2014 provides that every seafarer is entitled to at least 30 days leave per year of employment, or pro rata if the seafarer is not employed for a full year, within each year of employment. Seafarers will also be entitled to 8 days public holidays per year, or pro rata if the seafarer is not employed for a full year, within each year of employment. Repatriation: The Merchant Shipping (Maritime Labour Convention) (Repatriation) Regulations, 2014 provide that a seafarer has a right to be returned to their home country: • when their employment contract ends or is cancelled; • when they're no longer able to carry out their duties; • in the event of shipwreck; • if their ship is bound for a war zone they haven't agreed to go to. In addition: • Owners of Cayman Islands ships are required to provide financial security to ensure that seafarers are duly repatriated in accordance with the MLC; • Shipowners are prohibited from requiring seafarers to make an advance payment towards the cost of repatriation at the beginning of their employment; • Where the shipowner fails to arrange or pay for repatriation, the Flag State has to do so. Where a seafarer's employment is terminated on grounds of misconduct on the part of the seafarer, the shipowner may recover repatriation and ancillary costs from the seafarer up to $1000.

Declaration of Maritime Labour Compliance – Part I   Page 3 of 10   Cert 3903 Rev 4

APPENDIX XI(B)

Name of Ship: **   DMLC 400 / 2017**

Title	National Legislation
	Financial security: for compensation in case of death or long term disability of seafarers due to occupational injury, illness or hazard is the responsibility of the shipowner.
5. Use of any licensed or certified or regulated private recruitment and placement service (Regulation 1.4)	The Merchant Shipping (Maritime Labour Convention)(Survey and Certification) Regulations, 2014, require that Cayman Islands flagged ships using private recruitment and placement services may recruit only from crewing agencies which meet MLC requirements.
6. Hours of work or rest (Regulation 2.3)	Merchant Shipping (Certification, Safe Manning, Hours of Work and Watchkeeping) Regulations, 2004, provide for minimum rest of at least 10 hours in any 24 hour period, which may be divided into no more than two (2) periods – one of which shall be at least six (6) hours in length, and no more than 14 hours between any consecutive periods; and 77 hours an any 7 day period.

Any exception from the above requirements authorised by MACI must be recorded in the DMLC Part 2.

More information is provided in Shipping Notice CISN 05/2014 (as amended). |
| 7. Manning levels for the ship (Regulation 2.7) | Merchant Shipping (Certification, Safe Manning, Hours of Work and Watchkeeping) Regulations, 2004 require a MSMD for all ships of 500 GT and above.

Owners of ships under 500 GT may also choose to hold a MSMD.

The MSMD must be carried on board the ship and be made available for inspection.

The number of seafarers on board must comply with or exceed the MSMD in terms of both the number and qualifications of seafarers.

If a ship changes trading area, construction, machinery or equipment, operation and/or method of maintenance, or seafarers persistently fail to comply with hours of rest requirements, the MSMD should be reviewed. |
| 8. Accommodation (Regulation 3.1) | **For existing ships:** Merchant Shipping (Crew Accommodation) Regulations, 1988, set standards for ships with keels laid before 20 August 2013.

Accommodation shall be inspected at least weekly.

For Ships with a keel laid after 20 August 2013: the standards are set by the Merchant Shipping (Maritime Labour Convention) (Crew Accommodation) Regulations, 2014, and Shipping Notice CISN 03/2014 (as amended) and require the shipowner to comply with regulations with regard to –
• The size of rooms and other accommodation spaces;
• Heating and ventilation;
• Noise, vibration and other ambient factors; |

Declaration of Maritime Labour Compliance – Part I   Page 4 of 10   Cert 3903 Rev 4

389

APPENDIX XI(B)

Name of Ship: _____ DMLC **400 / 2017**

Title	National Legislation
	• Sanitary facilities; • Lighting; • Hospital accommodation. Commercial Yachts: For yachts constructed prior to MLC entering into force the crew accommodation has been constructed in accordance with the Large Commercial Yacht Code and as far as practical in accordance with ILO92/133.
9. On-board recreational facilities (Regulation 3.1)	**For existing ships:** Merchant Shipping (Crew Accommodation) Regulations, 1988, set standards for ships with keels laid before 20 August 2013. For Ships with a keel laid after 20 August 2013: the standards are set by the Merchant Shipping (Maritime Labour Convention) (Crew Accommodation) Regulations, 2014, and Shipping Notice CISN 03/2014 (as amended) and requires shipowners to provide appropriate seafarers' recreational facilities, amenities and services, as adapted to meet the special needs of seafarers who must live and work on ships. Furnishings for recreational facilities should as a minimum include a bookcase and facilities for reading, writing and, where practicable, games.
10. Food and catering (Regulation 3.2)	Merchant Shipping (Maritime Labour Convention) (Food and Catering) Regulations, 2014 and Shipping Notice CISN 07/2014 (as amended) set standards for food and water which must be free of charge to seafarers and suitable in terms of quantity, nutritional value, quality and variety. Merchant Shipping (Crew Accommodation) Regulations, 1988, set standards for galley requirements for ships with keels laid before 20 August 2013. For Ships with a keel laid after 20 August 2013: the galley requirements are set by the Merchant Shipping (Maritime Labour Convention) (Crew Accommodation) Regulations, 2014, and Shipping Notice CISN 03/2014 (as amended). Merchant Shipping (Maritime Labour Convention) (Food and Catering) Regulations, 2014 requires carriage of a fully certified ship's cook on all vessels with ten or more seafarers. Any substantial equivalence to this requirement must be recorded below. Cooks shall be trained and qualified and all catering staff shall have evidence of completion of a training course or of being instructed in food and personal hygiene and handling and storage of food. Catering departments shall be inspected at least weekly. Seafarers under 18 years of age shall not be employed as ships cooks.
11. Health and Safety and accident prevention (Regulation 4.3)	The Merchant Shipping (Maritime Labour Convention) (Health and Safety) Regulations, 2014 places a responsibility on the employer to provide a safe working environment and: • Requires the appointment of safety officers and safety representatives;

Declaration of Maritime Labour Compliance – Part I   Page 5 of 10   Cert 3903 Rev 4

APPENDIX XI(B)

Name of Ship: **DMLC 400 / 2017**

Title	National Legislation
	• Requires holding of regular safety committees on all vessels with five or more seafarers; • Requires suitable personal protective equipment to be provided; • Requires seafarers to be provided with adequate and appropriate health and safety training and instruction; • Sets the minimum requirements for risk assessments and health surveillance; • Sets safety requirements for equipment and machinery on ships; • Requires reasonable precautions to be taken for the prevention of risk of exposure to harmful levels of noise, vibration and chemicals. The Merchant Shipping (Maritime Labour Convention) (Health and Safety) Regulations, 2014 requires that the Code of Safe Working Practices for Merchant Seamen is taken into account at all times. The Merchant Shipping (Maritime Labour Convention) (Health and Safety) Regulations, 2014 requires reporting of occupational accidents, injuries and diseases.
12. On-board medical care (Regulation 4.1)	The Merchant Shipping (Maritime Labour Convention) (Medical Care) Regulations, 2014, requires that the cost of medical and emergency dental treatment for seafarers to be borne by the employer regardless of location. Ships with 100 or more persons on board operating on international voyages of more than 3 days shall carry a qualified medical doctor who is responsible for providing medical care. All other ships are required to have either at least one seafarer on board who is in charge of medical care or at least one seafarer on board competent to provide medical first aid. Seafarers have the right to visit a qualified medical doctor or dentist without delay in ports of call, where practicable. All ships shall carry a medicine chest, medical equipment and a medical guide (see Shipping Notice CISN 06/2014 (as amended)). The system for obtaining Radio Medical Advice to be used by Cayman Islands ships is detailed in Shipping Notice CISN 06/2014 (as amended). Confidential Medical Report Form (MRF3906) or similar shall be completed in all cases of illness or injury. The shipowner is required to provide financial security for compensation for death or long-term disability of seafarers due to an occupational injury, illness or hazard.
13. Onboard Complaint Procedure (Regulation 5.1.5)	The Merchant Shipping (Maritime Labour Convention)(Survey and Certification Regulations, 2014, requires the maintenance of a procedure for on board investigation of complaints. Shipping Notice CISN 04/2014 (as amended) provides more information.

Declaration of Maritime Labour Compliance – Part I   Page 6 of 10   Cert 3903 Rev 4

APPENDIX XI(B)

Name of Ship: _____ DMLC **400 / 2017**

Title	National Legislation
14. Payment of wages (Regulation 2.2)	Merchant Shipping (Maritime Labour Convention)(Seafarer Employment Agreement, Shipowner's Liabilities and Wages) Regulations, 2014 defines the principles applying to the payment and calculation of basic pay and wages which are partially or fully consolidated. All seafarers shall receive a monthly account of their wages. Shipowners are required to take measures to provide seafarers with a means to transmit all or part of their earnings to their families or dependants or legal beneficiaries. The following deductions from seafarer's wages are permitted – • Deductions permitted in relevant national laws, or agreed to in a Collective Bargaining Agreement (CBA); • on-board purchases, telecommunication calls and internet access; • cash advances, allotments, contributions by the seafarer in relation to any pension fund, charity, and in respect of membership of a body to any trade union and friendly society. No deductions can be made from a seafarer's wage in respect of obtaining or retaining employment. Monetary fines against seafarers other than those authorised in a CBA are prohibited.
15. Financial Security for repatriation (Regulation 2.5)	Shipping Notice CISN 01/2017 (as amended) requires a shipowner to provide a financial security system sufficient to meet his obligations in the event of abandonment of a seafarer. A seafarer is deemed to be abandoned if the ship owner: ☒ fails to cover the costs of the seafarers repatriation; or ☒ has left the seafarer without necessary maintenance and support; or ☒ has otherwise unilaterally severed their ties with the seafarer including failure to pay contractual wages for a period of at least two months. A ship must carry on board a certificate or other documentary evidence of financial security issued by the financial security provider and a copy of this document must be posted in a conspicuous place on board where it is available to the seafarers. The provider of the financial security shall inform the Maritime Authority of the Cayman Islands in all cases where the financial security is to be cancelled or terminated. This notification shall be made at least 30 days prior to the cancellation or termination. The certificates or other documentary evidence of financial security shall be in English or accompanied by an English translation. Where more than one financial security provider provides cover, the documents provided by each provider shall be carried on board.

Declaration of Maritime Labour Compliance – Part I Cert 3903 Rev 4

APPENDIX XI(B)

Name of Ship: _____ DMLC **400 / 2017**

Title	National Legislation
16. Financial Security for Shipowner's Liability (Regulation 4.2)	The Merchant Shipping (Maritime Labour Convention)(Seafarer Employment Agreement, Shipowner's Liabilities and Wages) Regulations, 2014 and Shipping Notice CISN 01/2017 (as amended) requires that a shipowner to provide a financial security system to assure compensation in the event of a seafarer's death or long term disability of a seafarer due to an occupational injury, illness. A ship must carry on board a certificate or other documentary evidence of financial security issued by the financial security provider and a copy of this document must be posted in a conspicuous place on board where it is available to the seafarers. If the financial security is to be cancelled or terminated, the shipowner shall ensure that seafarers are notified of the cancellation or termination at least 30 days prior to the cancellation or termination taking effect. The provider of the financial security shall inform the Maritime Authority of the Cayman Islands in all cases where the financial security is to be cancelled or terminated. This notification shall be made at least 30 days prior to the cancellation or termination. The certificates or other documentary evidence of financial security shall be in English or accompanied by an English translation. Where more than one financial security provider provides cover, the documents provided by each provider shall be carried on board.

Signed: ....
(Signature of authorized official)

Name:

Title: Surveyor of Ships

Place: Southampton, United Kingdom

Date: 16 January 2017

Official Stamp

APPENDIX XI(B)

Name of Ship: DMLC **400 / 2017**

SUBSTANTIAL EQUIVALENCIES AND EXEMPTIONS

SUBSTANTIAL EQUIVALENCIES

(Note: strike out any statement which is not applicable)

The following substantial equivalencies, as provided under Article VI, paragraphs 3 and 4, of the Convention, except where stated above, are noted *(insert description if applicable):*

~~**Substantial equivalencies for medical certification (Regulation 1.2):**~~

~~MACI accepts the following equivalent to the ENG 1 or non-UK equivalent in particular circumstances:~~

~~(a)   for the master and crew of a small commercial vessel operating under the appropriate MCA Code of Practice which goes no more than 60 miles from shore, a ML5. (See MGN 264 (Medical Fitness Requirements for Those Employed on Boats Certificated under MCA Codes of Practice, Crew of Seagoing Local Passenger Vessels and Non-seagoing Boatmasters);~~
~~(b)   for divers working in the offshore industry, where their place of work is for the time being a ship, e.g. on a short transit between working stations, but where the work activity takes place only on a working station, a National Commercial Diver medical~~
~~(c)   for helicopter pilots working in the offshore industry, where their place of work is for the time being a ship, e.g. on a short transit between working stations, but where the work activity takes place only on a working station, a National Commercial Pilot Medical Certificate;~~
~~(d)   for offshore workers working in the offshore industry, where their place of work is for the time being a ship, e.g. on a short transit between working stations, but where the work activity takes place only on a working station, a National Offshore Worker's Medical Certificate.~~

Substantial equivalency for hours of rest records: electronic records (Regulation 2.3):

Electronic record keeping of hours of work may be accepted provided that the system provides satisfactory security, audit and access arrangements. For full details contact MACI.

Substantial equivalency for ships cooks (Regulation 3.2)

MACI will accept a recognised chef on the basis of their experience and standing as a ships' cook in compliance with A3.2.3 provided that they have a certificate in food hygiene.

~~**Substantial equivalencies for crew accommodation (Regulation 3.1):**~~

~~•   Yachts over 24m in length holding a certificate of compliance with the Large Commercial Yacht Code: Standards agreed with MLC Tripartite Working Group and Large Yacht Sub-Group will become Chapter 21 of LY3. Separate guidance to be issued.~~

~~•   Ships under 24m in length holding a certificate of compliance with the Code of Practice for the safety of small commercial vessels (sailing, motor, or workboat) operating on domestic voyages: MGN 280 Chapter 21 to be amended to address MLC requirements. Separate guidance to be issued.~~

Substantial equivalence for crew accommodation for cadets (Regulation 3.1):

MACI will consider case by case applications from a shipowner for a dispensation allowing him to accommodate maximum of two officer trainees in one cabin, subject to the following conditions:

- the floor space of the cabin in question must be at least 12 m^2;
- officer trainees sharing a cabin must be of the same gender;

Declaration of Maritime Labour Compliance – Part I   Page 9 of 10   Cert 3903 Rev 4

APPENDIX XI(B)

Name of Ship: DMLC **400 / 2017**

- the cabin must contain sufficient integral desk space for the two officer trainees or provide access to a separate study space on board the ship.
- The shipowner should avoid placing two officer trainees who undertake watchkeeping training in the same cabin at the same time, unless the shipowner can show that such will not be detrimental to the officer trainees concerned. In particular, the shipowner must take steps to ensure that a trainee's hours of rest are not unduly disturbed.
- Shipowners seeking dispensations should take account of relevant guidance from the Merchant Navy Training Board (MNTB), from the Maritime Training Trust and Maritime Educational Foundation and relevant surveys undertaken by Nautilus International.

EXEMPTIONS
(Note: strike out the statement which is not applicable)

The following exemptions granted by the competent authority as provided in Title 3 of the Convention are noted:

No exemption has been granted

Signed: ....
(Signature of authorized official)

Name:

Title: Surveyor of Ships

Place: Southampton, UK

Date: 16 January 2017

Official Stamp

Declaration of Maritime Labour Compliance – Part I
Rev 4

APPENDIX XI(C)

Gibraltar forms

(1) Application for survey and inspection, form RA-09-F002
(2) Application to bareboat register a ship, form RA-09-F003
(3) Application to transfer out, form RA-09-F004
(4) Application to register a ship, form RA-09-F005
(5) Appointment of registered agent, form RA-09-F006
(6) Appointment of representative person, form RA-09-F007
(7) Bill of sale, form RA-09-F008

Note

Reproduced courtesy of the Gibraltar Maritime Administration.
For additional and updated forms see: www.gibraltarship.com

APPENDIX XI(C)

FR BB

Gibraltar Ship Registry
APPLICATION FOR SURVEY AND INSPECTION OF SHIPS
Guidance Notes overleaf. Complete form using BLOCK CAPITALS

1. APPLICANT DETAILS:

Name:		Company:	
Address:		Telephone:	
		Fax or email:	
		Country:	

NAME AND ADDRESS OF OWNER / OPERATOR IF DIFFERENT FROM ABOVE:

Name:		Company:	
Address:		Telephone:	
		Fax or email:	
		Country:	

2. PARTICULARS OF SURVEY / INSPECTION APPLIED FOR:

Ship Name:		Ship Type:	
Official Number:		IMO No.:	
Year of Build:			

| Requested date of Survey: | | Fax or email: | |
| Time of Survey: | | | |

| Where ship can be seen: | |

| Name of contact: | | Telephone: | |

Nature of survey / inspection:

I apply for the survey / inspection described above and enclose a deposit of £..................... and agree to pay additional fees.

| Name: | | Position in company: | |
| Signature: | | Date: | |

RA-09-F002 FR BB Appl for Survey & Inspection of Ships   Last Revised 3rd June 2009   1

APPENDIX XI(C)

FR BB

GUIDANCE NOTES

1. When you have completed this form, please send it together with the appropriate deposit / fee to the Gibraltar Ship Registry from where you can get information on the level of fees. Additional charges may be levied for overtime, surveys abroad, waiting time and abortive time.

2. You should pay by cheque made payable to 'Government General Account'. Cheques should be paid in Sterling. Credit transfers can be accepted by prior arrangement; contact the Gibraltar Ship Registry for details.

3. Any refunds or requests for additional fees will be made to the applicant or through the applicant's representatives in Gibraltar, in whose name the account will be held.

4. Work will not start until this form has been completed, signed, and the deposit / fee received.

GIBRALTAR SHIP REGISTRY
WATERGATE HOUSE
2/8 CASEMATES
GIBRALTAR

Tel: +350 200 46862
Fax: +350 200 47770

OFFICIAL USE ONLY:

The sum of .... has been received today.

Date: _____

Signed:

RA-09-F002 FR BB Appl for Survey & Inspection of Ships   Last Revised 3rd June 2009

APPENDIX XI(C)

BB

Gibraltar Ship Registry

APPLICATION TO BAREBOAT REGISTER A SHIP

- Warning: the ship is not registered until a 'Certificate of Bareboat Registry' has been issued.
- Please write in black ink using BLOCK CAPITALS and tick boxes where appropriate.

SECTION 1: THE SHIP

PROPOSED NAME OF SHIP
(several names should be entered in order of preference)

1)

2)

3)

Signal Letters*/
Radio Call Sign
(if known)

IMO Number

APPROXIMATE DIMENSIONS (in metres)

LENGTH   BREADTH   DEPTH

Approximate Gross Tonnage

Approximate Net Tonnage

Name & Address of Builder

Country of Build   Year of Build   Number of Engines

Estimated Speed (Knots)

---

* Kindly note that the Call Sign / Signal Letters, Ship Station Licence and MMSI Numbers are obtained from the Gibraltar Regulatory Authority (www.gra.gi)

RA-09-F003 BB Appl to Bareboat Register a Ship   Last Revised 3rd June 2009   1

APPENDIX XI(C)

BB

SECTION 2: EXISTING REGISTRATION OUTSIDE GIBRALTAR

Name of Ship

Country of Registration   Registration Number

Official Number

Is there an outstanding Mortgage recorded   YES   NO
in respect of the ship? (Tick box)

Does the present registry permit Bareboat   YES   NO
Registration to Gibraltar? (Tick box)

SECTION 3: REGISTERED AGENT

A Registered Agent must be appointed if the Charterer: a) Does not hold 64 out of 64 shares, and/ or b) Is not an individual resident in Gibraltar / Body Corporate having its principal place of business in Gibraltar, and / or, c) Is a Foreign Maritime Entity.

Full Name of the Registered Agent

Address

Tel No.

Fax   or
email

I herewith consent to act as registered agent, on behalf of the bareboat charterer, in respect of the ship which is applying to register on this form.

Signature   Date

Notes:
1. So long as the ship remains registered, a registered agent shall be appointed;
2. If there is a change to the details in this section, the Registrar must be informed within 7 days of the change occurring.

RA-09-F003 BB Appl to Bareboat Register a Ship   Last Revised 3rd June 2009   2

APPENDIX XI(C)

BB

SECTION 4: THE APPLICANT

FULL NAME AND ADDRESS (Please state whether you are the bareboat charterer or representative person, delete as appropriate)

	Tel No.	
	Fax No.	
	E-Mail	
BAREBOAT CHARTERER / REP. PERSON		

I enclose the fee of	£	NB: See below for fees applicable. Cheques drawn from a Bank in Gibraltar, cheques drawn from a UK Clearing Bank or International Bank Drafts should be made payable to 'GOVERNMENT GENERAL ACCOUNT'

Signature		Date	

Details of Fees:

Bareboat Registration Fee:	£550.00
NB: On registration, Annual Tonnage Tax will become payable	

Send this form, in original (and electronically, if you wish), to:

The Registrar of Ships
Gibraltar Ship Registry
Watergate House
2/8 Casemates Square
Gibraltar

Tel: +350 200 47771
Fax: +350 200 47770
Email: maritime.registry@gibraltar.gov.gi

Documents to be submitted:

Use The Gibraltar Ship Registry's checklist **RA-09-F012 'BB Documents required for Bareboat Reg (New Reg.)'** for guidance on what documents and certificates are required for Registration.

RA-09-F003 BB Appl to Bareboat Register a Ship   Last Revised 3rd June 2009

APPENDIX XI(C)

FR BB

Gibraltar Ship Registry

TRANSFER OF REGISTRY

To the Registrar of British Ships, Port of ....

Name of Vessel: _____

Official Number: _____

IMO Number: _____

Signal Letters: _____

Enclosed documents:
- Transcript of Register
- Copy of Certificate of Survey

Signed: .... Date: ....

Designation: REGISTRAR OF SHIPS

CONFIRMATION OF TRANSFER OF REGISTRY

To: Gibraltar Ship Registry
    Registry of Ships
    Watergate House
    2/8 Casemates Square
    Gibraltar

Fax: +350 200 47770
e-mail: maritime.registry@gibraltar.gov.gi

Name of Vessel: _____

Official Number: _____

IMO Number: _____

A Certificate of Registry has been issued by us   YES / NO

Signed: .... Date: ....

Designation: ....

RA-09-F004 FR BB Application to Transfer Out Last Revised: 3rd June 2009   1

402

APPENDIX XI(C)

FR

Gibraltar Ship Registry

APPLICATION TO REGISTER A SHIP (Full Registration)

- Warning: the ship is not registered until a 'Provisional Certificate' or a 'Certificate of Registry' has been issued.
- Please write in black ink using BLOCK CAPITALS, and tick boxes where appropriate.
- Do not use this form if you are seeking to register a ship under construction or a ship bareboat chartered.

SECTION 1: THE SHIP

PROPOSED NAME OF SHIP
(several names should be entered in order of preference)

1)

2)

3)

Signal Letters*/
Radio Call Sign
(if known)

IMO Number

APPROXIMATE DIMENSIONS (in metres)

LENGTH	BREADTH	DEPTH

Approximate Gross Tonnage

Approximate Net Tonnage

Name & Address of Builder

Country of Build

Year of Build

Number of Engines

Estimated Speed (Knots)

---

* Kindly note that the Call Sign / Signal Letters, Ship Station Licence and MMSI Numbers are obtained from the Gibraltar Regulatory Authority (www.gra.gi)

RA-09-F005 FR Appl Register a Ship   Last Revised 3rd June 2009   1

APPENDIX XI(C)

FR

SECTION 2: PREVIOUS REGISTRATION DETAILS

Previous Name of Ship

Country of Registration

Registration Number

IF THE SHIP HAS BEEN PREVIOUSLY REGISTERED IN A **RED ENSIGN REGISTRY (e.g. the UK, IoM, et al)** a transfer of registration to Gibraltar is required and you must still complete this form):

Is there an outstanding Mortgage recorded in respect of the ship? (Tick box)   YES   NO

SECTION 3: REGISTERED AGENT

A Registered Agent must be appointed if the Owner: a) Does not hold 64 out of 64 shares, and/ or b) Is not an individual resident in Gibraltar / Body Corporate having its principal place of business in Gibraltar, and / or, c) Is a Foreign Maritime Entity.

Full Name of the Registered Agent

Address

Tel No.

Fax No. or email

I herewith consent to act as registered agent, on behalf of the owner or owners, in respect of the ship which is applying to register on this form

Signature   Date

Notes:
1. So long as the ship remains registered, a Registered Agent shall be appointed;
2. If there is a change to the details in this section, the Registrar must be informed within 7 days of the change occurring.
3. Where there is more than one owner and one of them is a resident of Gibraltar and is appointed to act on behalf of the others as Registered Agent please attach to this application the written confirmation of all other owners that they consent that the Resident Owner act as Registered Agent.

RA-09-F005 FR Appl Register a Ship   Last Revised 3rd June 2009   2

APPENDIX XI(C)

FR

SECTION 4: THE APPLICANT

FULL NAME AND ADDRESS (Please state whether you are owner or representative person, delete as appropriate)

	Tel No.	
	Fax No.	
	E-Mail	
OWNER / REPRESENTATIVE PERSON		

I enclose the fee of £ | NB: See below for fees applicable. Cheques drawn from a Bank in Gibraltar, cheques drawn from a UK Clearing Bank or International Bank Drafts should be made payable to 'GOVERNMENT GENERAL ACCOUNT'

All correspondence will be sent to the Registered Agent unless you request otherwise.

Signature | | Date | |

Details of Fees:

Full Registration Fee	**£550.00**
Provisional Registration	**£450.00**
Registration following Provisional Registration	**£350.00**

Send this form, in original (and electronically, if you wish), to:

The Registrar of Ships
Gibraltar Ship Registry
Watergate House
2/8 Casemates Square
Gibraltar

Tel: +350 200 47771
Fax: +350 200 47770
Email: maritime.registry@gibraltar.gov.gi

Documents to be submitted:

Use The Gibraltar Ship Registry's checklist **RA-09-F013 'FR Documents required for Full Registration (New Reg.)'** for guidance on what documents and certificates are required for Registration.

RA-09-F005 FR Appl Register a Ship   Last Revised 3rd June 2009   3

APPENDIX XI(C)

FR BB UC

Gibraltar Ship Registry

APPOINTMENT OF REGISTERED AGENT

Name of Ship	
Official Number	
Port of Registry	**GIBRALTAR**

The under mentioned is hereby appointed Registered Agent.

Full name of individual or Body Corporate	
Full address (for body corporates give principal place of business)	

_____   *Consent of Registered Agent*
Signature of Owner / Charterer

_____   _____
Name in Block Capitals   Signature of Registered Agent

_____   _____
Date   Date

RA-09-F006 FR BB UC Appointment of Registered Agent   Last Revised 3rd June 2009

APPENDIX XI(C)

FR BB UC

Gibraltar Ship Registry

APPOINTMENT OF REPRESENTATIVE PERSON

Name of Ship	
Official Number	
Port of Registry	**GIBRALTAR**

The under mentioned is hereby appointed Representative Person.

Full name of individual or Body Corporate	
Full address (for body corporates give principal place of business)	

_____
Signature of Owner / Charterer

Consent of Representative Person

_____
Name in Block Capitals

_____
Signature of Representative Person

_____
Date

_____
Date

RA-09-F007 FR BB UC Appoint of Rep Person   Last Revised 3rd June 2009

1

407

APPENDIX XI(C)

FR UC

Gibraltar Ship Registry
BILL OF SALE

- **Warning:** A purchaser of a ship does not obtain a complete title until the appropriate Bill(s) of Sale has / have been recorded with the Registry, and a new Certificate issued.
- Registered owners or mortgagors *must* inform the Registry of any change of address.
- Where one owner is selling to two or more owners, separate forms are required unless they are buying as joint owners.
- Unless application to transfer the registration of the ship to the new ownership is received at the Registry within 30 days of the change, re-registration fees will be payable.
- A Declaration of Ownership in respect of each new owner must be submitted with this document when registering the transfer of ownership; Bodies Corporate must also provide a copy of the Certificate of Incorporation and Certificate of Good Standing; Foreign Maritime Entities must provide a copy of the Certificate of Registration as a Foreign Maritime Entity.
- Please write in black ink using **BLOCK CAPITALS**, and tick boxes where appropriate.

SECTION 1 - DETAILS OF THE SHIP REGISTERED OR TO BE REGISTERED AS A SHIP:

NAME OF SHIP

OFFICIAL NUMBER

SECTION 2 - DETAILS OF THE SALE:

Body Corporate give:	Company name	Registered office	Place of registration	Description
Individuals give:	Full name(s)	Address(es)	Nationality	Occupation(s)
I / We* the transferor(s) ☐ as joint owners Tick box if you are joint owners *(delete as appropriate)				

In consideration of (* the Sum of)

*Paid / given to *me / us on (date)   At (place)   By:

Body Corporate give:	Company name	Registered office	Place of registration	Description
Individuals give:	Full name(s)	Address(es)	Nationality	Occupation(s)
I / We* the transferor(s) ☐ as joint owners Tick box if you are joint owners				

*Delete as appropriate   RA-09-F008 FR UC BILL OF SALE   Last Revised 3rd June   1
2009

408

APPENDIX XI(C)

FR UC

SECTION 2: DETAILS OF THE SALE (Continued):

The receipt of which is acknowledged, transfer [   ] Shares in the above ship and in its

appurtenances to the transferee(s).   *(figures and words)*

Further, *I / we the said transferor(s) for *myself / ourselves, hereby declare that *I / we have the power to transfer in the manner aforesaid the above-mentioned shares, and that they are free from encumbrances.

If any recorded mortgage(s) *is / are outstanding, please tick the following box:

"Save as appears by the registry of the above ship" [   ]

SECTION 3: FOR COMPLETION WHEN TRANSFERORS IS A BODY CORPORATE OR A FOREIGN MARITIME ENTITY:

Executed by the transferor as a deed on this

.......................day of
...   .200   by:

(a) The affixing of the common seal of the transferor in the
     presence of the following persons signing; or

(b) Signing by the following persons:

Director ....

Director / Secretary...

SEAL

Authorised Signatory ....   Authorised Signatory ....

SECTION 4: FOR COMPLETION WHEN TRANSFEROR IS / ARE INDIVIDUAL(S):

Signed, sealed and delivered

...   .day of...   .200   ....
by the following person(s) signing as transferor(s)

Signature(s) of transferor(s) ....

Full name of witness(es)   ....
Signature of witness(es) ....

Occupation of witness(es)   ....

Address of witness(es)   ....

SEAL

When completed, you should send this form, together with the appropriate fee and supporting documents to:

The Registrar of Ships,	**Telephone: (+350) 200 47771**
Watergate House, 2/8 Casemates	**Fax: (+350) 200 47770**
Gibraltar	**Email:** maritime.registry@gibraltar.gov.gi

*Delete as appropriate   RA-09-F008 FR UC BILL OF SALE   Last Revised 3rd June   2
2009

APPENDIX XI(D)

Isle of Man forms

(1) Application to register a ship, form REG 1
(2) Appointment of authorised officer(s) for a body corporate, form REG 3
(3) Declaration of ownership on behalf of a body corporate, form REG 4
(4) Advice of appointment of ship's manager, managing owner etc., form REG 6
(5) Bill of sale, form REG 11
(6) Builder's certificate, form REG 12
(7) Application for registration on demise charter register, form DCR 3
(8) Owner consent to registry, form DCR 4
(9) Mortgagee's consent to registry, form DCR 5
(10) Notice of mortgage intent, form MORT 1

Note

Reproduced courtesy of Isle of Man Ship Registry.
For additional and updated forms see: www.iomshipregistry.com

APPENDIX XI(D)

Reg 1

The Merchant Shipping Registration Act 1991
Application to Register a Ship

NOTE: Please complete in BLOCK CAPITALS

Vessel details

Proposed name of ship and alternative name(s) in order of preference, in case your first choice cannot be authorised.

1.   3.
2.   4.

You should note that once a name has been approved, it may not be possible to change to an alternative name

If ship is new, please give:

Name and address of builder

Yard Number allocated to the ship

If the Ship is not new and if the ship has at any time been on the British Register, please give:

The last British name

The official number

If the ship last sailed under a foreign flag, please give:

the last foreign name		Proposed port of registry	
Nationality		Type of vessel	
At which port is the ship now lying?		Intended date of registry	
Tonnage (Gross)		Tonnage (Net)	

Method of propulsion (please tick)   steam [ ]   motor [ ]   sail [ ]

In support of my application, I enclose the following documents : (please tick appropriate boxes)

All applicants	Also required when applicant is a Body Corporate
Title documents (e.g. Builders certificate, Bill of Sale, transcript) [ ]	Appointment of Manager (not yachts under 24 metres) [ ]
Declaration of Ownership [ ]	Certificate(s) of Incorporation (copy) & Change of company name (if applicable) [ ]
Fee of £ [ ]	Appointment of Authorised Officer Reg 3) [ ]
Also required vessel is a pleasure yacht	Also required when Mortgage to be registered
Declaration of Registration as Pleasure Yacht (Reg 15) [ ]	Mortgage Deed [ ]

411

APPENDIX XI(D)

Reg 1

Details of Owner(s)

Please enter below the names, addresses and nationalities of all the owners of the ship. – If you need more continue on an additional sheet and affix to this form. Your own details should be entered last.

Name	
Address	
E-mail address	Phone No
Nationality	
Name of applicant	
Signature	
Date	
Name	
Address	
E-mail address	Phone No
Nationality	
Signature	
Date	

Notes – Application for Registration should be made by

a. In the case of an individual, by the individual requiring to be registered as owner or by his agent; or

b. In the case of joint owners, by any one of those owners; or

c. In the case of a body corporate, by a duly authorised officer (Form REG 3) of that body

If the ship is not registered within 12 months of the date of this application, the authority will be considered to have lapsed. The authority may however be renewed if you can show sufficient cause. If you have any queries about this form please telephone 01624 688500.

412

APPENDIX XI(D)

Reg 3

The Merchant Shipping Registration Act 1991
Appointment of Authorised Officer(s) for a Body Corporate

NOTE: Please complete in BLOCK CAPITALS

Ship Name

Port of Registry

Full Company Name

Full address of Principal Place of Business

The Following Officer(s) of the Company are hereby authorised to make and sign all declarations of ownership or otherwise for and on behalf of the said Company, as required under the provisions of the Merchant Shipping Registration Act 1991.

Please give full names	Signature of Officer

Signature of Director/Secretary

Full Name (in BLOCK CAPITALS)

Date

Signature of Director/Secretary

Full Name (in BLOCK CAPITALS)

Date

413

APPENDIX XI(D)

Reg 4

The Merchant Shipping Registration Act 1991

Declaration of Ownership On Behalf of a Body Corporate

Notes:

1. This form is to be completed by an authorised officer for the Company, who must be appointed using Form Reg 3.
2. Please ensure that you complete all three parts of this form.
3. After completion of Part 3, send this form, together with the documents specified in that part to Isle of Man Ship Registry, Department of Trade & Industry.
4. A ship is entitled to be registered if 33 of the 64 shares are legally and beneficially owned by qualified persons (defined in Part 2). Joint owners of a share must all be qualified persons for that share to count towards the 33 shares required.
5. If the vessel is currently registered abroad you must take all reasonable steps to remove the vessel from the foreign register before completing registration under the above Act. Failure to comply with this requirement can result in a fine.

PART 1

Official Number/IMO No   Name of Ship   Port of Registry

Length   Breadth   Depth

Sailing, Steam or Motor   Horse power of engines (if any)

Gross Tonnage   Net Tonnage   (for dual tonnages state the higher)

The ship was built at [   ] Year of build [   ]
and as described in more detail in the Certificate of Survey.

PART 2

Full Name   Address   Occupation

of (Company Name) [   ]   [   ] Shares in the ship
Individual Owner – The
Company is the legal
and beneficial owner of
OR
Joint Owner – The   [   ]   [   ] Shares in the ship
Company is the legal   together with the person(s) /Companies
and beneficial owner of   listed below.

414

APPENDIX XI(D)

Reg 4

Full Name(s)	Address(es)

(Each joint owner must complete a separate Form REG 4)

Is the Company a qualified person? (see below)

If NO, what is the country of incorporation and principal place of business?

Is the vessel under 24 metres (78.7 feet)?

If the vessel is over 24 metres and the owning company not an Isle of Man resident, you must appoint a representative person (RAN 15)

Specify details (name and address)

A qualified person is a citizen/subject/body corporate as defined in the categories below:

A A British citizen;
B A British Dependent Territory citizen;
C A British Overseas citizen;
D A British citizen under the 1981 Act;
E A British National overseas;
F A citizen of the Republic of Ireland;
G A citizen of the EU or EEA
H Bodies corporate incorporated in the Isle of Man or in any relevant country and having their principal place of business in the Isle of Man or any other relevant country.
I In addition: Prescribed relevant countries (see RAN 02 no.3)

} As defined Act Within the British Nationality 1981

Joint owners must appoint the same Representative Person.

A Representative Person can be an individual resident in the Isle of man or a body corporate incorporated in the island and having its principal place of business there.

The Department must be kept informed of all changes of Representative Person(s) including changes in name, address and new appointments.

The relevant country is Anguilla, Bermuda, Cayman Islands, Channel Islands, Falkland Islands and Dependencies, Gibraltar, united Kingdom, Montserrat, Pitcairn Islands, St Helena and Dependencies, Turks and Caicos Islands, Virgin Islands, the Republic of Ireland, EU Member States and EEA countries.

An Isle of Man Resident in the case of an individual is a person residing, that is living and sleeping, in the Isle of Man for a significant part of the year. If a person is resident in the Isle of Man for tax purposes, they will be regarded as resident for the purposes of the Merchant Shipping Registration Act 1991. An Isle of Man Resident in the case of a body corporate is a company incorporated in, and having its principal place of business in the Isle of Man.

Insert for example:
"An act of Parliament of the United Kingdom" (cite year in which Act was passed, its chapter and title)
OR
"A charter granted by her Majesty and dated ....
"An Act of Ordinance of the legislation of .... "(cite year in which Act of Ordnance was passed, its chapter and title)

on

Insert date of incorporation of the Company

APPENDIX XI(D)

Reg 4

And subject to the laws of			Insert 'The Isle of Man' or as the case maybe
And its registered office at			To be completed in the case of a Company Incorporated by virtue of the Companies Acts.

And its principal place of business is at (insert address)

Where all the important business of the Company is, in fact, controlled and managed at meetings of Directors or Representative Person(s) of the Company.

PART 3
I declare that:-

WARNING
There are heavy penalties for making a false declaration and under section 72 of the Merchant Shipping Registration Act 1991 the ship or share may be subject to forfeiture.

- The information given by me in this form is true to the best of my knowledge and belief;
- The ship is not fishing for profit;
- The ship is not registered under Part II of the Merchant Registration Act 1991 (Small Ships Register);
- The ship is not registered under Part III of the Merchant Shipping Registration Act 1991 (Fishing Vessel Register);
- The company is entitled to be registered as owner/joint owner of the shares specified in Part 2 of this form;
- To the best of my knowledge and belief a majority interest in the ship is owned by persons qualified to be owners of British ships and the ship is otherwise entitled to be registered under Part I of the Merchant Shipping Registration Act 1991;
- If the ship is registered under the law of any country outside the Isle of Man and still so registered when it becomes registered under Part I of the Merchant Shipping Registration Act 1991, the company will take all reasonable steps to secure termination of the ship's registration outside the Isle of Man.

Signature of authorised officer

Full Name (in BLOCK CAPITALS)

Date

Please send this completed form to the Department together with:-

For Initial Registry		For a change of Ownership	
Formal application to Register		Bill of Sale	
Title documents		Certificate of Registry	
Closed transcript/Deletion Certificate		The fee	
Appointment of Authorised Officer (Reg 3)		Copy of Certificate of Incorporation	
The fee			
In addition, you must have: A survey of vessels' particulars by an approved Classification society surveyor			
Copy of Certificate of Incorporation			

Page 3 of 3

22/06/12

APPENDIX XI(D)

REG 6

The Merchant Shipping Registration Act 1991
Advice of Appointment of Ship's Representative Person

1. The Merchant Shipping Registration Act 1991[1] requires owners of vessels of 24 metres in length or more to be either resident in the Isle of Man or if not resident, to appoint a Representative Person.
(a) In the case of a Manx Merchant Ship, the representative person must be a body corporate incorporated in and having its principal place of business in the Isle of Man.
(b) In the case of a pleasure yacht the representative person can either be an individual or a body corporate resident in the Isle of Man.
2. The Department must be kept informed of all changes Representative person including changes in names, addresses and new appointments.
3. The Representative Person should be guided by Registry Advice Note number 15.

REQUIREMENTS
The function of a Representative Person as set out in the 1991 Registration Act is to enable the Department to serve the following documents in relation to a ship for which they are appointed:
 ☒ Notice of the Department's intention to de-register a ship; and
 ☒ Papers for the purpose of the institution of, or otherwise in connection with, any criminal or civil proceedings.
In addition, Representative Persons are required, under Merchant Shipping (Crew Agreements, Lists of Crew and Discharge of Seamen) Regulations 1991 to retain a current crew list in the Isle of Man for each ship they represent.

Official/IMO Number	Name of Ship	Port of Registry

The under mentioned is/are hereby appointed:

Representative Person

Full Name	
Full Address	

Signature of owner (Director/Secretary) or Authorised Officer

Date	
Full Name & Signature	
Company Name	

I/we the undersigned, hereby agree to act as Representative Person of the above mentioned

03/10

APPENDIX XI(D)

Reg 11

The Merchant Shipping Registration Act 1991
Bill of Sale

1. Warning: A purchaser of a British registered ship does not obtain a complete title until the appropriate Bill(s) of Sale has been recorded with the Registry, and the certificate amended or a new one issued.
2. Registered owners or mortgagees must inform the Registry of any changes of address.
3. Where one owner is selling to two or more owners, separate forms are required unless they are buying as joint owners.
4. Please write in black in k using BLOCK CAPITALS, and tick boxes where appropriate.

Section 1: Details of the Ship

Name of Ship [ ]

Official Number (if any) [ ]   Length [ ] metres

Section 2: Details of the sale (*Delete as necessary)

Body Corporate, please give Individuals, please give	Company Name Full Name(s)	Principal Place of Business Address(es)	Occupation(s)
*I/We the transferor(s)As joint owners ☐ (please tick box if you are joint owners)			

In consideration of (*the sum of) [ ]

*paid/given to *me/us by:

Body Corporate, please give Individuals, please give	Company Name Full Name(s)	Principal Place of Business Address(es)	Occupation(s)
*I/We the transferee(s)As joint owners ☐ (please tick box if you are joint owners)			

Page 1 of 3   08/2013

APPENDIX XI(D)

Reg 11
(figures & words)

the receipt of which is
acknowledged, transfer
Shares in the above ship and in its appurtenances to the transferee(s)

Further, *I/we the said transferor(s) for *myself/ourselves, hereby declare that *I/we have the power to transfer in the manner aforesaid the above-mentioned shares, and that they are free from encumbrances

If any registered mortgage is outstanding, please tick the following box

"SAVE AS APPEARS BY THE REGISTRY OF THE ABOVE SHIP"

SECTION 3: For Completion when sale is by a company

Executed by the transferor as a deed on this

| | Day of | | By:- |

*(a)   the affixing of the common seal of the transferor in the presence of the following persons signing; or

*(b)   signing by the following persons;

Director

Director/Secretary

Authorised Signatory

Authorised Signatory

NOTE: IN SCOTLAND – signature may be by: two directors OR by a director and the secretary of the company; OR by any two persons authorised to sign and subscribe the documents on behalf of the company.

EXCEPT IN SCOTLAND – signature may be by two directors: OR by a director and the secretary of the company;; If the common seal is affixed, any special requirements of the company's articles about signing must be complied with.

SECTION 4: For completion when sale is by individual(s)

*Executed as a deed (in England or Wales)

*Signed (in Scotland)

*Signed, sealed and delivered (in Northern Ireland)

On this   Day of
By the following person(s) signing as transferor(s)

**Signature of
transferor(s)**

**Full name of
witness(es)**

Page 2 of 3

08/2013

APPENDIX XI(D)

Reg 11

Occupation of witness(es)		
Address of witness(es)		

PLEASE NOTE:

DOCUMENTS EXECUTED OUTSIDE THE ISLE OF MAN, UNITED KINGDOM OR A RELEVANT BRITISH POSSESSION MUST BE CERTIFIED BY A NOTARY ESTABLISHED IN THAT COUNTRY.

APPENDIX XI(D)

REG 12

The Merchant Shipping Registration Act 1991

Builder's Certificate

Yard/IMO Number	Name of Vessel	Date of Build

Details of Vessel

Length	metres	Method of propulsion (sail, motor or both)	
Breadth	metres	Make of engine (KW to be stated)	
Depth	metres	Estimated tonnage of vessel	

Builder's Name	Builder's Address	Place of Build (if different from builder's address)

*I/We hereby certify that *I/We *built/moulded/fitted out the vessel described above to the order of:

Full Name(s)	Full Address(es)	Occupation(s)

NOTE: If two or more persons are to own the vessel jointly, please give all their details in full and add the words "as Joint Owners"

Date	Signature of Builder

In the case of a body corporate, this certificate must be sealed and witnessed.

Date	Signature of Builder

Page 1 of 1

10/14

APPENDIX XI(D)

The Merchant Shipping Registration Act 1991
Demise Charter Registration
Application for Registration

NOTE: Please complete in BLOCK CAPITALS
SECTION A – DETAILS OF SHIP

Ships Name
(Undesirable names will not be accepted)

Existing Flag & Port of Registry

Type

Date & Place of Build

Tonnage   Gross   Net

SECTION B – DETAILS OF PRESENT OWNERSHIP

Total number of PRESENT owners

Please enter the name, address and where ordinarily resident and the nationality of every present owner

Body Corporate Individuals	Company Name Full Name	Principal Place of Business Address	Nationality

Share Holding   /64 (sixty-four)
In the case of multiple ownership please give details of all joint owners on a continuation sheet

SECTION C – DETAILS OF CHARTERER AND CHARTER

Intended period of Demise Charter

Details of Charterer

Body Corporate Individuals	Company Name Full Name	Principal Place of Business Address	Nationality

Page 1 of 3   DCR 3   03/10

APPENDIX XI(D)

SECTION D – MANAGER'S DETAILS, QUESTIONNAIRE AND CERTIFICATE

Body Corporate	Company Name	Principal Place of Business

Management Questionnaire

Please give:-

A. The Directors' names, permanent addresses, nationality and shareholding of director

B. Where and how frequently Directors' meetings are normally held;

C. Where the annual general meeting is normally held;

D. Address where the company's accounts are maintained (if different from Principal Place of Business);

E. The number of technical personnel employed by the company;

F. The address in the Isle of Man where a copy of the crew list is lodged in accordance with regulation 16 (1) of the Merchant Shipping (Crew Agreements, Lists of Crew and Discharge of Seamen) Regulations 1972.

If certain management functions are sub-delegated to persons other than the appointed manager please give the name of the person or company who:

A. Excercises direct control over the movement of the ship

B. Is responsible for technical management – i.e. Statutory Surveys;

C. Is responsible for the employment and recruitment of the crew;

D. Pays the crew's wages

CERTIFICATE OF AGREEMENT BY MANAGER

APPENDIX XI(D)

I [ ]   Signature [ ]
Certify that the above management company agrees to act as the Manager of the above ship.
Dated: [ ]

SECTION E – DETAILS OF MORTGAGEES etc

Body Corporate Individuals	Company Name Full Name	Principal Place of Business Address	Mortgage

SECTION F – ADDITIONAL DOCUMENTS

In support of the application, the following documents are enclosed (please tick appropriate boxes)

- Certified copy of charter party [ ]
- Certified copy of entries in underlying register [ ]
- Written consent of
  a. Underlying registry authorities [ ]
  b. Owner [ ]
  c. Mortgagees (if any) [ ]
- Arrangements have been made for a tonnage measurement survey [ ]
- Certificate of Incorporation (and change of company name if applicable) from manager [ ]

Also required if the applicant is a Body Corporate:-

- Certificate of Incorporation (and change of company name if applicable) for charterer [ ]
- Appointment of authorised officer of charterer [ ]

SECTION G - APPLICATION

I understand it is an offence knowingly or recklessly to make a false statement in order to obtain registration and hereby declare that, to the best of my knowledge, the details given in this application are correct.

Signature	
Name in full	
For and on behalf of	
Date	

APPENDIX XI(D)

The Merchant Shipping (Demise Charter Register)
Registration Act 1991

**Owner Consent to Registry
(Individual/Body Corporate)**

NOTE: Please complete in BLOCK CAPITALS

Official Number	
Name of Ship	
Flag & Port of Registry	
I (Full Name)	*Director/Secretary/Authorised Officer/Individual Owner

*Delete as necessary

Of Company Name	
Address	
Registered owner of	Shares in the above ship, consent to the Registry of the said ship on the Demise Charter Register at the port of Douglas, Isle of Man

BODY CORPORATE

Signature of *Director/Secretary			
Full name (in BLOCK CAPITALS)			
Signature of *Director/Secretary			
Full name (in BLOCK CAPTIALS)		Date	

Or

Signature of authorised officer			
Full name (in BLOCK CAPTITALS)		Date	

INDIVIDUAL

Signature			
Full name (in BLOCK CAPTITALS)		Date	

NOTE: Each Owner must complete a separate form DCR4)

Page 1 of 1   DCR 4   03/10

425

APPENDIX XI(D)

The Merchant Shipping (Demise Charter Register)
Registration Act 1991

Mortgagee's Consent to Registry
(Individual/Body Corporate)

NOTE: Please complete in BLOCK CAPITALS

Official Number	
Name of Ship	
Flag & Port of Registry	
I (Full Name)		*Director/Secretary/Authorised Officer/Individual Owner
		*Delete as necessary
Of Company Name	
Address	

Registered mortgagee of [   ] Shares in the above ship, consent to the Registry of the said ship on the Demise Charter Register at the port of Douglas, Isle of Man

BODY CORPORATE

EITHER

Signature of *Director/Secretary	
Full name (in BLOCK CAPTIALS)	
Signature of *Director/Secretary	
Full name (in BLOCK CAPTIALS)		Date

Or

| Signature of authorised officer | |
| Full name (in BLOCK CAPTITALS) | | Date |

INDIVIDUAL

| Signature | |
| Full name (in BLOCK CAPTITALS) | | Date |

NOTE: Each mortgagee must complete a separate form DCR5

Page 1 of 1   DCR 5   03/10

426

APPENDIX XI(D)

Notice of Mortgage Intent

Notice of Mortgage of Intent

- If more than one mortgagor (borrower) then a separate form is required, unless shares are held jointly.
- The notice of mortgage intent is recorded on the Register for a period of 30 days, unless it is withdrawn within that time.
- The notice may be renewed or further renewed for a period of 30 days, by notice in writing to the Registry. The relevant fee is required each time.
- Section 1 must be completed if the ship is already registered in the UK.
- Section 2 must be completed if the ship is not currently registered in the UK.
- Sections 3 & 4 must be completed in all cases.

SECTION 1: DETAILS OF THE SHIP (complete if the ship is currently registered in the UK)

| Name of Ship | |
| Official Number | |

SECTION 2: DETAILS OF THE SHIP (complete if the ship is not currently registered in the UK)

Present Name of Ship	
Intended Name of Ship	
Intended Port of Choice	
Details of any permanent marks	
Approximate Length	metres

If the ship is new, please attach the Builder's Certificate. If it is not available, complete the following:

| Name & Address of Builder | |

If the ship is registered outside the UK, please attach the certificate of Registry, and give:

| Port of Registration | |

Page 1 of 2

03/10

APPENDIX XI(D)

Notice of Mortgage Intent

SECTION 3: MORTGAGOR(S) (to be completed in all cases)

Full Name(s)	Address(es)	Signature(s)	No. of shares affected

SECTION 4: MORTAGEE(S) (to be completed in all cases)

Mortgagee's Reference No. or Bank Sort Code

Name & Address

Signature

Full Name

Date

The fee of £ _____ is enclosed

Branch Stamp

Official Use Only

Mortgage intent _____ (priority) recorded on the register
(date) _____ expiry date _____

Renewal of Intent

Renewal Date	Expiry Date

Page 2 of 2   03/10

428

APPENDIX XI(E)

Liberia forms

(1) Application for official number, call sign and registration of vessel, form RLM – 101A
(2) Application for newbuilding registration, form RLM – 101B
(3) ISM Code declarations of company and designated person, form RLM 297
(4) ISPS Code declaration by company security officer, form ISP-002
(5) Application for minimum safe manning certificate, form MSD 336RL

Note

Reproduced courtesy of LISCR, LLC.
For additional and updated forms see: www.liscr.com

APPENDIX XI(E)

RLM-101A

The Republic of Liberia
Liberia Maritime Authority

THIS SPACE FOR OFFICIAL USE ONLY	
OFFICIAL NO.	
CALL SIGN	

APPLICATION FOR VESSEL REGISTRATION, OFFICIAL NUMBER, CALL SIGN, TEMPORARY AUTHORITY RADIO STATION LICENSE AND WAIVERS

PART 1. TYPE AND DATE OF REGISTRATION (Check as appropriate)

[ ] Newbuilding   [ ] Transfer from another flag   [ ] Re-registration   [ ] Bareboat Charter Registration   [ ] Laid up

Estimated Registration Date   yyyy / mm / dd   / /

PART 2. VESSEL AND OWNER(S) PARTICULARS (Follow guidelines below)

01. NEW NAME	02. IMO NUMBER	03. PRESENT NAME	04. PRESENT FLAG
05. VESSEL TYPE	06. YEAR BUILT	07. BUILDER/SHIPYARD	08. COUNTRY BUILT
09. HULL MATERIAL	10. DECKS	11. MASTS	12. CLASSIFICATION SOCIETY	13. DATE AND PLACE OF CONVERSION
14. LENGTH - LOA	15. LENGTH REGISTERED	16. BREADTH	17. DEPTH	18. NET TONS	19. GROSS TONS	20. DEADWEIGHT
21. PROPELLING POWER KW	22. NUMBER AND TYPE OF ENGINES	23. ENGINE MAKER

24. NAME OF OWNER(S)	25. OWNER IMO ID.	26. RESIDENCE	27. CITIZENSHIP	28. OWNERSHIP %
		80 Broad Street, Monrovia, Liberia		
		80 Broad Street, Monrovia, Liberia		
			TOTAL	100%

(If more than two Owners, please attach extra sheet, signed and notarized)

Guidelines:
Box 01 – Name vessel will use under Liberian Flag
Box 02 – Vessel IMO ID number issued by IHS-Fairplay
Box 03 – Name under the current Flag or Hull Number (newbuilding)
Box 04 – Flag the Vessel is transferring from or 'Newbuilding' if applicable
Box 05 – As per Class Certificate, Class Statement or Confirmation of Class
Box 06 – Year delivered from shipyard (not keel laid year)
Box 09 – E.g. STEEL (covers also High Tensile or SS etc.)
Box 10 – Number of continuous decks only
Box 12 – Must be a full IACS member
Box 13 – Applies only if confirmed by classification documents

Box 14 – Length Overall (LOA)
Box 15 – As per International Tonnage Cert. (ITC)
Box 16, 17, 18, 19 – As per ITC
Box 20 – DWT SSW (Summer Salt Water)
Box 21 – Maximum power. Combined Main Propulsion Units only (Gen-sets do not apply).
(PS or BHP must be converted into Kilo Watts)
Box 22 – Can be exact model/type or a general description
e.g. One Sulzer 4RTA58 or One Diesel Engine
Box 23 – Name only. Address is not required

Box 24 – Name of Liberian Corporation or Foreign Maritime Entity (FME) as registered in Liberian Corporate Registry. Note: if BCR – it is the bareboat charterer registering the Vessel in Liberia (not the name of Owner registered in the underlying registry).
Box 25 – Owning Company IMO ID number issued by IHS-Fairplay
Box 26 – Registered office (also for FME) at 80 Broad Street, Monrovia, Liberia c/o The LISCR Trust Company acting as agent
Box 27 – If FME, country of the original jurisdiction
Box 28 – Proportion of Ownership

PART 3. RADIO COMMUNICATIONS /Radio Accounting Authority

A contract has been (or will be) entered into with the following Radio Accounting Authority (RAA): AAIC (code):_____,
Name:_____, which Accounting Authority will be responsible for all communications accounts. Pending the effective date of such contract, responsibility for payment of accounts and correspondence relative to the radiotelegraphy/telephony service of the vessel is hereby assumed by applicant Owner(s).

(!) Note: Temporary Authority Radio Station License issued based on RLM-101A will be valid for 3 months. The Owner must submit the Radio License Application (RLM-104) prior to expiration of the temporary license to obtain a full term Liberian Radio Station License.

PART 4. MORTGAGE

Mortgage to be recorded at vessel registration   check as appropriate: [ ] YES   or   [ ] NO   or   [ ] TBD

RLM-101A Page 1 of 2   10/13

APPENDIX XI(E)

RLM 101A

PART 5. CORRESPONDENCE AND BILLING AGENT

General Correspondence and Billing including annual tax invoices should be sent to the following address(s):

Full name and address of the responsible company(s) - (not an individual's name)

1. General Correspondence:	2. Billing/Annual Tonnage Fees:	Phone	
Address:	Address:	Fax	
		Email	
	3. Billing/Miscellaneous Invoices:		
Phone		Phone	
Fax	Address:	Fax	
Email		Email	

PART 6. WAIVERS

Declaration and Affidavit of the need for waiver of Liberian Requirements with regard to Ownership and/or Age and/or Tonnage under respective Sections of the Liberian Maritime Law;

OWNERSHIP *(not a Liberian Entity)*	Waiver of Section 51(2)	Under Section 51(5)	*Check as appropriate*	**YES**	or		**N/A**
AGE *(above 20 years)*	Waiver of Section 51(4)	Under Section 51(6)	*Check as appropriate*	**YES**	or		**N/A**
TONNAGE *(less than 500 net tons)*	Waiver of Section 51(2)	Under Section 51(2)(a)	*Check as appropriate*	**YES**	or		**N/A**

The application for waiver(s) is made because the Owner and/or the Vessel does not meet requirements of Ownership and/or Age and/or Tonnage as described in the Liberian Maritime Law, however the Owner desires to fly the Liberian flag and declare that all other requirements to register the vessel will be met.

OATH OF APPLICANT OWNER and
AFFIRMATION OF SURRENDER OF FOREIGN DOCUMENTS AND MAKING OF MARKINGS

I do hereby swear and affirm, as required by Section 57 of the Liberian Maritime Law, that I am duly authorized in writing by the Owner(s) [bareboat charterer] or prospective Owner(s) [bareboat charterer] of the Vessel as described in Part 2 "Vessel and Owner(s) Particulars" of this Application, that all information and particulars of the Vessel and the Owner(s) [bareboat charterer] or prospective Owner(s) [bareboat charterer] contained herein are true and correct and that the present or prospective Master of the said Vessel has been ordered or will be ordered and instructed, upon receipt of the vessel's Liberian Certificate of Registry and other Liberian Documents, to surrender the vessel previous documents issued by the Government of the Flag State as declared in Box 4 and to make the Vessel Markings required by Section 75 (1), (2) and (4), of the Liberian Maritime Law, as amended.

Submitted by:

Full Name *(Print)*	
Citizen of	
Residing at[1]	
Title[2]	

_____   _____
Signature   *Date*

ACKNOWLEDGEMENT

Subscribed and Sworn Before me

this ___ day of _____ _____ *(Year)*

at _____

_____
*Signature and Seal of Notary Public or other Officer
authorized by Liberian Law to administer oaths*

Notes:
1. Enter street address, city and country of residence or place of business.
2. Enter President, Vice-President, Director, Secretary, Attorney-in-Fact, etc whichever title applies.

RLM-101A Page 2 of 2   10/13

APPENDIX XI(E)

RLM 101B

The Republic of Liberia Liberia Maritime Authority	THIS SPACE FOR OFFICIAL USE ONLY	
	OFFICIAL NO.	
	CALL SIGN	

APPLICATION FOR REGISTRATION OF A NEWBUILDING DURING CONSTRUCTION AT BUILDER'S YARD, OFFICIAL NUMBER, CALL SIGN AND WAIVERS

PART 1. TYPE AND DATE OF REGISTRATION

| X | Newbuilding Under Construction | | Estimated Registration Date | yyyy/ mm/ dd | / / |

PART 2. VESSEL AND OWNER(S) PARTICULARS *(Follow guidelines below)*

01. PROPOSED NAME OF VESSEL	02. IMO NUMBER	03. HULL NO.	04. KEEL LAYING DATE

05. VESSEL TYPE	06. EST. BUILT DATE	07. BUILDER'S NAME/SHIPYARD	08. YARD LOCATION

09. HULL MATERIAL	10. DECKS	11. MASTS	12. CLASSIFICATION SOCIETY

13. LENGTH - LOA	14. LENGTH - REG'D	15. BREADTH	16. DEPTH	17. NET TONS	18. GROSS TONS	19. DEADWEIGHT

20. PROPELLING POWER KW	21. NUMBER AND TYPE OF ENGINES	22. ENGINE MAKER

23. NAME OF OWNER(S)	24. OWNER IMO ID.	25. RESIDENCE	26. CITIZENSHIP	27. OWNERSHIP %
		80 Broad Street, Monrovia, Liberia		
		80 Broad Street, Monrovia, Liberia		
(If more than two Owners , please attach extra sheet, signed and notarized)			TOTAL	100%

Guidelines:
Box 01 – Name vessel will use under Liberian Flag
Box 02 – Vessel IMO ID number issued by IHS-Fairplay
Box 05 – As per Class Statement or Confirmation of Class
Box 09 – E.g. STEEL (covers also High Tensile or SS etc.)
Box 10 – Number of continuous decks only
Box 12 – Must be a full IACS member
Box 13 – Length Overall (LOA)
Box 14 – As per International Tonnage Cert (ITC) or estimated
Box 15, 16, 17, 18 – As per ITC or estimated
Box 20 – Maximum power. Combined Main Propulsion Units only.
 (Gen-sets do not apply). PS or BHP must be converted into Kilo Watts
Box 21 – Can be an exact model/type or general description
 e.g. One Sulzer 4RTA58 or One Diesel Engine
Box 22 – Name only. Address is not required
Box 23 – Name of Liberian Corporation or Foreign Maritime Entity (FME)
 as registered in Liberian Corporate Registry.
Box 24 – Owning Company IMO ID number issued by IHS-Fairplay
Box 25 – Registered office (also for FME) at 80 Broad Street, Monrovia,
 Liberia c/o The LISCR Trust Company acting as agent
Box 26 – If FME, country of the original jurisdiction
Box 27 – Proportion of Ownership of the vessel

PART 3. MORTGAGE

| Mortgage to be recorded at vessel registration | *check as appropriate:* | YES | or | NO | or | TBD |

RLM-101B Page 1 of 2   10/13

432

APPENDIX XI(E)

RLM 101B

PART 4. CORRESPONDENCE AND BILLING AGENT

General Correspondence and Billing should be sent to the following address(es):

Full name and address of the responsible company(s) - (not an individual's name)

1. General Correspondence: Address:			2. Billing: Address:		
Phone		Fax	Phone		Fax
Email			Email		

PART 5. WAIVERS

Declaration and Affidavit of the need for waiver of Liberian Requirements with regard to Ownership and/or Tonnage under respective Section of the Liberian Maritime Law;

OWNERSHIP *(not a Liberian Entity)*	Waiver of Section 51(2)	Under Section 51(5)	*Check as appropriate*	**YES**	or	**N/A**
TONNAGE *(less than 500 net tons)*	Waiver of Section 51(2)	Under Section 51(2)(a)	*Check as appropriate*	**YES**	or	**N/A**

The application for waiver(s) is made because the Owner and/or the Vessel does not meet requirements of Ownership and/or Tonnage as described in the Liberian Maritime Law, however the Owner desires to fly the Liberian flag and declare that all other requirements to register the vessel will be met.

OATH OF APPLICANT OWNER and
AFFIRMATION OF SURRENDER OF FOREIGN DOCUMENTS AND MAKING OF MARKINGS

I do hereby swear and affirm, as required by Section 57 of the Liberian Maritime Law, that I am duly authorized in writing by the Owner(s) [bareboat charterer] or prospective Owner(s) [bareboat charterer] of the Vessel as described in Part 2 "Vessel and Owner(s) Particulars" of this Application, that all information and particulars of the Vessel and the Owner(s) [bareboat charterer] or prospective Owner(s) [bareboat charterer] contained herein are true and correct and that the present or prospective Master of the said Vessel has been ordered or will be ordered and instructed, upon receipt of the vessel's Liberian Certificate of Registry and other Liberian Documents, to surrender the vessel previous documents issued by the Government of the Flag State as declared in Box 4 and to make the Vessel Markings required by Section 75 (1), (2) and (4) of the Liberian Maritime Law, as amended.

Submitted by:

Full Name	*(Print)*	
Citizen of		
Residing at[1]		
Title[2]		

_____   _____
Signature   *Date*

ACKNOWLEDGEMENT

Subscribed and Sworn Before me

this ___ day of _____ _____ (Year)

at _____

_____
Signature and Seal of Notary Public or other Officer
authorized by Liberian Law to administer oaths

Notes:
1.   Enter street address, city and country of residence or place of business.
2.   Enter President, Vice-President, Director, Secretary, Attorney-in-Fact, etc whichever title applies.

APPENDIX XI(E)

THE REPUBLIC OF LIBERIA
LIBERIA MARITIME AUTHORITY

8619 Westwood Center Drive
Suite 300
Vienna, Virginia 22182, USA
Tel: +1 703 790 3434
Fax: +1 703 790 5655
Email: safety@liscr.com
Web: www.liscr.com

Office of
Deputy Commissioner
of Maritime Affairs

INTERNATIONAL SAFETY MANAGEMENT (ISM) CODE
DECLARATION OF COMPANY

Under the ISM Code, the declared Safety Management Company must provide contact information to the Administration. In accordance with Section 1.1.2 of the ISM Code, "Company" means the Owner of a ship or any other organization or person such as the Manager, or the Bareboat Charter, who has assumed the responsibility for operation of the ship from the Shipowner and who on assuming such responsibility has agreed to take over all the duties and responsibility imposed by the Code. The undersigned affirms that:

Name:
Address:

Telephone: Fax:
E-Mail:

is the Owner of record of the following Liberian registered Ship(s):*

Ship Name:	Official Number:	IMO Number:

In accordance with Section 3.1 of the ISM Code, if the entity responsible for the operation of the ship is other than the above stated Owner, the Owner must report the full name and details of such entity to the Administration. If such is the case here, the undersigned affirms that the "Company" responsible for all the requirements imposed by the Code for the Liberian registered Ship(s) listed above is:

Company: Company IMO Number:
Address:
Telephone/ Work: Fax:
E-Mail:

The undersigned further understands that any change in "Company" must be reported in writing by facsimile or email to: safety@liscr.com within two full business days to the Deputy Commissioner of Maritime Affairs.

Chairman or C.E.O. of Shipowner
Date:_____

* Additional sheets may be attached if needed.

RLM-297   Rev. 10/13

434

APPENDIX XI(E)

THE REPUBLIC OF LIBERIA
LIBERIA MARITIME AUTHORITY

8619 Westwood Center Drive
Suite 300
Vienna, Virginia 22182, USA
Tel: +1 703 790 3434
Fax: +1 703 790 5655
Email: safety@liscr.com
Web: www.liscr.com

Office of
Deputy Commissioner
of Maritime Affairs

INTERNATIONAL SAFETY MANAGEMENT (ISM) CODE
DECLARATION OF DESIGNATED PERSON ASHORE

To ensure the safe operation of each ship and to provide a link between the "Company" and those onboard, every "Company", as appropriate, shall designate a person or persons ashore having direct access to the highest level of management. The responsibility and authority of the designated person or persons shall include monitoring the safety and pollution prevention aspects of the operation of each ship and to ensure that adequate resources and shore based support are applied, as required.

The undersigned affirms that (1) _____
(name of Designated Person Ashore)

and (2), as alternate, _____
(name of alternate Designated Person Ashore)

has(ve) been assigned pursuant to Liberian Maritime Regulation 2.35 and Section 4, of the ISM Code, as the "Designated Person(s) Ashore" for the following Liberian registered Ship(s):*

Ship Name:	Official Number:	IMO Number:

The undersigned has also undertaken that the said "Designated Person(s)" will be available to the Office of the Deputy Commissioner of Maritime Affairs for Marine Safety at any time, as follows:

Name:	
Address**:	
Telephone/ Work:	Fax:
Telephone After Hours:	Cell Phone/Pager:
E-Mail:	

The undersigned further understand that any change in the said "Designated Person(s)" must be reported in writing by facsimile or email to: safety@liscr.com within two full business days.

_____
Chairman or C.E.O. of "Company
Date: _____

* Additional sheets may be attached if needed.
** Full street address of the "Designated Person(s)" to which official correspondence and materials may be sent.

RLM-297   Rev. 10/13

APPENDIX XI(E)

APPENDIX V

DECLARATION OF COMPANY SECURITY OFFICER

(To be filled out by the Company Security Officer)

Dates should be in the format yyyy/mm/dd

	Information		
1	This will apply from (date):		
2	Name of ship:	IMO Number:	
	Name of ship:	IMO Number:	
	Name of ship:	IMO Number:	
	Name of ship:	IMO Number:	
	Name of ship:	IMO Number:	
	Name of ship:	IMO Number:	
	Name of ship:	IMO Number:	
	Name of ship:	IMO Number:	
3	Name of registered owner(s):		
4	Name of Company Security Officer, and Alternate CSO, Address(es) of its safety management activities if different form above: Phone: Fax: Mobil Phone: 24 hour number: Email:		

THIS IS TO CERTIFY THAT this record is correct in all respects
Issued by the Company: _____ Date of issue: _____

Signature of authorized person: _____

Name of authorized person: _____

RL 5004

ISP-002 **1 of 1** 04/04
The Republic of Liberia

APPENDIX XI(E)

ANNEX 3

THE REPUBLIC OF LIBERIA

APPLICATION FOR MINIMUM SAFE MANNING CERTIFICATE FOR

SHIPS WHICH MUST COMPLY WITH THE STCW REQUIREMENTS

NAME OF OWNER/OPERATOR:	PRESENT SHIP NAME:		
ADDRESSS:	PREVIOUS SHIP NAME:		
	O.N:	IMO NUMBER:	
PHONE: FAX: EMAIL:	DATE BUILT:	GROSS TONS:	NET TONS:
VESSEL TYPE:			
TRADING AREA(S):			

NUMBER OF MAIN ENGINES:	⊠ STEAM:⊠ or ⊠ MOTOR	TYPE OF BOILERS:
TYPE OF MOTOR:		TOTAL KW PROPULSION:
NO. OF GENERATORS:		TOTAL KW GENERATORS:
CLASSIFICATION SOCIETY:		
INDICATE CLASS NOTATIONS FOR UNATTENDED MACHINERY OPERATION, IF ANY:		
INDICATE CLASS NOTATION FOR INTEGRATED BRIDGE SYSTEMS, IF ANY:		
NO. OF LIFEBOATS:		NO. OF RESCUE BOATS:
NO. OF LIFERAFTS:		LIFERAFTS WITH LAUNCHING APPLIANCES:

OWNERS MINIMUM MANNING PROPOSAL

___Master ___ Chief Mate ___ Navigational Watch Officer ___Other (Describe) _____	___Able Seaman/Able Seafarer Deck ___ Ordinary Seaman ___ Other (Describe) _____	___Chief Engineer ___ Second Engineer ___Engineering Watch Officer ___Other (Describe) _____	___ Oilers/Motorman/Able Seafarer Engine ___ Fitter ___ Other (Describe) _____

The proposal shall take into account IMO Assembly resolution A.1047(27) and will be reviewed by Marine Safety Division. A minimum Safe Manning Certificate will be issued under authority of Maritime Regulation 10.292(5), provided all necessary information requested of owner has been provided. Proposals for reduced manning should attach additional information the owner feels supports his proposal. Catering Department personnel are not included in minimum safe manning unless they are trained general purpose personnel.

Print Name of Submitter: _____
(Applicant should be a nominated Decision Maker for the above Vessel).
Signature of Submitter: _____
Title: _____ DATE: _____

Mail Application To: Liberia Maritime Authority
c/o Liberian International Ship and Corporate Registry
Attn: Marine Safety Division
8619 Westwood Center Dr., Suite 300, Vienna, VA 22182, USA
Telephone: (703) 790-3434   Fax: (703) 790-5655

MSD 336RL   **5/13**

APPENDIX XI(F)

Malta forms

(1)   Application for the registration of a ship, form MS(R) 21
(2)   Declaration of ownership on behalf of a body corporate, form MS(R) 5
(3)   Bill of sale (body corporate), form MS(R) 11
(4)   Application for minimum safe manning certificate, form MSD 01
(5)   Application for bareboat charter registration of a ship, form MS(R) 21A

Note

Reproduced courtesy of Transport Malta.
For additional and updated forms see: www.transport.gov.mt/ship-registration

APPENDIX XI(F)

APPLICATION FOR THE REGISTRATION OF A SHIP
UNDER THE
(MALTA) MERCHANT SHIPPING ACT, 1973

A. GENERAL — IMO No *(if applicable):*

1. Proposed Name (a)	2. Propulsion (Sailing, Steam or Motor)	3. Service (B/Carrier, Cargo, Tanker, Pleasure Yacht, etc.)
4. If the ship has been anytime on the Malta Register State the Name under which it was registered and the Official Number	5. Country under laws of which Ship was last documented and present name of vessel	6. Proposed date of registry
7. Classification Society/Issuing Authority, if applicable (a) Class. Society: (c) SMC (ISM Code): (b) DOC (ISM code): (d) ISSC (ISPS Code):	8. Port where Ship will be at time of registry	9. Number of Seamen and Apprentices for whom accommodation is certified

B. TONNAGE AND REGISTER DIMENSIONS - *According to ITC 1969 (if applicable)*

10. Gross Tonnage	11. Net Tonnage	12. Length (metres) Art 2(8)	13. Breadth (metres) Reg 2(3)	14. Depth (metres) Reg 2(2)

C. HULL DESCRIPTION

15. Number of Decks	16. Number of Masts	17. Stem	18. Stern	19. Rigged	20. Build (Carvel/Clencher)	21. Framework (Steel, GRP etc)	22. Number of Bulkheads
23. Builders: Name			Address				24. When Built

D. PROPELLING ENGINES

25. Number	26. Description of Engines	27. Year of Make	28. Number of Cylinders	29. Horsepower (KW)
30. Makers: Name		Address		

E. OWNER/S

31. Name (b)	32. Passport No. (Individual) Partnership No. (Body Corporate)
33. Residence/Registered Office	34. Telephone No: Fax No:
35. Details of Ship's Manager (ISM Code)	36. Telephone No: Fax No: Telex No: Email: AOH No: Contact Person:
37. Details of Ship's Manager Agents	38. Telephone No: Fax No: Telex No: Email: AOH No: Contact Person:

39. I hereby declare that the vessel is fitted with a radio equipment. (c)

Application is hereby made for the registration of the above-described vessel as a Maltese ship under Part II of the Merchant Shipping Act, 1973. This vessel is documented under the laws of the country indicated in Item 5 above and evidence of the consent of that Government to the transfer of the vessel to Maltese Registry is enclosed herewith/will be produced within thirty days from the issue of a provisional Certificate of Malta Registry. (c)

Signature ....
Owner or duly authorised Agent

Date: .... Name and Description: ....

(a) Give alternative name/s in order of preference in case the first cannot be authorised.
(b) In case of body corporate give full title of company.
(c) Delete whichever is inapplicable.

MS(R) 21A

APPENDIX XI(F)

Form No. 8

Declaration of Ownership
on behalf of a Body Corporate as Owner or Transferee

Official Number	Name of Ship	Home Port	No., Year and Port of Registry
		VALLETTA	

Whether a Sailing, Steam or Motor Ship	Power of Engines, if any

	Metres	Centimetres
Length Article 2(8)		
Length Overall (in case where Article 2(8) of ITC does not apply)		
Breadth Regulation 2(3)		
Depth Regulation 2(2)		

NUMBER OF TONS		
Gross	Net	

and as described in more detail in the Certificate of the Surveyor and the Register Book.

I, the undersigned ....

of (a) ....

(b) .... of (c) ....

declare as follows :-

(i) The said body corporate, which has its registered office at ....
.... was established under the Laws of .... on the ....
day of .... 20 ....

(ii) The above general description of the ship is correct.

(iii) The said ship was built at .... in 20 ____ The time and place of her building are not known to me (d).

(iv) The said body corporate is entitled to be registered as owner of .... shares in the said Ship.

(v) To the best of my knowledge and belief, no person or body of persons other than such persons or body of persons as are by the Merchant Shipping Act, 1973 qualified to be owners of Maltese Ships, is entitled as owner, to any interest in the said ship or any share therein.

(vi) The said ship is free from Registered encumbrances.

I make this declaration conscientiously believing the same to be true.

Signature of Declarant ....

Made and subscribed the _____ day of .... 20 ____ by the above named ....

in the presence of (e) ....

Signature ....

(a) Address of person making the declaration.
(b) Office of person making declaration, Secretary or otherwise.
(c) Name of Body Corporate.
(d) Delete whichever is inapplicable
(e) Declarations must be made before a Registrar of Maltese Ships, a Commisioner for Oaths or a Maltese Consular Officer.
 The qualification of the persons taking the declaration, and the place of attestation, are to be added to his signature.

M.S. (R) 5.

APPENDIX XI(F)

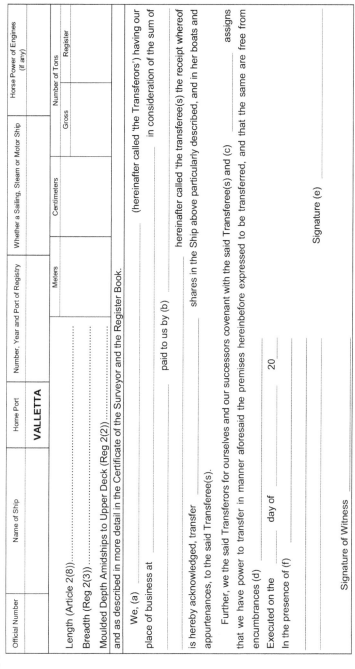

APPENDIX XI(F)

**APPLICATION FOR
MINIMUM SAFE MANNING CERTIFICATE**

Merchant Shipping Directorate

A. GENERAL

1. Name of Ship	2. Official Number	3. IMO Number
4. Type of Ship	5. Year of Build	

6. Area of Navigation (a)

Unlimited: ☐   Restricted: ☐

B. REGISTER DIMENSIONS

7. Length Overall	8. Beam	9. Certified Crew Accommodation
10. Gross Tonnage (ITC'69)	11. Gross Tonnage (Prior to ITC'69), if applicable	

C. PROPELLING ENGINES

12. Number and Description of Engine/s	13. BHP / KW	14. Speed (Knots)

15. Does vessel hold a valid Unmanned Machinery Space (UMS) documentary evidence	Yes ☐	No ☐	16. Bridge Control	Yes ☐	No ☐

D. LIFE SAVING APPLIANCES

17. Lifeboats

Type: Total Number: Total Capacity:

18. Thrown – In Type Liferafts	19. Davit Launched Liferafts
Total Number: Total Capacity:	Total Number: Total Capacity:

E. OTHER DETAILS

20. Type of Mooring Winches	21. External Communications
	WT ☐ RT ☐ GMDSS ☐

22. Unusual Characteristics or Special Features of Ship or Other Details

F. APPLICABLE ONLY FOR PASSENGER SHIPS

23. Number of Passengers that ship is certified to carry	24. Area of Navigation (b)

G. OWNER/CHARTERER/S AND MANAGERS

25. Name & Address of Registered Owners/Charterers	26. Telephone No: Fax No:

27. Name and Address of Managers	28. Telephone No:
	    Fax No:
	    E-Mail:
	    AOH No:
	    Contact Person:

I certify that to the best of my knowledge the particulars given by me in this form are correct.

Date _____   ....

(a) Where applicable, indicate Restricted Area of Navigation   Signature of Owner/Charterer/Manager/Authorised Agent
(b) If Restricted, indicate Consecutive Ports of Call

*Merchant Shipping Directorate Malta Transport Centre, Marsa MRS1917 Malta
Voice: +356 21 250360, 99494317 Fax: +356 21 241460 E-Mail: mershipmalta@transport.gov.mt*

APPENDIX XI(F)

**APPLICATION FOR BAREBOAT CHARTER REGISTRATION OF A SHIP
UNDER THE MERCHANT SHIPPING ACT**

A. GENERAL   IMO No:

1. Present Name	2. Where Built	3. When	4. Propulsion (Steam or Motor)
5. Port where ship will be at time of registry	6. If previously registered in Malta state Official Number		7. Underlying Registry

8. Classification Society/Issuing Authority, if applicable

(a) Classification Society   (b) DOC (ISM Code)   (c) SMC (ISM Code)   (d) ISSC (ISPS Code)   (e) MLC (Maritime Labour Convention)

B. HULL DESCRIPTION AND REGISTER DIMENSIONS

9. Name and Address of Builders	10. Description of Vessel

11. Number of Decks	12. Number of Masts	13. Stem	14. Stern	15. Build	16. Framework	17. Number of Bulkheads

18. Length (metres) Art 2(8) of ITC	19. Length Overall (in case where Art 2(8) does not apply)	20. Breadth (metres) Reg 2(3)	21. Depth (metres) Reg

C. PROPELLING ENGINES

22. Number and Description of Engines	23. When Built	24. Number of Cylinders	25. Main Propulsion Power

26. Name and Address of Makers

D. TONNAGE AND ACCOMMODATION

27. Gross Tonnage	28. Net Tonnage	29. Number of seafarers for whom accommodation is provided

E. CHARTERER

30. Name	31. Passport No. (Individual) Partnership No. (Body Corporate)
32. Residence/Registered Office	33. Telephone No:
34. Details of Ship's Manager (ISM Code) & Company Identification Number	35. Telephone No: Fax No: Email: AOH No: Contact Person:
36. Details of Ship's Manager Agents	37. Telephone No: Fax No: Email: AOH No: Contact Person:

Application is hereby made for the registration of the above-described vessel as a Maltese ship under Part IIA of the Merchant Shipping Act. This vessel is documented under the laws of the country indicated in item 7 above evidence of the consent of that Government/ registered owners/ and mortgagees to the registration of the vessel is enclosed herewith. (a)

Signature ....
Charterer or duly authorised Agent

Date ....   Name and Description ....
(a) Delete whichever is inapplicable.

MS(R) 21A

APPENDIX XI(G)

Marshall Islands forms

(1) Application for registration, form MI-101A
(2) Application for registration of newbuilding during construction, form MI-101B
(3) Application for bareboat charter registration, form MI – 101BCR
(4) Application for yacht registration, form MI-101Y
(5) ISM Code declaration of company, form MI-297A
(6) MLC/ISM/ISPS combined declaration, form MI-297-B
(7) Application for minimum safe manning certificate, form MI-336
(8) Application for minimum safe manning certificate – yachts, form MI-336Y

Note

Reproduced courtesy of International Registries, Inc.
For additional and updated forms see: www.register-iri.com

APPENDIX XI(G)

REPUBLIC OF THE MARSHALL ISLANDS
MARITIME ADMINISTRATOR
APPLICATION FOR REGISTRATION

Check all that apply:

Newbuilding ☐   Transfer from another flag ☐   Re-registration ☐   Laid-up ☐   Self-Propelled ☐   Non-Self-Propelled ☐

PART 1. GENERAL

NEW NAME	PRESENT NAME	IMO NUMBER

PRESENT COUNTRY OF REGISTRY	SERVICE TYPE	EXPECTED DATE OF REGISTRATION

PRESENT CLASSIFICATION SOCIETY	INTENDED CLASSIFICATION SOCIETY (only if changing at registration)

NAME OF REGISTERED OWNER(S)[1]	DOMICILE / ADDRESS (full address)	OWNER IMO NO.	CITIZENSHIP	OWNERSHIP %

[1] If more than one (1) Registered Owner, please attach an extra sheet.

PART 2. VESSEL PARTICULARS

BUILT BY	HULL NO.	YEAR BUILT	PLACE BUILT (City, Country)

KEEL LAYING DATE	DATE AND PLACE OF CONVERSION (if applicable)

DYNAMIC POSITIONING FITTED (if applicable)	TOTAL PROPELLING POWER	DEADWEIGHT TONS
☐ Yes ☐ No	KW	

AS PER ITC '69:

LENGTH	BREADTH	DEPTH	GROSS TONS	NET TONS

PART 3. INTERNATIONAL SAFETY MANAGEMENT (ISM) CODE DECLARATION OF COMPANY

Is the ISM Code applicable?   ☐ Yes   ☐ No   ☐ Voluntary
IMO ISM Code Company Number (if applicable):   Recognized Organization (RO) for Document of Compliance

If Yes/Voluntary, name the organization that has assumed the responsibility and duties for operation of the vessel and has agreed in writing to take over the duties and responsibilities imposed by the ISM Code from the owner or if No, name the organization responsible for the vessel: *(if unknown at the time of application, please complete form MI-297A prior to the date of registration).* [2]

Company Name [3]:
Address [3]:
Telephone: Facsimile: Email:

[2] Any change in ISM Code Company must be made in writing by submitting form MI-297A to the Republic of the Marshall Islands Maritime Administrator.
[3] Company Name and Address should be identical as per ISM Document of Compliance.

PART 4. BILLING PARTICULARS

Billing, including annual tonnage tax and maritime invoices, after vessel registration should be sent to the following address(es):

☐ Check if Maritime Invoices information is same as Annual Tonnage Tax Invoice information.

ANNUAL TONNAGE TAX INVOICES	MARITIME INVOICES
Company:	Company:
Attention:	Attention:
Address:	Address:
Telephone:	Telephone:
Email:	Email:

1 of 2   MI-101A (Rev. 8/15)

APPENDIX XI(G)

PART 5. INSTRUMENT RECORDATION

Do you intend to record a mortgage ($\square$), financing charter ($\square$), bill of sale[5] ($\square$), or builder's certificate ($\square$)?
[5] Required for re-registration.

PART 6. OATH OF OWNER OR AUTHORIZED AGENT

I _____ , a citizen of _____ ,
hereby swear and affirm, in accordance with Section 209(1) of the Republic of the Marshall Islands (RMI) Maritime Act, that I am a duly authorized agent or officer of the owner(s), managing owner(s), or part owner(s) of the vessel as described in Part 1 herein and declare that all information contained in Parts 1 through 5 herein are true and correct and that, pursuant to Section 214(1) of the RMI Maritime Act, the Master has been ordered and instructed, upon receipt of the vessel's RMI Provisional Certificate of Registry, to make the markings required by Section 230 of the RMI Maritime Act, and when transferring from another flag, to surrender the vessel's documents issued by the Government of the Present Country of Registry as declared in Part 1 herein. I further hereby swear and affirm that the official tonnage of the vessel shall be the tonnage as calculated in accordance with the International Convention on Tonnage Measurement of Ships, 1969, ifsuch calculation is different than as declared hereinabove.

Subscribed and Sworn Before me

this _____ day of _____ 20 ____   _____
at _____   (SIGNATURE)

_____   _____
SIGNATURE OF NOTARY PUBLIC, OR OTHER OFFICER AUTHORIZED   (TITLE)
BY RMI LAW TO ADMINISTER OATHS

SECTIONS 7, 8 AND 9 MAY BE COMPLETED IF INFORMATION IS AVAILABLE AT THE TIME OF APPLICATION.
IF UNKNOWN AT THE TIME OF APPLICATION DECLARATION FORM MI-297B MUST BE COMPLETED

PART 7. DECLARATION OF RO FOR THE MARITIME LABOUR CONVENTION, 2006 (MLC, 2006)

Is MLC, 2006 Certification applicable? $\square$ Yes $\square$ No $\square$ Voluntary	
Is a National Statement of Compliance being requested for mobile offshore units? $\square$ Yes $\square$ No	
The RO appointed for the issuance of a Maritime Labour Certificate (MLC) to the vessel is:	

PART 8. DECLARATION OF DESIGNATED PERSON ASHORE (DPA), DESIGNATED PERSON (DP), RO

Ifthe ISM Code is Yes/Voluntary, name ofthe RO appointed for the issuance of a Safety Management Certificate (SMC):

Pursuant to RMI Maritime Regulation 1.07, the DPA(s) (for ISM Code vessels) or DP(s) (for non-ISM Code vessels) is/are:

Name of $\square$ DPA or $\square$ DP:		
Telephone:	24-hour Mobile Telephone:	Email:
Name of $\square$ Alternate DPA or $\square$ Alternate DP:		
Telephone:	24-hour Mobile Telephone:	Email:

PART 9. DECLARATIONOFRECOGNIZEDSECURITYORGANIZATION(RSO)/COMPANYSECURITYOFFICER (CSO)

Is the International Ship and Port Facility Security (ISPS) Code applicable? $\square$ Yes $\square$ No $\square$ Voluntary	
IfYes/Voluntary, name the RSO appointed for the issuance of an International Ship Security Certificate (ISSC):	

Pursuant to Chapter XI-2, Regulation 4, of the International Convention for the Safety of Life at Sea, 1974, as amended, and the ISPS Code the CSO(s) is/are:

Name of CSO:		
Telephone:	24-hour Mobile Telephone:	Email:
Name of Alternate CSO:		
Telephone:	24-hour Mobile Telephone:	Email:

The undersigned affirms that he/she is authorized to act on behalf of the Company and that the information contained in Parts 7, 8 and 9 herein are true and correct and that any change in DPA(s), DP(s), CSO(s), (RO)s or RSO(s) must immediately be made in writing by submitting the appropriate form(s) to the Administrator, electronically or otherwise.

_____   _____   _____
Print Name & Title   Signature   Date

2 of 2   MI-101A (Rev. 8/15)

446

APPENDIX XI(G)

REPUBLIC OF THE MARSHALL ISLANDS
MARITIME ADMINISTRATOR

APPLICATION FOR OFFICIAL NUMBER, CALL SIGN AND PROVISIONAL CERTIFICATE OF INTENDED REGISTRATION OF NEWBUILDING, DURING CONSTRUCTION AT BUILDER'S YARD

Check all that apply:

Self-Propelled ☐   Non-Self-Propelled ☐   Commercial Yacht ☐   Private Yacht ☐   Passenger Yacht ☐
For Yachts Only – Desired Port of Registry: (Select One)   Jaluit ☐   Bikini ☐

PART 1. GENERAL

PROPOSED NAME OF VESSEL			IMO NUMBER	
START DATE OF PHYSICAL CONSTRUCTION OR ASSEMBLY		SERVICE TYPE	EXPECTED DATE OF DELIVERY	
PRESENT CLASSIFICATION SOCIETY		INTENDED CLASSIFICATION SOCIETY (only if changing at registration)		
NAME OF REGISTERED OWNER[1]	DOMICILE / ADDRESS (full address)	OWNER IMO NO.	CITIZENSHIP	OWNERSHIP %

[1] List the Registered Owner in accordance with §203(f) of the Republic of the Marshall Islands Maritime Act. If more than one (1) Registered Owner, please attach an extra sheet.

PART 2. VESSEL PARTICULARS

BUILT BY			PLACE BUILT (City, Country)		
HULL NO.	DYNAMIC POSITIONING FITTED LEVEL (if applicable) ☐ Yes ☐ No		TOTAL PROPELLING POWER KW	DEADWEIGHT TONS	
AS PER ITC '69 OR ESTIMATES:					
LENGTH	BREADTH	DEPTH		GROSS TONS	NET TONS

PART 3. BILLING PARTICULARS

Billing, including annual tonnage tax and maritime invoices, after vessel registration should be sent to the following address(es):
☐ Check if Maritime Invoices information is same as Annual Tonnage Tax Invoice information.

ANNUAL TONNAGE TAX INVOICES	MARITIME INVOICES
Company:	Company:
Attention:	Attention:
Address:	Address:
Telephone:	Telephone:
Email:	Email:

1 of 2   MI-101B (Rev. 7/15)

APPENDIX XI(G)

PART 4. OATH OF OWNER OR AUTHORIZED AGENT

I _____ , a citizen of _____ ,
hereby swear and affirm, in accordance with Section 209(1) of the Republic of the Marshall Islands (RMI) Maritime Act, that I am a duly authorized agent or officer of the owner(s), managing owner(s), or part owner(s) of the vessel as described in Part 1 herein and declare that all information contained in Parts 1 through 3 herein are true and correct and that, pursuant to Section 214(1) of the RMI Maritime Act, in the event the vessel receives a RMI Provisional Certificate of Registry, the Master shall be ordered and instructed to make the markings required by Section 230 of the RMI Maritime Act. I further hereby swear and affirm that the official tonnage of the vessel shall be the tonnage as calculated in accordance with the International Convention on Tonnage Measurement of Ships, 1969, if such calculation is different than as declared hereinabove.

Subscribed and Sworn Before me
this _____ day of _____ 20 _____   _____
                                                                                                                  (SIGNATURE)

at _____

_____   _____
SIGNATURE OF NOTARY PUBLIC, OR OTHER OFFICER AUTHORIZED   (TITLE)
BY RMI LAW TO ADMINISTER OATHS

2 of 2   MI-101B (Rev. 7/15)

APPENDIX XI(G)

REPUBLIC OF THE MARSHALL ISLANDS
MARITIME ADMINISTRATOR

APPLICATION FOR BAREBOAT CHARTER REGISTRATION

Check if applicable: ☐ Self-propelled   ☐ Non-self-propelled

PART 1. GENERAL

NEW NAME	PRESENT NAME	IMO NUMBER

PRESENT COUNTRY OF REGISTRY	SERVICE TYPE	EXPECTED DATE OF REGISTRATION

PRESENT CLASSIFICATION SOCIETY	INTENDED CLASSIFICATION SOCIETY (only if changing at registration)

NAME OF REGISTERED OWNER[1]	DOMICILE / ADDRESS (full address)	OWNER IMO NO.	CITIZENSHIP	OWNERSHIP %

NAME OF BAREBOAT CHARTERER[1]	DOMICILE / ADDRESS (full address)	CITIZENSHIP	OWNERSHIP %

[1] If more than one (1) Registered Owner or Bareboat Charterer, please attach an extra sheet.

PART 2. VESSEL PARTICULARS

BUILT BY	HULL NO.	YEAR BUILT	PLACE BUILT (City, Country)

KEEL LAYING DATE	DATE AND PLACE OF CONVERSION (if applicable)

DYNAMIC POSITIONING FITTED (if applicable) ☐ Yes ☐ No	TOTAL PROPELLING POWER KW	DEADWEIGHT TONS

AS PER ITC '69:

LENGTH	BREADTH	DEPTH	GROSS TONS	NET TONS

PART 3. INTERNATIONAL SAFETY MANAGEMENT (ISM) CODE DECLARATION OF COMPANY

Is the ISM Code applicable?   ☐ Yes   ☐ No   ☐ Voluntary
IMO ISM Code Company Number (if applicable):   Recognized Organization (RO) for Document of Compliance

If Yes/Voluntary, name the organization that has assumed the responsibility and duties for operation of the vessel and has agreed in writing to take over the duties and responsibilities imposed by the ISM Code from the owner or if No, name the organization responsible for the vessel: *(if unknown at the time of application, please complete form MI-297A prior to the date of registration).* [2]

Company Name:[3]
Address:[3]
Telephone: Facsimile: Email:

[2] Any change in ISM Code Company must be made in writing by submitting form MI-297A to the Republic of the Marshall Islands Maritime Administrator.
[3] Company Name and Address should be identical as per ISM Document of Compliance.

PART 4. BILLING PARTICULARS

Billing, including annual tonnage tax and maritime invoices after vessel registration, should be sent to the following address(es):
☐ Check if Maritime Invoices information is same as Annual Tonnage Tax Invoice information.

ANNUAL TONNAGE TAX INVOICES	MARITIME INVOICES
Company:	Company:
Attention:	Attention:
Address:	Address:
Telephone:	Telephone:
Email:	Email:

1 of 2   MI-101BCR (Rev. 7/15)

449

APPENDIX XI(G)

PART 5. INSTRUMENT RECORDATION

Do you intend to record a Notice of Foreign mortgage (☐) or a Notice of Foreign Finance Lease/Charter (☐)?

PART 6. OATH OF BAREBOAT CHARTER OR AUTHORIZED AGENT

I _____ , a citizen of _____ , hereby swear and affirm, in accordance with Sections 209(1) and 260(1) of the Republic of the Marshall Islands (RMI) Maritime Act, that I am a duly authorized agent or officer of the bareboat charterer(s) of the vessel as described in Part 1 herein and declare that all information contained in Parts 1 through 5 herein are true and correct and that, pursuant to Section 214(1) of the RMI Maritime Act, the Master has been ordered and instructed, upon receipt of the vessel's RMI Provisional Certificate of Registry, to make the markings required by Section 230 of the RMI Maritime Act, and when transferring from another flag, to surrender the vessel's documents issued by the Government of the Present Country of Registry as declared in Part 1 herein. I further hereby swear and affirm that the official tonnage of the vessel shall be the tonnage as calculated in accordance with the International Convention on Tonnage Measurement of Ships, 1969, if such calculation is different than as declared hereinabove.

Subscribed and Sworn Before me
this _____ day of _____ 20 ____   _____
at _____   (SIGNATURE)

_____   _____
SIGNATURE OF NOTARY PUBLIC, OR OTHER OFFICER AUTHORIZED   (TITLE)
BY RMI LAW TO ADMINISTER OATHS

SECTIONS 7, 8 AND 9 MAY BE COMPLETED IF INFORMATION IS AVAILABLE AT THE TIME OF APPLICATION.
IF UNKNOWN AT THE TIME OF APPLICATION DECLARATION FORM MI-297B MUST BE COMPLETED

PART 7. DECLARATION OF RO FOR THE MARITIME LABOUR CONVENTION, 2006 (MLC, 2006)

Is MLC, 2006 Certification applicable? ☐ Yes ☐ No ☐ Voluntary	
Is a National Statement of Compliance being requested for mobile offshore units? ☐ Yes ☐ No	
The RO appointed for the issuance of a Maritime Labour Certificate (MLC) to the vessel is:	

PART 8. DECLARATION OF DESIGNATED PERSON ASHORE (DPA), DESIGNATED PERSON (DP), RO

If the ISM Code is Yes/Voluntary, name of the RO appointed for the issuance of a Safety Management Certificate (SMC):

Pursuant to RMI Maritime Regulation 1.07, the DPA(s) (for ISM Code vessels) or DP(s) (for non-ISM Code vessels) is/are:

Name of ☐ DPA or ☐ DP:		
Telephone:	24-hour Mobile Telephone:	Email:
Name of ☐ Alternate DPA or ☐ Alternate DP:		
Telephone:	24-hour Mobile Telephone:	Email:

PART 9. DECLARATION OF RECOGNIZED SECURITY ORGANIZATION (RSO)/COMPANY SECURITY OFFICER (CSO)

Is the International Ship and Port Facility Security (ISPS) Code applicable? ☐ Yes ☐ No ☐ Voluntary

If Yes/Voluntary, name the RSO appointed for the issuance of an International Ship Security Certificate (ISSC):

Pursuant to Chapter XI-2, Regulation 4, of the International Convention for the Safety of Life at Sea, 1974, as amended, and the ISPS Code the CSO(s) is/are:

Name of CSO:		
Telephone:	24-hour Mobile Telephone:	Email:
Name of Alternate CSO:		
Telephone:	24-hour Mobile Telephone:	Email:

The undersigned affirms that he/she is authorized to act on behalf of the Company and that the information contained in Parts 7, 8 and 9 herein are true and correct and that any change in DPA(s), DP(s), CSO(s), (RO)s or RSO(s) must immediately be made in writing by submitting the appropriate form(s) to the Administrator, electronically or otherwise.

Print Name & Title	Signature	Date

MI-101BCR (Rev. 7/15)

APPENDIX XI(G)

REPUBLIC OF THE MARSHALL ISLANDS
MARITIME ADMINISTRATOR
APPLICATION FOR YACHT REGISTRATION

Service Type: Private Yacht (PY): ☐   Commercial Yacht (CY): ☐   Passenger Yacht (PAXY): ☐
(Application must be accompanied by the appropriate MI-127 Declaration)

DESIRED PORT OF REGISTRY (SELECT ONE):   JALUIT ☐   BIKINI ☐
PAYMENT TERM (SELECT ONE):   ONE YEAR ☐   THREE YEARS ☐

PART 1. GENERAL

NEW NAME	PRESENT NAME	IMO NUMBER (required if ≥300 GT):

PRESENT COUNTRY OF REGISTRY	YACHT TYPE Sail ☐ / Motor ☐	EXPECTED DATE OF REGISTRATION
PRESENT CLASSIFICATION SOCIETY (if applicable)	INTENDED CLASSIFICATION SOCIETY (only if applicable and changing at registration)	

NAME OF REGISTERED OWNER[1]	DOMICILE / ADDRESS (full address)	OWNER IMO NO. (optional)	CITIZENSHIP	OWNERSHIP %

[1] If more than one (1) Registered Owner, please attach an extra sheet.

PART 2. YACHT PARTICULARS

BUILT BY	HULL NO.	YEAR BUILT	PLACE BUILT (City, Country)
KEEL LAYING DATE	DATE AND PLACE OF CONVERSION (if applicable)	MAX. NO. OF PERSONS TO BE CARRIED INCL. CREW	

DYNAMIC POSITIONING FITTED (if applicable) ☐ Yes ☐ No	TOTAL PROPELLING POWER KW	DEADWEIGHT TONS (if known)	LENGTH OVERALL (LOA)

PER INTERNATIONAL / NATIONAL TONNAGE CERTIFICATE (in Meters)

LENGTH	BREADTH	DEPTH	GROSS TONS	NET TONS

NO. OF MAIN ENGINES:	KW PROPULSION PER ENGINE:

PART 3. INTERNATIONAL SAFETY MANAGEMENT (ISM) CODE DECLARATION OF COMPANY

Is the ISM Code applicable?   ☐ Yes   ☐ No   ☐ Voluntary
IMO ISM Code Company Number (if applicable):   Recognized Organization (RO) for Document of Compliance

If Yes/Voluntary, name the organization that has assumed the responsibility and duties for operation of the yacht and has agreed in writing to take over the duties and responsibilities imposed by the ISM Code from the owner or if No, name the organization responsible for the yacht: *(if unknown at the time of application, please complete form MI-297A prior to the date of registration).*[2]

Company Name [3]:
Address [3]:
Telephone: Facsimile: Email:

[2] Any change in ISM Code Company must be made in writing by submitting form MI-297A to the Republic of the Marshall Islands Maritime Administrator.
[3] Company Name and Address should be identical as per ISM Document of Compliance.

PART 4. BILLING PARTICULARS

Billing, including annual tonnage tax and maritime invoices, after yacht registration should be sent to the following address(es):
☐ Check if Maritime Invoices information is same as Annual Tonnage Tax Invoice information.

ANNUAL TONNAGE TAX INVOICES	MARITIME INVOICES
Company:	Company:
Attention:	Attention:
Address:	Address:
Telephone:	Telephone:
Email:	Email:

1 of 2   MI-101Y (8/15)

APPENDIX XI(G)

PART 5. INSTRUMENT RECORDATION

Do you intend to record a mortgage (☐), financing charter (☐), bill of sale[5] (☐), or builder's certificate (☐)?
[5] Required for re-registration.

PART 6. OATH OF OWNER OR AUTHORIZED AGENT

I _____ , a citizen of _____ , hereby swear and affirm, in accordance with Section 209(1) of the Republic of the Marshall Islands (RMI) Maritime Act, that I am a duly authorized agent or officer of the owner(s), managing owner(s), or part owner(s) of the yacht as described in Part 1 herein and declare that all information contained in Parts 1 through 5 herein are true and correct and that, pursuant to Section 214(1) of the RMI Maritime Act, the Master has been ordered and instructed, upon receipt of the yacht's RMI Certificate of Registry, to make the markings required by Section 230 of the RMI Maritime Act, and when transferring from another flag, to surrender the yacht's documents issued by the Government of the Present Country of Registry as declared in Part 1 herein. I further hereby swear and affirm that, the official tonnage of the yacht shall be the tonnage as calculated in accordance with the International Convention on Tonnage Measurement of Ships, 1969 or as stated on the National Tonnage Certificate, if such calculation or stated tonnage is different than as declared hereinabove.

Subscribed and Sworn Before me

this _____ day of _____ 20 _____

at _____

_____
(SIGNATURE)

_____
SIGNATURE OF NOTARY PUBLIC, OR OTHER OFFICER AUTHORIZED
BY RMI LAW TO ADMINISTER OATHS

_____
(TITLE)

===

SECTIONS 7, 8 AND 9 MAY BE COMPLETED IF INFORMATION IS AVAILABLE AT THE TIME OF APPLICATION.
IF UNKNOWN AT THE TIME OF APPLICATION DECLARATION FORM MI-297B MUST BE COMPLETED

PART 7. DECLARATION OF RO FOR THE MARITIME LABOUR CONVENTION, 2006 (MLC, 2006)

Is MLC, 2006 Certification applicable? ☐ Yes ☐ No ☐ Voluntary
The RO appointed for the issuance of a Maritime Labour Certificate (MLC) to the yacht is:

PART 8. DECLARATION OF DESIGNATED PERSON ASHORE (DPA), DESIGNATED PERSON (DP), RO

If the ISM Code is Yes/Voluntary, name of the RO appointed for the issuance of a Safety Management Certificate (SMC):
Pursuant to RMI Maritime Regulation 1.07, the DPA(s) (for ISM Code vessels) or DP(s) (for non-ISM Code vessels) is/are:

Name of ☐ DPA or ☐ DP:		
Telephone:	24-hour Mobile Telephone:	Email:
Name of ☐ Alternate DPA or ☐ Alternate DP:		
Telephone:	24-hour Mobile Telephone:	Email:

PART 9. DECLARATION OF RECOGNIZED SECURITY ORGANIZATION (RSO)/COMPANY SECURITY OFFICER (CSO)

Is the International Ship and Port Facility Security (ISPS) Code applicable? ☐ Yes ☐ No ☐ Voluntary
If Yes/Voluntary, name the RSO appointed for the issuance of an International Ship Security Certificate (ISSC):

Pursuant to Chapter XI-2, Regulation 4, of the International Convention for the Safety of Life at Sea, 1974, as amended, and the ISPS Code the CSO(s) is/are:

Name of CSO:		
Telephone:	24-hour Mobile Telephone:	Email:
Name of Alternate CSO:		
Telephone:	24-hour Mobile Telephone:	Email:

The undersigned affirms that he/she is authorized to act on behalf of the Company and that the information contained in Parts 7 and 8 herein are true and correct and that any change in DPA(s), DP(s), CSO(s), (RO)s or RSO(s) must immediately be made in writing by submitting the appropriate form(s) to the Administrator, electronically or otherwise.

Print Name & Title	Signature	Date

APPENDIX XI(G)

REPUBLIC OF THE MARSHALL ISLANDS
MARITIME ADMINISTRATOR

11495 Commerce Park Drive
Reston, Virginia 20191-1506 USA
Tel: +1-703-620-4880
Fax: +1-703-476-8522
Email: maritime@register-iri.com

DECLARATION OF COMPANY

Is the International Safety Management (ISM) Code applicable? ☐ Yes   ☐ No   ☐ Voluntary

International Maritime Organization (IMO) ISM Code Company Number (if applicable):

Recognized Organization (RO) for ISM Document of Compliance:

If Yes/Voluntary, name the organization that has assumed the responsibility and duties for operation of the below listed vessel(s) and has agreed in writing to take over the duties and responsibilities imposed by the ISM Code from the owner or if No, name the organization responsible for the below listed vessel(s):

Company Name: [1]
Address: [1]

Telephone: **Facsimile:**   **Email:** [2]

Vessel Name(s)[3]	Official Number(s)	IMO Number(s)

The undersigned affirms that the Company listed above has agreed in writing to assume all of the duties and responsibilities for the Republic of the Marshall Islands (RMI) registered vessel(s) listed above or as attached hereto, that the information contained herein is true and correct and that the undersigned is authorized to act on behalf of the Registered Owner, _____ ,
and acknowledges that any change in Company must be made in writing by submitting this form to the RMI Maritime Administrator, electronically or otherwise.

_____
Print Name & Title (on behalf of Registered Owner)   Signature   Date

---

[1] Company Name and Address should be identical as per ISM Document of Compliance.
[2] **Email is the primary mode of communication of vital and necessary information between the RMI MaritimeAdministrator and the Company. Maintenance of a viable email address is a requirement for registration under the flag.**
[3] For more than six (6) vessels, attach additional sheets.

MI-297A (Rev 8/15)

APPENDIX XI(G)

REPUBLIC OF THE MARSHALL ISLANDS
MARITIME ADMINISTRATOR

11495 Commerce Park Drive
Reston, Virginia 20191-1506 USA
Tel: +1-703-620-4880
Fax: +1-703-476-8522
Email: maritime@register-iri.com

COMBINED DECLARATION FORM
For the purpose of changing or adding information
(Excluding Declaration of Company)[1]

Vessel Name(s) [2]	Official Number(s)	IMO Number(s)

Maritime Labour Convention, 2006 (MLC, 2006)

Is MLC, 2006 Certification applicable? ☐ Yes ☐ No ☐ Voluntary	
Is a National Statement of Compliance being requested for a mobile offshore unit? ☐ Yes ☐ No	
The Recognized Organization (RO) appointed for the issuance of a Maritime Labour Certificate (MLC) to the vessel is:	

International Safety Management (ISM) Code[3]

Is the ISM Code applicable? ☐ Yes ☐ No ☐ Voluntary
The RO appointed for the issuance of a Safety Management Certificate (SMC) to the vessel is:

Designated Person Ashore (DPA) (for ISM Code vessels) / Designated Person (DP) (for non-ISM Code vessels)

Name of ☐ DPA or ☐ DP:	
Daytime Telephone:	Nighttime Telephone:
24-hour Mobile Telephone:	Email:[4]
Name of ☐ Alternate DPA or ☐ Alternate DP:	
Telephone:	Email:[4]

International Ship and Port Facility Security (ISPS) Code[5]

Is the ISPS Code applicable? ☐ Yes ☐ No ☐ Voluntary
The Recognized Security Organization (RSO) appointed for the issuance of an International Ship Security Certificate (ISSC) is:

Company Security Officer (CSO)

Name of CSO:	
Daytime Telephone:	Nighttime Telephone:
24-hour Mobile Telephone:	Email:[4]
Name of Alternate CSO:	
Telephone:	Email:[4]

The undersigned affirms that he/she is authorized to act on behalf of the below Company:

Company Name:	IMO Company Number (if applicable):

and that the information contained herein is true and correct and that any change in DPA(s), DP(s), CSO(s), RO(s) or RSO(s) must immediately be made in writing by submitting this form to the Republic of the Marshall Islands Maritime Administrator, electronically or otherwise.

Print Name & Title (on behalf of the Company)   Signature   Date

---

[1] See Declaration of Company form MI-297A.
[2] For more than three (3) vessels, one (1) Alternate DPA and/or one (1) Alternate CSO, attach additional sheets.
[3] To ensure the safe operation of each vessel and to provide a link between the Company and those on board, every Company, as defined in the ISM Code, shall designate a DPA, the responsibilities of which are addressed in Marine Notice 2-011-13, having direct access to the highest level of management.
[4] Email is the primary mode of communication of vital and necessary information between the Republic of the Marshall Islands Maritime Administrator and the DPA(s)/CSO(s). Maintenance of a viable email address is a requirement for registration under the flag.
[5] To ensure maritime security aboard vessels operated by the Company and to fulfill the obligations set forth in Part A, Section 11, of the ISPS Code, each Company shall designate a CSO the responsibilities of which are addressed in Marine Notice 2-011-16.

MI-297B (Rev. 8/15)

APPENDIX XI(G)

Republic of the Marshall Islands
Office of the Maritime Administrator

APPLICATION FOR MINIMUM SAFE MANNING CERTIFICATE

Owner/Operator Name:	Address:
Point of Contact Name:	
Phone Number:	Email:
Vessel Name:	Previous Vessel Name:
Official Number:	IMO Number:
Type:	Delivery Date:
Gross Tonnage:	Net Tonnage:
Trading Route:	
Number of Main Engines:	Type of Boilers:
KW Propulsion:	Periodically Unattended Machinery Space: ☐ Yes ☐ No
Steam: ☐ Yes ☐ No	Motor: ☐ Yes ☐ No
Indicate Class Notations for Unattended Machinery Operation if any:	
Classification Society:	
Number of Lifeboats:	Number of Rescue Boats:
Number of Life Rafts:	Life Rafts with Launching Appliances:

<u>**FOR NEW REGISTRATIONS ONLY**</u>

Expected Date of Registration: _____

Expected Location of Registration: _____

Comments/Special operational considerations or vessel configurations that may affect manning:

This application will be reviewed by the Maritime Administrator and a Minimum Manning Certificate under the authority of Maritime Regulation 7.38.6, will be issued, subject to all necessary information requested being provided. Special proposals or requests for non-standard manning should be attached to this application with complete support documentation.

Print Name of Applicant: _____

Title: _____   Date: _____

Signature of Applicant: _____

Questions regarding manning and training requirements may be addressed to: seafarers@register-iri.com.

Rev. 12/13   MI-336

APPENDIX XI(G)

Republic of the Marshall Islands
Maritime Administrator

APPLICATION FOR MINIMUM SAFE MANNING CERTIFICATE - YACHT

Owner/Operator Name:	Address:
Point of Contact Name:	
Phone Number:	Email:
Name of Yacht:	Previous Name of Yacht (if applicable):
Official Number:	IMO Number:
Length (LWL):	Delivery Date:
Gross Tonnage:	Material of Hull:
Area of Operation: ☐ <60 nm (2)　　　☐ 60 – 150 nm (1)　　　☐ unlimited (0)	
Number of Main Engines:	Number of Crew Berths:
KW Propulsion per Engine:	Number of Guest/Passenger Berths:
Motor: ☐　　　　Sail: ☐	
Classification Society and/or Appointed Representative:	
Type of Registry:	

FOR NEW REGISTRATIONS ONLY

Expected Date of Registration: _____

Expected Location of Registration: _____

Comments / Special operational considerations or vessel configurations that may affect manning:

This application will be reviewed by the Maritime Administrator and a Minimum Safe Manning Certificate will be issued under the authority of Maritime Regulation 7.38.6, subject to all necessary information requested being provided. Special proposals or requests for non-standard manning should be attached to this application with complete supporting documentation.

Print Name of Applicant: _____

Title: _____　　Date: _____

Signature of Applicant: _____

Questions regarding manning and training requirements may be addressed to: seafarers@register-iri.com.

Rev. 10/15　　　　　　　　　　　　　　　　　　　　　　　　　　　　　　　　MI-336Y

APPENDIX XI(H)

Norway forms

(1) Application for certificate of name, form KR – 0019/E
(2) Notification of registration, form KR – 0010/E
(3) Declaration concerning nationality – limited company or equivalent, form KR 0002/E
(4) Declaration concerning nationality – s.33 Norwegian Maritime Act, form KR – 0005/E
(5) Appointment of process agent/Norwegian representative, form KR – 0060E
(6) Bill of sale, form KR – 0020E
(7) Notification of amendment, form KR – 0008E
(8) Notification of deletion, form KR – 0009/E
(9) Notification of assignment of responsibilities – Ship Safety Act, form KR – 0061E
(10) Notification of assignment of responsibilities – ISM Code, form KR – 0014E

Note

Reproduced courtesy of the Norwegian Maritime Authority.
For additional and updated forms see: www.sdir.no/en/forms-directory/

APPENDIX XI(H)

Sjøfartsdirektoratet
Norwegian Maritime Authority

NIS // NOR

APPLICATION FOR CERTIFICATE OF NAME

THE VESSEL IS TO BE REGISTERED IN/ IS REGISTERED IN:

☐ THE NORWEGIAN INTERNATIONAL SHIP REGISTER - NIS

☐ THE NORWEGIAN SHIP REGISTER (NOR) - applicable for vessels 15 metres or more

DESIRED NAME, PRIORITIZED:	
1.	
2.	
3.	
PREVIOUS NAME:	
NORWEGIAN CALL SIGN:	(If allocated/)
IMO NO:	(If allocated)
FOR SIGNATURES- PLEASE SEE PAGE 2	

FOR INTERNAL USE BY THE SHIP REGISTER:	
SHIP NAME APPROVED/ DATE:	
CASE OFFICER:	
ENDORSED BY:	

ONLY TO BE COMPLETED FOR NEW REGISTRATIONS:

VESSEL	THE VESSEL HAS PREVIOUSLY BEEN REGISTERED IN:	☐ NIS ☐ NOR ☐ THE NORWEGIAN SHIPBUILDING REGISTER ☐ OTHER
	Approved HOME PORT in Norway	
	HULL NO:	
	HULL BUILT BY: (name, address, country)	
	YARD NO. FOR THE COMPLETED SHIP:	
	SHIPBUILDING COMPLETED BY YARD (name, address, country)	
	YEAR BUILT:	
	SHIP TYPE:	
	BUILDING MATERIAL	☐ ALUMINIUM ☐ IRON ☐ CONCRETE ☐ COMPOSITE ☐ FERROCEMENT ☐ PLASTIC ☐ GLASS FIBRE ☐ STEEL ☐ RUBBER CANVAS ☐ WOOD ☐ OTHER:

SEND DIRECTLY TO
The Norwegian Maritime Authority, Ship Registers (Nis/Nor)
P.O. Box 73, Nygårdstangen
N-5838 BERGEN

(SIDE 1 AV 3 SIDER)

KR-0019/E Amended 12/2011

SEND DIRECTLY TO
The Norwegian Maritime Authority, Ship Registers (Nis/Nor)
P.O. Box 73, Nygårdstangen
N-5838 BERGEN

APPENDIX XI(H)

Sjøfartsdirektoratet
Norwegian Maritime Authority

NIS // NOR

VESSEL	PROPULSION	☐ ENGINE ☐ SAILS ☐ NO MEANS OF PROPULSION
		☐ STEAM ☐ TURBINE
		☐ OTHER
	CLASSIFICATION SOCIETY (if applicable)	
	GROSS TONNAGE	
	EXPECTED TIME OF DELIVERY:	

☐ The ship is abroad. A Provisional Certificate of Nationality is needed. Please use form KR-0011 (available in Norwegian only)

1.

OWNER:	NAME:	
	ORG.NO./ PERSONAL ID.NO (11 digits)	
	E-MAIL:	
	PHONE:	FAX:

2.

APPLICATION FOR NAME MADE BY:	NAME:	
	ORG.NO/ PERSONAL ID.NO (11 digits)	
	E-MAIL:	
	PHONE:	FAX:

Signature (owner or applicant)

_____   _____
Place   Date

_____
Signature: to be repeated in capital letters

Application should be forwarded to: post@nis-nor.no, marked "Application for Name"

PLEASE NOTE:
- Certificate of *Name* is a reservation, valid for 5 years
- Owner must send a written request to the register when the change of name is to be registered

If this application is also to be used as a request for imminent change
- see next page

SEND DIRECTLY TO
The Norwegian Maritime Authority, Ship Registers (Nis/Nor)
P.O. Box 73, Nygårdstangen
N-5838 BERGEN

(SIDE 2 AV 3 SIDER)   KR-0019/E Amended 12/2011

APPENDIX XI(H)

SENDER / REQUISITIONER is responsible for the fee related to the registration. An invoice will be forwarded		JOURNAL STAMP
Name		
Organisation number or National identity number (11 digits)		

REQUEST FOR REGISTRATION OF CHANGE OF NAME
REGISTRATION IS TO TAKE PLACE AS SOON AS THE NAME HAS BEEN APPROVED

Signature

_____   _____
Place   Date

_____
Owner's binding signature (for companies: pursuant to Certificate of Company registration)
- to be repeated in capital letters

The Register's stamp and signature

NOTE! THE ORIGINAL APPLICATION IS TO BE FORWARDED TO THE SHIP REGISTER PRIOR TO REGISTRATION

SEND DIRECTLY TO
The Norwegian Maritime Authority, Ship Registers (Nis/Nor)
P.O. Box 73, Nygårdstangen
N-5838 BERGEN

(SIDE 3 AV 3 SIDER)

KR-0019/E Amended 12/2011

460

APPENDIX XI(H)

SEND DIRECTLY TO The Norwegian Maritime Authority, Ship Registers (Nis/Nor) P.O. Box 73, Nygårdstangen N-5838 BERGEN	JOURNAL NUMBER/ STAMP

NOTIFICATION

The vessel is to be registered in:

☐ THE NORWEGIAN INTERNATIONAL SHIP REGISTER - NIS

☐ THE NORWEGIAN SHIP REGISTER - NOR (FOR SHIPS SUBJECT TO MANDATORY REGISTRATION)

NAME:	
CALL SIGN (Norwegian)	
FORMER NAME:	
IMO NUMBER:	
Registration No. in The Register of Norwegian Fishing Vessels	

☐ The ship is abroad. A Provisional Certificate of Nationality is needed. Please use form KR-0011 (available in Norwegian only)

OWNER'S NATIONALITY (To be completed for registration in **NOR**)	OWNER'S NATIONALITY (To be completed for registration in **NIS**)
The owner satisfies the requirements to nationality set out in the Maritime Act	The owner satisfies the requirements to nationality set out in the Act relating to NIS,
☐ § 1, S.1 Norwegian citizen (Fill in 1)	☐ § 1 no. 1. (Fill in 1 and 3)
☐ § 1, S.1 Norwegian citizen resident abroad (Fill in 1 and 4)	☐ § 1 no.1. (Fill in 1, 3 and 6)- unlimited partnership
☐ § 1, S. 1 Unlimited partnership or other general partnership (Fill in 1 and 6)	☐ § 1 no. 2A. (Fill in 1, 3 and 5)
☐ § 1, S. 1 Limited partnership (Fill in 1)	☐ § 1 no. 2B. (Fill in 1, 3, 5 and 6)
☐ § 1, S. 1 company with limited liability (Fill in 1 and 3)	☐ § 1 no 3. (Fill in 1, 2, 3, 4 and 5)
☐ § 1, S. 3 (Fill in 1,2,3,4-as appropriate). EEA person/ company (on equal footing with a Norwegian national)	**Foreign trade union(-s):** **(Only applicable for ships registered in the NIS)**

(PAGE 1)

KR-0010E Amended 12/2011

APPENDIX XI(H)

 NIS // NOR

PLEASE FILL IN APPLICABLE ALTERNATIVE (-S)
- see under Owner's Nationality

1) OWNER:	NAME:			
	ORG.NO./ PERSONAL ID.NO. (11 didgits)		OWNERS IMO ID.NO. (7 didgits)	
	NATIONALITY:			
	E-MAIL:			
	PHONE:		FAX:	

2) HEAD OFFICE:	NAME:		
	ORG.NO./ PERSONAL ID.NO. (11 didgits)		
	E-MAIL:		
	PHONE:		FAX:

3) BUSINESS ADDRESS:	NAME:		
	ORG.NO./ PERSONAL ID.NO. (11 didgits)		
	E-MAIL:		
	PHONE:		FAX:

4) NORWEGIAN REPRESENTATIVE pursuant to: S.1 (1) no.3 of the NIS Act/ S. 1 no. 3 of the Maritime Act	NAME:		
	ORG.NO./ PERSONAL ID.NO. (11 didgits)		
	E-MAIL:		
	PHONE:		FAX:

5) MANAGING COMPANY: pursuant to: S.1 (1) no.3 of the NIS Act/ S. 1 no. 3 of the Maritime Act	NAME:		
	ORG.NO.		
	E-MAIL:		
	PHONE:		FAX:

ISM-liable company pursuant to the ISM-Code: Please see separate form, KR-0014	

6) MANAGING OWNER:	NAME:		
	ORG.NO./ PERSONAL ID.NO. (11 didgits)		
	E-MAIL:		
	PHONE:		FAX:

(PAGE 2)

KR-0010E Amended 12/2011

APPENDIX XI(H)

 NIS // NOR

OTHER

BODY WITHOUT ORG. NO.	NAME:	
	ADDRESS:	
	E-MAIL:	
	PHONE:	FAX:

Signature

Owner

Place: Date:

Binding signature (for companies- pursuant to Certificate of Company Registration)
- to be repeated in capital letters-

If other invoicing address than owner:
Alternatively, use separate form, KR-0070

Place: Date:

Name:

Org.nr./personal ID.no. (11digits):

I/we hereby confirm that I/we may be invoiced for this registration. To be signed with binding signature by the invoice recipient. Kindly repeat with capital letters.

The Register's stamp and signature

KR-0010E Amended 12/2011   (PAGE 3)

APPENDIX XI(H)

 **Sjøfartsdirektoratet**
Norwegian Maritime Authority

NIS // NOR

**DECLARATION CONCERNING NATIONALITY
LIMITED LIABILITY COMPANY OR EQUIVALENT
COMPANY WITH LIMITED LIABILITY**

NAME OF VESSEL:	
CALL SIGN:	
IMO NO. (if allocated):	

The undersigned member(s) of the Board of Directors, empowered to sign for:

COMPANY NAME:			
NATIONALITY:			
ADDRESS:			
POSTAL CODE:			
POSTAL ADDRESS:			
ORG. NO.			
PHONE:		FAX:	
E-MAIL:			

confirm that the company is **(tick one of the alternatives):**

☐ the owner of the above vessel

☐ a representative of the owner pursuant to S. 1 (1) no. 3 of the Act relating to a Norwegian International Ship Register (the NIS Act) / § 1, S. 3 of The Norwegian Maritime Act

☐ a representative of the owner, ref. (Declaration Concerning the Nationality of Limited Partnerships, No. KR-0004)

☐ part owner in the shipping partnership _____
                                                        Name of the shipping partnership

I/We confirm further that the company: (tick one of the alternatives)
1) ☐ has its head office and the seat of the Board of Directors in Norway
and that the majority of the members of the Board – including its Chair – is made up of Norwegian subjects who reside in Norway and have lived here for the past two years, and that Norwegian subjects or their equivalents. (S. 1 (2) of the Norwegian Maritime Act) own stocks or shares corresponding to at least 6/10 of the company's capital and can exercise voting rights in the company with at least 6/10 of the votes (S. 1, pt 4, of the Maritime Act).

or

if the conditions in point 1 have not been satisfied,
2) ☐ has its head office and the seat of the Board of Directors in a country affiliated to the EEA agreement, and that the majority of the members of the Board – including its Chair – is made up of citizens from countries affiliated with the EEA agreement and that they have lived there for the past two years and that citizens from EEA countries or companies or businesses encompassed by EEA countries, own stocks or shares corresponding to at least 6/10 of the votes, cp. S, 1 (3) of the Maritime Act.

For owner(s):
For the latter alternative (alt. 2), a Norwegian operating company must be appointed and this company is required to register with the Ship Register, cp. S. 13 of the Maritime Act.
If the controlling company is not registered as a Norwegian company in the Register of Business Enterprises, a representative resident in Norway is to be appointed, cp. S. 1, last sub-section of the Maritime Act.

_____ , _____
place   date

_____
Binding signature pursuant to the Certificate of Company Registration- to be repeated in capital letters

SEND DIRECTLY TO
The Norwegian Maritime Authority, Dep. of Ship Registration by email,   KR-0002/E Amended 12/2011
post@nis-nor.no
Alternatively,
PO Box 73 Nygårdstangen
N-5838 BERGEN, NORWAY

APPENDIX XI(H)

DECLARATION CONCERNING NATIONALITY DEVICE AS DESCRIBED IN S. 33 OF THE NORWEGIAN MARITIME ACT

NIS // NOR

NAME OF THE DEVICE:	
CALL SIGN:	
IMO NO. (if allocated)	

I, the undersigned, empowered to sign for:

NAME:	
NATIONALITY:	
ADDRESS:	
POSTAL CODE:	
POSTAL ADDRESS:	
ORG.NO.	
PHONE:	FAX:
E-MAIL:	

hereby confirm that the company is the owner of
☐ the above device
☐ a share in the above device

Moreover, I confirm: (tick one of the alternatives)

1) ☐ that my/our enterprise has its registered office in Norway with its head office in:

or

2) ☐ has its head office and the seat of its Board of Directors in a country affiliated with the EEA agreement, cp. S. 1 (3), of the Norwegian Maritime Act, and its head office in:

For the latter alternative (alt. 2), a Norwegian operating company must be appointed and this company is required to register with the Ship Register, cp S. 13 of the Norwegian Maritime Act.
Any special information:

_____ , _____
place   date

_____
Binding signature pursuant to the Certificate of Company Registration

This form is to be used for devices listed in S. 33 (1), nos. 1-2, of the Norwegian Maritime Act.
(For hovercraft (no. 3), use the same form as for ships).

SEND DIRECTLY TO
The Norwegian Maritime Authority, Ship Registers (Nis/Nor)
P.O. Box 73, Nygårdstangen
N-5838 BERGEN

KR-0005/E Amended 12/2011

APPENDIX XI(H)

APPOINTMENT OF PROCESS AGENT / NORWEGIAN REPRESENTATIVE

☐ THE NORWEGIAN INTERNATIONAL SHIP REGISTER - NIS (NIS-Act § 1, nr. 3)

☐ THE NORWEGIAN SHIP REGISTER - NOR (Maritime Act § 1, 3.section)

NAME:	
NORWEGIAN CALL SIGN:	
IMO NUMBER:	

REPRESENTATIVE'S NATIONALITY
The process agent satisfies the nationality requirements in the Norwegian Maritime Act:
☐ Norwegian or EU citizen, resident in Norway   ☐ Company with unlimited liability
☐ Company with limited liability

OWNER:	NAME:	
	ORG.NO./ PERSONAL ID.NO. (11 didgits)	
	E-MAIL:	
	PHONE:	FAX:

PROCESS AGENT:	NAME:	
	ORG.NO./ PERSONAL ID.NO. (11 didgits)	
	E-MAIL:	
	PHONE:	FAX:

Signatures

_____ the _____
place   date

_____
Owners binding signature - to be repeated in capital letters

_____ the _____
place   date

_____
Representatives binding signature - to be repeated in capital letters

SEND DIRECTLY TO
The Norwegian Maritime Authority, Ship Registers (Nis/Nor)
P.O. Box 73, Nygårdstangen
N-5838 BERGEN

KR-0060 E Amended 12-2011

APPENDIX XI(H)

Sjøfartsdirektoratet
Norwegian Maritime Authority

NIS // NOR

BILL OF SALE

Vessel	
Name	Call Sign
IMO No.	Reg.no., Register of Norwegian Fishing Vessels	HIN-/CIN-/WIN-Code	Other
Vessel Type/ Model	Length

Transferor *
Personal Id. (11 digits)/ Organisation no.	Name (in full)

Transferee *
Personal Id. (11 digits)/ Organisation no.	Name (in full)

The purchase price
Currency:	has been settled between the parties

Signature(-s)
Date (dd/mm/yyyy)	Place
Personal Id. (11 digits)/ Organisation no.	Tranferor's name
Transferor's binding signature (s) (for companies: pursuant to the company certificate)	To be repeated in capital letters

Witnesses *
We hereby confirm that the signatory(ies) has/have signed or acknowledged his/their signature(-s) on this document in our presence and that he/they are over 18 years old. We are of age and residents of Norway.
1. Witness' signature	To be repeted in capital letters
Date of Birth	Address
2. Witness' signature	To be repeted in capital letters
Date of Birth	Address

*) If the transferor and/or transferee is a sole proprietorship, the full Personal ID Number (11 digits) shall be inserted. We kindly ask that the Organisation Number is inserted as well.
If the transferor is a foreign body, the two witnesses must be replaced by a Notary Public. The Notary has to confirm both the identity and the power to sign on behalf of the company. The Notary's signature is then to be legalized either by a Norwegian Foreign Service Station or by an Apostille - please contact the register directly for further information.

SEND DIRECTLY TO
The Norwegian Maritime Authority, Dep. of Ship Registration
PO Box 73 Nygårdstangen
N-5838 BERGEN, NORWAY

KR-0020E (Godkj. 12-2011/09-2017)

APPENDIX XI(H)

 NIS // NOR

SEND DIRECTLY TO The Norwegian Maritime Authority, Ship Registers (Nis/Nor) P.O. Box 73, Nygårdstangen N-5838 BERGEN	JOURNAL NUMBER/ STAMP

NOTIFICATION OF AMENDMENT TO:

☐ THE NORWEGIAN INTERNATIONAL SHIP REGISTER – NIS
☐ THE NORWEGIAN SHIP REGISTER – NOR
☐ THE NORWEGIAN SHIPBUILDING REGISTER

The amendment concerns (check the appropriate alternative):

☐ New owner	☐ New ship name
☐ New home port	☐ Owner's new name
☐ New managing owner	☐ New business address
☐ New Norwegian representative	☐ New managing company
☐ Owner's new address	☐ Other change, please specify:

CALL SIGN :	
NAME OF SHIP:	
NEW NAME:	
IMO NO.:	
NEW REGISTRATION NO. IN THE REGISTER OF FISHING VESSELS	
NEW HOME PORT: Cf. Approved list which appears automatically if the word-document is filled in electronically. If in doubt, please see www.sjofartsdir.no, "NOR/case officers and home ports" or contact us directly.	
OTHER CHANGE – PLEASE SPECIFY:	
COMMENTS:	

☐ The ship is abroad: Contact the Ship Registers for issuance of a **Provisional Certificate of Nationality**. Please use form KR-0011 (available in Norwegian only)

(PAGE 1)

KR-0008E Amended 12/2011

APPENDIX XI(H)

Sjøfartsdirektoratet
Norwegian Maritime Authority

NIS // NOR

Information on owner's nationality is only to be completed for the following changes to the register:
- Owner/ managing owner/ business address or
- Norwegian Representative/ managing company

OWNER'S NATIONALITY (To be completed for changes to **NOR**)	OWNER'S NATIONALITY (To be completed for changes to **NIS**)
The owner satisfies the requirements to nationality set out in the Maritime Act	The owner satisfies the requirements to nationality set out in the Act relating to NIS,
☐ § 1, S.1 Norwegian citizen (Fill in 1)	☐ § 1 no. 1. (Fill in 1 and 3)
☐ § 1, S.1 Norwegian citizen resident abroad (Fill in 1 and 4)	☐ § 1 no.1. (Fill in 1, 3 and 6)- unlimited partnership
☐ § 1, S. 1 Unlimited partnership or other general partnership	☐ § 1 no. 2A. (Fill in 1, 3 and 5)
☐ § 1, S. 1 Limited partnership (Fill in 1)	☐ § 1 no. 2B. (Fill in 1, 3, 5 and 6)
☐ § 1, S. 1 company with limited liability (Fill in 1 and 3)	☐ § 1 no 3. (Fill in 1, 2, 3, 4 and 5)
☐ § 1, S. 3 (Fill in 1,2,3,4-as appropriate). EEA person/ company (on equal footing with a Norwegian national)	

ONLY FILL IN APPLICABLE ITEMS (1-6, other:

1) OWNER	NAME			
	ORG.NO./ PERSONAL ID.NO (11 digits)		OWNERS IMO ID.NO (7 digits)	
	NATIONALITY			
	E-MAIL			
	PHONE		FAX	

2) HEAD OFFICE	NAME			
	ORG.NO./ PERSONAL ID.NO (11 digits)			
	E-MAIL			
	PHONE		FAX	

3) BUSINESS ADDRESS	NAME			
	ORG.NO./ PERSONAL ID.NO (11 digits)			
	E-MAIL			
	PHONE		FAX	

4) NORWEGIAN REPRESENTATIVE	NAME			
pursuant to *) S.1(1) No.3 of the NIS Act/ *) S.1 no. 3 of the Maritime Act	ORG.NO./ PERSONAL ID.NO (11 digits)			
	E-MAIL			
	PHONE		FAX	

(PAGE 2)

KR-0008E Amended 12/2011

APPENDIX XI(H)

5) MANAGING COMPANY pursuant to *) S.1(1) No. 3 of the NIS Act *) S.1 No. 3 of the Maritime Act	NAME			
	ORG.NO./ PERSONAL ID.NO (11 digits)			
	E-MAIL			
	PHONE		FAX	

ISM-liable company pursuant to the ISM-Code: Please see separate form, KR-0014E	

6) MANAGING OWNER	NAME			
	ORG.NO./ PERSONAL ID.NO (11 digits)			
	E-MAIL			
	PHONE		FAX	

OTHER

BODY WITHOUT ORG.NO.	NAME			
	ADDRESS			
	E-MAIL			
	PHONE		FAX	

If two or more private persons are joint owners of a pleasure vessel, kindly confirm:
☐ The vessel is not involved in any shipping partnership activities. The owners have agreed upon shared use of the vessel
- all owners need to sign the application -

Signature

Owner	If other invoicing address than owner: Alternatively, use separate form, KR-0070
Place:　　　　　　Date:	Place:　　　　　　Date: Name: Org.nr./personal ID.no. (11digits):
Binding signature (for companies- pursuant to Certificate of Company Registration) - to be repeated in capital letters-	I/we hereby confirm that I/we may be invoiced for this registration. To be signed with binding signature by the invoice recipient. Kindly repeat with capital letters.

The Register's stamp and signature

(PAGE 3)

KR-0008E Amended 12/2011

APPENDIX XI(H)

NIS // NOR

PLEASE SEND DIRECTLY TO: The Norwegian Maritime Authority, Dep. of Ship Registration by email, post@nis-nor.no Alternatively, PO Box 73 Nygårdstangen N-5838 BERGEN, NORWAY	JOURNAL NUMBER/ STAMP

NOTIFICATION OF DELETION TO:

☐ NORWEGIAN INTERNATIONAL SHIP REGISTER - NIS

☐ NORWEGIAN SHIP REGISTER – NOR

☐ NORWEGIAN SHIPBUILDING REGISTER

INORMATION CONCERNING VESSEL	CALL SIGN:	
	NAME OF VESSEL:	
	IMO NO.:	
	YARD NO.:	
	AT YARD:	

REASON FOR DELETION:	☐ SOLD TO NORWEGIAN OWNER AND TRANSFERRED TO NEW REGISTER
	☐ SOLD TO FOREIGN OWNER AND TRANSFERRED TO NEW REGISTER
	☐ TRANSFERRED TO NEW REGISTER BY NORWEGIAN OWNER WITHOUT CHANGE OF OWNERSHIP Please specify:
	☐ TRANSFERRED TO NEW REGISTER BY FOREIGN OWNER WITHOUT CHANGE OF OWNERSHIP Please specify:
	☐ CUSTOM BUILT FOR NORWEGIAN PRINCIPAL. THE NEWBUILDING HAS BEEN DELIVERED TO THE BUYER.
	☐ CUSTOM BUILT FOR FOREIGN PRINCIPAL. THE NEWBUILDING HAS BEEN DELIVERED TO THE BUYER.
	☐ THE NEWBUILDING ORDER WAS NOT COMPLETED
	☐ DELETION OF VESSEL NOT UNDER OBLIGATION TO REGISTER (LENGTH LESS THAN 15M)
	☐ SOLD TO FOREIGN OWNER FOR BREAKING UP
	☐ SOLD TO NORWEGIAN OWNER FOR BREAKING UP
	☐ BROKEN UP
	☐ CONDEMNED
	☐ LOST AT SEA

KR-0009 ENG - SR   Revised 01.02.2016

APPENDIX XI(H)

DELETED TO: (COUNTRY)	☐
	☐ WITHOUT BEING TRANSFERRED TO NEW REGISTER

The below questions are relevant for NIS and NOR-vessels subject to mandatory registration (15 m or more) only:

YOUR FEEDBACK ON YOUR EXPERIENCE WITH OUR ADMINISTRATION DURING THE TIME THE SHIP HAS BEEN UNDER THE NORWEGIAN FLAG IS OF GREAT VALUE TO US.

Your comments help us provide the best possible service and we would be most grateful if you would take the time to answer the questions below. Both positive and negative feedback is of importance.

THE DEPARTMENT OF SHIP REGISTRATION	Always	Most of the time	Some times	Never
Provides good customer service. I feel that the staff provide «that little extra».				
The staff have a professional attitude.				
The staff possess the necessary expertise.				
Comments:				

OTHER DEPARMENT WITHIN THE NMA (please specify):	Always	Most of the time	Some times	Never
Provides good customer service. I feel that the staff provide «that little extra».				
The staff have a professional attitude.				
The staff possess the necessary expertise.				
Comments:				

Signature

Owner	If other invoicing address than owner: Alternatively, use separate form, KR-0070
Place: Date:	Place: Date:
	Name:
	Org.nr./personal ID.no. (11digits):
Binding signature (for companies- pursuant to Certificate of Company Registration) - to be repeated in capital letters-	I/we hereby confirm that I/we may be invoiced for this registration. To be signed with binding signature by the invoice recipient. Kindly repeat with capital letters.

The Register's stamp and signature

KR-0009 ENG - SR   Revised 01.02.2016

APPENDIX XI(H)

NIS // NOR

Notification of assignment of responsibilities according to the
Ship Safety Act

Date:

SEND DIRECTLY TO
The Norwegian Maritime Authority, Ship Registers (Nis/Nor)
P.O. Box 73, Nygårdstangen
N-5838 BERGEN

☐ NIS
☐ NOR
☐ Shipbuilding Register - BYGG
☐ The vessel is not registered

Please be advised that:
(Name of managing company or Company responsible for building)

has assumed the responsibility according to the Ship Safety Act to §§ 4 and 5, and has agreed to take over all duties and responsibilities imposed by the Ship Safety Act of the following vessel

(Identified either by name/ call sign/ IMO or name of yard/ yard no.):

Name of vessel
Call sign
IMO number
- or -   Name of yard
Yard number

Full details of owner
Name

Address

Full details of managing company/Company responsible for building
Name

Address

_____   _____
(Owner's signature)   (Managing company's signature)

KR-0061E/ Approved 06/2007

473

APPENDIX XI(H)

 NIS//NOR

Notification of assignment of responsibilities imposed by the **ISM-Code**

To: Date:

SEND DIRECTLY TO
The Norwegian Maritime Authority, Ship Registers (Nis/Nor)
P.O. Box 73, Nygårdstangen
N-5838 BERGEN

Please be advised that:

(Manager's name)

has assumed the responsibility for the Safe Operation and Pollution Prevention aspects and has agreed to take over all duties and responsibilities imposed by the International Safety Management (ISM) Code (IMO Res. A.741(18)) of the following vessel owned by:

(Owner's name)

Name of vessel	Call sign	IMO number

The manager is responsible for all duties imposed by the ISM Code, including the implementation and maintenance of the ISM Code, on board the above mentioned vessel

Where Management Company other than the above has been registered according to the NIS-Act § 1,2, 1.3, or Maritime Act § 1, 3.section, the owner of the vessel hereby confirms that this manager performs the main part of either the technical or commercial activity

Full details of OWNER
Registered Owner's IMO Identification Number:
Name:
Address:

Full details of MANAGING COMPANY
Company IMO Identification Number:
Name:
Address:

_____   _____
(Owner's signature)   (Managing company's signature)

KR-0014E Amended 10/2007

474

APPENDIX XI(I)

Singapore forms

(1) Application for registration as a Singapore ship
(2) Appointment of manager
(3) Appointment of agent
(4) Bill of sale
(5) Application for suspension of a Singapore ship's registry
(6) Application to reactivate a Singapore ship's registry
(7) Application form for multiple transactions

Note

Reproduced courtesy of Maritime and Port Authority of Singapore (MPA). Copyright MPA.
For additional and updated forms see:

www.mpa.gov.sg/web/portal/home/finance-e-services/forms/singapore-registry-of-ships/
ship-registration

APPENDIX XI(I)

Merchant Shipping Act
(Chap 179)
APPLICATION FOR REGISTRATION AS A SINGAPORE SHIP

This form will take approximately 30 minutes to fill in, provided you have the necessary supporting information ready.

1. SHIP'S PARTICULARS

Official Number	Name of Ship(2)		Type of Ship Code(3) ☐☐☐
IMO Number(4)	Gross Tonnage	Net Tonnage	Date Keel Laid Day Month Year
(5) Length in metres Breadth in metres Depth in metres	Name & address of shipyard where built		Hull Material ☐ Steel ☐ Aluminium ☐ -------------------- (please specify)
Country of previous registration Code(6) ☐☐☐	Name of Previous Owner(7)		Previous name of ship

2. ENGINE PARTICULARS

	Name & address of maker	Type
Number of engines Number of shafts BHP in kilo Watts		☐ Diesel ☐ Steam ☐ -------------------- (please specify)
Year made	Make and Model of each engine	Estimated speed of ship

3. OWNER'S/ BAREBOAT CHARTERER'S PARTICULARS

Full Name	Address	Nationality/ Place of incorporation(8)	Number of shares in ship owned(7)
		Total number of shares(7)	

Nature of Interest(7)   ☐ Sole Ownership   ☐ Joint Ownership   ☐ Ownership in severalty

APPENDIX XI(I)

4. EQUITY OF OWNING CORPORATION

Name of corporation	Paid-up capital	Local equity(10)	Foreign equity(11)
		Total: %	Total: %

5. OWNER OF BAREBOAT CHARTERED SHIP (12)

Full Name	Address	Nationality/ Place of incorporation(8)
Date of charter party	Charter period	Preferred date of termination of Singapore registration(13)

6. DECLARANT'S PARTICULARS

Full name(s)	Address	Nationality

Status of declarant

☐ Director of owning corporation   ☐ Secretary of owning corporation   ☐ Individual/ joint owner(s)   ☐ Appointed agent

I/ We*, whose name(s) *is/ are** hereunto subscribed, hereby declare that:

.1   all the particulars stated hereon are correct;

.2   the person(s) mentioned in section 3 *is/are** qualified to own a Singapore ship

.3   the property in the ship is divided into ………..shares; (15)

.4   no person, other than those mentioned in section 3 *is/are** entitled to be registered as owner(s) of the ship and no unqualified person is entitled as owner to any legal or beneficial interest in the ship or any share therein.(15)

And *I/we** make this solemn Declaration conscientiously believing the same to be true.

Name(s) and signature(s) of declarant(s)	Declared before me at Singapore on (date)…………………………………
	(Signature) (Qualification)…………………………………….. (The Director of Marine, a Surveyor of Ships, a Commissioner for Oaths, a Notary Public or other person empowered by law to administer oaths, affirmations or affidavits. The qualification of the person taking the declaration is to be stated.)
Indicate preferred date of registration(16):	Indicate date for collection of certificate of registry(17):

*Delete whichever are inapplicable.

APPENDIX XI(I)

Explanatory Notes

1. This form may be used for the registration of a ship as a Singapore ship in the ordinary register or register of bareboat charter ships.
2. Applicants are advised to seek prior approval for the name to avoid delay in case it cannot be used.
3. Enter the 3-digit code as indicated in the "Codes for Types of Ship & Countries" (available on request)
4. Not required for a ship which is less than 100 gross tons or if it is not self-propelled.
5. Give the dimensions as shown in the tonnage certificate
6. Enter the 4-digit code as indicated in the "Codes for Types of Ships & Countries" (available on request). Leave it blank if the country is not found on the list.
7. Not required for the registration of a bareboat charter ship.
8. Give the nationality in respect of individuals and place of incorporation for bodies corporate.
9. This section must be completed if the owner or bareboat charterer is a body corporate.
10. Give the name and percentage of equity owned by each and every person who is a citizen or permanent resident of Singapore. Affix a separate list if the space is insufficient. Also give the address and nationality of each person if this information is not contained in the computer printout on the company from the Registry of Companies and Businesses' Instant Information Service or equivalent. The printout must be accompanied by a "Certificate of Production of Statement by Computer".
11. Give the information as specified in item (10) above for each person who is not a citizen or permanent resident of Singapore. Affix a separate list if space is insufficient.
12. Not required for a ship which is to be registered in the ordinary register.
13. The date must be within 60 days of the date of termination of the charter party.
14. If the declaration is made by an appointed agent, the appointment must be made in the "Appointment of Agent" form and submitted with this application. This is not required for other declarants.
15. Delete this statement if the application is for the registration of a bareboat charter ship.
16. Applicants must ensure that all the required documents will be complete and in order, that all the requirements are met, and that the necessary formalities will be completed before or on this date, so that the ship can be registered on this date.
17. A certificate of registry may be collected up to one week in advance of the preferred registration date. This form, except for the signature(s) of the declarant(s) and the date, must be completed and submitted at least 3 working days before the date on which the certificate of registry is to be collected. On the date of registration the declarant(s) must be present to attest his/ their signature(s) and date the declaration.

APPENDIX XI(I)

VESSEL TYPE	CODE NO.	VESSEL TYPE	CODE NO.
Crude Oil Tanker	101	Pusher Tug	211
Petroleum Product Tanker (Below 60c)	102	Salvage Vessel	212
Petroleum Product Tanker (60c & Above)	103	Tug/Supply Vessel	215
Tanker	104	Offshore Supply Vessel	220
VLCC	106	Utility Vessel	230
Chemical Tanker	110	Dredger	231
LPG	121	Cable laying Ship	233
LNG	122	Heavyload Semi-Submersible Vessel	243
Chemical/ Gas Tanker	131	Barge	250
Oil/ Chemical/ Gas Tanker	133	Flat Top Deck Cargo Barge	251
Petroleum/Chemical Tanker	134	Hopper Barge	253
Bulk Carrier	140	Pilling Barge	254
Ore/Bulk Carrier	141	Dredger Barge	255
Car Carrier	150	Crane Barge	257
Roro Car Carrier	151	Semi-Submersible Rig	262
Cement Carrier	152	Jack-Up Rig	263
Live-Stock Vessel	160	Accomodation Rig	264
Container Ship	170	Tender Rig	265
General Cargo	180	FPSO Vessel	268
Reefer Vessel	181	Floating Storage Offshore	269
Roro Cargo	183	Drill Ship	270
Passenger Vessel	190	Accomodation/Pipe Laying Barge	273
Ferry Boat	193	Others	900
Tug Boat	210		

APPENDIX XI(I)

COUNTRY	CODE NO	COUNTRY	CODE NO.
Antigua & Barbuda	1160	Malaysia	2120
Australia	1190	Malta	2150
Bahamas	1220	Marshall Islands	2155
Bahrain	1230	Mexico	2180
Belgium	1260	Netherlands	2280
Belize	1270	Nigeria	2320
Bermuda	1290	Norway	2370
Brazil	1330	Oman	2380
Brunei	1340	Panama	2400
Canada	1400	Phillippines	2440
Cayman Islands	1420	Portugal	2460
Chile	1450	Russia	2500
China	1460	Saudi Arabia	2540
Cook Islands	1480	Sierra Leone	2560
Croatia	1500	Singapore	2580
Cyprus	1520	South Korea	2630
Denmark	1540	Spain	2650
Finland	1660	St Kitts & Nevis	2680
France	1670	St Vincents & Grenadines	2700
Germany	1690	Sweden	2740
Gibraltar	1710	Switzerland	2760
Greece	1720	Taiwan	2780
Honduras	1810	Thailand	2800
Hong Kong	1820	Turkey	2820
India	1850	Tuvalu	2840
Indonesia	1860	Ukraine	2860
Isle of Man	1880	United Arab Emirates	2880
Israel	1900	United Kingdom	2890
Italy	1910	United States of America	2900
Japan	1940	Unregistered	2920
Kiribati	1980	Vanuatu	2950
Liberia	2040	Vietnam	2970
Luxembourg	2060	Others	9000

APPENDIX XI(I)

Merchant Shipping Act
(Chap 179)

APPOINTMENT OF MANAGER (1)

This form will take approximately 10 minutes to fill in, provided you have the necessary supporting information ready.

SHIP & OWNER

Name of Ship	Name of Owner

MANAGER'S PARTICULARS

Full Name of manager (2)	Address (3)
Tel: Fax:	
Full Name of Person (4)	Status in Company (4)

CONFIRMATION BY MANAGER

I hereby confirm my appointment as manager of the above ship and my particulars as given above are correct (5).

Full name	Signature	Date

CERTIFICATION BY OWNER

I hereby certify that:

1. I am a Director/the Secretary* of the owning company (6):
2. the manager of the above ship is as given above; and
3. the particulars given above are correct.

Full name	Signature	Date

* Delete whichever is inapplicable.

Explanatory Notes

1. This form is to be completed and submitted to the Registrar of Singapore Ships when applying to register a ship and immediately on every occasion the manager is changed.
2. The manager may be a company or an individual. An owner may appoint itself as manager.
3. The manager must be resident in Singapore and is responsible for the operations of the ship, in particular for all matters related to the crew, safety and environmental protection. All communications relating to the ship will be directed to the manager.
4. If the manager is a company, the name and status or title of the person in the company with the ultimate responsibility for the ship must be given.
5. The confirmation must be made by the *person* appointed as manager.
6. Delete this statement if the owner of the ship is an individual.

481

APPENDIX XI(I)

Merchant Shipping Act
(Chap 179)

APPOINTMENT OF AGENT

This form will take approximately 10 minutes to fill in, provided you have the necessary supporting information ready.

OWNER

Name of Owner

I/We* hereby authorise the following agent to make and sign declarations and other documents for and on behalf of myself/ the said company* as required under the provisions of the Merchant Shipping Act.

AGENT'S PARTICULARS

Full Name of Agent	NRIC/ Passport No.
Address	

For use by individual(s)/joint owners	For use by body corporate owner(s)	
In witness whereof I/ we* have hereunto subscribed my/ our* name(s) and affixed my/ our* seal(s) on .... in the presence of: .... Signature(s) of Signature(s) & Owner(s) Name(s) of Witness(es)	In witness whereof we have affixed our common seal on .... in the presence of: .... Director .... Director/ Secretary	Common Seal

Explanatory Notes

1. An individual owner may appoint an agent to make and sign the declaration of ownership for the registration of a ship as a Singapore ship
2. A corporate owner **must** appoint an agent if the declaration of ownership is <u>NOT</u> made and signed by a Director or Secretary of the corporation
3. The appointed agent must be a natural person of legal age

FORM 5

APPENDIX XI(I)

The Merchant Shipping Act
(Chapter 179)

BILL OF SALE

SHIP'S PARTICULARS

Official Number	Name of Ship		Port Number	
GRT	Registered Length	metres	Description of Ship	
	Registered Breadth	metres		
NRT	Registered Depth	metres	BHP	

TRANSFEROR/TRANSFEREE

Full Name and Address of Registered Owner(s)/Transferor(s)	Full Name and Address of Purchaser(s)/Transferee(s)	
Amount Paid/Consideration	Nationality or Country of Incorporation	Singapore Permanent Resident: Yes/No/Not applicable*
Details of Encumbrance(s)	Total Number of Shares in the Ship	Number of Shares Transferred

I/We*, the transferor(s), in consideration of the amount shown above paid to me/us* by the transferee(s) and the receipt whereof is hereby acknowledged, transfer the number of share(s) shown above in the above described ship to the transferee(s).

Further, for myself/ourselves* and my/our* successors I/we* covenant with the transferee(s) and his/her/their* assigns, that I/we* have power to transfer the abovementioned share(s) and that the same is/are* free of encumbrances save as shown above.

For use by individual(s)/joint transferors	For use by body corporate transferor(s)	
In witness whereof I/we* have hereunto subscribed my/our* name(s) and affixed my/our* seal(s) on .... in the presence of:	In witness whereof we have affixed our common seal on .... in the presence of: .... Director	Seal
.... Signature(s) of Signature(s) & Name(s) Transferor(s) of Witness(es)	.... Director/Secretary*	

*Delete whichever are inapplicable.

Please read the explanatory notes overleaf carefully as they contain important information.

For Official Use	Registration of Bill of Sale	
Bill of Sale Recorded on .... at .... Registrar of Singapore Ships	Ship Registered as a Singapore Ship on .... Registrar of Singapore Ships	

FORM 3

483

APPENDIX XI(I)

Explanatory Notes

1. Every transfer of a Singapore ship or any share therein to a person who is qualified to own a Singapore ship (ie a citizen or permanent resident of Singapore or a body corporate incorporated in Singapore) must be made in this form.

2. Every bill of sale of a Singapore ship or any share therein must be produced to the Registrar of Singapore Ships for registration. If there are more than one bill of sale, they will be recorded in the order they are produced.

3. Where a Singapore ship or any share therein is transferred to a person qualified to own a Singapore ship, registration anew or closure of the ship's registry must be effected within 60 days of the date the first bill of sale is recorded, failing which the ship's registry will close by operation of the law. An application to close the ship's registry may be made by the registered owner or the transferee.

4. Where a Singapore ship or any share therein is transferred to a person not qualified to own a Singapore ship, the bill of sale will not be accepted for registration if the ship is not free of encumbrances. On the registration of such a bill of sale, the ship's registry will close by operation of the law and the registered owner has 60 days to surrender the ship's Certificate of Singapore Registry. Failure to do so is an offence.

5. A bill of sale which is signed by a person under power will not be accepted for registration unless accompanied by the power of attorney and a copy of it.

6. Owners are advised that entries (including those relating to bills of sale) in a Singapore ship's register, except for clerical or obvious mistakes, may not be corrected without an order of the High Court.

APPENDIX XI(I)

Merchant Shipping Act
(Chap 179)
APPLICATION FOR SUSPENSION OF A SINGAPORE SHIP'S REGISTRY

This form will take approximately 10 minutes to fill in, provided you have the necessary supporting information ready.

SHIP'S PARTICULARS

Name of Ship	Name of Owner	Official Number
		Port Number

BAREBOAT CHARTERER'S PARTICULARS

Full Name	Address
Date of charter party	Charter period

BAREBOAT REGISTRY

Port and Country of Registry	Name and Address of Registration Authority	Name under which ship is registered
	Tel: Fax:	Termination date

SUSPENSION OF SINGAPORE REGISTRY

Commencement Date	Termination Date

APPLICANT'S PARTICULARS

Full Name(s)	Address(es)

Status of applicant

☐ Director of owning corporation ☐ Secretary of owning corporation ☐ Individual/ joint owner(s) ☐ Authorised Person#

I/ We*, whose name(s) is/are* hereunto subscribed, hereby confirm that:
1. all the particulars stated hereon are correct;
2. a certified copy of the charter-party is attached;
3. a certified transcript of the register or similar document showing the bareboat registration of the ship *is attached/ will be produced within 60 days from the date of suspension*; and
4. the Singapore certificate of registry of the ship *is attached/ will be produced within 60 days from the date of suspension*.

Name(s) and signature(s) of applicant(s)

Date:

#Attach authorisation letter from owner(s)
*Delete whichever are inapplicable

APPENDIX XI(I)

Merchant Shipping Act
(Chap 179)
APPLICATION TO REACTIVATE A SINGAPORE SHIP'S REGISTRY

This form will take approximately 5 minutes to fill in, provided you have the necessary supporting information ready.

SHIP'S PARTICULARS

Name of Ship	Name of Owner	Official Number
		Port Number

APPLICANT'S PARTICULARS

Full Name(s)	Address(es)

Status of applicant

☐ Director of owning corporation   ☐ Secretary of owning corporation   ☐ Individual/ joint owner(s)   ☐ Authorised Person#

I/ We*, whose name(s) *is/are** hereunto subscribed, hereby confirm that:
1. the registry is to be reactivated on ....
2. the closure certificate or similar document in respect of the bareboat registration of the ship *is attached/ will be submitted within 60 days of this date**;
3. a statement from the classification society that this class is maintained *is attached/ will be submitted within 60 days of this date**; and
4. copies of the valid statutory certificates *are attached/ will be submitted within 60 days of this date**.

Name(s) and signature(s) of applicant(s)

Date:

#Attach authorisation letter from owner(s)
Delete whichever are inapplicable

486

APPENDIX XI(I)

The Merchant Shipping Act
(Chapter 179)
SINGAPORE REGISTRY OF SHIPS
APPLICATION FORM FOR
MULTIPLE TRANSACTIONS

| Vessel Name: _____ | Official No.: _____ | Port No.: _____ |

Tick & delete as appropriate **(For Transaction 1 & 4 is subjected to GST)**:

1. Mortgage ($48 Plus $1.00 per 100 gross tons or part thereof)
- [ ] * Initial registration of a mortgage.
- [ ] * Transfer/ transmission of a registered mortgage
- [ ] * Discharge of a registered mortgage

2. Closure (Deletion Certificate $14 per vessel)
- [ ] Do you require a Deletion certificate?

Reason:
- [ ] # Sale of vessel. (Owners **must** submit original bill of sale for recording)
- [ ] # Change of vessel flag
- [ ] # Registration no longer required.
- [ ] # Others: _____

3. Registration of Bill of Sale ($50 for Recording a Bill of Sale)
- [ ] * Transferee qualified to own a Singapore ship.
- [ ] * Transferee not qualified to own a Singapore ship. (Registration will result in closure of ship's registry)

4. Replacement of Cert. of Registry/ CLC 92 ($30 for Cert. of Registry and $24 for Cert. of CLC 92)
Reason:
- [ ] # Loss (Application to be accompanied with Statutory Declaration)
- [ ] # Certificate deteriorated

5. Amendments of particulars (Attached documentary evidence as appropriate)
- [ ] Ship's particulars _____
- [ ] Owner's particulars _____

6. Ship's name ($26 for change of ship's name only)
- [ ] Approval of ship's name and allocation of Official No. (Applicable even if there is no change in the name of the previous registry. An approved name is valid for one year)
- [ ] Approval & Change of ship's name.

(1) Proposed 1st name : _____ (2) Proposed 2nd name: _____ Existing name: _____

7. Allocation of Call Sign (Applicable to self-propelled ships. When applying, owners should state clearly the gross tonnage of the vessel)
Gross Tonnage : _____

8. RCB printout ($5 per copy) (1) _____ (2) _____

9. [ ] Application for Ship Station Licence

10. [ ] Application for Assignment of Maritime Mobile Service Identity (MMSI) Number
Ship's name: _____ Call Sign: _____
- [ ] Regional - Please indicate: [ ] With AAIC [ ] Without AAIC
- [ ] Worldwide Please include AAIC _____

11. [ ] Application for Appointment of RS01 as Accounting Authority
12. [ ] Application for Service Activation of Maritime Mobile Earth Station

* A mortgage, its transfer or discharge, or a Bill of Sale which is executed by a person under power, must be accompanied by the Power of Attorney and a copy of it. A Power of Attorney which is executed outside Singapore must be attested by a notary public & legalised. A certified true copy of a Power of Attorney may be accepted only for the discharge of a mortgage.

Original Certificate of Registry must be returned or an undertaking letter to surrender the Certificate of Registry within 30 days from the date of registration. Failure to do so is an offence.

Name of Applicant:	Status of applicant (Tick as appropriate.):	Official use:
Name of Company:	[ ] Owner	Fee paid:
Signature & Company Stamp:	[ ] Manager	Cheque/Receipt no:
	[ ] Owner's Lawyer	Received and Checked by:
	[ ] Mortgagee's Lawyer	
Date:	[ ] Others :	
Contact No: Fax No:	(Please Specify)	Date:

APPENDIX XI(J)

UK forms

(1) Application to register a British ship (Commercial vessels > 500GT), form MSF 4740A
(2) Builder's certificate, form MSF 4743
(3) Bill of sale, form MSF 4705
(4) Declaration of eligibility (merchant ships & pleasure vessels), form MSF 4727
(5) Mortgage of a ship (account current), form MSF 4736
(6) Notice of mortgage intent, form MSF 4739
(7) Application for safe manning document, form MSF 4227

Note

Reproduced courtesy of Maritime and Coastguard Agency (MCA) under the Open Government License v3.0: www.nationalarchives.gov.uk/doc/open-government-licence/version/3/

Copyright MCA.

For additional and updated forms see: www.ukshipregister.co.uk/registration/

APPENDIX XI(J)

APPLICATION TO REGISTER A BRITISH SHIP
(Commercial Vessels over 500 gt)

Merchant Shipping Act 1995

READ THE GUIDANCE LEAFLET AND THE FOLLOWING NOTES BEFORE COMPLETING THIS FORM
- **The Register is a Public Register from which any person can obtain a Transcript of entries in the Register.**
- *Warning*: the ship is not registered until a Certificate of Registry has been issued.
- Please write in black ink using BLOCK CAPITALS and tick the boxes where appropriate.
- Section 1 and 4 must be completed in all cases.
- Section 2 must be completed if the ship has been registered before in any way or in any country.
- Section 3 must be completed if the ship is a commercial vessel over 500gt.

SECTION 1: DETAILS OF THE SHIP

PROPOSED NAME OF SHIP (several names should be entered in order of preference)	

PORT OF CHOICE	

RADIO CALL SIGNS (if known)		IMO/HIN (if known)	
APPROXIMATE LENGTH (in metres)		YEAR OF BUILD	
TYPE OF SHIP		CONSTRUCTION MATERIAL	

NAME AND ADDRESS OF BUILDER	

COUNTRY OF BUILD	

SECTION 2: PREVIOUS REGISTRATION DETAILS

NAME OF SHIP (if different from section 1)	

REGISTRATION NUMBER		PORT OF REGISTRATION		REGISTERED LENGTH	

WHERE WAS THE SHIP REGISTERED?

In the UK		No & Year of registry (if applicable)		Port letters & number (if applicable)	
* An EU or EEA country		Which Country?		* EU Number	
Elsewhere		Which Country?			

HAS THE SHIP AN OUTSTANDING MORTGAGE?   Yes ☐   No ☐

---
* EU – European Union   EEA European Economic Area

MSF 4740 A Rev 01/15

APPENDIX XI(J)

SECTION 3: COMPLETE FOR COMMERCIAL VESSELS OVER 500 GT

NAME OF CLASSIFICATION SOCIETIES WITH WHICH THE SHIP IS CLASSED	

NAME AND ADDRESS OF COMPANIES INTERNATIONAL SAFETY MANAGEMENT	

SECTION 4: DETAILS OF THE APPLICANT

FULL NAME AND ADDRESS (please include the postcode)

	TEL NO:	
	FAX NO:	

I enclose the fee of   £   :   Cheques to be made payable to 'MCA'.   Please print name of vessel on reverse of cheque

If you are the agent for the owner please tick this box. ☐   NOTE: All correspondence will be sent to the owner/managing owner unless the owner requests the registry to send it to a specified person.

Signature: _____   Date: _____

I/we* being the owner (s) of the above ship request that all correspondence including the Certificate of Registry be sent to :

....

my/our * registration agent/agent*   * delete as necessary

Signature of Owner (s) _____

YOU SHOULD NOW SEND THIS FORM TOGETHER WITH:
- ☒ The correct fee, if you do now know the fee contact the registry on the number below.
- ☒ The Declaration of Eligibility
- ☒ In the case of companies, a copy of any Certificate of Incorporation.
- ☒ Builders Certificate and/or Bills of Sale.
- ☒ Ships to be registered on Part I and IV will need a survey for tonnage and measurement.

TO: REGISTRY OF SHIPPING AND SEAMEN
         ANCHOR COURT
         KEEN ROAD
           CARDIFF, CF24 5JW   Tel: 02920 448800   Fax 02920 448820
E-mail: part1_registry@mcga.gov.uk   or   comm_registry@mcga.gov.uk

NOTE: If your vessel carries a 406MHz EPIRB it is important to register your beacon with the MCA 406 EPIRB Registry and also to inform them of any future changes.

The contact details are as follows:
MXA 406MHz EPIRB Registry, Pendennis Point, Castle Drive, Falmouth, Cornwall, TR11 4WZ
Tel: (UK) 01326 211569   Fax: (UK) 01326 319264

MSF 4740 A Rev 01/15

APPENDIX XI(J)

DEPARTMENT FOR TRANSPORT

BUILDER'S CERTIFICATE
Merchant Shipping Act 1995

Builder can use their own printed form, provided that the details required below are included.

SECTION 1: DETAILS OF THE SHIP

NAME OF SHIP

DATE OF BUILD

YARD NUMBER

LENGTH (metres)

BREADTH (metres)

DEPTH (metres)

ESTIMATED TONNAGE

CONSTRUCTION MATERIAL

SECTION 2: DETAILS OF THE BUILDER

BUILDER'S NAME

FULL ADDRESS

PLACE OF BUILD
(if different from above)
(include country)

SECTION 3: CERTIFICATION

*I/we hereby certify that *I/we *built/moulded/fitted out the ship described above to the order of:
(*Delete as necessary)

FULL NAME(S) OF OWNER(S)	ADDRESS(ES) OF OWNER(S)

Signature of builder

Date

Position in company (if ship is built by a company)

When completed, send this form to: REGISTRY OF SHIPPING & SEAMEN
ANCHOR COURT,
KEEN ROAD   Tel: 029 20448800
CARDIFF CF24 5JW   Fax: 029 20448820

MSF 4743 Rev 11/14

OFFICIAL USE ONLY: This Builder's Certificate has been used to register a British ship, and the details entered in the Register on: The ship's Official Number is:

Officer's Initials:

491

APPENDIX XI(J)

Department of Transport
Merchant Shipping Act 1995

Bill of Sale

Warning: A purchaser of a British registered ship does not obtain complete title until the appropriate Bill(s) of Sale has been recorded with the Registry, and a new Certificate issued.

*Registered owners who are mortgagees *must* inform the Registry of any change of address. *Where one owner is selling to two or more owners, separate forms are required unless they are buying as joint owners. *Applications to change ownership received within 30 days of the change attract a 'transfer fee' rather than the more expensive 'full registration' fees. *Please write in black ink using BLOCK CAPITALS, and tick boxes where appropriate.

SECTION 1 : DETAILS OF THE SHIP

Name of ship

Official number (if any)   Length (metres)

SECTION 2 : DETAILS OF THE SALE

Body Corporate / LLP please give	Company or LLP name	Principal place of business[1]	
Individuals please give	Full name(s)	Address(es)	Occupation(s)

* I/we the transferor(s)

☐ as joint owners

(Please tick box if you are joint owners)

In consideration of (*the sum of)
*paid/given to *me/us by:

Body Corporate / LLP please give	Company or LLP name	Principal place of business [1]	
Individuals please give	Full name(s)	Address(es)	Occupation(s)

* I/we the transferee(s)

☐ as joint owners

(Please tick box if you are joint owners)

[1]Companies incorporated other than in the UK or British Dependant Territories – enter place of business   *Delete as necessary

the receipt of which is acknowledged, transfer

share in the above ship and its appurtenances to the transferee(s).   (figures & words)

IF ANY REGISTERED MORTGAGE IS OUTSTANDING YOU MUST TICK THIS BOX   ☐

Further, * I/we, as transferor(s), hereby declare that * I/we have the power to transfer in the manner described above the above mentioned shares, and that they are free from encumbrances ** save as appears by the registry of the above ship.

*** delete and initial the deletion if there are NO outstanding mortgages*

| When completed you should send this form, together with the appropriate fee and supporting documents (if required) to:
REGISTRY OF SHIPPING & SEAMEN
ANCHOR COURT, KEEN ROAD, CARDIFF, CF24 5JW | OFFICIAL USE ONLY
Entry in Register made on _____ (date)
at _____ (time)
Officer's Initials _____ |

MSF 4705 REV 02/14

APPENDIX XI(J)

SECTION 3 : FOR COMPLETION WHEN SALE IS BY A COMPANY OR LLP

☒ **Executed by the transferor as a deed (in England, Wales and Northern Ireland)**
☒ **Subscribed by the transferor (in Scotland)**

COMPANY SEAL

_____ day of _____ month of _____ year by:-

** (a) **the affixing of the common seal of the transferor in the presence of the following persons signing;** *or*
** (b) **signing by the following persons;**

Director _____

Director or Secretary _____

Authorised Signatory _____

Authorised Signatory _____

Member _____

Member _____

Witnessed by _____

Name (print) _____

Address (print) _____

** Delete as appropriate.   # If the signature must be witnessed the name and address of the witness must be given.
Note: IN ENGLAND, WALES & NORTHERN IRELAND – signature may be by (a) two directors, (b) by a company secretary and a director, or   (c) by a director in the presence of a witness who completes the details above to attest the signature. If the common seal is affixed any special requirement of the company's articles about signing must be complied with.
IN SCOTLAND – signature may be by one director or the secretary of the company or one person authorised to sign the document on behalf of the company, or one member of the Limited Liability Partnership, provided such single signature is witnessed. Alternatively, signature may be effected without a witness by two directors, or a director and the secretary, or two persons authorised to sign the document on behalf of the company, or two members of the Limited Liability Partnership. Note that signature by one authorised signatory and either a director or the secretary of the company is not valid.

SECTION 4 : FOR COMPLETION WHEN SALE IS BY INDIVIDUALS

* **Executed as deed** (England or Wales)   * **Subscribed** (Scotland)   * **Signed, sealed and delivered** (Northern Ireland)   * Delete as appropriate

on this _____ day of _____ month of _____ year

By the following person(s) signing as transferor(s)

Signature(s) of Transferor(s) *number each signature (ie 1, 2, 3) and print name after signature*

_____

_____

_____

In the presence of the following witness(es) *each witness must sign then print their name and address and occupation and number their entry to show which signature above they are witnessing. There must be a separate witness for each transferor.*

Witnessed by _____

_____

_____

_____

_____

_____

MSF 4705 REV 02/14

APPENDIX XI(J)

Maritime & Coastguard Agency

**MERCHANT & PLEASURE VESSELS
DECLARATION OF ELIGIBILITY**

TO REGISTER A BRITISH SHIP ON PART 1 OF THE REGISTER
Merchant Shipping Act 1995
A Public Register from which any person can obtain a Transcript of the entries in the Register.

* Part 1 of the register is for merchant and pleasure vessels

* For Part 1 registration, the property in a ship is divided into 64 shares.

* A share can be jointly owned by no more than 5 people.

SECTION 1: DETAILS OF THE SHIP (to be completed in all cases)

IS THIS AN APPLICATION TO REGISTER A MERCHANT VESSEL? ☐ *OR* A PLEASURE VESSEL? ☐ (please tick the appropriate box)

Name / proposed name of ship

Official number (if any)

Length (metres)

SECTION 2: LEGAL OWNERSHIP (the 64 shares are legally owned as follows)

For ships to be registered on Part 1, please list the qualified owners first and draw a line under them, before entering the unqualified owners.
A ship can be registered on Part 1 if the majority interest (i.e. 33 shares) is owned by persons qualified to be owners of British ships. **Please refer to the *Notes* overleaf.**

Owner Number *	Mr, Mrs, Miss other	Surname/ Company Name/ Limited Liability Partnership Name	Forename (s) / Registered Office	Address / Companies incorporated in the UK and British Dependent Territories must enter their principal place of business, all other companies must enter their place of business in the UK.	Nationality / Country of Incorporation	Status # See notes overleaf	No of shares held outright	No of shares held jointly	With owner number

* Please number each owner consecutively

Continue on a separate page if necessary and tick the box ☐

MSF 4727 Rev 02/15

SECTION 3: REPRESENTATIVE PERSON / MANAGING OWNER

* If none of the owners making up the majority interest is resident in the UK, a representative person must be appointed. (A body corporate is treated as resident if it has a place of business in the UK)	* A representative person is either an individual resident in the UK, or a body corporate incorporated in an EEA country which has a place of business in the UK.	* If more than 1 owner is resident in the UK one of them must be appointed as the managing owner. This must be one of the owners in the majority interest.

either: I/we appoint the following to be the ship's Representative person

Full Name / Company Name

Address / Place of Business in UK

NB: If there is a change to the details in this section, the Registrar must be informed within 7 days of the change occurring.

or: I/we appoint the following to be the ship's managing owner

Name in full.

SECTION 4: DECLARATION (must be signed by all those named in section 2)

I / we declare that:	Owner No	Signature	Date
• **I / we understand that The Register is a Public Register from which any person can obtain a Transcript of the entries in the Register;** • the information given by me / us in this form is true to the best of my / our knowledge and belief; • I am / we are the legal owner (s) of the shares as set out in section 2 of this form; • the ship is not fishing for profit; • to the best of my / our knowledge and belief, a majority interest in the ship is owned by persons qualified to be owners of British ships, and the ship is otherwise entitled to be registered on Part 1; • any Nationals of an EEA country other than the UK, who are represented in the majority interest are established (within the meaning of Article 48 or 52 of the EEC Treaty or Article 28 or 31 of the EEA Agreement) in the UK; **N.B.** **For companies and European Economic Interest Groupings, an authorized officer of each of the companies or groupings must sign this form.**			

 # NOTE ON STATUS -   qualified owners are:

a	British citizens or non-United Kingdom nationals exercising their right of freedom of movement of workers or right of establishment under Article 48 or 52 of the EEC Treaty or Article 28 or 31 of the EEA Agreement;	d	Persons who under the British Nationality Order 1981 are British subjects;	g	Bodies corporate incorporated in any relevant British Possession and having their principal place of business in the UK or any such possession;
b	British Dependant Territories citizens;	e	Persons who under the Hong Kong (British Nationality) Order 1986 are British Nationals (Overseas):	h	European Economic Interest Groupings formed in pursuance in the UK.
c	British Overseas citizens:	f	Bodies corporate incorporated in an EEA State;		

When completed you should send this form, together with the appropriate fee and supporting documents to:
THE REGISTRY OF SHIPPING AND SEAMEN, ANCHOR COURT, KEEN ROAD, CARDIFF, CF24 5JW. TEL: 02920 448800

Continue on a separate page if necessary and tick the box

MSF 4727 Rev 02/15

APPENDIX XI(J)

Maritime & Coastguard Agency

An Executive Agency of the Department for Transport
Merchant Shipping Act 1995

Mortgage of a Ship
to secure Account Current etc/other obligation

- If more than one mortgagor then a separate mortgage is required from each mortgagor, unless shares are jointly held.
- In respect of fishing vessels, mortgages may be registered only against those registered with FULL registration.
- The prompt registration of a mortgage deed with the Registry is essential to establish the priority of the mortgage. This is because the priority of the mortgage is determined by the date on which it is produced for registration and not from the date of the mortgage itself.
- If the mortgagor is a company the mortgage must be registered with the Registrar of Companies within 21 days of its execution.
- It is important that the Registry is informed of any changes.
- Please write in black ink using BLOCK CAPITALS, and tick boxes where appropriate.

The mortgage reference no. (issued by the mortgagee) is: [ ]

SECTION 1 : DETAILS OF THE SHIP

IS THIS MORTGAGE IN RESPECT OF A FISHING VESSEL?   Yes [ ]   No [ ]

Name of ship [ ]

Official number [ ]

SECTION 2 : THE MORTGAGE

Whereas there is [1]

between [2]

* as joint mortgagors (hereinafter called "**the mortgagors**")

and [2]

* as joint mortgagees (hereinafter called "**the mortgagee**")

[3]

*Delete as necessary

OFFICIAL USE ONLY
Mortgage
entered in the Register on (date) at (priority)
officer's initials (time)

[1] State "an account current" or write in a short description of the obligation.
[2] Give full name and address, with place of business in respect of a company.
[3] Describe fully the nature of the liabilities secured. You may refer to another document.

MSF 4736 REV 02/14

APPENDIX XI(J)

SECTION 2 : THE MORTGAGE *(continued)*

* **_Complete in respect of "account current"_**:
Now *I/we the mortgagor(s) in consideration of the advance made or to be made to *me/us by the mortagee(s), bind *myself/ourselves to pay to the mortgagee(s) the sums for the time being due on this security whether by way of principal, interest or otherwise at the time(s) and in the manner mentioned above.

* **_Complete in respect of "other obligation"_**:
Now *I/we the mortgagor(s) in consideration _____

bind *myself/ourselves to _____

For the purpose of better securing to the mortgagee(s) the *sums/obligation mentioned above. *I/we hereby mortgage to the mortgagee(s)

[   ] *(figures & words)*

shares of which *I/we are the owners in the ship described above and in its appurtenances.
Lastly, *I/we for *myself/ourselves hereby declare that *I/we have the power to mortgage in the manner aforesaid the above-mentioned shares and that they are free from encumbrances **save as appears by the registry of the above ship.*

COMPLETE IF THE MORTGAGOR IS A COMPANY

☒   **Executed by the mortgagor as a deed (in England, Wales and Northern Ireland)**   *COMPANY SEAL*
☒   **Subscribed by the mortgagor (in Scotland)**

_____ day of _____ 20 _____ by:-

** **(a)   the affixing of the common seal of the mortgagor in the presence of the following persons signing;** *or*
** **(b)   signing by the following persons;**

Director _____

Director or Secretary _____

Authorised Signatory _____

Authorised Signatory _____

\# Witnessed by _____

Name (Print) _____

Address (Print) _____

Address _____

** Delete as appropriate.   \# If the signature must be witnessed the name and address of the witness must be given.

Note: IN ENGLAND, WALES & NORTHERN IRELAND – signature may be by (a) two directors; (b) by the company secretary and a director, or (c) by a director in the presence of a witness who completes the details above to attest the signature. If the common seal is affixed any special requirement of the company's articles about signing must be complied with.

IN SCOTLAND – signature may be by one director or the secretary of the company or one person authorised to sign the document on behalf of the company, or one member of the Limited Liability Partnership, provided such single signature is witnessed. Alternatively, signature may be effected without a witness by two directors, or a director and the secretary, or two persons authorised to sign the document on behalf of the company, or two members of the Limited Liability Partnership.
Note that signature by one authorised signatory and either a director or the secretary of the company is not valid.

COMPLETE IF THE MORTGAGOR(S) IS/ARE ONE OR MORE INDIVIDUAL

*   **Executed as a deed** (in England or Wales)
*   **Subscribed** (in Scotland)   Seal(s) if
*   **Signed, sealed and delivered** (in Northern Ireland)   *Delete as appropriate   executed in
                                                                                           Northern
on this _____ day of _____ 20 _____ by :-   Ireland

by the following person(s) signing as mortgagor(s)

Signature(s) of mortgagor(s)		
In the presence of:		
Name(s) of witness(es)		
Address(es) of witness(es)		
Occupation(s) of witness(es)		

NOTE: Every signature must have one witness

MSF 4736 REV 02/14

APPENDIX XI(J)

SECTION 2 : THE MORTGAGE *(continued)*

COMPLETE IF THE MORTGAGOR(S) ARE A LIMITED LIABILITY PARTNERSHIP

* **Executed by the mortgagor as a deed (in England, Wales & Northern Ireland)**
* **Subscribed by the mortgagor (in Scotland)**   **Delete as appropriate*

on this _____ day of _____ 20 _____ by signing by the following persons

Member _____

Member _____

Witnessed by _____

Name (Print) _____

Address (Print) _____

_____

Note: IN SCOTLAND subscription may be by one member of the Limited Liability Partnership and one witness, or by two members of the Limited Liability Partnership.

SECTION 3 : TRANSFER OF MORTGAGE

*I/we, the above mentioned mortgagee(s), in consideration of [1]

this day [2]

by [3]

hereby transfer to *him/her/them the benefit of the within written security

COMPLETE IF THE TRANSFEROR IS A COMPANY

☒ **Executed by the transferor as a deed (in England, Wales and Northern Ireland)**   *COMPANY SEAL*
☒ **Subscribed by the transferor (in Scotland)**

_____ day of _____20 ____ by:-

**(a)   the affixing of the common seal of the transferor in the presence of the following persons signing; *or*
** (b)   signing by the following persons;

Director _____

Director or Secretary _____

Authorised Signatory _____

Authorised Signatory _____

\# Witnessed by _____

Name (Print) _____

Address (Print) _____

Address _____

** Delete as appropriate.   \# If the signature must be witnessed the name and address of the witness must be given.

Note: IN ENGLAND, WALES & NORTHERN IRELAND – signature may be by (a) two directors, (b) by the company secretary and a director, or (c) by a director in the presence of a witness who completes the details above to attest the signature. If the common seal is affixed any special requirement of the company's articles about signing must be complied with.

IN SCOTLAND – signature may be by one director or the secretary of the company or one person authorised to sign the document on behalf of the company, or one member of the Limited Liability Partnership, provided such single signature is witnessed. Alternatively, signature may be effected without a witness by two directors, or a director and the secretary, or two persons authorised to sign the document on behalf of the company, or two members of the Limited Liability Partnership. Note that signature by one authorised signatory and either a director or the secretary of the company is not valid.

Left margin (vertical text):
OFFICIAL USE ONLY
Transfer of mortgage

(priority)   entered in the Register on   (date)   at   official's initials
(time)

MSF 4736 REV 02/14

APPENDIX XI(J)

SECTION 3 : TRANSFER OF MORTGAGE *(continued)*

COMPLETE IF THE TRANSFEROR(S) IS/ARE ONE OR MORE INDIVIDUAL

* **Executed as a deed** (in England or Wales)
* **Subscribed** (in Scotland)
* **Signed, sealed and delivered** (in Northern Ireland)   **Delete as appropriate*

Seal(s) if executed in Northern Ireland

on this _____ day of _____ 20 _____

by the following person(s) signing as transferor(s)

Signature(s) of transferor(s)		
In the presence of:		
Name(s) of witness(es)		
Address(es) of witness(es)		
Occupation(s) of witness(es)		

NOTE: Every signature must have one witness

[1] Enter the sum of money or the nature of the obligation.
[2] Enter "paid to *me/us", or narrative suitable to the obligation.

[3] Give full name and address of the transferree, with place of business in respect of a company.

* Delete as necessary

COMPLETE IF THE TRANSFEROR(S) ARE A LIMITED LIABILITY PARTNERSHIP

* **Executed by the transferor as a deed (in England, Wales & Northern Ireland)**
* **Subscribed by the transferor (in Scotland)**   **Delete as appropriate*

on this _____ day of _____ 20 _____ **by signing by the following persons**

Member _____

Member _____

Witnessed by _____

Name (Print) _____

Address (Print) _____

_____

Note: IN SCOTLAND subscription may be by one member of the Limited Liability Partnership and one witness, or by two members of the Limited Liability Partnership.

MSF 4736 REV 02/14

APPENDIX XI(J)

SECTION 4 : DISCHARGE OF MORTGAGE

* Received by the within-mentioned *mortgage(s)/transferee(s) of the mortgage.

¹

This within written security is now discharged.

---

* The within-mentioned *mortgagee(s)/transferee(s) have agreed to discharge this within written security and it is therefore discharged.

COMPLETE IF DISCHARGE IS GIVEN BY A COMPANY

☒ **Executed by the mortgagee/transferee as a deed (in England, Wales and Northern Ireland)**
☒ **Subscribed by the mortgagee/transferee (in Scotland)**

_____ day of _____ 20 ___ by:-

COMPANY SEAL

(a) **the affixing of the common seal of the mortgagee/transferee in the presence of the following persons signing; *or*
** (b) **signing by the following persons;**

Director _____

Director or Secretary _____

Authorised Signatory _____

Authorised Signatory _____

Witnessed by _____

Name (Print) _____

Address (Print) _____

Address _____

** Delete as appropriate.   # If the signature must be witnessed and the name and address of the witness must be given.

Note: IN ENGLAND, WALES & NORTHERN IRELAND – signature may be by (a) two directors; (b) by the company secretary and a director, or (c) by a director in the presence of a witness who completes the details above to attest the signature. If the common seal is affixed any special requirement of the company's articles about signing must be complied with.

IN SCOTLAND – signature may be by one director or the secretary of the company or one person authorised to sign the document on behalf of the company, or one member of the Limited Liability Partnership, provided such single signature is witnessed. Alternatively, signature may be effected without a witness by two directors, or a director and the secretary, or two persons authorised to sign the document on behalf of the company, or two members of the Limited Liability Partnership. Note that signature by one authorised signatory and either a director or the secretary of the company is not valid.

COMPLETE IF THE DISCHARGE IS GIVEN BY ONE OR MORE INDIVIDUALS

* **Executed as a deed** (in England or Wales)
* **Subscribed** (in Scotland)
* **Signed, sealed and delivered** (in Northern Ireland)

* Delete as appropriate

Seal(s) if executed in Northern Ireland

on this _____ day of _____ 20 ____

by the following person(s) signing as mortgagee(s)/transferee(s)

Signature(s) of mortgagee(s)/transferee(s)		
In the presence of:		
Name(s) of witness(es)		
Address(es) of witness(es)		
Occupation(s) of witness(es)		

NOTE: Every signature must have one witness

¹ Enter "the sum of _____", or narrative suitable to the obligation

WARNING: **If the discharged deed is not presented to the Registry the mortgage will remain registered against the ship.**

(Left margin, bottom to top:) OFFICIAL USE ONLY Discharge of mortgage — entered in the Register on — at — officer's initials — (priority) — (date) — (time)

MSF 4736 REV 02/14

500

APPENDIX XI(J)

SECTION 4 : DISCHARGE OF MORTGAGE *(continued)*

COMPLETE IF THE DISCHARGE IS GIVEN BY A LIMITED LIABILITY PARTNERSHIP

* Executed by the mortgagor as a deed (in England, Wales & Northern Ireland)
* Subscribed by the mortgagor (in Scotland)
*Delete as appropriate

on this _____ day of _____ 20 _____ by signing by the following persons

Member _____

Member _____

Witnessed by _____

Name (Print) _____

Address (Print) _____

_____

Note: IN SCOTLAND subscription may be by one member of the Limited Liability Partnership and one witness, or by two members of the Limited Liability Partnership.

When the mortgage is originally executed you should send
this deed with the correct fee to:

When a transfer or discharge of mortgage is executed you
should send this deed (without a fee) to:

REGISTRY OF SHIPPING & SEAMEN
ANCHOR COURT, KEEN ROAD,
CARDIFF, CF24 5JW.

MSF 4736 REV 02/14

APPENDIX XI(J)

DEPARTMENT FOR TRANSPORT

NOTICE OF MORTGAGE INTENT

Maritime & Coastguard Agency

MSF 4739 Rev 11/14

- If more than one mortgagor (borrower) then a separate form is required, unless shares are held jointly.
- The notice of mortgage intent is recorded on the Register for a period of 30 days, unless it is withdrawn within that time.
- The notice may be renewed or further renewed for a period of 30 days, by notice in writing to the Registry. The relevant fee is required each time.
- Section 1 **must** be completed if the ship is already registered in the UK.
- Section 2 **must** be completed if the ship is **not** currently registered in the UK.
- Sections 3 and 4 **must** be completed in all cases.

SECTION 1: DETAILS OF THE SHIP (complete if the ship is currently registered in the UK)

NAME OF SHIP

OFFICIAL NUMBER

SECTION 2: DETAILS OF THE SHIP (complete if the ship is **not** currently registered in the UK)

PRESENT NAME OF SHIP

INTENDED NAME OF SHIP

INTENDED PORT OF CHOICE

DETAILS OF ANY PERMANENT MARKS

APPROXIMATE LENGTH (metres)

IF THE SHIP IS NEW, PLEASE ATTACH THE BUILDER'S CERTIFICATE. IF IT IS NOT AVAILABLE, COMPLETE THE FOLLOWING

NAME AND ADDRESS OF BUILDER

IF THE SHIP IS REGISTERED OUTSIDE THE UK, PLEASE ATTACH THE CERTIFICATE OF REGISTRY, AND GIVE:

PORT OF REGISTRATION

SECTION 3: MORTGAGOR(S) (To be completed in all cases)

FULL NAME(S)	ADDRESS(ES)	SIGNATURE(S)	No. of shares affected

SECTION 4: MORTGAGEE (to be completed in all cases)

MORTGAGEE'S REFERENCE No. *or* BANK SORTING CODE

NAME AND ADDRESS

Branch stamp

SIGNATURE

FULL NAME

DATE   The fee of £   :   is enclosed

When completed you should send this form to:
REGISTRY OF SHIPPING & SEAMEN,
ANCHOR COURT, KEEN ROAD, CARDIFF, CF24 5JW

OFFICIAL USE ONLY

Mortgage intent_____recorded on the Register
(priority)
_____ expiry date _____
(date)

RENEWAL OF INTENT	
renewal date	expiry date

APPENDIX XI(J)

MSF 4227/ REV 0607

 APPLICATION FOR A SAFE MANNING DOCUMENT

Maritime and Coastguard Agency

EXPLANATORY NOTES

With effect from 1 February 1997, the revised IMO Convention on Standards of Training, Certification and Watchkeeping (STCW 95) came into force. New UK merchant Shipping (Safe Manning, Hours of Work and Watchkeeping) Regulations 2002 specify the revised requirements for safe manning of ships over 500gt and you are advised to read these and the advice given in Merchant Shipping Notice MSN 1767 and Parts 5, 6 and 10 of the Guidance on Training and Certification before completing this application.

PLEASE COMPLETE IN BLOCK CAPITALS

1. PARTICULARS OF APPLICANT

Full name of owner

Address

Postcode

Name of applicant if not the owner

Address of applicant if not the owner

Postcode

2. PARTICULARS OF THE SHIP

Any further relevant details not adequately covered below should be included in a separate letter

Name of ship

Port of Registry   Official Number

Year of build   IMO Number

Type of ship

Principal dimensions (LOA x B x draught)

Unusual characteristics / features of ship

Tonnage 1. Gross   2. Max. summer deadweight

Auto Steering   Yes / No*   Details of hatch covers

External communications   (tick as appropriate)   W/T   R/T   VHF

Details of internal communications

* Delete as appropriate

1/7   **Formerly MAN 1**

APPENDIX XI(J)

MSF 4227/ REV 0607

2. PARTICULARS OF THE SHIP (continued)

LSA class		Number of Lifeboats	
Area of Operation (tick as appropriate)	Near-Coastal (UK)	Number of ILRs	
	Unlimited	Number of ILR Davits	
Number of Passengers		Number of Rescue Boats	

Restricted conditions (please specify)

Bow thruster	Yes / No*
CP propeller	Yes / No*
Number of main engines	
Type of engines	Steam / Motor*
Steam Boilers (tick as appropriate)	
High bilge alarm system	Yes / No*
Unattended Machinery Space (UMS) Certificate	Yes / No*

Stern thruster	Yes / No*
Number of engine-room spaces	
Registered power per engine (kW)	
None	Auto	Manual
Bridge Control	Yes / No*
Engine-room fire detection fitted	Yes / No*

* Delete as appropriate

Details of engine-room / bridge communication system

3. INTENDED SERVICE

Please give details of the intended nature of service of the ship

4. MANNING SYSTEM (See Marine Guidance Note MSG 97(M) - Training and Certification Guidance - Part 10)

Please give details of the type of manning system
i.e. Conventional, General Purpose, Share System, Interdepartmental Flexibility or other

APPENDIX XI(J)

MSF 4227/ REV 0607

5. Please submit your proposals for the safe manning of the above ship in the table below. (The tables at Annex 1 of MSN 1682 provide guidance on the numbers of certificated deck and engineer officers appropriate to different sizes of ships, tonnages and trading areas).

	Near-Coastal*	Unlimited
Master		
Chief Mate		
OOW (Deck)		
Rating (Deck) Grade 1		
Rating (Deck) Grade 2		
Chief Engineer		
2nd Engineer		
OOW (Engineer)		
Rating (Engine)		
Cook		
Doctor		
Other (specify)		
Rating (GP) Grade 1		
Rating (GP) Grade 2		
TOTAL (Minimum number of crew to be		

* **Near-Coastal -** within 150 miles from a safe haven in the UK or 30 miles from a safe haven in Eire.

6. SUPPLEMENTARY INFORMATION

Merchant Shipping Notice MSN1767 must be read in conjunction with the details required in this section. This section of the form is to be used by owners and managing operators as guidance in the assessment of proposed safe manning levels, especially in relation to paras 2.2 and 2.3 of MSN1767.

(Additional sheets should be attached if the space provided is insufficient)

Describe anticipated trade or trades

Describe anticipated length and nature of voyages

Describe the anticipated geographical trade areas

APPENDIX XI(J)

MSF 4227/ REV 0607

6. SUPPLEMENTARY INFORMATION (Continued)

Detail how the following capabilities will be covered:

1. Maintain a safe bridge watch at sea in accordance with Regulation VIII/2 of STCW 95, which includes general surveillance of the vessel.

Which watch system will be adopted?	TWO / THREE*	(* Delete as appropriate)
Will the Master undertake a navigational watch?	YES / NO*	
Will the Master be required to undertake his/her own pilotage?	YES / NO*	
Are office to ship communications handled only by the Master?	YES / NO*	
What is the communication system between bridge & watch rating?		

2. Moor and unmoor the vessel effectively and safely

Are self-tension mooring winches fitted to the vessel?	YES / NO*

Detail mooring station equipment and manning requirements for peak workload situation:

Forward

Aft

3. Operate and, when practicable, maintain efficiently, all watertight closing arrangements, fire equipment and life-saving appliances provided, including the ability to muster and disembark passengers and non-essential personnel (as appropriate), and mount an effective damage control party.

Is the vessel fitted with an accommodation fire detection system?	YES / NO*
Are fire pumps started remotely?	YES / NO*

Who is responsible for equipment maintenance?

Describe the lifeboat and rescue boat launching systems (as appropriate)

State how fire/damage control/LSA requirements are covered

4. Manage the safety functions of the vessel at sea, when not under way.

Does the vessel have DP capability?	YES / NO*

4/7

APPENDIX XI(J)

MSF 4227/ REV 0607

6. SUPPLEMENTARY INFORMATION (Continued)

5. Maintain a safe engineering watch at sea in accordance with Regulation VIII/2 of STCW 95, and also maintain general surveillance of spaces containing main propulsion and auxiliary machinery.

Will a watch system be adopted?   YES / NO*   (* Delete as appropriate)

Which watch system will be adopted?   TWO /

Is there a UMS Certificate in operation? YES / NO*

Are all machinery spaces covered by a fire detection system? YES / NO*

Are all machinery spaces covered by a bilge alarm system? YES / NO*

Will the Chief Engineer undertake a watch? YES / NO*

Can emergency steering be engaged by one person? YES / NO*

How will the engineer watch rating duties be covered?

6. Operate and maintain in a safe condition, the main propulsion and auxiliary machinery to enable the ship to overcome the foreseeable perils of the voyage, and maintain the safety arrangements and cleanliness of machinery spaces to minimise the risk of fire.

Who will undertake machinery space cleaning?

Who will assist in the event of breakdowns?

7. Provide for medical care onboard.

How is the provision satisfied?

8. Maintain a safe radio watch in accordance with 1974 SOLAS and ITU Regulations, as amended.

What is the radio equipment maintenance agreement?   ONBOARD / SHORE BASED*

Who will be the primary GMDSS operator?

9. Maintain the precautions and safeguards necessary to protect the marine environment in accordance with MARPOL 73/78, as amended.

What personnel are necessary to cover the vessels SOPEP requirements?

APPENDIX XI(J)

MSF 4227/ REV 0607

6. SUPPLEMENTARY INFORMATION (Continued)

10. Maintain safety in all ship operations whilst in port.

What cargo handling gear is fitted to the vessel and who operates it?

Who undertakes hold/tank cleaning?

11. Ships Cook

Will a certificated ships cook be carried?   YES / NO*   (* Delete as appropriate)

If not, how will the cooking duties be covered?

12. Ships Doctor

With respect to the M.S. (Ships Doctors) Regulations 1995, S.I. 1995/1803, state compliance (as appropriate):

(UK ships are required to have a doctor on board if carrying 100 or more persons on an international voyage of more than three days, or on a voyage during which it is more than one and a half day's sailing time from a port with adequate medical equipment)

HOURS OF WORK PROVISION

Provide an explanation of how the proposed manning level takes account of the requirements contained in the M.S. (Safe Manning, Hours of Work and Watchkeeping) Regulations 2002, ensuring that the working arrangements allow for sufficient rest periods to avoid fatigue:

7. PLANS SUBMITTED WITH THIS APPLICATION (tick ✓ as appropriate)

Fire   Mooring & equipment   Escape (Passenger ships only)

Schedule of duties   General arrangement   Engine-room arrangement

509

APPENDIX XI(J)

MSF 4227/ REV 0607

8. DECLARATION (The maximum penalty for a false entry is £5000)

I declare that to the best of my knowledge, the particulars given by me on this form are correct.

Signed (on behalf of the owners) | | Date |

Please now complete the PAYMENT DETAILS in Section 8 below

The completed form together with the appropriate fee and enclosures should be sent to:

Maritime and Coastguard Agency
Seafarer Training and Certification
Spring Place
105 Commercial Road   **Tel 02380 329231**
Southampton SO15 1EG   **Fax 02380 329252**

9. PAYMENT DETAILS (To be completed by applicant)

Please tick (✓) the appropriate box below to indicate your chosen method of payment. **CASH WILL NOT BE ACCEPTED**

Maestro ☐   Visa ☐   Mastercard / Access ☐   Delta ☐   Cheque/bankers draft ☐   Postal Orders ☐

		Security Code
Name of Card Holder		☐☐☐
Card Number		(The Security Code is the last three digits of the numbers on the reverse of the card, near to the signature
Start Date		
Expiry Date		
Maestro Issue Number (Maestro Cards only)		

Signature | | **Date** |

ALTERNATIVELY - If you have a Rolling Account with the MCA, please provide the following information:-

Client Reference Number

Marine Office where
Account is held

Customer Service

FOR OFFICIAL USE ONLY

Fee received by

File reference   MC49/48/

F264   Official Stamp

An Executive Agency of the Department for Transport

INDEX

administration of register
    Bahamas, 7.2
    Barbados, 8.2
    Bermuda, 9.2
    British Virgin Islands, 10.2
    Cayman Islands, 11.2
    Cyprus, 12.2
    Gibraltar, 13.2
    Hong Kong, 14.2
    Isle of Man, 15.2
    Jamaica, 16.2
    Liberia, 17.2
    Malta, 18.2
    Marshall Islands, 19.2
    Norway, 20.2
    Panama, 21.2
    Singapore, 22.2
    St Vincent and the Grenadines, 23.2
    United Kingdom, 24.2
    Vanuatu, 25.2
age of vessel
    eligibility for registration
        Bahamas, 7.5
        Barbados, 8.6
        Bermuda, 9.5
        British Virgin Islands, 10.5
        Cayman Islands, 11.5
        Cyprus, 12.5–12.14
        Gibraltar, 13.5
        Hong Kong, 14.5
        Isle of Man, 15.5
        Jamaica, 16.4
        Liberia, 17.5
        Malta, 18.5
        Marshall Islands, 19.5
        Norway, 20.5
        Panama, 21.5
        Singapore, 22.5
        St Vincent and the Grenadines, 23.5
        United Kingdom, 24.5
        Vanuatu, 25.5
annual returns. *See* returns

Bahamas
    bareboat charter registration, 7.6
        foreign charter, 7.7
    classification societies, 7.13
    crew certification, 7.9
        competency certificates, 7.10
        nationality of crew, 7.11
    deregistration
        procedure for, 7.22
    eligibility for registration
        age limit, 7.5
        vessel type, 7.4
    fees, 7.17, 7.22
    fishing vessels, 7.4
    fleet, 7.2
    geography of, 7.1
    manning requirements, 7.8
        safe manning documents, 7.12
    mortgages
        registration of, 7.20
    permanent registration, 7.17
        age limit, 7.19
        forms, 7.18
    procedure for registration, 7.15
    provisional registration, 7.15
        extension of, 7.16
        validity of, 7.16
    radio traffic accounting authorities, 7.14
    register, administration of, 7.2
    registration
        bareboat charter, 7.6
        deregistration, 7.22
        eligibility for, 7.4. 7.5
        mortgages, 7.20
        permanent registration, 7.17
        permanent registration, age limit, 7.19
        permanent registration, forms, 7.18
        procedure for, 7.15
        provisional registration, 7.15
        provisional, extension of, 7.16
        provisional, validity of, 7.16
        register, administration of, 7.2

security interests, 7.20
survey, 7.21
yachts, 7.23
security interests
registration of, 7.20
source of law, 7.3
survey
requirement of, 7.21
trading limits, 7.8
yachts
registration of, 7.23
Barbados
bareboat charter registration, 8.9–8.10
foreign charter, 8.11
classification societies, 8.17
crew certification, 8.13
competency certificates, 8.13. 8.14
nationality of crew, 8.15
deregistration
procedure for, 8.25
eligibility for registration
age limit, 8.6
vessel type, 8.4. 8.5
fees, 8.3, 8.19, 8.25
fishing vessels, 8.8
fleet, 8.2
geography of, 8.1
manning requirements, 8.13
safe manning documents, 8.16
mortgages
registration of, 8.23
ownership
requirements of, 8.7–8.8
permanent registration, 8.22
forms, 8.22
provisional registration, 8.18–8.20
extension of, 8.21
validity of, 8.21
register, administration of, 8.2
registration
bareboat charter, 8.9–8.10
deregistration, 8.25
eligibility for, 8.4–8.6
mortgages, 8.23
permanent registration, 8.22
permanent registration, forms, 8.22
procedure for, 8.18
provisional registration, 8.18–8.20
provisional, extension of, 8.21
provisional, validity of, 8.21
register, administration of, 8.2
security interests, 8.23
survey, 8.24
yachts, 8.26
security interests
registration of, 8.23

source of law, 8.3
survey
requirement of, 8.24
trading limits, 8.12
yachts
registration of, 8.26
bareboat charter
foreign charter, registration of
Bahamas, 7.7
Barbados, 8.11
Bermuda, 9.12–9.14
British Virgin Islands, 10.9
Cayman Islands, 11.9
Cyprus, 12.17
Gibraltar, 13.14–13.15
Isle of Man, 15.9
Jamaica, 16.13
Liberia, 17.11
Malta, 18.8
Marshall Islands, 19.13
Norway, 20.7
Panama, 21.13
Singapore, 22.13
St Vincent and the Grenadines, 23.12
United Kingdom, 24.11
Vanuatu, 25.9
mortgages
convention on, 5.32–5.34
protection of mortgagees, 5.26–5.31
registration
Barbados, 8.9–8.10
Bermuda, 9.8–9.11
British Virgin Islands, 10.8
Cayman Islands, 11.8
Convention on Conditions for Registration
of Ships 1986 5.24–5.25
Convention on Maritime Liens and
Mortgages 1993 5.32–5.34
Cyprus, 12.16
development of, 5.1–5.18
Gibraltar, 13.10–13.13
Hong Kong, 14.7–14.8
in practice, 5.19–5.23
Isle of Man, 15.8
Jamaica, 16.12
Liberia, 17.9–17.11
Malta, 18.6–18.8
Marshall Islands, 19.12
Norway, 20.7
Panama, 21.11–21.12
protection of mortgagees, 5.26–5.31
Singapore, 22.12
St Vincent and the Grenadines,
23.11
United Kingdom, 24.9–24.10
Vanuatu, 25.8

INDEX

bearer shares, 6.6
beneficial ownership, 6.8
Bermuda
  bareboat charter registration, 9.8–9.11
    foreign charter, 9.12–9.14
  classification societies, 9.19
  crew certification, 9.13
    competency certificates, 9.16
    nationality of crew, 9.17
  deregistration
    procedure for, 9.26
  eligibility for registration
    age limit, 9.5
    vessel type, 9.4
  fees, 9.14, 9.27
  fleet, 9.2
  geography of, 9.1
  manning requirements, 9.16
    safe manning documents, 9.18
  mortgages
    registration of, 9.23–9.24
  ownership
    requirements of, 9.6–9.7
  permanent registration, 9.21–9.22
    forms, 9.21–9.22
  provisional registration, 9.18–9.20
    extension of, 9.20
    validity of, 9.20
  register, administration of, 9.2
  registration
    bareboat charter, 9.9–9.10
    deregistration, 9.26
    eligibility for, 9.4–9.5
    mortgages, 9.23–9.24
    permanent registration, 9.21–9.22
    permanent registration, forms,
      9.21–9.22
    procedure for, 9.20
    provisional registration, 9.18–9.20
    provisional, extension of, 9.20
    provisional, validity of, 9.20
    register, administration of, 9.2
    security interests, 9.25
    survey, 9.24
    yachts, 9.27
  security interests
    registration of, 9.25
  source of law, 9.3
  survey
    requirement of, 9.24
  trading limits, 9.15
  yachts
    registration of, 9.27
blacklists, 3.47
boycotts, 6.17
Britain. *See* United Kingdom

British Virgin Islands
  bareboat charter registration, 10.8
    foreign charter, 10.9
  classification societies, 10.15
  crew certification, 10.12
    competency certificates, 10.12
    nationality of crew, 10.13
  deregistration
    procedure for, 10.30
  eligibility for registration
    age limit, 10.5
    vessel type, 10.4
  fees, 10.30
  fleet, 10.2
  geography of, 10.1
  interim registration, 10.21
  manning requirements, 10.11
    safe manning documents, 10.14
  mortgages
    registration of, 10.25–10.28
  ownership
    requirements of, 10.6–10.7
  permanent registration, 10.17–10.20
    forms, 10.18
  provisional registration, 10.22
    extension of, 10.23
    validity of, 10.23
  radio traffic accounting authorities,
    10.16
  register, administration of, 10.2
  registration
    bareboat charter, 10.8–10.9
    deregistration, 10.30
    eligibility for, 10.4–10.5
    interim registration, 10.21
    mortgages, 10.25–10.28
    permanent registration, 10.17–10.20
    permanent registration, forms, 10.18
    procedure for, 10.17
    provisional registration, 10.22
    provisional, extension of, 10.23
    provisional, validity of, 10.23
    register, administration of, 10.2
    security interests, 10.25–10.28
    ships under construction, 10.24
    survey, 10.19–10.20. 10.29
    yachts, 10.31–10.33
  sanctions, 10.10
  security interests
    registration of, 10.25–10.28
  ships under construction
    registration of, 10.24
  source of law, 10.3
  survey
    requirement of, 10.19–10.20. 10.29
  trading limits, 10.10

513

yachts
registration of, 10.31–10.33
BVI. *See* British Virgin Islands

capital markets
access to, 6.15
categories of ship. *See* Vessels
Cayman Islands
bareboat charter registration, 11.8
foreign charter, 11.9
classification societies, 11.15
crew certification, 11.13
competency certificates, 11.12
nationality of crew, 11.13
deregistration
procedure for, 11.29
eligibility for registration
age limit, 11.5
vessel type, 11.4
fees, 11.29, 11.33
fleet, 11.2
geography of, 11.1
interim registration, 11.20
manning requirements, 11.11
safe manning documents, 11.14
mortgages
registration of, 11.24–11.27
ownership
requirements of, 11.6–11.7
permanent registration, 11.17–11.19
forms, 11.21–11.22
provisional registration, 11.21
extension of, 11.22
validity of, 11.22
radio traffic accounting authorities, 11.16
register, administration of, 11.2
registration
bareboat charter, 11.8–11.9
deregistration, 11.29
eligibility for, 11.4–11.5
interim registration, 11.20
mortgages, 11.24–11.27
permanent registration, 11.17–11.19
permanent registration, forms, 11.21–11.22
procedure for, 11.17
provisional registration, 11.21
provisional, extension of, 11.22
provisional, validity of, 11.22
register, administration of, 11.2
security interests, 11.24–11.27
ships under construction, 11.23
survey, 11.18. 11.28
yachts, 11.30–11.34
sanctions, 11.10

security interests
registration of, 11.24–11.27
ships under construction
registration of, 11.23
source of law, 11.3
survey
requirement of, 11.18. 11.28
trading limits, 11.10
yachts
registration of, 11.30–11.34
certification
International Convention on Standards of
Training, Certification and Watchkeeping
for Seafarers, 2.37–2.39
charges. *See* Mortgages
choice of flag
access to markets, 6.15–6.16
economic factors, 6.3–6.11
factors influencing, 6.15–6.17
operating costs, 6.12–6.14
political factors, 6.17
choice of international registers. *See* international
registers, choice of, 6.18
choice of law, 1.32–1.33
classification societies
Bahamas, 7.13
Barbados, 8.17
Bermuda, 9.19
British Virgin Islands, 10.15
Cayman Islands, 11.15
Cyprus, 12.24
flag states, 2.11, 3.50
Gibraltar, 13.21
Hong Kong, 14.11
Isle of Man, 15.15
Jamaica, 16.19
Liberia, 17.17
Malta, 18.13
Marshall Islands, 19.19
Norway, 20.13
Panama, 21.20
Singapore, 22.19
St Vincent and the Grenadines, 23.18
United Kingdom, 24.17
Vanuatu, 25.15
collective agreements, 4.42
collisions, 10.9, 11.9. 18.22
common law, 5.15
company formation
accounts
Singapore, 22.11
company officers
Jamaica, 16.10
Marshall Islands, 19.10–19.11

INDEX

Panama, 21.9–21.10
Singapore, 22.8–22.10
St Vincent and the Grenadines, 23.9–23.10
Gibraltar, 13.7–13.9
Jamaica, 16.6
Liberia, 17.7
Marshall Islands, 19.7
non-resident status
Jamaica, 16.8
Marshall Islands, 19.8
Panama, 21.8
United Kingdom, 24.8
Vanuatu, 25.7
overseas company
Jamaica, 16.7
Panama, 21.7
Panama, 21.7
registered agent
Liberia, 17.8
Marshall Islands, 19.9
registered office
Jamaica, 16.9
Liberia, 17.8
Panama, 21.8
St Vincent and the Grenadines, 23.8
Returns
Jamaica, 16.11
Singapore, 22.11
Singapore, 22.7
St Vincent and the Grenadines, 23.7
United Kingdom, 24.7
Vanuatu, 25.7
company officers
Jamaica, 16.10
Marshall Islands, 19.10–19.11
Panama, 21.9–21.10
Singapore, 22.8–22.10
St Vincent and the Grenadines, 23.9–23.10
company secretary. See company officers
company security officer
appointment of, 2.35
competency certificates
Bahamas, 7.10
Barbados, 8.13. 8.14
Bermuda, 9.16
British Virgin Islands, 10.12
Cayman Islands, 11.12
crew certification
Bahamas, 7.10
Barbados, 8.13. 8.14
Bermuda, 9.16
British Virgin Islands, 10.12
Cayman Islands, 11.12
Cyprus, 12.20

Gibraltar, 13.17
Hong Kong, 14.10
Isle of Man, 15.12
Jamaica, 16.16
Liberia, 17.14
Malta, 18.10
Marshall Islands, 19.16
Norway, 20.10
Panama, 21.17
Singapore, 22.16
St Vincent and the Grenadines, 23.15
United Kingdom, 24.14
Vanuatu, 25.12
Cyprus, 12.20
Gibraltar, 13.17
Hong Kong, 14.10
Isle of Man, 15.12
Jamaica, 16.16
Liberia, 17.14
Malta, 18.10
Marshall Islands, 19.16
Norway, 20.10
Panama, 21.17
Singapore, 22.16
St Vincent and the Grenadines, 23.15
United Kingdom, 24.14
Vanuatu, 25.12
competition, 6.1–6.2
conditions for registration of ships.
See registration
connecting factors, 1.15
nationality of crew
Bahamas, 7.11
Barbados, 8.15
Bermuda, 9.17
British Virgin Islands, 10.13
Cayman Islands, 11.13
Cyprus, 12.21
Gibraltar, 13.19
Hong Kong, 14.10
Isle of Man, 15.13
Jamaica, 16.17
Liberia, 17.15
Malta, 18.11
Marshall Islands, 19.17
Norway, 20.11
Panama, 21.18
Singapore, 22.17
St Vincent and the Grenadines, 23.16
United Kingdom, 24.15
Vanuatu, 25.13
Norway, 20.10
Panama, 21.17
Singapore, 22.16

INDEX

St Vincent and the Grenadines, 23.15
United Kingdom, 24.14
Vanuatu, 25.12
currency
Bahamas, 7.1
Barbados, 8.1
Bermuda, 9.1
British Virgin Islands, 10.1
Cayman Islands, 11.1
Cyprus, 12.1
Gibraltar, 13.1
Hong Kong, 14.1
Isle of Man, 15.1
Jamaica, 16.1
Liberia, 17.1
Malta, 18.1
Marshall Islands, 19.1
Norway, 20.1
Panama, 21.1
Singapore, 22.1
St Vincent and the Grenadines, 23.1
United Kingdom, 24.1
Vanuatu, 25.1
Cyprus
bareboat charter registration, 12.16
foreign charter, 12.17
classification societies, 12.24
crew certification, 12.20
competency certificates, 12.20
nationality of crew, 12.21
deregistration
procedure for, 12.31
eligibility for registration
age limit, 12.5–12.14
eligibility for registration
vessel type, 12.4
fees, 12.3, 12.27, 12.28
fishing vessels, 12.13
fleet, 12.2
geography of, 12.1
manning requirements, 12.19
safe manning documents, 12.22–12.23
mortgages
registration of, 12.29
ownership
requirements of, 12.15
permanent registration, 12.28
forms, 12.28
provisional registration, 12.25–12.26
extension of, 12.27
validity of, 12.27
register, administration of, 12.2
registration
bareboat charter, 12.16–12.17
deregistration, 12.31

eligibility for, 12.4
mortgages, 12.29
permanent registration, 12.28
permanent registration, forms, 12.28
procedure for, 12.25
provisional registration, 12.25–12.26
provisional, extension of, 12.27
provisional, validity of, 12.27
register, administration of, 12.2
security interests, 12.29
survey, 12.30
security interests
registration of, 12.29
source of law, 12.3
survey
requirement of, 12.30
tonnage tax, 12.3
trading limits, 12.18

Danish International Ship Register, 4.14, 4.44
deregistration, procedure for
Bahamas, 7.22
Barbados, 8.25
Bermuda, 9.26
British Virgin Islands, 10.30
Cayman Islands, 11.29
Cyprus, 12.31
Gibraltar, 13.27
Hong Kong, 14.20
Isle of Man, 15.22
Jamaica, 16.27
Liberia, 17.26
Malta, 18.23
Marshall Islands, 19.26
Norway, 20.19
Panama, 21.29
Singapore, 22.26
St Vincent and the Grenadines, 23.25
United Kingdom, 24.31
Vanuatu, 25.22
detention, 2.16–2.22
developing countries, 6.15
discrimination, 3.50, 6.17
documentation. *See* forms
double tax treaties
Marshall Islands, 19.20
Panama, 21.22
drilling platform, 4.41
dual registry, 21.11
duties of flag state. *See* flag states, duties of

economic factors
choice of flag, 6.3–6.11
electronic certificates
international registers, 6.31

INDEX

eligibility for registration
  age of vessel
    Bahamas, 7.5
    Barbados, 8.6
    Bermuda, 9.5
    British Virgin Islands, 10.5
    Cayman Islands, 11.5
    Cyprus, 12.5–12.14
    Gibraltar, 13.5
    Hong Kong, 14.5
    Isle of Man, 15.5
    Jamaica, 16.4
    Liberia, 17.5
    Malta, 18.5
    Marshall Islands, 19.5
    Norway, 20.5
    Panama, 21.5
    Singapore, 22.5
    St Vincent and the Grenadines, 23.5
    United Kingdom, 24.5
    Vanuatu, 25.5
  type of vessel
    Bahamas, 7.4
    Barbados, 8.4. 8.5
    Bermuda, 9.4
    British Virgin Islands, 10.4
    Cayman Islands, 11.4
    Cyprus, 12.4
    Gibraltar, 13.4
    Hong Kong, 14.4
    Isle of Man, 15.4
    Jamaica, 16.3
    Liberia, 17.4
    Malta, 18.4
    Marshall Islands, 19.4
    Norway, 20.4
    Panama, 21.4
    Singapore, 22.4
    St Vincent and the Grenadines, 23.4
    United Kingdom, 24.4
    Vanuatu, 25.4
exchange control, 19.8, 23.23, 25.16
extension of provisional registration
  Bahamas, 7.16
  Barbados, 8.21
  Bermuda, 9.20
  British Virgin Islands, 10.23
  Cayman Islands, 11.22
  Cyprus, 12.27
  Gibraltar, 13.22
  Hong Kong, 14.13
  Jamaica, 16.23
  Liberia, 17.21
  Malta, 18.17. 18.19
  Marshall Islands, 19.22

  Panama, 21.25
  Singapore, 22.23
  St Vincent and the Grenadines, 23.21
  United Kingdom, 24.21
  Vanuatu, 25.18

fees, 1.21, 4.18, 4.45, 5.19, 5.29, 6.3, 6.19, 6.25, 6.26
  Bahamas, 7.17, 7.22
  Barbados, 8.3, 8.19, 8.25
  Bermuda, 9.14, 9.27
  British Virgin Islands, 10.30
  Cayman Islands, 11.29, 11.33
  Cyprus, 12.3, 12.27, 12.28
  Gibraltar, 13.13, 13.23
  Hong Kong, 14.3
  Jamaica, 16.2, 16.26
  Liberia, 17.20, 17.26
  Malta, 18.7, 18.15, 18.18
  Marshall Islands, 19.12, 19.26
  Panama, 21.14, 21.19, 21.24
  Singapore, 22.26
  St Vincent and the Grenadines, 23.11, 23.20,
    23.22, 23.23, 23.25
  Vanuatu, 25.2, 25.8, 25.17, 25.19
fishing vessels, 3.26, 3.32, 3.43, 4.41, 4.43,
  4.45, 6.32
  Bahamas, 7.4
  Barbados, 8.8
  Cyprus, 12.13
  Gibraltar, 13.4
  Hong Kong, 14.4
  Isle of Man, 15.14
  Jamaica, 16.3
  Liberia, 17.22
  Marshall Islands, 19.4
  St Vincent and the Grenadines, 23.4
  United Kingdom, 24.4, 24.6, 24.15, 24.19,
    24.22, 24.24, 24.30
flag of convenience
  international registers, 4.14–4.36
  See also registration, flag of convenience
flag states
  choice of flag, 6.1–6.2
    access to markets, 6.15–6.16
    economic factors, 6.3–6.11
    operating costs, 6.12–6.14
    political factors, 6.17
  classification societies, 2.11
  duties of
    general principles, 2.1–2.4
    implementation of mandatory instruments,
      2.5–2.15
  port state control, 2.16–2.28
  quality control system
    Hong Kong, 14.17–14.18

INDEX

sovereignty
  registration, 3.1–3.7
survey, 2.12–2.15
fleet
  Bahamas, 7.2
  Barbados, 8.2
  Bermuda, 9.2
  British Virgin Islands, 10.2
  Cayman Islands, 11.2
  Cyprus, 12.2
  Gibraltar, 13.2
  Hong Kong, 14.2
  Isle of Man, 15.2
  Liberia, 17.2
  Malta, 18.2
  Marshall Islands, 19.2
  Norway, 20.2
foreign charter
  registration of bareboat charter
    Bahamas, 7.7
    Barbados, 8.11
    Bermuda, 9.12–9.14
    British Virgin Islands, 10.9
    Cayman Islands, 11.9
    Cyprus, 12.17
    Gibraltar, 13.14–13.15
    Isle of Man, 15.9
    Jamaica, 16.13
    Liberia, 17.11
    Malta, 18.8
    Marshall Islands, 19.13
    Norway, 20.7
    Panama, 21.13
    Singapore, 22.13
    St Vincent and the Grenadines, 23.12
    United Kingdom, 24.11
    Vanuatu, 25.9
forms
  permanent registration, 1.20–1.24
    Bahamas, 7.18
    Barbados, 8.22
    Bermuda, 9.21–9.22
    British Virgin Islands, 10.18
    Cayman Islands, 11.21–11.22
    Cyprus, 12.28
    Gibraltar, 13.23
    Hong Kong, 14.14
    Isle of Man, 15.18
    Jamaica, 16.24
    Liberia, 17.22
    Malta, 18.20
    Marshall Islands, 19.23
    Norway, 20.16
    Panama, 21.26
    Singapore, 22.24

St Vincent and the Grenadines, 23.22
United Kingdom, 24.22–24.23
Vanuatu, 25.19

geography
  Bahamas, 7.1
  Barbados, 8.1
  Bermuda, 9.1
  British Virgin Islands, 10.1
  Cayman Islands, 11.1
  Cyprus, 12.1
  Gibraltar, 13.1
  Hong Kong, 14.1
  Isle of Man, 15.1
  Jamaica, 16.1
  Liberia, 17.1
  Malta, 18.1
  Marshall Islands, 19.1
  Norway, 20.1
  Panama, 21.1
  Singapore, 22.1
  St Vincent and the Grenadines, 23.1
  United Kingdom, 24.1
  Vanuatu, 25.1
Gibraltar
  bareboat charter registration,
    13.10–13.13
    foreign charter, 13.14–13.15
  classification societies, 13.21
  company formation, 13.7–13.9
  crew certification, 13.17
    competency certificates, 13.17
    nationality of crew, 13.19
  deregistration
    procedure for, 13.27
  eligibility for registration
    age limit, 13.5
    vessel type, 13.4
  fees, 13.13, 13.23
  fishing vessels, 13.4
  fleet, 13.2
  geography of, 13.1
  manning requirements, 13.17–13.18
    safe manning documents, 13.20
  mortgages
    registration of, 13.24–13.25
  ownership
    requirements of, 13.6
  permanent registration, 13.23
    forms, 13.23
  pleasure craft, 13.4
  provisional registration, 13.22
    extension of, 13.22
    validity of, 13.22
  register, administration of, 13.2

INDEX

registration
    bareboat charter, 13.10–13.13
    deregistration, 13.27
    eligibility for, 13.4–13.5
    mortgages, 13.24–13.25
    permanent registration, 13.23
    permanent registration, forms, 13.23
    procedure for, 13.22
    provisional registration, 13.22
    provisional, extension of, 13.22
    provisional, validity of, 13.22
    register, administration of, 13.2
    security interests, 13.24–13.25
    survey, 13.26
    yachts, 13.28
security interests
    registration of, 13.24–13.25
source of law, 13.3
survey
    requirement of, 13.26
trading limits, 13.16
yachts
    registration of, 13.28
Great Britain. *See* United Kingdom

high seas
    definition, 1.2
    jurisdiction, 1.3
    vessels
        nationality of, 1.3, 1.4
        protection of, 1.4
        registration of, 1.4, 1.5, 1.6
        registration of, 1.4–1.19
Hong Kong
    bareboat charter registration, 14.7–14.8
    classification societies, 14.11
    crew certification, 14.10
        competency certificates, 14.10
    crew certification
        nationality of crew, 14.10
    deregistration
        procedure for, 14.20
    eligibility for registration
        age limit, 14.5
    eligibility for registration
        vessel type, 14.4
    fees, 14.3
    fishing vessels, 14.4
    flag State quality control system, 14.17–14.18
    fleet, 14.2
    geography of, 14.1
    manning requirements, 14.10
        safe manning documents, 14.2
    mortgages
        registration of, 14.15–14.16

ownership
    requirements of, 14.6
permanent registration, 14.14
    forms, 14.14
provisional registration, 14.13
    extension of, 14.13
    validity of, 14.13
register, administration of, 14.2
registration
    bareboat charter, 14.7–14.8
    deregistration, 14.20
    eligibility for, 14.4–14.5
    flag State quality control system,
        14.17–14.18
    mortgages, 14.15–14.16
    permanent registration, 14.14
    permanent registration, forms, 14.14
    procedure for, 14.13
    provisional registration, 14.13
    provisional, extension of, 14.13
    provisional, validity of, 14.13
    register, administration of, 14.2
    security interests, 14.15–14.16
    survey, 14.19
security interests
    registration of, 14.15–14.16
self-propelled vessels, 14.4
source of law, 14.2. 14.3
survey
    requirement of, 14.19
taxation, 14.12
trading limits, 14.9
hypothèques. *See* mortgages

in rem rights, 1.23, 1.38, 5.12, 5.22
inspections. *See* surveys
interim registration
    British Virgin Islands, 10.21
    Cayman Islands, 11.20
International Association of Classification
    Societies, 2.11
International Maritime Organization, 2.34
international registers, 4.14–4.36, 6.16
    choice of, 6.18
        accessibility, 6.29–6.30
        costs, 6.25–6.26
        electronic certificates, 6.31
        fishing vessels, 6.32
        government stability, 6.22
        labour relations, 6.23
        manning and certification, 6.24
        national preference, 6.27
        ownership restrictions, 6.21
        reputation, 6.40
        technical expertise, 6.28

INDEX

vessel eligibility, 6.19–6.20
yachts, 6.33–6.39
labour rights, 4.30–4.36
opposition to, 4.20
safety, 4.21–4.24
second registers, 4.37–4.46
transparency, 4.25–4.29
International Ship Security Certificate,
2.35
Isle of Man
bareboat charter registration, 15.8
foreign charter, 15.9
classification societies, 15.15
crew certification, 15.11
competency certificates, 15.12
nationality of crew, 15.13
deregistration
procedure for, 15.22
eligibility for registration
age limit, 15.5
vessel type, 15.4
fishing vessels, 15.14
fleet, 15.2
geography of, 15.1
manning requirements, 15.11
safe manning documents, 15.14
mortgages
registration of, 15.19–15.20
ownership
requirements of, 15.6–15.7
permanent registration, 15.18
forms, 15.18
pleasure craft, 15.14
provisional registration, 15.17
register, administration of, 15.2
registration
bareboat charter, 15.8–15.9
deregistration, 15.22
eligibility for, 15.4
mortgages, 15.19–15.20
permanent registration, 15.18
permanent registration, forms, 15.18
procedure for, 15.25
provisional registration, 15.17
register, administration of, 15.2
security interests, 15.19–15.20
survey, 15.21
yachts, 15.23–15.24
sanctions, 15.10
security interests
registration of, 15.19–15.20
source of law, 15.3
survey
requirement of, 15.21
taxation, 15.16

trading limits, 15.10
Jamaica
bareboat charter registration, 16.12
foreign charter, 16.13
classification societies, 16.19
company formation, 16.6
company officers, 16.10
non-resident status, 16.8
overseas company, 16.7
registered office, 16.9
returns, 16.11
crew certification, 16.16
competency certificates, 16.16
nationality of crew, 16.17
deregistration
procedure for, 16.27
eligibility for registration
age limit, 16.4
vessel type, 16.3
fees, 16.2, 16.26
fishing vessels, 16.3
geography of, 16.1
manning requirements, 16.15
safe manning documents, 16.18
mortgages
registration of, 16.25
ownership
requirements of, 16.5
permanent registration, 16.24
forms, 16.24
pleasure craft, 16.3
provisional registration, 16.22
extension of, 16.23
validity of, 16.23
register, administration of, 16.2
registration
bareboat charter, 16.12
deregistration, 16.27
eligibility for, 16.3–16.4
mortgages, 16.25
permanent registration, 16.24
permanent registration, forms, 16.24
procedure for, 16.22
provisional registration, 16.22
provisional, extension of, 16.23
provisional, validity of, 16.23
register, administration of, 16.2
security interests, 16.25
survey, 16.26
security interests
registration of, 16.25
source of law, 16.2
survey
requirement of, 16.26
taxation, 16.20–16.21

INDEX

trading limits, 16.14
jet skis and similar craft, 3.39, 3.42

Kerguelen register, 4.39

labour relations. *See* certificates of competency;
international registers; manning; nationality
of crew
law merchant, 1.9
leisure craft, 3.42, 3.43
Liberia
bareboat charter registration, 17.9–17.11
foreign charter, 17.11
classification societies, 17.17
company formation, 17.7
registered agent, 17.8
registered office, 17.8
crew certification, 17.14
competency certificates, 17.14
nationality of crew, 17.15
deregistration
procedure for, 17.26
eligibility for registration
age limit, 17.5
vessel type, 17.4
fees, 17.20, 17.26
fishing vessels, 17.22
fleet, 17.2
geography of, 17.1
manning requirements, 17.13
safe manning documents, 17.16
mortgages
registration of, 17.23–17.24
ownership
requirements of, 17.6
permanent registration, 17.22
forms, 17.22
provisional registration, 17.20
extension of, 17.21
validity of, 17.21
register, administration of, 17.2
registration
bareboat charter, 17.9–17.11
deregistration, 17.26
eligibility for, 17.4–17.5
mortgages, 17.23–17.24
permanent registration, 17.22
permanent registration, forms, 17.22
procedure for, 17.19
provisional registration, 17.20
provisional, extension of, 17.21
provisional, validity of, 17.21
register, administration of, 17.2
security interests, 17.23–17.24
survey, 17.25

security interests
registration of, 17.23–17.24
self-propelled vessels, 17.4
source of law, 17.3
survey
requirement of, 17.25
taxation, 17.18
tonnage tax, 17.18, 17.20
trading limits, 17.12
liens, 5.5, 5.11, 5.13, 5.14, 5.21, 5.27, 5.32–5.34

maintenance of the register, 2.2
Malta
bareboat charter registration, 18.6–18.8
foreign charter, 18.8
classification societies, 18.13
crew certification, 18.10
competency certificates, 18.10
nationality of crew, 18.11
deregistration
procedure for, 18.23
eligibility for registration
age limit, 18.5
vessel type, 18.4
fees, 18.7, 18.15, 18.18
fleet, 18.2
geography of, 18.1
manning requirements, 18.10
safe manning documents, 18.12
mortgages
requirement of, 18.22
permanent registration, 18.18
forms, 18.20
pleasure craft, 18.15
provisional registration, 18.15
extension of, 18.17. 18.19
validity of, 18.16. 18.19
radio licence
registration of, 18.21
register, administration of, 18.2
registration
bareboat charter, 18.6–18.8
deregistration, 18.23
eligibility for, 18.4–18.5
mortgages, 18.22
permanent registration, 18.18
permanent registration, forms, 18.20
procedure for, 18.14
provisional registration, 18.15
provisional, extension of, 18.17. 18.19
provisional, validity of, 18.16. 18.19
radio licence, 18.21
register, administration of, 18.2
security interests, 18.22
survey, 18.19

521

INDEX

security interests
requirement of, 18.22
source of law, 18.3
survey
requirement of, 18.19
trading limits, 18.9
manning
requirements of
Bahamas, 7.8
Barbados, 8.13
Bermuda, 9.16
British Virgin Islands, 10.11
Cayman Islands, 11.11
Cyprus, 12.19
Gibraltar, 13.17–13.18
Hong Kong, 14.10
Isle of Man, 15.11
Jamaica, 16.15
Liberia, 17.13
Malta, 18.10
Marshall Islands, 19.15
Norway, 20.9
Panama, 21.16
Singapore, 22.15
St Vincent and the Grenadines, 23.14
United Kingdom, 24.13
Vanuatu, 25.11
safe manning documents
Bahamas, 7.12
Barbados, 8.16
Bermuda, 9.18
British Virgin Islands, 10.14
Cayman Islands, 11.14
Cyprus, 12.22–12.23
Gibraltar, 13.20
Hong Kong, 14.2
Isle of Man, 15.14
Jamaica, 16.18
Liberia, 17.16
Malta, 18.12
Marshall Islands, 19.18
Norway, 20.12
Panama, 21.19
Singapore, 22.18
St Vincent and the Grenadines, 23.17
United Kingdom, 24.16
Vanuatu, 25.14
maritime security
International Ship and Port Facility Security
Code, 2.34–2.36
Marshall Islands
bareboat charter registration, 19.12
foreign charter, 19.13
classification societies, 19.19
company formation, 19.7

company officers, 19.10–19.11
non-resident status, 19.8
registered agent, 19.9
crew certification, 19.16
competency certificates, 19.16
nationality of crew, 19.17
deregistration
procedure for, 19.26
eligibility for registration
age limit, 19.5
vessel type, 19.4
fees, 19.12, 19.26
fishing vessels, 19.4
fleet, 19.2
geography of, 19.1
manning requirements, 19.15
safe manning documents, 19.18
mortgages
registration of, 19.24
ownership
requirements of, 19.6
permanent registration, 19.23
forms, 19.23
provisional registration, 19.21
extension of, 19.22
validity of, 19.22
register, administration of, 19.2
registration
bareboat charter, 19.12–19.13
deregistration, 19.26
eligibility for, 19.4–19.5
mortgages, 19.24
permanent registration, 19.23
permanent registration, forms, 19.23
procedure for, 19.21
provisional registration, 19.21
provisional registration, 19.21
provisional, extension of, 19.22
provisional, validity of, 19.22
radio licence, 19.21
radio licence, 19.21
register, administration of, 19.2
security interests, 19.24
survey, 19.25
yachts, 19.27–19.29
security interests
registration of, 19.24
source of law, 19.3
survey
requirement of, 19.25
taxation, 19.20
tonnage tax, 19.21
trading limits, 19.14
yachts
registration of, 19.27–19.29

INDEX

merchant fleet. *See* fleet
mortgages, 6.15
  applicable law, 3.46, 5.5
  bareboat charter
    convention on, 5.32–5.34
    protection of mortgagees, 5.26–5.31
  enforcement, 5.12
  registration of, 1.38
    Bahamas, 7.20
    Barbados, 8.23
    Bermuda, 9.23–9.24
    British Virgin Islands, 10.25–10.28
    Cayman Islands, 11.24–11.27
    Cyprus, 12.29
    Gibraltar, 13.24–13.25
    Hong Kong, 14.15–14.16
    Isle of Man, 15.19–15.20
    Jamaica, 16.25
    Liberia, 17.23–17.24
    Malta, 18.22
    Marshall Islands, 19.24
    Norway, 20.18
    Panama, 21.27
    Singapore, 22.25
    St Vincent and the Grenadines, 23.23
    United Kingdom, 24.27–24.29
    Vanuatu, 25.20

nationality of crew
  crew certification
    Bahamas, 7.11
    Barbados, 8.15
    Bermuda, 9.17
    British Virgin Islands, 10.13
    Cayman Islands, 11.13
    Cyprus, 12.21
    Gibraltar, 13.19
    Hong Kong, 14.10
    Isle of Man, 15.13
    Jamaica, 16.17
    Liberia, 17.15
    Malta, 18.11
    Marshall Islands, 19.17
    Norway, 20.11
    Panama, 21.18
    Singapore, 22.17
    St Vincent and the Grenadines, 23.16
    United Kingdom, 24.15
    Vanuatu, 25.13
naval protection of vessels, 1.29, 4.6, 6.17
non-resident status
  company formation
    Jamaica, 16.8
    Marshall Islands, 19.8
    Panama, 21.8

United Kingdom, 24.8
Vanuatu, 25.7
Norway
  bareboat charter registration, 20.7
    foreign charter, 20.7
  classification societies, 20.13
  crew certification, 20.10
    competency certificates, 20.10
    nationality of crew, 20.11
  deregistration
    procedure for, 20.19
  eligibility for registration
    age limit, 20.5
    vessel type, 20.4
  fleet, 20.2
  geography of, 20.1
  manning requirements, 20.9
    safe manning documents, 20.12
  mortgages
    registration of, 20.18
  ownership
    requirements of, 20.6
  permanent registration, 20.17
    forms, 20.16
  register, administration of, 20.2
  registration
    bareboat charter, 20.7
    deregistration, 20.19
    eligibility for, 20.4–20.5
    mortgages, 20.18
    permanent registration, 20.17
    permanent registration, forms, 20.16
    procedure for, 20.15
    register, administration of, 20.2
    security interests, 20.18
    survey, 20.15
  security interests
    registration of, 20.18
  self-propelled vessels, 20.4
  source of law, 20.3
  survey
    requirement of, 20.15
  taxation, 20.14
  tonnage tax, 20.14
  trading limits, 20.8

offshore drilling platforms, 3.41, 3.43
open registries. *See* International registers
operating costs
  choice of flag, 6.12–6.14
overseas company. *See* company formation,
  overseas company
ownership
  co-owners, 1.37
  permitted categories, 3.8–3.12

registration
  genuine link, 3.13–3.36
requirements of
  Barbados, 8.7–8.8
  Bermuda, 9.6–9.7
  British Virgin Islands, 10.6–10.7
  Cayman Islands, 11.6–11.7
  Cyprus, 12.15
  Gibraltar, 13.6
  Hong Kong, 14.6
  Isle of Man, 15.6–15.7
  Jamaica, 16.5
  Liberia, 17.6
  Marshall Islands, 19.6
  Norway, 20.6
  Panama, 21.6
  Singapore, 22.6
  St Vincent and the Grenadines, 23.6
  United Kingdom, 24.6
  Vanuatu, 25.6

Panama
  bareboat charter registration, 21.11–21.12
    foreign charter, 21.13
  classification societies, 21.20
  company formation, 21.7
    company officers, 21.9–21.10
    non-resident status, 21.8
    overseas company, 21.7
    registered office, 21.8
  crew certification, 21.17
    competency certificates, 21.17
    nationality of crew, 21.18
  deregistration
    procedure for, 21.29
  eligibility for registration
    age limit, 21.5
    vessel type, 21.4
  fees, 21.14, 21.19, 21.24
  geography of, 21.1
  manning requirements, 21.16
    safe manning documents, 21.19
  mortgages
    registration of, 21.27
  ownership
    requirements of, 21.6
  permanent registration, 21.26
    forms, 21.26
  provisional registration, 21.23–21.24
    extension of, 21.25
    validity of, 21.25
  register, administration of, 21.2
  registration
    bareboat charter, 21.11–21.12
    deregistration, 21.29

eligibility for, 21.4–21.5
mortgages, 21.27
permanent registration, 21.26
permanent registration, forms, 21.26
procedure for, 21.23
provisional registration, 21.23–21.24
provisional, extension of, 21.25
provisional, validity of, 21.25
register, administration of, 21.2
security interests, 21.27
short-term registration, 21.14
survey, 21.28
security interests
  registration of, 21.27
short-term registration, 21.14
source of law, 21.3
survey
  requirement of, 21.28
taxation, 21.21
  double tax treaties, 21.22
trading limits, 21.15
parallel registration. *See* bareboat charter
part-owners, 1.37
permanent registration
  age limit
    Bahamas, 7.19
  Bahamas, 7.17
  Barbados, 8.22
  Bermuda, 9.21–9.22
  British Virgin Islands, 10.17–10.20
  Cayman Islands, 11.17–11.19
  Cyprus, 12.28
  forms, 1.20–1.24
    Bahamas, 7.18
    Barbados, 8.22
    Bermuda, 9.21–9.22
    British Virgin Islands, 10.18
    Cayman Islands, 11.21–11.22
    Cyprus, 12.28
    Gibraltar, 13.23
    Hong Kong, 14.14
    Isle of Man, 15.18
    Jamaica, 16.24
    Liberia, 17.22
    Malta, 18.20
    Marshall Islands, 19.23
    Norway, 20.16
    Panama, 21.26
    Singapore, 22.24
    St Vincent and the Grenadines, 23.22
    United Kingdom, 24.22–24.23
    Vanuatu, 25.19
  Gibraltar, 13.23
  Hong Kong, 14.14
  Isle of Man, 15.18

INDEX

Jamaica, 16.24
Liberia, 17.22
Malta, 18.18
Marshall Islands, 19.23
Norway, 20.17
Panama, 21.26
Singapore, 22.24
St Vincent and the Grenadines, 23.22
United Kingdom, 24.22–24.26
Vanuatu, 25.19
permitted categories of ships. *See* vessel
pleasure craft
Gibraltar, 13.4
Isle of Man, 15.14
Jamaica, 16.3
Malta, 18.15
United Kingdom, 24.19, 24.30
political factors
choice of flag, 6.17
port state control
duties relating to, 2.16–2.28
flag states, 2.16–2.28
survey, 2.16–2.28
procedure for deregistration. *See* deregistration, procedure for
procedure for registration. *See* registration, procedure for
provisional registration
Bahamas, 7.15
Barbados, 8.18–8.20
Bermuda, 9.18–9.20
British Virgin Islands, 10.22
Cayman Islands, 11.21
Cyprus, 12.25–12.26
extension of
Bahamas, 7.16
Barbados, 8.21
Bermuda, 9.20
British Virgin Islands, 10.23
Cayman Islands, 11.22
Cyprus, 12.27
Gibraltar, 13.22
Hong Kong, 14.13
Jamaica, 16.23
Liberia, 17.21
Malta, 18.17. 18.19
Marshall Islands, 19.22
Panama, 21.25
Singapore, 22.23
St Vincent and the Grenadines, 23.21
United Kingdom, 24.21
Vanuatu, 25.18
Gibraltar, 13.22
Hong Kong, 14.13
Isle of Man, 15.17

Jamaica, 16.22
Liberia, 17.20
Malta, 18.15
Marshall Islands, 19.21
Panama, 21.23–21.24
Singapore, 22.22
St Vincent and the Grenadines, 23.20
United Kingdom, 24.20
validity of
Bahamas, 7.16
Barbados, 8.21
Bermuda, 9.20
British Virgin Islands, 10.23
Cayman Islands, 11.22
Cyprus, 12.27
Gibraltar, 13.22
Hong Kong, 14.13
Jamaica, 16.23
Liberia, 17.21
Malta, 18.16. 18.19
Marshall Islands, 19.22
Panama, 21.25
Singapore, 22.23
St Vincent and the Grenadines, 23.21
United Kingdom, 24.21
Vanuatu, 25.18
Vanuatu, 25.17

radio licence
registration
Malta, 18.21
Marshall Islands, 19.21
radio traffic accounting authorities
Bahamas, 7.14
British Virgin Islands, 10.16
Cayman Islands, 11.16
registered agent
company formation
Liberia, 17.8
Marshall Islands, 19.9
registered office
company formation
Jamaica, 16.9
Liberia, 17.8
Panama, 21.8
St Vincent and the Grenadines, 23.8
registration
bareboat charter
Bahamas, 7.6
Barbados, 8.9–8.10
Bermuda, 9.9–9.10
British Virgin Islands, 10.8–10.9
Cayman Islands, 11.8–11.9
Cyprus, 12.16–12.17
Gibraltar, 13.10–13.13

525

INDEX

Hong Kong, 14.7–14.8
Isle of Man, 15.8–15.9
Jamaica, 16.12
Liberia, 17.9–17.11
Malta, 18.6–18.8
Marshall Islands, 19.12–19.13
Norway, 20.7
Panama, 21.11–21.12
Singapore, 22.12–22.13
St Vincent and the Grenadines, 23.11–23.12
United Kingdom, 24.11–24.12
Vanuatu, 25.8–25.9
choice of law, 1.32–1.33
deregistration
  Bahamas, 7.22
  Barbados, 8.25
  Bermuda, 9.26
  British Virgin Islands, 10.30
  Cayman Islands, 11.29
  Cyprus, 12.31
  Gibraltar, 13.27
  Hong Kong, 14.20
  Isle of Man, 15.22
  Jamaica, 16.27
  Liberia, 17.26
  Malta, 18.23
  Marshall Islands, 19.26
  Norway, 20.19
  Panama, 21.29
  Singapore, 22.26
  St Vincent and the Grenadines, 23.25
  United Kingdom, 24.31
  Vanuatu, 25.22
effect of, 1.29–1.40
eligibility for
  age limit, 3.45–3.50
  Bahamas, 7.4. 7.5
  Barbados, 8.4–8.6
  Bermuda, 9.4–9.5
  British Virgin Islands, 10.4–10.5
  Cayman Islands, 11.4–11.5
  Cyprus, 12.4
  general principles, 3.37–3.44
  Gibraltar, 13.4–13.5
  Hong Kong, 14.4–14.5
  Isle of Man, 15.4
  Jamaica, 16.3–16.4
  Liberia, 17.4–17.5
  Malta, 18.4–18.5
  Marshall Islands, 19.4–19.5
  Norway, 20.4–20.5
  Panama, 21.4–21.5
  Singapore, 22.4–22.5
  St Vincent and the Grenadines, 23.4–23.5
  United Kingdom, 24.4–24.5

Vanuatu, 25.4–25.5
vessel type, 3.45–3.50
flag, 1.25-.127
flag of convenience
  international registers, 4.14–4.36
  meaning, 4.1–4.13
flag State quality control system
  Hong Kong, 14.17–14.18
forms, 1.20–1.24
general principles, 1.1
interim registration
  British Virgin Islands, 10.21
  Cayman Islands, 11.20
international registers, 4.14–4.36
  choice of, 6.18–6.40
  labour rights, 4.30–4.36
  opposition to, 4.20
  safety, 4.21–4.24
  second registers, 4.37–4.46
  transparency, 4.25–4.29
mortgages, 1.38
  Bahamas, 7.20
  Barbados, 8.23
  Bermuda, 9.23–9.24
  British Virgin Islands, 10.25–10.28
  Cayman Islands, 11.24–11.27
  Cyprus, 12.29
  Gibraltar, 13.24–13.25
  Hong Kong, 14.15–14.16
  Isle of Man, 15.19–15.20
  Jamaica, 16.25
  Liberia, 17.23–17.24
  Malta, 18.22
  Marshall Islands, 19.24
  Norway, 20.18
  Panama, 21.27
  Singapore, 22.25
  St Vincent and the Grenadines, 23.23
  United Kingdom, 24.27–24.29
  Vanuatu, 25.20
obligations on flag states, 1.29–1.40
ownership
  genuine link, 3.13–3.36
permanent registration
  Bahamas, 7.17
  Barbados, 8.22
  Bermuda, 9.21–9.22
  British Virgin Islands, 10.17–10.20
  Cayman Islands, 11.17–11.19
  Cyprus, 12.28
  Gibraltar, 13.23
  Hong Kong, 14.14
  Isle of Man, 15.18
  Jamaica, 16.24
  Liberia, 17.22

Malta, 18.18
Marshall Islands, 19.23
Norway, 20.17
Panama, 21.26
Singapore, 22.24
St Vincent and the Grenadines, 23.22
United Kingdom, 24.22–24.26
Vanuatu, 25.19
permanent registration, age limit
Bahamas, 7.19
Bahamas, 7.18
Barbados, 8.22
Bermuda, 9.21–9.22
British Virgin Islands, 10.18
Cayman Islands, 11.21–11.22
Cyprus, 12.28
Gibraltar, 13.23
Hong Kong, 14.14
Isle of Man, 15.18
Jamaica, 16.24
Liberia, 17.22
Malta, 18.20
Marshall Islands, 19.23
Norway, 20.16
Panama, 21.26
Singapore, 22.24
St Vincent and the Grenadines, 23.22
United Kingdom, 24.22–24.23
Vanuatu, 25.19
procedure for
Bahamas, 7.15
Barbados, 8.18
Bermuda, 9.20
British Virgin Islands, 10.17
Cayman Islands, 11.17
Cyprus, 12.25
Gibraltar, 13.22
Hong Kong, 14.13
Isle of Man, 15.25
Jamaica, 16.22
Liberia, 17.19
Malta, 18.14
Marshall Islands, 19.21
Norway, 20.15
Panama, 21.23
Singapore, 22.21
St Vincent and the Grenadines, 23.20
state sovereignty, 3.1–3.7
United Kingdom, 24.20
Vanuatu, 25.17
provisional registration
Bahamas, 7.15
Barbados, 8.18–8.20
Bermuda, 9.18–9.20
British Virgin Islands, 10.22

Cayman Islands, 11.21
Cyprus, 12.25–12.26
Gibraltar, 13.22
Hong Kong, 14.13
Isle of Man, 15.17
Jamaica, 16.22
Liberia, 17.20
Malta, 18.15
Marshall Islands, 19.21
Marshall Islands, 19.21
Panama, 21.23–21.24
Singapore, 22.22
St Vincent and the Grenadines, 23.20
United Kingdom, 24.20
Vanuatu, 25.17
provisional registration, extension of
Bahamas, 7.16
Barbados, 8.21
Bermuda, 9.20
British Virgin Islands, 10.23
Cayman Islands, 11.22
Cyprus, 12.27
Gibraltar, 13.22
Hong Kong, 14.13
Jamaica, 16.23
Liberia, 17.21
Malta, 18.17. 18.19
Marshall Islands, 19.22
Panama, 21.25
Singapore, 22.23
St Vincent and the Grenadines, 23.21
United Kingdom, 24.21
Vanuatu, 25.18
provisional registration, validity of
Bahamas, 7.16
Barbados, 8.21
Bermuda, 9.20
British Virgin Islands, 10.23
Cayman Islands, 11.22
Cyprus, 12.27
Gibraltar, 13.22
Hong Kong, 14.13
Jamaica, 16.23
Liberia, 17.21
Malta, 18.16. 18.19
Marshall Islands, 19.22
Panama, 21.25
Singapore, 22.23
St Vincent and the Grenadines,
23.21
United Kingdom, 24.21
Vanuatu, 25.18
radio licence
Malta, 18.21
Marshall Islands, 19.21

INDEX

register, administration of, 1.7–1.19
  Bahamas, 7.2
  Barbados, 8.2
  Bermuda, 9.2
  British Virgin Islands, 10.2
  Cayman Islands, 11.2
  Cyprus, 12.2
  Gibraltar, 13.2
  Hong Kong, 14.2
  Isle of Man, 15.2
  Jamaica, 16.2
  Liberia, 17.2
  Malta, 18.2
  Marshall Islands, 19.2
  Norway, 20.2
  Panama, 21.2
  Singapore, 22.2
  St Vincent and the Grenadines, 23.2
  United Kingdom, 24.2
  Vanuatu, 25.2
security interests, 1.38
  Bahamas, 7.20
  Barbados, 8.23
  Bermuda, 9.25
  British Virgin Islands, 10.25–10.28
  Cayman Islands, 11.24–11.27
  Cyprus, 12.29
  Gibraltar, 13.24–13.25
  Hong Kong, 14.15–14.16
  Isle of Man, 15.19–15.20
  Jamaica, 16.25
  Liberia, 17.23–17.24
  Malta, 18.22
  Marshall Islands, 19.24
  Norway, 20.18
  Panama, 21.27
  Singapore, 22.25
  St Vincent and the Grenadines, 23.23
  United Kingdom, 24.27–24.29
  Vanuatu, 25.20
ships under construction
  British Virgin Islands, 10.24
  Cayman Islands, 11.23
short-term registration
  Panama, 21.14
survey, 2.12–2.15
  Bahamas, 7.21
  Barbados, 8.24
  Bermuda, 9.24
  British Virgin Islands, 10.19–10.20. 10.29
  Cayman Islands, 11.18. 11.28
  Cyprus, 12.30
  Gibraltar, 13.26
  Hong Kong, 14.19
  Isle of Man, 15.21

  Jamaica, 16.26
  Liberia, 17.25
  Malta, 18.19
  Marshall Islands, 19.25
  Norway, 20.15
  Panama, 21.28
  Singapore, 22.24
  St Vincent and the Grenadines, 23.24
  United Kingdom, 24.30
  Vanuatu, 25.21
yachts
  Bahamas, 7.23
  Barbados, 8.26
  Bermuda, 9.27
  British Virgin Islands, 10.31–10.33
  Cayman Islands, 11.30–11.34
  Gibraltar, 13.28
  Isle of Man, 15.23–15.24
  Marshall Islands, 19.27–19.29
  St Vincent and the Grenadines, 23.26–23.28
  United Kingdom, 24.32–24.34
renvoi, 5.26
returns. *See* company formation, returns
Roman law, 1.9

safe manning documents. *See* manning,
  requirements of
safety
  competency certificates
    Bahamas, 7.10
    Barbados, 8.13. 8.14
    Bermuda, 9.16
    British Virgin Islands, 10.12
    Cayman Islands, 11.12
    Cyprus, 12.20
    Gibraltar, 13.17
    Hong Kong, 14.10
    Isle of Man, 15.12
    Jamaica, 16.16
    Liberia, 17.14
    Malta, 18.10
    Marshall Islands, 19.16
    Norway, 20.10
    Panama, 21.17
    Singapore, 22.16
    St Vincent and the Grenadines, 23.15
    United Kingdom, 24.14
    Vanuatu, 25.12
  international registers, 4.21–4.24
safe manning documents
    Bahamas, 7.12
    Barbados, 8.16
    Bermuda, 9.18
    British Virgin Islands, 10.14
    Cayman Islands, 11.14

INDEX

Cyprus, 12.22–12.23
Gibraltar, 13.20
Hong Kong, 14.2
Isle of Man, 15.14
Jamaica, 16.18
Liberia, 17.16
Malta, 18.12
Marshall Islands, 19.18
Norway, 20.12
Panama, 21.19
Singapore, 22.18
St Vincent and the Grenadines, 23.17
United Kingdom, 24.16
Vanuatu, 25.14
safety management
international safety management code,
2.29–2.33
survey, 2.12–2.15
Bahamas, 7.21
Barbados, 8.24
Bermuda, 9.24
British Virgin Islands, 10.19–10.20. 10.29
Cayman Islands, 11.18. 11.28
Cyprus, 12.30
Gibraltar, 13.26
Hong Kong, 14.19
Isle of Man, 15.21
Jamaica, 16.26
Liberia, 17.25
Malta, 18.19
Marshall Islands, 19.25
Norway, 20.15
Panama, 21.28
Singapore, 22.24
St Vincent and the Grenadines, 23.24
United Kingdom, 24.30
Vanuatu, 25.21
sanctions, 2.6, 2.7, 3.14, 4.13, 6.17
British Virgin Islands, 10.10
Cayman Islands, 11.10
Isle of Man, 15.10
United Kingdom, 24.12
second registers
international registers, 4.37–4.46
security interests
registration of, 1.38
Bahamas, 7.20
Barbados, 8.23
Bermuda, 9.25
British Virgin Islands, 10.25–10.28
Cayman Islands, 11.24–11.27
Cyprus, 12.29
Gibraltar, 13.24–13.25
Hong Kong, 14.15–14.16
Isle of Man, 15.19–15.20

Jamaica, 16.25
Liberia, 17.23–17.24
Marshall Islands, 19.24
Norway, 20.18
Panama, 21.27
Singapore, 22.25
St Vincent and the Grenadines, 23.23
United Kingdom, 24.27–24.29
Vanuatu, 25.20
Malta, 18.22
security, enforcement of, 6.16
seizure of stateless ships, 1.4, 1.38, 3.28
self-propelled vessels, 4.41, 6.19
Hong Kong, 14.4
Liberia, 17.4
Norway, 20.4
Singapore, 22.6, 22.8
United Kingdom, 24.19
semi-submersible rigs, 3.39, 3.41
ship security officer
appointment of, 2.35
shipowners. *See* Ownership
ships under construction
registration of
British Virgin Islands, 10.24
Cayman Islands, 11.23
short-term registration
Panama, 21.14
Singapore
bareboat charter registration, 22.12
foreign charter, 22.13
classification societies, 22.19
company formation, 22.7
accounts, 22.11
company officers, 22.8–22.10
returns, 22.11
crew certification, 22.16
competency certificates, 22.16
nationality of crew, 22.17
deregistration
procedure for, 22.26
eligibility for registration
age limit, 22.5
vessel type, 22.4
fees, 22.26
geography of, 22.1
manning requirements, 22.15
safe manning documents, 22.18
mortgages
registration of, 22.25
ownership
requirements of, 22.6
permanent registration, 22.24
forms, 22.24
provisional registration, 22.22

INDEX

provisional registration
   extension of, 22.23
   validity of, 22.23
register, administration of, 22.2
registration
   bareboat charter, 22.12–22.13
   deregistration, 22.26
   eligibility for, 22.4–22.5
   mortgages, 22.25
   permanent registration, 22.24
   permanent registration, forms, 22.24
   procedure for, 22.21
   provisional registration, 22.22
   provisional, extension of, 22.23
   provisional, validity of, 22.23
   register, administration of, 22.2
   security interests, 22.25
   survey, 22.24
security interests
   registration of, 22.25
self-propelled vessels, 22.6, 22.8
source of law, 22.3
survey
   requirement of, 22.24
taxation, 22.20
tonnage tax, 22.13, 22.22
trading limits, 22.14
size of vessel
   Bermuda, 9.4
   British Virgin Islands, 10.4
   Cayman Islands, 11.4
   Cyprus, 12.4
   Gibraltar, 13.4
   Hong Kong, 14.4
   Isle of Man, 15.4
   Jamaica, 16.3
   Liberia, 17.4
   Malta, 18.4
   Marshall Islands, 19.4
   Norway, 20.4
   Panama, 21.4
   Singapore, 22.4
   small ships, 3.46, 6.19, 6.32
   St Vincent and the Grenadines, 23.4
   United Kingdom, 24.4
   Vanuatu, 25.4
small ships
   size of vessel, 3.46, 6.19, 6.32
source of law
   Bahamas, 7.3
   Barbados, 8.3
   Bermuda, 9.3
   British Virgin Islands, 10.3
   Cayman Islands, 11.3

Cyprus, 12.3
Gibraltar, 13.3
Hong Kong, 14.2. 14.3
Isle of Man, 15.3
Jamaica, 16.2
Liberia, 17.3
Malta, 18.3
Marshall Islands, 19.3
Norway, 20.3
Panama, 21.3
Singapore, 22.3
St Vincent and the Grenadines, 23.3
United Kingdom, 24.3
Vanuatu, 25.3
St Vincent and the Grenadines
   bareboat charter registration, 23.11
     foreign charter, 23.12
   classification societies, 23.18
   company formation, 23.7
     company officers, 23.9–23.10
     registered office, 23.8
   crew certification, 23.15
     competency certificates, 23.15
     nationality of crew, 23.16
   deregistration
     procedure for, 23.25
   eligibility for registration
     age limit, 23.5
     vessel type, 23.4
   fees, 23.11, 23.20, 23.22, 23.23, 23.25
   fishing vessels, 23.4
   geography of, 23.1
   manning requirements, 23.14
     safe manning documents, 23.17
   mortgages
     registration of, 23.23
   ownership
     requirements of, 23.6
   permanent registration, 23.22
     forms, 23.22
   provisional registration, 23.20
     extension of, 23.21
     validity of, 23.21
   register, administration of, 23.2
   registration
     bareboat charter, 23.11–23.12
     deregistration, 23.25
     eligibility for, 23.4–23.5
     mortgages, 23.23
     permanent registration, 23.22
     permanent registration, forms, 23.22
     procedure for, 23.20
     provisional registration, 23.20
     provisional, extension of, 23.21

INDEX

provisional, validity of, 23.21
register, administration of, 23.2
security interests, 23.23
survey, 23.24
yachts, 23.26–23.28
security interests
registration of, 23.23
source of law, 23.3
survey
requirement of, 23.24
taxation, 23.19
trading limits, 23.13
yachts
registration of, 23.26–23.28
state sovereignty, 3.2
subsidies, 4.6, 4.38, 4.39, 5.10
survey
port state control, 2.16–2.28
requirement of, 2.12–2.15
Bahamas, 7.21
Barbados, 8.24
Bermuda, 9.24
British Virgin Islands, 10.19–10.20. 10.29
Cayman Islands, 11.18. 11.28
Cyprus, 12.30
Gibraltar, 13.26
Hong Kong, 14.19
Isle of Man, 15.21
Jamaica, 16.26
Liberia, 17.25
Malta, 18.19
Marshall Islands, 19.25
Norway, 20.15
Panama, 21.28
Singapore, 22.24
St Vincent and the Grenadines, 23.24
Vanuatu, 25.21
United Kingdom, 24.30

taxation
double tax treaties
Marshall Islands, 19.20
Panama, 21.22
Hong Kong, 14.12
Isle of Man, 15.16
Jamaica, 16.20–16.21
Liberia, 17.18
Marshall Islands, 19.20
Norway, 20.14
Panama, 21.21
Singapore, 22.20
St Vincent and the Grenadines, 23.19
tonnage tax, 4.44, 6.9–6.11, 6.25
Cyprus, 12.3

Liberia, 17.18, 17.20
Marshall Islands, 19.21
Norway, 20.14
Singapore, 22.13, 22.22
United Kingdom, 24.18, 24.19
United Kingdom, 24.18–24.19
Vanuatu, 25.16
terrorism, 2.34, 2.36
tonnage tax, 4.44, 6.9–6.11, 6.25
Cyprus, 12.3
Liberia, 17.18, 17.20
Marshall Islands, 19.21
Norway, 20.14
Singapore, 22.13, 22.22
United Kingdom, 24.18, 24.19
trading limits
Bahamas, 7.8
Barbados, 8.12
Bermuda, 9.15
British Virgin Islands, 10.10
Cayman Islands, 11.10
Cyprus, 12.18
Gibraltar, 13.16
Hong Kong, 14.9
Isle of Man, 15.10
Jamaica, 16.14
Liberia, 17.12
Malta, 18.9
Marshall Islands, 19.14
Norway, 20.8
Panama, 21.15
Singapore, 22.14
St Vincent and the Grenadines, 23.13
United Kingdom, 24.12
Vanuatu, 25.10
training
International Convention on Standards
of Training, Certification and
Watchkeeping, 2.37–2.39
transfers, 4.17, 5.16, 5.27
transparency
international registers, 4.25–4.29

United Kingdom
bareboat charter registration, 24.9–24.10
foreign charter, 24.11
classification societies, 24.17
company formation, 24.7
non-resident status, 24.8
crew certification, 24.14
competency certificates, 24.14
nationality of crew, 24.15
deregistration
procedure for, 24.31

531

INDEX

eligibility for registration
  age limit, 24.5
  vessel type, 24.4
fishing vessels, 24.4, 24.6, 24.15, 24.19,
  24.22, 24.24, 24.30
geography of, 24.1
manning requirements, 24.13
  safe manning documents, 24.16
mortgages
  registration of, 24.27–24.29
ownership
  requirements of, 24.6
permanent registration, 24.22–24.26
  forms, 24.22–24.23
pleasure craft, 24.19, 24.30
provisional registration, 24.20
  extension of, 24.21
  validity of, 24.21
register, administration of, 24.2
registration
  bareboat charter, 24.11–24.12
  deregistration, 24.31
  eligibility for, 24.4–24.5
  mortgages, 24.27–24.29
  permanent registration, 24.22–24.26
  permanent registration, forms, 24.22–24.23
  procedure for, 24.20
  provisional registration, 24.20
  provisional, extension of, 24.21
  provisional, validity of, 24.21
  register, administration of, 24.2
  security interests, 24.27–24.29
  survey, 24.30
  yachts, 24.32–24.34
sanctions, 24.12
security interests
  registration of, 24.27–24.29
self-propelled vessels, 24.19
source of law, 24.3
survey
  requirement of, 24.30
taxation, 24.18–24.19
tonnage tax, 24.18, 24.19
trading limits, 24.12
yachts
  registration of, 24.32–24.34

validity of provisional registration. *See*
  provisional registration, validity of
Vanuatu
  bareboat charter registration, 25.8
    foreign charter, 25.9
  classification societies, 25.15
  company formation, 25.7
    non-resident status, 25.7

crew certification, 25.12
  competency certificates, 25.12
  nationality of crew, 25.13
deregistration
  procedure for, 25.22
eligibility for registration
  age limit, 25.5
  vessel type, 25.4
fees, 25.2, 25.8, 25.17, 25.19
geography of, 25.1
manning requirements, 25.11
  safe manning documents, 25.14
mortgages
  registration of, 25.20
ownership
  requirements of, 25.6
permanent registration, 25.19
  forms, 25.19
provisional registration, 25.17
  extension of, 25.18
  validity of, 25.18
register, administration of, 25.2
registration
  bareboat charter, 25.8–25.9
  deregistration, 25.22
  eligibility for, 25.4–25.5
  mortgages, 25.20
  permanent registration, 25.19
  permanent registration, forms, 25.19
  procedure for, 25.17
  provisional registration, 25.17
  provisional, extension of, 25.18
  provisional, validity of, 25.18
  register, administration of, 25.2
  security interests, 25.20
  survey, 25.21
security interests
  registration of, 25.20
source of law, 25.3
survey
  requirement of, 25.21
taxation, 25.16
trading limits, 25.10
vessel
  age of vessel
    eligibility for registration, 7.5, 8.6, 9.5,
      10.5, 11.5, 12.5–12.14, 13.5, 14.5,
      15,5, 16.4, 17.5, 18.5, 19.5, 20.5,
      21.5, 22.5, 23.5, 24.5, 25.5
  eligibility for registration
    Bahamas, 7.4
    Barbados, 8.4. 8.5
    Bermuda, 9.4
    British Virgin Islands, 10.4
    Cayman Islands, 11.4

INDEX

Cyprus, 12.4
Gibraltar, 13.4
Hong Kong, 14.4
Isle of Man, 15.4
Jamaica, 16.3
Liberia, 17.4
Malta, 18.4
Marshall Islands, 19.4
Norway, 20.4
Panama, 21.4
Singapore, 22.4
St Vincent and the Grenadines, 23.4
United Kingdom, 24.4
Vanuatu, 25.4
nationality of, 1.3, 1.4, 1.12–1.19
  flag, 1.25–1.27
protection of, 1.4
registration of, 1.4–1.19

watchkeeping
  International Convention on Standards
    of Training, Certification and
    Watchkeeping 1978, 2.37–2.39

yachts
  effect of non-registration, 1.5
  registration of
    Bahamas, 7.23
    Barbados, 8.26
    Bermuda, 9.27
    British Virgin Islands, 10.31–10.33
    Cayman Islands, 11.30–11.34
    effect of non-registration, 1.5
    Gibraltar, 13.28
    Marshall Islands, 19.27–19.29
    St Vincent and the Grenadines, 23.26–23.28
    United Kingdom, 24.32–24.34